MASTERPLOTS II

WORLD FICTION
SERIES

MASTERPLOTS II

WORLD FICTION SERIES

2

Fer-Lov

Edited by

FRANK N. MAGILL

SALEM PRESS

Pasadena, California   Englewood Cliffs, New Jersey

Library of Congress Cataloging-in-Publication Data
Masterplots II: world fiction series.
    Bibliography: p.
    Includes index.
    Summary: Examines the themes, characters,
plots, style, and technique of 347 works by authors
from the non-English speaking countries of the
world, including Poland, France, Czechoslovakia,
Austria, Germany, and Russia.
    1. Fiction—19th century—Stories, plots, etc. 2.
Fiction—19th century—History and criticism. 3.
Fiction—20th century—Stories, plots, etc. 4. Fic-
tion—20th century—History and criticism. [1. Fic-
tion—Stories, plots, etc. 2. Fiction—History and
criticism] I. Magill, Frank Northen, 1907-   . II.
Title: Masterplots 2. III. Title: Masterplots two.
PN3326.M28   1988   809.3   87-33695
ISBN 0-89356-473-7 (set)
ISBN 0-89356-475-3 (volume 2)

90-2969

LIST OF TITLES IN VOLUME 2

MASTERPLOTS II

LIST OF TITLES IN VOLUME 2

MASTERPLOTS II

WORLD FICTION
SERIES

FERDYDURKE

Author: Witold Gombrowicz (1904-1969)
Type of plot: Philosophical fantasy
Time of plot: The mid-1930's
Locale: Poland
First published: 1937 (English translation, 1961)

> *Principal characters:*
> JOHNNIE, the narrator
> MIENTUS, Johnnie's schoolmate
> SIPHON, Johnnie's schoolmate and Mientus' opponent
> PROFESSOR PIMKO, Johnnie's schoolmaster
> ZUTA YOUTHFUL, Johnnie's beloved, who disdains him
> MR. and MRS. YOUTHFUL, Zuta Youthful's modern parents

The Novel

Johnnie is a thirty-year-old author who is disappointed over the reception of his writing. Critics have called his work immature and he, in turn, complains of the power they have over his reputation. Why should these "cultural aunts and uncles" be in a position to define literature? Johnnie is outraged that people whose intellects he cannot respect have so much say over the course of his career, yet he realizes that it is in the nature of things that the individual's self is defined by others.

Unaccountably, Johnnie suddenly finds that his life is no longer his own. He is taken in hand by Professor Pimko, a distinguished scholar who puts Johnnie back in school. Strangely enough, no one seems to notice that Johnnie is much older than his fellow pupils. Indeed, they welcome him as though he fit right in. At school, the tyranny of the teacher's opinions is even worse than the literary critics Johnnie attacked earlier in the novel. Pupils are expected to cherish great writers, such as the nineteenth century Romantic poet Juliusz Slowacki, just because the teacher says that they are great. What is at stake is not really the greatness of the literature which the students study but rather the opinions of the teacher.

The same is true for the society of students. The students are led by the boy who can establish himself as an authority and not necessarily by the one who has the better argument. Mientus and Siphon fight over whether the students are innocent. Their means of combat is the making of faces. Siphon is to make beautiful faces, and Mientus is to respond with ugly faces. What counts, in other words, are the poses they strike and not the substance of their arguments. Professor Pimko has tried to indoctrinate them into the idea of innocence—a notion that the crude Mientus rejects and that the better-mannered Siphon tries to defend. The students take sides and herd around their heroes without giving much consideration to what they really think of these opposing positions.

Johnnie is trapped in a world of doctrines and finds himself in the home of Mr. and Mrs. Youthful, who are rearing their daughter, Zuta, as the perfect modern girl. Like Professor Pimko, who has arranged for Johnnie's board there, Mr. and Mrs. Youthful are ideologues. They stoutly believe in progress and that they can make their daughter the embodiment of progressive social ideals. Johnnie's every approach to this cool, modern girl is thwarted. He cannot penetrate her aloofness or speak to her in a tone that is truly his own.

Eventually, Johnnie is able to escape from the tyranny of the Youthfuls and is accompanied to the countryside by Mientus. They visit Johnnie's relatives, who are anything but modern. The relatives beat and abuse their servants; they believe in the traditional class structure. Mientus proves to be a problem, because he has come to fraternize with the lower classes. He believes that a stable boy would be a more authentic companion than anyone he has ever known at school. Mientus' efforts to befriend a stable boy, however, are clumsy and ludicrous; the boy has no idea what Mientus means by his familiarity. After a brutal scene in which the stable boy is beaten nearly to death by his master (one of Johnnie's relatives) for fraternizing with Mientus, Johnnie and Mientus flee. The novel ends with Mientus' quest frustrated and with Johnnie just as much a fugitive from society as he was at the beginning.

The Characters

Witold Gombrowicz's characters very clearly reflect his skeptical view of life and the human personality. In one sense, the author does not believe that there is such a thing as "character"—if what is meant by that term is a fixed personal essence, a set of qualities that do not change. The author quite explicitly rejects what he would call the romantic notion of the self as a unique entity. Human beings, in his view, are the sum of what has been said about them, their actions, and environmental influences. For example, when the schoolboys argue and fight with one another, Johnnie observes, "All of them were the slaves of the faces they were making." Human behavior, in other words, is not guided by some internal motivation. On the contrary, people act the way they do because of the behavior that has been imposed upon them or that they impose upon themselves.

Thus, Johnnie's efforts to attract Zuta are a dismal failure. She has been programmed to be entirely self-assured. She knows what the correct behavior is, and when Johnnie comes into her room unannounced, all she can think to say is that he has transgressed the boundaries of proper behavior. She never lets down her guard, and he never is able to elicit even one spontaneous action from her.

Professor Pimko is the architect of this modern behavior. He tries to keep all of his students "youthful" by insisting on their innocence. He fits them with fannies, or little behinds, because he wants them to feel insecure and immature. Gombrowicz depicts modern schooling—indeed much of modern life—as demeaning and deforming the personality. The lascivious Pimko is hardly mature himself, and Johnnie relishes tricking him into visiting Zuta's bedroom at night and then making sure that her parents catch him at it. Professors are no more mature than their students—a point Gombrowicz emphasizes by including two parables in his novel about learned men who are rivals and whose behavior is as childish as the schoolboy fights depicted in the first part of the novel.

Themes and Meanings

Gombrowicz's novel attacks the idea that human beings are the masters of their destinies. Most people are immature; they do what they have been taught by family, society, and school. Much of the author's humor derives from exposing human pretensions and conventionality. People believe that they are acting on their own and in the interest of the highest ideals when, in fact, they are usually motivated by urges they cannot control. Professor Pimko says that he has brought Johnnie to the Youthful household to learn how a modern home and family are managed. In truth, Pimko is obsessed with Zuta and is looking for ways to be intimate with her. His concerns are sensual, not intellectual. Yet the professor is so bound by the rhetoric of schooling that he cannot see the lie in what he professes. He does not really want to teach children; he wants to be a child again. His advanced age makes youth all the more desirable. While his façade is one of a confident, urbane intellectual, his true state reflects an instability that is characteristic of human life in general. As the critic Robert Boyers suggests, "what *Ferdydurke* enforces ultimately is an existentialist view of man as perpetually in the act of becoming, perpetually insecure and filled with that neurotic dread of extinction that is a visible component of works by Sartre, Beckett, and others."

It takes a considerable adjustment to read Gombrowicz because, unlike most novelists, he is not interested in presenting well-rounded characters. Mientus, the Youthfuls, and Pimko do not have psychological depth; they are types and react to other people as types. Their psychologies are a matter of conditioning and form. Once life takes a certain form, Gombrowicz argues, it cannot change. Human beings are under the illusion that they create form, that they shape life. It is, alas, exactly the opposite. As Johnnie realizes, "[T]he fundamental grief is purely and simply, in my opinion, the agony of bad outward form, defective appearance, the agony of phraseology, grimaces, faces." People cannot help the way they look or, by extension, the way they behave. This is why Gombrowicz uses the term "bad outward form." Life is external to human beings, even though they often think just the opposite. Just as the hapless Johnnie becomes the victim of Pimko's schoolmaster tyranny, so human beings in general inhibit one another. Gombrowicz writes, "[T]he primary and fundamental agony is that born of the constraint of man by man . . . i.e. from the fact that we suffocate and stifle in the narrow and rigid idea of ourselves that others have of us."

Critical Context

Gombrowicz has been a difficult writer to assimilate into Western literature. When his novel first appeared in Polish in 1937, it created a sensation. Critics quickly recognized that he was writing something quite new. He was attacking Polish Romanticism of the nineteenth century, in which the figure of the great hero, the great poet, was predominant. He was most skeptical of these noble qualities and believed that much of Polish Romanticism fostered illusions about human nature. How far had the human race really progressed? Written on the eve of World War II, this novel seems particularly prophetic. He knew that the so-called great philosophy and literature had made virtually no difference in the way people lived their lives or in the way the world was organized. By and large, people are unprepared to face this truth about themselves and their world, and Gombrowicz has been accused of asserting a cynical, nihilistic point of view.

Gombrowicz once said that he was not a political writer. It is true that his work does not deal explicitly with politics, and the novelist did not then take an active role in political matters. He was traveling outside Poland in 1939, when World War II began, and he never returned to his native land. Except for a brief period of liberalization from 1956 to 1957, when most of his work was published in Poland, he has been a proscribed writer there. The Communist government has rightly viewed Gombrowicz's writing as subversive and may have been alarmed when editions of his work sold out quickly during the political thaw. *Ferdydurke* is, above all, an attack on indoctrination, and there is very little place in Poland for writers who are so original and uncompromising in their thinking.

In later novels, Gombrowicz uses his own name for the narrator. He must have realized after writing *Ferdydurke* how autobiographical his fiction had become. Like Johnnie, Gombrowicz came from a family that claimed to be aristocratic. While he was disdainful of its pretenses, he could not idealize the peasantry or think of the lower class as closer to reality. Unlike Fyodor Dostoevski, for example, Gombrowicz finds no particular spiritual value in the common man. In his published journal, Gombrowicz comments on his reading, and it is clear that he has been deeply influenced by Friedrich Nietzsche. While hardly a follower of the German philosopher, Gombrowicz shares Nietzsche's merciless probing of the emptiness of modern man. In *Pornografia* (1960; English translation, 1966), he acknowledges that *Ferdydurke*, with its emphasis on immaturity, is the key to his subsequent work. Gombrowicz himself had been criticized for his early immature work. The criticism obviously rankled, and he set out in *Ferdydurke* not only to have his revenge on critics but also to insist that humankind was basically unable to grow psychologically. Yet reading Gombrowicz is not merely a negative experience, for his revelation of human inadequacy is often amusing and instructive. He proves to be a wise counsel against complacency and a shrewd guide through the absurdity of life.

Sources for Further Study

Boyers, Robert. "Gombrowicz and *Ferdydurke*: The Tyranny of Form," in *Centennial Review*. XIV (1970), pp. 284-312.

Fletcher, John. "Witold Gombrowicz," in *New Directions in Literature: Critical Approaches to a Contemporary Phenomenon*, 1968.

Jelenski, Constantin. "Witold Gombrowicz," in *TriQuarterly*. No. 9 (Spring, 1967), pp. 37-42.

Miłosz, Czesław. *A History of Polish Literature*, 1983.

Thompson, Ewa W. *Witold Gombrowicz*, 1979.

Updike, John. Review in *The New Yorker*. XLIII (September 23, 1967), p. 169.

Carl E. Rollyson, Jr.

FIASCO

Author: Stanisław Lem (1921-   )
Type of plot: Philosophical science fiction
Time of plot: The future
Locale: Titan, a moon of Saturn, and Quinta, a planet in the Harpy System
First published: Fiasko, 1986 (English translation, 1987)

> *Principal characters:*
> ANGUS PARVIS, a spaceship pilot
> MARK TEMPE, a pilot, who may be Parvis resurrected a
>   century after his death
> FATHER ARAGO, a Dominican monk
> STEERGARD, the captain of the Quinta mission

The Novel

Fiasco tells of mankind's first contact with an alien civilization. Having searched the heavens for centuries, scientists finally discover, on distant Quinta, an intelligent species at roughly the same technological level as humanity. The attempt to visit them becomes a fiasco. The novel explores the many barriers to communicating with aliens.

Fiasco opens with a small-scale fiasco, set in a time (perhaps the twenty-first century) previous to the main action of the novel. Angus Parvis arrives on Titan, a moon of Saturn which is being developed as a source of minerals. He discovers that his teacher and friend, Pirx, is among a group of men who disappeared while attempting to move materials between two bases. Parvis takes a giant machine across the alien, unpredictable, and dangerous landscape to attempt a rescue, but the combination of human error and the hostility of the landscape causes the rescue's failure and his death.

The failure on Titan foreshadows the later fiasco that gives the novel its title: Both spring from human nature and from the relationship of humans to the cosmos. At the center of Parvis' personal failure are love, pride, and ignorance. He attempts the rescue out of affection and loyalty to Pirx and his fellow workers. These admirable but irrational passions override his ignorance of the terrain and his inexperience with the machine he uses. His pride in his ability to operate the machine and in the power of human technology over nature leads him into a death trap.

More general failures contribute to his personal failure. Mistakes and bureaucratic rivalries have produced two bases on the treacherous moon, when only one was desirable. Continued mistakes and rivalries produce the need for the surface travel between bases that, in turn, leads to accident and death.

From this small fiasco, Parvis may be saved for a greater catastrophe, the journey of the space ship *Eurydice* to an alien civilization. When he learns that he will die on Titan, Parvis uses an emergency machine that vitrifies him instantaneously. In a future century, when the technology for reviving frozen people is developed, he finds himself on the *Eurydice*, where he has been revived and rechristened Mark Tempe. The relation between Parvis and Tempe is not one of simple identity, however, for in order to come up with a subject capable of functioning fully when revived, the medical technicians of the *Eurydice* have had to choose between two of the men who were vitrified on Titan, both of whom are viable candidates for resurrection. The identity of the revived pilot remains a tantalizing—and disturbing—puzzle, for the technicians have had to exercise powers traditionally reserved for God.

When the *Eurydice* arrives at the Quinta system, it must undergo a complex series of maneuvers that accomplish a form of time travel. Meanwhile, a smaller ship with a crew of ten, the *Hermes*, undertakes the specific mission of visiting Quinta. Just before the *Hermes*, arrives, Quinta takes actions that suggest it is aware of an alien approach. As a result, Steergard and his crew become extremely cautious, and the fiasco begins.

Father Arago participates in this expedition as a physician and as a moral adviser. He elicits from Steergard the initial intention of the mission, to establish contact peaceably. If the aliens do not want contact, then the *Hermes* has no choice but to go home. This intention is gradually displaced.

From hiding, the *Hermes* collects space artifacts that appear to be military equipment. Though alien technology is incomprehensible without knowledge of its use, the men assume human purposes and use human analogies to develop elaborate hypotheses about the civilization they wish to contact.

There are several signs that Quinta does not want contact. As the *Hermes* approaches, all Quintan radio sources enter a jamming mode. Though there is evidence of activity on the Quintan moon, no Quintans and no space travel are observed there. Also, to the variety of signals sent by the *Hermes* there is no reply.

Although there is no way of knowing what the Quintans want, the expedition crew never entertains the possibility that they may simply want to be left alone. Instead, the men continue to develop and elaborate on various hypotheses about national powers, arms races, and levels of war. They read into their scanty evidence about Quintan intentions an extrapolation of Earth's twentieth century arms race. Thus, Stanisław Lem comments on the multiple forms such a competition may take, all of which lead to a dead end.

The Quintans' silence brings out anxiety and aggression in the men, intensifying their collective desire to make contact. Admirable desires lead to mistaken actions. These passions are focused when the men send the *Gabriel*, an unmanned communications probe, to the surface. This probe is pursued by four missiles from the planet. The probe's computer is programmed to prevent the capture of its main propulsion unit because the humans believe that this gives them a technological edge over the Quintans. When capture seems imminent, the computer improvises a means of self-destruction that also destroys the approaching missiles. Thus, because of a technical failure, a peaceable attempt at contact becomes interpretable as an act of aggression. Though the humans do not know whether the approaching missiles were exploratory, like their own, or hostile, they are inclined to interpret them as hostile and to blame the Quintans for this failure.

Continued attempts to contact the Quintans produce more ambiguous events that are interpreted as hostile. This escalates the *Hermes* crew's insistence upon contact. Eventually, the crew has moved from its original intention of humbly requesting conversation to insisting on contact at any price— including destruction.

When a large mass instantaneously coalesces near the *Hermes*, the ship automatically defends itself with a shield that jerks it away. The sudden move from zero to high gravity helps convince the crew members that they have been attacked. This event leads them to decide that they must show their strength, that they cannot simply be driven away. They destroy Quinta's moon. Quinta interferes with this act in such a way that large fragments fall onto the planet, causing great destruction. Again, the crew blames the Quintans for causing themselves suffering and works their interference into the hypothesis of a planet at war with itself.

Though there are always dissenting voices, the dominant motion of the *Hermes* is toward greater violence to force contact. Father Arago and Tempe suggest projecting "cartoons" on the planet's clouds to communicate. This attempt produces an invitation to land. An unmanned mock *Hermes* is sent down, and the Quintans apparently incapacitate it. In response, the *Hermes* destroys the giant ice ring the Quintans have created around their planet. Massive planetary destruction follows.

Steergard then issues an ultimatum: Communicate, or all life on the planet will be destroyed. Feeling guilt for the destruction that the crew has already caused, Steergard says that he would not really destroy Quinta. The Quintans respond, however, and Tempe descends to the planet. He is sent under the condition that if he fails to answer a regular call signal during his stay, Steergard will attack again.

On the surface, Tempe becomes fascinated with his attempts to discover something about the Quintans, who, though present, seem invisible. He discovers living objects that seem to be a cross between trees and fungus. He is busily exploring them when he realizes that he has been ignoring his signal to contact the *Hermes*, and he is far from his radio equipment. Before he can act, he and the area of his landing are destroyed by the *Hermes*' attack.

The Characters

As in most of Lem's works, characters are not very important in *Fiasco*.

Lem does not create characters and relationships that lead the reader to be concerned about their fates. Instead, characters are mainly voices for ideas and approaches to problems.

Fiasco is a realistic look at the romantic desire for contact with alien civilizations. Lem plays upon this desire, tantalizing the reader with a few suggestive details about the Quintans but never allowing the quantity of information that might make understanding possible. The typical reader is likely to identify most closely with Tempe, who tries to steer a middle course between Father Arago's Christian approach to contact with aliens and the militaristic approach the crew actually follows. Having a romantic desire "to see the Quintans," Tempe looks for a workable plan. Though he may finally see them, Tempe finds that merely seeing is not enough. He really wants communication. As Father Arago intimates, however, even if meaningful communication between the two worlds is possible—and there is significant doubt of this—it must be voluntary on both sides. Any other approach will fail.

Themes and Meanings

Fiasco shares situations, themes, and meanings with most of Lem's other works. A central theme is humanity's desire to make contact with an intelligence other than itself, whether that be God or aliens. As in his most famous novel, *Solaris* (1961; English translation, 1970), an important aspect of this theme is the difficulty, perhaps the impossibility, of humans to see anything other than themselves.

An alien civilization with a different biology, evolution, geology, history, and environment must almost certainly be different from humanity in every other conceivable way. From the few verbal messages that pass between Quinta and the *Hermes*, it becomes clear that the more abstract their languages become, the more they diverge from each other. They can communicate precisely about the measurement of space and time, but they cannot communicate their most elementary needs and desires—except for survival. Nevertheless, out of a need to understand driven by the desire to communicate, the crew of the *Hermes* writes and rewrites a speculative account of Quinta in which the planet's history mirrors aspects of Earth's history almost exactly. Humans can only see themselves; yet the true Quintans remain invisible. Even the supposedly objective computer seems to "think" in human terms because its programs and information are provided by human minds.

The order humanity sees in the universe is created and imposed by the human mind. These ideas of order serve human purposes well enough, but they provide no way of stepping outside the human perspective to see alien ways of creating and imposing order for alien purposes.

With mythical and religious names, Lem underlines the unconscious arrogance of the expedition's expectation of successful contact. For example, the spaceship is named for *Hermes*, the messenger of the gods, and is controlled by DEUS, the computer (from *deus ex machina*, a "god from a machine"). Among other attempts at communication, the crew sends the probe *Gabriel*, which recalls God's messenger to Mary. The mission becomes a godlike attempt to impose human order on an alien culture.

Critical Context

Fiasco presents themes that pervade Lem's fiction: themes of alien contact, cybernetics, and artificial intelligence, as well as themes of the human hunger for absolute knowledge, the limits of knowing, and the slavery of reason to human biology. Distinctive to this novel is the emphasis on Christianity in the character of Father Arago. Although Lem has often affirmed his atheism, he has also affirmed the human need for faith, as the expression of preference for specific values. Father Arago's faith leads to the only admirable ethical position in *Fiasco*, even though that position does not prevail.

Like Lem's other works, this novel is rich in invention. Reviewers, though they acknowledged its lack of interesting characters, were enthusiastic about the novel's engaging plot, vivid description, and intellectual weight.

Sources for Further Study

Delaney, Paul. "*Fiasco* by Stanisław Lem," in *The New York Times Book Review*. XCII (June 7, 1987), p. 1.

Engel, Peter, and John Sigda. "An Interview with Stanisław Lem," in *The Missouri Review*. VII (1984), pp. 218-237.

Lem, Stanisław. *Microworlds: Writings on Science Fiction and Fantasy*, 1984.

Potts, Stephen W. "Dialogues Concerning Human Understanding: Empirical Views of God from Locke to Lem," in *Bridges to Science Fiction*, 1980.

Tierney, John. "A Mundane Master of Cosmic Visions," in *Discover*. VII (December, 1986), pp. 56-62.

Ziegfeld, Richard E. *Stanisław Lem*, 1985.

Terry Heller

THE FIFTH SON

Author: Elie Wiesel (1928-   )
Type of plot: Historical realism
Time of plot: The 1960's to the 1980's
Locale: New York City and Reshastadt, Germany
First published: Le Cinquième Fils, 1983 (English translation, 1985)

Principal characters:

THE NARRATOR, the Brooklyn-born son of Holocaust survivors
REUVEN TAMIROFF, the narrator's father
SIMHA-THE-DARK, a Holocaust survivor and Reuven's
  companion in philosophical discussions
BONTCHEK, another survivor, excluded from the discussions
LISA, the narrator's girlfriend
THE ANGEL, a sadistic Nazi officer
ARIEL, an older Tamiroff son, who is killed by The Angel

The Novel

The Fifth Son describes a journey into the past, a pilgrimage that leads the narrator, the son of Holocaust survivors, to an understanding of his father. Although written from the narrator's point of view, the novel has three other voices: Reuven Tamiroff, the narrator's father, whose reminiscences and letters provide glimpses of a tortured man; Bontchek, another survivor, whose recollections reveal more about Reuven; and Simha-the-Dark, also a survivor, who finally unlocks Reuven's past.

The novel begins with the narrator's dream; in Reshastadt, he sees his father, who tells him that the trip to Germany is a mistake. The dream fades, and the narrator begins to piece together twenty years of reminiscences about his attempts to understand his father's silence.

As the narrator assembles the vignettes about his life, he remembers his father as silent and his mother as an unhappy woman who withdrew into a private world when he was only six. He is reminded of a Passover during which Simha demanded that Reuven remember his duty to the living. Simha then told the folktale about the four sons and The Question. The first son knows and assumes The Question, the second knows and rejects it, the third is indifferent to it, and the fourth is ignorant of it. The fifth son, not mentioned in the tale, is gone.

Few vignettes involve Reuven's descriptions of his own life, but the narrator recalls that Bontchek "brought to life . . . an entire society with its heroes and villains, its giants and its dwarfs." He particularly remembered the sadistic Nazi called The Angel and recalled The Angel's murder of fifty men, an act which the survivors protested by going on strike. In retaliation, The

Angel executed half of the Jewish Council, sparing Simha and Reuven. Intermittently, the narrator analyzes his relationship with Lisa, a banker's daughter whom he met in a philosophy class. He recounts his seduction by Lisa, his obsession with her sensuality, her frenetic existence, and her political activism. Simha completes Reuven's story by remembering the shooting of more than two hundred people (among them, Simha's wife, Hanna) for defying The Angel's orders that they pray in public so that he could prove that God did not hear them. Several men swore that if they survived the war, they would execute The Angel.

Throughout *The Fifth Son* are Reuven's secret letters to an absent son named Ariel. In them, Reuven questions God and existence and reveals his remorse at the deaths of his fellow councillors. (He admits that he feels responsible because he supported the strike.) Finally, he tells Ariel that he and several others found The Angel after the war and killed him. Reuven confides that he and Simha are still disturbed by their action; revenge is the sole topic of their monthly discussions. He wonders how he would have acted in different circumstances.

The narrator eventually remembers his discovery of the Ariel letters, his reading of the letter in which Reuven relived Ariel's last day. The letter contained Reuven's cry to Ariel: "[T]hat night you left us, you were six years old; you are still six years old." Ariel, son of Reuven and Regina, was tortured to death by The Angel. Obsessed with Ariel, the narrator attempted to learn everything about The Angel and finally discovered that The Angel, still alive, became Wolfgang Berger, a businessman and a respected citizen of Reshastadt. In his own attempt at revenge, the narrator traveled to Reshastadt, but the encounter between former Nazi and survivors' son was anticlimactic: The narrator could only tell Berger who he was and threaten Berger with the curse of the dead. Assassination was impossible.

Years later, the narrator ends his quest with a meditation on his life. He has assimilated his father's lost years and Ariel's lost life into his own existence; he has finally connected with his father. His life has purpose and form but no meaning: "[W]hen," he asks, "yes, when, shall I finally begin to live my life, my own?"

The Characters

Although the narrator provides brief physical descriptions of the other characters, he himself remains indistinct, exhibiting the same absence from life that he deplores in his father. Content to watch rather than to experience life, the narrator spends his childhood and adolescence as his father's assistant, instead of participating in games with his peers. In college, he drifts into philosophy, again demonstrating his preference for abstractions. With Lisa, he is passive, allowing her to initiate him into new experiences. Despite (or maybe because of) the barriers he has erected between himself and life, he is attracted to those who are his opposites—Lisa and Bontchek—perhaps hoping to discover life through them.

Trained in economy of emotion, the narrator reveals his capacity for passion only in his persistent attempts to know his father. Convinced that his father's history has the answers to his questions, he searches for information about his parents and their life before him. Later, having exhausted Bontchek's and Simha's store of recollections and having heard his father's vague tales, the narrator turns to libraries for information that will substantiate his family history.

Reuven Tamiroff shares himself only minimally with his son, slightly more with Simha. Reuven lives a narrow life defined by two concerns: his act of revenge and his attempt to write a commentary on the work of Paritus.

The other major characters are little more than substantial shadows. Simha-the-Dark and Bontchek are figures from Reuven's past, survivors of The Angel's regime. Bontchek is more talkative, more practical; he inhabits the world of action rather than the world of discussion. While in the ghetto, he traveled secretly, smuggling Jews to friendly countries. Bontchek's stories reveal the events that shaped the brooding man that Reuven has become. It is significant that the narrator provides a vivid description of this garrulous man: "a mixture of martyr and hedonist. A black . . . face as though covered with soot, flattened nose, powerful neck, square chest. . . ." Simha is "a nocturnal character attracted by darkness and its ghosts. . . . He buys and sells shadows." A shadow himself, Simha lives alone and spends his free hours calculating the time that separates the Jews from messianic deliverance. He and Reuven spend hours together in philosophical debates, from which they exclude Bontchek.

Themes and Meanings

At one point, the narrator remembers Simha's explanation of his occupation as a merchant of shadows: "Most people think that shadows follow, precede, or surround beings or objects; the truth is that they also surround words, ideas, desires, deeds, impulses, and memories." *The Fifth Son* is about shadows: shadows of the Holocaust, of Ariel and Hanna, and of others who died at The Angel's orders. The characters are all shadows, their lives outlined by the past. Reuven, in particular, cannot separate himself from the past, and he passes on his preoccupations to his son.

Two concerns inform the novel. First is the narrator's story; second is the question of revenge. The two concerns intersect and parallel, often forming one narrative thread. As he becomes acquainted with his father's past, the narrator learns that Reuven is obsessed with revenge because he is guilty of it. Overcome with the enormity of his action, Reuven engages in endless discussions with Simha, always on the same question: Is revenge ever justified? The theme of revenge comes full circle when, discovering that The

Angel is not dead, the narrator decides to finish what his father started.

Although Ariel clearly is the "fifth son" of both folktale and novel, Simha's reminder to Reuven of his duty to the living indicates that the narrator is also a "fifth son." Indeed, in the epilogue, the narrator reveals that his name is Ariel; he represents both the dead and the living.

Critical Context

The Fifth Son has elicited mixed commentary. Critics generally agree that the work is almost a poem, with its strong imagery, its terseness, and its carefully handled language. Praised for its sympathetic treatment of a sensitive subject—the feelings of children born to Holocaust survivors—Elie Wiesel's novel has also been hailed for its ambition of purpose, its poetry, its spare characterization, its brilliant use of novelistic techniques, and its masterly construction.

It is ironic that *The Fifth Son* has also been strongly criticized for those qualities often singled out as its strengths. Yet there are elements of truth in the criticism. To a certain extent, the structure is ill-conceived, the characters are almost faceless, and the novel's ambition goes largely unrealized. Occasionally, the novel is overwhelmed by its own technique. Oddest of all is the suspenseful unveiling of Ariel's identity and fate. Reuven's letters to Ariel slowly become more specific, slowly provide more information about who Ariel is; yet the final revelation is only a vague reference to the execution of a child.

Flaws of construction aside, what Elie Wiesel has produced in *The Fifth Son* is a thoughtful study of the least-known Holocaust victims: the children of survivors. How accurate that study is, only those children can say. Wiesel's book, however, is valuable because it makes all readers "children" of the Holocaust through its sympathetic portrayal of the feelings that isolate the survivors from the rest of society.

Sources for Further Study

Abrahamson, Irving, ed. *Against Silence: The Voice and Vision of Elie Wiesel*, 1985 (three volumes).
Brown, Robert McAfee. *Elie Wiesel: Messenger to All Humanity*, 1983.
Fine, Ellen S. *Legacy of Night: The Literary Universe of Elie Wiesel*, 1982.
Mano, D. Keith. "An Omen or Three," in *The National Review*. XXXVII (July 12, 1985), pp. 57-59.
Morton, Frederic. "Execution as an Act of Intimacy," in *The New York Times Book Review*. XC (March 24, 1985), p. 8.

Edelma Huntley

THE FIRST CIRCLE

Author: Aleksandr Solzhenitsyn (1918-   )
Type of plot: Historical realism
Time of plot: December, 1949
Locale: Suburban Moscow
First published: V kruge pervom, 1968 (English translation, 1968)

Principal characters:
GLEB NERZHIN, an unyielding prisoner who battles the system
LEV RUBIN, a dedicated Communist who has trouble reconciling the prisons and the ideals of the Party
DMITRI SOLOGDIN, a cunning prisoner who tries to trade his knowledge for his freedom
COLONEL YAKANOV, who is in charge of the research laboratory and fearful of failing Stalin

The Novel

The First Circle takes place over four days at the end of 1949. The novel is a virtual anatomy of Russian society in the late 1940's. Solzhenitsyn dissects a wide range of social and character types within that society, including the prisoners, guards, free workers, prosecutors, government officials and ministers, and even the supreme ruler of that society, Joseph Stalin. The center of this society, however, is, for Aleksandr Solzhenitsyn, not the political or social leader but the prison, the gulag system established by Stalin. All other characters and levels of society are tested by the standard of the moral and realistic vision of the *zek*, the familiar term for a prisoner.

The novel is set in the hell of the Stalinist prison system, but it begins in the "first circle" of that hell; Solzhenitsyn applies the categories of Dante's *Inferno* to the extensive prison system, and the "first circle" is easier and pleasanter than the usual labor camp, but it is still hell. The prisoners are deprived of their freedom of movement, of ownership of all but their meager clothes, of visits and letters from their loved ones. It is a psychological rather than a physical prison and is called a *sharaska*, which means a fake or sham. Paradoxically, since they are already in hell, they have more freedom to think, speak, and resist threats than those above them who fear the descent into the underworld.

In this privileged first circle, the prisoners are engaged in electronic work; predictably, that work has been perverted from its original purpose, and they are trying to find a safe phone for Stalin and a method of identifying "voice prints" on telephone calls for the secret police. The plot of the novel begins with a telephone call by Innokenty Volodin to warn Professor Dobroumov not to pass on medical information to the West. The seemingly aimless and unproductive work in the laboratory then takes on a sinister meaning. Will the prisoners create a system that will entrap Volodin? Will they manage to produce a "safe" phone for Stalin? At the end of the novel, the phone may be the means to freedom for one prisoner, Sologdin, but Volodin is captured and condemned to the "hell" of the gulag. In another allusion to Dante, the chapter in which Volodin is captured is called, "Abandon All Hope Ye Who Enter Here"—the words which greet those who enter Dante's Inferno.

The other plot interest in the novel is whether the main characters will remain in the sheltered alcove of the first circle of Marvino Laboratory or return to the hard labor of a Siberian camp. The three characters that are most at risk are Gleb Nerzhin, Lev Rubin, and Dmitri Sologdin. In his years in the prison system, Nerzhin has been writing a historical account of that system; clearly he is a spokesman for Solzhenitsyn, who suffered in the same prisons only to come out with the material for *Odin den Ivana Denisovicha* (1962; *One Day in the Life of Ivan Denisovich*, 1963) and other novels and historical writings. Nerzhin is an attractive character while, in contrast, Lev is more argumentative and dogmatic. His battles with Nerzhin and Sologdin lead to ruptures between them, especially when Rubin is trying to prove that the "Plowman," Stalin, is right to imprison so many people. Sologdin is more cunning than the other two. He is attempting to use the system against itself, while Nerzhin is writing a history of it and Rubin is supporting it.

The upper reaches of Soviet society are also precarious. The supervisor of Marvino is a Colonel Yakanov; he is being threatened by his superiors, who in turn are being threatened by Stalin. All of them, even the Minister of Security, Abakumov, fear becoming prisoners if they displease or annoy Stalin. This fear leads to rigid rules and classifications that stifle any creativity or dissent.

The center of this web and terror is Stalin, and Solzhenitsyn's portrait of the old and paranoid tyrant is memorable. He mocks Stalin's turgid style and shows him working at night alone and planning the destruction of others whom he fears. Stalin's final perception is that he can trust no one in the Soviet Union, and that distrust filters down to those who oversee the prisoners.

Despite this hierarchy of paranoia, Solzhenitsyn makes it clear that the fate of the prisoners is determined not by those who are placed over them but by the choices they themselves make. Rubin, for example, is forced to identify the voice of the man who warned Dobroumov about the danger of passing on medical knowledge. He narrows it to two persons, and in typical Stalinist fashion the two are arrested and sentenced. Rubin believes, however, that he has saved the lives of three other suspects who might have been arrested as well were it not for his voice identification, so his knowledge and dedication produce a small benefit.

Another type of choice is made by Sologdin. He has produced the solution of a safe phone for Stalin, but he burns the plans because he knows his superiors will claim the device as their own. Confronting Yakanov, Sologdin forces the colonel to give him credit and his freedom if he agrees to re-create his work. It is a wonderful example of the cunning of the prisoners in their dealings with their guards and superiors.

Nerzhin is offered a different sort of choice: He has the opportunity to join a mathematics group, and if the group discovers anything, he will be freed and returned to his earlier status. He refuses because the work would be abstract and interfere with his historical studies and because it is of no use to humanity. His experience in prison has led him to value the simple things in life. His rejection of an easier life and possible freedom results in his being sent back to a labor camp at the end of the novel. Although he has to destroy his historical writings, this is not a defeat but a victory of the spirit of the *zek*; Nerzhin knows that he can withstand the worst that the state can offer and survive, even triumph. A deeper and more important brotherhood between the prisoners arises when Nerzhin and the others are sent away, and he repeats the proverb: "It's not the sea that drowns you, it's the puddle." Leaving the sheltered but tempting laboratory for the harshness of the camp is a victory, and Nerzhin's return to the simplest and most important acts and feelings will help him grow as a human being.

The Characters

One important aspect of Solzhenitsyn's method of characterization is the brief history he provides for the prisoners and their superiors. These histories are often ironic: Those who have performed heroic deeds have been imprisoned, and those who are brutal and cruel are rewarded. For example, Rubin became a hero in World War II by convincing two towns to capitulate, but his sympathies for those people he captured led to his own arrest and sentence; as a good Communist, supporting the system that oppresses him, he awaits his acquittal. Nerzhin is in prison because he fought on the front against the Germans and therefore became suspect for his contacts with the West. The story of the janitor Spirodin is the most remarkable. He is a typical peasant who resists any attempt to sever him from his small plot of land; he will not fight for an abstraction called the state. He is loyal to his family and the older values of the Russian peasant. As a result, he has spent years in a prison camp and may never be released. His simple wisdom, which intrigues Nerzhin, is: "The wolfhound is right and the cannibal is wrong." (Spirodin contrasts the natural killer of wolves with the unnatural killer and devourer of men.)

While these and other characters in the novel are vividly realized, they are subordinate to Solzhenitsyn's larger design: *The First Circle* is intended to be a study of a system and a whole society.

Themes and Meanings

The First Circle portrays an upside-down society. In this strange world, the prisoners, the supposed Fascist scum, are the true communists, and the leaders are the ones who are cheating and benefiting from the unequal system. The debate between Clara Makarygin and her father, who is a prosecutor, reveals this paradox most clearly: He defends the benefits he receives as "accumulated labor," but he knows his answer is inadequate and he refuses to relinquish the benefits he receives from the system. The contrast between these two worlds is also shown in the way the prisoners help and care for one another; the few informers are exposed and ridiculed near the end of the novel, and they do not belong to the family of *zeks*. The leaders of the society do not act in this altruistic fashion; Yakanov obstructs the work at the laboratory so that his rival, Roitman, will not be victorious.

Another theme grows out of the many references to Dante. The prison may be only the "first circle" of hell, but the whole society is surely a hell, a kind of parody of the promised withering-away of the state in Marxist theory. In the center of the deepest circle of this hell is Joseph Stalin and not the *sharaska* or even a Siberian labor camp.

The gulag may be a hell, but it also is an opportunity to sort out what is important in life. Nerzhin sees his experience as a means of becoming an individual in the midst of a collective society. He first must develop a personal point of view and then "polish [his] soul so as to become *a human being*." That assertion of individuality does not, however, end within oneself; it will lead Nerzhin to become "a tiny particle of [his] own people." It is impossible for the leaders to become individuals; they have surrendered their individuality to the positions they hold, refusing the opportunity for suffering and growth. As one of the prisoners says, "Only a zek is certain to have an immortal soul."

Critical Context

The First Circle has a complex history. Although not Solzhenitsyn's first novel to be published, it was his first to be completed. He began it in 1955, while in exile in Kazakhstan, completing the first version in 1957. Despite the liberalization that followed Stalin's death, there was no hope at that time of publishing *The First Circle* in the Soviet Union; in fact, Solzhenitsyn destroyed several drafts of the novel rather than risk premature exposure. By 1962, when he published *One Day in the Life of Ivan Denisovich*, he had completed another redaction of *The First Circle*. This ninety-six-chapter version, however, contained material which, he believed, would still prevent its publication in the Soviet Union, so in submitting the novel for approval he prepared a self-censored eighty-seven-chapter version. When, after much debate, the novel was rejected for publication in the Soviet Union, it was this truncated version which appeared in the West. A restored text of the ninety-six-chapter version, with some additional changes made by Solzhenitsyn, was published in Russian in 1978 in the ongoing edition of his complete works which he is issuing from Vermont.

While there are significant differences between the version of *The First Circle* available in the West and the novel as Solzhenitsyn intended it, the substance of the work is intact. Earlier critical responses to the novel stressed its ideological content rather than its artistry, acknowledging the power of Solzhenitsyn's indictment of the Soviet system. Now, however, there is greater critical appreciation of Solzhenitsyn's art. Particularly noteworthy is what Solzhenitsyn himself has described as the novel's "polyphonic" style, in which no single character is at the center of the action; in Solzhenitsyn's words, "Each person becomes the main hero as soon as the action reverts to him." This approach allows Solzhenitsyn to present the conflicting world-views of an extraordinarily diverse range of characters.

Sources for Further Study
Ericson, Edward E., Jr. *Solzhenitsyn: The Moral Vision*, 1980.
Kodjak, Andrej. *Alexander Solzhenitsyn*, 1978.
Krasnov, Vladislav. *Solzhenitsyn and Dostoevsky: A Study in the Polyphonic Novel*, 1980.
Lukács, Georg. *Solzhenitsyn*, 1969.
Rothberg, Abraham. *Aleksandr Solzhenitsyn*, 1971.

James Sullivan

FIRST LOVE

Author: Ivan Turgenev (1818-1883)
Type of plot: Psychological realism
Time of plot: 1833
Locale: Moscow, a summer home near the Neskutchny gardens, and St.
  Petersburg
First published: Pervaya lyubov, 1860 (English translation, 1884)

> *Principal characters:*
> VLADIMIR PETROVICH, the romantic sixteen-year-old
>   protagonist
> PIOTR VASSILICH, Vladimir's father
> PRINCESS ZASYEKIN, the impoverished and widowed mother
>   of Zinaida
> ZINAIDA ALEXANDROVNA ZASYEKIN, a twenty-one-year-old
>   beauty

The Novel

Ivan Turgenev's *First Love* opens with a brief scene in which three apparently prosperous Russian gentlemen of the 1850's propose to amuse themselves by recounting the stories of their first loves. Although they are seen but briefly, these phlegmatic characters can be identified as "superfluous men," Turgenev's phrase for those who exist comfortably without awareness or purpose. Indeed, only Vladimir Petrovich, a middle-aged bachelor, has anything of interest to say on this romantic topic, reluctantly admitting that his first love "was not quite an ordinary one." He cautiously refuses to recount the tale to his companions immediately, insisting upon writing it out first and then reading it to them at a subsequent meeting. The first-person narrative that describes Vladimir Petrovich's experience during the summer of his sixteenth year is framed by Turgenev's introductory scene, thus presenting the story of Vladimir's love for Zinaida as a remembrance of a vanished past and underscoring the tension between the naïve youth whom the reader sees in the narrative and the mature man who tells the tale.

In the narrative, Vladimir Petrovich is portrayed as a sensitive and somewhat confused sixteen-year-old filled with a "delicious sense of youth and effervescent life." He accompanies his parents to their summer home outside Moscow with the intention of studying for his university entrance examinations. Vladimir is distracted, however, by awakening romantic yearnings: "a half-conscious, shamefaced presentiment of something new, unutterably sweet, feminine. . . ."

This presentiment becomes incarnate when Princess Zasyekin, a vulgar and impoverished widow, rents the dilapidated home next to his family's, and

Vladimir has the opportunity to meet Zinaida, Princess Zasyekin's beautiful twenty-one-year-old daughter. Almost immediately, Zinaida becomes the focus of Vladimir's romantic obsession. His adolescent desire is encouraged when Zinaida allows him to join in her nightly entertainment of an entourage of older courtiers. Although this odd assortment of suitors, who represent a variety of military, intellectual, and artistic accomplishments, are considerably older than Vladimir, they repeatedly display a humiliatingly adolescent devotion to Zinaida, humoring her whims and playing parlor games in which she toys with their emotions.

Zinaida treats Vladimir affectionately, but it is impossible for him to overcome his sense of immaturity. She playfully names Vladimir her page, a title which gives him a special place in her chivalric fantasy while simultaneously emphasizing his youth. His frustrating sense of inexperience is heightened when he gradually realizes that she is in love, a realization that becomes evident when she recounts her dream of meeting a romantic and dominating stranger in a garden. Vladimir tortures himself over the identity of Zinaida's lover, and lost in the grip of his romantic passion, he even considers murder and stations himself with a knife outside Zinaida's home. His bloody intentions are shattered by the appearance of his father and the revelation that Piotr Vassilich is Zinaida's lover. This unexpected knowledge throws Vladimir into a painful state of emotional confusion.

The family's stay in the country is cut short by Maria Nikolevna's discovery of her husband's infidelity. The bitter recriminations that follow show Vladimir the lovelessness of his parents' marriage, but their return to Moscow shows that the pragmatic concerns of appearance and money continue to hold them together.

The climactic scene in the novella occurs shortly after the family's return to Moscow. Vladimir goes riding with his father and inadvertently witnesses a secretive meeting between Piotr and Zinaida. In a revelatory moment, he sees his father become angry and strike Zinaida with his riding crop only to rush into her arms subsequently. This reversal of control—the Zinaida who once ruled over her parlor suitors now accepts physical abuse—forces Vladimir to realize that experiential passion is more complex than romantic fiction. It makes Vladimir feel that his love "with all its transports and sufferings" had been "something small and childish and pitiful beside this other unimagined something. . . ."

The concluding chapter of *First Love* recounts the early death of Piotr, who warns his son on his deathbed to "'fear the love of woman; fear that bliss, that poison. . . .'" It then tells of Vladimir's unexpected opportunity to see Zinaida four years later, after she has married. His emotional uncertainty repeatedly causes him to delay his visit to her hotel. When he eventually calls on her, he discovers that she died in childbirth a few days before. Although this final chapter does not describe the middle-aged Vladimir reading to his companions, its tone of regret, despair, and even horror effectively completes the narrative frame by reminding the reader of the aging narrator.

The Characters

Turgenev modestly claimed that a lack of imagination always forced him to work from known characters. He also wrote that *First Love* was largely autobiographical, based on an affair his father carried on with a beautiful neighbor. To whatever extent the novella accurately portrays the adolescent experiences of Turgenev, the subtle exploration of character is central to *First Love*, which focuses on the love triangle of Piotr, Vladimir, and Zinaida.

Piotr believes in will and the power of the individual to act. He rejects responsibilities to family or to abstract codes of behavior. He is a creature of passion, but he never seems out of control. Just as he has a rare knack for breaking horses, he is able to dominate the people and situations around him. In a rare communicative moment, Piotr advises his son to "[t]ake for yourself what you can, and don't be ruled by others; to belong to oneself— the whole savour of life lies in that. . . ." His willful independence parallels that of Bazarov in *Ottsy i deti* (1862; *Fathers and Sons*, 1867), the novel Turgenev finished soon after publishing *First Love*. Unlike Bazarov, Turgenev's best-known protagonist, who adheres to a nihilistic rationalism, Piotr pursues the ephemeral ideal of passion. Eventually this unending pursuit consumes him, as his deathbed warning indicates.

Like Piotr, Zinaida is a willful character. Part saint and part temptress, she uses her beauty to escape the vulgarity and limitations of her situation. Her frivolity contrasts with the litigious and financial preoccupations of her mother. Her teasing games allow her to assert control over her suitors, and she seems to enjoy their helpless humiliation as much as she enjoys their companionship. The novella reveals, however, that her careless independence disguises a desire to be mastered: "[O]ut there . . . waits he whom I love, who holds me in his power." This hidden need to be conquered is graphically revealed in the scene in which Piotr strikes her with his riding crop as though he were reprimanding an unruly mount.

Because of Turgenev's narrative frame, Vladimir exists as two separate characters: the young protagonist of the novella and the middle-aged narrator. The youthful Vladimir is a creation of his own reading, trying to live through his first love as though it were a romantic novel, continually imagining himself in the role of hero and idealizing the object of his love: "I began picturing to myself how I would save her from the hands of enemies; how, covered with blood I would tear her by force from prison, and expire at her feet." As Zinaida's page, Vladimir imagines winning her according to the code of chivalry, but despite his dreams of heroic victory, he is incapable of decisive action when presented with evidence of Zinaida's true nature. He enacts an imitation of adult passion without understanding it. He reacts to the climactic scene in which his father strikes Zinaida by recognizing the childish simplicity of his own love, but he still cannot understand fully the contradictions of the passion he witnesses. To him it seems "like an unknown, beautiful, but menacing face, which one strives in vain to make out clearly in the half-darkness. . . ."

The middle-aged Vladimir who narrates the story has never fully recovered from the disillusionment of his youth. Although his maturity has enabled him to sympathize with the passion of his father and Zinaida, he has not experienced it himself. Indeed, he implies that such love is tragically doomed, a bright flame that must burn itself out. His only response to the contemplation of life's beauty and brevity is a concluding desire to pray.

Themes and Meanings

First Love is a story of maturation in which the naïve protagonist is initiated into the painful ironies of adult life and love. At the start of the narrative, Vladimir's emotions and behavior are shaped by the romantic fiction he has read. He is blinded to the complexities of experience by his naïve idealism, but he learns a more mature sight through two painful, revelatory experiences: the discovery that his father is Zinaida's lover and his observation of his father striking Zinaida. These experiences show Vladimir the limitations of his own romantic illusions and intimate that mature love is psychologically mysterious, a risky emotional state that is full of both appeal and threat.

First Love is, thus, a commentary on romanticism, a story that defines romantic idealism's failure to describe experiential reality. The code of chivalry is shown to be an inadequate guide to the labyrinth of love, but the alternative, Piotr and Zinaida's hedonistic passion, is shown to be inevitably destructive. Both the adolescent and mature forms of love are ephemeral, and Turgenev's story offers no other happy path to follow. When the middle-aged Vladimir considers the intense emotions of his youth, he realizes that nothing else in his life has equaled them: "I should not wish it ever to come again: but I should think myself unfortunate had I never experienced such an emotion." The story condemns neither Vladimir's naïve idealism nor Piotr and Zinaida's self-justifying hedonism; instead, the middle-aged Vladimir expresses sympathy for all who experience love, for life and love eventually end: "[I] longed to pray for her, for my father—and for myself." Thus, *First Love* expands from a discussion of a particular youth's maturation to become a poignant statement about the human condition.

Psychologically, *First Love* explores the theme of dominance and subjugation. The central characters compete for control of their relationships, and the novella effectively displays the ironies of such competition: Zinaida manipulates her suitors while secretly longing to be dominated; Piotr conquers Zinaida only to find himself consumed by the poison of passion; Maria uses financial threats to force Piotr to maintain outward appearances but wins only a loveless marriage.

Critical Context

Turgenev categorized his fiction according to length, but these two types also differ in purpose. His major novels—*Rudin* (1856; *Dimitri Roudine*, 1873; better known as *Rudin*, 1947), *Dvoryanskoye gnezdo* (1859; *Liza*, 1869; also as *A Nobleman's Nest*, 1869; better known as *A House of Gentlefolk*, 1894), *Nakanune* (1860; *On the Eve*, 1871), *Ottsy i deti* (1862; *Fathers and Sons*, 1867), *Dym* (1867; *Smoke*, 1868), and *Nov* (1877; *Virgin Soil*, 1877)—are clearly preoccupied with social issues. Turgenev's novels effectively present the social structures and concerns of Russian society in the middle of the nineteenth century. Turgenev's shorter novellas are more personal and universal, focusing on the timeless themes of love and maturation. They are stories of emotional incident, and, of these, *First Love* and *Veshniye vody* (1872; *Spring Floods*, 1874; better known as *The Torrents of Spring*, 1897) are Turgenev's most enduring.

Because of its inclusion in many college-level literature anthologies, *First Love* is better known to American readers than any of Turgenev's other works, with the possible exception of *Fathers and Sons*. While the social commentary of Turgenev's novels has lessened their interest for some modern readers, the universality of *First Love* has helped maintain its popularity.

Sources for Further Study

Hart, Pierre R. "The Passionate Page: Turgenev's *First Love* and Dostoevsky's *The Little Hero*," in *New Perspectives on Nineteenth-century Russian Prose*, 1982.

Mirsky, Dmitry S. *A History of Russian Literature*, 1949.

Pritchett, V. S. *The Gentle Barbarian: The Life and Work of Turgenev*, 1977.

Schapiro, Leonard. *Turgenev: His Life and Times*, 1979.

Carl Brucker

THE FLANDERS ROAD

Author: Claude Simon (1913-   )
Type of plot: Romance
Time of plot: From 1940 to 1945
Locale: Northeastern France, Nazi Germany, and Paris
First published: La Route des Flandres, 1960 (English translation, 1961)

> *Principal characters:*
> GEORGES, the narrator, a solider and prisoner of war who is
>   obsessed with Corinne
> DE REIXACH, Georges's commanding officer and Corinne's
>   cuckolded husband
> CORINNE, de Reixach's wife, the object of Georges's desire,
>   and Iglesia's mistress
> IGLESIA, a jockey employed by de Reixach and a member of
>   de Reixach's ill-fated military detachment
> BLUM, Georges's Jewish comrade and fellow prisoner of war

The Novel

   The Flanders Road, the work for which Claude Simon, the winner of the 1985 Nobel Prize for Literature, is best known in the English-speaking world, is a brilliant and satisfying novel on a number of levels. The novel appeals to the reader not least because of its dazzling demonstration of the ways in which various facets of public, private, historical, and erotic experience can be associated, dissociated, unexpectedly and exhilaratingly combined, and tragically divorced. The germ of the novel's inspiration is Simon's own family history and, to a greater extent, his experiences during the fall of France in 1940.

   The novel's plot, though the least obvious and to some extent the least significant aspect of the whole work, deals with the narrator, Georges, and his reactions to the death from a sniper's bullet of his military commander, de Reixach, during an ambush into which de Reixach has perhaps knowingly gone. This event leads to Georges's capture by the advancing German troops and to his incarceration in a prison camp for the remainder of the war. During that time, Georges's mind plays back and forth on de Reixach's action, on the commander's family history, and particularly on de Reixach's wife, the alluring Corinne. The novel concludes with Georges's erotic assignation with Corinne after the war is over.

   The fabric of the novel is suspended between two climactic events, the first being the killing by sniper of the narrator's commanding officer, and the second being a night of love shared by the narrator and that officer's wife immediately after the liberation of France. Between these two events, the novel weaves its complex, exploratory texture, invoking memory, desire, varieties of history, and contemporary exigencies in what becomes an embarrassment of imagistic, symbolic, and philosophical riches. Readers familiar with the narrative methods of Marcel Proust, William Faulkner, and James Joyce— novelists whom Simon has acknowledged as his major influences—will have some inkling of what to expect, though added to the lessons of these masters in *The Flanders Road* is strong and arresting evidence of the author's prolonged involvement with the visual arts, particularly painting. There are moments in this novel when the only word sufficient to describe the effects being created is "ravishing." Given Simon's preoccupation with repetition and the ambiguity which is the inevitable result of his narrator's all-too-human instability of perspective, it is appropriate to consider ravishment itself as a double entendre expressing the impact of beauty and the effect of violence— a term applicable to the novel's two definitive realities, love and war.

The interval between the death of de Reixach, under whom the narrator, Georges, has been serving, and the erotic encounter between Georges and Corinne, is spent, for the most part (in a physical sense), in a Nazi prisoner-of-war camp. Nevertheless, the obvious physical constraint of such a context, while periodically intruding on the narrative, functions also as a pretext for Georges's inner life to assume preeminence. It is not the dehumanizing conditions of the prison that claim the reader's most intense concern. Rather, it is to those elements of the individual's makeup which are so uniquely and distinctively human to which the narrative and the narrator turn. In Simon's terms, these elements are expressed by Georges's twin capacities to remember and to desire, capacities which are given free rein by the novel's stream-of-consciousness narrative technique.

Georges's thoughts are largely consumed with de Reixach, to whom he is distantly related and who carries an ancient and honorable name. There is enough evidence from the incident in which de Reixach was killed to suggest that he went knowingly to his death and in effect committed suicide. A reason for his doing so is the disgrace he had sustained because his wife was having an affair with a lowly employee, Iglesia the jockey. The willfulness of Corinne's behavior, its challenge to the politesse embodied by her husband's name and heritage, is as much a source of ardent reflection for Georges as is de Reixach's final act. Georges's consciousness, which is the signature of his humanity and his means of sustaining himself in the dark days of imprisonment, has been authorized by, and seeks authentication in, the experiences of this couple. Thus, *The Flanders Road* attains its power not because of the dramatic nature of its narrative material but because of that material's effect on a consciousness which is seduced by it.

This novel's elevation of aftermath over motive, and of the mind's rhythms over the body's stagnation, is not given its most crucial expression by a character's specific action or statement, since every action or statement in the novel exists in the shadow of its opposite. What gives *The Flanders Road* its characteristic priorities is its formal nature. The novel begins as if it were a complex, but nevertheless direct, reflective account of Georges's wartime experience, but the reader soon realizes that it may be more accurately read as an explosion of memory ignited by Georges's night with Corinne. The interchangeability and interdependence of these two narrative perspectives provide the reader's potential, temporary disorientation, placing the experience of the text on the same provisional but engrossing level as Georges's restless analysis of de Reixach and Corinne. In the enactment of the fundamentally tentative and experimental procedures of consciousness lies this novel's unique reality.

The Characters

Despite the fact that the main characters, except Georges, are filtered through Georges's consciousness, *The Flanders Road* conveys a strong sense of character. This is particularly true of de Reixach, who emerges as a formidable web of complex issues concerning human nature and historical destiny. Severe and punctilious to a fault in maintaining the social position which his name and heritage commands, de Reixach is also perceived to be inscrutable. Did he, or did he not, allow his death to occur in the ambush? What exactly was his attitude toward Corinne's infidelity? De Reixach's inscrutability—which seemingly exists between the folds of an ambiguity embraced by cowardice and its opposite, stoicism—can be readily seen to be the product of his aristocratic demeanor, all the more so since his own end parallels that of one of his eighteenth century forebears.

In the case of Corinne, however, Simon alters his approach, or rather gives Georges a different mode of perception. In contrast to de Reixach, Corinne is seen in glimpses, at a distance, posed, suggestive. She remains an object of desire, whereas her husband is an emblem of that desire's defeat and of other defeats which ensue. In depicting Corinne, the author's painterly training is seen to spectacular advantage. The pictorializing effects have a peculiar appropriateness in the portrayal of Corinne, however, as they release vividly and persuasively the sensuality which she embodies. While de Reixach, Corinne, and the state of their marriage were vaguely known to Georges prior to de Reixach's death, Corinne is kept at a distance until the climax of her brief, troubling erotic encounter with Georges. Thus, it is not necessarily the physical reality of Corinne which is the object of Georges's preoccupations. It is the potential for love, for beauty, for pleasure which she embodies for him which sustains him. She is the counterpart to her husband's militarism. Her commitment to living in the present, typified by her affair with Iglesia, is the opposite of her husband's historical inheritance. Yet the two are indissolubly linked, each inescapably implicated in the other's fate.

Both de Reixach and Corinne are animated by the intensity of Georges's quest for the truth about them. In contrast, therefore—or as a means of enacting through the cast of characters the sense of doubleness which pervades *The Flanders Road*—the reader is also provided with characters lacking in mystery. These are Iglesia and Blum. Both characters serve to remind Georges that the world is also a material entity. Blum performs this service in the prison camp; Iglesia performs it in the de Reixach household. The ability to face and accommodate a given reality, to exist within and abide by the opportunities of the here and now, are what both these characters personify, each functioning as an antidote to the more internalized reality represented by the central trio of characters.

The crucial figure of that trio is Georges. Not only do the actual physical realities of both de Reixach and Corinne affect him profoundly, but also the readings which he conjures up out of the unadorned fact of the physical being affect him just as much, if not more. It is these readings, however, insatiably scanning the spectrum of experience embraced by de Reixach and Corinne (war and love) in order to discern motivation, certainty, and understanding, which sustain Georges and which give him the authoritative reality of the novel's narrator. Georges embodies the spirit and value of quest, of the mind's invincibility, and of the salvific nature of desire. Because of his mind's restlessness, Georges is the novel's most changeable character, and the shifts in narrative perspective which he brings about and to which he is subjected underline his mutability. Yet the very openness which the mutability brings about places him at the human, problematical center of the novel.

Themes and Meanings

Commenting on *The Flanders Road*, Claude Simon has drawn attention to its cloverleaf structure, thereby underlining the principles of doubling and repetition upon which this novel is structured. The physical presence around which the cloverleaf is drawn is the corpse of a horse killed in the ambush in which de Reixach dies. As in other instances in *The Flanders Road*, however, physicality is both a reality in its own right and the pretext for the mind's efforts and anxiety to give form to the abstract. Thus, while the horse's remains have significance as a casualty of war, and are the occasion for some striking meditations on the depredations of warfare, they also achieve greater significance by facilitating motifs of recurrence and duality.

These motifs are given their most sustained force in the manner in which the novel deals with time, a manner which provides the most obvious basis for its kinship with some of the great works of modernist fiction. Time is experienced in two ways in the novel. As a general, abstract phenomenon, it is present—to Georges, particularly—as an ineluctable, irreversible force whose iron path is starkly denoted by Georges's rail journey to the prison camp.

That journey shows Georges in the grip of time, at the disposal of an agency which he cannot control: It is noteworthy that his condition is made synonymous with defeat and with the impotence that defeat confers. In the camp, however, Georges rehabilitates himself thanks to his memory, or, in effect, experiences time as relative, subjective, malleable. The coexistence of both views of time, the interplay between them, and the fact that not only Georges but also de Reixach and Corinne experience time in the same way create the source of the novel's conceptual and psychological richness. While the last word of *The Flanders Road* is a grim tribute to the indifference and destructiveness of time in its objective character, there has been enough during the course of the novel to suggest that the alternative version of time has something of a saving grace.

The novel's other main themes, concerning the operation of history and the force of desire, stem essentially from Simon's investigation of time. A distinctive feature of the undertaking, however, is the degree to which cause, effect, intention, and accident are relativized, preventing the reader from eliciting any one solution to the problems adumbrated. The novel's relativity supports its sense of the tentative and unknowable, a sense which both validates and frustrates the questing mind that keeps Georges alive.

Critical Context

Claude Simon is one of the foremost practitioners of the experimental fiction which came to the fore in France immediately after World War II, known as *le nouveau roman* (the New Novel). The basic objective of this approach to fiction, as set forth by the most noted theoretician among its practitioners, Alain Robbe-Grillet, was to create fiction which would eschew the debts to documentation and photography incurred by realist fiction. While none of the New Novelists necessarily agreed as to the specific direction such a development might take, their diverse works have had a considerable influence on contemporary fiction and narrative theory.

The fiction of Claude Simon is worthy of special attention, however, and will continue to command notice when the works of some of his fellow New Novelists have come to be regarded as literary curiosities. The lushness of his imagery, the passion of his attentiveness, his psychological suppleness and narrative flexibility, and his profound and unrelenting exposure of man's existential frailty and persistence—these qualities mark Simon as a great writer.

Sources for Further Study

Birn, Randi, and Karen Gould, eds. *Orion Blinded: Essays on Claude Simon*, 1981.

Gould, Karen L. *Claude Simon's Mythic Muse*, 1979.

Levin, Martin. Review in *The New York Times Book Review*. LXVI (May 21, 1961), p. 5.

Loubere, J. A. E. *The Novels of Claude Simon*, 1975.
Mercier, Vivian. *A Reader's Guide to the New Novel*, 1971.
Sturrock, John. *The French New Novel: Claude Simon, Michel Butor, Alain Robbe-Grillet*, 1969.

George O'Brien

THE FLOUNDER

Author: Günter Grass (1927-　　)
Type of plot: Magical realism
Time of plot: From the neolithic period to the late 1970's
Locale: Germany and Poland
First published: Der Butt, 1977 (English translation, 1978)

> *Principal characters:*
> THE NARRATOR, a writer who has lived many lives throughout
> 　history
> ILSEBILL, his wife
> THE FLOUNDER, the mythical fish who has advised men
> 　throughout history
> THE NINE COOKS, the women who have cooked for the nar-
> 　rator during his many lives

The Novel

　The Flounder examines the issues inherent in the age-old war between the sexes. Written in the first person, the novel is a long chronicle in which every aspect of this war is examined by the author. Beginning with the neolithic period and proceeding through modern times, Günter Grass leaves no feminist issue unchallenged, no sexist stone unturned. Even the way in which the chapters are arranged (in nine monthly headings signifying the pregnancy of the narrator's current wife, Ilsebill) indicates that the war has not abated, that it will continue long after the novel has finished.

　The novel begins in the neolithic period, with the catching of a flounder by a primitive fisherman. This flatfish is no ordinary fish but a magical entity who teaches the primitive fisherman many things: how to count on his fingers, how to explore outside his local domain, and how to subjugate the womenfolk of his clan.

　The neolithic fisherman, the reader is informed, is only one of the many lives of the narrator. In fact, by the end of the novel, this same narrator has passed through at least nine different periods of history under dozens of guises and occupations. Throughout this time, the Flounder remains his spiritual adviser, ready at any moment to be summoned from the sea for advice on how to run the world. This arrangement continues for centuries.

　One day, in the late 1970's, three feminists who are fishing in Lübeck Bay catch the Flounder—or rather, he allows himself to be caught. The fish, to their surprise, bluntly informs them that he is tired of serving men, that men have ruined the world. He now wants to help women run things. Women, he insists, are the only salvation of the world.

　The feminists, instead of accepting his offer, decide that the Flounder should be tried as a criminal, a war criminal, for his many offenses against womankind. They drop him into a tank of seawater and ship him back to Berlin to stand trial before a tribunal of women.

The remainder of the book, its bulk, alternates between the many different lives of the narrator and the trial of the Flounder. The way in which the book moves between historical periods serves as a means of seeing both the past and the present. The narrator might talk about himself, for example, as a sword-smith in the Middle Ages and expound on what the relationship with his wife was like. Then he will invariably turn to the women's tribunal to get the views of that time period. This device allows the narrator to view the historical differences and relationships between the sexes from a variety of perspectives.

The narrator proceeds in great detail, following each of his lives more or less in historical order but always returning to the tribunal to gain the women's opinions. He also manages to balance his own views with those of whatever woman happens to be his cook at the time. Although seemingly a sexist label, "cook" is probably the most appropriate term for these women simply because that was the only thing they all had in common. Not all were wives, lovers, or even companions to the narrator. Yet all of them cooked for him.

The cooks vary greatly between historical periods. In the neolithic period, his cook is named Awa. She is ruler of the tribe, possessor of three breasts. This is a point in history when matriarchy is in the ascendancy, when men serve women in blissful ignorance. This is also the time when the Flounder enters the scene, advising the narrator on how to forge iron, make axes, and start war. Soon thereafter, Awa loses her third breast, and the matriarchy begins to crumble.

The cooks serve as links to the history of women. There is Metswina, who lives in the pagan Europe of the sixth century and is hanged for the murder of a dour Christian missionary. There is Fat Gret, a plump abbess in a medieval convent, who rules the town with her wit and cast-iron pot of soup. There is Dorothea, the narrator's wife at the time of the Crusades, who indulges in acts of masochism in the name of Christ; it is her hope to be canonized eventually. There is Sophie, a Prussian cook who poisons five officers of Napoleon's army because they were holding her betrothed in prison. Finally, there is Lena Stubbe, the wife of a Danzig dockyard worker; she invented the proletarian cookbook at the beginning of the twentieth century.

One by one, the narrator writes about his cooks, often devoting more space to their stories than to his own. His most important cook, however, is his late wife, Ilsebill. She is the woman carrying his child. Much of the narrative is an ongoing argument between Ilsebill and the narrator about the inherent differences between the sexes. This argument seems to have no end.

In the meantime, the woman's tribunal is also examining the lives of these women, attempting to determine whether the Flounder is guilty of helping the male to oppress them. The cooks take affidavits, they submit documents, and they file motions. The Flounder makes long, rhetorical speeches about the differences between the sexes; the prosecutor objects to these speeches; and the defense lawyer objects to her objections. In the end, the trial becomes a media circus.

In the process, the group raises questions about fundamental issues such as domesticity, romantic love, strength, masculinity, and femininity. In addition it manages to make its own survey of history, as a counterpoint to the character-lives of the narrator. When the stories are all told and the closing arguments are made, the tribunal renders its verdict against the Flounder: guilty on all counts. The group sentences the guilty flatfish to a huge banquet held in front of him in which the main course is baked flounder. The tribunal eats the meal with relish and then, as a final gesture of contempt, throws the bare fish bones into the Flounder's tank.

Eventually, despite an assassination attempt by a group of radical feminists, the Flounder is dumped back into the Baltic Sea by members of the tribunal, with his promise that he will serve womankind forever. He is, one might say, on parole.

The Characters

The narrative stance and characterization of this book are quite clever. By claiming to have passed through so many lives, the narrator can not only write in the first person but also maintain an omniscient viewpoint. He has seen history not through the eyes of God but through a number of different characters. He has the best of both narrative worlds. By virtue of having lived so many lives, the narrator can also take on a variety of personalities. He is a simpering, young boy in one life and a brutal wife-beating husband in another. He moves like a specter across the spectrum of possible personalities, becoming one type then transforming into another. He is never constricted by his characters, for they change with the era in which they live and with their station in life. Some are bishops, others fishermen. All are shaped by the circumstances of their lives. In this way, the narrator can be both himself and any other man he chooses.

Similarly, the female characters vary greatly. Some are kind. Others are cruel. Still others show elements of both qualities. Even though there are probably thirty different women in this book (the vast majority of characters are women), Grass manages to draw a distinct personality for each one. None, not even the most minor of characters, seems like an archetype. All have their quirks, foibles, and idiosyncrasies.

With so many characters, Grass is able to look at women in many different stations and personalities. By the same token, depicting so many different women precludes any one woman from becoming a major character. While there are those—Awa, Dorothea, Sophie, and Fat Gret—who have their stories told at length, none of them appears more than briefly over the whole span of the novel. For the many times her name is mentioned, there is little told about the narrator's beloved Ilsebill. In the end, Ilsebill becomes little more than the person to whom the narrator is directing his long narrative.

In fact, apart from the narrator, the Flounder is the only major character who appears regularly throughout the novel. In contrast to the narrator, however, the character of the mythical flatfish does not change as the centuries pass. He simply stays what he has always been: a magical, pompous, and long-winded fish who often gives bad advice.

As a character, the Flounder is both human and godlike. He is capable of making mistakes as his service to the male species reveals. Yet he is capable of rectifying his mistakes. His advice to women and his magic will redeem him. In a sense, the mythical flatfish (first made famous by the Brothers Grimm) is the perfect symbol for the war between the sexes. Neither man nor woman, he is neutral in the struggle but is slippery enough to take sides.

Themes and Meanings

The fairy tale upon which this novel is based, "The Fisherman and His Wife," is a story of the war between the sexes. In it, the wife is eventually done in by the flounder because of her incessant greed. The moral of the story is that women are essentially self-indulgent, dissatisfied beings who deserve no better status than what history has accorded them.

The Flounder sets out to reinterpret history through this same fairy tale, again using the flounder as its main metaphor. This time, however, instead of denouncing the greed of women, the Flounder decries the travesties—wars, starvation, and pollution—that men have brought upon the world. He is, in a sense, the conscience of humankind, ready to swing his magical powers in favor of the sex that can change the world.

It is little wonder that the Flounder takes this position, for throughout the novel, women nourish the world. Whenever food is mentioned—and it is mentioned often—it is the women who are cooking it and thereby providing their menfolk with sustenance. While the men talk about such things as religion, war, and plagues, the women do the practical chores of daily life— chores which keep those around them alive.

Symbols such as churches, castles, and political offices are always important to the men. These symbols, which determine ways of life, have often been associated with violence: early Christian crusades that brought wholesale slaughter to villages, Socialist riots that sparked vengeful shootings, and male festivities that inspired gang rapes. Yet, food, in its many guises, has always meant happiness and fulfillment. This basic symbol, always associated with the women, the providers, is the one symbol that has lasted throughout history, lasted longer than even the wars, the plagues, and the famines. If, as the Flounder would have it, women begin to rule the world, then this food, this sustenance, will replace democracy, capitalism, and socialism and become the symbol of a new dawn—not only for women but also for all humankind.

Critical Context

The Flounder is Grass's most important work, and it represents a new height in the literature of postwar Germany. Two of Grass's other novels, *Die Blechtrommel* (1959; *The Tin Drum*, 1961) and *Hundejahre* (1963; *Dog Years*, 1965) were successful literary endeavors in a Germany that had focused its view on World War II. Both are written in a style which straddles realism and fantasy, and both deal with the war. *The Flounder*, however, was written in the late 1970's and broke this fixation on World War II. This novel took on an even older war, the war between the sexes. Observing the growing feminist movement in Germany, Grass sought to grapple with the fundamental issues facing both genders. He was not content, however, to view these issues with the myopia common to most of his contemporaries. Instead, he wanted to go back to the root of the struggle, back to the dawn of history.

With this in mind, he delved into the history of his native northern Germany to show both the male and female perspectives through specific characters. This undertaking, to retell history through characters without rendering them mere archtypes, would be too ambitious for most writers. For Grass, it was clearly a success.

Sources for Further Study

Hayman, Ronald. *Günter Grass*, 1985.
Hunt, Irmgard Elsner. *Mutter und Muttermythose in Günter Grass' Roman "Der Butt,"* 1983.
Keele, Alan Frank. *Understanding Günter Grass*, 1987.
Mews, Siegfried. *"The Fisherman and His Wife": Günter Grass's "The Flounder" in Critical Perspective*, 1983.
Pickar, Gertrud Bauer. *Adventures of a Flounder: Critical Essays on Günter Grass's "Der Butt,"* 1982.

Michael Verdon

"FOOLS SAY"

Author: Nathalie Sarraute (1900-   )
Type of plot: New Novel
Time of plot: Unspecified
Locale: Unspecified
First published: "*Disent les imbéciles,*" 1976 (English translation, 1977)

> *Principal characters:*
> This Sarrautean *nouveau roman*, or New Novel, offers nei-
> ther the characters nor the plot of the traditional novel. In-
> stead, a number of different unidentified voices speak in
> reaction to one another and in unspecified contexts.

The Novel

"*Fools Say*" is composed of thirteen sections which embody the subdia-
logue or subconversation of unidentified individuals. Nathalie Sarraute deals
with what she calls "tropisms," which may be defined as one's immediate reactions, in all of their minutiae, to outside stimuli. ("Tropism" is a biological
term which refers to an organism being either attracted to or repelled by a
stimulus.) These tropisms, substrata of psychological reactions, constitute a
nonverbal reality to which Sarraute assigns words. The hidden depths of a
person's emotional or psychological complexity lie far beneath any rational
patterns of behavior. At this level, human psychology is in constant flux.
Sarraute focuses on these ephemeral responses because human beings—
regardless of group, gender, creed, color, or nationality—participate in this
tropistic realm.

In re-creating such subtle psychological data, Sarraute ignores the fully
developed characters which, in a traditional novel, provide readers with a
sense of reality. She eliminates any appeal to outside or verifiable reality
through her use of shifting voices in contexts which are completely open to
speculation and interpretation. While the pronouns shift dizzyingly, each
voice in "*Fools Say*" seems to exist because of a need to find a secure place
amid the voices in conflict. Only glimpses of relationships are perceived. The
progression of the novel is circular; from the fears in adolescence to the fears
of so-called adulthood, the nightmarish suspicion persists that one does not
exist or will not be heard. Subtle fusions of thought and feeling at the level of
the tropism constitute human reality for this author. Because of the constant
shift of voices, there is no way of rephrasing the experience that each reader
will have when plunged into this intangible, always malleable reality as re-
created by Sarraute.

For Sarraute, man's linguistic arsenals, all of his categories, theories, and
systems, lead him to conclude falsely that there is a word for everything. Fur-

thermore, man argues—again falsely—that anything which does not fit into his linguistic schemes is not real. He has created a grid of platitudes and clichés by which he categorizes and judges others, but which he insists cannot be applied to himself. Thus, man's willingness to define others but not himself reveals the pretension and hypocrisy which make him vulnerable to Sarraute's lethal irony. Each person's attempt to create a harmonious world for himself, by allotting roles for others to play, can lead to nothing but one more cage created by words.

Each voice or idea might be secure in its own narrated construct, but it would cease to exist, as ideas atrophy if they are not exposed. Yet an idea might be destroyed in free discussion. Thus, the lure of imposing or attempting to impose one's ideas on others is clearly irresistible. To attempt to define the world on one's own terms leads to an ongoing struggle, in which some voices will prevail and others will be canceled, and everything will be altered by clamoring demands for acceptance and recognition. In the conflict of voices as each seeks to make his use of words the accepted ones, any idea which does not serve some entrenched power is irrelevant. In the context of this novel, those who seek to maintain power by controlling the use of words, those who insist that anyone who disputes this power is a fool, are fools. Political dictators are not as powerful as the established arbiters of words.

There is no resolution to this ongoing battle; there are no victories in humanity's conflict over words. If people control words, they are also controlled by words. If reality is defined by words, even the arbiters or supporters of hierarchy are vulnerable, regardless of whether they know it. If one does not accept the status quo and authority, one is pilloried as a fool. If one argues that those who function within categories and hierarchies are themselves fools, one will be attacked. To be silent is to give consent to a petrified and self-serving power structure. To find that one has no words which are effective is to find that one is crazy.

The voices in this novel emit opinions, promote incomplete arguments, and struggle to escape inner conflicts; generally, outside authority prevails in what must be described as a terrorist world. The novel begins with a grandson ordering others away because they have reduced his grandmother to an object. He is accused of jealousy, of believing that his grandmother belongs solely to him (he is told that authorities have proved that jealousy and hatred always go together), and he recants in horror, pleading madness. As the novel ends, with a voice protesting, "no, he didn't think, he can't think, he must have gotten the words from someone else, he can't remember," it is clear that fear knows no age, that all people, in their fears, are equally defenseless.

Authority reigns in this novel and to no good effect. Judgments are made on the basis of personality by some external authority. Judgments and endless assumptions—which are false or unverifiable—are based on the slightest of actions. Hence, the creation of any personality—the creator's or that of another—is constantly in question and certainly not to be trusted.

The Characters

Because Sarraute is not dealing with individual characters, the reader is prevented from making the customary judgments by which any member of the human species is classified. Here, human voices are heard, but the rest of their beings remains amorphous at best. The voices and the ideas that they express can be discussed only in their relationship to one another.

Appearances never cease to provoke questions. Can one's temperament be deduced from one's forehead, chin, eyes, nose, or hands? For what traits is one responsible: for those traits perceived and therefore developed, or for those traits which are less practiced but developed against the odds? Can emotional states or stages be deduced from physical appearance? When are children real children and when are they only acting like children? Can one ever know with cats? Can one be sure that they are not simply acting like cats?

Sarraute forces the reader to question the nature of human personality. What is actually known about any individual? How can the endless assumptions and conclusions that are drawn be anything less than ludicrously inaccurate? From a photograph, a personality is perceived; from personal papers, a character is constructed. Everyone knows how to do it, and whatever does not fit or cannot be explained will be ignored. From one slight word or action, a whole character is revealed. A pair of newlyweds is blissful, until she notices the care with which he counts a tip into the waiting palm. She suddenly knows that she has married a stingy miser, and that she has no choice except to divorce him or go through life knowing that people will say, "there goes the poor bride who married a miser." By one mark of one claw, the lion shall be known.

The false authority of words results in an emotional tyranny from which there seems to be no exit. A grandmother cannot swallow the image of "sweet," applied to her by her grandchildren, but cannot avoid it, either. When told by his relatives that he will grow to be as ugly as his uncle, a boy knows terror. An adolescent who believed that he was nothing before he was bound by the words of others is incapable of freeing himself, of returning the ball, of saying, "If I'm a fool, you're another." He does not know how to defend himself.

If one really believes in perfect equality and is not merely mouthing witty nonsense, one is obviously to be pitied. To retreat with one's idea, to keep it out of the fray, is to watch it atrophy and die. To decide that one is nothing but a construct built by others is to lose all sense of identity. To find that everything else is moving and that one's words are incomprehensible is to find that one is invalidated and in need of rehabilitation. One must accept one's intelligence as less than, more than, or equal to Descartes'. "Different from" will not do. One offends against law and order, if one does not accept an assigned place in the established hierarchies.

Themes and Meanings

This novel explores what is true in human personality. If tropistic reality represents the ultimate, universal reality of the species, truth—for Sarraute—must be found there. By applying the word tropisms to human beings, Sarraute creates a world in which people's deep subconscious responses to one another, which cannot be fully articulated, seem to be based on the fear of social ostracism. Thus, in seeking security and order amid conflicting voices, a person is not likely to find that he is seeking the truth: Truth is usually painful, and at the level of tropisms, one seeks to gain acceptance and to avoid emotional pain.

In assigning words to human reality at this subterranean level, Sarraute makes clear that the conscious use of words is motivated by a need for personal recognition rather than by a need for disinterested truth. Hence, words become the means to self-aggrandizement. Once the fixed reputation of the few is institutionalized, the bureaucracy seeks to perpetuate itself by endowing its words with the authority of rational order and permanence. In response, individuals assert their freedom only by forcing that static language of hierarchy to yield to a newly articulated reality. Only then, in Sarraute's view, are they at least trying to use words, though not necessarily to wield them over others. Thus, *"Fools Say"* is wonderfully subversive and antiauthoritarian. Why should one not believe in a saint as one's savior or in a heavenly apparition so purely absentminded that he was once observed staring at an "egg while his watch was cooking in boiling water"?

Surely, one of the most subversive aspects of this novel is Sarraute's use of multiple voices in place of a traditional narrator whose single voice delineates reality for the reader. The reader must listen to many voices, many perceptions of reality, and realize that he cannot credit truth to any one voice—for, in assigning words to perceptions, every narrator inevitably alters that which is perceived, as well as that which is communicated to the reader. Implicit in this novel is the hope that the reader will abandon any attempt to construct an edifice of character out of the quicksand of human voices. Is there any human truth which can be secured? To search for a truth—instead of a fixed security with everything in its place—is not only hazardous but also fraught with difficulty. In Sarraute's world, as the reader listens to the conflicts of the multiple voices, he realizes that he might approach a truth, but that the truth is beyond any human comprehension.

Critical Context

"Fools Say," Sarraute's seventh novel, may well be her most abstract, but

her dense, precise prose has always focused on the most fundamental of human emotions. Her first volume was *Tropismes* (1938, 1957; *Tropisms*, 1963), a collection of sketches. Her first two novels, *Portrait d'un inconnu* (1948; *Portrait of a Man Unknown*, 1958) and *Martereau* (1953; English translation, 1959), with first-person narrators, were followed by the essays in *L'Ère du soupçon* (1956; *The Age of Suspicion*, 1963); these essays were used as a manifesto for what has been called the New Novel. More significant, it is in these essays that Sarraute discusses subconversation and what she is trying to do in her fiction. She accepts Fyodor Dostoevski and Marcel Proust as her predecessors and begins where Proust ended. Her work is distinct from that of New Novelists such as Alain Robbe-Grillet and Michel Butor, in that however experimental it may be, it belongs to the realist tradition.

Sarraute's other novels include *Le Planétarium* (1959; *The Planetarium*, 1960); *Les Fruits d'or* (1963; *The Golden Fruits*, 1964), in which there is a discussion by many voices of the literary value of a novel titled *The Golden Fruits*; *Entre la vie et la mort* (1968; *Between Life and Death*, 1969), which presents the vacillating consciousness of a writer in the process of writing; and *Vous les entendez?* (1972; *Do You Hear Them?*, 1973), which focuses on the reactions of a devoted father hearing and trying to interpret his children's laughter. *L'Usage de la parole* (1980; *The Uses of Speech*, 1980), like *Tropisms*, is a collection. Sarraute has also written five plays, which have been successful both on the radio and in stage productions.

In contrast to the isolation and alienation of Samuel Beckett's world, Sarraute creates a community of voices. Her insistence on the validity of tropistic reality, despite the ever-present threat of misinterpretation, makes it clear that human significance, for this author, can be found only amid the cacophony of other voices.

Sources for Further Study
Besser, Gretchen Rous. *Nathalie Sarraute*, 1979.
Bory, Jean-Louis. "Le Sapeur Sarraute," in *Le Nouvel Observateur*, December 6, 1976, pp. 86-88.
Davin, Antonia. "Nathalie Sarraute's '*Disent les imbéciles*': The Critic's Dilemma," in *New Zealand Journal of French Studies*, May, 1981, pp. 56-79.
Minogue, Valerie. *Nathalie Sarraute: The War of the Words*, 1981.
Temple, Ruth Z. *Nathalie Sarraute*, 1968.
Watson-Williams, Helen. *The Novels of Nathalie Sarraute: Towards an Aesthetic*, 1981.

Carol Bishop

THE FORBIDDEN FOREST

Author: Mircea Eliade (1907-1986)
Type of plot: Psychological realism, with elements of fantasy
Time of plot: 1936-1948
Locale: Romania (mainly Bucharest), London, Lisbon, and Paris
First published: La Forêt interdite, 1955 (English translation, 1978)

> *Principal characters:*
> STEFAN VIZIRU, a political economist working for the
>   Romanian Ministry of National Economy, thirty-four
>   years old when the novel opens
> IOANA VIZIRU, his wife, a homemaker, age twenty-six
> ILEANA SIDERI, a young woman with whom Stefan falls in love
> CIRU PARTENIE, a writer to whom Stefan bears a striking
>   resemblance who was formerly engaged to Ioana
> SPIRIDON VADASTRA, a young attorney with limited talents
>   and unlimited ambitions
> GHEORGHE VASILE, Vadastra's father, a retired provincial
>   schoolteacher
> IRINA IVASCU, a deeply religious young woman who marries
>   Vadastra
> PETRE BIRIS, a poor, tubercular professor of philosophy,
>   Stefan's friend and confidant
> CATALINA, an actress with whom Biris is in love
> DAN BIBICESCU, an intelligent, egotistic playwright, actor,
>   and director
> MISU WEISSMAN, a wealthy Jewish patron of Bibicescu
> BURSUC, a cynical, amoral, opportunistic graduate of a
>   theological school who becomes a monk under the
>   Communist regime

The Novel

Spanning the twelve years from 1936 to 1948, which were so tragically decisive for the Romanian people, *The Forbidden Forest* is, on one level, a chronicle of the sad events of that era. These events are presented as the experiences of a rather large number of interrelated characters whose personal biographies constitute the intricate web of the plot. At another level, the book is a vehicle for examining and testing a variety of philosophies about time, history, fate, and the meaning of life. Beginning and ending on a Midsummer's Night (also known as St. John's Eve and the summer solstice), when "the heavens open" and miracles can occur, the novel is pervaded by a subtle atmosphere of the fantastic.

The fantastic element is embodied in two mysteries that obsess the central character, Stefan, throughout the novel: The first is that of *doamna* (Mrs.) Zissu, whose name has haunted him ever since he overheard it spoken by Vadastra, his neighbor in a cheap hotel with thin walls; the second is that of "the car that ought to have disappeared," seen in a vision on June 23, 1936, which is connected with Ileana, whom Stefan met that same night in a forest to which he was mysteriously drawn. Scattered throughout the novel are episodes which reveal bits of information about *doamna* Zissu or in which an automobile figures—episodes marking crucial events in Stefan's life. Only at the conclusion of the book are the mysteries resolved, when *doamna* Zissu is disclosed to have been a woman romantically involved with four men, all of whom are significant in Stefan's life, and when the car materializes as Ileana's automobile on St. John's Eve, 1948, in France, becoming the vehicle in which the two will die in a plunge off a mountain road.

There is little action in the first three chapters, which serve mainly to introduce most of the leading characters and their problems. Stefan dearly loves his wife, Ioana, who is going to have a baby, but he has also fallen in love with Ileana, who at first finds him bizarre but later realizes that she loves him in spite of herself. Stefan and Ileana meet only rarely and without prearrangement; their friendship is platonic, except when once, impulsively, he kisses her. Stefan maintains a "secret room" in a hotel to which he retreats to experience "another time," while painting. He envies the saints for their abilities to transcend time while still living on earth and to love all persons equally. If he could love both Ileana and Ioana simultaneously, he thinks, he would achieve a transcendence of the human condition. Unfortunately, his feelings vacillate and he seems always to love one woman more than the other.

After the appearance of a car in chapter 4, history begins to intrude upon the story. It is 1938 and Stefan is mistakenly arrested as an Iron Guardist (a Christian Fascist) and is interned in a concentration camp. He endures by living in his memories of moments spent with Ileana, whom he now believes he loves. Nevertheless, when released six months later, he finds that he loves Ioana more. Partenie, a writer who resembles Stefan and whom Ioana loved before meeting Stefan, is shot by police while talking with a Guardist who mistook him for Stefan. Stefan, who already blames himself for having taken Ioana away from Partenie, now feels responsible for the writer's death and becomes deeply depressed. At length, he "receives a message" that enables him to "come out of the labyrinth." The message is that Ileana's car is real and that there are openings in the iron shell that imprisons mankind.

In April, 1940, Stefan is sent on a government economic assignment to London, where he again encounters his neighbor, Vadastra, who is in Great Britain on "official business." Stefan experiences the blitz in which Vadastra apparently perishes—although his body is never found. As diplomatic relations between Great Britain and Romania deteriorate in the winter of 1941, Stefan is sent to Lisbon. Meanwhile, the Iron Guard rebellion of January, 1941, is taking place in Romania, affecting the lives of several of Stefan's friends. In Lisbon, Stefan becomes involved in a torrid affair with a young Romanian woman, having been attracted to her by her name: Stella Zissu. Stella is not, however, the Zissu woman for whom he is searching, but instead is a combination of Circe and Calypso; he breaks with her after another appearance of a car.

Stefan returns home briefly, then volunteers for duty on the Russian front as a supply officer. That same winter, he is returned to Lisbon, where Ileana now lives as a legation employee. They spend a romantic New Year's Eve together, consummating their love for the first time. When he learns that Ileana had slept with her fiancé, who died in an auto crash, Stefan is angry and leaves the room. Ileana warns him that he will never see her again—and in the morning she is gone.

Stefan returns to the front, in what he will later call a suicide attempt. He survives, but his wife and son die in an American air raid on Easter Day, 1944. Plunged into grief, he is helped back to normalcy by Vadastra's widow, the saintly Irina, who was also Ioana's friend.

The Russian Occupation begins in August, 1944, and the war ends the following spring. Stefan's life is rather uneventful; he continues to work for the Ministry of Economy but believes that since 1936 he has not been living the life for which he was destined. He begins searching for Ileana but can find no trace of her in Romania.

In the summer of 1947, Stefan defects to Paris with a briefcase of government papers. He has fled, he insists, primarily to search for Ileana. He suspects (correctly) that she is in Switzerland, but he is unable to obtain a Swiss visa. The following spring, he acquires from another refugee one of Partenie's diaries which reveals the identity of *doamna* Zissu. That same night Vadastra appears, alive, but he refuses to explain anything that has happened to him.

Then, on the eve of the summer solstice, Stefan finds Ileana—standing beside her car in a forest (at a monastery), just as he visualized the scene twelve years earlier. They confess their love, though Ileana is now married to her former psychiatrist. Stefan tells her part of the riddle of *doamna* Zissu, without disclosing that Ileana's father was one of *doamna* Zissu's lovers. He tries to explain the meaning of the car, to warn her—but she refuses to listen. As the car leaves the highway, Ileana looks at him lovingly—and Stefan knows the bliss which he has sought for so many years.

The Characters

While Mircea Eliade on several occasions cautioned readers against identifying him with Stefan, it is clear that the hero's experiences at many points parallel those of the author. Eliade was interned in 1938 for Guardist associations, he went to London in 1940 on government service and experienced the blitz, he spent 1942 through 1945 in Lisbon, his wife died in 1944, and he became a refugee in Paris after the war. More important, Stefan's apolitical nature, his longing to escape history and experience another dimension of time, his agony over Romania's fate, his optimistic faith that for the individual "an exit exits," and his certainty that life has a transhistorical meaning were Eliade's as well. Moreover, several characters are modeled on persons of the author's acquaintance. Nevertheless, Eliade felt free to invent most of their biographies, even as he did that of Stefan.

The novel is populated with a large cast of finely drawn characters who play important, supporting roles in the labyrinthine plot and whose own stories are engrossing in themselves. Vadastra, whom Eliade took from an earlier, aborted novel, is one of several humorous personages. His vanity and bombast, his grandiose ambitions, his pitiful efforts to impress others, his bungling attempts to gain wealth and power, capped with his surprising "return from the dead" as an apparently successful secret agent, mark him as an archetypal trickster. His father, Gheorghe Vasile, the semicultured village schoolmaster, retired, is equally comical as he sells precious Romanian antiques to buy booze and popular books to furnish a "great library" that he intends to found for the common folk of his village. Dan Bibicescu, a third comic egotist, is, however, more pitiful than amusing in most of his appearances.

Petre Biris, the philosopher with whom Stefan holds many lengthy and profound discussions, emerges as the most memorable of the secondary male characters and is, perhaps, more likable than is Stefan. A stoic and a historicist, he nevertheless becomes the recipient of a "revelation" (in a dream) while being tortured in a Communist prison and thus is able to die serenely, quoting from the *Miorița* (a classical Romanian folk ballad). Catalina, his sweetheart, also undergoes an impressive character development in the course of the novel. Irina (Vadastra's wife) and Colonel Baleanu are "near saints," gifted with suprahuman spiritual qualities. In contrast, Bursuc, the "unworthy monk," who readily cooperates with the Communist government (though rumored to be a double agent), remains an enigma: Does he perhaps, after all, truly believe? In part 2, the secondary characters and their stories come to the forefront, while Stefan is reduced to the role of "witness" up to the time when he leaves to seek Ileana.

Themes and Meanings

In broadest terms, *The Forbidden Forest* is a novel about the meaning of life, or, more specifically, how to discern meaning in the seemingly random, tragic series of events that comprises the histories of individuals and nations. Subsidiary, complementary themes are time, history, death, and fate.

Stefan attempts to hold himself aloof from history (politics) as much as possible; he withdraws into his secret room to paint, or into literature or his memories of privileged occasions—childhood, moments of love—when time stood still. These methods of evading historical time afford but temporary relief, nor are they foolproof (for example, during the London blitz). Stefan seeks the ability to live permanently in "eternal time"—while still continuing his existence in the historical duration, "as the saints do." Otherwise, history would have no meaning, he says. In the mountains, he meets an educated man, Anise, who has adopted the life of a peasant and is living in harmony with "cosmic rhythms," nature's cyclical time. Stefan is attracted to this lifestyle but becomes disillusioned with it when he learns that both Anise and his farm were swept away by the war. Biris regards history stoically as leading only to death, until late in the book when he comes to believe that there is more. Irina, a firm believer in Orthodoxy, promises Stefan that all he has experienced sequentially on earth will be his simultaneously in Heaven, where time will be no more. Catalina, enamored of Oriental philosophy, believes that life is illusory, the purposeless play of maya (though later she seems to find purpose in unselfish service). Bibicescu, the playwright, thinks that history and fate can be conquered only by compressing time into the dramatic spectacle and "exorcising" it.

Rejecting all these views of historical time, as well as those of Marxism and existentialism, Stefan is convinced that for those who are alert, "signs" can be perceived amid commonplace events, and that by following these signs one can discover the purpose of one's personal life. This discovery is possible because life is predetermined by fate—a thing that several characters in fact believe. For Stefan, *doamna* Zissu is a clue as to the course which his life should take, or should have taken. When he discovers that this long-dead woman is a kind of "common denominator" in his life and those of several others, including Ioana and Ileana, he exclaims humbly, "Thy will be done!" Thus, like Jesus in Gethsemane, Stefan accepts his destiny.

Though this life is governed by fate, is there perhaps also a transcendent meaning to history, an existence beyond in which all enigmas are resolved? Stefan dares to believe that there is, and for him its proof is Ileana's car. The car is, clearly, the vehicle that effects the "rupture of planes," the passage to the "other life." Ileana, as one sees in the end, is Stefan's "angel of death."

Critical Context

Eliade was a unique and isolated figure in Romanian and world literature, resisting attempts to be classified or associated with schools or models. Among his acknowledged idols were Johann Wolfgang von Goethe, Honoré de Balzac, Fyodor Dostoevski, James Joyce, and William Faulkner. Having begun in his youth to write autobiographical and semiautobiographical novels (his first published novel appeared in 1930, when he was twenty-three), he next experimented with the interior monologue, stream of consciousness, and the "journal novel" while in pursuit of "authenticity." From here, Eliade evolved a third-person narrative style resembling that of *The Forbidden Forest* in which the reader follows the thoughts of the characters thanks to the omniscient narrator. A stylistic peculiarity of this novel, related undoubtedly to its theme of time, is the flashback technique, in which past events are presented, apparently, as thoughts of the characters.

The Forbidden Forest was written between 1949 and 1954 in Paris when Eliade was establishing his reputation in the scholarly world as a historian of religions, his "other vocation," in which he achieved worldwide recognition. The novel reflects themes familiar to readers of Eliade's nonfiction, especially his *Le Mythe de l'éternel retour* (1949; *The Myth of the Eternal Return*, 1955). *The Forbidden Forest*, written in Romanian, was immediately translated and published in French, being offered to a public for whom existentialism and plotless novels were in vogue. (It was not published in its original form, as *Noaptea de Sânziene*, until 1971.) Eliade expected his work to be viewed as old-fashioned, but it was his conviction that narrative, a form as old as the myth and fairy tale, fulfills an inherent human need and would, in time, be appreciated again.

While in one sense *The Forbidden Forest* is a patriotic Romanian novel voicing the sorrows and hopes of a people who have known for millennia the "terror of history," in another sense, it is a universal work with themes that are concerns of all human beings in all times and places.

Sources for Further Study
Calinescu, Matei. "Between History and Paradise: Initiation Trials," in *Journal of Religion*. LIX, no. 2 (1978), pp. 218-223.
_____. "The Disguises of Miracle: Notes on Mircea Eliade's Fiction," in *World Literature Today*. LII (Autumn, 1978), pp. 558-564.
Girardot, Norman, and Mac Linscott Ricketts, eds. *Imagination and Meaning: The Scholarly and Literary Worlds of Mircea Eliade*, 1982.
Kitagawa, Joseph, and Charles H. Long, eds. *Myths and Symbols: Studies in Honor of Mircea Eliade*, 1969.
Ricketts, Mac Linscott. "Fate in *The Forbidden Forest*," in *Dialogue*. VIII (1982), pp. 101-119.

Mac Linscott Ricketts

THE FOUNDATION PIT

Author: Andrei Platonov (Andrei Platonovich Klimentov, 1899-1951)
Type of plot: Satire / surrealism
Time of plot: The early 1930's
Locale: An unnamed provincial city in central Russia and a nearby village
First published: Kotlovan, 1973 (English translation, 1973)

> *Principal characters:*
> VOSHCHEV, a former machinist, now a laborer in the pit crew
> CHIKLIN, one of the diggers
> ZHACHEV, a cripple, wounded in World War I
> NASTYA, an orphan adopted by the digging crew

The Novel

Set somewhere in the early 1930's, *The Foundation Pit* seems to have all the components of the canonical construction novel: a huge project, Party activists, marching pioneers, collectivizing peasants, a random assortment of workers come together to build the foundations for a bright Communist future. Although the novel follows the digging of the foundation pit and the collectivizing of a nearby village, it is worlds apart from anything resembling Socialist Realism.

As the novel begins, Voshchev arrives at the outskirts of a provincial Russian city. Fired from his machine-shop job for "pensiveness in the midst of the general tempo of labor," he has gone in search of a plan for life—life as a whole, that is, since his own life is not a puzzle to him. He lives merely because, like any other creature, he happened to be born. As he makes his way to the city's center, his loneliness and isolation never leave him but instead grow as he watches the construction projects rising all around him. He has the uncomfortable sense that when humans put together a building, they manage to fall apart themselves. He wanders back to the empty lots and wasteland at the city's edge and, more or less by accident, joins the crew of an enormous construction project.

Although the project is enormous, the crew is not: A motley assortment, they all sleep in a garden shack converted into barracks. They are digging a foundation pit for no ordinary apartment building, though, but for an enormous all-proletarian "home," a true communal residence unlike the separated, fenced-off houses of the old city. The building is the brainchild of Engineer Prushevsky, who, suffering from the same puzzled melancholy as Voshchev, comforts himself with the resolution to die in the near future.

Hereafter, the novel simply follows the course of the digging, and the life of the crew itself, the "artel"—Chiklin the tireless laborer, Safronov the

Party activist, Pashkin the trade-union secretary, and Zhachev the sadistic cripple, who takes it upon himself to wreak revolutionary vengeance by bullying and robbing anyone who seems bourgeois. As plans progress, Engineer Prushevsky and Chiklin discover something in common—a lost sweetheart, daughter of the former owner of a nearby Dutch tile factory. In the ruins of that same factory they discover a ragged woman and a small child. The woman, whom they take to be that same girl from their youth, dies of starvation. They take the girl with them, and she becomes their mascot, the symbol of the young proletarian future.

More than that, she becomes their oracle, the voice of that future, as she mouths slogans and watchwords of the Revolution. Nastya, the child, is the only pure proletarian among them, since she, as she says, refused to be born until Lenin appeared on the scene. The workers dote on her, try to make her as comfortable as possible, find a bed her size—a child-sized coffin, one among many tucked away in a cave near the foundation pit.

It turns out that the peasants from a nearby village own these coffins and demand them all back, at which point the Party activists realize that the village is yearning for collectivization and needs the encouragement of the local proletariat. Kozlov, a tubercular digger turned bureaucrat, and Safronov, the Party activist, are dispatched by the artel as messengers and emissaries to the peasants. At the same time Voshchev again wanders off, vaguely on the peasants' trail, in search of direction in a different place, since none of the workers has any clearer idea than he does about their reason for living. Prushevsky is ordered (on Pashkin's initiative) to expand the size of the pit sixfold, lest Socialist children "live out in the open air, in the midst of the unorganized weather. . . ."

It is the child Nastya who informs Chiklin that Safronov and Kozlov are dead, and so Chiklin and Voshchev, now returned, set off for the village to investigate. They find the murdered pair laid out on a table in the village Soviet, and there Chiklin almost accidentally kills a peasant with a single blow; murdered or not, the yellow-eyed peasant becomes the third corpse on display. The real murderer, or "wrecker," eventually climbs up on the table and dies for solidarity's sake.

Chiklin and Voshchev stay in the village to help dispose of the wealthy peasants, or kulaks, to confiscate their hoarded grain and livestock, and to build for the poor peasants a raft. The poor peasants plan to liquidate the kulaks as a class by simply launching them downriver, *en masse*. Prushevsky, Nastya, and Zhachev (who has taken on the task of educating Nastya) arrive to act as cadres of the Cultural Revolution, as does Pashkin, who has discovered the last "most oppressed landless hired laborer" in the district. The laborer, who had once been paid nothing but who now works in the village smithy, is a bear, the most politically conscious creature of the whole lot. The diggers take the bear on the rounds of the village to identify the kulaks marked for liquidation, and his instinctive sense tallies perfectly with the Party activists' list.

The poor peasants celebrate the launching, Voshchev wanders off in search of discarded objects symbolic of the old life. In one of the hovels that very night the striker bear wakes the entire village with his hammering; while Chiklin works the bellows, the bear frenziedly works the iron, and gradually the entire village joins in until all the charcoal is gone, all possible repairs made, and all tools supplied.

As the diggers prepare to return to the foundation pit, the Party activist is declared a saboteur and a wrecker by a directive brought from outside—and he, too, dies from one of Chiklin's mighty blows, although as much because he has taken his jacket away from feverish Nastya as for any ideological reason. On the snowy winter road back to the future home of the proletariat, Nastya weakens and, in the morning, she dies. Voshchev arrives a short time later, along with the entire collective farm and bear in tow—they want to enlist in the proletariat and help dig the foundation pit even wider and deeper. The novel ends as Chiklin digs a special grave for Nastya and carves a special stone. At night, when everyone in the barracks except for the striker bear is asleep, he buries her.

The Characters

In this Utopia-in-the-making, the hole in the ground which is to underlie a new society, the characters all share two things: an all-encompassing sadness and a strangely altered language. Whether it be Voshchev the truth seeker or Zhachev the malicious vigilante, or even Nastya the small girl (none has a full name), they all seem to operate in a daze, an expectation of death in the midst of life. They are unsurprised by the strangest of events—horses foraging collectively, bears belonging to trade unions—so violence and death are hardly anything new. Yet Andrei Platonov's characters are not callous: Humans, animals, and objects seem to deserve pity and compassion in equal measure, since all three seem to be identically wasted, impoverished, and discarded. What is so disturbing in Platonov's characters is that their very compassion seems as impersonal as their anger. It has nothing to do with specific people or traits.

The characters, then, are motivated by physical need, by ideological dictates, and by "what used to be called the soul." Platonov is dealing with body and with consciousness, not realistic psychological motivation. Hence, the seeming aimlessness and randomness of their actions; there are Party directives which they fulfill, they are believers, but their melancholy puzzlement suggests that they are moving out of inertia rather than will.

The vocabulary of the revolutionary era has for them become a vocabulary of the spirit. Their language—common to all the characters as well as the author-narrator—is a complex mixture of clichés, slogans, revolutionary buzzwords, abstractions visited on concrete, and colloquial turns of phrase. Voshchev sees nothing absurd in his dismissal for "the growth of the strength of his weakness and of pensiveness in the midst of the general tempo of labor" but instead goes off to try to understand what has made him this way. A man about to make love to his wife speaks of her "gigantic feeling for the masses" and plans to "organize himself up close to her." He is not self-conscious, not joking—nor, perhaps, is Platonov.

Themes and Meanings

The search for truth and an earthly paradise are well-worn themes in nineteenth century Russian literature, and *The Foundation Pit* owes something both to Nikolai Leskov's eccentric folk geniuses and provincial settings and to Fyodor Dostoevski's dreams (or nightmares) of the Golden Age. Still, there is an eerie, surreal quality to Platonov's new world, a pervasive hopelessness and desolation that those two masters lack.

A grandiose project on the edge of a nameless provincial city in the heart of Russia, the foundation pit would seem to hold the promise of a Utopia—Dostoevski's Crystal Palace, the workers' paradise, a massive home for the masses. That is how Engineer Prushevsky sees it. Yet its projected dimensions keep expanding while its work crew keeps shrinking, and it seems unlikely ever to reverse its direction—to grow up instead of down. The Utopia is not only unfinished but also is in the process of becoming its own vertical opposite.

What makes the novel alternately dreamlike and nightmarish is the irony of theory versus practice but, more than that, the uncertainty of time and space. The city, village, and river are all unnamed, the landscape a lunar wasteland where, despite the presence of buildings and houses, the characters seem isolated and homeless in the middle of the windy steppe, sheltered only by their scanty clothing and occasionally by one another. Voshchev and the others follow Party directives and exhortations, but even while doing so they give the impression of random movement in space: either that, or they are moved by a mechanism so much larger than themselves that they have no idea of its workings. Cause and effect seem curiously out of joint, and there is a sense of discontinuity and alogic about the novel, even as Nastya pursues logic to an inevitable end with her assumption that from now on only the bourgeois will die—hence anyone who dies must be a class enemy.

Time passes, and Voshchev muses on its "longness," but although there is some reference to the characters' various past lives, they are all figures in an eternal present. Fall turns to winter, Nastya grows cold and dies, but there is little sense of linear movement—yet this is a novel about inevitable progress toward the future. Platonov's language, the narrator's and the characters' language, has created a universe in limbo, where the characters operate according to mangled constructs, where perfect logic becomes no logic at all. What results from abstractions taken literally is the absurdity of the foundation pit.

Critical Context

Although *The Foundation Pit* is one of Andrei Platonov's most important works, it has never been published in the Soviet Union. This does not mean, however, that it has not influenced the course of Soviet prose. The work was circulated in manuscript long before its publication abroad in the 1970's. Platonov's experiments with language and his vision of the absurd have helped shape some of the best of post-Stalin prose, official and unofficial.

Platonov first began to gain fame in the 1920's. Stories that would eventually go into his first collection, *Epifanskie shlyunzy* (1927; epiphany), attracted attention for the cleverness of their style. Platonov's original use of language, as well as his intense focus on the relationship between humans and their machines (he himself was an engineer) earned for him a place among the emerging young writers who were exploring the effects on an old rural consciousness of a new ideology and technology.

Neither Platonov's idiosyncratic use of language nor his bleak portrayal of rural life was easily accepted in the 1930's. He became an object of derision for his attitudes and anti-Soviet slander. Platonov, however, had many defenders and managed to publish such powerful stories as "Usomnivshiysya Makar" ("Makar the Doubtful"), "Vprok" (for the future good), and "Fro." Hostile criticism, however, as well as the arrest of his only son, effectively ended his writing career by 1940. Platonov continued to write, however— journalistic reworkings of folktales—until his death in 1951. Platonov's best work, which includes *The Foundation Pit* and his novel *Chevengur* (1972; English translation, 1978) is more than simply satire; it is the purest example of surrealism and the absurd in Russian literature.

Sources for Further Study

Bayley, John. Review of *Collected Works, "Chevengur,"* in *The New York Review of Books.* XXVI (May 3, 1979), p. 37.
Brodsky, Joseph. "Catastrophes in the Air," in *Less than One*, 1985.
───────────. Preface to *The Foundation Pit*, 1973.
Jordan, Marion. *Andrei Platonov*, 1973.
Olcott, Anthony. Foreword to *Chevengur*, 1978.

Jane Ann Miller

FRIDAY
Or, The Other Island

Author: Michel Tournier (1924-   )
Type of plot: Mythological re-creation
Time of plot: 1759-1787
Locale: "Speranza," an island located off the coast of Chile
First published: Vendredi: Ou, Les Limbes du Pacifique, 1967; revised, 1972
   (English translation, 1969)

> *Principal characters:*
> ROBINSON, a Puritan English fortune seeker stranded on
>   Speranza
> FRIDAY, a mestizo servant, companion, mentor, and alter ego
>   to Robinson

The Novel

Michel Tournier's *Friday* adapts Daniel Defoe's original masterpiece *Robinson Crusoe* (1719) and re-creates the whole myth of Robinson Crusoe as it also appears in Johann Wyss's *Der schweizerische Robinson* (1812-1827; *The Swiss Family Robinson*, 1814, 1818, 1820) and Jules Verne's *L'Île mystérieuse* (1874-1875; *Mysterious Island*, 1875). Tournier retains the adventure story of his predecessors but alters their system of values and makes significant additions of an ethnological and psychological nature. Where his sources focused on environmental conquest and social conformity, Tournier emphasizes Robinson's personal experience of solitude, his dejection, and the rediscovery of his youthful virility through exposure to the alien perceptions of Friday.

The novel opens with a prologue at sea. Robinson is aboard the brig *Virginia*, en route from Lima. He has abandoned his wife and children in England to seek his fortune in the New World. In the midst of a formidable tempest, the ship's captain, Van Deyssel, reads his passenger's future from the tarot: "Crusoe, . . . take heed of what I say. Beware of purity. It is the vitriol of the soul."

The storm wrecks the ship two hundred miles off the South American coast. Save for the ship's dog, Tenn, Robinson is the sole survivor. He surveys his new home and labels it "Desolation." Later, he rechristens the island "Speranza," naming it for an Italian lover whose name means "hope" and calls to mind the philosopher Baruch Spinoza.

Robinson domesticates the island. He breeds goats; grows crops; catalogs the flora and fauna; maps the terrain; constructs a mock municipality complete with private villa, storage depot, town hall, temple, and fortress; and writes legislation for a population of one. In short, he is master of his universe: Governor, Pastor, Engineer, and Defense Minister combined. His life is rigidly controlled by the dripping of a water clock.

One day, some Araucanian Indians land on the island to rid themselves of a presumed evil influence. Their intended victim is Friday. Robinson rescues the crossbreed and "cultivates" him as he did the island. Friday must wear clothing, respect the Sabbath, and polish the flagstones. Friday is docile but considers his master to be a "madman." Robinson views Friday as a "devil" but, at the same time, sees in him the possibility of a completely different world. When Friday accidentally touches off an explosion that destroys the entire artificial township, Robinson recognizes that it is a blessing in disguise and yields to his other self. Henceforth, Robinson is Friday's attentive pupil. He learns to live as a subject of the sun and in symbiosis with the island.

After twenty-eight years, the English schooner *Whitebird*, a slave trader, lands on the island. Robinson, shocked by the coarseness of the crew and alarmed by the prospect of sudden aging, elects to stay. Friday, intrigued by the speed and airiness of the boat, chooses to depart. Jaan Neljapaëv, a mistreated galley boy who sees kindness in Robinson, steals ashore and takes Friday's place. "I shall call you Sunday," determines Robinson. It "is the day of the resurrection, of the youth of all things, and the day of our master, the Sun." The two remain on the island, frozen in eternity.

The Characters

Tournier's published commentary and the novel's title would argue that Friday is the primary character, but this conclusion is not supported by the novel itself. There is quantitatively less material devoted to Friday. Friday does not have his own narrative voice and is seen only in Robinson's terms; Robinson keeps the logbook; Friday's identity is constructed in counterpoint to that of Robinson; Friday's longest episode with Andoar the he-goat is designed to kill the old Robinson and empower the new; and finally, Friday was replaced. Nevertheless, Friday's role is massively greater than it was in Defoe's work, and it is not unfair to think of Friday as the "hero" of the novel, since it is he who wins the internal battle under way within Robinson.

Robinson is a red-haired, light-skinned English Quaker, twenty-two years old at the beginning of the story and fifty at the end. At first, his morals are the sum of his Puritan virtues, and his functions are programmed by societal stereotypes. Production is good, consumption is bad, and nonprocreative sex is punished. He can play supply clerk, census taker, cartographer, and stenographer with equal ease. Very early in the novel, however, another person begins gestating inside Robinson. This other expresses itself through behavioral leakages: Robinson's first nudity on the island is joyful; his first journal entry replaces Christian virtue with male virility; he mocks John Bunyan's Slough of Despond by wallowing in a slime bog; he has sex with plants. His psyche is composed of a few childhood images: the taboo on wearing (ocean) blue, his longing to be a baker, the sensual sight of his mother kneading dough, his father impotently praying while the house burns, his desire to be the bean baked inside his mother's Epiphany cake. Friday's arrival merely actualizes a strong potential for subversion that was already implicit in Robinson.

Friday is fifteen years old when rescued, a half-caste (or "twin blood"), named for the day he was found, for the day of Venus, and for the day of the death of Christ. As seen by Robinson on first encounter, Friday is "the most rudimentary form of companion, midway between person and object." He is as loyal a subject of Robinson as Robinson is of civilization. Nevertheless, Friday also shows early signs of breakaway originality: He uses a red-ant nest for garbage disposal, is adept at the bola, and makes a shield by cooking a turtle alive. Friday is a wonderful clown and satirist: He dresses flowers in Robinson's clothes, smokes Robinson's pipe, and enrages Robinson by sleeping in the latter's conjugal flower bed. In the end, Robinson comes to appreciate and emulate Friday's own brand of culture and integration with the animal world and sees in him a condenser of possible embodiments of otherness: father, son, neighbor, and brother. As a paired unit, Friday and Robinson reflect Cain and Abel, Castor and Pollux, and Tournier's own Jean and Paul from the novel *Les Météores* (1975; *Gemini*, 1981).

Themes and Meanings

Important keys to interpretation lie in the novel's full title: in French, *Vendredi: Ou, Les Limbes du Pacifique*; in translation, *Friday: Or, The Other Island*. Both versions reflect an intent to shift Friday's status from a secondary to primary one. The French subtitle means "the limbo of the Pacific," but the episode in which Robinson fornicates with quillam flowers suggests a comparison of *limbes* to *lombes* (loins). "This Island" is the one that Robinson sees with civilized eyes, as mother, bride, or object to be domesticated. "The Other Island" is the one indifferent to human projections of language, religion, and culture. Interesting readings of the title are "Friday: Or, The Loins of the Pacific" and "Friday: Or, The Other Robinson."

Within this framework, the themes of time, provincialism, and subversion are essential. Robinson and Friday were divided by a time barrier. The Robinson of York had only the past (the baggage of family, Bible, and *Poor Richard's Almanack*) and the future (the stubborn goal-orientedness of technology). Friday has no past or future but teaches Robinson to live in the present. To arrive at the present, Robinson must age backward. His personal transformation is a sort of Pilgrim's Regress.

Provincialism is denounced in the novel on the levels of country (isolationism), race (xenophobia), and self (solipsism). Purity—not the morally upright abstinence but the crippling absence of otherness—is indeed a corrosive milieu. Purity is dirty. Thus, when Robinson soils himself in the mire, or Friday sullies Robinson's mandrake grove, they perform positive acts of purification by inversion.

Ultimately, then, the novel is quite subversive. Friday does not merely undermine Robinson's clockwork order; he literally blows it to kingdom come. Robinson is a man who takes a permanent vacation from his wife, family, and country, and enjoys it. He worships the sun, acquires blond hair and a nice tan, grows younger with the years, has no briefcase or bank account, and has gained a son without investing any biological resources in the maintenance of the species. One need only imagine what would happen if Robinson were to be held up in Sunday school as an example of a model citizen.

Critical Context

Tournier's original version of *Friday* won the esteemed French Academy Prize for best novel in 1967. It is often considered to be the first installment of a trilogy including *Le Roi des aulnes* (1970; *The Ogre*, 1972) and *Gemini*. *Vendredi: Ou, La Vie sauvage* (1971; *Friday and Robinson: Life on Esperanza Island*, 1972), an important adaptation created for children, deletes Robinson's private journal and adds seven scenes of interpersonal exchange in which Friday transfers to Robinson his knowledge of gourmet cooking, metaphor, and mime. These modifications strengthen Friday's role as mentor and mirror. Tournier's autobiographical essay *Le Vent Paraclet* (1977) includes comments on *Friday* in terms of urban isolation and problems of the Third World.

The novel is highly discussable, and comparison to *Gemini* is especially indicated. Friday and Robinson become twins with two bodies and two souls, whereas Jean and Paul have two bodies and one soul. Important theories of morality, perception, and sexual composition can be extracted from the novel. Speranza can be studied independently as an ecological system, and each of the behaviors exhibited by its two main inhabitants (nudity, urination, mimicry, mating, signal systems, death rituals, and so on) count as formal objects of ethnological inquiry. Most important, through its case history of solitude, its laboratory encounter between two cultures, and its structure of creation through compensation, Tournier's *Friday* continues Freudian thinking on the origins of neurosis in technological societies. As Sigmund Freud wrote, "It is easy. . . for the barbarian to be healthy; for the civilized man, the task is a hard one."

Sources for Further Study

Cloonan, William. "*Vendredi: Ou, Les Limbes du Pacifique,*" in *Michel Tournier*, 1985.
Koster, Serge. *Michel Tournier*, 1986.

Shattuck, Roger. "Locating Michel Tournier," in *The Innocent Eye: On Modern Literature and the Arts*, 1984.

Stirn, François. *Vendredi: Ou, Les Limbes du Pacifique, Tournier*, 1984.

Sud. January, 1986. Special Tournier issue.

Frank Coppay

GARDEN, ASHES

Author: Danilo Kiš (1935-   )
Type of plot: Impressionistic realism
Time of plot: The late 1930's and early 1940's
Locale: Northern Yugoslavia (Voyvodina)
First published: Bašta, pepeo, 1965 (English translation, 1975)

> *Principal characters:*
> EDUARD SCHAM, a railway official, poet, and world traveler
> MARIA SCHAM, his wife
> ANDREAS "ANDI" SCHAM, their son
> ANNA SCHAM, their daughter

The Novel

The story of *Garden, Ashes* is narrated by Andreas ("Andi") Scham in a series of loosely connected reminiscences about his childhood. At the beginning of the novel, he is a five-year-old boy who remembers vividly the incomprehensible happenings around him: the constant comings and goings, the changing places in which he lives, the numerous older relatives whom he cannot quite remember, and the mysterious disappearances of his father, Eduard Scham. Only later does Andi fully understand these happenings; at the time, surrounded by an aura of anxiety and even fear, he tries simply to cope with them and to understand their meaning, though the fact that his fertile imagination frequently blows things out of proportion does not help. As an obedient child, he follows the adults' orders instinctively, aware of the fateful nature of the happenings around him. Andi never mentions explicitly the war going on around him, yet he senses that his Jewish father, a former railroad official, is being harassed and hunted for reasons the child cannot yet understand.

Andi is comforted by his steadfast mother, Maria Scham, and his older sister, Anna, who, though yet a child herself, is able to cope slightly better with the ominous events. It is his mother whom he trusts and understands. Although Maria never tries to explain the true nature of the traumatic events happening to them, the two tacitly understand each other. In such a gloomy atmosphere, however, even an innocent "love" between Andi and Julia, a Gentile girl, assumes overtones of forbidden fruit.

Throughout these events, Andi is aware of one constant in his young life—his father. Aside from his love for his father, Andi is fascinated by his eccentricity and originality, by his intelligence which borders on genius, and by his father's strange aloofness toward him. As if forewarned of events to come, Eduard seems to avoid becoming too close to his son; the more he tries to maintain his distance, however, the more his son wants to be close to him. When Eduard is humiliated—as he is, many times—he pretends otherwise, blaming his problems on the inability of others to understand him. He hopes that Andi will understand his father's singularity and his role as a sacrificial lamb selected by uncontrollable celestial forces. Just when the two seem to have drawn closer together, the inevitable happens, and Eduard is swept away in a pogrom.

Long after his father's departure, Andi (now eleven) often thinks about him, no longer trying to understand him but instead accepting him as he was. More important, Andi discovers that he has inherited many of his father's traits. He has just as exuberant an imagination, he feels the same urge to travel to exotic places, and he has begun to write poetry. Above all, Andi senses that the shadow of his father will accompany him into manhood. "Above the forest hovered the spirit of our father," he says before leaving home. "Haven't we heard him clearing his nose into a newspaper and the forest echoing threefold?"

The Characters

Although the novel is narrated by Andi, relating his childhood impressions, the true protagonist is his father, Eduard. Eduard occupies the central position in the rather diffused plot, and he is constantly on his son's mind, an eccentric and incorrigible dreamer, a frustrated genius, a poet, a philosopher, a drunkard, a proud squanderer of his many gifts, a misplaced wanderer from some mysterious, exotic land. In real life, Eduard is a railroad inspector, as if to symbolize one of his constant urges—to disappear every now and then, to travel without any apparent goal or direction and without the knowledge of his family. (It was this urge which inspired him to write his magnum opus, *A Railroad, Bus, and Airline Schedule*, into which he infused his considerable poetic talent.) Eduard is always reaching for the stars, desiring the unattainable and setting his goals higher and higher; the more unlikely the achievement, the better. An amateur philosopher, he adopts a fatalistic point of view. In his words, "There are people who are born to be unhappy and to make others unhappy, who are the victims of celestial intrigues incomprehensible to us. . . . I look at myself in the role forced on me by the heavens and by fate, conscious of my role at all times yet at the same time unable to resist it with the force of logic or will."

Eduard's relationship with his family is quite vague and similarly fatalistic. He acts as though he could live without them, yet he always returns from his wandering. He is aloof from his wife without being guilty of infidelity. He absentmindedly calls his son "young man," yet he is anxious to secure Andi's respect and admiration. Eduard's premonition of his tragic fate makes him hide his feelings, as if to spare his family grief after his final departure. Above all, he is a victim of circumstances in the colossal dance of death that was World War II. As a Jew and an intelligent man, he cannot help but see what the future holds for him, and this vision saps his strength, no matter how much he struggles to accomplish his goals in his remaining time.

Andi is too young to understand fully his father's predicament; nevertheless, he feels the magnitude of the loss, for he misses his father at the time when he needs him the most—in his formative years. Perhaps for this reason, father and son share an almost mystical bond, as may be seen in the early development of their similar, and at times identical, traits. At the end of the novel, Andi is determined to follow in his father's footsteps, to reach, through his poetry, the same star his father saw. In other respects, Andi shows the traits of any boy between the ages of five and eleven: playfulness, imagination, anxiety, and a tendency to live in a world of his own. His parents differ greatly, and Andi has inherited from them a remarkable balance of traits—from his mother, sensitivity and confidence, from his father, wild imagination and the desire to excel.

Maria is a rock of granite amid the surrounding misfortune. Her love for her husband is not clear from Andi's reminiscences, although that can be assumed because she stands by him throughout the turmoil. She also has much to give to her son through her tales of her past, which are perhaps not as colorful as those of her husband, but which nevertheless nourish the young child's imagination. Between the two of them, the parents give their boy a good start on the road to manhood.

Themes and Meanings

The main theme of the novel is that of a boy's childhood under most difficult circumstances. Indeed, up to a point, *Garden, Ashes* is a *Bildungsroman*; although the book covers only a short period in the boy's life, the quantity of tragic experiences packed in those few years had a powerful impact on his psyche. Andi's knowledge comes from his experiences, not from any conscious effort on the part of his elders, and the lessons learned thus have a much greater value to him.

The value of such an education can be questioned because of what may be considered to be the second important theme of the novel, the inhumanity of man to man. Andi is faced with a tragic reality too early in life, with potentially devastating consequences. While it is true that neither he nor his family, aside from his father and several other older relatives, is subjected directly to the cruelty of the pogroms, horror, no matter how muted, lurks in the background throughout the novel as a constant reminder of the times. Yet Andi is not destroyed by it; on the contrary, he salvages from the tragedy a glorious, perhaps overly idealized, image of his father that will nourish him for the rest of his life.

The horrors of World War II are best illustrated in *Garden, Ashes* by the persecution of the Jews; this is the one facet that ties the book directly to historical reality. Yet Danilo Kiš writes very little about it directly. Instead, he allows the impact of the age's cruelty to sink slowly into the minds and hearts of those affected—and into those of the readers. The author firmly believes in understatement, knowing that the full force of horror will break through.

Critical Context

In 1965, when it was first published, *Garden, Ashes* announced the arrival of a young and unmistakable talent in Serbian and Yugoslav literature, Danilo Kiš. Kiš's two previous novels, *Mansarda* and *Psalam 44* (both published in 1962), were only harbingers of his mature achievements. With *Garden, Ashes*, Kiš stepped to the front of a promising new generation of writers, and he has remained there ever since.

Kiš's stature among his contemporaries can be attributed in part to his surprising maturity in matters of style. *Garden, Ashes* is written in both a realistic and a somewhat impressionistic style, imbued with poetry all the more effective because of its unassuming gentleness. Another striking feature of his style is the richness of his vocabulary, which is a well-balanced mixture of Serbian and international expressions normally shunned by most writers. In this respect, Kiš is provocatively modern. Modern, also, is a certain experimentation in style, such as his inclusion of a drawing of a Singer sewing machine and his avoidance of straight plot; in fact, the novel has hardly any distinct plot or even a chronological sequence of events. Even though the novel is basically realistic, it requires the reader's efforts to supply the missing links. The abundance of rich metaphors and images, coupled with cultural and historical allusions, adds to the artistic quality of *Garden, Ashes*, making it one of the best novels in the second half of the twentieth century.

Sources for Further Study

Czarny, Norbert. "Imaginary-Real Lives: On Danilo Kiš," in *Cross-Currents*. III (1984), pp. 279-284.

Mihailovich, Vasa D. "Serbian Fiction 1965," in *Books Abroad*. XL (1966), pp. 281-283.

Pawel, Ernst. "*Garden, Ashes*," in *The Nation*. CCVII (September 16, 1978), p. 246.

White, Edmund. "Danilo Kiš: The Obligations of Form," in *Southwest Review*. LXXI (Summer, 1986), pp. 363-377.

Vasa D. Mihailovich

THE GARDEN OF THE FINZI-CONTINIS

Author: Giorgio Bassani (1916-   )
Type of plot: Social criticism
Time of plot: Primarily fall, 1938, to summer, 1939
Locale: Ferrara, Italy
First published: Il giardino dei Finzi-Contini, 1962 (English translation, 1965)

Principal characters:
> THE NARRATOR, a young, middle-class Jewish man who falls in
> love with Micòl
> MICÒL FINZI-CONTINI, a rich Jewess
> ALBERTO, Micòl's brother
> PROFESSOR ERMANNO, Micòl's father
> GIAMPIERO MALNATE, Alberto's friend from Milan

The Novel

The Garden of the Finzi-Continis is an elegy about the Finzi-Continis, Ferrara's richest Jewish family, all of whom died soon after their deportation to Germany in 1943. As seen through the eyes of the narrator, a middle-class Jewish boy, the exclusive Finzi-Continis are the source of much wonder. He is fascinated by their possessions—from their imposing but tasteless family tomb to their stately, ornate carriage and their gloomy, neo-Gothic mansion surrounded by a huge park. He is even more fascinated by the Finzi-Contini children, who are tutored at home instead of attending the Jewish primary school and state high school and who speak in accents like those of no one else. On the other hand, the Finzi-Continis' self-imposed isolation disgusts the narrator's father, especially when the family withdraws from the Jewish community by ceasing to worship in the thriving Italian synagogue and by beginning to worship in the tiny Spanish synagogue which had not been used for more than three hundred years. The narrator's father charges that the Finzi-Continis are guilty of an "aristocratic-type anti-semitism."

In part 1, the novel traces the history of the Finzi-Contini family from the patriarch, Moisè Finzi-Contini, who amassed the huge family fortune, to Moisè's great-grandchildren, who prove to be the end of the Finzi-Contini line. Part 2 begins in October, 1938, two months after the imposition of the first of what was to become a series of racial laws which forbade, among other things, Jews from marrying Gentiles and from employing Gentiles as servants. One result of the racial laws is that all the Jews are forced to resign from Eleonora d'Este, a private tennis club, when a mixed doubles team consisting of a Gentile woman and a Jewish man appear to be winning the club's doubles championship. As a result, Alberto and Micòl Finzi-Contini, who are in their early twenties, invite the ostracized club members to play on the private Finzi-Contini court. The narrator, who is about the same age as Alberto and Micòl, is included in the group even though he does not know either very well and has had no contact with the Finzi-Contini family for more than five years. Giampiero Malnate, a Gentile whom Alberto befriended while the two young men were studying at the Polytechnic in Milan, also joins the group from time to time.

This clutch of tennis players enjoys several weeks of fellowship during late autumn, 1938, before the winter rains begin. Micòl often pulls the narrator away from the group, ostensibly to show him the grounds of the estate. The turning point of their relationship occurs one day when the young couple escapes to the coach house, but the narrator cannot find the words to tell Micòl of his love for her, and the moment passes forever.

Part 3 chronicles the winter of 1938-1939, during which the narrator falls in love with Micòl more desperately while Micòl draws further away from her lover. The vivacious Micòl, who is writing her thesis on the poetry of Emily Dickinson at the university in Venice, insists that she will die, like Dickinson, an old maid.

Juxtaposed against what quickly becomes a hopeless, even painful, love affair is a catalog of the various ways that loyal Jewish-Italian citizens are gradually losing their rights, all the more horrifying because the tone is so matter-of-fact. The narrator's father is expelled from the Fascist Party, the narrator's younger brother Ernesto is forced to leave Italy in order to go to a university, and thirteen-year-old Fanny is banned from attending public school. In addition, the narrator is told that he can no longer study at the city library, a place that he has frequented since he was a very young boy.

Part 4 covers the period from mid-April, 1939, to August, 1939, during which the narrator's hopeless love for Micòl grows still more hopeless and even embarrassing. In frustration, the narrator alternates between stealing kisses at inopportune moments and picking fights. Instead of making a clean break, Micòl simply orders her admirer to stay away for a few days, then a few weeks. Finally, the narrator's pride allows him no more humiliation, and after one last surreptitious, nocturnal visit to the Finzi-Contini garden, he never returns.

Paralleling the disintegrating relationship of Micòl and the narrator is the worsening political situation of the Farrarese Jews in general and the Finzi-Contini family in particular. The Fascist federal secretary decrees that the Finzi-Continis must stop the gatherings at their private tennis court. Failure to abide by the order will be cause for deportation to a concentration camp. As the epilogue states, deportation is precisely the fate that awaited Micòl and her family. The time and place of their deaths are unknown. Only Alberto, who suffocated to death from a disease called malignant lymphogranuloma, is buried in the family tomb in the Jewish cemetery.

The Characters

The unnamed narrator of *The Garden of the Finzi-Continis* shares several important characteristics with the author, Giorgio Bassani. Both were born in 1916 to Jewish fathers who had studied medicine, both grew up in Ferrara, and both were imprisoned during the Nazi Holocaust.

As a young boy, the narrator stands in awe of the Finzi-Continis. As a literate, sensitive young man, he is invited into their private world, but for him, the relationship means only heartache. His obsessive love for Micòl leads him into nightmares of jealousy. He also seems paralyzed by the same stasis that engulfs the Finzi-Continis; after he receives his degree from the university in Bologna, he seems neither to write nor to look for a job, although the latter would have been very difficult considering the rampant anti-Semitism in Ferrara at the time.

Micòl, a kind of Jewish Scarlett O'Hara, encourages the narrator by selecting him to give tours of the grounds, by encouraging him to develop a relationship with her brother while she is away in Venice, and by inviting him into her bedroom. Then she torments her young lover by pretending to have become engaged in Venice and by talking about the non-Jewish students with whom she has flirted.

In relation to Micòl, the Finzi-Contini men seem lifeless. Once the racial laws are passed, Alberto never leaves the family grounds except to go to the synagogue. He never returns to Milan to finish his degree, he seems to know nothing about the family business, he shows no interest in women, and he takes no part in the heated political discussions between the narrator and Malnate. Although Alberto's father, Professor Ermanno, shows great kindness to the narrator by inviting him to use the Finzi-Contini private collection when the city library closes its doors to the young man, the professor does not teach or do research, excepting two thin pamphlets written years before.

In contrast to the dreamy, impractical Jewish characters in the novel is the no-nonsense Giampiero Malnate, who has come to Ferrara to work as a chemist in the local synthetic rubber factory. He satisfies his lust by visiting brothels instead of getting entangled in romantic relationships. It is he who warns of the treachery of the Fascists while his Jewish friends try to remain faithful to the Italian government.

Themes and Meanings

In *The Garden of the Finzi-Continis*, the events in Ferrara are symbolic of the madness spreading all over Europe during the years leading up to World War II. As Jews begin losing their rights, the aloof Finzi-Continis invite some of their coreligionists to share the family's rather paradisiacal existence in the garden of the novel's title. Yet even that little corner of the world is, at best, only a momentary stay against the hatred and envy of the outside world.

Prejudice, its practices and effects, is the main theme of the novel. The theme is all the more effective because the tone is devoid of rancor and sometimes even a bit amused. Furthermore, Bassani shows that prejudice exists on many levels, not the least of which is within the Jewish community itself. The narrator's father, a landowner, objects to the Finzi-Continis' vast holdings and complains that the family is entirely too ostentatious in its religious practices. At least part of Micòl's rejection of the narrator is a result of their common Jewish heritage.

The central irony lies in the fact that the super-rich Finzi-Continis, who can, as late as 1942, corner the market in oxygen cylinders to help the dying Alberto breathe, cannot, in the end, help their fellow Jews, or even themselves, to escape Adolf Hitler's war machine.

Critical Context

An Italian poet, critic, and editor, Bassani is best known for his novels and short stories set in Ferrara, his childhood home. Within the confines of Ferrara, the protagonist typically searches for self-discovery amid various types of prejudice. In the novella *Gli occhiali d'oro* (1958; *The Gold-Rimmed Spectacles*, 1960; also as *The Gold-Rimmed Eyeglasses*, 1975), the prejudice is directed against the once-respected physician Dr. Fadigati, whose homosexuality, when revealed, drives him to suicide. The novel *Dietro la porta* (1964; *Behind the Door*, 1972) depicts the corruption of a sixteen-year-old Jewish boy who seeks acceptance from his Catholic schoolmates. *L'airone* (1968; *The Heron*, 1970) employs a middle-aged protagonist whose hunting expedition becomes a symbolic journey through the political and social conditions of postwar Italy.

The Garden of the Finzi-Continis, which continues the theme of the ostracism of the outsider, is Bassani's most popular work. It is also his most critically acclaimed novel, having been awarded the Viareggio Prize in 1962. In 1970, *The Garden of the Finzi-Continis* was adapted for the screen by the highly respected film director Vittorio De Sica and cinematographer Ennio Guarnieri.

Bassani's fiction is distinguished above all by its realistic treatment of self-discovery. Understanding in Bassani's Ferrara, as in real life, often does not pave the way to happiness. Further, self-discovery seldom leads to an understanding of the actions of others, even when those actions are particularly vicious. What makes this point palpable and even intriguing is Bassani's narrative technique, in which the story is not told directly but is filtered through memory. Memory reshapes experience as one forgets important events and overemphasizes ordinary ones. The result is not fact but essence. This technique is reinforced by Bassani's classical, restrained prose style.

Sources for Further Study

De Charmant, Elizabeth. "Bassani *Il giardino dei Finzi-Contini,*" in *Eu-*

ropean Patterns: Contemporary Patterns in European Writing, 1964. Edited by T. B. Harward.

Lavorato, Rachele Longo. "Thematic Aspects of the Works of Giorgio Bassani," in *Dissertation Abstracts International*. XLIV (March, 1984), p. 2784.

Mitgang, Herbert. Review in *The New York Times Book Review*. LXX (August 1, 1965), p. 4.

Newsweek. Review. LXVI (August 30, 1965), p. 83.

Radcliff-Umsted, Douglas. "Bassani: The Motivation of Language," in *Italica*. LXII (Summer, 1985), pp. 116-125.

Time. Review. LXXXVI (August 6, 1965), p. 86.

Sandra Hanby Harris

GARGOYLES

Author: Thomas Bernhard (1931-   )
Type of plot: Psychological realism
Time of plot: After World War I
Locale: The Austrian Alps
First published: Verstörung, 1967 (English translation, 1970)

Principal characters:
THE NARRATOR, a student home from Leoben to visit his father
THE DOCTOR, the narrator's father, a country doctor
PRINCE SAURAU, a mad patient

The Novel

Gargoyles chronicles a day in the life of an unnamed Austrian country doctor as he travels from patient to patient in the company of his son, an engineering student home for a visit. Although the son, who narrates the day's events, remains an uninvolved observer, the stories of the people whom he watches his father treat reflect his own family's alienation from one another. While the day's journey could perhaps have provided both father and son with some understanding of each other, the book's ending suggests that nothing will change.

The novel opens in the early morning as the father and son set off to treat an innkeeper's wife who has been mortally wounded by a drunken miner in an early morning tavern brawl. As they ride in the innkeeper's wagon, the father describes the life such people lead: one of anger, despair, and enslavement—a life that goes nowhere and provides no satisfaction or worthwhile human contact. Estrangement and betrayal are the fate of all the people in the doctor's region. By the time the pair reaches the innkeeper's wife, it is too late. The doctor's only reaction is that, given the squalid nature of the woman's marriage, murder was inevitable. This detachment sets the tone for the day's visits.

Back on the road, the father and son discuss the death of the doctor's wife, yet they never express their inner feelings about this woman. It becomes clear from the beginning that these two men do not know each other and probably never will. The next patient is a Frau Ebenhöh, a woman slowly dying of cancer and whose dull-witted son works in a tannery. Like the other patients in the novel, Frau Ebenhöh is estranged from her family, and she is convinced that her son and his wife will squander the inheritance that she will shortly leave him.

The doctor and his son next see a diabetic industrialist who lives in a decaying, empty hunting lodge, isolated from the rest of the world—except for his half-sister, with whom he conducts an incestuous relationship. Kept outside, the doctor's son overhears the ravings of this crazed philosopher, who destroys every text he writes only to write each over again in search of the perfect statement concerning an undisclosed subject. When the doctor concludes this visit, the two men make their way up a narrow valley toward Hochgobernitz, the castle of Prince Saurau, stopping along the way to see more patients.

At a mill, the doctor looks in on an aging couple, the man ailing from gangrene, the woman immobilized by dropsy and incipient tuberculosis. Trapped in their fetid room with a Russian wolfhound that refuses to go outside without them, they oversee the workings of their mill. The doctor's son stays outside, a witness to the equally bizarre events there: The couple's sons and Turkish hired hand have been wringing the necks of dozens of exotic birds in an effort to silence their frenzied cries. It seems that the birds' owner, the boys' uncle, had died several weeks earlier, and since then the birds have been frantic, their cries becoming intolerable to the inhabitants of the mill. Creating a museum of stuffed, rare birds seems to be the only solution.

On the way out of the oppressive valley, the two men stop at the home of an incurable cripple, a gifted musician who had played the music of Wolfgang Amadeus Mozart at the age of four but who is now a physically twisted, frenzied lunatic, confined to his room. His sister, also his caretaker, lives in the same room with him, a room filled with reminders of his lost promise: countless musical instruments as well as paintings of the composers whose works he used to play.

The final patient whom the doctor and his son see is Prince Saurau, whose fractured monologue takes up more than half of the book. Isolated within his castle, the prince is a prisoner of his delusions, hearing inaudible sounds and imagining impossible intrigues plotted against him. Perhaps the most important thing the narrator hears during this visit is the prince's account of his ungrateful son, a student in London. Part truth and part nightmare, the prince's story tells of his son's plot to destroy his inheritance once the prince has died. The novel concludes as the two men prepare to leave for home; nothing is resolved.

The Characters

The narrator is a passive observer of his father's interactions with patients and friends, yet the scenes that he has chosen to report tell the reader much about him, his family, and his relationship with his father. The world of which he gives readers a glimpse is one filled with grotesques, dying husbands and wives both physically and psychically deformed. Like the sons of the patients and of Prince Saurau, the doctor's son is emotionally estranged from his father. The narrator believes that his "real" life is in Leoben, where he studies mining engineering; Prince Saurau's son studies in London and refuses to come home.

The narrator has come home to try to establish a deeper contact with his father. To that end, he has written a letter—unacknowledged by the father—concerning the family's inability to make contact with one another and proposing reasons why this should be so. His mother has wasted away and died, his sister makes frequent suicide attempts, and his father treats the sick but seems able to heal no one. It is clear that Bernhard intends for the events of the narrator's journey to serve as a commentary on the narrator's family as well as on the lives of the people whom the young man meets.

The father, a detached observer of those whom he treats, is mirrored in his insane double, Prince Saurau. Both men are disappointed in their children and see no hope either for reconciliation before their death or for compassionate understanding after they die. Yet neither seems able to speak directly to their sons, to express his fears or his hopes. The journey on which the doctor and his son go and the extended narrative of Prince Saurau serve as the only means by which the doctor can communicate his thoughts to his dispassionate son.

All the other characters reflect or share the same anxieties concerning their families, and all the people whom the doctor and his son visit on their day's excursion live lives of crazed isolation, even when other members of their families are close at hand.

Themes and Meanings

By creating a story whose narrator and main characters are so detached from one another and, consequently, unable to express their real feelings, Bernhard presents a world of isolated, frightened, and frightening people. Aside from the doctor and his son, all the people in this novel are grotesques—gargoyles—misshapen physically and mentally. The journey symbolizes the father's failed attempt to communicate with his son. The conclusion leaves the reader with no sense of resolution or closure, just as the two men have reached no understanding despite the horrors that they have seen and heard as they visited each patient. By visiting each of these diseased patients during the height of his suffering, the author forces the reader and the narrator to view the grotesques in passing, as if they are fixed forever in their suffering. Bernhard offers no hope that any of these people will improve or that the rift between the doctor and his son will be bridged.

Much of the novel is devoted to the ramblings of Prince Saurau in his castle at Hochgobernitz, where he reveals his paranoid delusions regarding his son, his employees, and other members of his family, all of whom seem only to be doubles for the members of the narrator's own family. The characters in this novel are unable to relate in any meaningful way to the people who matter the most to them: Parents are estranged from children, siblings hate one another or are cut off by insanity, and townspeople hate and fear one another. All these exterior circumstances seem only to duplicate the essential fractures evident in the narrator's own family.

The physical journey he takes with his father to the prince's castle—deep in the mountains beyond a narrow, gloomy ravine, isolated from everyone— parallels the interior probings deeper and deeper into the relationship between the narrator and the doctor. Finally, the incipient madness in the narrator's family is externalized in the person of Prince Saurau, who articulates problems remarkably similar to those experienced by the narrator and his family.

Critical Context

Gargoyles was Thomas Bernhard's first novel and, in its bleak portrait of the human condition, closely resembles the work of Albert Camus, Franz Kafka, and Jean-Paul Sartre. In particular, Bernhard's style is reminiscent of that of Kafka, whose settings were often the eternally depressing present of places, recognizable yet unfamiliar. Similar to the settings of these three authors, Bernhard's landscapes are spare and gloomy, with the darkness originating from within the characters rather than emanating from the landscape itself. The tone of the fiction is one of menace, a menace that never fully manifests itself. The reader cannot identify this menace and, therefore, fails to deal with it satisfactorily; thus Bernhard increases the tension. He depicts a world whose barren landscape and lonely people are more horrifying because he demands that the reader see beyond a character's immediate plight to the horror within, to the terror stemming from alienation, madness, and isolation—a spiritual condition explicitly identified in the novel's German title, which means "derangement."

While *Gargoyles* introduced the themes that have continued to obsess Bernhard throughout his career, this novel differs noticeably from his later works. The episodes prior to the encounter with Prince Saurau are darkly grotesque, yet they remain within the boundaries of conventional narrative, and the prince's extended monologue is framed by the narrator's comments (though in fact the prince has the last word). Bernhard's later novels, in contrast, are monologues unbounded by any narrative frame; from the first sentence, one is in the grip of a relentless voice.

Sources for Further Study

Domandi, Agnes, ed. "Thomas Bernhard," in *Modern German Literature*, 1972.

Gamper, H. *Thomas Bernhard*, 1977.

Riley, Carolyn, ed. "Thomas Bernhard," in *Contemporary Literary Criticism*. III (1975), pp. 64-65.

Schwedler, Wilfried. "Thomas Bernhard," in *Handbook of Austrian Literature*, 1973. Edited by Frederick Ungar.

Sorg, B. *Thomas Bernhard*, 1977.

Melissa E. Barth

THE GATES OF THE FOREST

Author: Elie Wiesel (1928-   )
Type of plot: Psychological realism
Time of plot: The 1940's and early 1950's
Locale: Hungarian forests and villages, Paris, and Brooklyn
First published: Les Portes de la forêt, 1964 (English translation, 1966)

> *Principal characters:*
> GREGOR, whose real name is GAVRIEL, the protagonist, a
>   young Hungarian Jew who has escaped the Holocaust
> GAVRIEL, a mysterious, unnamed Jew who borrows the
>   protagonist's name and sacrifices himself for him
> MARIA, formerly a servant in the home of Gregor's family
> LEIB THE LION, the leader of the Jewish partisans
> CLARA, Leib's lover and, after his death, Gregor's wife

The Novel

Beginning with spring and ending with winter, *The Gates of the Forest* is divided into four parts, each standing for a season in its natural order. The first and last parts concentrate on the inner self and the middle two on action. The novel first introduces Gregor, a Hungarian Jew in his late teens who, without his family, has escaped the Holocaust. While Gregor hides from the Nazis in a village forest, another Jew, a mysterious man of about thirty, happens upon his hiding place. Since this stranger has no name, Gregor gives him his own name, Gavriel, which Gregor had abandoned because it was too conspicuously Jewish. The two Jews hide in a cave whose entrance is concealed by a large boulder. There, they pass many days together, sharing their beliefs and stories with each other. From Gavriel, Gregor learns of the hideous facts of the war, especially information about the cruelties of the Nazis against the Jews. Gavriel comes to be seen as a lunatic philosopher-saint who sometimes reacts to the Holocaust with insane laughter.

The search by the Nazis intensifies outside the hideout; getting away from them seems impossible to the two men. Just as the Nazis are upon the site, Gavriel gives himself up. The Nazis have no reason to believe that there is more than one Jew in the forest area, and so they are satisfied. The sacrifice of Gavriel leaves Gregor with a moral obligation to which he totally commits himself.

In a nearby village, he finds refuge in the home of Maria, a Christian and an old servant of his family. She has him pretend to be a deaf-mute and the son of her sister Ileana, who has departed the village, leaving behind a reputation for looseness. Unaware of Gregor's pretense, the village folk take him into their confidences, many of the men confessing to illicit relations with Ileana. The parish priest, "against sin, but not against crime," confesses to having betrayed a Jew because the Jew refused to accept Christianity as a condition of refuge. What is for Elie Wiesel a thematic analogy between the Crucifixion of Jesus and the annihilation of the Jews is brought out dramatically. Against Maria's protests, Gregor is cast as Judas in a school play about the passion of Christ. Becoming caught up in the drama as it is performed, members of the cast and the audience, also, verbally and then physically attack Gregor. He stuns them to temporary inaction by declaring, first, that he is not Judas and second, that he is not the son of Ileana. When at last he tells them that he is not Gregor, that he is a Jew whose name is Gavriel, the villagers are prepared to cut out his tongue. They despise him because he is a Jew and fear him because he knows their secrets. The mayor of the town, Petruskanu, who suspects that he may have fathered Gregor, rescues him and helps him make contact with Jewish partisans in the forest.

As Gavriel had informed Gregor about the concentration camps and the crematoria, Gregor now tells the partisans. They are led by Leib the Lion, who was a boyhood friend of Gregor; at ten years of age, the two stood up against Christian bullies. Hearing from Gregor of Gavriel's imprisonment, Leib says that the prisoner must be set free in order for him to communicate what he has seen as a victim of the Holocaust. The plan to get Gavriel out of prison backfires, however, and Leib is captured by the Nazis. Once more, Gregor, who was the central figure in the escape plan, believes that he has betrayed another. The partisans, suspicious of him, put him through an intense grilling that ends only when Clara, Leib's lover, intervenes.

Yehuda, a young partisan, now befriends Gregor. Putting aside his feeling that his own death is imminent, Yehuda tells Gregor that he should make known to Clara the obvious truth that he loves her. In an inhumane world, Yehuda declares, love is a bridge against solitude. It is the great reward, the greatest victory. Gregor admits to Yehuda that indeed he does love Clara. A few days later, Yehuda is stabbed to death, the partisans shoot his killer, and Gregor tells Clara that he loves her.

After a chance meeting in Paris following the war, Gregor and Clara are married. The marriage is a failure, however, because Clara, haunted by a past of death and destruction, acts as if Gregor is Leib, her dead lover. Just when Gregor is about to give up on his marriage and leave Clara, he is drawn into a relationship with a rebbe who helps him rediscover his Jewish past. A man who may or may not be Gavriel appears at the rebbe's synagogue. After a long conversation with this mysterious man, Gregor comes to realize that he cannot, after all, leave Clara. To do so would be to return to solitude and thus betray her as he has, at least by omission, betrayed others. Once more, Gregor assumes the name of Gavriel. Asked by a young boy to serve as the tenth man necessary to say morning prayers, Gregor consents. While reciting the prayer for the dead, he turns the moment into an occasion to pray for the soul of Leib and to ask God to arrange an end to the suffering of those who loved, and still love, the dead hero.

The Characters

The central character, Gavriel, changes his name to Gregor and then, at the end of the novel, back to Gavriel. Furthermore, he uses the name Judas temporarily, if only for the purpose of a play. For Wiesel, the name choices and name exchanges in his novel clearly serve as devices that underscore the themes of sacrifice and suffering. An angel, Gabriel, comes to earth in the person of the mysterious Gavriel, who risks his life for Gregor. Gregor, in turn, takes on the suffering of all the Jews of history by becoming Judas. Other biblical names, notably Maria and Petruskanu (Peter), are given to characters who, though Christian, take great risks for the Jews.

Elie Wiesel himself is very much a part of his story. Like his protagonist, he lost his family in the Holocaust and, like Gregor, survived it and experienced the suffering and guilt that many Holocaust survivors have felt. Wiesel's story allows him, a witness to Nazi crimes, to be a messenger to the world; thus, *The Gates of the Forest* seems more than a mere work of fiction, and its characters seem more than figures from the author's imagination.

Themes and Meanings

The Gates of the Forest begins with a Jewish tale, essentially an epigraph, illustrating the vitality of storytelling. The facts of the Holocaust, all the horrors, must be told as many times and in as many ways as are necessary to make the story known; Wiesel's novel is another attempt to convey that story so that readers will be as haunted by it, as unable to forget it as he himself has been. Leib the Lion, as the last line of the novel indicates, is a messenger to heaven just as, in Wiesel's *Le Jour* (1961; *The Accident*, 1962) Eliezer is a living messenger from the dead. A central theme of *The Gates of the Forest* is that the Jews, though deserted by God during the Holocaust, have no alternative but to tell their tragic story and to recover their faith. "After what has happened, how believe in God?" is answered by "After what has happened, how *not* believe in God?"

Along with the theme of faith is that of friendship, oneness, and community. If the Messiah has not come to the Jews, the novel says, then let every Jew, every individual, be the Messiah to everyone else. Christians must do their part to bring humanity together; one way is to end their persecution of Jews as descendants of Judas, to cease making Jews take the place of Christ on the Cross.

Like Eliezer in *The Accident*, Clara in *The Gates of the Forest* is immobilized by the dead, by the past. She gives her love to Gregor only when she pretends that he is Leib the Lion, the lover she has lost to the Holocaust.

Symbolically, Leib not only defends Gregor but also sacrifices himself for him, as Gavriel does at the beginning of the novel. Sacrifice, or courageous and unselfish risk-taking such as that of Maria or Petruskanu, is a recurring theme of great substance in this novel. Guilt—both as a survivor and as the recipient of another's sacrifice—is still another controlling and pervasive theme. Instead of living with guilt, Gregor learns to love, to affirm the present and put the past behind. He even learns to change places with another, which is something like returning one's life to both the giver and the receiver. To love the living is not to forget the dead; to pay homage to the dead is not to lay aside an obligation to the living.

Critical Context

The Gates of the Forest, Wiesel's fourth novel, should be read chronologically, after *L'Aube* (1960; *Dawn*, 1961), *The Accident*, and *La Ville de la chance* (1962; *The Town Beyond the Wall*, 1964) and before *Le Mendiant de Jérusalem* (1968; *A Beggar in Jerusalem*, 1970). This order is important because of the thematic development in Wiesel's first five novels—from annihilation to affirmation, from solitude to community. Having lost his entire family and many other loved ones in the monstrous Holocaust, Wiesel came to know that there are countless ways to record or interpret such an event. Each of Wiesel's novels may be seen, then, as a circle which shares a center with the other novels; that center is the Holocaust. Along with other writers—notably, Primo Levi, Nelly Sachs, Robert Donat, Paul Celan, Ernst Weichert, Vladka Meed, Pierre Gascar, André Schwarz-Bart, and Tadeusz Borowski—Wiesel is a sensitive and bold interpreter of the Jewish experience. As the winner of the Nobel Peace Prize in 1986, Wiesel has enhanced an already considerable reputation worldwide. He has given his life to creating a literature assuring his readers that victims of inhumanity, both living and dead, will never be forgotten.

Sources for Further Study

Brown, Robert McAfee. *Elie Wiesel: Messenger to All Humanity*, 1983.

Estees, Ted L. *Elie Wiesel*, 1980.

Fine, Ellen S. *Legacy of Night: The Literary Universe of Elie Wiesel*, 1982.

Knopp, Josephine. "Wiesel and the Absurd," in *Contemporary Literature*. XV (Spring, 1974), pp. 212-220.

Wiesel, Elie. Interview in *The Paris Review*. XXVI (Spring, 1984), pp. 130-178.

David Powell

GEMINI

Author: Michel Tournier (1924-   )
Type of plot: Philosophical naturalism
Time of plot: 1918-1961
Locale: Various locations in France and throughout the world
First published: Les Météores, 1975 (English translation, 1981)

> *Principal characters:*
> ÉDOUARD SURIN, the father of identical twins, owner of a
>   textile mill, and volunteer soldier
> MARIA-BARBARA, his fertile wife, the mother of eleven and a
>   clandestine anti-Nazi insurgent
> JEAN-PAUL, the collective name of his twin sons: Jean, the
>   rebel individualist, and Paul, the dominating idealist
> FLORENCE, Édouard's Jewish mistress in Paris, who is
>   captured and sent to Buchenwald
> ANGELICA, Édouard's Flemish mistress, killed by German
>   shelling
> ALEXANDRE, Édouard's younger brother, the scandalous
>   uncle of the twins, director of a garbage-reclaiming
>   empire, and a homosexual gadabout
> FRANZ, an idiot savant, the only boy to understand the twins'
>   private language
> THOMAS KOUSSEK, a Benedictine schoolmate of Alexandre,
>   now a Catholic priest
> SOPHIE, Jean's fiancée, an interloper between Paul and Jean

The Novel

Gemini is two stories in one; it is the story of Alexandre Surin and his generation, and it is the story of the twins, Alexandre's nephews, collectively known as Jean-Paul, and their generation. The two stories are separate, but they are told simultaneously and overlap in the middle. The first part, covering the period from 1918 to 1950, relates Édouard's marital and extramarital life, the twins' boyhood togetherness, and the personal and professional scandals of Alexandre. This section of the book ends in quadruple disaster: Maria-Barbara, Édouard's wife, is arrested and deported; Alexandre is murdered; Édouard dies of diabetes; and the arrival of Sophie, Jean's fiancée, fatally compromises the twins' fraternal pact. The second part, covering roughly the period from 1950 to 1961, includes Sophie's break with Jean, Jean's flight from Paul on an extended solo honeymoon around the world, and Paul's failed attempt to catch up to his brother and recement the bond of twinship. These two chronological divisions can also be viewed as Jean-

Paul's successive phases of adolescence and maturity; as the presence, then absence, of a father in the Surin family; as the country of France followed by the context of Europe; and as a sequel to the adventures of Michel Tournier's Robinson and Friday from his earlier book, *Vendredi: Ou, Les Limbes du Pacifique* (1967, revised 1972; *Friday: Or, The Other Island*, 1969).

The novel opens in the year 1937, when the twins are seven and their father is thirty. Édouard leads a divided life between the city of Florence and Maria-Barbara in France, but Jean and Paul are inseparable. Their mother, divorced from her own body by repeated childbirth, has become sterile. The name of their hometown in Britanny, Pierres Sonnantes, French for "Chiming Stones," seems to echo the Japanese rock gardens visited by Paul some twenty years later. The town's main road divides La Cassine, the home of the Surin brood, from the grounds of the old Charterhouse of Guildo, which is now shared by Sainte-Brigitte (an establishment for retarded children) and Édouard's weaving workshops.

Some years earlier, at the Catholic Collège du Thabor, Alexandre joined a homosexual band called "The Foils." Later, when a twist of fate kills his older brother Gustave, Alexandre falls heir to a garbage empire and is transformed from family black sheep to a sort of inverted prodigal son. In a subplot reminiscent of William Golding's *Lord of the Flies* (1954) and the Italian film *Mondo Cane* (1961), "Monsieur Surin" directs six landfill sites with cynical competence, while "Monsieur Alexandre" loses his heart successively to Eustache Lafille, Daniel, Fabienne, and Murillo, constructed homosexual stereotypes with symbolic names. As Adolf Hitler looms in the background, this "dandy of sewage" provokes his own end on the docks of Casablanca.

The voice of Paul, narrating retrospectively, unveils the inner mystery of identical twins and chronicles the major stages in the development of the pair. These stages can be summarized in three steps: Jean-Paul, Paul minus Jean, and Paul equals Jean. The whole of this movement might be called, "Genesis of a Meteor," the anthropocentric creation of a brother to earth and sky. Paul discloses the outstandingly formative moments of his shared life. Franz, the only one who understands Jean-Paul's private communications, and an innocent band of handicapped girls drown like lemmings. A pair of binoculars (trade-named JUMO, "Gemini"), a present, suggests to Paul a cinema experience of life. An angle and a reverse angle together make for a spherical panorama. Paul has instructed Jean in playing at "Bep," a ritualized game of role reversal first seen in Tournier's *Friday*. The two go shopping independently, buy the same clothes, and shock each other in the dressing-room mirror. Unfortunately, Jean suffocates in his brother's embrace and progresses to exogamy via three betrayals: When he rides the Centrifuge with a strong garageman at the county fair; when he sows his wild oats with Denise Malacanthe, the leader of the mill-working girls; and when he brings Sophie home with him to a house empty of parents. Maria-Barbara has now been added to the account of Buchenwald. Édouard, having lost both his lovers and his chance to be a war hero, exhausts his health in a pointless search for his wife.

The story seems to be over, but it is relaunched when Sophie breaks away from her engagement with Jean under the influence of the sinister housekeeper, Méline. Jean feels compelled to embark on a solo honeymoon around the world, after the manner of Jules Verne. Paul desperately retraces his twin's exact itinerary, covering Venice, Iceland, Djerba, Tokyo, Vancouver, Montreal, and finally Berlin. While in Berlin, Paul's left side is crushed in a tunnel collapse as he tries to crawl from the Soviet sector to the French sector of the walled city. Doubly amputated, he "grows" phantom limbs to replace the lost members. This imaginary prosthesis is both an extension of Jean and a sensor through which Paul can become one with the elemental forces of nature, the "meteors." As the novel closes, Paul convalesces on the bay near his old home, his silent reflections accounting for the pages just read. He is alone with Méline.

The Characters

The most immediate defining feature of all the characters is their paradoxical sexual status. Édouard is the straight man of the novel, the only married heterosexual male with children. He is likably polygamous but feels redundant in the all-female group of mill workers. Maria-Barbara is first described as an *alma genitrix*, or pure womb. Later, she symbolically castrates her husband by stealing his glory in the Resistance. Paul is specifically sexed—a monogamous homosexual unique to his type, with the important exception that he once acts as incubus to Sophie. Jean is nervously sexed. He sleeps with Denise out of spite, because she is a wayward aristocrat stooping to common labor, and becomes engaged to Sophie after one party favor. After Sophie, there is no one, implying that Jean is a kind of stillborn heterosexual. Sophie knowingly acts against her own feminine interests in attaching herself to a male whose "matrimonial prospects" are "nil." Alexandre is the prototypical male predator. His holy trinity is "an erect penis and two testicles." He considers himself to be a sort of superman, with eyes and ears like radar for the detection of suitable young men. The only woman who smites him is Fabienne de Ribeauvillé, a lesbian amazon who, like Alexandre, excretes tapeworms in public. She dances the first dance with Alexandre at her travesty wedding to a homosexual fop.

The characters' names are usually a form of wordplay. Alexander the Great was a pupil of Aristotle, the author of the *Meteorologica* (in French, also *Les Météores*). "Jean-Paul" recalls both Jean-Paul Sartre and the corresponding saints. "Beatrice," who watches over the handicapped of Sainte-Brigitte, also served as a guide in Dante's Purgatory. "Méline" is a surrealist figure and a near homonym of the French *maligne*, malign(ant). Thomas

Koussek's last name comes from *coup sec*, French for a putative dry ejaculation. Alexandre's protégé "Daniel" has biblical connotations. "D'Urfé", the last name of Fabienne's fiancé, also refers to Honoré d'Urfé, the author of *L'Astrée*, (1607-1628, 1925; *Astrea*, 1657-1658), a romantic pastoral. "Sophie" connotes wisdom. Entire chapters are based on this kind of word derivation, as in "The Philippine Pearls," which are, in a sense, "cast before the swine."

Most important, every character belongs to a composite figure. To compose the figure of Édouard from scratch, for example, one needs to combine his absolute personality (mild and approachable) with his mirror image (Gustave), plus his reverse mirror image (Alexandre), plus his inner drives (lust, embodied in Florence, and affection, in the person of Maria-Barbara), plus his storybook counterpart (the Bumpkin), plus his biological avatar (the "useless drone in between the queen bee and the workers"). A similar configuration exists for each of the characters, who consequently resemble literary and philosophical dossiers more than fictionalized individuals.

Themes and Meanings

Clearly, the theme of "the couple" and its variants (copulation, conjunction, recombination) is paramount—so much so that the novel can usefully be considered as an experiment in generating dyadic structures of social interaction. No fewer than thirty couples populate the novel: Édouard plus (Maria-Barbara, Florence, Angelica); Alexandre plus (his mother, Eustache, Daniel, Sam, Murillo); Thomas plus (Christ, Alexandre); Jean plus (Paul, Denise, Sophie); Paul plus (Jean, Sophie, Shonin, himself); Méline plus (Justin, Paul); Fabienne plus (Alexandre, Alexis); Deborah and Ralph; Olivier and Selma; and more. Each couple represents not only a different pairing but also a different type of pairing, based on such variables as anatomical sex, erotic preference, demography, intellect, and age group. Some couples, such as East and West, Time and Weather, Christ and Spirit, Venice and Constantinople, bind philosophical categories rather than people.

In order to interpret this exploratory formation of novel couples, many levels must be coordinated. First, the mere act of manufacturing so many different couples expresses some desire for fulfillment. The novel's last word suggests a sublimated desire for autosodomy. The key episode of the Gemini binoculars militates for a stereoscopic vision of life: one framework enhanced or adjusted by another, an "objective" correlated with a "perspective." Alternating voice narration dubs this idea of perceptual accommodation—as does the repeated conjunction of bisymmetric geographies—and creates an adversarial atmosphere of witnesses and testifying. In treasuring rubbish and scorning valuables, Alexandre inverts the social hierarchy of Majority and Minority. The proliferation of nonstandard pairings suggests a groping for a new order. Pairings are created, tested, and extinguished as they prove nonviable. Of all these pairings, none is "normal," and only the last survives. In the terminal pairing, Paul's mind absorbs that of Jean, then pushes it out as an extrusion, from Paul's own side, to act as a bridge with nature: Genesis retold, with Eve as a man.

Critical Context

Critics often conceive of *Gemini* as the third installment of a three-part series including *Friday* and *Le Roi des aulnes* (1970; *The Ogre*, 1972). Certainly, *Gemini* is the product of many readings, but the list should also include "Le Nain rouge" (1975), *Gilles et Jeanne* (1983), Dante, the Bible, the life and works of Pierre Loti, and Tournier's autobiographical essay *Le Vent Paraclet* (1977). Thus, *Gemini* is one part of a vast "parallel edition" in which each character, twinned within the novel, is also twinned without it. Jean is joined to Paul, but Jean-Paul reflects Friday-Robinson; Édouard loves Angelica, his Flemish mistress, but Édouard-Angelica mirrors François Jaubert and Marthe Grangier of Raymond Radiguet's *Le Diable au corps* (1923; *Devil in the Flesh*, 1932). Many of these couples are socially interdicted: the teenage youth and the older married woman, the female soldier and the male valet, the single parent and the adopted child. To condone or not to condone is the reader's decision, but the overall Tournier enterprise clearly seems to be a form of social engineering in which the elementary unit, the pair, is examined through disassembly and reassembly, and affinity groups are created where impossible matings once existed. The ultimate couple is Heredity plus Environment. For Tournier, the confines of this dual prison, though not escapable, can be expanded.

Sources for Further Study

Cloonan, William. "*Les Météores*," in *Michel Tournier*, 1985.
Koster, Serge. *Michel Tournier*, 1986.
Redfern, W. D. "Approximating Man: Michel Tournier and Play in Language," in *Modern Language Review*. LXXX (1985), pp. 304-319.
Rushdie, Salman. "The Stuff of Marvels: *Gemini*," in *The New York Times Book Review*. LXXXVI (October 4, 1981), pp. 12, 31-32.
Sud. January, 1986. Special Tournier issue.

Frank Coppay

A GHOST AT NOON

Author: Alberto Moravia (1907-   )
Type of plot: Psychological novel
Time of plot: Postwar Italy
Locale: Rome, Capri, and the coast of southwest Italy
First published: Il disprezzo, 1954 (English translation, 1955)

> *Principal characters:*
> MOLENI, the narrator, a struggling author who becomes a
>   writer of film scripts
> EMILIA, his wife, formerly a typist, now a housewife
> BATTISTA, the head of Triumph Films, Moleni's employer
> RHEINGOLD, a German director hired by Battista

The Novel

A *Ghost at Noon* is a subtle book about the death of a marriage. Moleni, the narrator, an intellectual who wishes to write for the theater, is married to Emilia, the beautiful daughter of an old Roman family which has become poverty-stricken. She is not highly educated and has devoted herself to caring for her husband and the one furnished room in which they live. They were blissfully happy for two years. Then, Moleni claims, his wife changed, judged him, ceased to love him. The book is both the reconstruction of this decline and an attempt to make sense of it.

Ironically, the first step in the deterioration of the marriage seems to be the result of the narrator's effort to provide a better home for his wife. After buying the lease of an apartment he cannot afford, he perceives himself as "a poor devil," isolated in financial anxiety from a domestically inclined, working-class woman who cannot understand his unhappiness. He has incurred debts on her behalf, he believes; to pay them he must prostitute his talent and become a scriptwriter.

The reader wonders if it is, in fact, Emilia who first becomes judgmental. Why do Moleni's debts involve payments on a car as well as on the apartment? Purchasing a car was not a sacrifice made for Emilia. The reader can see throughout the book Moleni's confused pattern of behavior. He ignores the indications Emilia gives of her feelings; he constructs what he believes that she feels, acts accordingly, and then blames her for the result.

The struggling author obtains work from Battista, whose company, Triumph Films, occupies an ancient palace: Pictures of film stars are pinned on walls where great, mythological paintings once hung. Emilia detests and distrusts Battista from the time when the three first dine together. On this occasion, in spite of her objections, Moleni lets Battista drive Emilia home while he follows in a taxi. He sees the producer every day. Emilia is always included in their social activities; although she is unwilling, her husband pressures her into joining them.

Yet when Emilia moves into a separate bedroom Moleni is hurt and angry. She becomes unresponsive and uncommunicative, and he desperately tries to discover why her feelings have altered. Her attempts to create physical and emotional space between them drive him to frenzy and ultimately to violence. She wishes to leave but has nowhere to go.

Without her love, Moleni detests scriptwriting even more. He hates its collaborative and anonymous nature, and he hates working for mediocrities such as the director Pasetti, who has, nevertheless, a doting wife and a happy home.

The couple have reached an impasse when Battista proposes to make a film of Homer's *Odyssey*. Moleni will write the script; Rheingold, a German who looks like Johann Wolfgang von Goethe, will direct it.

Against Emilia's wishes, the four travel to Battista's villa on Capri. As before, the men determine that Emilia will travel with Battista. She goes unwillingly, making the same objections about his fast driving and her wish to stay with her husband. After narrowly missing an oxcart, Rheingold and Moleni are surprised to catch up with Battista and Emilia at a beach near Naples. Moleni notices Battista's exaggerated assurance and Emilia's bewilderment and disgust. He is angry without recognizing why.

At the villa the situation worsens. Moleni sees Battista kiss Emilia and becomes increasingly desperate about his marriage, increasingly disgusted with his scriptwriting, and less and less able to work with Rheingold.

The German director's version of the *Odyssey* begins with a question: Why should a shrewd and civilized man such as Ulysses come home and commit such a barbarous act as killing all of Penelope's suitors? Rheingold's answer is a reconstruction: Penelope is a simple, traditional woman. When a man who desired her was accepted by her husband as a guest, she considered her honor impugned and her house polluted. Her contempt for Ulysses made the marriage so unhappy that he was glad to leave for Troy. His wanderings in the *Odyssey* resulted from his unwillingness to return to an unhappy home.

While refusing to accept this modern travesty of Homer, Moleni sees its application to his own marriage. Like Penelope, Emilia is a traditional woman. Does she despise him because she believes he wished her to encourage Battista?

In what is perhaps the central scene of the novel, Moleni asks his wife to decide if he should break his contract. To him his work is a test of his love, not of his professional integrity. As always, he is seeking not an answer but reassurance, "corroboration of her feeling for me." When Emilia says, "There are things that one can't allow other people to decide," he merely becomes more insistent. When she admits to despising him because he does not "behave like a man," he thinks of Penelope and Ulysses and Battista. When she spells it out, "It is not manly to make all your life decisions to please someone else and blame someone else when they are wrong," he still misses the point.

Yet he loves her. Finding her sunbathing on the beach, he sleeps beside her and dreams of a kiss which reunites them. He confronts Rheingold and resigns. The German claims that Battista and Moleni are on the same side: "To you Art does not matter; all you want is to be paid." Unimpressed, Emilia says that she will go back to Rome with Battista and try to become independent. Even when Moleni states that he will no longer work for a man who wishes to seduce his wife, Emilia is unmoved. Finally, he realizes that her contempt is not produced by his actions but by his character.

Seeking distraction after his wife and Battista leave, Moleni goes to the beach to hire a boat. When he reaches the boat, Emilia is sitting in the stern. All misunderstandings are resolved, and Moleni rows to a grotto where they can make love, but when he turns to help her from the boat it is empty. The happy ending was a hallucination: "Noon is the hour for ghosts."

Moleni is informed that Emilia is seriously hurt and on his way home is met by news of his wife's death. Driving at his usual speed, Battista had braked suddenly to avoid an oxcart, and Emilia, asleep at the time, had her neck broken.

The obvious assumption—that the dead Emilia appeared to her husband and sought a reconciliation—is rejected. She was probably alive at the time of the apparition, says the narrator. Unless he can find her again, he fears that he will be forever exiled from "the world in which people loved without misunderstandings and were loved in return and lived peaceful lives." He returns to Capri seeking to contact her and realizes that, like Penelope and Ulysses, she is now fixed in "the great spaces of the sea," changelessly what she was in life. Having seen his wife only in relation to himself, only as his feelings created her, he must now discover her reality. This narrative is his attempt to reach Emilia.

The Characters

The three male characters are defined by their attitudes toward success, Emilia, and the *Odyssey*. The personality of the film magnate is shown by his possessions, his films, and the tasteless desecration of the palace in which he works. Battista is apelike in appearance and drives a luxurious red sportscar. His fast driving, his womanizing, his villa on Capri, his habit of judging everything ultimately by the profit it will make are used by Moravia to establish the contrast between the superficial and amoral "glitz" which marks modern success and the ancient traditions and simplicities of Mediterranean life, which live on in Emilia.

The fact that Emilia comes from an old Roman family in decline immediately suggests the fate of tradition and older values in the modern world. Emilia's beauty, her struggle against the mode of life and the friend her husband has chosen, her love of home, of integrity, her sound instincts and the uneducated and uncorrupted simplicity of her judgment give her dignity. Her husband's incomprehension, hysteria, and self-pity arouse the reader's sympathy for her. Her largely passive resistance, her entrapment, and her occasional telling statements enable the reader to understand her, though the narrator does not.

Moleni is not an attractive character. He is arrogant, chauvinistic, and largely incapable of self-criticism. Ultimately, perhaps, he is childish; for him everyone exists solely in relation to himself. Yet he does love Emilia, and he has a real appreciation of the *Odyssey*, of the lands of antiquity, and of ancient honor and faithful love.

In these traits he is opposed to Rheingold, the nattily attired, arty, blond German just back from America. Rheingold represents the Freudian, psychologically reductive aspect of modern thought, its lack of respect for tradition and its pursuit of novelty. It may be that the narrator, while functioning primarily as a vehicle for the story and as the husband of Emilia, should also be seen as a representative modern man, seeking his way in a world of conflicting values, living in a society which offers substantial rewards for the meretricious.

Only Emilia has a counterpart in the *Odyssey*: Penelope, the Queen, the keeper of the house, the child, and the Kingdom. Emilia is killed because an oxcart gets in the way of a fast car driven by Battista, who represents the tawdriness of the modern world.

Themes and Meanings

The novel is concerned with conflicting values. The old society, marked by sacred duties, honor, and simplicity, is contrasted with the modern world. The characters evidence their different values, and the narrator moves confusedly among them. The palace which Triumph Films uses and debases, the cars disputing with oxcarts the right to the road, and, above all, the use of the *Odyssey* and the death of Emilia make the theme plain.

Much of the interest of the novel lies in the reader's participation in the puzzle: Why did the marriage of Moleni and Emilia fail? The reader's ability to participate depends on his detachment from the narrator, and even on his ability to compete with the narrator in reaching a solution. The author's technical skill ensures that the narrator, seeking the truth himself, reports conversations, behavior, and feelings as fully and as accurately as possible. Consequently, readers are able to follow the events without adopting the narrator's interpretation of them and may, indeed, construct from Moleni's story the solution Moleni himself cannot find.

Critical Context

Like many of Moravia's works, *A Ghost at Noon* has been adapted for film, serving as the basis for Jean-Luc Godard's *Le Mépris* (1963; *Contempt*, 1964). Chronologically it belongs to the period of *L'amore coniugale* (1949; *Conjugal Love*, 1951) and *Il conformista* (1951; *The Conformist*, 1952).

A Ghost at Noon is marked by many of the features that characterize Moravia's body of work. It is typical of his fiction both in its journalistic or documentary style and in its visual acuity—in part, perhaps, a reflection of his long career as a film critic. It evidences the author's conviction that character is shaped by the things people have to do, rather than by those which they choose to do. It offers a psychologically acute analysis of the subtle corruptions of an affluent society. *A Ghost at Noon* is also representative of Moravia's fiction in its deeper vision of the malaise of the modern world—a vision which made him a forerunner of the existentialist school of novelists.

Sources for Further Study

Cottrell, Jane. *Alberto Moravia*, 1974.
Heiney, Donald. *Three Italian Novelists: Moravia, Pavese, Vittorini*, 1968.
Pacifici, Sergio. *The Modern Italian Novel: From Pea to Moravia*, 1967.
Ross, Joan, and Donald Freed. *The Existentialism of Alberto Moravia*, 1972.

Jocelyn Creigh Cass

THE GIFT

Author: Vladimir Nabokov (1899-1977)
Type of plot: Parody of realism
Time of plot: 1926-1929
Locale: Berlin
First published: Dar, 1937-1938, serial, expurgated; 1952, book, unexpurgated
  (English translation, 1963)

> *Principal characters:*
>> FYODOR KONSTANTINOVICH GODUNOV-CHERDYNTSEV, a young
>>   Russian émigré poet and prose writer
>> ZINA MERTZ, his beloved
>> ALEXANDER and ALEXANDRA CHERNYSHEVSKI, friends whose
>>   son Yasha has committed suicide
>> NIKOLAY CHERNYSHEVSKI, a nineteenth century radical
>>   journalist, the subject of a biography by Fyodor
>> KONCHEYEV, an émigré poet and critic who is much admired
>>   by Fyodor

The Novel

The Gift is the dual story of the evolution of Fyodor Konstantinovich Godunov-Cherdyntsev's literary gifts and his love affair with Zina Mertz. The lovers are part of the large émigré colony in Berlin following the Russian Revolution. The young poet and writer, a former aristocrat, leads a happy, if straitened, existence giving lessons, doing translations, and selling an occasional poem to the émigré press while searching for his true literary voice and for his love.

The novel opens on April 1, 1926. Fyodor has just moved into a new room and is basking in the glow of his first book of poems. The exquisitely perceptive review that he mentally composes while skimming through the slender volume is, alas, the only review it is destined to receive. That evening, he sets out to visit his friends, the Chernyshevskis, where he has been promised the first, flattering newspaper review of his poems—a promise that turns out to be an "April fool's" jest. The chagrined poet passes the evening watching the guests and imagining the scene as each of them sees it. Through Alexander Chernyshevski's troubled eyes, he sees a shadowy figure sitting in the corner. This image is a projection of Chernyshevski's incipient madness resulting from the bizarre suicide of his son Yasha, an inept aspiring poet. Fyodor's mental game revives his spirits, and he strolls home composing a poem. On his arrival, he discovers that he, the eternal exile, has the wrong house key.

The summer passes pleasantly, ending in a satirically described émigré literary evening during which the young hero is offered some translation work.

He fails to pursue the matter, however, and misses meeting Zina, the woman he will love. As Fyodor leaves the gathering, he falls into a long discussion with the poet and critic Koncheyev, whom he knows slightly. Only at the end of their brilliantly incisive survey of Russian literature does the reader learn that the entire discussion has taken place in Fyodor's mind.

That Christmas, Fyodor's mother, Elizaveta Pavlovna, who lives in Paris, pays a visit, and they reminisce about their idyllic family life in Russia. Most of all, they muse on the fate of Fyodor's father, a famous entomologist and explorer who disappeared in 1918 while returning from a collecting expedition to Tibet. His death is uncertain, and both mother and son are haunted by dreams of his return. So strong is the aura of his adored father that Fyodor undertakes a biography, which he eventually abandons. Neither it nor his earlier poems are his true voice.

The young writer's living quarters, where he has spent two years, prove unsatisfactory, and he sets out to find more suitable accommodations with the help of Alexandra Chernyshevski. At length a room is located in the apartment of the Shchyogolev family. Although Fyodor is dismayed by his interview with Boris Shchyogolev, the cheerful, vulgarian apartment owner, he takes the room, having unconsciously noticed a young woman's blue ball dress spread on a chair. The Shchyogolev apartment is also the home of Zina Mertz, Mrs. Shchyogolev's daughter from an earlier marriage. The romance which develops between the young people is conducted on street corners and in cafés, for Zina refuses to acknowledge their love in the blighted atmosphere of her odious stepfather's apartment. Meanwhile, Fyodor, an ardent composer of chess problems, has stumbled upon an article in a Soviet chess magazine about Nikolay Chernyshevski, the radical nineteenth century Russian literary and political journalist. Exiled by the czar, Chernyshevski became a political martyr and sacred cow of the Russian intelligentsia. So potent was his influence that his primitivist, social utilitarian aesthetic views dictated the main trend of Russia's cultural development from the 1860's onward. Fyodor, the young aesthete, finds Chernyshevski's writings so logically and stylistically inept that he becomes perversely enchanted with their author. Chernyshevski becomes the subject of Fyodor's new book, an iconoclastic exercise in wit and stylistic elegance, that subtly evokes its sainted antihero as the bad seed in Russia's cultural and political development. Reproduced in full as chapter 4 of *The Gift*, the short book is anathema to almost all Russian readers, and the barrage of outraged reviews gains for Fyodor a certain visibility.

The impecunious lovers, never alone together, ponder their plight. Fate lends a hand. Shchyogolev, who has fallen on hard times, unexpectedly obtains a job in Copenhagen. He plans to take his wife, leaving the apartment to Zina and Fyodor until the arrival of the new tenants. The young couple eagerly await the Shchyogolevs' departure, seeing them off at the train station.

Having spent the last of their money on dinner in a sidewalk café, Fyodor outlines to Zina the plan of his projected novel, which proves to be *The Gift*. They wend their way home, blissfully unaware that in the last-minute confusion their keys were locked inside the apartment. The novel's last day ends as did the first, with Fyodor locked out. Nevertheless, Fyodor has found Zina and his literary voice.

The Characters

Vladimir Nabokov's disclaimer to the contrary, Fyodor is in part an autobiographical figure. The young Russian émigré poet and writer in 1920's Berlin, the aesthete, the admirer of butterflies, the composer of chess problems, the lover—all are recut facets of Nabokov's life. Although the novel was written only ten years after the period described, Nabokov looks back on his young hero with gentle, often wry bemusement. Fyodor, dreamy, impractical about mundane matters such as money and keys, is preoccupied with absorbing the perceptions and finding the form best suited to his literary gift. The news of the day, the vulgarity of his Berlin surroundings, catch his derisive attention only fleetingly, if at all. Although reverent toward the memory of his beloved father, the family, and the settings of his Russian childhood (memorialized in his poems), Fyodor, unlike most of the émigrés, is perfectly happy with his marginal, alien existence. Exile affords him a unique freedom for his life and art.

Zina's lot is less happy. Although she is the daughter of a cultivated, idolized Russian-Jewish father, her stepfather Shchyogolev, a jocular and anti-Semitic philistine, makes her home life oppressive. Employed as a typist in a law office, she loathes the burgeois atmosphere of her surroundings. Like Fyodor, she carries the treasures of an idyllic past in her memory. Strong-willed and resolute, she is direct, almost imperious. A longtime admirer of Fyodor's poetry, she quite literally becomes his muse. The dedicatee of one of Fyodor's finest poems, her "perfect pitch" for Russian prose makes her the ideal auditor for Fyodor's nightly readings of his Chernyshevski biography as the homeless lovers sit in corner cafés. She is also the heroine of Fyodor's projected novel, *The Gift*.

The poet and critic Koncheyev plays a role out of all proportion to the number of his appearances. A "lonely, unpleasant, myopic man, with some kind of unpleasant defect in the reciprocal position of his shoulder blades," Koncheyev is Fyodor's envied rival, the sole critic whose esteem he craves. Curiously, the only extended conversations between the two men, both stunning literary critiques, are imaginary. Koncheyev is the secret sounding board for Fyodor's evaluation of his own work and his reevaluation of all Russian literature. He is Fyodor's alter ego.

The lovingly portrayed Chernyshevskis are among Fyodor's few friends. Fyodor's obvious affection is surprising, for the aging couple represent a very different outlook on life from that of the young aesthete. The Chernyshevskis take their name from the radical, atheist social critic's father, an Orthodox priest, who converted their Jewish forebears to Christianity. It is they who first propose that Fyodor write about the famous Chernyshevski. Fyodor's old friend, who dies just as the book about his namesake appears, is the center of one of the novel's themes: the puzzle of death and immortality. The demented old man believes that he is in touch with the other world. As he lies dying, listening to water drumming outside the heavily curtained window, he murmurs, "What nonsense. Of course there is nothing afterwards. . . . It is as clear as the fact that it is raining." In fact, the sun is shining, and a neighbor is watering her plants.

The Gift, Nabokov's longest Russian novel, contains a rich gallery of human portraits. Each is carefully individuated. In addition to full-length studies of such secondary characters as the vile Boris Shchyogolev, and Fyodor's adored mother, Elizaveta Pavlovna, there are marvelous thumbnail sketches of dozens of minor figures, the denizens of the world of the Russian émigré intelligentsia—Nabokov's presciently nostalgic portrait of a world soon fated to disappear.

Themes and Meanings

The Gift is a study of the creative process enveloped in a brilliant display of Nabokovian structural and stylistic pyrotechnics. The theme is elaborated in two parallel plot lines: the gradual coming together of Fyodor and Zina, and the ripening of Fyodor's talent, leading to the creation of *The Gift*. The basic plan of the novel is circular, the legendary snake swallowing its own tail.

The "gift" of the title has several meanings. The most central is Fyodor's talent. His very name, the Russian form of Theodore, means "God's gift." The word also refers to the Russian literary heritage. Fyodor's biography of his father and his study of Chernyshevski are written under the respective stars of Alexander Pushkin and Nikolai Gogol, the founding fathers of modern Russian literature. *The Gift* is Fyodor's (and Nabokov's) original contribution to that heritage and also a provocative reevaluation of Russian cultural history.

The Gift has a leitmotif that echoes and augments the book's theme of art and the artist. Keys play an important role in the plot and also have symbolic meaning. Although an exile, locked out from his native land, Fyodor retains its keys, the Russian language and cultural tradition. The Russian word for "key" (*klyuch*) also means "spring," suggesting the Castalian Spring of Greek mythology from which artists drink in inspiration. Yet another association is the crucial "key move" in the solution of chess problems. Nabokov's seemingly realistic novel, like Fyodor's projected work, is designed or plotted on the model of a chess problem which Fyodor composes in the course of the book. Nabokov has repeatedly remarked on the parallels between the composition of novels and his beloved hobby of composing chess problems. *The Gift* is both a loving tribute to, and a parody of the traditional Russian realistic novel.

Critical Context

The Gift, Nabokov's last Russian novel, is reckoned by its author and by many of his readers as his finest contribution to his native literature. By far the longest and most complex of his Russian works, it is his nearest approach to the tradition of the classical nineteenth century Russian novel. As its protagonist Fyodor says, it is "a novel with 'types,' love, fate, conversations . . . and with descriptions of nature." It is Nabokov's farewell to his native literary tradition, a summing up before launching his new career as an American writer in 1940. Only after Nabokov's international fame for his American novels such as *Lolita* (1955), *Pale Fire* (1962), and *Ada or Ardor: A Family Chronicle* (1969) did his Russian works, belatedly translated into English, win the attention they richly deserve. *The Gift* is a fitting monument to Nabokov's Russian career.

Sources for Further Study

Davydov, Sergei. "Nabokov's Aesthetic Exorcism of Chernyshevskii," in *Canadian-American Slavic Studies*. XIX (Fall, 1985), pp. 357-374.

Johnson, D. Barton. "The Chess Key to *The Gift*," in *Worlds in Regression: Some Novels of Vladimir Nabokov*, 1985.

Karlinsky, Simon. "Vladimir Nabokov's Novel *Dar* as a Work of Literary Criticism," in *Slavic and East European Journal*. VII (Fall, 1963), pp. 284-290.

Rampton, David. "*The Gift*," in *Vladimir Nabokov: A Critical Study of the Novels*, 1984.

Salomon, Roger B. "*The Gift*: Nabokov's Portrait of the Artist," in *Critical Essays on Vladimir Nabokov*, 1984. Edited by Phyllis A. Roth.

D. Barton Johnson

GIGI

Author: Colette (Sidonie-Gabrielle Colette; 1873-1954)
Type of plot: Comedy of manners
Time of plot: 1899
Locale: Paris
First published: 1944 (English translation, 1952)

> *Principal characters:*
> GIGI, a charming and independent fifteen-year-old girl
> ANDRÉE, Gigi's mother, a singer in musicals
> MADAME ALVAREZ, Gigi's maternal grandmother, who primarily supervises her granddaughter's rearing
> AUNT ALICIA, Gigi's maternal great-aunt, who helps to supervise the girl's education
> GASTON LACHAILLE, a rich young man who falls in love with Gigi

The Novel

Gigi is a simply narrated fairy tale based on the Cinderella motif. Her maternal grandmother and great-aunt carefully control Gigi's education, while her mother, Andrée, is busy singing in secondary roles in musicals; her father has deserted the family. The two elderly sisters, both retired courtesans, seek to coach their charge in how to embark on a successful career as the kept mistress of wealthy admirers.

Gigi is taught to lower her knees, pull down her skirts, and keep legs and knees close together. She is also taught to keep her stomach in, not to wear stays because they would spoil her figure, and to be sure to wear gloves. She is taught the supreme importance of table manners: how to dismember a lobster; how to enjoy various omelets; how to eat and speak clearly at the same time. Her sophisticated great-aunt, Alicia, proffers detailed instructions on the selection of jewelry; above all, "Never wear second-rate jewels. Wait till the really good ones come to you." Gigi is, moreover, strongly advised to avoid blackheads, uncooked pork, and too many almonds, which "add weight to the breasts." The girl must also indulge men's foibles and superstitions and know how to choose their cigars. Concludes Alicia, "Once a woman understands the tastes of a man, cigars included, and once a man knows what pleases a woman, they may be said to be well matched."

Her grandmother and great-aunt both seek to impress upon Gigi the cardinal principle of a courtesan's career, which is not to marry—or, at least, not to do so as long as she remains erotically attractive. Madame Alvarez failed a generation earlier with her daughter, Andrée, who married badly; after her husband's desertion, she perversely preferred a tiring and mediocre career onstage to the leisurely life of a kept woman. Alicia sums up the protocol of the demimonde: "Instead of marrying 'at once' it sometimes happens that we marry 'at last.'"

An occasional visitor to Madame Alvarez's apartment is thirty-two-year-old Gaston Lachaille, the bored, single, extremely rich son of one of her former lovers. When Gaston lends Gigi, with whom he plays cards, his luxurious automobile, Alicia originates the plot of having Gigi initiated into a courtesan's career by the charming Gaston, who has just been jilted by a histrionic mistress. Madame Alvarez and Gaston agree to the plans, with the grandmother cautioning the young man, "I shall do my best to entrust Gigi only to the care of a man capable of saying, 'I take charge of her and answer for her future.'"

Surprisingly, the usually obedient Gigi rebels at the scheme, stubbornly resisting the combined pressure of her grandmother and great-aunt. She tells Gaston that his offer "to make me my fortune" means she will sleep with him, accompany him to various pleasure spots, be photographed by the sensational press, and then be discarded when he tires of her, as he has tired of a gallery of previous mistresses. She firmly refuses him. They quarrel, and he furiously leaves her.

Gigi broods sadly. Astoundingly, Gaston reappears the next day. Even more surprising, Gigi has changed her mind: She now realizes that she loves him and would rather be miserable with him than do without him. Gaston thereupon asks for Gigi's hand in marriage.

The Characters

Gigi is a simple, direct, piquantly provocative girl-woman, a lily in a garden of weeds, a moral exception to her immoral environment. Her youthful exuberance and innocence contrast sharply with the jaded, cynical worldliness of the older generations. Her coltish energy and unmeditated impertinence smash the carefully arranged furnishings of an artificial, febrile, *fin de siècle* society. She is a seductive, singular wonder, perhaps too marvelous to be believed by experienced readers, but nevertheless a charming princess for Colette's fantasy.

The two elderly sisters are carefully differentiated. Madame Alvarez dotes on Gigi and means to do her best for her granddaughter. She is invariably courteous, kind, firm, and correct. Her older sister, Alicia, once a great beauty, has been the more successful courtesan, and possibly the more cunning as well. Described as "the perfect stage marquise," she is more awesome than lovable. Colette reserves for Alicia the role of pedagogue in a lecture regarding the distinctions between bearable and unbearable jewelry. Together, the sisters comprise a formidably expert brace of amoral deities.

Gaston joins Colette's long list of slightly ridiculous, manipulable lovers. He is sketched rather than fully portrayed and is immature, weak, and far from bright. Andrée, Gigi's mother, is remarkably uninvolved in the planning of her daughter's future.

Themes and Meanings

The main theme is the triumph of love and innocence in an elegantly corrupt world. Despite her careful upbringing in demimonde decadence, Gigi prefers the integrity of possibly penurious but bourgeois virtue to a richly compensated promiscuity, only to gain love, money, and respectability. Incredible? Yes. Beguiling? Also, yes.

The double surprise of both the man and the woman finding themselves in love and willing to marry is beautifully fashioned as the compact climax and resolution of a tautly controlled and tightly written short novel. Colette concentrates on quickly establishing her world's turn-of-the-century manners and morals. Dialogue dominates; descriptions are employed only to promote the plot; and the tone is mordantly witty and biting for the sisters, exuberantly bubbly for Gigi.

Another, underlying theme also deserves notice, that of advice, which pervades many of Colette's works. Advice becomes the agenda of *Gigi*, with both grandmother and great-aunt showering the girl with sententious, often sound, directions as they supervise her maturation. Madame Alvarez, faced with their apparent failure as guardians, cannot resist the sally, "You'll never be able to say you didn't have good advice, and the very best at that." Her older sister sagely stops her: "Don't meddle any more. Can't you see she is way beyond us?" The child's instincts have proved wiser than her protectors' knowledge. *Gigi* is a parable on the nature of love, whose wisdom cannot be taught.

Critical Context

Like François Montaigne and Jean-Jacques Rousseau, Marcel Proust and André Gide, Colette is a superb expositor of herself in her writing. The most important influence on her was that of her mother, Sido, whose Demeter she followed by playing Persephone. Her Sido-self became a personal version of the Garden of Eden, pure and soundly instinctual. The character of Gigi is a reincarnation of this undefiled, uninitiated stage. Significantly, the tale ends before the lovers are married—for marriage, Colette came to discover, usually is a time of trouble and disillusionment.

Colette's first marriage proved to be particularly painful. It was in 1893, to a man fifteen years her senior named Henry Gauthier-Villars, whom everyone called Willy. She had fallen in love with Willy when she was seventeen; her mother never approved of him. The attraction was largely sexual, in a somewhat masochistic way: Colette was fascinated by the fantasy of becoming the willing plaything of a dissolute older man. Later, she came to distrust erotic desire as a demoniac drive that was usually fulfilled in sorrow and subjugation. Willy, while witty and erudite, soon shamed her with his cruelty, coarseness, and chronic adulteries, yet she remained with him for thirteen tormented years, during which she founded her literary career. She began by setting down thinly fictionalized accounts of her schoolgirl memories. Willy decided that they were salable. Her first novel, *Claudine à l'école* (1900; *Claudine at School*, 1956), became popular, so Willy ordered a series of *Claudine* sequels, ensuring that she would write them by locking his young wife into a room for four hours daily. Colette did not really mind: She had become addicted to writing. Nevertheless, these experiences motivated her conviction that the relationship between men and women was frequently that of jailer and prisoner.

Claudine at School is written in diary form and veers from titillating scenes of sexual provocation to relative innocence. The novel follows the autumn-to-summer cycle of one year in a girls' school. Most of Claudine's friends and acquaintances engage in either heterosexual or lesbian intrigues. They are, like all adolescents, troubled by the awakening demands of their senses. Claudine, however, refrains from expressing her sensuality in any affair. Fifteen years old, she is curious but virginal, precocious yet pure, tomboyish and high spirited—the first model for Gigi's integrity and essential sweetness, her desire for independence yet her yearning for love.

It is to Claudine and other heroines of her earlier fiction, then, that Colette returns in *Gigi*. It is also to the fashionable, perverse *fin de siècle* society to which Willy introduced her, and the polarizing dilemma of independence opposed to submission which Colette's Sido-self battled against her Willy-self—the symbols that establish the basic structure of her private and fictive worlds. Colette wrote *Gigi* in 1942, in her seventieth year, a few months after her third husband, Maurice Goudeket, whom she dearly loved, had been arrested by the Germans and sent to a concentration camp. Colette was herself in great pain from arthritis.

Considering these circumstances, it is not at all surprising that Colette indulged herself in a hard-to-credit romance when she composed *Gigi* as an escape from her harrowing reality, as a puff-pastry exercise in slyly satiric humor and benignly optimistic wishfulness. What is surprising and delightful is that she carries off her confection so masterfully.

Sources for Further Study
Crosland, Margaret. *Colette: A Provincial in Paris*, 1954.
Davies, Margaret. *Colette*, 1961.
Goudeket, Maurice. *Close to Colette*, 1957.
Marks, Elaine. *Colette*, 1960.
Richardson, Joanna. *Colette*, 1983.

Gerhard Brand

THE GLASS BEAD GAME

Author: Hermann Hesse (1877-1962)
Type of plot: Bildungsroman
Time of plot: Possibly the year 2400
Locale: Castalia, the "pedagogical province"
First published: Das Glasperlenspiel: Versuch einer Lebensbeschreibung des
  Magister Ludi Josef Knecht samt Knechts hinterlassenen Schriften, 1943
  (*Magister Ludi,* 1949; better known as *The Glass Bead Game*)

> *Principal characters:*
> JOSEPH KNECHT, a student of the Glass Bead Game, later
>   Magister Ludi, Master of the Game
> THE MAGISTER MUSICAE, Knecht's music tutor and lifelong
>   counselor
> PLINIO DESIGNORI, Knecht's worldly friend
> FRITZ TEGULARIUS, the zealous pro-Castalian intellectual
> PATER JACOBUS, a historian and monk
> THE ELDER BROTHER, master of the *I Ching*
> THOMAS VON DER TRAVE, Magister Ludi before Knecht

The Novel

Hermann Hesse's last novel, his most ambitious in scope and theme, traces the growth of the youth Joseph Knecht from early studies through maturing philosophical discovery to the office of Magister Ludi and past it, to his voluntary retirement and death. At once a *Bildungsroman,* a *roman à clef,* and a philosophical utopian novel, *The Glass Bead Game* ranks with a handful of other twentieth century novels as one of the most complex expressions of the modernist sensibility in prose literature.

Told by an anonymous narrator, possibly Knecht's successor to the title of Magister Ludi, the story of Knecht's absorption with the Glass Bead Game begins with early school successes at the violin. Discovered by an ancient musician who travels from school to school and is known only as the Magister Musicae, Knecht demonstrates an aesthetic sensitivity, a technical skill, and an ability to improvise on musical themes that convince the Master of the young man's promising future as one of the elitist members of the Order of Castalia. The Order is partly a monastic and reclusive quasi-religious sect, partly a musician's conservatory, and partly a think tank for the ongoing study of universal correspondences articulated through mathematics, history, logic, and the literary arts.

Knecht's initiation into the mainstream of Castalian life comes at two schools: Eschholz, a clearing ground to determine the students' special strengths, and Waldzell, for students demonstrating an affinity for the Glass

Bead Game, a mysteriously eclectic intellectual exercise incorporating all the human disciplines.

As Knecht moves through his education, he meets various masters and peers, each of whom advances his general knowledge not only about a specialty—*I Ching*, music, history, mathematics, and so on—but also about the pluralistic nature of the world. Certain exercises required by his apprenticeship, notably the fictitious autobiographies that Knecht places in the past, form an appendix to the novel.

Although his experiences at Waldzell introduce Knecht to the Glass Bead Game indirectly, he resists a total commitment to this great intellectual game. His first assignment as a tutor is to mend fences between Castalia and a neighboring Catholic monastery devoted to good works and the relieving of human suffering. There he engages in a friendly debate over several months' time with Pater Jacobus, a historian who adds yet another dimension to Knecht's studies. Discovering that his old school chum Plinio Designori is responsible for the rift between the two orders, Knecht repairs the differences and is commended for his work by the people of Castalia. The episode serves the narrator's purpose of describing Knecht's growing involvement with worldly as well as intellectual and monastic matters.

As Knecht's successes grow, and as his fascination for the Glass Bead Game turns into total absorption, his credentials for higher office in Castalia become unassailable. After the death of the current Magister Ludi, Thomas von der Trave, with whom Knecht enjoyed a warm personal relationship, Knecht assumes the office and duties of the Master of the Game. For eight years he represents the height of the mastery of the Glass Bead Game, composing, studying, and conducting games. Yet, unexpectedly, he resigns his position in order to return to the real world, leaving behind him the ascetic life of the Order to become private tutor to Tito, Plinio's son. On the second day of this new association, however, while swimming in a cold lake, Knecht drowns.

The novel's narrative element ends here, but the supplementary documents, which constitute about one-third of the novel, support the narrator's conclusions. The longest of these sections are the fictitious autobiographies that Knecht wrote as exercises while he was a student at Waldzell. They mirror in many interesting ways the dualities set up by the combinations of characters in the main body of the novel and allow the narrator to comment on the habits of mind that Knecht reflected in his work as a student. Almost as a reminder that not all Knecht's student hours were filled with intellectual exercises, the supplement contains a handful of poems as well, mostly in imitation of the poetic styles of others.

The Characters

Through a complex literary style that places *The Glass Bead Game* squarely in the modernist camp, Hesse gives first attention not to Knecht, the subject of the biography, but to the narrator composing the biography for the reader. This narrator, by the careful use of detail and by reporting only incidents supported or at least hinted at in the Castalian records (including Knecht's own writings) comes to life for the reader as the novel progresses through Knecht's career. It is the narrator's duty to describe Castalian life as Knecht lived it and to do so in the measured, neutral tones appropriate to the principles of Castalian intellectual discourse. Nevertheless, the narrator reveals an affection for and an indebtedness to Joseph Knecht that, together with a hint at the very end of the novel, suggest that Tito, the young son of Plinio, grows up to become a Magister Ludi and is, in fact, the narrator himself.

The object of the narrator's biography, however, is the central figure in the novel. Joseph Knecht is more than the sum of his accomplishments as listed by his biographer, because Hesse's style offers ironical interpretations of the events in the story. What is reported as warm discussion is understood by the reader to have been heated argument; what is described as an inquisitive and curious temperament is understood by the reader to be a bold, questioning, even challenging, young student spirit, one which must be tamed from time to time by the even-tempered admonishments of his tutors. Knecht's resistance to but eventual fascination with the Glass Bead Game is interpreted by the careful reader as the reluctance of the normal, bright student to sacrifice the pleasures of youthful arrogance to the sedulous study of orderly disciplines, along with the kind of grudging admission of the value of knowledge that comes only with maturity. Part of Knecht's success in Castalia is a result of the combination of quickness of mind and independence of spirit, neither of which alone makes genius. In short, Knecht (whose name means "servant") is anything but a servant: He is a student Everyman, perhaps more intelligent than most but with the same eagerness to know everything, to experience everything, to live every life (while at the same time knowing that childish things must eventually be put away in deference to the complexities and demands of reality). Knecht is more than a three-dimensional, psychologically believable person: He stands for the inquiring mind as it passes through the stages of adolescence and youth (what is called the *flos juventutis* or the "flow of youth") into a growing maturity and responsibility. Insofar as biographers have recounted Hesse's education at special schools with increasingly greater concentration on the arts, Knecht can be seen as a thinly disguised, fanciful, idealized, but still accurate, portrait of the author.

The support characters to Knecht's *Bildungsroman* constitute the cast of a *roman à clef*, as so many scholars have noted. Each major contact along Knecht's path toward mastery of the Glass Bead Game shows three sides: the fictive personality, who answers to psychological characterization; the Hegelian representative of an argumentative thesis or antithesis; and the actual contemporary or historical figure whom Hesse honors or mocks by placing him in the novel.

Easily recognizable are the pair of Pater Jacobus and Fritz Tegularius, representing the two opposing sides of the ongoing struggle between body and mind. Jacobus, a Benedictine devoted to earthly good works, is a portrait of the philosopher Jacob Burckhardt, who influenced Hesse's later philosophical views. His opponent, Fritz Tegularius (a portrait of the hypertense Friedrich Nietzsche), is all mind, the ideal of Castalian scholarship and intellectualization. More difficult to discern is the duality of Plinio Designori and the Elder Brother, the first a man of the world and the second an Oriental contemplative given over to the impressionistic instructions of the *I Ching*. Designori is more than a mere spokesperson for the secular pleasures of free enterprise. He has yet to be identified in the *roman à clef* matrix and represents for Knecht an alternative to Castalian life itself, a return to the realities of nonelitism, an alternative that Knecht eventually chooses. By denying a name to the Elder Brother (a composite of the Eastern philosophers whom Hesse studied during his research for earlier novels), Hesse further abstracts his meditative nature, reducing him to yet another alternative for Knecht, a retreat into a totally unrealistic existence. Thomas von der Trave is acknowledged to be a tribute to Hesse's contemporary, Thomas Mann, whose novel *Doktor Faustus* (1947; *Doctor Faustus*, 1948) bears undeniable similarities to *The Glass Bead Game*. Finally, the Magister Musicae may be Hesse's homage to any number of historical geniuses, from Johann Sebastian Bach to Johann Wolfgang von Goethe to Ludwig van Beethoven.

Themes and Meanings

In a novel of this size and scope, a kaleidoscope of ideas illuminates every page, but the major theme is the universality of human experience. By a Hegelian dialectic, in which the clash between thesis and antithesis yields a synthesis of ideas, Hesse presents to the reader virtually all the major aesthetic disciplines embodied in one or another of Knecht's companions. The Glass Bead Game, itself infinite in possibility, is in fact a concretization of all human activity stored in humankind's collective memories, libraries, universities, and books. It is a metaphor for all human interaction, particularly that aspect of human study that measures accomplishment by accretion of skill, knowledge, talent, even instinct. The Game is the game of human intellectual activity, including but not limited to history, music, mathematics, literary scholarship, chess, Oriental disciplines such as the study of the *I Ching* and meditation, philosophy, classic studies, languages, symbolic and linguistic logic, religion, mythology, anthropology, and, most especially, the uniquely human practice of game playing.

Woven through the fabric of all this human activity are two major threads in European intellectual history. As the narrator tells the reader, "The first of these was the liberation of thought and belief from the sway of all authority. In practice this meant the struggle of Reason, which at last felt it had come of age and won its independence. . . ." The second thread, however, a necessary corollary to any rejection of pure faith, is "the covert but passionate search for a means to confer legitimacy on this freedom, for a new and sufficient authority arising out of Reason itself." The synthesis of these two historic human activities is, according to Hesse in the voice of the narrator, the Mind. In this respect the book is a utopian novel, set in a future well past the "Age of the Feuilleton," a war-filled era in which great foolish battles raged, not unlike the period of European history in which Hesse was writing his novel (1934-1943). The Intellect, that most successful manifestation of Mind, has not prevailed, and the elitist culture of Castalia rules in peace, playing the Glass Bead Game like an organ that "has attained an almost unimaginable perfection; its manuals and pedals range over the entire intellectual cosmos; its stops are almost beyond number. . . reproducing in the Game the entire intellectual content of the universe."

Critical Context

Hesse's massive novel belongs among the great works of twentieth century literature that mark the height of the modern age. Often compared with the masterpieces of his contemporaries—Thomas Mann's *Der Zauberberg* (1924; *The Magic Mountain*, 1927) and *Doctor Faustus*, Hermann Broch's *Die Schlafwandler* (1931-1932; *The Sleepwalkers*, 1932), the Austrian Robert Musil's *Der Mann ohne Eigenschaften* (1930-1943; revised 1952, 1978; *The Man Without Qualities*, 1953-1960), and even the Irishman James Joyce's *Ulysses* (1922)—*The Glass Bead Game* has been much read and more often misread by the youthful intellectuals of post-World War II America. Seeing in Hesse's novel a justification of an adolescent intellectualism that was part of the rise of the working classes into the educated classes, college students in the 1950's and the 1960's embraced the work with a zeal and humorlessness not shared by readers in Europe, where Hesse's work was seen as part of a larger modernist statement that included condemnation of totalitarianism.

The Glass Bead Game gained popularity, too, as the culmination of a series of novels by Hesse, notably *Die Morgenlandfahrt* (1932; *The Journey to the East*, 1956) and *Siddhartha* (1922; English translation, 1951), which helped to introduce Eastern religion to young American readers, many of whom also shared a drug-culture appreciation of the arts fueled by another Hesse novel, *Der Steppenwolf* (1927; *Steppenwolf*, 1929). *The Glass Bead Game*'s more enduring reputation, however, rests on Hesse's adroit manipulation of several literary genres at the same time, as well as on the boldness of Hesse's defense of the joy of intellectual and artistic pursuits.

Sources for Further Study

Freedman, Ralph. *Hermann Hesse: Pilgrim of Crisis*, 1978.

Marrer-Tising, Carlee. *The Reception of Hermann Hesse by the Youth in the United States*, 1982.

Mileck, Joseph. *Hermann Hesse: Life and Art*, 1978.

Sorell, Walter. *Hermann Hesse: A Man Who Sought and Found Himself*, 1974.

Ziolkowski, Theodore. *The Novels of Hermann Hesse: A Study in Theme and Structure*, 1965.

Thomas J. Taylor

THE GOALIE'S ANXIETY AT THE PENALTY KICK

Author: Peter Handke (1942-   )
Type of plot: Psychological realism
Time of plot: The late 1960's
Locale: Vienna and a small Austrian village bordering on Yugoslavia
First published: Die Angst des Tormanns beim Elfmeter, 1970 (English
   translation, 1972)

> *Principal characters:*
> JOSEPH BLOCH, a former soccer goalie now working as a
>   construction worker
> GERDA, a film-theater cashier

The Novel

   The Goalie's Anxiety at the Penalty Kick presents, on one level, a psychological case study of a man undergoing an apparent schizophrenic breakdown. The novel, which is written in the third person, follows the former soccer goalie turned construction worker, Joseph Bloch, as he wanders around the city of Vienna, commits a senseless murder of a cashier, and finally flees to a small Austrian border village. The plot is minimal, and the narrative focuses primarily on the character's disturbed perceptions of his surroundings.

   The novel begins as Bloch enters the workers' hut on the construction site where he has been employed. It becomes immediately clear that his perception of reality is disturbed. The former goalie interprets an insignificant occurrence—that no one looks up to greet him when he walks in—to mean that he has been fired from the job, and he goes to collect his final paycheck. He tends to find meaning in random objects and gestures. A woman adjusting her skirt as she sits in a car is read as being some kind of answer or reply to him. In his agitated and disoriented state, Bloch walks around the city, compulsively reading newspapers and sitting in motion-picture theaters. These activities seem to make him feel more comfortable.

   He follows Gerda, a theater cashier, home, and they spend the night together. In the morning, Bloch is extremely disturbed, unable to visualize the objects in his surroundings or carry on even a simple conversation. Suddenly and without reason, he strangles the young woman. After the murder, he buys a bus ticket to the border town where a former girlfriend owns a small inn. The difficulties with the perception and interpretation of his environment continue. As a drop of water rolls down the side of a glass, for example, he feels compelled to gaze not at the drop as most would do, but at the spot where it will land. On another occasion, he perceives a plate of fish-shaped crackers as a kind of special message that he should be silent as a fish. He tends, in general, to see various objects as metaphors or signs that carry a special meaning for him. He is often jolted out of sleep by loud, abrupt noises.

At the conclusion of the novel, Bloch attends a soccer game, where he discusses with another man his past experiences as a goalie. He explains how the goalie, in order to block the penalty shot, must intensely observe every gesture and movement of the kicker so that he might predict where the ball will land. He says that the anxiety for the goalie is tremendous. Although Bloch has not been found by the police, it is clear that his capture is imminent.

The Characters

The figure of Joseph Bloch has several sources. The character is based, in part, on a psychiatric study of schizophrenia which Peter Handke read in 1968. This work describes a type of disturbed thought process called apophanic perception, in which the patient perceives random objects as having some secret meaning, usually of paranoid significance. The usual contexts that establish meaning in the everyday world are lost during this state of mental delusion, and the patient's environment becomes a shifting complex of hostile and threatening dimensions. In an interview, Handke claimed that this was one of the best books he had read that year.

Bloch's character is also intended to represent certain ideas Handke came across in his readings of structuralist and semiological thinkers and writers such as Roland Barthes and Alain Robbe-Grillet. The central notion here is that reality, or rather one's perception of it, is deeply influenced by language. Discussing this novel in another interview, Handke claimed that Bloch's behavior is only an exaggerated form of what is found in everyday perception, that his tendency to construct reality is essentially typical of all people.

A third source for the figure of Joseph Bloch is Handke's own experience. According to Handke, all writers have occasional schizophreniclike states of mind, almost mystical moments of transcendence when they are transported from the regularity of the everyday world. The world of the imagination is one of "unreality" or fantasy. Such moments are often the origin for the creative energy that fuels artistic activity. Bloch, in this work, exhibits extreme versions of tendencies present in the author himself.

Themes and Meanings

The Goalie's Anxiety at the Penalty Kick deals with the themes of language and the nature of perception. Philosophers of the twentieth century have been very much concerned with the issue of language and the degree to which notions of "reality" or "truth" are shaped by the linguistic forms and signs of culture. Semiology, the study of signs, indicates that one's environment is full of seemingly simple objects that represent meanings and convey messages: There is nothing that is merely what it appears to be. The clothes a person wears, for example, are not merely functional; they are signs that represent a certain economic class or social affiliation, an attitude toward life. The reality one perceives is the product of numerous subtle messages suggested by one's environment. Joseph Bloch's bizarre compulsion to transform random objects and details into metaphors, into signs, is merely an exaggeration of what occurs in normal perception of the world. Handke's novel addresses a fundamental modern philosophical theme about the nature of reality.

Bloch's tendency to perceive his surroundings as if they were metaphors or symbols also suggests the sensibility of a poet or writer who views the world as a source for the creation of fictions. In a novel or poem, an object is often not simply the thing itself but rather stands for something else, an idea or concept. A tree in a literary text, for example, is not merely a tree but a symbol or metaphor for life, nature, strength, rootedness, or some other quality. The goalie's perceptions also resemble the kind of reality found in dreams, where objects assume symbolic values. Sigmund Freud explained in his theories, the mind's activity in the dream state is very close to what occurs in the creative imagination and the daydream. Bloch serves, although in a distorted fashion, as a model of the poetic sensibility. In essence, he is the creator of his own symbolic world; the world becomes a "text" or a "dream" which he must interpret.

For Handke in particular and, one might surmise, for creative writers in general, art becomes a way of transcending the existential fact of fundamental human estrangement and isolation. Creativity and the imagination allow for a momentary escape from the sufferings that inevitably come with existence. Art is, in the best sense of the term, an escape from the pain of life. Fictions are a "flight" from reality, but they also allow one to envision other possibilities of living; therefore, they connect people in a more authentic manner to what is —or what can be. Art gives one the freedom, the vision, to change one's life. Joseph Bloch is clearly an extremely alienated character, and his compulsion to ascribe symbolic meaning to objects represents his attempt to relate himself in some way to the world around him.

In one passage, for example, Bloch awakes from a deep sleep and is overcome by feelings of self-disgust and self-estrangement. He feels completely alienated from life. Suddenly, he hears the sound of a coin rolling under the bed and he tries to read that event as if it were a symbol or metaphor. In doing this, Bloch seeks to connect himself to the world, to generate a meaning that will relate him to existence. For that moment, he might transcend the pain of his isolation. On this existential level, Handke's novel illustrates mankind as the one animal that tries to give meaning to suffering through the creation of art.

Critical Context

   The Goalie's Anxiety at the Penalty Kick was Handke's first commercially successful novel. His earlier two narratives, *Die Hornissen* (1966; the hornets) and *Der Hausierer* (1967; the peddler) were experimental texts and rather inaccessible to the general public. This third work evidences, in the character of Joseph Bloch, a concern with issues of language and perception. These ideas are prominent in Handke's early writings—the plays *Publikums-beschimpfung* (1966; *Offending the Audience*, 1969) and *Kaspar* (1968; English translation, 1969), for example. Handke clearly proves here that he is a major postmodernist author, whose writing seeks to illuminate the ways in which meaning is constructed.

   The autobiographical and existential themes which predominate in the author's later texts are also apparent in *The Goalie's Anxiety at the Penalty Kick* but are not as pronounced. Because of its concern with seemingly abstract issues of language theory and psychology, the novel drew criticism from those who, during the 1960's, demanded that all literature be socially concrete and politically relevant.

   The personal themes of isolation and alienation and the notion of art as transcendence in this novel clearly place Handke in the tradition of modern existential fiction. He stands in the company of writers such as Franz Kafka, Thomas Bernhard, Jean-Paul Sartre, and Albert Camus.

Sources for Further Study

Barry, Thomas F. "Language, Self, and the Other in Peter Handke's *The Goalie's Anxiety at the Penalty Kick*," in *South Atlantic Review*. LI (1986), pp. 93-105.

Heintz, Günter. *Peter Handke*, 1974.

Klinkowitz, Jerome, and James Knowlton. *The Goalie's Journey Home: Peter Handke and the Postmodern Transformation*, 1983.

Mixner, Manfred. *Peter Handke*, 1977.

Schlueter, June. *The Plays and Novels of Peter Handke*, 1981.

Thomas F. Barry

GOD'S BITS OF WOOD

Author: Ousmane Sembène (1923-   )
Type of plot: Social criticism
Time of plot: 1947-1948
Locale: Senegal
First published: Les Bouts de bois de Dieu, 1960 (English translation, 1962)

Principal characters:
>RAMATOULAYE, a strong African woman who becomes the
>leader of the other women
>BEAUGOSSE, one of the union leaders, an educated and
>Europeanized African
>BAKAYOKO, the union's primary leader, a new African devoted
>to bettering his fellow Africans
>N'DEYE TOUTI, a young woman torn between her African
>heritage and her European fantasies
>MONSIEUR DEJEAN, the regional director of the railway
>company and a Frenchman

The Novel

Based on the events surrounding an actual strike by African railway workers, *God's Bits of Wood* presents a dramatic fictionalized account of the way in which the strike in 1947 and 1948 must have affected the lives of the African union leaders, workers, and their families, as well as the French managers of the railroad. The novel, set along the Dakar-Niger railway line in Senegal (at that time a French colony), employs a large cast of characters, moves from city to village to countryside, and develops a variety of situations. The central conflict, which stems from the strike itself, serves to unify these often disparate characters, places, and narrative strands.

The opening chapter introduces the set of characters who initiate the workers' walkout. Soon, as their defiance of the French-owned railroad spreads along the line, the trains stop running. Once determined to stand united against the foreign management and to carry the strike to its resolution (and in a sense to reclaim their own country), the Africans resign themselves to a long period of hardship. Food becomes scarce, then the water does the same, and both are rationed by the officials. Before long, the euphoria that first filled the idle workers turns into discouragement. Faced with the struggle for survival, friends and relatives turn on one another, making cruelty and violence commonplace. The strikers and their families also face random acts of retribution and punishment carried out by the railway's private police and strikebreakers. Even the revered family life of the largely Muslim population disintegrates.

Amid all the disruption, however, some of the strikers display heroism and kindness. In addition, the traditionally homebound women start to play a larger role in the affairs of the world. One of the most memorable sections of the novel depicts the women's march to the city to make known the suffering they and their children have endured and the wrongs inflicted on them.

Each of these narrative elements develops through tautly constructed scenes in which numerous characters participate. These characters sometimes appear only once, in other instances several times. Although economic and political theory emerges, the narrative never descends to didacticism but at all times displays a dramatic and graphic reality; nor do the numerous characters forsake their humanity in order to mouth messages. Instead, the agony, brutality, humiliation, and torment they face with such courage make them all the more human.

Eventually, the strike ends in victory for the workers. As the novel closes, it expresses this victory in the words of a song from the native oral tradition, thus asserting the African pride for which the strike had stood:

> *From one sun to another,*
> *The combat lasted,*
> *And fighting together, blood-covered,*
> *They transfixed their enemies.*
> *But happy is the man who does battle without hatred.*

The Characters

Considering the number of characters, Ousmane Sembène's development of them is admirable for its economy. Each one assumes his individuality not so much through description as through actions and reactions. In some cases, interior monologues serve to tell more about the characters' inner lives. All of them, caught up in this event, which is like no other in their experience as a people subjected to colonial rule, show their true mettle, whether it be indestructible or weak.

Of the many people who weave their way in and out of the narrative, certain ones emerge as more memorable. These personalities, to an extent, represent an entire group of lesser characters. Such a one is Ramatoulaye, a typical African woman who is devoted to her family and faithful to the restrictions that the Muslim religion places on her. Yet when the survival of the family lies in her hands, she meets the needs of everyone. As she changes, she does so in a way altogether natural, sometimes comic, always touching.

Both Beaugosse and N'Deye Touti portray another kind of African, one with education, the ability to speak the conqueror's language and a longing to trade African tradition for European ways. Inner conflict accompanies such a division of loyalty, and the private battles that these two fight lend them a distinction in their portrayal.

Yet another sort is represented by Bakayoko, the union's leader. Not as fully or as realistically developed as the others, Bakayoko assumes a shadowy presence. Possibly too noble in motive, too elevated in stature, he lacks the shortcomings that provide the others with humanity. Portraying the new African who unselfishly gives all for the good of his people, this hero appears in a succession of African novels. Nevertheless, the person who shows imperfections always seems more believable than the one who appears to have risen above all human follies.

Monsieur Dejean, one of several French men and women who appear at intervals, suffers from the same one-dimensional development of all the European characters. They often were a despicable lot as they exploited the country's people and resources, treating both as commodities that were rightfully theirs. Nevertheless, they must have shown some favorable characteristics, but Sembène does not permit such traits to emerge among his French colonials. So one-sided a portrayal marks the novel's major weakness in characterization.

In spite of this prejudice against the Europeans and the large cast he has assembled, Sembène performs an admirable feat by making most of the characters real, these "God's bits of wood"—that is, these humans that God sends to struggle in a world beset by cruelty, injustice, and pain. Once determined to face the struggle, they discover the inner strength that allows them to triumph over the trials God has given them.

Themes and Meanings

Like many of the novels written while colonialism withered during the two decades after World War II, *God's Bits of Wood* records the exploitation and inhumane treatment of the Africans by their colonizers. In one respect, Sembène has rewritten history to show the African side of the colonial experience. In re-creating an actual and significant strike that took place early during the struggle for independence, he attempts to show the Africans that they, once united, can continue to vanquish those who have seized their land and made them virtual slaves. In Sembène's hands, the strike carries a symbolic note as one of the first African triumphs over colonialism. Writing at a time when negritude, the pride of being African, has developed from a concept into a reality, Sembène focuses on the Africans' capacity to endure in order to overcome the obstacles that block their way to selfhood. He also examines those who sacrifice their negritude and turn into mere mimics of Europeans.

While Sembène relies on the Western novelistic tradition—the book suggests at times Émile Zola's *Germinal* (1885; English translation, 1885)—he has managed to imbue *God's Bits of Wood* with an African quality through the characters, the use of the native oral tradition, and the recorded history of the struggle against colonialism.

Critical Context

Sembène's first novel, *Le Docker noir* (1956; the black dock worker), reflected his experiences as an African dock worker in France; his second novel, *Ô pays, mon beau peuple!* (1957; o my country, my beautiful people), chronicled the return of a Senegalese war veteran to his native village and his attempts to modernize the villagers' farming techniques. Neither of these works gained the wide acceptance of *God's Bits of Wood*, which launched his literary career, first in France and then abroad. This novel remains one of the major works of the postcolonial literature that focused on the wrongs of colonialism. Sembène moved next into this fiction's second stage: the exposure of the political and social chaos that followed independence. *Xala* (1973; English translation, 1976) is considered to be the best of the novels he has written on this theme.

When Sembène returned to Senegal in 1961, he saw the limited impact African writing had on Africans and decided that the masses could be influenced more effectively through film. After studying cinematography abroad, he began to bring his own novels and other works to the screen. Sembène is recognized not only as one of the major African novelists of the twentieth century but also as a brilliant filmmaker.

Sources for Further Study

Blair, Dorothy S. *African Literature in French: A History of Creative Writing in French from West and Equatorial Africa*, 1976.

Brench, Anthony C. *Novelists' Inheritance in French Africa*, 1976.

Killam, G.D., ed. *African Writers on African Writing*, 1973.

Ogungbesan, Kolawole. *New West African Literature*, 1979.

Wauthier, Claude. *The Literature and Thought of Modern Africa*, 1966.

Robert Ross

THE GOLD-RIMMED EYEGLASSES

Author: Giorgio Bassani (1916-   )
Type of plot: Tragedy
Time of plot: The late 1930's
Locale: Ferrara and Rimini, Italy
First published: Gli occhiali d'oro, 1958 (*The Gold-Rimmed Spectacles*, 1960;
   revised as *The Gold-Rimmed Eyeglasses*, 1975)

> *Principal characters:*
> THE NARRATOR, a male literature student, twenty years old,
>   from a middle-class Jewish family
> DR. ATHOS FADIGATI, a distinguished ear, nose, and throat
>   specialist, born in Venice but practicing in Ferrara
> ERALDO DELILIERS, a fellow student of the narrator and the
>   companion of Fadigati

The Novel

   The Gold-Rimmed Eyeglasses is above all a precise reconstruction of the
time and place that provide the background for all Giorgio Bassani's major
fiction: the middle class and professional world of Ferrara, as seen from the
vantage point of a member of the city's well-established Jewish community.
Fascism was at its height during the last years of the 1930's, a period marked
by the cementing of the ties between Italy and Nazi Germany, and the passing of the Special Laws against the Jews. The mounting climate of intolerance takes its psychic and physical toll on the characters in the novel.
   Dr. Athos Fadigati is a distinguished physician, with a flourishing practice
in Ferrara, as well as being the head of the ear, nose, and throat department
of the city's main hospital. The children of most of the best families in Ferrara have been under his care, and even the narrator remembers having his
tonsils removed by Fadigati. Since the early 1920's (and coinciding with the
new order imposed by the Fascist regime on Italian society), Fadigati's life
has been one of unruffled professional advancement. Nevertheless, Fadigati
has a weakness that threatens his seemingly impregnable social status. He is
to be found during the evening frequenting the stalls, and not the balconies,
of the local cinemas, or favoring the more popular and lower-class areas of
town rather than the cafés of the major boulevards; wherever, in short,
groups of proletarian youths, soldiers, perhaps, or knots of soccer fans may
be gathered. Imperceptibly, Bassani brings his respectable bourgeois chorus,
which has hitherto been preoccupied with finding the doctor a suitable wife,
to the conclusion that Fadigati prefers men to women.
   In the second section of the novel, Fadigati comes to the fore, as he
befriends a group of university students who take the early morning train

from Ferrara to Bologna. He gradually establishes himself as an avuncular companion, a man of culture, and an occasional counselor. He manages to break down the reserve that naturally divides the generations, but on some of those train journeys, he must submit to the undisguised insults of Eraldo Deliliers, not only the most handsome member of the group but also the most arrogant and dangerous.

The summer of 1937, at Rimini, marks the decline and fall of Fadigati. On his arrival at the resort to spend his summer vacation with his family, the narrator learns that Fadigati and Deliliers are sharing a room at the Grand-Hôtel, and that they have been seen at all the most fashionable resorts along the Adriatic coast, traveling in an Alfa Romeo sports car. This scandal naturally is the main topic of conversation among the respectable Ferraresi gathered on the Rimini beachfront, and Fadigati is ostracized by virtually everyone except the narrator and his family, with whom he establishes a close friendship. The relationship with Deliliers can only end in disaster. Fadigati is left more and more to his own devices, while Deliliers shamelessly exploits the older man's good nature and imprudent generosity. Following a violent scene at the hotel, Deliliers finally leaves, taking with him the car and most of his benefactor's money and valuables. The summer is over, the weather changes for the worse, and everyone returns to Ferrara.

In the last four chapters of the book, the destinies of Fadigati and the narrator are more closely intertwined. Fadigati loses his post at the hospital and almost all of his patients, and the narrator observes with mounting despair the government's well-orchestrated anti-Semitic campaign (which culminated in the introduction of racial laws in 1938). He can hardly bear to have a cup of coffee in the cafés in the center of town or talk with his university companions. With Fadigati, he shares a sense of persecution: the unjust isolation of the innocent. Unlike his father, he refuses to be consoled by bland reassurances from well-placed acquaintances that no racial laws will ever come to pass in Italy. A meeting tentatively arranged between the two friends does not take place, probably as the result of a weekend of torrential rain, and on Sunday, the narrator reads that the Fadigati's body was found in the river. He was the victim of an accident, according to the paper.

The Characters

Like other men in his situation with a professional reputation to uphold, Fadigati must live a dual life, divided between day and night: by day, the concerned throat specialist; by night, a lonely man withdrawing into the shadows of the ill-lit popular quarters of the city and the cheaper seats at the cinema. It is when Bassani draws his tragic victim out of the nocturnal shadows of Ferrara, and even out of the discreet monotones of the winter train journeys, into the blinding summer sun that bakes the bathers at Rimini that the reader knows that Fadigati's collapse is imminent. Light is the medium of exposure, and from exposure to public disgrace is but a step. Fadigati's decision to appear openly at Rimini with Deliliers seems such a calculated affront to public opinion, and so out of character, that the narrator rightly attributes it to Fadigati's shameless companion. The narrator also discerns in Fadigati's nature another quality that leads to his demise. When Fadigati shows his young friend the curt note left by his departed lover, he seems to revel in his own humiliation. The exultant tone in his voice reveals a self-destructive desire, derived perhaps from a corrosive guilt that demands some kind of expiation.

The narrator of the story is not a distant bystander but a participant drawn into the action by moral compulsion. It is not only his reputation as a dreamer (a "poet") that sets him apart from his companions. It is also the fact that he is a Jew. He shares this isolation with Fadigati, and this melancholy similarity of experience develops into the book's central relationship and illuminates its major theme. Apart from Deliliers, the narrator is the only member of the crowd on the train who turns up at Rimini, and it is he and his family (his father is an amiable *naïf*) who offer the only companionship Fadigati can find in his enforced solitude. This is to be the last summer of relative tranquillity. Winter announces darkness and despair, and the narrative tone grows bleaker with the change in the weather. It is significant that the narrator and Fadigati encounter each other at night in the fog, that rain prevents their final rendezvous, and that only the narrator seems to be aware of Fadigati's suicide.

Deliliers is not so much a character as a nemesis, a destructive force whose single function is Fadigati's downfall. Naturally, the young man combines demoniac calculation with Apollonian beauty. A perfect physical specimen, and an amateur middle-weight boxing champion, Deliliers is an extremist in both his decadent beauty and his cynicism, inspiring in others no mere love or affection but instead blind infatuation. He will use his physical beauty as a means of blackmail and seduction, with the pathetic Fadigati perhaps only the first of a long trail of victims. Deliliers is an exact product of his time, or any time that reveres the cult of the body without any corresponding dose of moral awareness. In his cynicism and brutality, and his exalted egotism, he is a born Fascist, but without the political affiliation.

A minor character, Nino Bottecchiari, the acknowledged intellectual of the group of students on the Bologna train, is also worth noting. Bottecchiari comes from a family of established Socialists (his uncle is an ex-Socialist deputy). When the narrator runs into Bottecchiari on his return from vacation, however, Bottecchiari informs him that he has been offered a job as chief cultural officer for the district by one of the leaders of the local Fascist Party. Should he accept? The narrator bitterly tells him to do so and without a moment's hesitation. For the narrator, it is all of a piece: the humiliation of Fadigati, the anti-Semitic campaign, the brutality of Deliliers, the cynical ambition of this former student. Bottecchiari may pretend to despise his fellow Italians and the present political leadership, but while the Fascists are in power, they command the jobs. At the start of what promises to be a successful political career, Bottecchiari is a representative figure, a man prepared to jettison moral tradition when it suits his interests.

Themes and Meanings

Bassani prefaced *The Gold-Rimmed Eyeglasses* with a quotation from Sophocles, and structured his novel as a tragedy, more or less respectful of the conventions of time, place, and action. The three "acts" are largely complete in themselves (train, Rimini, Ferrara). The action is limited to one slim drama, and the spotlight falls on only three characters. The fate of the protagonist is inevitable, born of a fatal flaw and the flouting of a sexual taboo no less damnable than in the case of Oedipus. Bassani has chosen the tragic genre to discern, in the ruins of one man's life, a metaphor for a tragic age. Fadigati is doomed, because he is a deviant figure, and no society will tolerate those who are "different." This has always been true, but under Fascism the state applied the standards of uniform behavior, and the pressures to conform reached the breaking point.

Intolerance, however, is not the main theme of *The Gold-Rimmed Eyeglasses*. That is to be found in the parallel lives of Fadigati and the Jewish narrator who befriends him. The page following the news of Deliliers' betrayal announces the start of the concerted anti-Semitic campaign in the newspapers, and the similarities of fates are made explicit. The homosexual offends the virile masculine norms of Mediterranean society, as the Jew stains the purity of the Latin (or Aryan) race. The former will be driven to suicide just as surely as the latter will be deported to the prison camps. In the interim, they are drawn together in a despairing solitude in the gathering darkness of a Ferrara winter. Finally, they seem to be the only remaining characters in the novel. The narrator is more and more removed from his family's preoccupations. His last conversation with Fadigati is on the telephone, and he alone reads of Fadigati's death in the paper, announcing it as if talking to himself.

Critical Context

Bassani's fiction is deliberately limited to the experience of the Jewish community in Ferrara and largely to the few years that correspond to the most formative period of his own life, from the late 1930's until the end of the war. In those years, he was graduated from the university, embarked on a literary career, witnessed the local effects of the Holocaust, and joined the Italian Resistance. Only upon entering this seemingly narrow world, and surrendering to Bassani's language, can one appreciate the richness of a narrative experience set in a narrow compass. Bassani's genius is to evoke, in the microcosm that he creates, the connecting links between the tragedies and struggles endured by his characters and those of coreligionists in a host of other communities beyond Ferrara, and beyond Italy itself. To have been a part of a well-established Jewish community in that time and place was not only a personal misfortune; it was also, for the writer, a kind of historical gift, for it presented him with a local and universal theme and allowed him to link the fate of *his* Jews with that of all victims of the Holocaust.

The fiction of Bassani is of a piece, and *The Gold-Rimmed Eyeglasses* should be read along with the collection of tales in which it was published, in 1956, *Cinque storie ferraresi* (*Five Stories of Ferrara*, 1971). The stories follow the experiences of the Jews during World War II. The narrator of *The Gold-Rimmed Eyeglasses* anticipates the Special Laws and their consequences. Ninety-year-old Doctor Elias Corcos from "La passeggiate prima di cena" ("A Walk Before Supper") is rounded up with 182 other Jewish victims and shipped off to Germany. In "Una lapide in Via Mazzini" ("A Plaque in Via Mazzini"), Geo Josz, the single survivor of that group of victims, returns from Auschwitz. Also among that group, and mentioned in passing in *The Gold-Rimmed Eyeglasses*, are the Finzi-Continis, the subject of Bassani's most famous novel, *Il giardino dei Finzi-Contini* (1962; *The Garden of the Finzi-Continis*, 1965). This recapitulation of themes and the reappearance of characters gives Bassani's oeuvre the unity of the saga novel. A writer who worked miniature in a provincial corner of Italy, Bassani nevertheless belongs to the European tradition.

Sources for Further Study
Clay, G. R. Review in *The New York Times Book Review*. LXV (October 9, 1960), p. 54.
Grillandi, Massimo. *Invito alla lettura di Giorgio Bassani*, 1972.
The New Yorker. Review. XXXVI (December 24, 1960), p. 61.
Pacifici, Sergio. Review in *Saturday Review*. XLIII (August 20, 1960), p. 16.
Trevelyan, R., ed. *Italian Writing Today*, 1967.

Harry Lawton

GROUP PORTRAIT WITH LADY

Author: Heinrich Böll (1917-1985)
Type of plot: Social realism
Time of plot: c. 1923-1971
Locale: Cologne, West Germany
First published: Gruppenbild mit Dame, 1971 (English translation, 1973)

> *Principal characters:*
> THE AU., the narrator, who has an objective interest in Leni
>   Pfeiffer's life
> LENI PFEIFFER, a woman of forty-eight, a passive resister of
>   injustice and inhumanity, and a romantic
> MARGRET SCHLÖMER, Leni's best friend, a modest woman who
>   comes to a bad end
> BORIS LVOVICH, a young Russian prisoner of war, the father of
>   Leni's son
> WALTER PELZER, Leni's boss
> SISTER RAHEL, a brilliant Jewish woman who has converted to
>   Catholicism and is ill-treated in a convent
> MARJA VAN DOORN, Leni's parents' loyal housekeeper

The Novel

Heinrich Böll's massive novel manages to integrate its in-depth portrait of a woman into a broad picture of postwar German society. Organized like a collage by the unnamed, imaginary author, "the Au.," the novel is a vast collection of impressions, reports, and interrogations that, at its best, transcends the voluminous mass of facts and presents precisely what its title suggests: a group portrait with a particular individual at its center. The novel unfolds much like a detective story, except that its "crimes" are not sensational or lurid but rather deep and fundamental wrongs against the universal values of justice and charity. The novel's painstaking dating of material is augmented by the fragmented recollections of numerous characters who give the reader a sense of social, political, cultural, and moral texture.

Leni Pfeiffer, the protagonist, is a forty-eight-year-old woman whose striking physical attributes are in marked contrast to her tainted reputation and her economic straits. Having been an unskilled worker for most of her life, she is now without large financial resources, so she rents rooms to lodgers. Her old-fashioned dress marks her as someone out of place in a world that requires male protection. The novel is composed of the testimony of those who have known her; what emerges is a picture of a survivor. Leni lives in the house where she was born. Enormously sensual, she is laconic, though not bitter, about her troubles. Life has brought her many tests, and she has survived them all, though the emotional costs have sometimes been great.

Böll's picture of German society contains several factors that account for the peculiarities of Leni's story. Swept by the political climate into joining a Nazi organization while still young, she lacks awareness of its political dimensions and finds its "den evenings" reminiscent of the oppressive convent piety that plagued her as a girl. Her brilliant older brother is killed in Denmark, and this tragedy is coupled with a family atmosphere riddled with anomalies. Her father, Hubert Gruyten, a mason by trade, becomes a successful construction manager but remains a pathological brooder. Her mother, Helene, a highly literate woman, lacks conjugal harmony and dies in pain.

Leni yields to her cousin, Erhard Schweigert, a nervous and inferior person, but Erhard is shot by a German firing squad. Leni loses weight, turns tearful, and appears to be in an irreversible decline. She does marry Alois Pfeiffer, a man plagued by his own unrealistic expectations, but this marriage abruptly ends with Alois' death. Leni, however, refuses to mourn for him because he had forced her to have sex against her will just prior to his recall by his army division. Leni experiences two and a half years of tranquillity: She goes to films, practices the piano, takes loving care of her mother, and visits Sister Rahel, the brilliant nun who imparts to her near-mystical notions of sex. Leni learns to think of love as a laying-on of hands and develops a passion for enlarged drawings of human organs, particularly genitalia. She devotes years of effort to a large, uncompleted picture titled "Part of the Retina of the Left Eye of the Virgin Mary alias Rahel."

The heart of her story is her love affair with Boris Lvovich, a Soviet prisoner of war. She meets him while working for Walter Pelzer's thriving wreath business, and, ironically, the devastation of war gives birth to their intense passion. Daylight raids allow her a chance to get away from her supervisors and escape into the fields with her lover. She runs enormous risks in sharing food and intimacy with a potential enemy of the German republic, especially as Boris is far from reticent about his behavior. The provocatively fun-loving Boris acquires a taste for German authors and songs. Ironically, his taste incriminates him one day when he is mistaken for a German by American soldiers and captured. The legacy of his love for Leni is a son, who is born in catacomb-like conditions under the municipal cemetery.

A strong narrative pattern becomes quite evident: the continuation of existence amid destruction and debris. The novel is like a kaleidoscope of minibiographies. Although Leni is the main figure, she is by no means the only important one. Her difficult romance with Boris is, perhaps, the most heartwarming section, but there are so many other figures who also suffer and who also compound the question of the inhumanity of postwar German society. By the end of the novel, Leni's son is a deliberate rebel, and Leni struggles with a quirky, unresolved enigma. She is made pregnant by a Turk, and her life is still without a coherent shape.

The Characters

Leni Pfeiffer's history ostensibly motivates "the Au." to interview a vast number of other characters and organize a collection of life stories. The "heroine" is presented as an anomalous, puzzling figure, who raises several (ultimately unanswered) questions about herself. The plain facts of her case are easy to organize, but the underlying metaphysical questions about her innocence, romanticism, and realism are more difficult.

Leni's sensuality is also the cause of her tainted moral reputation. An amateur pianist and artist, she also has a scatological interest which seems pornographic. She is reviled by strangers because of an apparent isensitivity. She refuses to mourn Alois' death so she is said to be devoid of feeling. The truth, however, is that she is without remorse. She regrets nothing— especially not her love affair with the Russian Boris, a dangerous act that brings her vile accusations of whoredom.

Although she does not go to church, she believes in visions and visitations of the Virgin Mary. She does not enjoy sex at first, although her mind appears to be obsessed with sexual images and sensations. In wartime, she drives around the countryside, a vigorous blonde in a snappy car, bribing gardeners to take food to her lifelong friend, Sister Rahel. She dances while others are dying heroically. She goes to the cinema while bombs fall. She allows herself to be seduced by an unimpressive fellow and, when he dies a few days after their marriage, she holds his parents in contempt for having arranged a widow's pension for her.

Politically naïve, she seems to be at the mercy of unfolding events, yet she is tough enough to resist asking for pity. Her genuine love and sympathy for displaced exiles and other victims such as Sister Rahel, Boris, and Margret Schlömer, her best friend, impel her to risk her own safety and deny her own comfort. She is so proletarian that she seems incapable of adopting the bourgeois profit mentality. Yet she is not a true rebel, for her method is not radical protest; she is a passive resister, drawn to acts of charity and justice. She seeks to act positively rather than negatively, and so, in a world of often bitter recrimination and sordid struggle, she is a puzzling curiosity. The overwhelming question concerns her innocence: Is she a pure, humane being, or is she a shrewd manipulator? The preponderant evidence lies on the side of her lack of cognizance.

There is a serious flaw in Böll's presentation of Leni's character, for the sheer mass of evidence and testimony sometimes buries the outline of the story, and she disappears. This technique of collage, however, is what holds the novel together and allows opportunities for satire. The other informants are all strikingly individualistic and range from the iconolatrous former housekeeper, Marja van Doorn; the music critic, Dr. Schirtenstein; the bookkeeper, Otto Hoyser; and the unconscionably sly Pelzer to a sensual nun, Sister Klementina; a victim of venereal disease, Margret Schlömer; a Soviet prisoner of war, Bogakov; and an anonymous, exalted personage.

Controlling all this material, "the Au." is a lively narrator and editor, who is candid about his own peculiarities and biases without interrupting the flow of the story. In the course of his tireless research, he sets eyes on Leni only twice yet is able to document her life very credibly. His voice is questioning and meditative, sometimes shallow but always aimed at taking in a large picture of humans under stress. He is a man who obviously cares about people and their problems, yet he shapes his story without overt propaganda or didacticism. By allowing his witnesses to evaluate, reevaluate, and justify their lives at various moments, the narrator achieves a balanced impressionism.

Themes and Meanings

Heinrich Böll's novels tend to consist of situations reported by second or third parties. They usually include a Catholic spirit of compassion for the wounded and defenseless, a thirst for justice, and a curiosity about virtue and vice. His plots function as machinery in a literature of debris, *Trümmerliteratur* (literally "rubble literature"), for his are novels of the destruction caused by war.

In order to tell a story that covers the rise of Nazism, World War II, an economic boom, and a subsequent economic collapse, Böll makes skillful use of "the Au." as a researcher. Yet politics, as such, are not the prime focus; the unvarnished realism is designed to create a portrait of humans—some maladjusted, some privileged, but all caught up in a materialistic world where spiritual values are increasingly weakened. The most important question is: What has happened to justice and compassion? Margret Schlömer dies of venereal disease after having put a foreign statesman into a "treaty mood," an act that befitted the very society that despises her. An intrinsically modest woman, she dies of blushing. Sister Rahel, the Jewish convert to Catholicism, is relegated to the status of a neglected hideaway in a convent. Her intellectual brilliance and defiance are nullified by the degrading treatment given her. Ilse Kremer, Leni's fellow worker, dies in despair, with no belongings other than a recently paid-up television set, half a bottle of vinegar, a few cigarette papers, and a rent receipt-book. Boris is caught up in the web of politics, which allows no room for love. Lev, the son born to Boris and Leni, is a deliberate criminal in protest against his cousins who manipulate family fortunes in their favor. Finally Leni, the trammeled heroine, never appears to have a life of unambiguous hope. She can be certain of only one thing: more duress. Yet her romanticism and her son's unrest signal an emerging opposition to society. Their anomalies are an anarchic resistance to life's injustices.

Critical Context

Heinrich Böll, winner of the Nobel Prize for Literature in 1972, built a reputation for realism and satire. Böll's links to Ernest Hemingway are evidenced by his interest in character and in prose of unvarnished plainness. His work is also close to that of Graham Greene and Evelyn Waugh, among English-language writers, for he was a notable satirist of a victimizing society. His Catholicism was not as explicit as Greene's or Waugh's, for he used religious symbols to explore their effects on character rather than for any overt theological significance. His moral universe often has a Dickensian simplicity in that his good and evil characters are easily distinguished by stereotypical virtues and vices. The good stay together in a homogeneous world because they fear contamination. Consequently, they are removed from direct political activity, which accounts for their ostensible passivity in the face of broad political events.

Böll is most aptly linked to postwar German writers who have found it difficult to deal with the past for both factual and literary reasons. Oppressive memories of suffering and destruction often make it difficult to write with clarity. Moreover, what literary technique to use becomes a problem. Böll allied himself to the movement known as Gruppe 47 because of its express purpose of attempting to use language as a straightforward instrument. Along with members such as poet Günter Eich, fiction writer Hans Werner Richter, and playwright Peter Weiss, Böll attempted to use clean, nonvisionary language for his realism. He began as an exponent of *Trümmerliteratur*, and his satire is notably critical of materialism and the high-pressure economic competitiveness of modern society.

Böll assumed that the reader has an insatiable interest in facts, and implicit in his approach is the belief that the same story should be able to be told numerous times and in various ways. His arduous attention to details gives his fiction mass and weight, but sometimes the result is a negative one, a blurring of the outlines of his story. Moreover, his long-winded attempts to present all the available evidence dissipate some of the suspense. His satire and wit, however, leaven the heaviness and sharpen his moral directness.

Sources for Further Study
Bauke, Joseph P. "Another Tentative Start," in *On Contemporary Literature*, 1969. Edited by Richard Kostelanetz.
Böll, Heinrich. "The 'How' and the 'What,'" in *Missing Persons and Other Essays*, 1977.
_____. "In Defense of 'Rubble Literature,'" in *Missing Persons and Other Essays*, 1977.
Demetz, Peter. *Postwar German Literature*, 1970.
Magill, C. P. *German Literature*, 1974.
Seymour-Smith, Martin. *Guide to Modern World Literature*. Vol. 2, 1975.

Keith Garebian

THE GUARDIAN OF THE WORD

Author: Camara Laye (1928-1980)
Type of plot: Adventure romance
Time of plot: The thirteenth century
Locale: Ancient West Africa
First published: Le Maître de la parole, 1978 (English translation, 1984)

>   *Principal characters:*
>   SUNDIATA, the great ruler and warrior who brought order to
>   his part of West Africa
>   MAGHAN KÖN FATTA, Sundiata's father and a powerful king
>   SOGOLON CONDÉ, Sundiata's mother
>   FATUMATA BÉRÉTÉ, Sogolon Condé's rival wife, who plots
>   against her and Sundiata
>   SUMAORO, a tyrant who sets out to conquer the other
>   kingdoms

The Novel

The Guardian of the Word relates the events surrounding the rise and reign of Sundiata, a thirteenth century Africa leader. The story was told to Camara Laye by a noted *griot,* a traditional storyteller in Guinea, in West Africa. Literally "the guardian of the word," the *griot* has long played an important role for his people by keeping alive their political and social history. This oral tradition, handed down from generation to generation, survived the colonial period and, since independence, has been revived by Africans seeking to understand their past more fully. Laye's novel is one such effort; during 1963, he recorded the words of a modern *griot* named Babu Condé, then transcribed them into a purely African work. The voice of Babu Condé speaks throughout the tale; thus the narrative style belongs to him, not to Laye's inventiveness.

After framing the central story with genealogy and a history of earlier rulers, the *griot* tells of the miracles and adventures that made Sundiata's life legendary. He begins by revealing how Sundiata's mother, Sogolon, ugly and hunchbacked, marries Maghan Kön Fatta. To this aging ruler and his mysterious second wife Sundiata is born, during a violent storm, but, in spite of the prophecies heralding his birth, Sundiata appears at first to be a disappointment. Unable to walk until he reaches the age of ten, the boy only then begins to fulfill his destined promise.

Not long thereafter, with his father dead and his father's first wife jealous, Sundiata and his mother, along with her younger children, go into exile; various rulers give them shelter. By the time that Sundiata has reached eighteen years of age and proved himself to be an able warrior, he hears of the evil exploits of the tyrant Sumaoro and of the cruelties that his armies are inflicting on innocent people. To right these wrongs, Sundiata raises an army of his own, and other kings join him with theirs to destroy Sumaoro. After learning Sumaoro's secret, that he can be killed with a white rooster's spur, Sundiata chases this perpetrator of destruction into a cave. There Sumaoro dies, ending his reign of terror.

Triumphant, Sundiata then unites the various kingdoms and assigns authority to those who fought with him, creating a great empire where "carefree mothers gave birth to happy children, and desolation, the sign of Sumaoro's passage through the savanna, gave place to prosperity which burst forth everywhere."

The narrative first covers events that lead up to Sundiata's triumph and introduces a number of characters who serve to fulfill the prophecies surrounding him. Then, its structure entirely in the tradition of the *griot*, the story moves into a rehearsal of Sundiata's preparation as a warrior, his demonstrations of courage, and his practice of wise and fair government. Economical in its telling, dependent on magic spells and other such devices, fiery in its depiction of battles, fixed in its assurance that evil yields to good, *The Guardian of the Word* resembles any number of epics from world literature.

The Characters

Following the demands of the epic tradition, the *griot* does not develop characters as the novelist might but relies instead on broad strokes, especially those derived from action, to bring the story's figures to life. Although it may sometimes be difficult to believe in Sundiata as a flesh-and-blood person, considering the number of advantageous interventions he enjoys from mystical sources, the great warrior emerges as a memorable hero who takes his proper place alongside the Zulu's Chaka, Beowulf, King Arthur, Sir Gawain, the mythological Greeks and Romans, and the Old Testament heroes. The fact that he loves his mother and shows devotion to his younger siblings, and that he even falls in love, gives Sundiata human dimensions, while his fearless fight on the side of good to destroy the forces of evil lends him ideal dimensions.

Sundiata's father, Maghan Kön Fatta, a powerful king whose son is destined to be even greater, also faces human problems, including confrontations with his jealous first wife after he marries Sogolon. Even his stormy relationship with Sogolon, who at first refuses his romantic advances, helps to turn him into more than simply an abstract instrument of prophecy. When the much-touted son proves to be an embarrassment, the disappointed father again shows his human fallibility.

Although ugly and deformed, Sogolon not only fulfills the role that supernatural forces had ordained for her but also evolves into a warm, touching character. She becomes a devoted wife and mother whose personal traits shine so beautifully that they obliterate her outward ugliness. When she dies in exile on the eve of her son's triumph, her death causes far more sorrow for the reader than would that of a stick figure, for she has developed into much more than a mere fulfiller of prophecy.

One of those distinctive evil heroines, Maghan Kön Fatta's first wife, Fatumata Bérété, does not calmly accept her demotion from the position of favorite wife but reacts to the situation as such a woman might, with cunning and cruelty. Her intense jealousy is understandable, for she intends to protect not only her personal interests but also those of her children. Disappointed in her son's weakness, she again shows the way in which the mind of such a woman works when she displays her human side as well as her stereotypical villainy.

Sumaoro, depraved and ambitious to the exclusion of all else, succumbs to the wiles of a beautiful woman in a weak moment that leads to his downfall. Reveling in evil and barbarity, Sumaoro murders at will, engages in unspeakable rites, and exults in destruction. Yet, like Fatumata Bérété, he shows a human side which is subject to fear and jealousy.

These major characters, as do all the others who weave their way through the narrative, emerge both as symbolic personages in the unfolding of the epic and as actual people caught in the web of timeless human events. The guardian of the word understands the demands of characterization; he knows that stereotypes will not gain his listeners' (and in this case, his readers') attention and sympathy. Only those with human traits can do that.

Themes and Meanings

Laye studies the tales of the *griot* not as accurate historical documents but as artistic preservations of the values found in a traditional culture. One authority in the oral tradition of West Africa has noted that the stories, although entertaining, have as their primary purpose the revelation of moral truths. Research has shown that the Sundiata legend probably gained its form around the end of the seventeenth century, a time of political crisis; by telling such a story, the *griot* hoped to present an image of the perfect ruler and kingdom in order to construct an ideal for those who ruled at that time.

Three centuries later, Laye makes a similar use of the Sundiata material. In the chapters that introduce the tale, Laye points out that destiny finds its direction through spiritual forces on which Africans could draw, if only they would forsake the remnants of colonialism and found their nations on past glorious traditions, such as those exemplified in the Sundiata story.

Laye also indirectly criticizes the regime then ruling Guinea by comparing it to Sumaoro's dictatorship, which, like its modern counterpart relied on the terror and execution of its opponents for power. That such a leader as Sundiata might rise in modern Guinea appears to be Laye's hope, for the guardian of the word concludes the tale with this moral: "May the example of Sundiata and his family illuminate us in our progress along the slow and difficult road of African evolution!"

Critical Context

Laye's first novel, *L'Enfant noir* (1953; *The Dark Child*, 1954), ranks second only to Chinua Achebe's *Things Fall Apart* (1958) in international sales of a work by an African writer. A romantic evocation of what it is like to grow up in a West African village, *The Dark Child* presents Laye's strong belief in the importance of retaining traditional values. His next two works to appear, *Le Regard du roi* (1954; *The Radiance of the King*, 1956) and *Dramouss* (1966; *A Dream of Africa*, 1968), elaborate on this theme. Nevertheless, Laye's final novel may well contain the richest expression of his philosophy.

In all of his work, Laye attempted to blend European fictional forms with Africa's oral tradition, rather than depending solely on the realistic approach. He accomplishes this objective in *The Guardian of the Word* and fulfills as well his desire to preserve traditional culture in the hope that such a record might inspire contemporary Africans as they wrestle with their destiny.

Sources for Further Study

Blair, Dorothy. *African Literature in French*, 1976.

Gakwandi, Shatto Arthur. *The Novel and Contemporary Experience in Africa*, 1977.

King, Adele. *The Writings of Camara Laye*, 1981.

Ogungbesan, Kolawole. *New West African Literature*, 1979.

Robert Ross

HADJI MURAD

Author: Leo Tolstoy (1828-1910)
Type of plot: Historical realism
Time of plot: 1851-1852
Locale: The Caucasus Mountains
First published: Khadzi-Murat, 1911 (English translation, 1911)

>   *Principal characters:*
>   HADJI MURAD, a Moslem Caucasian warrior who defects to
>   the Russians
>   NICHOLAS I, the Czar of Russia
>   SHAMIL, the Imam (holy leader) of the Chechen
>   mountaineers
>   HAMZAD, Shamil's predecessor as Imam
>   PRINCE SIMON MIKHAILOVICH VORONTSOV, the Russian
>   commander at Vozdvighensk
>   PRINCESS MARYA VASILEVNA, his wife
>   MICHAEL SEMENOVICH VORONTSOV, his father, viceroy and
>   sirdar
>   LORIS-MELIKOV, the aide-de-camp to the viceroy and sirdar
>   CAPTAIN BUTLER, the commander of the Fifth Company
>   POLTORATSKY, the Russian company commander
>   PETER AVDEEV, a Russian soldier, killed in a skirmish
>   SADO, the man who shelters Hadji Murad in Makhmet
>   YUSUF, Hadji Murad's son

The Novel

  Hadji Murad takes place in the mid-nineteenth century Caucasus Mountains, where a religious civil war has been waged by the Tartar Moslem mountaineers, also known as the Chechen, against the Russian imperial army and Orthodox church, who are attempting to repress them and to extend the empire. As the story opens, Hadji Murad, a Tartar governor and a warrior of legendary prowess, has defected from the forces of Shamil, the Chechen holy leader (Imam), and is in flight. Hadji Murad is trying to negotiate with the Russians to join their forces and take revenge against Shamil, who has killed many of his kin and who holds his mother, two wives, and five children hostage. He finds refuge and hospitality in the home of Sado, who runs some risk because the rest of the village hope to capture his guest. Hadji Murad sends messengers to the Russians to offer his surrender on the condition that they accept him into their forces, help him regain his family, and let him fight with them to destroy Shamil.

  Meanwhile, the villagers try to capture Hadji Murad, who gallops through their barricade and escapes into the forest, where he finds the rest of his men waiting for him. The next day, he is received at Fort Vozdvighensk by Prince Vorontsov, whose father is the viceroy and sirdar in the Caucasus. Both father and son hope to benefit from Hadji Murad's defection, and they receive him with much ceremony.

Hadji Murad relates his past life to the sirdar's aide-de-camp, Loris-Melikov. As a child and young man, Hadji Murad was a close friend of the Khan family. When a holy war erupted between the Chechens and the Russians, the Moslem Imam, Hamzad, urged the Khans to join. When they asked him first to explain the war, he mutilated their messengers and betrayed and killed the Khans; his second-in-command, Shamil, threw the youngest son over a precipice. Hadji Murad fled. That was the only time in his life that he was afraid. In revenge, he and his brother killed Hamzad in the mosque. During the assassination, the brother was killed, but Hadji Murad escaped. When Shamil succeeded Hamzad, he invited Hadji Murad to join him, but the latter refused; the blood of his brother and the Khans was on Shamil's hands. Instead, Hadji Murad joined the Russians and was made governor of Avaria. A rival soon traduced him, had him imprisoned, and then had his men take him, as a bound prisoner, up a mountain pass— with orders to kill him if he tried to escape. From a height of 120 yards, Hadji Murad jumped off a cliff, pulling a soldier with him. Though his skull, ribs, arms, and a leg were fractured, he survived. Feeling betrayed by the Russians, he finally joined Shamil, who promised to make him ruler of Avaria again. For years, Hadji Murad fought the Russians in a series of bold raids and campaigns. Yet all this time, he hated Shamil, and when Shamil learned that Hadji Murad expected to succeed him, he confiscated his property and attempted to capture and kill him. At that point, Hadji Murad once again went over to the Russians.

Because of Hadji Murad's past, the Russians are not sure that they can trust him. While they treat him as an honored guest, they also restrict his freedom and keep him guarded. When he defected, Hadji Murad had to leave his family behind, and they became prisoners of Shamil. Until they are freed, Hadji Murad cannot fully help the Russians overthrow Shamil. He urges them to negotiate with the Imam, to arrange an exchange of prisoners or, failing that, to undertake a rescue operation. Instead of giving Hadji Murad a command, the Russians, from the czar down, dawdle and play politics, with Hadji Murad as a pawn. Meanwhile, Shamil has threatened to give Hadji Murad's mother and wives to various villages and to blind his eldest son, Yusuf. By terrorizing the mountaineers who are sympathetic to Hadji Murad, Shamil eliminates the possibility of their helping in a rescue attempt.

Finding that the Russians show no serious interest in freeing his family, that they waste time with bureaucratic trifles, Hadji Murad decides to escape and rescue his family himself. Hadji Murad is allowed a daily ride, with two of his men and a military escort. On the day of the escape, however, he takes all of his men. In a brief skirmish, his men kill several of the soldiers. When word reaches the fort, the commander sends his cossacks and the local militia in pursuit. Figuring that the pursuers will expect him to go right, to the mountains, Hadji Murad turns left, hoping to cross the river, go downstream, and cross back to the mountains by an unanticipated route, but he makes a fatal blunder, for the rice fields between him and the river have flooded and turned into a bog in which the horses flounder helplessly. By nightfall, the fugitives have reached a small patch of scrubby higher ground, where the troops catch them. Though vastly outnumbered, Hadji Murad refuses to surrender; he and his five men put up a heroic defense, but they are overwhelmed. Mortally wounded, Hadji Murad fights until he can no longer move. He can still fell pain when one of his enemies stabs him in the head. Then, the enemy beheads him.

The Characters
  Though *Hadji Murad* is a short novel or novella, it has a panoramic scope and a large cast of characters. Writing as a detached omniscient third-person narrator, Leo Tolstoy moves among the characters freely. Hadji Murad, although the title figure, is present in only about half the novella, but his character dominates the narrative. A devout Moslem (a *Hadji* is one who has made the pilgrimage to Mecca), he never fails to make the prescribed Islamic prayers. In one sense, he is a turncoat and renegade. Yet, he also appears as a man of honor, driven twice into defection through betrayal by his allies. As a warrior, he is bold, resolute, and fearless; his prowess is legendary. In person, he is tall and slender, with a shaved head and black wide-set eyes. Despite his limp, he moves with the sinuous grace of an untamed panther. He is a man of action rather than contemplation. Thus, the reader rarely gets into his mind. Charismatic, Hadji Murad is a natural leader: haughty and contemptuous toward those he scorns, charming toward those he admires. His generosity and courtesy are Homeric. Whatever his faults, he is more admirable than either the czar or Shamil, to whose power plays he is victim.
  Czar Nicholas I, who appears in several chapters, and Shamil, who makes only a brief appearance when he threatens to mutilate Hadji Murad's son, but whose presence is felt throughout the narrative, are both evil manipulators of power. As the critic Henri Troyat observes, they resemble each other in many ways; each is tall, with a pale face, "big white hands," and a cold, lifeless expression. The czar, however, is obese whereas Shamil is powerfully built. Each believes that he receives divine inspiration for his deeds of cruelty. Both are absolute despots. The czar is a hypocrite as well. Committing adultery and thanking God that Russia has no death penalty, he sentences a student accused of striking his master to twelve thousand strokes in the gauntlet—tantamount to death by torture. He orders all peasants who balk

at baptism to be court-martialed and justifies any crime by the sanctity of his imperial office. Shamil uses his role as religious leader only to inflame his followers for a fanatical holy war. His is a religion of hatred, not love.

The large breadth of characters expands the novella's setting to encompass all Russia. One sees the mountain people—Hadji Murad's followers—brave, rash, and blindly loyal; the villagers, hating the Russians, who have burned and looted their community; the Russian officers, flirting, fornicating, drinking themselves senseless, gambling recklessly, and going into battle casually, as if to a hunt; the soldiers killed abruptly and pointlessly; their families mourning them; and the politicians caught in the web of their own intrigue. Among the soldiers, Captain Butler is much like young Tolstoy, who served with the Russian army in the Caucasus at the time of his narrative's plot. He, too, flirts, drinks to excess, ruins himself at cards, and goes blithely into battle as if senseless of the danger. Poltoratsky, in turn, is much like Captain Butler. During an evening of cards with his commander, Prince Vorontsov, he flirts with the princess. In the morning, he gets one of his men killed in an unnecessary skirmish. The victim, Peter Avdeev, is a likable fellow who enlisted to save his married brother with children from being conscripted; his death means nothing to the officers but is devastating to his parents. His wife, though, is rather relieved, because she has been made pregnant by another man.

Themes and Meanings

In *Hadji Murad*, the narrator seems detached; the novella is free from the didacticism of most of Tolstoy's later work. Yet, though its themes are not overt, it is not without values and implicit meanings. One of these is the tyranny of unbridled power, whether wielded by the czar or the Moslem Imam—both of whom are ruthless and treacherous. Contrasted to this power are the values of loyalty, honor, courtesy, and generosity generally shown by the mountain people. The freedom of their wild way of life is threatened by the encroachment of the Russian empire, as well as by the fanaticism of Shamil. Though Hadji Murad twice changes sides, he does so only under extreme provocation; otherwise, he is intensely loyal to his family, friends, and followers, and the Caucasians hold him in great respect. On the other hand, the Russian soldiers spend much of their time in debauchery, while the self-serving Russian leaders maneuver for personal advancement. Czar Nicholas I, with his adulterous, sanctimonious, and cruel behavior, is absolutely unfit to rule. As in most of Tolstoy's later work, the best people are the peasants, who are close to the soil, devout, kind, and live from day to day without the canker of ambition.

Another implied theme is the horror of warfare. By the time he wrote *Hadji Murad*, Tolstoy was a pacifist, and though there are few combat scenes in the novella, the scenes included make a powerful case against war. One episode is a skirmish that occurs when a Russian troop on a tree-felling expedition (one Russian tactic against the mountaineers is to destroy their forest) is fired upon by the Chechen that had pursued Hadji Murad. The Russian commander, Poltoratsky, sees war as a lark and, for sport, pursues the fleeing Chechen, who fire back and hit one of his men in the stomach. The victim is Avdeev, whom the reader saw the night before, smoking his pipe and chatting with his friends while keeping watch. A kindly man, Avdeev is mortally wounded in a meaningless encounter that could have been avoided had the commander been less immature. Later, when Hadji Murad tries to escape from the Russians, a young officer gallops after him, feeling the joyous play of life as he rides his fine horse on a beautiful morning, never thinking that anything dreadful may happen to him. Suddenly, Hadji Murad turns and shoots him. "What are you doing?" screams the officer in shock as he falls mortally wounded. In war, death is unexpected and savage. During another skirmish, Captain Butler, who shares with Poltoratsky the naïve belief that war is a game, has his men burn, loot, and destroy a Chechen village—with no concern for the villagers or their future. Innocent civilians suffer along with the warriors, and the survivors are filled with bitter hatred because of this casual and indiscriminate carnage. In short, war may be exciting, but it exists for only one reason—to kill and destroy. Tolstoy never lets the reader forget the suffering. A final theme in *Hadji Murad* is simply the intensity of life. Tolstoy manages to re-create the scenes of his youth in vivid detail.

The story of *Hadji Murad* came to Tolstoy one evening in July of 1898. He was walking along a fallow field and saw nothing but black earth—except for a thistle with three shoots: one broken, with its flower hanging down; another bent, its stem soiled with dirt; the third run over by a cartwheel but rising up again. In his diary Tolstoy noted, "It reminded me of Hadji Murad. I want to write. Life asserts itself to the very end, and here in the midst of this whole field it has somehow asserted itself." In the opening of the novella he amplified this incident, recalling both man's destructiveness and his unconquerable vitality and explaining how the thistle caused him to remember "a Caucasian episode of years ago, which I had partly seen myself, partly heard of from eyewitnesses, and in part imagined." The thistle, emblematic of the tenacious but doomed mountain leader, is one recurring symbol in the book; the other is the nightingales' song of love and death, functioning as a musical motif of the rhythms of nature and the cycles of life.

Critical Context

After the publication of *Anna Karenina* (1875-1877; English translation, 1886), Tolstoy experienced a brief bout of profound depression, followed, in 1879, by a religious conversion. The conversion caused him to reject the concept of art for aesthetic or entertainment value and to endorse only that art which advanced a high moral purpose and could be understood by the simplest people. Thereafter, he wrote comparatively little fiction, devoting himself more to religious, philosophical, and political essays; his short stories were often parables aimed at a popular audience. In 1898, he published his literary manifesto, "What Is Art?" In it, he maintains that people have no real need for most music, painting, and literature—which are mere idle distractions—and that the true artist should be a prophet, preaching moral values and confronting urgent problems of politics, economics, and human relations.

Yet, in the same year, he began *Hadji Murad*, which is free from this sort of didacticism and is generally considered one of his supreme artistic works. Written between 1898 and 1904 and published posthumously in 1911, *Hadji Murad* is Tolstoy's last major work of fiction. In it, he returns to the manner and subject matter of such youthful stories of Caucasian adventure as "Nabeg: Razskaz volontera" ("The Raid: A Volunteer's Story"), "Rubka lesa" ("The Wood-Felling"), and *Kazaki* (1863; *The Cossacks*, 1872). From 1851 to 1854, Tolstoy served in the Caucasus as an officer in the Russian army and took part in numerous raids against Shamil and the Chechen. The major events and characters in *Hadji Murad*, including Hadji Murad himself, are historically accurate, drawn from firsthand experience and observation. In addition, Tolstoy did extensive research on the Caucasus and the war between Shamil and the Russians. One of the merits of *Hadji Murad* is the vividness with which Tolstoy reconstructs the sense of time, place, customs, and conflicting cultures of the mountain people and the Russian soldiers and imperialists. Tolstoy the young officer who fought carelessly in the Caucasus and was repeatedly cited for bravery, however, was quite different from Tolstoy the aged moralist, who is critical of the debauchery and immaturity of such soldiers as Butler and Poltoratsky and who sees war not as a youthful diversion but as the grim reaper.

Usually Tolstoy is thought of as a realist; in *Hadji Murad*, he combines a realistic technique with the romantic and exotic subject matter of the Caucasus that earlier appeared in fiction by Alexander Pushkin and Mikhail Lermontov. In structure, *Hadji Murad* is cinematic, cutting abruptly from one quick, vivid scene to another. The novella stresses a visual quality, minimizes dialogue, and avoids authorial editorializing.

The aged Tolstoy, torn between conflicting claims of morality and art, sometimes dismissed *Hadji Murad* as rubbish. "If that is so," asked one guest, "why did you write it?" "But it is not finished yet," replied Tolstoy. "You came into my kitchen and no wonder it stinks with the smell of cooking." The critical consensus is that *Hadji Murad* is a small masterpiece; critic Ernest J. Simmons calls it "almost a perfect example of the 'good universal art' that Tolstoy had acclaimed."

Sources for Further Study

Bayley, John. *Tolstoy and the Novel*, 1966.
Crankshaw, Edward. *Tolstoy: The Making of a Novelist*, 1974.
Simmons, Ernest J. *Leo Tolstoy*, 1946.
Tolstoy, Leo. *The Portable Tolstoy*, 1978. Edited by John Bayley.
Troyat, Henri. *Tolstoy*, 1967.

Robert E. Morsberger

HEADBIRTHS
Or, The Germans Are Dying Out

Author: Günter Grass (1927-   )
Type of plot: Social criticism
Time of plot: 1979 and 1980
Locale: Germany and Asia
First published: Kopfgeburten: Oder, Die Deutschen sterben aus, 1980 (English translation, 1982)

> *Principal characters:*
> GÜNTER GRASS, the (nonfictional) author
> HARM PETERS, Günter Grass's (fictional) alter ego
> DÖRTE PETERS, Harm's wife
> DR. KONRAD WENTHIEN, an Asia specialist employed by the Sisyphus Travel Agency

The Novel

Headbirths: Or, The Germans Are Dying Out is a fictionalized account of Günter Grass's reading tour of China in the fall of 1979, with stops in Singapore and Indonesia. The trip was sponsored by the Federal Republic of Germany under the auspices of the Goethe Institute.

Grass and his wife, Ute, are accompanied on portions of their monthlong journey by the director Volker Schlöndorff, who had recently made an award-winning film based on Grass's novel *Die Blechtrommel* (1959; *The Tin Drum*, 1961), and by Schlöndorff's wife, the actress and director Margarethe von Trotta. As a gesture to them, and because Grass was obviously hoping to make a film about Asia with Schlöndorff, the narrative is written in the style of notes for a potential film script.

Meanwhile, back in the Federal Republic of Germany, where an election campaign is in full swing, Grass's archenemy, the ultraconservative Bavarian Franz Josef Strauss, has been delivering political speeches which Grass considers blatantly xenophobic and racist, distant echoes of the speeches of Adolf Hitler. Strauss warns that the Germans are dying out, that Turks and other foreigners are taking over the country, and that Germans must increase their birth rate.

Standing in Shanghai, surrounded by hordes of bicyclists, Grass tries to imagine what it would be like if this happened. What if the First and the Third Worlds were reversed? What if there were nearly a billion Germans and less than eighty million Chinese? How does German efficiency compare with Chinese efficiency? Could the Germans feed people as efficiently as they can make and sell weapons to kill them?

To help answer these questions, Grass creates two characters for his tentative film script, a married couple named Harm and Dörte Peters. In the film, they also make a journey to Asia. They travel later than Grass does, in the summer of 1980, and they will go where there are slums and starvation: to India, where Grass had traveled in 1975, as well as to Thailand and Indonesia.

The Peterses are both former 1960's radicals, now secondary-school teachers of foreign languages and geography and hence well-read in such matters as global population trends. Through them, Grass exposes his readers to the facts and figures of widespread poverty and world hunger. Grass provides the Peterses—and his readers—with an almost omniscient tour guide, Dr. Konrad Wenthien, who offers further informed commentary on the problems of the world.

The couple have been trying to decide whether to have a child. Concerned about nuclear war and the building of a nuclear power plant near their home in Germany, Dörte has already had one abortion. Their experiences in the slums of Asia only add to the arguments on the side of remaining childless.

Primitive rituals associated with various mother goddesses they encounter, however, awaken deep maternal instincts in Dörte. Over Harm's rational objections, she throws her birth-control pills into the bat-infested fertility shrine of a serpent goddess. Later, Harm yields to his paternal instincts and throws more of the pills into the toilet. They consider adopting an Asian child, but they fear that it would be treated badly by other children in Germany, so they return from their trip with the problem unresolved.

One detail of Grass's trip which becomes a subplot in the tentative film script concerns a liverwurst which Grass delivers to a German diplomat residing in China. In this episode's fictionalized transmogrification for the film script, Harm tries—unsuccessfully—to deliver the sausage to an old schoolmate named Uwe Jensen, who is now living in Bali. In the film script, Harm's mysterious friend appears to be an arms merchant who has made a fortune smuggling weapons for use in local conflicts.

Meanwhile, Grass tells a bit more about his reading tour. In addition to sections of his most recent novel, *Der Butt* (1977; *The Flounder*, 1978), he reads a paper about his efforts to establish ties between East German and West German authors. He argues that it is the authors, perhaps more than any other Germans, who have been able to transcend their differences and make an attempt at a cultural reunification of their fatherland.

At the end of the book, with tongue in cheek, Grass wonders what would have happened if his bugbear, Franz Josef Strauss, had become a writer, rather than a politician, something which would have allowed him to give his strange fantasy free rein without endangering the world.

The Characters

Harm Peters, while clearly a fictional extension of Günter Grass himself, is not merely that. He is also an archetypal European: liberal, rational, well-informed, and concerned about such issues as world hunger, nuclear power, and arms merchandizing. Yet he is trapped by wants which have become needs: a rich diet, a large, warm home, an automobile, air conditioning, jet travel, and a child of his own. Impaled on the horns of this dilemma, his frustration grows until he begins to fantasize about becoming a dictator who solves all the world's problems with the stroke of a pen. He becomes fascinated by violence, as he reveals when he enthusiastically films an illegal cockfight in Bali, ostensibly to show the local chapter of his political party back home how bread and circuses are used to keep the Asians in subjugation.

Dörte is a kind of European Everywoman: liberated and enlightened, yet susceptible to the most atavistic religious cults, such as that of the serpent goddess. She, too, is immobilized by frustration. She is unable to do rational things, to adopt an Asian child, for example, because she wants so badly to be big, round, and pregnant, like a cow, she says, and say "Moo!"

Dr. Konrad Wenthien is a figure imbued with almost supernatural powers, a demiurge—as Grass at one point refers to him—who instructs Dörte, the latter-day Eve, and Harm, the latter-day Adam, not to be fruitful and multiply and replenish the earth, but to do something fruitful to help replenish and balance Earth's resources. The godlike Dr. Wenthien is employed by the Sisyphus Travel Agency, a mythic name reflecting Grass's belief that the fight against world hunger is comparable to rolling a great stone uphill, only to have it roll down again. Yet Grass also cites Albert Camus to show that Sisyphus is really a happy figure; his work, though strenuous and never-ending, is rewarding and important.

If there is a devil in this mythical configuration of characters it is Uwe Jensen, the archetypal European profiteer. He sells the products of the West, technological instruments of death, to underdeveloped Asian countries which so badly need enlightened help and technological instruments to preserve life: schools, water purification systems, sewage treatment plants, agricultural machines, medicines, and family planning.

Themes and Meanings

Headbirths, as the main word in its title implies, is an appeal for a new Adam and Eve, for mankind, to give birth not to more children but to radically new ideas, to a new world order, one which would transcend traditional nationalism, racism, and militarism. Its most important priority would be to feed the human race.

The early 1980's, the beginning of George Orwell's decade, as Grass chooses to call it, is the ideal time for Germany—the European country with the most infamous history of nationalism, racism, and the exportation of death—to transcend itself and begin to exist on a global scale for the first time, thus setting the example for other industrialized countries. Led in this effort by its authors and united under a National Endowment of German Culture envisioned by Grass's idol, Willy Brandt, Germans should turn from war and harness their efficiency to help fight world hunger. They should stop worrying about dying out and should begin to prevent dying. They should stop worrying about having a child and begin to worry about children.

The last paragraph of the book is a symbolic cinematographic summary of Grass's vision: Back home in Germany, as they drive along in their Volkswagen, Harm and Dörte almost hit a small Turkish boy who runs in front of their car. They manage to stop in time, and he and his friends, other Turkish boys, celebrate his survival with him.

Children then stream out from all the neighboring streets and yards, all of them foreigners: Indian, Chinese, and African, all happy children. Their numbers increase. They all celebrate with the little Turk who has been lucky once again. As the children cheerfully knock on the Volkswagen, the childless couple does not know what to say in German. The very language Grass uses to describe their speechlessness is pidginized, pulled away from standard German in the direction of the language of the children. It is a subtle beginning away from nationalism and toward globalism, but it is a beginning.

Critical Context

To be fully appreciated, the relatively small and tentative *Headbirths* must be read in the context of other works by Günter Grass. His first books, including *The Tin Drum*, *Katz und Maus* (1961; *Cat and Mouse*, 1963), and *Hundejahre* (1963; *Dog Years*, 1965), came to grips with the evil of Hitler's Third Reich by capturing it in a mythical paradigm of life-giving good versus life-taking evil.

Subsequent books, such as *Örtlich betäubt* (1969; *Local Anaesthetic*, 1969), applied this same mythic paradigm to the modern, postwar world, seeking the heirs of Nazism, evils in their most primal forms, and attempting to exorcise them. *Aus dem Tagebuch einer Schnecke* (1972; *From the Diary of a Snail*, 1973) further explored the political possibilities for creating a more humane world without yielding to frustration and resorting to inhumane means. Similar themes and characters in all these novels illuminate those in *Headbirths*. Many of the characters imagine themselves to be enlightened liberals, for example, and not a few, like the Peterses, are teachers.

The Flounder is particularly helpful in understanding *Headbirths*. A voluminous history of the world from Neolithic times to the present, told as a history of nutrition and of the battle of the sexes, it posits a coming new age of the earth, a great "headbirth" of humankind. Typical male patterns of behavior—the creation of weapons of war and oppression, including starvation, of the weak—will give way to a new, balanced culture. Under the aegis of a new *Weltanschaung* from a blend of archetypal mother goddesses, the innate female impulse to nourish and nurture will again be given free rein.

In this context, the mythic dimensions of such figures as Dörte, Harm, and Dr. Wenthien, only sketched out in *Headbirths*, become abundantly clear. Dörte's involvement with the serpent goddess and her impulse to nurture life take on deeper meaning, as do Harm's frustrations as a male, liberal European who, deep down, desires to become a violent dictator in order to solve the world's problems. The demiurge Dr. Wenthien, like the flounder, is a harbinger of a new era.

Headbirths, though a short book, is important as a succinct reiteration of Günter Grass's deep concern about world hunger and related issues. If Grass has taken literary risks, writing a didactic work replete with current events which could easily date it, it is because he is willing to enlist even his fame in the fight against famine.

Sources for Further Study
Hayman, Ronald. *Günter Grass*, 1985.
Irving, John. Review in *Saturday Review*. IX (March, 1982), p. 59.
Lawson, Richard H. *"Headbirths: Or, The Germans Are Dying Out,"* in *Günter Grass*, 1985.
Rohlfs, J.W. "Chaos or Order? Günter Grass's *Kopfgeburten*," in *Critical Essays on Günter Grass*, 1987. Edited by Patrick O'Neill.
Ryan, Judith. "'Into the Orwellian Decade': Günter Grass's Dystopian Trilogy," in *Critical Essays on Günter Grass*, 1987. Edited by Patrick O'Neill.
Updike, John. Review in *The New Yorker*. LVIII (June 14, 1982), p. 129.

Alan Frank Keele

THE HEART OF A DOG

Author: Mikhail Bulgakov (1891-1940)
Type of plot: Satiric allegory
Time of plot: The early 1920's
Locale: Moscow
First published: Sobache serdtse, 1968; revised, 1969 (English translation, 1968)

> *Principal characters:*
> PROFESSOR PHILIP PHILIPPOVICH PREOBRAZHENSKY, a research physician engaged in rejuvenation experiments
> SHARIK, a mongrel dog that is the subject of one of Philip Philippovich's experiments
> POLYGRAPH POLYGRAPHOVICH SHARIKOV, the dog-man Philip Philippovich creates
> DR. BORMENTHAL, Philip Philippovich's assistant
> SHVONDER, the head of the housing committee in the building where Philip Philippovich lives and works

The Novel

The Heart of a Dog recounts a scientific experiment and its unexpected result. Like Mary Shelley's *Frankenstein* (1818), Mikhail Bulgakov's novella describes a creator's rejection of the creature he brings into existence. Incorporating several narrators as well as elements of fantasy and surrealism, *The Heart of a Dog* is a sometimes comic, sometimes blackly humorous reminder of the limits of human perfectibility.

The action begins on a snow-swept Moscow street. An injured, starving dog—mistakenly perceived as a cuddly "Sharik" ("Little Ball") by passers-by—is lured into an apartment by a well-dressed man who offers him sausage. Sharik quickly learns to revere his master, who can provide good food, warm lodging, and medical care.

Sharik's benefactor is Philip Philippovich Preobrazhensky, a noted surgeon and researcher. Specializing in the rejuvenation of human organs, Philip Philippovich plans to transplant a dead man's testes and pituitary gland into Sharik. With little hope that the dog will survive, but convinced that the experiment will yield valuable data, Philip Philippovich performs the transplant.

Surprisingly, Sharik survives and flourishes. He rapidly takes on human appearance: He walks erect, fur falls from his body, his mouth makes speech. The dog-man is often caught between worlds, clumsily reacting with a dog's instincts to social situations which human beings habitually handle with common sense. Quickly Sharik, now calling himself Polygraph Polygraphovich

Sharikov, after a machine advertised on a medical calendar, grows restless. He is reluctant to obey as a man the master he worshipped as a dog.

His rebellion is aided by Shvonder, who chairs the housing committee in the apartment building where Philip Philippovich lives. Shvonder hates Philip Philippovich; he believes in the Communist equality which was won in the October Revolution of 1917, and regards Philip Philippovich as a counter-revolutionary who puts his own comfort and interests before social duty. With Shvonder's help, Sharikov gets official identity papers, goes to work for the local Soviet ministry, and finds a girlfriend. Sharikov even learns, like a good citizen, to inform against his benefactor by reporting antirevolutionary remarks or habits.

Appalled by the transformation he has wrought, Philip Philippovich orders Sharikov to move out of the house. A fight breaks out and the dog-man is subdued. With the help of Dr. Bormenthal, his assistant, Philip Philippovich retransplants the dog's original organs. Rapidly, Polygraph Polygraphovich Sharikov devolves into Sharik. When Shvonder comes looking for his friend, he finds only a dog—albeit an odd-looking one—seated at Philip Philippovich's feet.

The Characters

Sharik is an appealing mutt. Because the first chapter is told primarily through his eyes, the reader immediately senses that Sharik is a dog undeservedly down on his luck. Though he feels self-pity and curses the plight of dogs in general, he views his situation with humor. He notes that his cold and hungry state is shared by many humans, and he realizes that he is more fortunate than some people. When Philip Philippovich lures him home, Sharik willingly abandons the hard freedom of the streets for the comfortable dependency of the apartment. For Sharik it is natural that a dog be obedient to and fawn over his master. Though Sharik takes a jaundiced view of the activities in the apartment/clinic, he nevertheless considers the professor a superior being, even a god.

Philip Philippovich is singularly dedicated to his research. His dedication puts him at odds with the majority of his fellow citizens, who have embraced the Revolution. For Philip Philippovich the Revolution has destroyed the social amenities and creature comforts which made life refined and genteel. His desire to transcend his time and place is symbolized by his habit of humming lines from Giuseppe Verdi's opera *Aïda*. The reader's tendency to sympathize with the professor is tempered by the unsavory nature of his research. He rejuvenates the sexual organs of those who seem more desperate than deserving: The aging roué who longs for the hedonism of his youth; the lonely matron who wants to attract a younger man; the bureaucrat who wants to restore the virginity of a teenager he seduced, before he is arrested or exposed. The goal of Philip Philippovich's operation on Sharik, to implant the organs of a criminal into a dog, is also unsavory. The description of the procedure is gruesome: The doctor ferociously hacks, drills, and pummels the helpless creature.

The resulting dog-man is the predictable product of a thoughtless operation. Sharikov's rude, obnoxious behavior soon demonstrates that he no longer possesses the heart of a dog; he now has the heart of a criminal. Though some of his awkward adaptations to society are amusing, Sharikov never gains the reader's sympathy. He is as unattractive to the reader as to his creator.

Part of Sharikov's unattractiveness is physical: His body is an unnatural amalgam of species. Another part is psychological, because he takes on the personality and worldview of Shvonder, the young man who heads the housing committee. Shvonder is an ideologue, a committed Communist who unthinkingly accepts the premises of the Revolution, which makes him aggressive, harsh, and confrontational. Shvonder sees the world in opposites: good Reds versus bad Whites, revolutionary versus counterrevolutionary, proletarian versus bourgeois, documented citizen versus undocumented troublemakers.

None of Bulgakov's characters are full psychological portraits. They are representatives or types, who embody certain social and philosophical positions. After initially establishing the reader's identification with Sharik, Bulgakov keeps all subsequent characters at arm's length. Thus distanced, he can make readers laugh with or laugh at them, depending upon his purpose at any point in the text.

Themes and Meanings

Bulgakov's obvious satiric targets are the excesses of the Revolution as embodied in Shvonder and Sharikov, as well as in Philip Philippovich's complaints. The satirist comments on the shortage of housing and the resulting loss of privacy, the bureaucracy's need to define human existence by documents, and the intrusion of political ideology into everyday life. As one character wonders, "Does Karl Marx forbid rugs on the stairs?"

It is tempting to see the operation as a metaphor for the October Revolution, and Philip Philippovich as an image of its leader, Vladimir Ilich Lenin. Reading the political allegory thus, one appreciates why the novella's manuscript was refused publication in 1925 and confiscated by the police in 1926. Why should the Soviet authorities appreciate work that interprets the Revolution as an unthinking operation which merged and empowered the criminal, animal instincts of Russia's uneducated peasant classes?

Yet this interpretation may be too narrow. It emphasizes the negative connotation of the title, that is, that the heart of a dog is lower than the heart of a man. It also ignores Philip Philippovich's disgust with the Revolution, an odd detail if Philip Philippovich symbolizes Lenin, the Revolution's architect.

An alternate reading suggests that the heart of a dog is a normative value by which other values may be judged and that Philip Philippovich stands for a mindset rather than a historical individual.

Sharik's heart, as readers learn early in the narrative, is full of trust, sympathy for the downtrodden, and contentment with life's little pleasures: good sausage, warm lodging, and freedom from pain. By his empathy with Moscow's human poor, Bulgakov suggests that ordinary Russians have similar hearts. If there is a failing with a dog's heart, it is a dependency upon authority and a gullibility that authority is divinely ordained. Thus Sharik unhesitatingly thinks of Philip Philippovich as a "god" or "god head," even though he recognizes the tawdry, selfish aspects of the doctor's life and work.

Since Philip Philippovich prefers life before the Revolution to life after it, he apparently represents a line of nineteenth and twentieth century thinkers and reformers other than simply the archrevolutionary Lenin. From Russia's victory over Napoleon in 1815 until the Revolution in 1917, Russian intellectuals argued about the best way to lift the mass of the population from the medieval morass of agriculture, autocracy, and serfdom into the modern world of industrialization, representational government, and emancipation. Most reformers linked progress to technological development, believed that culture was subject to laws discoverable through scientific analysis, and assumed that social change would have to be forced upon a population inert from centuries of oppression. Philip Philippovich clearly works in this tradition: He cares little for the welfare of any individual and ignores the psychological or spiritual nature of humanity. Sadly, failure teaches him nothing; he returns immediately to the same path of experimentation. Unlike Victor Frankenstein, Philip Philippovich escapes poetic justice; his monster does not slaughter him for his hubris.

By abstract speculation and reckless experimentation, Philip Philippovich creates a being susceptible to the worst tendencies of the Revolution: ideology, violence, and self-aggrandizement. Thus he continues the line of Russian intelligentsia who, though well-meaning in working for modernity, forgot the important human qualities of their people. Thus Bulgakov appears in a conservative tradition which, though appalled at inequalities and injustices under the czar, or under the Communist Party, is more appalled at the destruction of spiritual values in the Russian character: the good humor, the capacity to suffer, and a simple, instinctual charity which mark the heart of a dog.

Critical Context

The Heart of a Dog is one of Bulgakov's major fictions about the October Revolution. The others are the realistic novel *Belaya gvardiya* (1927, 1929; *The White Guard*, 1973), the fantastic tales of *Diavoliada* (1925; *Diabolid and Other Stories*, 1972), and the lengthy surrealistic/realistic narrative *Mas-*

ter i Margarita (1966-1967, 1969; *The Master and Margarita*, 1967). These works express Bulgakov's nightmare vision of the Revolution: the bureaucrat's heaven which would be a citizen's hell. The four works may be viewed as stages in an evolving attitude toward the upheavals of the 1910's and 1920's. *The White Guard* sympathetically portrays prerevolutionary and antirevolutionary Russians through the genre of the family chronicle. *The Heart of a Dog* and *Diabolid and Other Stories* combine fantastic and comic elements to satirize the architects of violent revolution; they paint a gloomy picture of cultural and spiritual losses which no one knows how to repair. *The Master and Margarita*, equally surreal and no less caustic about the Revolution, envisions the hidden hand of Providence working toward good amid man-made evils.

For four decades, Bulgakov's fiction was suppressed in the Soviet Union and virtually unknown to foreign readers. Bulgakov had a reputation as a significant playwright whose always controversial, sometimes banned work enlivened the generally barren theater of the 1920's and 1930's. His plays lack, however, the comic and satiric inventiveness of his fiction. His rediscovery as a novelist and short story writer in the 1960's occurred first outside the Soviet Union. The publication in the West of Soviet writers such as Boris Pasternak, Yevgeny Yevtushenko, and Aleksandr Solzhenitsyn whetted appetites for more of the literature that Soviet politics had suppressed. The publication of Bulgakov's fiction in Russian and in other languages is belated recognition for one of the masters of twentieth century political satire. *The Heart of a Dog* ranks with George Orwell's *Animal Farm* (1945), Karel Čapek's *Válka s mloky* (1936; *The War with the Newts*, 1937), and Yevgeny Zamyatin's *My* (1952; *We*, 1924) as a classic exposure of humanity's infatuation with dangerous ideologies.

Sources for Further Study

Goscilo, Helena. "Point of View in Bulgakov's *Heart of a Dog*," in *Russian Literature Triquarterly*. XV (1976), pp. 281-291.

Proffer, Ellendea. *Mikhail Bulgakov: Life and Work*, 1984.

Rydel, Christine. "Bulgakov and H. G. Wells," in *Russian Literature Triquarterly*. XV (1976), pp. 293-311.

Wright, A. Colin. *Mikhail Bulgakov: Life and Interpretations*, 1978.

Robert M. Otten
Michael L. Otten

HIS MASTER'S VOICE

Author: Stanisław Lem (1921-   )
Type of plot: Science fiction
Time of plot: The 1960's
Locale: A huge science project center in the desert Southwest
First published: Głos pana, 1968 (English translation, 1983)

>*Principal characters:*
>PETER E. HOGARTH, a mathematician, author of the memoir
>   which comprises the bulk of the novel
>SAUL RAPPAPORT, the first legitimate scientist to obtain the
>   communication from space
>DONALD PROTHERO, a scientist who, with Hogarth, discovers
>   the weapons potential of the communication
>EUGENE NYE, the Pentagon's representative on the Project

The Novel

The title of Stanisław Lem's novel *His Master's Voice* is taken from a nickname given by scientists to a possible communication from outer space: a stream of subatomic particles (neutrinos) in a recurring pattern. The problem which the scientists face is to "read" the pattern, thereby determining its content, sender, and purpose. To accomplish this task, the United States government assembles the nation's best scientific minds in the desert Southwest, in a research facility once devoted to work on the atom bomb. The bulk of the novel is composed of a memoir of one of those scientists, the late mathematician Peter E. Hogarth. A brief "Editor's Note," written by Professor Thomas W. Warren, prefaces the memoir. Hogarth's memoir can, in fact, be read on at least three separate levels: as a simple history of the Project; as a meditation on the nature of the scientific process, especially when faced with uncertainty; and as a meditation on the interplay of communal pursuit and individual personality.

That Hogarth (as well as Stanisław Lem) is interested in more than a straightforward account of events is suggested by the rather lengthy preface to the memoir, in which crucial events in the history of the Project are virtually ignored in favor of more general speculation on the interplay of good/ evil and responsibility/lack of choice. Even in chapter 1 of the memoir, Hogarth seems in no hurry to discuss events or even to pique the reader's interest. Indeed, in violation of all rules of suspense-building, Hogarth announces at the outset that the Project was a failure, that the scientists learned nothing for certain about the communication—if, indeed, it was such. At this point in the novel, rather than speculating on the Project and its failure, Hogarth seems more interested in discoursing on the unwillingness of scientists (and people in general) to accept any phenomenon outside the realm of what they already know. This line of thought continues throughout the second chapter, in which Hogarth addresses the limits of science and the relationship between science and the scientist as a fallible human.

Not until chapter 3 does Hogarth turn his attention to the "letter from space" and the Project itself. The neutrino emission was discovered by accident, and the pattern detected in the emission seemed to indicate that it was created and sent by an intelligent life form. Once the implications of the discovery become clear, a massive research project is organized by the American government, and eventually Hogarth is asked to join the scientists, who, after a year of work, have reached no more than provocative dead ends.

Hogarth achieves a major success shortly after joining the Project by mathematically proving (or so it seems) that the pattern describes a phenomenon—as opposed to, for example, saying "Hello." It is characteristic of Hogarth's honesty that he himself is less taken with this success than others, and he finally acknowledges that he really accomplished very little.

Hogarth's theory, however, is applauded by others who have already attempted to use the emission as a tool. Working independently, physicists and chemical biologists have used the emission to create a substance—a sort of organic goo—whose properties defy some of nature's laws. Hogarth himself is more interested in a discovery made by the eminent biologist, Romney: that the emission when concentrated on certain macromolecules seems to make them more resistant to decay. The same macromolecules are the basis for living organisms; hence, the emission seems to propagate and enhance life. From this discovery Hogarth formulates the theory that he never really abandons: that the sender is a benevolent higher form who has, for eons perhaps, been sowing the seeds of life throughout the universe.

All previous theories are soon overshadowed by a discovery which is made by Donald Prothero: that "frog eggs"—the nickname given to the organic goo—appears to have frightening potential as a weapon. Prothero shares his findings with Hogarth, and the two are torn between the desire to verify the findings and the fear of how this weapon would be used by man. They try to work on the findings in secret, but inevitably their activities are discovered. Pentagon officials descend on the Project and take charge of all operations. In outrage, several of the top scientists, including Hogarth, resign, but they agree to return to the Project in exchange for token concessions.

The novel winds down quickly from this point. "Frog eggs," it turns out, has no potential as a weapon. Some of the new scientists on the Project offer original and interesting theories about the emission, but the very number and variety of theories reinforce the suspicion that the scientists will never know much at all, with certainty, about the emission. At the end, Hogarth clings to his theory of a benevolent higher civilization sending a life signal, but neither he nor the reader has great confidence in his belief.

The Characters

Even such a brief summary of the plot as the foregoing should suggest that Lem is not primarily interested in simply spinning a good yarn. It must be admitted that not much exciting action transpires in the novel; indeed, Lem's strategy seems to be to deflate potentially dramatic situations—the "frog eggs"-as-weapon scenario, for example. Lem is far more interested in the characters and how they react to events than in the events themselves.

Especially in the preface and the first two chapters but also elsewhere in the novel, Lem (or Hogarth) suspends discussion of the action to meditate on personality in general, especially the personality of scientists. For example, while the other scientists are studying the neutrino emission, Hogarth speculates that it might be equally productive to study the scientists themselves from an anthropological perspective. He concludes that while they thought that they were analyzing the "letter from space," the scientists were actually, intentionally or not, attempting "to discern the presence of what lay, first and foremost, within ourselves."

These speculations on the nature of the scientist are not at all irrelevant to the central action. The reader learns at the outset that the Project was a failure; what is not so clear is why it failed. Hogarth believes that the answer lies within the flawed nature of the scientist, whom "we must have . . . incorruptible, ideal." By implication, the scientist is far from incorruptible or ideal, and in analyzing the Project's failure one must consider if each scientist "represented only himself, with the inspiration for his hypotheses about the contents of the 'letter' being supplied by his own—possibly raving, possibly wounded—psyche in its uncontrollable regions."

Hogarth's interest in his fellow scientists is manifested in lengthy block descriptions of their physical appearance, intellectual capacity, mannerisms, emotional health, and personal histories. For all the description, however, the secondary characters never pulse with much life for the reader, perhaps because of the suspicion that Hogarth—in all of his speculations on a variety of persons and topics—is revealing more about himself than about others. Indeed, rather than asking why the Project failed, one might more properly ask, why did Hogarth fail?

Hogarth assesses himself with a surprising honesty: "The fundamental traits of my character I consider to be cowardice, malice, and pride." While one might applaud his honesty, one would not consider such traits desirable in a scientist or anyone else. Unfortunately, Hogarth's assessment is all too accurate, at least in regard to malice and pride.

It is significant that, brilliant mathematician though Hogarth is, the project directors wait more than a year—until the various specialists seem to be at an impasse—before inviting him to join. Their wariness no doubt stems from the fact that Hogarth's virtues as a scientist carry as many negative connotations as positive. He might help in breaking the impasse because

he is an "iconoclast." Seen in a positive light, Hogarth's iconoclasm allows
him to be less rigid, more receptive to theories that violate preconceived expectations. In practice, however, his iconoclasm is largely cynical and
supercilious.

The destructiveness of his method—based upon the destructiveness of his
personality—is most clearly seen in the absence of any significant contribution by Hogarth to the Project. He contributes, in fact, nothing of value. His
theory of the benevolent civilization is based entirely on Romney's research;
Hogarth offers no evidence of any nature to support his theory.

To his credit, Hogarth admits to all these failings and at the end returns to
and applies to himself his suspicion that the scientific method cannot be
divorced from or superior to the scientist wielding it:

> Can it simply be that, stung for so long by humiliations . . . I spun for myself—
> in the image and likeness of my own hopes—the only equivalent available to
> me of holiness: the myth of the Annunciation and Revelation, which I then—
> also to blame—rejected as much out of ignorance as ill will?

Themes and Meanings

Like all the best writers, Lem so integrates plot, characterization, and
theme that it is difficult to extract one from the others. The conflict (to solve
the riddle of His Master's Voice) transpires the way it does (that is, failure to
solve the riddle) because of the kind of characters which are involved: fallible
men too small for their huge undertaking. Plot, characterization, and other
facets of the novelist's craft are all in service of a broad theme: the pervasive
uncertainty of contemporary life. Indeed, the reader should consider himself
forewarned at the outset not to expect many answers, simply because of the
makeup of the human animal: "It is a curious thing that the marks of our imperfection, which identify the species, has never been, not by any faith, recognized for what they simply are, that is, the results of uncertain processes."

Uncertainty works its way into the most mechanical features of the novel.
Hogarth's memoir, for example, is only a fragment, unfinished. Had he lived
long enough to revise and finish it, it is possible that Hogarth would have
made important changes. Similarly, the method by which the tape of the
emission finds its way into the hands of legitimate scientists—only after
being fumbled from charlatan to crackpot and so on—seems inspired more
by the Keystone Cops than by dignified scholarly pursuit.

His Master's Voice is not a parody of scientific research, however, although
there is much wit in the novel. Rather, Lem's point is that uncertainty is the
inevitable legacy even of capably conducted research. To the scientist, for
example, raw data are "full of gaps and uncertainties," which only to the
uninformed layperson provide "an impression of tidiness." One might almost
conclude that the more one knows, the less certain one becomes. "Genius,"

says Hogarth, "is not so much a light as it is a constant awareness of the surrounding gloom."

The conflict of any novel is in a state of uncertainty until it passes through a climax to the resolution. Lem, however, underscores uncertainty as his theme by leaving the conflict—to find the meaning and source of the emission—pointedly unresolved.

Critical Context

His Master's Voice is a prime example of the intellectual vigor and honesty that have established Lem in the eyes of many as the greatest contemporary science-fiction writer. Unlike the "space operas" of early science fiction or the inferior efforts of many of his contemporaries, Lem's novels rest on a solid understanding of scientific principles; he has been able to extend science into imaginative dramatizations of the convincingly possible rather than willfully distorting science into fantasy and melodrama: no bug-eyed monsters for Lem, no cheap apocalypses.

At least as important as Lem's profound intellectual vigor is his honesty. Lem is one of the few science-fiction writers who have been brave and honest enough not to give the reader all the answers. He recognizes the limitations as well as the exhilarating potential of science, and he is imaginative enough to make limitation and failure interesting subjects for fiction—as *His Master's Voice* attests.

While these qualities are found in varying degrees in all Lem's novels, *His Master's Voice* may more specifically be seen as a companion piece to a later novel, *Fiasko* (1986; *Fiasco*, 1987). Here, a research team not unlike the one in *His Master's Voice* has found evidence of life on a distant planet, and a spaceship is sent out to make contact. The chief problem is how to communicate with the life form. Once again, the situation is complicated by politics, fear of the unknown, the limitations of science, and man's innate fallibility. And once again, Lem refuses to provide all the answers.

Sources for Further Study

Engel, Peter, and John Sigma. "An Interview with Stanisław Lem," in *The Missouri Review*. VII (1984), pp. 218-237.

Potts, Stephen W. "Dialogues Concerning Human Understanding: Empirical Views of God from Locke to Lem," in *Bridges to Science Fiction*, 1980.

Scarborough, John. "Stanisław Lem, 1921-   ," in *Science Fiction Writers: Critical Studies of the Major Authors from the Early Nineteenth Century to the Present Day*, 1982.

Ziegfeld, Richard E. *Stanisław Lem*, 1985.

Žirković, Zoran. "The Future Without a Future: An Interview with Stanisław Lem," in *The Pacific Quarterly*. IV (1979), pp. 255-259.

Dennis Vannatta

HISTORY

Author: Elsa Morante (1918-1985)
Type of plot: Historical realism
Time of plot: 1941-1947
Locale: Rome and its environs
First published: La storia, 1974 (English translation, 1977)

> *Principal characters:*
> IDA RAMUNDO, a widow and schoolteacher
> NINO, her teenage son
> GIUSEPPE (USEPPE), Ida's infant son by a German soldier
> DAVIDE SEGRE, also known by the alias CARLO VIVALDI, an
> escaped political prisoner

The Novel

History draws on the depth of Elsa Morante's personal knowledge of and research into the lives of the common people in Rome during World War II. Following the lives of two presumably fictional characters, Ida Ramundo and her son Giuseppe, the novel depicts the toll of suffering, fear, and deprivation inflicted by war on its innocent victims. Though each section of the novel is preceded by a capsule summary of the year's major events, the narrative concentrates with an attention bordering on moral outrage on the histories of ordinary individuals.

The novel begins with a German soldier named Gunther walking along the streets of Rome. His encounter with an Italian widow, Ida Ramundo, is preceded by a detailed description of her past and family history. Ida has carried with her since early childhood, almost like a racial memory, a *"sense of the sacred*: meaning by *sacred*, in [this] case, the universal power that can devour them and annihilate them, for their guilt in being born." In this immediate instance her foreknowledge is of being raped and impregnated by the German soldier, during the midst of which she suffers an epileptic fit. The soldier is never seen again and dies shortly thereafter in a plane crash.

The result of this violent encounter is Ida's child Giuseppe, or, as he comes to be called because he cannot pronounce his own name, Useppe. Despite the war and Ida's guilt over his birth, Useppe leads an almost idyllic existence described with the innocence of a child's point of view. His great friend is his brother Nino who in between frequent adolescent adventures always seems to have time, at least initially, for his younger brother. Together with Nino's dog, Blitz, who like Useppe is a bastard, as Nino points out to a horrified Ida, Nino and Useppe play and discover the joys of nature.

As the war progresses into the year 1943, the story becomes more bleak. Along with the air raids and wartime deprivation, there is Ida's continuing worry over her other great secret in addition to her epilepsy—her Jewish ancestry. Nino enlists and disappears, while Ida and Useppe are left homeless by the bombing. They move to temporary shelter where the deprivations of war are felt all the more strongly. Nino returns, having deserted, with several friends. Carlo Vivaldi, one of these friends, tells the horrified refugees of his experience in the "antechambers of death" while awaiting deportation to Germany for political crimes. Ida, in one of the central events of the novel, witnesses, by accident, the roundup and deportation from the Tiburtina train station of the major portion of Rome's Jewish population (of the 1,056 who leave, only fifteen will return). This event pushes Ida even further into a nearly paralyzing paranoia compounded of fear and guilt.

While Ida withdraws into her fearful isolation, Useppe's contact with the outside world comes primarily through Nino, who by this point is active with a group of partisan Resistance fighters. Several of the engagements with the Germans are described in graphic detail, culminating in the destruction of the group and the violent rape and murder of Nino's girlfriend, Maria. Particularly active in the Resistance action is Nino's friend Carlo, who seems to be all the bolder for having suffered at the hands of the Nazis. As Rome is declared an open city, Ida and Useppe move into an apartment with a family, though Useppe's health continues to suffer because of Ida's overwhelming guilt and secretiveness.

Once the war is over Ida and Useppe move to yet another apartment and Ida resumes her teaching. Useppe begins having terrible nightmares of people burning, and Ida takes him to a specialist in neurological disorders. Nino's postwar exploits take him from the Resistance to the black market, where he displays the same mix of street smarts, luck, and savvy. In one memorable episode, he gives Useppe a tour of Rome on the back of his motorcycle. They also receive a long letter from Davide Segre (the real name of Carlo Vivaldi, indicating his Jewish parentage), which contains a long discourse on his bourgeois background and subsequent rebellion against it. Nino brings Useppe another dog, Bella, to replace Blitz, who was killed in the bombings, but Useppe continues to have nightmares and—despite his precocity—trouble in school.

Ida receives the shocking news that Nino has been killed. After serving in the army and fighting the Germans as a Resistance fighter, he died when a truck he was driving overturned during a chase with police. Ida's troubled interior state now includes hallucinations of Nino as well as increased concern over Useppe, who has begun to suffer epileptic fits of increasing frequency and seriousness. Useppe and Bella, however, take advantage of Ida's work schedule to explore the city and meet with Davide, who has returned to Rome. Davide has become a drug addict and lives in a squalid room once inhabited by a prostitute, but he is Useppe's great friend and the two of them exchange poems and conversation. Just before Davide's death from a drug overdose, he yells at Useppe for the first time; soon, Useppe himself dies in his mother's arms after a severe epileptic fit. The story of Ida Ramundo, her family and circle, has been one of suffering, fear, and deprivation, caused by the larger forces of history and brightened only by the childish innocence and exuberance of the doomed Useppe.

The Characters

Ida Ramundo is a complex and tragic figure. A good and simple woman, Ida carries the burden of a double secret, her epilepsy and her Jewish heritage. Though in other times she might have lived and taught school in relative tranquillity, the war and its devastation touch Ida in both external and internal ways. While her daily life is changed, uprooted, and degraded as a result of the war, her inner life amounts to a crucible in which the most dehumanizing aspects of Nazism are compounded.

Morante gives careful attention to Ida's background, the lives of her parents and her husband, Alfio. Especially poignant is the story of Ida's mother, Nora, a story which prefigures Ida's fate. Nora marries and seeks to hide the fact that she is Jewish but eventually dies of exposure in a deluded nighttime flight from her enemies. Throughout the novel Ida is haunted by the racial laws and their baroque prescriptions, even going so far as to draw charts of her sons' lineages to determine their legal status (all the more ironic since Useppe is fathered by one of the Aryan conquerors).

As the war progresses and its deprivations increase, Ida's efforts to forage for her young son are poignant even in their ineptitude. Her own paranoid secretiveness effectually prevents her from making the most ordinary contacts with her fellow refugees that would ensure Useppe's basic nutrition. Later, his problems with school discipline are all the more perplexing to her because she is herself a schoolteacher. It is finally the hidden genetic link of epilepsy, compounded by malnutrition, that dooms her son to an early death.

If Ida is the novel's figure of unremitting tragedy, then Useppe is its figure of innocent joy and childish delight. In a story dominated by the fate of Rome's Jews and Ida's fears about her Jewish background, Useppe is a clear Christ symbol, from his not-so-immaculate conception to the Pietà typology of his death in his mother's arms. Morante does not insist on the religious aspect of this symbolism as much as its universal aspect. Useppe has the same joy and openness to life and nature that all children have, the same chance to start anew, but he is predestined to suffer the fate of a collective societal destiny. As Ida's character recedes into the externally imposed depths of guilt, Useppe's adventures with life begin to assume major importance in the work.

Useppe is small at birth and undernourished throughout his short life. Yet his ground's-eye view gives him a special appreciation for life's small joys. His brother Nino is his greatest joy but is only erratically present. During Nino's lengthening absences, Useppe's substitute friends are his dogs, Blitz and Bella, and the birds. Useppe is a natural poet, uttering verses about the birds and nature around him. This aspect of his personality draws him into an affinity with Davide, who is another kindred soul. Useppe's fate, like Ida's, is to be struck down by forces beyond his knowledge or control. Malnourished and subjected to virtual refugee status, he develops acute epilepsy of which he is incompletely aware. He is one of the simple and one of the doomed.

Nino seems to be one of the lucky and charmed. With a glib savvy and insouciance he moves easily from the black shirt of the Fascists to army gray, and from the partisan's irregular uniform to the sudden prosperity of the postwar black market. His erratic behavior, including sudden appearances and disappearances, causes anguish to his mother and a mixture of profound joy and disappointment to his little brother. Always an easy friend to his comrades and an instant success with women, he lives intensely until he is cut down by a violent death.

Violence is the sign of Davide Segre as well. He first appears as a troubled escapee from the death cells and then becomes vengeful as a particularly ruthless partisan. Through letters and flashbacks the reader learns of his Jewish middle-class background and his politically motivated rebellion against that. Davide ends his life as a haunted drug addict whose only friend is the precocious Useppe.

Themes and Meanings

Elsa Morante's theme in *History* is brutally straightforward and concerns the suffering of the innocent at the hands of larger historical forces. The novel begins with an epigraph taken from the words of a survivor of Hiroshima: "There is no word in the human language capable of consoling the guinea pigs who do not know the reason for their death." Morante herself was a survivor, having taken refuge from Rome with her husband, Alberto Moravia, in the mountains during the war years to escape deportation. In *History*, she reconstructed the experience of those who remained in Rome for the duration. The book's clear evil is Nazi domination, but even that is only a part of the geopolitical power structure her work indicts. She writes with the crystalline style of someone whose vision has been burned pure by anger.

The suffering and deprivation of Rome's population is portrayed through a scrupulous attention to a small group of characters. The central moment of the book is undoubtedly when Ida Ramundo, herself a Jew, witnesses the spectacle of the train cars filled with human beings at Tiburtina station. She hears their cries, she retrieves a scribbled message dropped from a slot in a car, she attempts in her confused and dazed way to decipher that message and deliver it to its addressee. Morante, too, bears witness through her writing, attempting to communicate this central fact of twentieth century history.

Though the book is dominated by the Holocaust and its destruction of human lives, Morante's strategy is to follow the fate of two characters who do not perish in the Nazi death camps but rather suffer through an internalization of the threat those camps represent. Ida's fear of someone discovering her Jewishness and denouncing her to the authorities drives her into a state of paranoia and quiet despair. Her fear in turn prevents her from making the human contacts necessary to maintain Useppe's health. Useppe suffers from the two deadly secrets he inherits from his mother, the Jewish background he never knows and the epilepsy which ultimately kills him. For Morante, the writing of history can be nothing less than bearing witness to this ultimate tragedy.

Critical Context

Morante's *History* follows and extends her earlier work in *L'isola di Arturo* (1957; *Arturo's Island*, 1959) and *Menzogna e sortilegio* (1948; *House of Liars*, 1951). It takes its place in the larger postwar Italian movement termed neorealism, but with a clear attempt to transcend the bounds of any particular school or style. Morante in *History* wishes to write using a transparency of style that will make the novel's content immediately accessible.

As the title of the work indicates, Morante's novel also represents an attempt to rethink the very concept of history. From a background that is clearly dialectical and historical, Morante moves to establish a position where one might realize that history is not only, or even primarily, a collection of facts concerning large-scale geopolitical events. Rather she seems to urge a reorientation of thinking and writing about history in such a way as to be able to see the suffering of the individual. From an eclectic blend of Jewish background, Christian symbolism, and leftist political orientation, Morante seeks to discover the meaning of history in individual lives along with the need to resist all large-scale political forces or entities.

Morante's work has long been prized and respected in Italian and European critical circles. In the United States it may well be that feminist literary approaches which share her distrust of male-dominated power structures and her belief in the necessity to concentrate on human values will succeed in integrating her vision into the critical canon. The power of Morante's vision in portraying the central tragedy of the twentieth century clearly succeeds in the only task that truly matters to her—bearing witness to human history.

Sources for Further Study

Caesar, Michael. "Elsa Morante," in *Writers and Society in Contemporary Italy: A Collection of Essays*, 1984. Edited by Michael Caesar and Peter Hainsworth.

Evans, Annette. "The Fiction of Family: Ideology and Narrative in Elsa

Morante," in *Theory and Practice of Feminist Literary Criticism*, 1982. Edited by Gabriela Mora and Karen S. Van Hooft.

Peter Baker

THE HOLY SINNER

Author: Thomas Mann (1875-1955)
Type of plot: Romance
Time of plot: The sixth century
Locale: Lands that were to become Belgium and France, the North Sea, and Rome
First published: Der Erwählte, 1951 (English translation, 1951)

Principal characters:
SIBYLLA, the daughter of Duke Grimald and Baduhenna
WILIGIS, the brother of Sibylla
GREGORIUS, also known as GRIGORSS, their son

The Novel

Based mainly on an epic poem of the twelfth century which was derived from a French chivalric romance, *The Holy Sinner* relates the lives of two legendary figures, the beautiful and noble twins Sibylla and Wiligis. Their mother having died at their birth, the two are devoted to each other and believe that no one else is equal to them in any way. Unable, therefore, to be parted in childhood and youth, the two become lovers when their father, Duke Grimald, dies. In time, Sibylla conceives a child. To do penance for their sinful attachment, Wiligis goes on a pilgrimage to Rome but dies before he achieves his goal. Sibylla, in the meantime, is taken to the home of the Sieur Eisengrein, a loyal baron and the counselor of their father. When her son is born, he is set adrift in a small boat, wrapped in rich cloths and identified on a small ivory tablet carved by his mother, telling only of his noble but sinful origin, not his name or place of birth.

Miraculously, the infant survives and is found by two fishing men from the imaginary village of St. Dunstan in a channel of the North Sea. He is adopted by the abbot Gregorius, who baptizes him and gives him his own name. The baby is reared by the wife of one of the fishermen. At the age of six, he moves to the monastery and becomes a scholar, studying Latin, grammar, theology, and law, all the while dreaming of becoming not a monk but a knight-errant. When at seventeen he learns of his origins by eavesdropping on his foster mother, he determines to leave the monastery, bearing the ivory tablet, in search of his parents.

Gregorius' ship brings him to Bruges, where the duchess Sibylla lives like a nun, refusing to give herself in marriage to any man. The most persistent suitor, King Roger of Arelat, has for years been conducting a war between Burgundy and Flaundres-Artoys. Thus Gregorius, without planning it, becomes Sibylla's knight, defeats King Roger, and marries the duchess.

Their life is blissful for three years. A daughter is born to them, named Harrad, and Duke Gregorius is known throughout the land for his mild and merciful judgment. Their happiness comes to an end when Sibylla's maid, having spied on the duke, tells her mistress of the ivory tablet. Revealing her knowledge to the duke, Sibylla must once again be parted from her lover, who is not only her son but also her husband.

Gregorius, dressed as a beggar, departs immediately to do penance wherever God may lead him until death. Again, a fisherman and his wife are the source of a turning point in his life. The wife pities the beggar and suspects that he may be a saint, but her rough and cruel husband provides him with what he wants: a high rock to which he is fastened with fetters. The fisherman then hurls the key into the sea. For seventeen years the beggar survives, nourished by a milklike substance provided by the earth, the ancient mother of all, and he gradually turns into a small, prickly, hedgehog-like creature.

Gregorius' life is again changed by war, this one caused by two factions in conflict over the choice of a pope; the two contenders die, and the Romans decide to leave the choice this time to God. A simultaneous dream vision is vouchsafed to two Romans, a wealthy man named Probus and a cardinal named Liberius. The two follow the instructions of the Lamb, who has appeared to them in their revelation, and after months of hard travel, arrive at the house of the poor woman and her fisherman husband, who has just caught an enormous pike. In the fish, the fisherman finds the key to the legiron with which he had locked the beggar to the rock. Terrified and abashed, he leads the two travelers to the rock, where they find the strange little creature, who is soon restored to his human form when the two travelers declare him Pope.

Now Pope Gregory I, Gregorius has been ruling for five years when Sibylla, old and grief-worn, comes on a pilgrimage to seek pardon for her sins. They recognize each other, and the Pope forgives her as God has forgiven him. Sibylla lives out her years as the honored abbess of a cloister in Rome, and the Pope becomes known throughout Christendom for his wisdom and justice.

The Characters

As legendary figures, the two main characters are more than human, not well-rounded, three-dimensional, and credible as ordinary persons. Their beauty, passion, singularity, and steadfastness are the qualities of which legendary tales are made. Extreme in everything they feel, say, and do, whether in love or penitence, pride or humility, they are appropriately astonishing.

Many secondary characters weave in and out of the story like figures in a tapestry. These persons are all entirely human and believable, ranging from the most aristocratic to the most humble. Mention should be made of at least a few of them. The stout-hearted and sensible Sieur Eisengrein helps the sinful twins with practical advice and genuine service, performing deeds of great sacrifice and courage. His wife, Dame Eisengrein, whose passion is motherhood (her own and that of every woman in her care), is memorable for her single-minded maternalism. The fishing folk of St. Dunstan are also completely acceptable as they are portrayed: simple, ignorant, canny, and strong. Their counterparts at the end of the story, the kindly woman of faith and her coarse and crude fisherman husband, are remarkably real. The wealthy man of faith and the cardinal who find Gregorius and bring him back to Rome are highly individualized and admirable. There are many others, too numerous to mention, who contribute to the richness of the story.

Themes and Meanings

The brother-sister mystique, the spiritual versus the physical, and the mysterious unity in duality are some of the themes found in many of Thomas Mann's works. In *The Holy Sinner*, these themes are expressed even in the English title; it suggests the ambiguities of such polarities as good and evil, holiness and sinfulness, and piety and sensuality.

The symbolic narcissism of incest and the sinfulness of pride furnish the novel with its central idea, but salvation through God's forgiveness and grace is the novel's primary focus. The self-love of "the bad children," the twins, was caused by pride and, in turn, resulted in the sin for which each, after brief joy, spends most of a lifetime in atonement. Even in their penances there is a duality, for while Sibylla cares for the sick and afflicted in the humblest circumstances, Gregorius, the product of a sinful relationship, is chosen to lead the Church in its highest position.

The tension between man and woman must also be recognized as important to the author's purpose in this novel. This tension is best expressed in the conversation between the wealthy, matter-of-fact Roman, Probus, and his intellectual wife, Faltonia, whose opinion and advice he seeks after his vision. Faltonia astutely analyzes his dream vision, and when Probus expresses disappointment that she has no advice for him, she replies with insight and some acerbity, pointing out that it is an ecclesiastical matter, in which the Church requires that women be silent. After suggesting that the Church might be better served if rational women had a voice in it, she declines to discuss the possibility but proceeds to give Probus some simple, straightforward advice.

In apparent and poignant contrast to this amusing scene is the second appearance of the fisherman and his wife. After finding the key to the fetter in the belly of the fish that he has caught, the arrogant fisherman is totally humbled and prostrate with fear of eternal damnation. Yet the heart of his wife is so filled with joy and faith that around her head there appears to be more light than anywhere else in the dark and humble room.

In these two brief scenes, Mann brings to his fantastic tale a human and realistic element that takes the novel out of its imaginary and medieval setting and places it where any modern reader can recognize its significance.

Critical Context

The purported narrator is the Irish monk Clemens, writing at the Benedictine cloister of Sankt Gallen. Representing the spirit of storytelling, as symbolized in the inexplicable ringing of the bells in the first chapter, he is almost a character in his own right. Claiming not to know in which language he writes because he knows so many, the narrator blends High German, Latin, Old French, Middle High German, Low German, and English. It is a linguistic medley that has many humorous implications.

The story is also enriched by numerous appurtenances of courtly life: furniture, weapons, musical instruments, costumes, and so on. While not so elaborately detailed, the atmosphere of the fishermen's huts is also graphically described. Mann handles the sexual encounters with delicacy, and there is much humor and wit throughout the book, particularly in the comments of the narrator, through whose voice Mann is able to inject an element of ironic parody.

The Holy Sinner (the original German title means "the chosen one") was the last work written in the United States by this prodigiously prolific and gifted writer. It has been called a humorous epilogue to Mann's greatest work, *Doktor Faustus* (1947; *Doctor Faustus*, 1948). For its ingenious, entertaining, and seriocomic qualities, many readers prefer it to Mann's more complex and profound writings.

Sources for Further Study
Apter, T. E. *Thomas Mann: The Devil's Advocate*, 1979.
Cleugh, James. *Thomas Mann*, 1933.
Feuerlicht, Ignace. *Thomas Mann*, 1968.
Heller, Erich. *The Ironic German*, 1958.
Lukács, Georg. *Essays on Thomas Mann*, 1964.

Natalie Harper

HOLZFÄLLEN
Eine Erregung

Author: Thomas Bernhard (1931-   )
Type of plot: Philosophical realism
Time of plot: The mid-1980's
Locale: Vienna
First published: 1984

Principal characters:
THE NARRATOR, a writer, who has just returned to Vienna
   from England
HERR AUERSBERGER, a composer
FRAU AUERSBERGER, his wife
AN ACTOR, a regular at the *Burgtheater*
JEANNIE BILLROTH, a writer

The Novel

Set in an upper-middle-class household in contemporary Vienna, where life revolves around the arts and the artistically pretentious, *Holzfällen* (woodcutting) focuses on a dinner party given for an actor of the prestigious *Burgtheater*. The actor's late arrival, after the evening's performance, delays the beginning of the actual meal until past midnight. Up to this midpoint in the novel, the narrator, a writer, observes the empty social chatter and ruminates on his past ties to the people around him from the vantage point of a comfortable chair at the outer edge of the activities. He ponders the circumstances which several days earlier brought him into renewed contact with his host and hostess, the Auersbergers, former friends whom he had abandoned twenty years ago. On the very morning when he learned of the suicide of Joana, a mutual friend from their past, he met the Auersbergers by accident on the street. In a state of emotional confusion, he accepted their invitation to the dinner party—despite the long estrangement and his declared loathing of them.

The party itself takes place on the evening following Joana's burial, almost all the guests still dressed in black. Particularly until the actor arrives, the narrative perspective is severely limited to his musings, and he catches only muffled echoes and sketchy shadows of the external world. Among these shadows the most prominent are the figures of the drunken host doing finger exercises on the piano and his wife constantly reassuring her hungry guests of the eminence of their guest of honor as well as the imminence of his arrival. From his seat in a dimly lit anteroom, the narrator watches others pass by him to the center of the party in the music room, consciously avoiding conversation and giving himself over to his reflections.

His failure to refuse the Auersbergers' invitation becomes a core question that he poses to himself over and over, each time adding associations that gradually accrete to form a larger, more detailed picture of their common past. This past had its roots thirty-five years before, following the narrator's graduation from the Mozarteum, an academy of music and the arts in Salzburg. Apparently jaded by his studies at the time, he had renounced his artistic ambitions until his acquaintance with the Auersbergers and, through them, with Joana. With Herr Auersberger accompanying him on the piano, he spent entire afternoons and evenings singing the classical repertories of Italian, German, and English arias and lieder. As a frequent guest at Joana's home, the nascent writer came into a setting supportive of intellectual and aesthetic growth, a setting populated by the elite of the Viennese artistic, scientific, and political worlds. Over the years, the lives of these charismatic figures deteriorated, however, and an increasing alienation set in between them and the narrator. With the Auersbergers, mutual accusations of betrayal and exploitation grew into bitterness, while the narrator seemed simply to have forgotten Joana. When he first learned of her suicide, he reacted with surprise that she had not been dead for some time.

By the time the actor arrives, two hours after the others and midway through the novel, the hostess has to rouse the narrator from a nap before he can follow her into the dining room. Seated at the table across from Jeannie Billroth (a writer who claims the reputation of a Viennese Virginia Woolf), the narrator has less chance for introspection, since the monologue of the long-awaited guest overwhelms even his attention. The actor expounds, practically without pause, on his current and past successes in the theater as well as on the demands and difficulties of his profession. Almost uninterrupted, except by the movement of his spoon and fork in and out of his mouth, he talks incessantly, well into the early morning hours.

As the monologue grows increasingly tedious, the narrator's focus turns inward once again, this time to the intimate details of his past relationship with Jeannie Billroth. Adhering to his convictions about his other relationships, the narrator also maintains that he broke with Jeannie at precisely the right moment in his life. He now holds her in complete contempt and believes that the feeling is mutual.

It is three o'clock in the morning by the time dinner is over, and the party moves back into the music room. Occasionally becoming lucid enough to stammer a few words into the conversation or to abuse his wife for her attempts to remove him from the scene into the bedroom, Herr Auersberger fades ever deeper into an intoxicated stupor. His embarrassing pranks reach a high point of tastelessness when he suddenly removes his lower dental plate and thrusts it under the nose of the actor as a graphic example, he remarks, of human frailty. Jeannie, her efforts to engage the guest of honor in intellectual discussion virtually ignored throughout the evening, presses the actor with increasingly personal challenges. Finally overstepping the limits of his tolerance and defenses by asking whether he had found "fulfillment" in the theater now at the "end of his life," she touches off an almost paranoid response. It is only in the fury of this totally honest response that the actor becomes a sympathetic figure in the narrator's eyes. As if mortally wounded, the enraged actor attacks Jeannie for her crassness and stupidity and laments the vulnerability of public figures such as himself to such insolence. His wish had always been, he claims, for the anonymity of a private existence, for the isolated peace of the *"forest, mountain forest, felling trees."* For the narrator, who years ago radically disconnected himself from most of the people in the room, these are profoundly philosophical words that set the direction of millions of lives.

The storm passes quickly, however, and the civilities of social life return to the Auersberger household. During the ritual of departure, the actor not only gallantly kisses the hand of his antagonist but also pays a superfluous compliment to her adventurous spirit. Even the narrator becomes caught up in the social hypocrisies and finds himself kissing the brow of the hostess as he had twenty years ago, assuring her of his delight in having made renewed contact after the long interval. Alone on the street in the final scene and in a manic state fueled by conflicting emotions, the narrator sets out not in the direction of his apartment but toward the heart of the city that he both hates and loves. His final thoughts are dominated by an urgent need to set the experiences of the evening to paper.

The Characters

The characters in Thomas Bernhard's novel have significance only in their relationship to the narrator's past. The two young writers, almost unseen and unheard in the background, are viewed as types, simply artistically ambitious people whom Herr Auersberger had always attracted to his home and into his bedroom. Auersberger recognizes the type so readily because he had himself once played the role. As the centerpiece of an Auersberger party, the actor, too, has typological rather than personal meaning for the narrator, although he had seen the actor perform onstage many years before. Recalling this performance leads into a litany of complaints about actors, particularly those at the *Burgtheater*, and about this revered establishment of Viennese cultural life itself, which he calls a "place for the destruction of writers."

Viewed through the misanthropic eye of the narrator, only Joana appears in a favorable light. Jeannie and Anna Schreker, a teacher at a *Gymnasium*, are writers with local talents but international aspirations who have been inflated by the state cultural apparatus. Long ago, they sold their artistic souls to a bureaucracy that has, in turn, rewarded them with official prizes and honors. Joana, a frustrated dancer, channeled her creative energies into building the reputation of her husband, whose artistic career blossomed with her help. Her husband, however, proved ungrateful and fled to Mexico with another woman.

Among the "artistic corpses" present, the narrator spends his harshest criticism on Herr Auersberger, whose unearned affluence he contrasts with Joana's undeserved poverty. This onetime reputed successor to Anton von Webern wasted his musical gift and became a ruinous influence on young talent. The Austrian composer Gerhard Lampersberg claimed to recognize his own reflection as well as that of his wife in the novel's central characters, a contention vehemently denied by Bernhard. Bernhard had collaborated with Lampersberg in the 1960's on operatic productions and was probably a guest at social gatherings given by the couple in the "Maria Saal," a location only slightly altered to "Maria Zaal" in the novel. In what sense and to what degree Bernhard's works are rooted in the author's personal history has varied from case to case. In this instance, Lampersberg felt sufficiently upset at what he believed to be the autobiographical basis of *Holzfällen* that he attempted to have the novel confiscated from the shelves of Austria's bookstores. The composer later took the author to court for slander.

Themes and Meanings

In neo-Romantic flight from social reality reminiscent of characters in the early prose of Thomas Mann, the narrator in Bernhard's novel has isolated himself in order to protect and nurture his artistic talent. Fundamental to the truth of his art, he believes, is his capacity for detached observation and contemplation of other human beings. The narrator had seen the talents of his former circle of friends, particularly the musical genius of Herr Auersberger, contaminated and ruined by the trivialities of Viennese society. Both by rejecting this past network and by isolating himself, the narrator demonstrates an extreme version of a romantic ethic which views social intercourse as inimical to artistic activity. On the final page, however, when the narrator realizes the truly ambivalent nature of his relationship with the city and the people he had loathed, Bernhard underlines the problem this ethic poses. Despite the parallels to Bernhard's life, *Holzfällen* is not an autobiographical truth but rather a fictional study of subjectivity that is fascinating in its hyperbole and linguistic grace.

Characterized by the absence of subdivisions into chapters or paragraphs and by sentences of breathtaking length and complexity, Bernhard's prose style accounts for much of the momentum that, in the traditional novel, is borne by the linear development of plot. The rhythms and pauses in the novel's language carry the reader forward as pieces of the narrator's past, out of sequence with the occurrences as they happened, accumulate rather than develop in his mind. Bernhard also uses language to reinforce the novel's thematic center, the isolation of the narrator. With his consciousness crowded with linguistic remnants of the past, he has little mind space to register the present. Through the dense web of memory, the dinner party appears strikingly remote.

Critical Context

Between 1975 and 1982, Bernhard published five volumes of autobiographical writings. In these works, he sketched the main mileposts of his life, from his illegitimate birth in Holland in 1931 to his experiences as a schoolboy in Nazi-occupied Salzburg. He also describes his life as a patient in a hospital and sanatorium in postwar Austria until about 1950. The memories of the narrator of *Holzfällen* continue this chronology, if only very loosely. Reference is made several times to the 1950's as the period of the narrator's involvement in the social life from which he later fled. Yet, in the sense that all imaginative literature is partly autobiographical and partly fiction, *Holzfällen* clearly belongs to the latter category. In *Holzfällen*, Bernhard creates a narrative voice quite different from the voice of his unconventional memoirs, where he is acutely aware of the pitfalls of autobiographical reconstruction. In contrast, only at the very end of *Holzfällen* does the fictitious "I" realize that he has always loved the objects of his tirades as much as he has hated them.

Whatever Bernhard writes, he continues to be the "mischief maker" that he declared himself to be in *Der Keller* (1976; the cellar), the second volume of his autobiography. Judging from the scandal surrounding the publication of *Holzfällen* in 1984, his talent for controversy appears to be undiminished.

Sources for Further Study

Domandi, Agnes, ed. "Thomas Bernhard," in *Modern German Literature*. 1972.

Fetz, Gerald A. "The Works of Thomas Bernhard: 'Austrian Literature,'" in *Modern Austrian Literature*. XVII, nos. 3/4 (1984), pp. 171-192.

Sharp, Francis Michael. "Literature as Self-reflection: Thomas Bernhard and Peter Handke," in *World Literature Today*. LV (Autumn, 1981), pp. 603-607.

Sorg, B. *Thomas Bernhard*, 1977.

Francis Michael Sharp

HOMO FABER
A Report

Author: Max Frisch (1911-   )
Type of plot: Psychological realism
Time of plot: April to July, 1957
Locale: New York, Mexico, Guatemala, Cuba, Venezuela, Zurich,
   Düsseldorf, France, Italy, and Greece
First published: Homo Faber: Ein Bericht, 1957 (English translation, 1959)

>   *Principal characters:*
>   WALTER FABER, a fifty-year-old UNESCO engineer
>   IVY, his mistress in New York
>   HANNA PIPER, Walter's former lover, whom he has not seen
>   for twenty-one years
>   ELISABETH (SABETH), Walter's attractive twenty-year-old
>   traveling companion
>   JOACHIM HENCKE, Hanna's former husband, whom Walter
>   finds dead in the Guatemalan jungle
>   HERBERT HENCKE, Joachim's brother, a fellow airplane
>   passenger who persuades Walter to accompany him to
>   Joachim's Guatemalan plantation

The Novel

Homo Faber describes the tragic disintegration of a man who presumes that he is in control of his own life. It follows the travels of Walter Faber, a Swiss technologist working for UNESCO in aid to underdeveloped nations, as he ingenuously moves toward catastrophe.

As the novel begins, Walter is flying from New York to Caracas to supervise the delivery of turbines in Venezuela. His plans go awry, however, when the plane is forced into an emergency landing in the desert of Tamaulipas and the passengers must spend eighty-four hours isolated from civilization. After they are rescued, a fellow passenger, also Swiss, persuades Walter to postpone his business and journey with him into the Guatemalan jungle to visit his brother, Walter's old friend Joachim Hencke. With great difficulty, the two men manage to traverse the forbidding terrain, but, when they arrive at Joachim's plantation, they discover that he is dead, his corpse still suspended from the rope with which he has hanged himself.

Back in New York, determined to break up with his twenty-six-year-old lover, Ivy, Walter impulsively books passage on a ship leaving for France the next morning. During the sea voyage, he becomes attracted to a young woman he calls Sabeth, and, when they run into each other again in Paris, Walter and Sabeth agree to travel together through Europe. The two become lovers during an idyllic journey through Italy and along the Greek coast. Disaster strikes, however, when Sabeth is bitten by a viper and falls over an embankment. Walter rushes her to a hospital in Athens, where she dies of a fractured skull. He later learns from Hanna Piper, a former lover, whom he has not seen for twenty-one years and who now works in the Athens Archaeological Institute, that Sabeth was his own daughter.

Walter flees Greece in desperation, returning first to New York and then retracing his journey into Guatemala. After four days in Cuba, he moves on to Düsseldorf and then to Zurich before returning to Athens. At the conclusion of the novel, Walter is in an Athenian hospital, awaiting surgery on a stomach tumor.

The Characters

The narrator and protagonist of *Homo Faber*, Walter, is indeed representative of man the maker, arrogantly confident of his abilities to shape his own life. Proud of modern civilization's triumph over nature, he proclaims: "We live technologically, with man as the master of nature, man as the engineer, and let anyone who raises his voice against it stop using bridges not built by nature." At the outset of the narrative, Walter, secure in his rational human faculties, refuses to recognize any forces beyond his control. "I don't believe in providence and fate, as a technologist I am used to reckoning with the formulas of probability," he proclaims. "What has providence to do with it?"

An engine failure in the Yucatán begins to demonstrate the inadequacy of Walter's view. Though he obsessively shaves himself, even in the desert, there are primitive natural forces over which even Walter Faber, the representative of modern cosmopolitan enlightenment, has no control. Walter, who hates perspiration, has, except for measles, never been sick a day in his life, but he concludes his narrative in a sickbed, his imperious will powerless against the organic processes that have taken charge of his body.

For Walter, "the profession of technologist, a man who masters matter, is a masculine profession, if not the only masculine profession there is." Intent on affirming his masculine sovereignty, Walter associates nature and femininity; both are elements to be subdued. "As far as I am concerned, every woman is clinging ivy," he insists, and he does his best to disengage himself from Ivy, his aptly named lover in New York. Because everyone is seen from Walter's perspective, the female characters are presented reductively, as untidy creatures of debilitating emotion.

With a doctorate in archaeology, Hanna is an eminently capable professional, but Walter knew her as a pregnant Jewish refugee from Nazi tyranny, and he abandoned her in order to pursue his engineering career. The feminine forces he has spent most of his life trying to repress now assert themselves in the reappearance of Hanna, who is more successful at handling things than Walter, and in the undeniable reality of their daughter, Sabeth.

Themes and Meanings

Like the tragic Theban Oedipus, who finds his fate in fleeing it, Walter Faber falls, in Greece, through an arrogant disregard of the pattern of circumstances that are impelling him toward destruction. Until it is too late, he refuses to recognize the chain of events culminating in the death of his daughter as anything but isolated coincidences. Walter would like to believe that it was mere happenstance that put him on the same transatlantic ship as his daughter and on the same defective airplane as Joachim Hencke's brother. The intricate plot of *Homo Faber* is a refutation of its own narrator's rejection of providence in favor of belief in his own free will. An elaborate structure of flashbacks, crosscuts, and other jumps in time implicates every detail in everything else. As in Greek tragedy, the denouement is apparent in the exposition. From the beginning, there is no question that, for all of his technological prowess, Walter Faber is enmeshed in a mechanism from which he is powerless to escape.

Appropriate to the style of a professional rationalist, *Homo Faber* is subtitled "A Report," but Walter, who dislikes novels and is uncomfortable with "literary" flourishes, is as unsuccessful in the role of verbal engineer as he is in designing his own life. The narrative is presented in two parts: The first, written in Caracas, where Walter has gone after the death of Sabeth, recounts the events from April through June, while the second, written in the Athens hospital while he awaits surgery, begins on July 19. Each section is a sort of diary, written almost concurrently with the events it details and thus emphasizing the fact that its narrator does not have sufficient distance from the experiences to understand them.

Nevertheless, there is a dramatic difference in style and tone between the two parts. The first part, composed of complete sentences and carefully organized paragraphs, projects the illusion of a rational author still in command of his material and of himself. The second part, however, recorded in feverish all-night sessions, consists of highly metaphorical sentence fragments linked through ostensibly random associations of ideas. By the time Walter, who is probably dying, comes to write the second part of his narrative, he has relinquished his position with UNESCO—and his confidence in the rational powers of man. Like Joachim Hencke, who ended up hanging himself in the primeval wilderness that he discovered he could not dominate, Walter has abandoned the pretenses of Aristotelian logic and linear chronology, acknowledging his implication in archetypal realities beyond his comprehension or control. The very form of the text documents the collapse of *Homo faber*.

Critical Context

Homo Faber was published at the end of the first decade of the East-West nuclear confrontation, when the possibility that the ingenious inventions wrought by the human race could be used to destroy their creators became an urgent concern. Some scientists were cautioning against the divorce of technological sophistication from ethical deliberations, and the English physicist and novelist C.P. Snow was bemoaning the development of "two cultures," the fact that scientists and humanists had become unintelligible to each other.

From the time he earned his degree from the Technical University of Zurich in 1941 until literary success freed him to concentrate on his writing in 1954, Max Frisch was an architect, a profession which links art to technology. He has, along with Friedrich Dürrenmatt, become one of the two most widely respected contemporary Swiss authors, and he has attracted more scholarly attention than has any other author writing in German since World War II.

Like *Homo Faber*, many of Frisch's most highly regarded works—the novels *Stiller* (1954; *I'm Not Stiller*, 1958), *Mein Name sei Gantenbein* (1964; *A Wilderness of Mirrors*, 1965), and *Der Mensch erscheint im Holozän* (1979; *Man in the Holocene*, 1980), and plays such as *Andorra* (1961; English translation, 1964) and *Biedermann und die Brandstifter* (1958; *The Firebugs*, 1963)—concentrate on a solitary man confronting the marginality of his individual existence. Perhaps this theme is a product of the author's vantage point in Switzerland, a fragmented society peripheral to the centers of contemporary cultural power. Yet Frisch's fictions have successfully embodied the anxieties of many who have had to learn to live in postindustrial society and cope with the ambiguous benefits of a triumphant civilization.

Sources for Further Study

Bradley, Brigitte. "Max Frisch's *Homo Faber*: Theme and Structural Devices," in *The Germanic Review*. XLI (1966), pp. 279-290.
Butler, Michael. *The Novels of Max Frisch*, 1976.
Petersen, Carol. *Max Frisch*, 1972.
Probst, Gerhard F., and Jay F. Bodine, eds. *Perspectives on Max Frisch*, 1982.
Weisstein, Ulrich. *Max Frisch*, 1967.

Steven G. Kellman

HORACKER

Author: Wilhelm Raabe (1831-1910)
Type of plot: Social realism
Time of plot: July 25, 1867
Locale: Two neighboring villages in the area of the Weser River in Germany, principally Gansewinckel
First published: 1876 (English translation, 1983)

> *Principal characters:*
> DR. WERNER ECKERBUSCH, the vice principal of the local school
> IDA, his wife
> VICTOR WINDWEBEL, the drawing master
> HEDWIG, his wife
> NEUBAUER, the assistant master at the school
> CHRISTIAN WINCKLER, the pastor of Gansewinckel
> BILLA, his wife
> CORD HORACKER, a young man who has escaped from reform school
> LOTTCHEN ACHTERHANG, his girlfriend

The Novel

   Horacker is a story told by an outside narrator, who leads the reader into the setting of the novel, descending from the area's highest mountain down into the hills, forest, and meadows. The reader first encounters Dr. Werner Eckerbusch, vice principal of the local school and the last of a dying breed, and is thus introduced to the rhythms of village life, where the most important thing for the inhabitants is the spate of rumors about Cord Horacker: "Horacker was rampant in the land."

   In this setting, Eckerbusch and Victor Windwebel, the drawing master, spend their last day of vacation before school starts again, hiking to the neighboring village of Gansewinckel to visit their friend, Pastor Christian Winckler. In the forest, the schoolmasters encounter Horacker's mother and finally Horacker himself. Up to this moment, the reader knows only the horrible rumors. Reality is restored as a young man of nineteen—"trembling, emaciated, ragged"—emerges from the forest with his suffering mother. The reader learns that Horacker grew up in abject poverty and was constantly harassed by the villagers. When he was driven to stealing and pranks, the authorities sent him to a reformatory—where he was learning to be a tailor—from which he escaped only after being told that Lottchen Achterhang, the girl he loves, would not wait for him.

Meanwhile, Lottchen, an orphan reared by the Wincklers, has been caught stealing carrots. She has run away from her job on the other side of Berlin with Pastor Nöleke, after hearing of Horacker's supposed crimes, and arrives on foot, ragged and hungry. After the Wincklers have taken her into their care once again, Eckerbusch arrives with the news that he and Windwebel have seen Horacker, who ran away in panic at the mention of the public prosecutor. Windwebel chases him, finally persuading the youth to return. Pastor Winckler himself goes out and brings Horacker to the parsonage, where he is reunited with Lottchen.

By five o'clock in the afternoon, the rumor that Horacker has murdered two schoolmasters is spreading. Hedwig Windwebel, nearly hysterical with grief, goes immediately to Ida Eckerbusch, a strong, sensible woman, who maintains that the rumor is nonsense. Unable to comfort Hedwig, however, Ida hires a coach and, accompanied by Assistant Master Neubauer, the women travel to Gansewinckel, where they surprise their husbands at the end of the story.

Just before they arrive, Eckerbusch disperses the assembled villagers by pointing out that their failings are greater than young Horacker's: "the night cannot grow black enough to cover your shame, you threefold Horackers of Gansewinckel!" He encourages each person to examine his own conscience and leave Horacker in the capable hands of the pastor and his wife. Soon the public prosecutor and his assistant arrive, in time to discover that Horacker has been found and that no murders have been committed. All join in drink and fellowship, and the women reassure Widow Horacker and the two young people that everything will turn out well.

The Characters

Eckerbusch is introduced in the first sentences of the novel as a creature like the kiwi of New Zealand, who "should be stuffed and revered as a species that one shall never again encounter." The narrator emphasizes that Eckerbusch is the last vice principal (*Konrektor*), since this position is being abolished. While these words have a humorous effect, they are not intended to mock the vice principal, except insofar as Wilhelm Raabe always gently mocks the absurdities of human beings. In this case, Raabe's ironic tone carries with it a very serious note: Eckerbusch is the representative of a type of humane individual who is gradually disappearing in favor of a new breed of men like Neubauer.

Eckerbusch is a product of his local village environment, beyond which he "never ventured, with the exception of three years spent at the university." He is a compassionate man, concerned about his students and others, but he is considered something of an odd character and often laughed at for his eccentricities. Raabe's portrait of him as a man "respected in the community as an authority on matters of weather" is gently humorous. Eckerbusch is a good-humored old man who does not seem to worry about upholding the image of a dignified vice principal.

Winckler also is a compassionate man, whose sympathy immediately goes out to Lottchen and Horacker. He is an old-fashioned pastor with "both the body and the spirit for the task" and is an admirer of the moralizing fables of Christian Fürchtegott Gellert. Outwardly, Winckler seems to be a rural pastor in an idyllic setting, but the undercurrents in the parish show this image to be an illusion. When there is need, he and his wife, having no children of their own, easily "adopt the cause of strangers," and they dedicate their lives to ministering to the Gansewinckel farmers.

Ida Eckerbusch and Billa Winckler are both strong-minded partners to their husbands. Realistic, sensible women, they know how to deal with others. Raabe's portrait of them is gently humorous and admiring. Memorable scenes occur when Billa deals firmly with the parishioners on the question of the quarter-money and when Ida lectures an unwilling Neubauer.

Windwebel is a younger man, under Eckerbusch's protective wing, with the same compassion and other humane qualities characteristic of both Eckerbusch and Winckler. The younger man takes genuine pleasure in his association with Eckerbusch and, when faced with Horacker's troubles, shows an immediate empathy based on his own struggles to succeed in a hostile world. Windwebel's handling of Horacker's return wins for him new respect from Eckerbusch.

In contrast to these men and women of the two villages, Neubauer represents the man of the future. He is a very serious young philologist who has recently been transferred from the city to the province, and he considers Windwebel "shallow" and "insignificant." Neubauer is a pedantic scholar, characterized by "the awful gravity of his character and views on life." When forced to accompany Ida and Hedwig to Gansewinckel, he shows no sympathy for their concern but worries instead about whether he looks ridiculous. Concerns about his image and dignity and a detached approach to the problems of others distinguish him as much as humane action based on real sympathy distinguishes the Eckerbusches and Wincklers. The two contrasting ways of dealing with life revolve around the decision to become personally involved or to keep all contact with poverty and troubled individuals on an impersonal level.

Themes and Meanings

Horacker is constructed around a deceptive idyll. The outward appearance of a gentle and charming life in the small town of Gansewinckel and the atmosphere of a late summer afternoon hide the undercurrent of "chaos, absurdity, and stupidity of this world." In this contrast lies a recognition of the conflict between reality and ideals, the conflict between selfish individual interests and concern for the community.

Social criticism surfaces in the petty argument by the local farmers over quarter-money, a small sum of money which the schoolmaster and pastor traditionally earned by making a personal visit to every head of family in the parish on New Year's Day; this custom has not been followed for more than a century, and the farmers now wish to reinstate it. More seriously, a criticism of the cruelty with which outcast individuals are treated by the community is illustrated by the central story of Horacker and Lottchen. The villagers look at suffering with the same detachment as Neubauer, or sometimes even with malicious enjoyment. The suffering of people such as Horacker and Lottchen is a reminder that not all is idyllic in the community, that the community has failed at least some of its members.

The value of the humane individual is upheld in such characters as Eckerbusch, who disperses the crowd gathered outside the parsonage by refusing to accept its judgment, relying instead on his own. He stands for that small circle of compassionate individuals which serves as a guide to the young people in their confusion and attempts to deal with society's demands. The digression on the word "one" (German *man*)—"Who is *one*?"—actually embodies this conflict. In the parsonage, Winckler sends Widow Horacker some trousers for Cord because "one simply cannot sit by and watch," while at the same time in the village, the loss of some cabbage and potatoes stolen by hungry people causes the reaction: "Oh, wouldn't one love to skin the scoundrels alive."

The idyllic small town pictured here is a lost paradise, just as Eckerbusch is the last of a dying breed. The contradictions of later nineteenth century society are reflected in the contrast between selfish materialism (often associated with city life) and unselfish humane action (associated with a small town or haven away from the city), even though the sympathy and desire to help of people like the Eckerbusches or Wincklers contrasts sharply with the average villager's detachment from all but his own suffering. Although humane intervention helped Horacker and Lottchen, it is the result of an individual response rather than of the concerted action of a humane village community. As such, it is clear that Wilhelm Raabe sees the ideal of humane action as something which is being eroded and will finally be lost in modern society.

Critical Context

Horacker is one of the mature works on which Raabe's reputation as a major German novelist of the nineteenth century rests. The novel falls within the period of German realism, sometimes referred to in German literary criticism as *poetischen* or *bürgerlichen Realismus*, and is realistic in contrast to the more idealistic classicism and Romanticism. *Horacker* focuses on the daily life experienced by the protagonists in a transitional society following the Revolution of 1848, a period when the German bourgeoisie (*Bürgertum*) was struggling vainly for more political rights. The book is regional only in the sense that it is firmly anchored to a specific geographical area, which Raabe knew well and portrayed with a sure touch.

The humorous, rambling style used by Raabe allows a comprehensive view of the society he describes. Plots are weakened—not much action occurs in *Horacker*—and suspense is diminished. Although many devices are used to delay the conclusion, all the elements are carefully woven into a well-orchestrated whole; for example, everyone arrives at the final scene in Gansewinckel at just the right moment. What appears to be merely purposeless digression contributes to the reader's understanding of the attitudes of the people and of the village environment. The structure, which superficially appears so very rambling and uninterrelated, turns out to be very carefully constructed.

Raabe's narrative technique became more complex as his work matured, probably reaching a high point in his masterpiece *Stopfkuchen: Eine See- und Mordgeschichte* (1891; *Tubby Schaumann: A Tale of Murder and the High Seas*, 1983). Various narrators bring their perspective to his later stories. This happens to a certain extent in *Horacker*; the narrator provides an overview, bringing the reader into the scene, while Eckerbusch and Windwebel, Ida, and the Wincklers contribute their views of "the Horacker Case." This unconventional way of telling a story is directed to the perceptive reader. In *Horacker*, Raabe identifies this individual as the one in a thousand, who, watching a house being built, "will be given to quiet and somewhat melancholy meditation, who will ask of himself and fate: 'What all do you suppose will happen in that new house?'" His style of writing demands participation and overturns the reader's expectation that the narration will build suspense and finally produce satisfaction at the capture of a criminal. This destruction of expectations is a particularly modern feature of this nineteenth century novelist.

Throughout his works, Raabe focuses on the question of human development, the struggle between an individual's dreams and the limiting effect of society. In *Horacker*, as in his other works, he considers the relationship between an individual and a society in transition. *Horacker* ends on a positive note, but with an individual solution to one problem that does not resolve the overall conflict of values. Later novels show more resignation and skepticism about man's ability to understand or control history; *Horacker* represents the high point of Raabe's vision of a more humane world established through the actions of single individuals.

Sources for Further Study
Daemmrich, Horst S. *Wilhelm Raabe*, 1981.
Fairley, Barker. *Wilhelm Raabe: An Introduction to His Novels*, 1961.
Helmers, Hermann. *Wilhelm Raabe*, 1968.

Pascal, Roy. "Wilhelm Raabe (1831-1910)," in *The German Novel: Studies*, 1956.

Stern, J. P. "Wilhelm Raabe: Home and Abroad," in *Idylls and Realities: Studies in Nineteenth-century German Literature*, 1976.

Susan Piepke

THE HORSEMAN ON THE ROOF

Author: Jean Giono (1895-1970)
Type of plot: Symbolic realism
Time of plot: 1838
Locale: Provence
First published: Le Hussard sur le toit, 1951 (*The Hussar on the Roof,* 1953;
better known as *The Horseman on the Roof*)

> *Principal characters:*
> ANGÉLO PARDI, the horseman of the title, a young Italian
> nobleman dedicated to the fight for liberty
> PAULINE, MARQUISE DE THEUS, Angélo's companion during
> the last part of his journey through cholera-ridden
> Provence
> GIUSEPPE, Angélo's foster brother

The Novel

As *The Horseman on the Roof* opens, Angélo Pardi is riding into the
Rhone valley during the summer of 1838. The heat is oppressive, and everyone suffers from thirst. Then people begin to die. At first, the deaths do not
draw unusual attention, but soon it becomes clear that a cholera epidemic
has begun. People become frightened, and their attempts to protect themselves make travel difficult. Angélo meets a young doctor who tries to save as
many lives as he can, even to the point of searching out cholera victims who
have hidden themselves away to die. Angélo helps him eagerly, though their
efforts fail time after time. Finally, the young doctor himself becomes a victim. Angélo is unable to keep him alive.

He takes up his travels again after the doctor's death. After getting past a
group of soldiers and several roadblocks manned by citizens, Angélo makes
his way into Manosque, where he expects to find his foster brother Giuseppe. Instead, he finds himself trapped by a mob; he is accused of poisoning
the well and his life is threatened. To escape the mob's wrath, Angélo makes
his way onto the rooftops, where he lives for the next several days.

From his position above the city, Angélo watches the progress of the epidemic. In a brief expedition into one of the houses, he meets Pauline,
Marquise de Theus, who—unafraid and clearly in control of the situation—
makes tea for him. Angélo, frightened that he might have brought cholera
into the house, leaves; he does not encounter Pauline again until much later.

When he finally comes down from the rooftops, the first person whom
Angélo meets is a nun, who has taken upon herself the job of washing the
dead bodies of cholera victims. Again, as with the young doctor, Angélo
cheerfully and energetically accepts the role of assistant.

Soon after, Angélo leaves the streets of Manosque, which are almost abandoned, and searches the surrounding hills for Giuseppe. Angélo finds his foster brother with several people who have taken refuge outdoors to escape the cholera; for a while it seems as if they have succeeded. When cholera begins to strike the community, however, Angélo and Giuseppe decide that they should make their separate ways back to Italy. They establish a rendezvous and set out on their journeys.

Angélo reencounters Pauline when they have both been stopped by a roadblock. The soldiers have orders to keep people off the roads, in order to prevent the spread of cholera. Traveling together, Angélo and Pauline make a formidable pair, however, and they are able to outwit, outfight, and outbluff any who try to stop them. Indeed, when they are captured and put into quarantine, they escape easily, although Angélo is disappointed that he did not get to display more of his soldierly skills in the escape.

Shortly before the end of the novel, Angélo and Pauline meet a country doctor whose explanation of cholera—he connects the disease to pride—helps make Jean Giono's symbolic intentions clearer. The two travelers, who have a great respect, admiration, and affection for each other, although they have not become lovers, set out on the final leg of their journey. Just when their spirits are highest, however, Pauline collapses: Cholera has finally caught up with her, too. Angélo ministers to her through the night, using all the skills he learned from the young doctor, and in the morning she is weak but clearly out of danger. Angélo sees that she arrives safely home, and as the novel ends, he is filled with joy that he will soon see Italy.

The Characters

There is almost no development of character in *The Horseman on the Roof*, nor is there any attempt at complex psychological realism. The reader's experience of characterization, then, becomes largely a matter of getting to know the two principal figures, who carry the symbolic weight of Giono's meaning. The main character, Angélo, is young, wealthy, charming, generous, idealistic, quick to defend himself and others from injustice, and proud of his military skills and idealistic values. His generosity is most evident in his willingness to care for victims of cholera and in his absolute lack of fear that he might die of the disease himself. On the other hand, his spirits rise highest whenever he is given an opportunity to demonstrate his horsemanship and swordcraft. One admires Angélo, but at times he seems like a proud child, eager to show off his skills. His pride is balanced throughout the novel, however, by his cheerfulness and high spirits, and in the end, he is thoroughly likable.

Even though she has an important role only in the last part of the novel, Pauline is clearly also a major character. In many ways she is like Angélo: young, intelligent, capable of taking care of herself. She is high-spirited and proud of her ability to handle the pistols she carries. Pauline appears in the other novels which make up the "Hussard Cycle," particularly *Mort d'un personnage* (1949); it seems clear that Giono modeled her on his own mother.

Several minor characters deserve mention, not only because they make very effective foils to set off the character of Angélo but also because Angélo himself thinks about them during moments of crisis. Giuseppe, for example, is important because, unlike Angélo, whose idealism drives him to kill the Austrian spy Baron Swartz in an open duel, he is practical: Giuseppe would have killed the baron with hired assassins. The altruistic are also important. Angélo admires the young doctor's zeal, his hopeless devotion to curing. He also admires the nun who takes the washing of the bodies of the dead to be her holy duty. Ironically, she seems to have no interest in saving the lives of the victims but insists instead that she is preparing their bodies for the last judgment.

Themes and Meanings

The themes of *The Horseman on the Roof* come directly out of the situation in which Angélo finds himself, and Giono's ideas about these themes can be found in his protagonist's response. Thus the novel is about nobility, courage in the face of natural catastrophe, cheerful willingness to serve others, and more specifically, the willingness to serve through healing even at some risk to oneself.

It is clear that Giono intended the cholera in *The Horseman on the Roof* to be both symbolic and real. Giono may have been influenced by Herman Melville, whose *Moby Dick* (1851) he admired greatly. There are suggestions throughout the novel that Giono would have cholera symbolize human pride, or the particular pessimism which lies at the heart of much fiction from early in the twentieth century, or the disaster of World War II. Nevertheless, Giono's research into the cholera epidemics that swept through Europe during the 1830's and 1840's was extensive, and, just as Melville took pains to make the whaling scenes in *Moby Dick* realistic, Giono took pains to make the cholera seem real to the reader.

This realism makes the symbolic force of the epidemic all the stronger. In the face of its realistic and symbolic force, Angélo's cheerful self-confidence, his willingness to risk his own life, and his eager but unsuccessful attempts to save victim after victim become even more admirable. Consequently, in Angélo's last struggle with cholera—his successful attempt to save Pauline's life when she, too, comes down with the disease—the reader understands that his success represents not a change in his medical technique or in the nature of the world but a just and appropriate reward for his attitude toward life. Thus, at the end of the novel, Angélo's optimism seems to reflect Giono's faith in the human ability to come through disaster with the virtues of hard work and fidelity to loved ones intact.

Critical Context

Jean Giono projected a sequence of novels which would deal both with the Angélo of *The Horseman on the Roof* and with another Angélo, the grandson of the first Angélo and Pauline. These novels would establish parallels not only between the characters of two generations but also between the eras of the 1840's and the 1940's. This Angélo, grandson of the hero of *The Horseman on the Roof*, becomes the narrator of *Mort d'un personnage* (1949), a novel which describes the death of Pauline de Theus in powerful detail.

At the time of his own death, Giono had finished four novels in the Hussard Cycle: *Mort d'un personnage*, *The Horseman on the Roof*, *Le Bonheur Fou* (1957; *The Straw Man*, 1959), and *Angélo* (1958; English translation, 1960). *Mort d'un personnage* deals with the most recent time period, even though it was the first of the four to be published. *Angélo*, the last of the novels published, was, according to Giono, the first written, a quick sketch made when he first envisioned the characters of Angélo and Pauline. *The Straw Man* takes Angélo (the hero of *The Horseman on the Roof*) back to Italy, where he finds himself involved in the war with Austria. Perhaps because Giono was unable to complete the sequence as originally planned, the connection between the published novels is not always clear, nor are the plot lines consistent. Nevertheless, Giono insisted before his death that these four works be published together as the Hussard Cycle when his writings were collected.

Much of the power of *The Horseman on the Roof* lies in its devastatingly realistic picture of the cholera epidemic of 1838, which Giono researched thoroughly before he began work on the final version of the novel. Angélo is a compelling character: naïve, accomplished, generous, always willing to help, and as devoted to liberty as he is to health. More than one critic has pointed out that for a novel filled with corpses, *The Horseman on the Roof* is, ultimately, a novel which celebrates life.

Part of the life of the novel is Provence itself. Giono was born and grew up in the village of Manosque. When he was able to support himself as a writer, he bought a house in the village and spent his working life there. Giono's descriptions of the geography, the hills and forests, and the villages and towns of Provence make the region come alive for the reader. Nature in the Provençal countryside takes on almost the quality of a character. This love of the area with which he was so familiar, and his return to it in book after book, have caused some critics to accuse Giono of being a regional novelist. If he was, however, he was a regional novelist in the same way that William Faulkner was, or in the way that Herman Melville was a novelist of the sea.

Some critics call *The Horseman on the Roof* an epic, and in many ways it does resemble a long heroic poem. Nevertheless, Norma L. Goodrich makes a strong argument that the literary form uppermost in Giono's mind as he worked on *The Horseman on the Roof* was the *roman courtois*, and to read the novel in the light of this suggestion makes it clear that Angélo most resembles a medieval chivalric knight. In this character, the novel celebrates the medieval ideal of courtesy as maintained by a modern hero within the context of horrifying conditions. To have created so modern a work from a form so ancient (and so ignored by most other modern writers) is a remarkable achievement. With this novel, Giono's literary reputation seems safely established.

Sources for Further Study
Chabot, Jacques. *La Provence de Giono*, 1980.
Goodrich, Norma L. *Giono: Master of Fictional Modes*, 1973.
Nadeau, Maurice. *The French Novel Since the War*, 1967.
Peyre, Henri. *French Novelists of Today*, 1967.
Redfern, W. D. *The Private World of Jean Giono*, 1967.
Smith, Maxwell A. *Jean Giono*, 1966.

Archibald E. Irwin

THE HOUSE OF THE DEAD

Author: Fyodor Dostoevski (1821-1881)
Type of plot: Autobiographical realism
Time of plot: The late 1840's to the early 1850's
Locale: A prison in Siberia (probably Omsk)
First published: Zapiski iz myortvogo doma, 1861-1862 (*Buried Alive: Or, Ten Years of Penal Servitude in Siberia*, 1881; better known as *The House of the Dead*)

Principal characters:
THE NARRATOR, perhaps a Siberian civil servant
ALEXANDER PETROVICH GORYANCHIKOV, an ex-convict
AKIM AKIMOVICH, an elder prisoner
ALEY, a young Tartar prisoner
PETROV, a prisoner who befriends Goryanchikov
ISAIAH FOMICH BUMSTEIN, a Jewish prisoner
ARISTOV, an informer
SUSHILOV, a prisoner who serves Goryanchikov
ORLOV, a prisoner who dies of flogging
THE MAJOR, the prison commandant

The Novel

The plot, a thinly veiled account of Fyodor Dostoevski's four years in a Siberian military prison, has little of the usual narrative structure. Instead, the author presents a series of scenes of prison life, disguised as the memoirs of Alexander Petrovich Goryanchikov, a wellborn young man who has served ten years at hard labor for killing his wife. In a sketchy frame story, an anonymous first-person narrator extols the many attractions of Siberian life, particularly in the small town where he met Goryanchikov, who was earning his living as a French tutor. The townspeople think the ex-prisoner a "terrible misanthrope," perhaps even a crazy man. After Goryanchikov's death, the narrator buys what remains of Goryanchikov's papers from the tutor's landlady. Among them is a bulky notebook, chiefly filled by prison memoirs: These the narrator offers for public judgment.

The main narrative begins as Goryanchikov arrives at the prison and depicts the grim fortress, containing about 250 prisoners from various classes of society, sent there for all sorts of crimes, criminal and political. After describing the stench, noise, and other terrible conditions of his barracks, he concludes, "Man is a creature who can get used to anything, and I believe that is the very best way of defining him." Goryanchikov briefly catalogs the kinds of prisoners sent there, paying particular attention to the Special Class—prisoners with indefinite sentences even more harsh than their fellows'. In sum, Goryanchikov thinks himself in Hell, "the nethermost pit and the outer darkness." The prisoners constantly fight, steal from one another— even Goryanchikov's Bible is quickly taken—and are subject to the sadistic whims of the prison's commandant, who has men flogged for the smallest offense. In this underworld, there is also underground activity: smuggling vodka, working to make money, even pawnbroking. Yet this first chapter ends on a curiously hopeful note: Goryanchikov recalls a small girl's giving him a kopeck, "in Christ's name."

Goryanchikov next introduces characters who illustrate prison life, an existence for which nothing could have prepared him. Being of the gentility, for example, worked against him for nearly two years, the other convicts watching this gentleman's sufferings with delight. Another Russian gentleman, Akim Akimovich, helps Goryanchikov understand their prejudice, which he has risen above by the strength of his character and his abilities as a craftsman. For the first two years, Goryanchikov finds himself "under the rule" of Akim Akimovich, who first warns him of the drunken major's fits. After a long digression on prisoners smuggling vodka, Goryanchikov introduces Gazin, a Tartar of enormous strength who flies into murderous rages when drunk. On one of these, he accosts and nearly kills Goryanchikov, who ends his first full day in prison sadly considering the inequality of the prisoners' punishments to their crimes, specifically the heavy flogging of prisoners for trivial offenses.

Lights out brings another description of two more aspects of prison life: the illegal plying of various crafts and the forbidden playing of cards. Goryanchikov also describes some of the other inmates of his barracks, focusing particularly upon Aley, a young Tartar, who exemplifies both the injustice of the penal system and the incredible ability of the human soul to survive it, relatively untouched and pure. Though a Muslim, Aley appreciates the word of Jesus. Goryanchikov contrasts him to another non-Christian, Isaiah Fomich Bumstein, a cunning Jew, the object of much fond amusement in the barracks. Continuing the character sketches, Goryanchikov sharply contrasts Sushilov and Aristov. Considered a fool, the former contents himself serving others, particularly Goryanchikov; the latter still practices what put him in prison: informing upon innocent people. A tool of the major, Aristov is atypical of the prisoners, among whom Goryanchikov eventually discovers a peculiar integrity, even honor. Goryanchikov sees that he himself has become one, legally and superficially, with these common people and meditates upon the importance of freedom, or its illusion, for the prisoners. It explains the sporadic binges during which they throw away all of their carefully hoarded money or the sudden violent outbursts from quiet men. He resolves neither to fear nor to pander to his fellows but to bear himself as simply and independently as possible. He closes the chapter describing his friendship with Sharik, a despised mongrel dog, whom he considers to be the only creature in the universe who loved him.

Sharik foreshadows Petrov, another creature who attaches himself to Goryanchikov. After noting the kinds of prison work he preferred—grinding gypsum, turning a lathe, shoveling snow—Goryanchikov singles out among his widening circle of acquaintances this man with whom he apparently has nothing in common. Others think him desperate and fearless, and Petrov readily admits to having stolen Goryanchikov's Bible, yet Goryanchikov maintains a friendship with him, in part because of Petrov's surprising intellectual curiosity.

The concluding chapters of part 1 cover the Christmas season. The prisoners are given a rare bath; paradoxically, the long-awaited event seems like a scene from Hell. On Christmas Eve and the feast day, the prisoners do little or no work. In their idleness, they painfully recall the holidays of their past, becoming unconsciously aware that observing this day brings them into contact with the rest of the world. Even in prison things are "the same as among real people." After preparing for the feast and its religious observance, the men slowly turn disappointed, morose, quarrelsome. The grim post-holiday spirit lifts only on the third day after Christmas, when the prisoners put on a theatrical evening, described at some length—and with a critic's eye—by Goryanchikov. He finds with surprise the normally hostile commoners deferring to him and salutes their ability to put aside their prejudices in search of his approval, claiming the gentility could learn from the common folk. He marvels at the skill of the musicians, asserts that the two principal actors are superior to those in Moscow and St. Petersburg, and meticulously describes the dramatic pieces, the audience's response, and the air of pleasure which prevails among the prisoners. Indeed, their moral character seems temporarily changed by this brief break from prison routine. That night, Goryanchikov reflects upon these extraordinary days, his companions, and his environment. Momentarily overcome by terror, he consoles himself that he will not be there forever.

Part 2 opens with three chapters on the hospital, where Goryanchikov spent an unusual amount of time. Though marginally more comfortable, it contains suffering and death not seen in the barracks, particularly among those convicts, such as Orlov, who have run the gauntlet. He reflects upon the common prisoners' reverence for the doctors, who temporarily shield them from such brutality. By contrast, he presents various officers who ordered or administered flogging, concluding that such punishment is "an ulcer on society" and that it destroys any civilization.

As summer approaches in Siberia, the men begin to long even more for freedom: The number of escape attempts dramatically increases in spring, as does Goryanchikov's melancholy amid the general gladness and renewal in nature. The celebration of Easter is like that of Christmas, only sadder because the days are longer. More daylight also means more and heavier work, such as making bricks, the heaviest work of all. Yet Goryanchikov grows stronger by such work, and it takes him to the banks of the Irtysh River, from which he can see the "free, lonely steppes."

The long days are enlivened only by events such as an impending inspector's visit (which proves anticlimactic), the buying of a new horse (which prompts Goryanchikov to discuss other prison animals), and a prisoners' grievance over the hard work and poor food (a protest that the common prisoners do not allow Goryanchikov to join). Primarily, however, Goryanchikov dreams of freedom and understands more fully the gulf between the common people and the gentility. He describes the other "gentleman exiles" and their relationship to the highest authorities, who sometimes temper the harshness inflicted by those beneath them. Goryanchikov's birth and education occasionally obtain for him lighter duties, such as working as a clerk for the military. More tangible relief comes when the major is replaced for flogging an impudent ex-professor.

Describing the new prison regime, Goryanchikov recognizes that his loosely chronological summary of his first months in prison has touched upon all the important matters of his stay. To repeat these would only become monotonous and depressing. He even begins to distrust his own memory, except for his "passionate longing for resurrection, renewal, a new life." Recollecting this longing for freedom leads to his final story, that of an abortive escape and the prisoners' shifting response to it. The attempt occurs during Goryanchikov's last year in prison, during which he realizes that he has many friends: The common people have at last accepted him. He gains new privileges, most important the right to read books and magazines which take him out of his torment. He also gains a new respect for the prisoners, whom he now regards as perhaps "the most highly gifted and strongest of all our people." He has learned the value of freedom: When his fetters are at last removed, he calls it "a resurrection from the dead."

The Characters

Through Goryanchikov, Dostoevski dramatizes his gradually changing attitude toward the Russian common man during his own four years in prison. At first repulsed by the prisoners, the wellborn young man comes to value their integrity and courage, endurance, and remarkable adaptability. Finally, he can admire the stoic acceptance of Akim Akimovich and the defiant courage of Orlov, as well as appreciate the kindness and charity of others inside and outside the prison walls. While he objectively depicts the prisoners' coarseness and laments their failure to repent of their crimes, even murder, he ultimately prefers these violent, passionate men to the effete, Europeanized gentility into which he was born.

His empathy for the commoners springs from his highly prizing freedom. The Special Class prisoners, with their doubly harsh, indefinite sentences, especially draw his attention and compassion. Their fate prompts him to speculate about injustice, freedom, and man's nature and condition and to criticize the penal system, especially its failure to fit the punishment to the crime. The major serves as the focus of this criticism, but Dostoevski makes it very clear that the system itself tolerates, perhaps even encourages, such monsters.

In two justly praised set pieces—the pre-Christmas bath and the post-holiday theatrical—Dostoevski demonstrates both his pity for the prisoners and his admiration for their talent and judgment, which he in many respects prefers to those of the sophisticated intellectual circles in which he traveled before his imprisonment in 1849 for illegal political activities. As Goryanchikov mentally takes leave of the prison the night before his release, he insists that "the whole truth must be told: these were no ordinary men. Perhaps, indeed, they were the most highly gifted and the strongest of all our people. But these powerful forces were condemned to perish uselessly, unnaturally, wrongfully, irrevocably. And whose is the blame?"

Themes and Meanings

The House of the Dead was originally published in *Vremia* (*The Time*), a magazine Dostoevski was editing: The serial publication perhaps encouraged the narrative's loose structure. Dostoevski takes advantage of it to enter into numerous "digressions" which are as significant as Goryanchikov's own story, though a contemporary reader may find them distracting, even as monotonous as prison life itself. The writer remains remarkably detached as he describes the horrors of prison life, though clearly Dostoevski himself was profoundly affected by it. When the tone does become more emotional, the reader senses more readily the importance of the topic.

As the discussions of plot and character indicate, much of Dostoevski's meaning is conveyed through his character sketches. The centrality of freedom to human dignity, the inherent strength and integrity of the Russian common man, the terrible injustices wrought by the penal system, the importance of Christianity as a response to a nightmarish existence—all these ideas are embodied in figures such as Akim Akimovich, Sushilov, the major, and, finally, Goryanchikov as he develops through the narrative. While only sketchily developed, the narrator of the frame story also contributes to the main story's meaning. His sympathetic but uncomprehending interest in Goryanchikov and his superficial, "progressive" outlook underscore Dostoevski's criticism of liberal, "Western" notions intruding into Russian culture.

The narrative outlines a descent into hell and a "resurrection" or return to the world. At points, such as the bath scene and the description of Christmas, the author's Dantesque intent becomes clear. Yet with no Vergil to guide him and no imposed structure, such as the circles of the Inferno, Goryanchikov must rely upon repetition of the central themes. With a censor to get around, the former radical Dostoevski must rely on the reader to infer the author's anger at the prison system; the book itself never explicitly calls for penal reform. Rather, it focuses upon the system's horrors and the prisoners' remarkable physical and spiritual resilience.

Critical Context

Though not exemplifying the "fantastic realism" of his more famous later novels, *The House of the Dead* anticipates strongly *Zapiski iz podpolya* (1864; *Notes from the Underground*, 1913). In its unorthodox narrative structure, its insistent concern with freedom, and its rejection of the Western or European elements creeping into Russian culture, this more realistic, objective novel paves the way for its subjective, fantastic successor.

The House of the Dead certainly demonstrates Dostoevski's switch from earlier, more conventional novels such as *Bednye lyudi* (1846; *Poor Folk*, 1887) and from his vaguely radical political leanings toward the mature style of the great novels—*Prestupleniye i nakazaniye* (1866; *Crime and Punishment*, 1886), *Idiot* (1868; *The Idiot*, 1887), *Besy* (1871-1872; *The Possessed*, 1913), and *Bratya Karamazovy* (1879-1880; *The Brothers Karamazov*, 1912)—and toward the political and religious conservatism of his later years. Though *The House of the Dead* contains little on the subject of religion, it illuminates a Christianity which accepts the worth of all people, no matter what their social station or history. In a famous letter sent to a friend in 1854, Dostoevski insisted that his prison experience had convinced him of the absolute, transcendent truth of Christ.

This novel perhaps most firmly marks Dostoevski's return to the Russian literary scene after an enforced absence of twelve years. While less bold and polished in its ideas and form than the major novels or *Notes from the Underground*, it remains important biographically, historically, and thematically to the serious student of Dostoevski.

Sources for Further Study
Mochulsky, K. V. *Dostoevsky: His Life and Work*, 1967.
Simmons, Ernest J. *Dostoevski: The Making of a Novelist*, 1940.
Wasiolek, Edward. *Dostoevsky: The Major Fiction*, 1964.
Wellek, René, ed. *Dostoevsky: A Collection of Critical Essays*, 1962.
Yarmolinsky, Avrahm. *Dostoevsky: His Life and Art*, 1957.

David E. Robinson

THE HOUSE OF THE SLEEPING BEAUTIES

Author: Yasunari Kawabata (1899-1972)
Type of plot: Psychological realism
Time of plot: 1960
Locale: An unnamed hot-spring resort in Japan
First published: Nemureru bijo, 1960-1961, serial; 1961, book (English
  translation, 1969)

> *Principal characters:*
> YOSHIO EGUCHI, a visitor to an inn at which older men pay to
>   sleep beside drugged young women
> KIGA, the friend who tells Eguchi about the inn
> THE WOMAN, the unnamed manager of the establishment
> SIX SLEEPING BEAUTIES, all anonymous, with whom Eguchi
>   spends five nights

The Novel

The House of the Sleeping Beauties focuses on Yoshio Eguchi, aged sixty-seven, who visits an inn at a Japanese hot-spring resort in order to sleep beside one or another beautiful young woman. The establishment caters to elderly gentlemen who have lost their sexual powers, and the rules of the place explicitly forbid a customer to initiate sexual contact. A girl is drugged, stripped naked, and put to bed in a room hung with red velvet curtains before an old man sees her, and she remains asleep until her customer leaves the next morning. The five chapters of Yasunari Kawabata's novella correspond to Eguchi's five visits to the inn. They trace his search, through memories prompted by the presence of each of the six girls beside whom he sleeps, for understanding of his own imperfect nature and for acceptance of his eventual death.

Eguchi's five visits to the inn occur from autumn to midwinter during a single year, reinforcing the metaphysical thrust of the novel. The girls next to whom he sleeps are alive, responsive to stimulus, but so heavily drugged that he cannot awaken them. Eguchi sees them as corpses; he calls their sleep a form of death. Sensitive to the color, texture, and scent of each girl's body, he finds the experience of lying next to the girls a stimulus to his memory. The patterning of Eguchi's recollections seems random, prompted by the process of association which causes him to think, for example, of the scent of a nursing mother when he joins the first girl in bed one stormy autumn evening. In fact, Eguchi's memories run roughly parallel to the stages of human life. His thoughts during his evening with the first girl relate to innocence, new life, and birth. The things Eguchi contemplates during his final evening at the inn, the one time he has two companions, center on death, life's final experience.

The men patronizing the inn, unlike the girls who work there, are alert throughout their hours in the curtained room. Nevertheless, they too are living corpses, as all men and women are, and it is only a matter of time before one of the inn's patrons dies in the bed of one of the young women. The body is removed to a neighboring inn, one with no secrets to hide, and the facts are concealed to protect the dead man's reputation and the feelings of his family. Eguchi's friend Kiga hears of the death, however, and so Eguchi discusses it with the manager on the evening of his fifth visit. This time, he finds two young women asleep in the curtained room, one of them dark and the other fair, and after Eguchi considers using force to prove his virility on the dark girl, he discovers that she seems to have stopped breathing. The manager removes the girl's body, denying that she is actually dead, and reminds Eguchi that the fair girl is still in bed. "The covers were as they had been, thrown back in confusion, and the naked form of the fair girl lay in shining beauty." The reader is not told if Eguchi gets back into bed with her.

The Characters

The significant action of *The House of the Sleeping Beauties* occurs within Eguchi's consciousness; the girls at the inn neither act nor speak. Eguchi assigns each one a personality based on her physical characteristics and the events in his past that she recalls for him. He does speak with the unnamed woman who runs the inn. The manager is a self-disciplined, unnaturally quiet person, more an emanation of the closely guarded house than an actual woman. She refuses Eguchi's repeated requests for the medication which puts the girls to sleep. This request, like his repeated fantasy of sexually assaulting one of the sleeping girls or strangling her, reflects the internal tensions at work in Eguchi's mind. Initially, he sees his visits to the inn as ways of both affirming and denying the fact that, like most of the place's customers, he is losing his sexual powers. Eguchi repeatedly insists that, unlike the other men, he is still virile and capable of sexual activity. As time passes and Eguchi encounters a different young woman on each of his visits, the emphasis shifts from the sexual dimension of his dilemma to its moral and spiritual ramifications.

Eguchi both fears death and is attracted to it. He uses his experiences at the inn, and the memories that the girls evoke, both to assert his own vitality and to face the emptiness of most of the encounters between men and women. He recalls a youthful trip to Kyoto with a girl he did not marry, an affair with a woman married to a foreigner, and his youngest daughter's marriage to the young man who did not take her virginity. Sexual activity, however pleasurable in itself, seems merely evidence of attachment to the world of human experience. Eguchi finds himself looking at the sleeping beauties beside him and speculating upon the motives leading girls in their teens and twenties to sell themselves to men such as him, and he considers the lives that these girls are likely to lead once they are too old for so innocent a form of prostitution. There is a tradition in Japanese folklore, and Eguchi refers to it, in which prostitutes are incarnations of the Buddha. If the dark girl to whom he is attracted at the end of the novel represents sensuality, the fair girl represents an inviolate purity with certain religious overtones. Eguchi may be choosing between them when he finds the dark girl dead beside him and turns from her to the shining, fair one asleep on his other side.

Kawabata's handling of the sleeping beauties (the literal meaning of the book's title in Japanese) is nothing short of masterful. Lacking knowledge of the men who kiss and fondle them, these girls remain uncorrupted by the experience. They vary in age and appearance, but all manifest the eternal woman. Eguchi sees them as embodiments of life's complexity. His memories of the women he has loved, prompted by the six girls, confirm both his pleasure in his own sexual capacity and his recognition of his moral and spiritual emptiness. Like the Buddha, the sleeping beauties lead Eguchi to self-knowledge. Unwaking themselves, they awaken him.

Themes and Meanings

The central point of *The House of the Sleeping Beauties* is Eguchi's acceptance of his aging body and eventual death. The memories he reviews suggest that, despite his pleasure in sexual activity with many women, he has not made his partners happy or himself achieved satisfaction. With the helping presence of the six sleeping beauties, he learns to accept the loss of this world's pleasures. The focus of the novel is profoundly moral, despite the details of Eguchi's erotic history. This emphasis emerges from Kawabata's typical rendering of action in terms of images and symbolic clues. The central motifs of the novel come together in the final chapter, when Eguchi dreams of the death of his tubercular mother. The details of this scene echo the images he uses to describe his various mistresses. Eguchi recalls the pale skin and dark hair of his dying mother, her cold hands, the redness of the blood she hemorrhages on the bedding, and the withered breasts he massages to relieve the pressure in her lungs. The dream verifies that the woman who brought Eguchi into this world is the most important one in his life, the woman he has always loved, and the one his other women must always fail to replace.

The red curtained chamber at the inn is a womb to which Eguchi retreats to achieve rebirth. The sea and wind he hears outside are the sounds of the body of the primal mother. When the dark girl dies, so does Eguchi's attachment to the world of passion. His association with the fair girl suggests spiritual transcendence. This reading, however, fails to do justice to Kawabata's skill as a writer. The imagery is highly allusive, and the interconnection of the sexual and spiritual dimensions of the motifs is handled more delicately than any paraphrase can suggest. Nevertheless, one theme running throughout nearly all Kawabata's fiction is the contention that life's value and meaning come clear when existence is examined from the perspective of a dying man. In this case, Eguchi's capacity to see truly comes from his use of the sleeping beauties as surrogates for the dying mother in his memory.

Critical Context

The process of Eguchi's enlightenment in this novel is typical of Kawabata's fiction. Similar old men struggle against aging and learn to welcome death in *Meijin* (1942-1954; *The Master of Go*, 1972) and *Yama no oto* (1954; *The Sound of the Mountain*, 1970). Also typical is Eguchi's wistful attraction to innocent young girls. This is the subject of *Izu no odoriko* (1926; *The Izu Dancer*, 1955), Kawabata's first novella, and he returned to it in *Yukiguni* (1947; *Snow Country*, 1956) and *Sembazuru* (1952; *Thousand Cranes*, 1958).

Less characteristic is the tightness of the novel's construction and its sense of completeness. Most of Kawabata's fiction was produced serially, often over long periods of time, and he often returned to earlier material to rework or add to it. *The House of the Sleeping Beauties*, by contrast, was written in a relatively short time, and it does not seem open-ended in the way that *Snow Country* and *Thousand Cranes* do. Eguchi's story is perhaps Kawabata's most thorough analysis, and certainly his most explicit, of the male character type he favored as protagonist. It is also a good example of his treatment of the effects of sexually innocent women on that kind of man.

When Kawabata was awarded the Nobel Prize for Literature in 1968, his ability to convey in fiction the feel of an older way of life in Japan was singled out for comment. On the surface, this is less true of *The House of the Sleeping Beauties*, with its emphasis on the psychology of sexual attraction, than of other of Kawabata's novels. Nevertheless, in the light of the explicitly Buddhist focus of Eguchi's growing understanding of himself, this novella also becomes a book about a traditional aspect of Japanese culture.

Sources for Further Study

Keene, Donald. *Dawn to the West: Japanese Literature in the Modern Era*, 1984.

Lippit, Noriko. *Reality and Fiction in Modern Japanese Literature*, 1980.

Petersen, Gwenn Boardman. *The Moon in the Water: Understanding Tanizaki, Kawabata, and Mishima*, 1979.

Ueda, Makoto. *Modern Japanese Writers and the Nature of Literature*, 1976.

Yamanouchi, Hisaaki. *The Search for Authenticity in Modern Japanese Literature*, 1978.

                                                                                   Robert C. Petersen

THE HOUSE ON THE EMBANKMENT

Author: Yury Trifonov (1925-1981)
Type of plot: Psychological realism
Time of plot: The late 1930's to the early 1970's
Locale: Moscow and Bruskovo
First published: Dom na naberezhnoi, 1976 (English translation, 1983)

> *Principal characters:*
> VADIM ALEXANDROVICH GLEBOV, a literary critic
> A NARRATOR, Glebov's childhood friend who is now a writer
> (and probably was Yura the Bear)
> LEV MIKHAILOVICH SHULEPNIKOV, a childhood friend who
> now holds menial jobs
> SONYA GANCHUK, a childhood friend who becomes Glebov's
> fiancée
> NIKOLIA VASILIEVICH GANCHUK, Sonya's father and a
> professor at the Literary Institute who becomes Glebov's
> dissertation adviser

The Novel

The House on the Embankment, told by two narrators, is a series of inter-twined reminiscences, flashbacks, and episodes, mainly of childhood and young adulthood in Moscow under Joseph Stalin. Most of the novella, told in the third person, relates incidents from the life of Vadim Alexandrovich Glebov. These portions alternate with short chapters told by an unidentified narrator who once knew Glebov.

When the novella begins, Glebov, an irritable middle-aged man, sees an alcoholic porter in a furniture store whom he recognizes as his old friend Lev Mikhailovich Shulepnikov or "Shulepa." At first, Glebov cannot remember his name. Surprisingly, Lev refuses to recognize him. Later that evening, Glebov receives a telephone call from Lev, who tells him that he is being sent "you-know-where" (that is, to prison) and that he used to dislike Glebov.

Lev's puzzling rebuff triggers Glebov's memories of youth and childhood and the luxurious apartment house on the embankment, where many of his childhood friends lived. Glebov was drawn to the house, with its mirrored elevator, balconies, antiques, and interesting books. Next to it and in its shadow was the dilapidated Deryugin Street house, where Glebov and his family lived in one room.

Glebov's childhood world includes Anton, Chemist, Walrus, Lev, Sonya Ganchuk, other classmates, and the belligerent Bychkov children. Nearly all the incidents that Glebov recalls involve fear, humiliation, resentment, or envy. He is intimidated by the elevator man in the apartment house and embarrassed by his anxious father, who treats Lev, the stepson of a powerful man, with respect and tries to impress him. The pain that Glebov senses even as an adult, the "agony from the unfairness of things," begins at approximately the time when Lev moves into the house on the embankment. Glebov is able to bring friends to the cinema without paying, because his mother works in a theater. This small amount of power in his class is demolished when Lev invites a group to his apartment and shows the same film with which Glebov has been tantalizing his classmates. To Glebov's chagrin, Lev also emerges triumphant from a boyish prank to humiliate him. Later, the elder Shulepnikov, learning that Glebov's family wants information, extorts the names of the ringleaders of the prank from Glebov. Believing that his uncle's fate depends on his answer, Glebov, who himself was one of the ringleaders, names Yura the Bear and Manyunya. Bear's parents are forced to leave Moscow, Manyunya is expelled, and Glebov's uncle is sent to prison despite Glebov's attempts to protect him. In another incident, Anton and Lev are attacked by the Deryugin Street gang, led by Minka Bychkov, and the boys' clothes are torn by the Bychkovs' dog. The next day, a mysterious man appears and shoots the dog. Minka is later arrested, and the Bychkovs vanish.

After World War II, Lev and Glebov meet again as graduate students. Lev now has a second stepfather, as powerful as the first. Glebov uses his old friendship with Sonya to develop a personal relationship with her influential father, Professor Nikolia Vasilievich Ganchuk. A crude remark at a party gives Glebov the idea of pursuing Sonya, who has always loved him.

Ironically, Glebov's hopeful alliance with the Ganchuks involves him in a moral dilemma that jeopardizes his future. He unwittingly becomes a pawn in a plot to oust Ganchuk, his dissertation adviser and future father-in-law. When questioned about Ganchuk's ideology, Glebov partially admits what the dean wants to hear. Finally, in effect ordered to speak out publicly against Ganchuk and pressured by Ganchuk's supporters to defend him, Glebov is in a turmoil. He is saved from having to make a decision at that time by the death of his grandmother on the day he is to appear in public. Although Sonya generously offers to release him from their commitment, he leaves her one time with the impression that he will return, but he never does. At another meeting, Glebov says something against Ganchuk, which he is later unable to recall. Lev shows up drunk and muttering at the meeting, and from that point forward, Lev's life goes downhill. When his second stepfather loses his influence, there is nothing to stop his precipitous fall. Both Ganchuk and his wife, Yulia Mikhailovna, lose their positions at the Institute. Ganchuk is later reinstated, his wife dies, and Sonya suffers emotional problems and dies.

Almost two years after seeing Lev in the furniture store, Glebov meets his aristocratic mother on a train to Paris. Although her position in life has suffered, she still retains her arrogance, and Glebov is disturbed by her indifference to him. He learns, however, that she has a widow's pension from her first husband.

Several short chapters are told by a narrator who was once one of the boys in the house on the embankment. His friends were the same children whom Glebov remembers, but he does not include Glebov as part of the group. The narrator was annoyed by Glebov's caution and resented him, partly because Sonya loved him. He believes that Glebov is "a *nothing person*" to the point of genius, and he considers this the key to his luck and later success. The narrator recalls several incidents which Glebov does not recall or remembers differently. The narrator includes himself in his version of the Deryugin gang attack, in which he, Anton, and Lev were beaten. On their next foray down Deryugin Street, neither the gang nor the dog appeared, and the narrator suspected that Glebov had fixed it. He also recalls the humiliation when his family moved from the apartment house, and Glebov's pleasure when he learned that they were moving to a single room in a house without an elevator.

Years later, the narrator interviews Professor Ganchuk for a book. On the anniversary of Sonya's death, they visit her grave near closing time. At first, they are prevented from entering by a surly gatekeeper, whom the narrator recognizes as Lev. The novella ends with Lev looking up at "the long, squat, ugly house on the embankment" and wondering if some miracle might change his life.

The Characters

Glebov is an individual who uses up his vitality achieving what he wants but then is too tired to enjoy it. He attends international literary congresses and has a dacha. The reader assumes that his wife, Marina, was once the student activist Marina Krasnikova, "a loud girl in a perpetual state of excitement," not unlike Glebov's daughter, Margot. Glebov changes from a timid, resentful child into a short-tempered, outwardly successful man. Along the way, he loses his integrity. He misses the opportunity to confront the past and himself with honesty. Although Glebov has some sympathy for others (he feels sorry for the Bychkovs) and a conscience, he rationalizes, fails to see connections, and conveniently forgets. He tells himself that Bear and Manyunya were "bad boys" and that nothing "very terrible" happened to them. Later, he rationalizes his semi-betrayal of Ganchuk by convincing himself that Ganchuk once behaved ruthlessly and that he cannot help him anyway.

As a child, Glebov lived in an atmosphere of anxiety. His father, whose motto was "Don't stick your head out," hid his fear under glib humor: "He seemed to feel suffocated as though by some ancient traumatic fear." Glebov's once understandable fear and resentment become a justification for opportunism and a lack of moral courage. Glebov does not crave power as much as he desires security, success, and genteel comfort. (He loves the old books and carpets in Ganchuk's study.) Glebov is dishonest with himself, about his motives and the harm to others that results. He does not consciously connect the beginning of his physical desire for Sonya with his desire for the Ganchuks' dacha in Bruskovo. When the Ganchuk relationship becomes a hindrance, he loses his desire for her and wonders if it was really love or a only physical attraction. He decides that it was the latter. Sonya is a rare and compassionate individual, with sympathy for everyone. Glebov considers her sympathy indiscriminate and is capable of appreciating Sonya only in a limited way, mainly in terms of how he benefits from her goodness. He cannot admit any connection between her breakdown and his betrayal. Although Glebov compromises himself, he arouses the reader's sympathy.

Lev's slide into obscurity parallels Glebov's rise to success. As an arrogant boy and young man, Lev impresses others with his boldness, lies, and material possessions. Whatever natural confidence he may have is enhanced by his two powerful stepfathers. Lev has a cynical awareness of the reality of power struggles that Glebov lacks. When Glebov asks his help in the Ganchuk affair, Lev becomes angry at his desire to avoid getting his hands dirty—the price of success. To his credit, Lev does not speak out against Ganchuk, but he remains a contemptuous, unpleasant individual.

Several characters represent the older generation that lived through the Bolshevik Revolution. Once a pitiless revolutionary, the old Marxist intellectual Ganchuk is an idealist, a bit self-important but kindly, unlike his mean-spirited enemies at the Institute. Interestingly, after his defeat at the Institute, Ganchuk begins to reassess the idea that troubled Fyodor Dostoevsky: If death is the end, "then *all is permitted.*" His wife, Yulia Mikhailovna, is almost a caricature. Enjoying comfort herself, she rages against the hypocrites who espouse Marxism and secretly harbor bourgeois ideas, and Glebov is one whom she has in mind. Lev's mother embodies some of the worst qualities associated with the czarist nobility: indifference and haughty superiority. In contrast, Glebov's grandmother, a peasant type, compassionately comforts Glebov on the last evening of her life.

The narrator may be identified as Yura the Bear and a persona of the author, Yury Trifonov. The narrator recalls feats of bravery (Bear was the strongest boy) and the shame of moving (Bear's family left Moscow). The novella is, in part, autobiographical. Yury Trifonov's father, like Lev's real father, fell from power and was imprisoned under Stalin in the 1930's. Like Bear, Trifonov would have known the humiliation of no longer belonging. The narrator is honest, for he admits at times that his memory and interpretation may be affected by his resentment of Glebov. He has strong affection for his friends, and his pain of moving is, in large part, the pain of losing his friends. As an adult, he is not afraid to look back.

Themes and Meanings

Reconstructing the past is a central theme in *The House on the Embankment*. While "reality looks different at different times," the outline of the past remains visible. The "skeletal pattern" appears. This theme is developed through the complex narrative structure of shifting time frames. By using two narrators, Trifonov creates a multiple perspective of the past: Glebov's thoughts as related by the narrator, the narrator's semi-detached, sometimes ironic view, and the view of the narrator, who is openly annoyed by Glebov. The structure also illustrates the difficulty in determining when a situation actually begins. Glebov's chance encounter with Lev occurs not in the present, but two years before he meets his mother on the train. In a sense, the action begins and ends with Glebov being snubbed, by Lev and his mother. Lev's hoping for a miracle at the end, a parody of the happy ending of Socialist Realism, is actually in the past. The reader is called upon to reconstruct the order of events and evaluate their meaning.

Another important and related theme is the brutalization of life under Stalin. Oppression is ever-present in Glebov's childhood and youth, even if only as a sinister threat in the background, and its insidious effect appears as fear, hypocrisy, compromise, betrayal, and guilt. The boys' war with the Deryugin Street gang, the literary battles of the 1920's which Ganchuk fought, and the plot at the Institute—all reflect and are metaphors of the larger political struggles. The end of the regime, noted only by a brief mention of Stalin's funeral, is a pivotal point. It accounts for the simultaneous rehabilitation of Lev's real father, the fall of his second stepfather, and the reinstatement of Ganchuk. Viewed against this background, Glebov's behavior, though unethical, appears understandable.

The gray, imposing apartment house on the embankment, which dominated Glebov's childhood and the landscape, is a symbol of the Stalinist regime. Outwardly dull and intimidating, the house contains bourgeois luxuries hypocritically enjoyed by the elite, the Communist bourgeoisie.

There are also allusions to Fyodor Dostoevski's *Prestupleniye i nakazaniye* (1866; *Crime and Punishment*, 1886). Both works contain a compassionate character named Sonya. When Glebov visits the Ganchuks during the plot at the Institute, Ganchuk makes a half-conscious comparison between Glebov and Raskolnikov, the murderer who returned to the scene of the crime in Dostoevski's novel.

The last episode is set symbolically in the monastery cemetery where Sonya is buried. The extinguished crematorium is a symbol of the finality of death; it is "dead death." The eerie cemetery in twilight and mist, with rooks cawing overhead, recalls classical descriptions of entrances to the underworld. Here, however, it is a universe without spiritual consolation.

Critical Context

The House on the Embankment is one of several thematically related works by Trifonov dealing with urban life, disappointments of middle age, grudges, and work and family problems. This group includes the three novellas collected in *Dolgoe proshchanie* (1973; *The Long Goodbye: Three Novellas*, 1978), comprising *Obmen* (1969; *The Exchange*, 1973), *Prevaritalnye itogi* (1970; *Taking Stock*, 1978), and the title piece, *Dolgoe proshchanie* (1971; *The Long Goodbye*, 1978); also in this group is the novella *Drugaya zhizn* (1975; *Another Life*, 1983). These works are part of the decanonization of Socialist Realism, which is characterized by a self-sacrificing, positive hero, an omniscient narrator who views the action from the Olympian vantage point of "history," and an inspirational theme in keeping with official ideology. *The House on the Embankment* may best be described as anti-Socialist Realism; it is marked by the most distinctive feature of Trifonov's works, his concern with *byt* (the trivia of ordinary life), a preoccupation which in large part accounts for the popularity of his works in the Soviet Union. Trifonov's early works include short stories and his first novel, *Studenty* (1950; *Students*, 1953), for which he won the Stalin Prize. His later novel *Starik* (1978; *The Old Man*, 1984), which some consider his masterpiece, continues the theme of confronting the past.

Sources for Further Study

Eberstadt, Fernanda. "Out of the Drawer and into the West," in *Commentary*. CXXIX (July, 1985), pp. 36-44.

Hosking, Geoffrey. "Yury Trifonov," in *Beyond Socialist Realism*, 1980.

McLaughlin, Sigrid. "Jurij Trifonov's *House on the Embankment*: Narration and Meaning," in *Slavic and East European Journal*. XXVI, no. 4 (1982), pp. 419-433.

Pankin, B. "A Circle or a Spiral? On Iurii Trifonov's Novels," in *Soviet Studies in Literature*. XIV (Fall, 1978), pp. 65-100.

Elizabeth Berlings

THE HOUSE ON THE HILL

Author: Cesare Pavese (1908-1950)
Type of plot: Symbolic realism
Time of plot: 1943-1944
Locale: The Piedmont region of Italy, in and around the city of Turin
First published: La casa in collina, 1949 (English translation, 1956)

> *Principal characters:*
> CORRADO, the narrator
> CATE, Corrado's former lover
> DINO, Cate's son

The Novel

The House on the Hill, set in northern Italy in the city of Turin and its surrounding hills, describes events in 1943-1944 as the Allies invade Italy, the
Germans occupy it, various Italian governments claim authority, and armed
partisans take to the hills. Anarchy exists outside the range of the guns of the
nearest political authority.

The narrator, Corrado, ceaselessly moves between the city of Turin, where
he teaches, and the nearby hills, where he lives in a villa owned by Elvira and
her mother. His movement matches that of the city dwellers who go into the
hills at night to escape air raids. There is a feeling of movement without
change as Corrado seeks a peace that always eludes him. At night, Turin
looks calm viewed from the hills; by day, the hills promise haven from dangers in the city.

In the first chapters of this relatively brief novel, Corrado introduces a
number of characters who will be eliminated, one by one, from his life. Some
of his friends have already been killed in the war or imprisoned by the Fascists. Several of his friends are anti-Fascist, especially Fonso, a young partisan who can commit himself to action in ways that Corrado cannot.

Cate, his lover eight or ten years earlier, reenters his life with her son,
Dino. Corrado soon realizes that Dino is probably his child. He reestablishes
his friendship with Cate and spends time talking, studying, and walking with
Dino. Elvira, a forty-year-old spinster, loves the narrator, but he rejects her
with contempt and pity. "We are born and die alone," Corrado tells her, and
she answers: "But we just want a little love. . . ."

In the summer of 1943, the Allies invade Italy, Benito Mussolini is over-
thrown, and the Germans tighten their grip on Turin. As the months pass,
the war becomes more brutal and more personal. Corrado becomes increasingly fearful, not of winter's approaching cold or death rained from bombers,
but because he grasps a secret: Amid the gentle hills and beautiful city,
which promise that the cycle of history will bring a brighter future, bestial

things still happen: "I was beginning to look round me, panting like a hare at its dying gasp." As Fonso and others prepare to go into the hills and join the resistance, Dino is pulled into their orbit, away from Corrado. Cate is imprisoned, perhaps to be shot. The Germans conduct a desultory search for Corrado, evidently wanting him only because of his association with Fonso and Cate. The Germans do not pay much attention to him; maybe, he thinks, because he alone is useless and does not even merit punishment. Elvira arranges for Corrado to hide in a seminary, the College of Chieri, where he is joined by Dino.

Even Chieri does not provide sanctuary. The student body, like the general society, is divided into factions, some students informing on others. In the spring of 1944, the Germans come to Chieri and Corrado flees. Dino has already disappeared, evidently to join the partisans.

Corrado moves to another range of hills, to his family's farm. He threads his way through Italian Fascists, Germans, partisans, and other bands of armed men. Violence is random. The last chapter opens six months after Corrado reaches the farm. Corrado, looking back, regards himself as having lived inauthentically. He has come to know that life consists of something else than what he has lived. The war continues; only for the dead is it really over.

The Characters

Unlike nineteenth century novelists who used the story to display character change and development, Cesare Pavese's concept of character is that of "static essentials." Character does not change but is revealed for what it is. Trapped by events and by his despair and indecision, Corrado is estranged from himself and from those around him. The war does not change him, nor is it the source of his problem, he realizes; it has only removed his already-fading scruples about living alone. It frees him to live for the moment without regrets for lost opportunities and without dwelling on future defeats: "The kind of dull bitterness which had hedged in my youth found a refuge and a horizon in the war."

Corrado's reacquaintance with Cate provides much of the drama of the novel. He loves her but is afraid to recognize his feelings and fears she will attempt to resume their love affair. Elvira loves him and takes risks for him that he could never take himself. He loves Dino but cannot assume a father's role. He cannot commit himself to involvement in the war that has consumed so many of his friends; it seems to be only a cruel and implacable force from which he tries to find a safe haven. He understands better than any of his partisan friends what is at stake, but he cannot act on his understanding, partly because of his intellectual need to resolve all contradictions before he acts. He cannot even blame the Germans for what they are doing; evil was loose in Italy before the Germans arrived.

Corrado only wants peace, a place of refuge, sanctuary. He fears the open horizon, wishing that the college at Chieri was walled in like a tomb. He fears even Dino, because in joining him the boy might give him away. He tries to find peace by separating himself from people, by withdrawing to church and prayer, and by immersing himself in nature. Yet there is no peace because the alienation is within him. Corrado runs not only from the Germans but from his own sorrow and remorse as well. He is nonjudgmental toward everyone except himself. He is the detached observer, who feels guilty for his detachment. He is self-centered; he does not pray for the peace of the world, he says, but for his own peace, and acts in a virtuous manner only in the hope that it will bring him safety. In despair, he regards people as a threat, while believing life to be meaningful only if lived with other people.

Cate, in contrast, is self-possessed, mature, independent, and at peace amid the chaos and danger. She does not expect perfection in herself or others. Although she had been betrayed by Corrado years earlier, she feels no anger toward him, only sorrow for his inability to live fully. Cate refuses to confirm to Corrado that Dino is his son because she realizes that Corrado cannot cope with that threat to his isolation. She encourages him to become friends with Dino, but on his own terms, allowing him to commit himself to the extent that he is capable. She tells Corrado that he is afraid not of the war but of other people, including even Dino. When Cate is captured and imprisoned by the Germans for her connection with the partisans, Corrado's first reaction is fear, terror so great that he dares not even think of Cate, hoping, he says, that that proves his innocence.

Fonso, a teenage boy, is a happy-go-lucky person, optimistic and joyous without engaging in bravado and without deluding himself about the seriousness and danger of his work with the partisans. He has a lightness of spirit and an ability to commit himself in ways that Corrado can admire but cannot emulate.

Corrado says that he does not love Italy, only Italians. In the minor characters, Pavese introduces Italians of every sort: teachers, students, peasants, priests, workers, Fascists, partisans, and the majority, who are simply trying to survive amid a storm of random violence, people who, like Corrado, flee before the implacable forces that threaten them.

Themes and Meanings

Cesare Pavese, like the narrator, Corrado, was born in Piedmont and lived most of his life there, in the hills and in the city of Turin. He was, like Corrado, attracted to the anti-Fascists and exiled himself to a family farm in 1944. Pavese's love affairs evidently were as unsatisfactory, even dangerous, to him as were Corrado's. Unlike Corrado, however, who seems almost paralyzed, Pavese was an immensely hard worker who turned out a large volume of excellent work before his carefully planned suicide in 1950.

Pavese did not regard his novels as "entertainments," entertaining though they were. He used them to explore the central existential concerns of humans in the twentieth century. His narrators, themselves flawed, are often individuals driven, like Pavese, to seek moral and ethical perfection in an imperfect world. In his various works, Pavese examined the meaning of myth, the need for work and solitude, the joy and menace of love, the role and nature of women, and the necessity of overcoming what he believed was traditional Italian misogyny.

In *The House on the Hill*, Pavese explores the tension between individual needs and social responsibility. Corrado requires solitude to maintain his sanity, even his will to live. He cannot cope with the intrusive bustle of the world around him or the ethical compromises required in everyday life. Corrado intellectually understands the need to assume responsibility that comes with his loving Cate and Dino and with his recognition of political evils in Italy, but he cannot reconcile his inner needs with his larger obligations. He, like Pavese, tortured by existential loneliness, can respond with understanding and compassion but not with action to join others in loving relationships or in resistance to evil. Corrado, and perhaps eventually Pavese, cannot find a path that allows one to maintain personal integrity while assuming social responsibility in a flawed world. He can, he finds, respond only by gaining self-knowledge and by honoring the dead—especially those who died because of commitments they made—with humility and compassion.

Critical Context

Pavese translated many American literary works into Italian and wrote extensively on the literature of Walt Whitman, Sherwood Anderson, and others. Captivated by the vigor of the American language, especially its slang and its connection with the life of the people, he wanted to use it as a base to reinvigorate Italian literary language and tried to connect the language of his writings with the everyday life of the Italians.

At the time of his death in 1950, Pavese had achieved recognition as one of the foremost Italian, and European, literary figures. His cool and detached style, and his exploration of alienation and despair fit the existential currents sweeping postwar Europe. *The House on the Hill* was, perhaps, his most fully realized work.

Pavese placed *The House on the Hill* in the category of "symbolic realism." His style, elliptic and oblique, fits the character of Corrado, an observer of life who is captivated, and perhaps trapped, by the ambiguity of his makeup and historical situation. Pavese's allusive language enhances and reinforces the ambience of ambiguity. Corrado is not an omniscient narrator who knows and tells all, but one who hints at certain truths while at the same time offering countersuggestions and ambiguities. Pavese uses dialogue to give flashes of insight into characters and situations, but these exchanges seldom exceed a few sentences; conversations are terse and enigmatic.

Pavese's quiet, objective tone reinforces the sense of estrangement emanating from Corrado, as he calmly and clearly describes the horrors and chaos about him. Pavese's style is earthy, but light and delicate rather than blunt and heavy. One senses Corrado's rootedness in the forests and wild lands of the Piedmontese hills and in the streets and suburbs of Turin, yet he remains the detached observer, turning nature, institutions, people, and even his own son, into symbols. He intellectualizes his experiences and cannot commit himself to one mode of existence or another.

Sources for Further Study
Biasin, Gian-Paolo. *The Smile of the Gods: A Thematic Study of Cesare Pavese's Works*, 1968.
Lajolo, Davide. *An Absurd Vice: A Biography of Cesare Pavese*, 1983.
Thompson, Doug. *Cesare Pavese: A Study of the Major Novels and Poems*, 1982.

William E. Pemberton

HOW IT IS

Author: Samuel Beckett (1906-   )
Type of plot: Existential allegory
Time of plot: Unspecified
Locale: A wasteland of mud
First published: Comment c'est, 1961 (English translation, 1964)

> *Principal characters:*
> BOM, the narrator, a wanderer across a surrealistic landscape
> of slime
> PIM, the narrator's companion during the middle third of the
> novel

The Novel

How It Is chronicles a journey which is, for the most part, maddeningly static. The tale is told in first person by the protagonist, who is crawling through the mud. He moves an arm, then a leg. He pushes, pulls, and laboriously progresses ten or fifteen yards. Over his shoulder he carries a sack, which he must constantly shift and rearrange. In the sack are tins, or cans, the contents of which he does not describe.

The setting is nightmarish. The entire terrain is mud, and the duration of the action is unmeasurable. The narrator speaks not in sentences but in fragments. Many of these fragments are repeated throughout the text, as if to give the impression that the journey keeps bending back upon itself. Other details combine to make the journey seem like frustrating dreams that all readers have experienced. The narrator is constantly aware of the vast stretch of time, which by implication dwarfs all of his efforts. He inserts the Latin term *quaqua* (in all directions) at various syntactical positions in his monologue, suggesting that these efforts are dispersed almost as soon as they are made.

The narrator struggles to complete an act in some satisfactory manner, but every action is frustratingly laborious: shifting the sack from one side to the other, loosening the cord at the mouth of the sack, reaching deep into the sack for a tin, finding an opener for the tin. Then he drops the opener into the mud and thrashes about in search of it. Periodically, he vomits and defecates into the mire; perhaps his vomit and excrement are the sources of the mire.

There is, however, a progression to the narrative. The protagonist is seeking after Pim, and this quest gives the novel its three formal divisions: the time before Pim, the time with Pim, and the time after Pim. The time before Pim has overtones of infancy and childhood. The protagonist has several fleeting memories of his mother. She is huge, because he is so small, and she offers him a love that is severe. She drones a snatch of the Apostles' Creed. Next comes the memory of a redheaded, pudding-faced girl with a protruding belly; under an April or May sky, she and the protagonist cross pastures hand in hand until the pair disappear from view. These images come and go quickly, providing the traveler with only a brief respite from his squalid trek.

In part 2, the narrator finds Pim. He also acquires a name, observing that Pim has chosen to call him Bom. Pim, holding a sack of his own, is lying face down in the mud. Bom throws his right leg across the other man's legs and pinions him. Pim is unresponsive; if he attempts to speak, his mouth fills with mud. Bom claws Pim's armpits with his fingernails. He thumps Pim on the skull. He fishes out the opener and stabs Pim in the buttock. He pounds Pim's kidney as with a pestle. Pim finally responds with a song, presumably wordless. Bom attempts to identify with Pim, and it becomes increasingly difficult for the reader to determine who is doing what to whom.

The narrator is abandoned by Pim in part 3 and is again alone. In this final section of the novel, the narrator becomes ruminative and discursive. He describes life's journey as a closed curve having four parts: First, the traveler seeks a victim; second, he finds and torments a victim; third, he loses his victim; fourth, he becomes a victim himself. Yet, since every traveler is both the seeker and the sought, the tormentor and the victim, parts 2 and 4 are actually the same part—thus, the tripartite structure of the novel.

Finally, the narrator shakes the reader's confidence in everything that has gone before. He denies the authenticity of the journey and of its formulation in part 3. He concludes that it was "all balls from start to finish."

The Characters

The characterization in *How It Is* is as circular as the plot. The narrator is Bom, the protagonist. Pim, the antagonist, is Bom's alter ego, his *Doppelgänger*. Perhaps they have no separate identities at all. In part 2, the narrator occasionally calls them Kram and Krim, as if to demonstrate how little of the self is revealed by arbitrary designations.

In a way, Bom embarks upon a very familiar literary journey. "Life" is surely the antecedent of the "It" in the title, so Bom is making the archetypal journey from the womb to the tomb. Indeed, he states repeatedly and overtly that his life is the thing under discussion. On several occasions in part 1, Bom assumes the fetal position, his knees drawn up, his back bent in a hoop. At this point in the narrative, the sack—an ambiguous symbol throughout—reinforces the womb motif.

Yet Bom's journey through life is markedly unlike that of Christian in John Bunyan's *The Pilgrim's Progress* (1678), for example. Whereas the traditional symbolic journey is from dawn to sunset, from east to west, Bom travels, rather perversely, from left to right, from west to east. The reversed direction underscores the futility of the quest. The setting is a landscape of the mind. It is reminiscent of Dante's terrain in the third circle of the Inferno, thus suggesting that consciousness is a kind of Hell. Bom's consistently scatological description of his journey emphasizes the perceived nastiness of physical experience: He is obsessed with the "arse," both Pim's and his own, and in describing his birth, he states that he was "shat" into the world.

Bom and Pim are, in the final analysis, representative characters. They are Everyman and his elusive sense of selfhood. Some critics have described the travels of Bom and Pim as a movement from macrocosm to microcosm, a journey toward the core of consciousness. The sacks that the characters wear around their necks hold the tins that, in turn, hold the meaning of existence. Yet Bom (consciousness) must fumble about deep in his sack, in search of the proper tin. Then he must find the opener with which he can unlock Pim's inner being (the self). This effort is constantly frustrated, and the implication of the journey as it is described is that the effort never can succeed.

The relationship between the characters Bom and Pim is succinctly expressed in part 3: They are "always two strangers uniting in the interests of torment."

Themes and Meanings

The theme of *How It Is* is the human being's quest for the core of selfhood. The discovery of this core—within one of the tins within the sack—would give life meaning. The insoluble problem, however, is that the self is simultaneously an entity and a duality. The fetid landscape of the narrative is the microcosm within which the perceiving self attempts to explore the objective self. The closer the perceiving self's approach to the objective self, the narrower and more distorted is the perspective. Each time the narrator thinks that he has experienced an insight, he immediately realizes that it will not serve, that something was wrong there.

The novel presents an absurdist view of existence. Because the narrator has consciousness, he is driven to understand "how it is." Because he never can understand, consciousness affords only mental anguish. The stream-of-consciousness narrative is appropriate to the setting, which is the human mind. The syntactical fragments, the repetitions, and the *non sequiturs* reflect the fits and starts of the narrator's journey of perception.

Samuel Beckett's view of life is unrelentingly pessimistic. Since true self-awareness can never be attained, talk about it (such as the narrator's rambling talk in this novel) is absurd. Beckett has the final voice in the narrative to cancel all the descriptions of movement that have gone before. All that has been told is negated, but the narrator has been preparing the reader for this conclusion throughout the telling. He repeatedly characterizes speech as merely a brief movement of the lower face, thus trivializing it. Toward the end of the novel, the narrator reflects upon "all we extort and endure from one another from the one to the other inconceivable end of this immeasurable wallow." If language is futile, is it not better to be silent? If the only end of striving is torment, is it not better to lie quietly, face down in the mud?

Critical Context

How It Is, Beckett's sixth novel and his fourth written originally in French, continues to develop his central theme of the meaninglessness of existence. Its initial publication in 1961, however, seemed to evidence some literary meaning since it, in part, occasioned the awarding of the International Publishers Prize to the author in that same year. The ten-thousand-dollar prize, which Beckett shared with Jorge Luis Borges, was for the body of his work, but *How It Is* was cited particularly, along with the novels *Molloy* (1951; English translation, 1955), *Malone meurt* (1951; *Malone Dies*, 1956), and *L'Innommable* (1953; *The Unnamable*, 1958).

Beckett is perhaps even better known as a dramatist, as a leading member of the Theater of the Absurd. In plays such as *En attendant Godot* (1952; *Waiting for Godot*, 1954) and *Fin de partie* (1957; *Endgame*, 1958), the denuded settings and laconic characters seem to be leading the drama toward silence. Certain critics insist that some hope can be found behind Beckett's black despair. Yet they are inevitably forced to use tenuous arguments—for example, that the very act of writing a novel or play is a refutation of total nihilism.

Throughout Beckett's career, stream of consciousness has been his habitual literary form. In the 1930's, he took dictation from a fellow Dubliner, the nearly blind James Joyce, and copied out parts of Joyce's *Finnegans Wake* (1939). Though the stream-of-consciousness technique may have derived from Joyce, Beckett's style is unmistakably his own. In *How It Is*, he takes Macbeth's observation that life "is a tale told by an idiot . . . signifying nothing" to its ultimate, disturbing conclusion.

Sources for Further Study

Abbot, H. Porter. "Other Worlds: The Artist as Planetary Engineer," in *The Fiction of Samuel Beckett: Form and Effect*, 1973.

Barnard, C. J. "The Thing Itself," in *Samuel Beckett, A New Approach: A Study of the Novels and Plays*, 1970.

Brée, Germaine. "The Strange World of Beckett's *Grands Articulés*," in *Samuel Beckett Now: Critical Approaches to His Novels, Poetry, and Plays*, 1970. Edited by Melvin J. Friedman.

Kenner, Hugh. *A Reader's Guide to Samuel Beckett*, 1973.

Rosen, Steven J. "Against Consolation," in *Samuel Beckett and the Pessimistic Tradition*, 1976.

Patrick Adcock

I AM A CAT

Author: Sōseki Natsume (Kinnosuke Natsume, 1867-1916)
Type of plot: Satiric novel
Time of plot: 1905-1906
Locale: The house and immediate neighborhood of a Japanese schoolteacher
First published: Wagahai wa Neko de aru, 1905-1906, 2 volumes (English
   translation, 1906, 1909)

Principal characters:
   THE NARRATOR, an unnamed cat
   KUSHAMI SENSEI, the cat's owner, a teacher of English
   MEITEI, a friend of Kushami
   KANGETSU, Kushami's former pupil, a graduate student in
      science
   KANEDA, a neighbor and businessman

The Novel

   I Am a Cat satirizes the life of Japanese intellectuals at the turn of the century. The episodic novel, narrated in the first person by a cat, proceeds as a
series of discussions on a variety of historical, artistic, and philosophical
topics, such as the history of peacocks as food, the mechanics of hanging, the
decline of traditional Japanese attitudes. These discussions are often sparked
by the personal experiences and memories of the main human characters or
the cat-narrator.
   The novel begins with the cat finding himself a home in the household of a
teacher. The first two chapters make the most use of the idiosyncratic point
of view of a cat. Thus, the first part of the narrative refers to the other cats in
the neighborhood, in particular his romantic interest in a female cat and his
strategy in dealing with a bully cat. The narrator, nimbly able to slip in un-
noticed anywhere he wishes, observes the peculiar habits of human beings,
leading to some sly, witty conclusions about the superiority of cats. At one
point, for example, the narrator ponders the possibility of organizing a cat
revolt against humanity.
   The third chapter, which starts with the announcement of the death of the
female cat, marks a shift, as if the author needed the stimulus of fresh characters to continue. The narrator states outright that he is inclined to forget
that he is a cat, a hint from the author that the focus will change. A slender
plot line is introduced when Mrs. Kaneda, also referred to as Mrs. Nose,
comes to the Kushami household to garner information about Kangetsu as a
possible husband for her daughter. Her husband, a wealthy businessman, will
allow the marriage if Kangetsu finishes his thesis and earns his Ph.D. This
proposal sets off another series of discussions, half serious, half comical, on

the functions of noses, the wisdom of marrying, the questionable ethics of businessmen, and the subject of Kangetsu's thesis.

The novel ambles along, alternating stretches of human conversations, which get longer, with the narrator's feline observations and antics. The seventh chapter, for example, starts with the cat's thoughts about sports and games and continues with a description of his favorite activities, such as jumping suddenly on a child's back, hunting praying mantises or cicadas, peering at naked bodies in public baths. The basic method of the novel, beginning with a specific act or thought which by association leads to more abstract and philosophical discussions, is maintained. When in chapter 8 neighborhood tensions rise between the passive intellectuals who gather at the teacher's house and the rambunctious students who cut through his property, the narrator observes that teasing monkeys and schoolteachers is a human way of showing superiority. He then falls into a meditation on frenzy, insanity, and thus back to the students' battle with authority.

Finally, in the eleventh chapter, the neighborhood battle ends when Kangetsu announces that he has married a hometown girl. A minor character, a former houseboy of the Kushami household, enters to announce his engagement to the businessman's daughter. The people who have gathered drink beer in celebration, an act which precipitates the abrupt ending. The cat sips the remaining beer; his intoxication makes him want to walk. He falls into a rain barrel and, unable to claw his way to the rim, he stops struggling and drowns. The novel ends with his dying prayer to Buddha.

The Characters

The title of the novel in Japanese, *Wagahai wa Neko de aru*, uses the formal first person pronoun to refer to a cat, bestowing on the animal narrator an ironically elevated status. Sōseki is evidently poking fun at himself and human beings in general on several levels, through the dual perspective of a cat who lives in the home of an English teacher.

First, the cat behaves and thinks like a cat. Some hilarious passages arise from the clash between the worlds of cats and humans, as when the narrator decides to try some leftover rice cakes and gets completely entangled in the sticky mess, or when he remarks on the superiority of cats who wear no clothes and yet are never naked.

Second, the cat has the characteristics not only of a human but also of a widely read, literate, and perceptive one, much like the author, who is able to read diaries and refer breezily to great historical figures in both Western and Eastern civilization. At the same time, the cat's master is an English teacher, as Sōseki himself was; the cat mercilessly mocks the habits of his master, who locks himself in his study after coming home from school, ostensibly to read and study, but who more often than not falls asleep over his book. The cat perceives his master as an ineffectual, introverted man who tries in vain to improve himself, trying the art of writing poetry or painting watercolors, but constantly subject to his physical ailments.

Third, the cat, a homeless orphan who must attach himself to a household, shares a similarity of background with the author, who himself had an unstable childhood. Sōseki was the youngest in a family of eight children; he was actually brought up by foster parents until he was nine, when he was returned to his parents. Other experiences influenced his independent outlook. After studying and teaching for several years, Sōseki went to England for two years to study English literature; though he studied hard, he made no friends and left England with a distinctly soured attitude toward the English. Even this miserable experience had a positive effect on his writing, an effect manifested in his choice of a cat, one of the more independent household pets, as a narrator. Unlike many of his Japanese contemporaries, Sōseki dared to form his own opinions of English literature and to view the influence of Western civilization in Japan with foreboding, a characteristic evident in the detached, mocking tone he gives to his cat narrator.

The other male characters in the novel serve primarily as mouthpieces for different points of view in the many conversations which are the main delight of the book. Women are minor characters, their function subservient to the comforts of the men. When they appear for any length of time, they are the objects of derision, from the point of view of both the cat and the male characters.

Themes and Meanings

The setting of the novel, contemporaneous with the Russo-Japanese War, in the late Meiji era, was a time of great change in Japan. New social classes were formed as the result of the rise of Japanese capitalism; the eagerness to adopt Western ways also led to social changes. Sōseki's personal experiences with the West convinced him that hasty changes motivated by the outside world were, if not dangerous, at least foolhardy. His own response, evident even in this early novel, is to achieve some balance between Eastern and Western cultures.

The choice of a cat narrator allows Sōseki to handle these serious themes lightly. The cat refers to himself proudly as a Japanese cat, prepared to join with other Japanese cats to fight in the Russo-Japanese War. When the female cat dies, the narrator observes that her owners buried her with the proper Buddhist rites, just as if she were a human being. The conflation of the cat world with the human world thus suggests a similar synthesis of two separate cultures.

The conversations which make up the bulk of *I Am a Cat* show at least the intellectual's attempt at this synthesis. References to the history and literature of both Western and Eastern cultures abound. The episodic nature of the novel and its satiric tone evoke the eighteenth century English tradition of Laurence Sterne in *Tristam Shandy* (1759-1767), Jonathan Swift in *Gulliver's Travels* (1726), and the Japanese tradition of *shaseibun* (sketch writing).

Yet Sōseki does not take the intelligentsia too seriously either. If the group of talkers who meet at the teacher's house feel superior to the businessman who grubs for money, they are made aware that intellectuals, too, must have a crass social value in this new world. The businessman will accept a scientist as a son-in-law provided he has the right degree; he wants only the worldly symbol of education, the degree of Ph.D. Sōseki slyly pokes fun at his own world; Kangetsu's thesis is "The Effects of Ultra-Violet Rays on the Electro Movement Action of the Frog's Eyeball." To analyze the effects, Kangetsu grinds away at crystal balls, trying to get the exact shape of a frog's eyeball, from morning until night, seven days a week, for months at a stretch. It is a devastating critique of the nature of scholarship.

A letter from the provinces to one of the characters inserts another serious note; it mentions the classmates who died or were injured in the war, contrasting that stark reality with the leisurely life of the central characters. The stimulating, original opinions voiced in the rambling conversations also contrast with the equally detailed descriptions of the teacher's physical ailments and his inability to act. When his wife finally persuades him to take her to a theater performance, for example, Kushami becomes ill and does not recover until it is too late to attend. Set against each other, the misfortunes of those who must leave their homes to fight and die for Japan with the intellectual who gets ill at the thought of any extra exertion even for entertainment, these incidents serve as Sōseki's critique of his own intellectual environment.

Ultimately, however, the lighthearted tone which permeates the book, and which is reinforced by the unusual point of view, blunts the effect of the satire. The abrupt death of the narrator suggests that Sōseki could find no other way to end a novel that, having no underlying structure or overall theme to carry it forward, could ramble on endlessly.

Critical Context

Though *I Am a Cat* was one of Sōseki's first publications, it is considered by some to be his masterpiece. The unusual point of view gives it a unique status not only in Japanese but also in world literature. The startling novelty of the narrative voice made the first chapter and its author an immediate success. Some critics find, however, that the looseness of the structure, inevitable given Sōseki's original intention of writing only one chapter but continuing to eleven because of popular demand, detracts from its appeal as a serious work.

Born a year before the Meiji Restoration of 1868, Sōseki grew up and wrote at a time when Japanese literature started flourishing again after a sterile period. The emperor Meiji's avowed intention was to open Japan to the knowledge of the rest of the world for the good of the nation. Japanese translations of works from all over the world were bountiful, giving the Japanese easy access to Western literature. Trained as a scholar in both the classical Chinese literature, which had dominated in Japan, and English literature, especially of the eighteenth century, Sōseki was also rare among Japanese scholars of his day in forming his own theories of literature in his classroom. Two of his lectures, *Bungakuron* (1907; a study of literature) and *Bungaku Hyōron* (1909; literary criticism), were published. As is apparent in the final chapter of *I Am a Cat*, Sōseki felt the tension between the traditional Japanese loyalty to the family, to the nation, to the larger group outside the self and the new sense of individualism. As is apparent from the title and the exploration of his personal opinions in the novel, he believed to some extent in the importance of the individual.

As he was finishing *I Am a Cat*, Sōseki was also writing what proved to be his most popular work, *Botchan* (1906; English translation, 1918). Sōseki's later and much more serious novels develop themes introduced in these two early works. His style varies considerably from book to book, making it impossible to classify his work as a whole; Sōseki himself did not belong to the schools of Romanticism or naturalism which dominated the literary scene. Yet the comic tone of his early work, especially *I Am a Cat*, his colloquial style, and his amusing philosophical discussions continue to attract a wide readership in Japan. Sōseki remains one of the most admired and influential writers in Japan.

Sources for Further Study
Doi, Takeo. *The Psychological World of Natsume Sōseki*, 1976.
Kato, Shuichi. "The Age of Meiji," in *The History of Japanese Literature.* Vol. 3, *The Modern Years*, 1983.
Keene, Donald. "Natsume Sōseki," in *Dawn to the West: Japanese Literature in the Modern Era*, 1984.
McClellan, Edwin. *Two Japanese Novelists: Sōseki and Tōson*, 1969.
Yamanouchi, Hisaaki. "The Agonies of Individualism: Natsume Sōseki," in *The Search for Authenticity in Modern Japanese Literature*, 1978.
Yu, Beongcheon. *Natsume Sōseki*, 1969.

Shakuntala Jayaswal

IF NOT NOW, WHEN?

Author: Primo Levi (1919-1987)
Type of plot: Wartime realism
Time of plot: 1943 to 1945
Locale: Russia, Poland, Germany, and Italy
First published: Se non ora, quando?, 1982 (English translation, 1985)

Principal characters:
> MENDEL, a Red Army gunner who has become detached
> from his regiment and joined the partisans
> LEONID, a Red Army soldier who has escaped from a
> concentration camp and joined the partisans
> GEDALEH, a legendary partisan hero and the leader of a
> Jewish partisan unit
> EMMELINE (LINE), a partisan with a strong political
> background as a Socialist, Zionist, and feminist
> ULYUBIN, the authoritarian leader of a highly trained Russian
> partisan unit

The Novel

If Not Now, When? chronicles the exploits, sufferings, fears, and hopes of a band of Jewish partisans behind enemy lines in Russia and Poland. Its twelve chapters run in chronological sequences, the first covering July, 1943, and the last July and August, 1945.

The wife, home, and village of Mendel, the principal character, have been wiped out by the Nazis, and Mendel himself has become separated from his frontline Red Army regiment in German-occupied territory. He is joined by Leonid, a Red Army soldier not yet twenty years old, who has escaped from a concentration camp. The two men tramp across country, cold, hungry, and continually on the alert. Mendel is determined to join a partisan group, and Leonid, whose experiences have enclosed him in a wall of silent bitterness, reluctantly follows. After being rejected by the first partisan group they contact because they are Jews, the two finally join a Jewish partisan unit in a ruined abbey surrounded by marshland, and Leonid finds new strength and hope, thanks to a young woman and fighter named Emmeline, known to everyone as "Line." To impress her, Leonid unexpectedly takes the lead in a sabotage mission, but he is disappointed when it is not completely successful.

At this point, the legendary violin-playing Jewish partisan leader, Gedaleh, who is temporarily working with a crack Russian group under the leadership of Ulyubin, invites the small Jewish group to join an ambush on a hunting party which includes important German officers. Gedaleh is anxious to prove to his highly trained non-Jewish comrades that Jews can match both their courage and their military skill. Unfortunately, the ambush goes tragically wrong, and the Germans attack the partisan's abbey retreat. Mendel, Leonid, and Line are among the few survivors.

Unwilling to stop fighting, the three companions manage to find and join Ulyubin's camp, which is hidden in a dense forest. They are amazed by its size, military organization, and discipline yet are disappointed to find that Gedaleh is away on a mission. Following a particularly daring sabotage exploit, they learn that the Germans are about to attack the camp. The unit is preparing to move when a group of tired and ragged men and women fighters—survivors of the ghettos of many different regions—arrives, headed by Gedaleh, whose flamboyant personality and flair for the unexpected dominate the rest of the book.

In the spring of 1944, the Russian front is rapidly advancing toward the Partisans. Near the Polish border, Ulyubin and Gedaleh part company. Mendel and the other Jews in Ulyubin's unit elect to go forward with Gedaleh into Poland, as all but one have lost home and family, and they hope to reach Palestine via Italy, to start a new life. The group is soon joined by Piotr, a Christian member of Ulyubin's unit who has quarreled with Ulyubin. Piotr's reappearance sparks off a high-spirited celebration, in which Gedaleh sings a song with the refrain, "If I'm not for myself, who will be for me? If not this way, how? And if not now, when?"

With typical panache, Gedaleh announces that they will enter Poland by train. The partisans capture a train and cross the border in it, with Mendel driving. This remarkable journey ends when the Gedalists dismount and send the locomotive crashing into a repair shed to remove its usefulness to the enemy. Now in Poland, the unit continues its sabotage of the Germans but meets with hostility from the local people. Even after they help a stricken peasant village with the harvest, the Jewish partisans' welcome is mixed. After a frank discussion about anti-Semitism, the mayor of the village tells them, "I'm glad I met you. . . . I'm glad I talked with you the way a man speaks with friends, but I am also glad you are going away."

At the end of the summer, Poland is in chaos. The Germans, retreating on all fronts, vent their fury against both peasants and partisans. The Gedalists become increasingly disgusted and weary of the war, especially when they have arrived too late on a rescue attempt at a small concentration camp. Sickened at the carnage, they mount an attack on the guards of the camp, trying to free the remaining prisoners, and Leonid, distraught after learning that Line is now sleeping with Mendel, fights heroically but suicidally and is killed. The Gedalists slay the guards and release the Jewish survivors—only ten out of a group of 120. Yet despite all the anguish and suffering, there is a camp wedding, at which the pregnant bride, Rokhele, has persuaded Mendel to officiate. For once, there is much gaiety and music.

The war in Europe is over by the time the group reaches Germany. Nevertheless, they meet with racist insults and open hostility. In a heated confrontation, a woman partisan is shot dead by an unidentifiable German, and the Gedalists, enraged by this gratuitous peacetime murder, attack the town hall, killing everyone. Later, they express mixed feelings about their spontaneous act of revenge. The partisans continue their journey to Palestine. Soon after reaching Italy, where they are received kindly, Rokhele goes into labor. Mendel and the others gather at the hospital, where the baby is born on August 7, 1945. Ironically, a doctor rushes in at the same time with a newspaper headlining the dropping of the first bomb on Hiroshima.

The Characters

The novel teems with colorfully drawn characters from Eastern Europe and the Soviet republics, both Jews and non-Jews, each with his or her own national political and personal history. These figures represent a complex interaction of contradictory forces, with the Jewish partisans at the center. Fifteen or more named Gedalists are given highly individualized personalities; their backgrounds and views may differ widely, but they are bound together by a shared heritage of age-old persecution, and by a common language (Yiddish), combined with a knowledge, no matter how slight it is in some cases, of Talmudic culture. These elements color everything they do and say.

One of the ways in which Levi achieves such convincing representations of "real" people is by having them talk and think in terms of their own work or skills. Mendel provides a particularly vivid example of this approach. A former watch mender, he observes people in terms of gears wrongly meshed, of springs too tightly wound, and he sums up situations by comparing their dynamics with those of a working watch. Mendel weaves this practical approach to life into a philosophical context gleaned from the Old Testament.

Gedaleh's points of reference are his love of poetry and music, particularly his violin, which, according to legend, once saved him from a bullet. He carries his beloved instrument with him everywhere and plays it in the most unexpected places. The violin is a symbol for him not merely of survival but of positive survival with a love of life. Gedaleh is the least theoretical of the group of Jews—a figure of spontaneity and a lover of simple pleasures.

As a leader, he does not plan ahead as does Ulyubin but relies instead on flashes of inspiration to flesh out a broad, overall plan. Gedaleh's intense interest in other people and his contempt for bureaucracy and the rigid discipline of the Russian and Polish units is contrasted, sometimes satirically, with Ulyubin's dry authoritarianism. This contrast also establishes the imaginative working style of the Jewish unit and the friendly, quarrelsome, and occasionally chaotic atmosphere of its camp.

Line, the daughter of revolutionaries who named her after Emmeline

Pankhurst, is an activist like her parents. She adds a political edge to the narrative. A committed Zionist and Socialist, she often adopts a sharper attitude than her comrades. When Mendel, after the vengeful attack on the German town, questions the morality of paying for blood with more blood, Line tells him he is counting wrongly. The ten they killed have to be accounted not against the death of one partisan but against the millions at Auschwitz. Strongly feminist, Line always insists that she should receive the same training as the men and demands the same right to sexual freedom which the men take for granted.

Leonid is the least resilient of the partisans. Childhood neglect and sufferings in the concentration camp have left him embittered, robbing him of the will to survive. Only his attachment to Line keeps him going. When he loses her, he too is lost.

Piotr, the Christian who remains with the Gedalists, plays an important role in helping the Jews to define themselves. His gruff questions and teasing force them to try to explain the essence of the convoluted, paradoxical, and self-mocking style of their thinking and their humor. Oddly enough, the least convincing of the characters are the Italians, whom Levi has depicted with a degree of sentimentality and idealization refreshingly absent from his pithy depiction of the Jews.

Themes and Meanings

Beneath the action of the book lies a turbulent complex of ideas and discussions on fundamental and interlinked themes, such as the nature of heroism and self-sacrifice; historic, political, and personal motivations; the insidious and destructive power of racism; and the reality of being Jewish in a hostile world. The exploits of the partisans are recounted with the breathtaking tension of a wartime thriller, but Primo Levi never lets them remain mere adventures. Every achievement carries elements of failure; every positive action has a negative reaction. Levi also refers in several different ways to the sense of freedom the Jewish fighters experience when, away from the atmosphere of suspicion and bigotry of the towns and villages, they take to the fields and woods, in control of their own destinies.

In the many discussions around the camp, the partisans ask themselves whether they are Russian Jews or Jewish Russians. Most of them had started with a Russian identity, but with their families and homes now destroyed and their continuing encounters with anti-Semitism, their Jewish identity becomes dominant. The watershed proves to be the crossing of the Polish border. Not long afterward, Gedaleh, who periodically disappears for secret meetings with nameless contacts, tells his followers that they are no longer under Russian command; the group will remain autonomous but is now working under the Jewish Combat Organization.

Levi's language is consistently simple and natural, but because he reinforces it with metaphor, unpretentious symbolism, and biblical allusion, it can comfortably encompass complex ideas. The contradictions and ambiguities which run throughout the book reach their culmination in the powerful final paragraph with the joyous birth of the baby and the dropping of the first atomic bomb. Nevertheless, Levi's affectionate appreciation of the human spirit lifts the book beyond its internal doubts into an overall spirit of optimism.

Critical Context

Primo Levi is best known for two autobiographical books: *Se questo è un uomo* (1947; *If This Is a Man*, 1959) describes his experiences in the concentration camp at Auschwitz, while *La tregua* (1963; *The Reawakening*, 1965) recounts his roundabout journey back to Italy. By profession, Levi was a research chemist, employed for many years at a paint factory of which he ultimately became the manager. Not until his retirement was he able to write full time. The publication of several of his later books in English translation, most notably *Il sistema periodico* (1975; *The Periodic Table*, 1984), sparked great interest in his work and prompted the reissue of his memoirs, retitled and combined in a single volume as *Survival in Auschwitz and The Reawakening* (1986). Thus it came as a shock to many readers when, early in 1987, Levi died in a fall in the stairwell of his apartment building, an apparent suicide.

If Not Now, When? is based on actual events as told to Levi by a friend, but the names and places have been changed. Levi, who himself fought with the Italian partisans before being captured and deported to Auschwitz, was also able to draw from his own experiences and spent months researching Yiddish culture and period detail before doing any writing. The song which supplies the title of the book, ascribed in the narrative to a wandering minstrel, was written by Levi himself. He adapted the refrain from a collection of sayings by famous rabbis, incorporated into the Talmud.

Although the events, seen mainly through Mendel's eyes, are evaluated entirely within the context of their period, some of its aspects, according to Levi, were inspired by the situation at the time of writing, in particular the continuing oppression in Poland and the contrast between the Gedalists' vision of an idyllic future in Palestine and the reality of the 1980's. Having dealt, in his two great autobiographical works, with Jewish men and women as victims, in *If Not Now, When?* Levi felt the need to pay tribute to them as fighters.

Sources for Further Study

Chanteau, Cara. "A Consoling Name," in *The Listener*. XIV (May 15, 1986), p. 30.

Clemons, Walter. Review in *Newsweek*. CV (May 6, 1985), p. 79.

Hughes, H. Stuart. Review in *The New York Times Book Review*. XC (April 21, 1985), p. 7.
MacLeod, Sheila. "Wide-angle Lens," in *The New Statesman*. CXI (April 18, 1986), p. 28.
The New Yorker. Review. LXI (July 15, 1985), p. 85.

Nina Hibbin

IF ON A WINTER'S NIGHT A TRAVELER

Author: Italo Calvino (1923-1985)
Type of plot: Antinovel
Time of plot: The late twentieth century
Locale: An unnamed city
First published: Se una notte d'inverno un viaggiatore, 1979 (English
   translation, 1981)

> *Principal characters:*
> THE NARRATOR, the often-whimsical, sometimes infuriating
>   voice who addresses the Reader throughout
> THE READER, a man who wishes to enjoy a good novel in his
>   spare time
> THE OTHER READER, or LUDMILLA, a woman who shares the
>   Reader's ambition
> LOTARIA, Ludmilla's sister, a relentless and pedantic critic

The Novel

The Reader—actually one of the central characters of the novel—is invited to relax and enjoy the narrative to come. The first story in the book is
"If on a Winter's Night a Traveler," which purports to be a cloak-and-dagger
mystery in which a man arrives at a railroad station for the purpose of
exchanging suitcases with another man, but the latter orders a change of
plans, and the first traveler departs, still holding the same suitcase. At this
point, corresponding to the end of a sixteen-page signature, the Reader
discovers that the book is defective, containing in fact nothing but repetitions
of the same pages. He goes to the shop where he purchased the book and
there meets the Other Reader, an attractive young woman named Ludmilla,
who is there on the same errand. They converse briefly, exchange their books
for presumably perfect copies, exchange telephone numbers, also, and go
home to continue the interrupted novel.

Unfortunately, the text turns out to be that of a completely different
novel, *Outside the Town of Malbork*, by another writer. The Reader telephones Ludmilla and discovers that her experience is again identical. The
Readers visit a university professor's office, a women's study group, the office of the original book's publisher—wherever they go, together or apart,
the trail leads to yet another novel, all of which, for one reason or another,
they cannot complete.

After beginning ten novels, the Reader visits a library and finds all ten
cataloged there, but is frustrated in his attempt to turn up a complete copy
of any of them. He talks to seven readers in the library on the general subject
of reading; each reads for a different purpose. The last of the seven questions

the validity of the Reader's attitude toward beginnings and endings. Either the hero and heroine marry, he points out, or they die. Contemplating these alternatives, the Reader decides to marry Ludmilla so that they might finish reading and life together. In a very brief final chapter, the newlyweds are reading together in bed, he vowing to finish *If on a Winter's Night a Traveler*, by Italo Calvino.

The Characters

Italo Calvino's two Readers, man and woman, reflect his previous attachment to allegory and fable. The Reader aggressively pursues the elusive complete novel and presses forward to resolve the confusion of the abortive novels to his own satisfaction. Concurrently he is pursuing Ludmilla, the Other Reader, carefully soliciting her telephone number at their first meeting and striving to know her better, although only at the end acknowledging that he wants her as his mate. Ludmilla represents the feminine approach to fiction and to life. She appreciates the "driving force" of a good novel and is content simply "to observe its own growth, like a tree, an entangling, as if of branches and leaves." Throughout the book, the woman reader, whether Ludmilla or an ideal reader imagined by one of the fictional authors of the aborted novels, is presented as receptive, unwilling to impose prejudgments, ready to follow where the story leads. As the Reader's beloved, Ludmilla responds decorously to his advances and eventually accepts him as husband.

The real readers of the book, whether male or female, are invited to identify with the (male) Reader, but it soon becomes clear that the true reader is a hermaphrodite. The Reader's and Other Reader's efforts complement each other, and their marriage is the logical resolution of their quest for an integral reading experience.

Ludmilla's sister, Lotaria, seems to represent the critical mentality at its most confident, categorical, and dogmatic. She is, in other words, not a reader at all, only a person using books to promote her own opinions and to provide fodder for study sessions with like-minded friends. As such, she represents a temptation to the Reader, who, being male, displays domineering tendencies. Inevitably he takes up with Lotaria, only to find their frantic and short-lived passion thoroughly unsatisfying, for she is all head and no heart, not even likable, much less lovable.

The narrator is a somewhat satirical portrait of the Author—that traditional, omniscient provider and director of the reading experience. The story "If on a Winter's Night a Traveler" for which he is responsible is only the first of the ten novel beginnings. It is as though "Calvino" has no more control over the situation than does the bewildered reader who cannot ever get on to the second chapter of the original story. Calvino is adapting to his own purposes a narrative stance resembling Geoffrey Chaucer's six centuries ago in another set of "framed" stories, *The Canterbury Tales* (1386-1390). Like

Chaucer the pilgrim, Calvino, or rather a version thereof, has become a character in his own work. Like Chaucer's persona (not only in *The Canterbury Tales* but in several of his other works), he has great difficulty getting his story told. The pilgrim Chaucer is the victim of impatient fellow travelers who, not seeing the satirical point of his "Tale of Sir Thopas," cut him short; Calvino is victimized by his publisher, whose supposed carelessness and general disorderliness prevent readers from finishing the story of the man with the suitcase. Chaucer, whose audience was accustomed to having stories read or recited to them, had to endure not being listened to; Calvino, not being read. Meanwhile, the real Chaucer and the real Calvino are getting the larger job done.

Themes and Meanings

Two related themes emerge in *If on a Winter's Night a Traveler*: the intimate relationship between reading and living, and the tension between the reader's expectations and the writer's quest for distinction and originality. Reading and living are metaphors for each other. Observations such as the narrator's "The lives of individuals of the human race form a constant plot" are frequent. The two Readers "read and review" each other in Ludmilla's home. The book resembles life in many ways, particularly in its unpredictability. In developing a thesis about Calvino's "narrative discourse" several years before the publication of this book, Teresa de Lauretis translated a passage from Calvino's preface to a 1964 novel thus:

> Readings and lived experiences are not two universes, but one. To be interpreted, every experience of life recalls certain readings and becomes fused with them. That books are always born of other books is a truth only seemingly contradictory to this other truth: that books are born of practical day-to-day life, and of the relationships among men.

Calvino never exemplified his theory of the "one universe" more strikingly than in *If on a Winter's Night a Traveler*.

The theme of life and reading leads Calvino to play continually with the conflict between the reader's demands and the author's intentions. The former is likely to want to immerse himself (or herself—Ludmilla particularly expresses this wish) in the narrative, to submit to being swept along to a satisfying conclusion. The writer counts on the ordinary expectations of the reader but defies these expectations to a greater or lesser extent, as daring and originality dictate. To conform completely would be to write pallid and imitative books; to defy all expectations would be to risk unintelligibility and alienation. Calvino takes a risk—not the minor risk of supplying an unexpected ending but the headier one of furnishing no ending at all, instead producing a series of beginnings that resembles neither life nor any of the usual forms of fiction.

The novel comments throughout on these tensions between writer and reader. Calvino's narrator is lured by the possibilities of the various counter-narratives that suggest themselves. As far back as Miguel de Cervantes, novelists have digressed from the main story, and not always irrelevantly. One of Calvino's fictional subnarrators is "always finding stories that cannot be told until other stories have been told first." The reader, however, may not share this penchant for literary sideshows.

Furthermore, readers have different expectations, some of them excruciatingly inapt to the writer. Some want only to escape from the world, an outright denial of Calvino's premise that life and reading are inseparable. When the Reader encounters the seven readers with different slants on their common interest, one, for example, reads each new book only until he is sure that it is not one which he read in his childhood but has not been able to locate since. Another reads in order to go off on a tangent; when he has succeeded, the book has served its purpose. Clearly, these are perverse readers, unwilling to receive the book as written, in Ludmilla's fashion. The Reader, in response to such vagaries, asserts his intention to read only what is in the book, to connect its parts with the whole, to acknowledge only certain readings as correct, to distinguish one book from another, and, most important, to read the complete book from first page to last.

This quest for unity, for the one complete book, is signaled in the first interpolated narrative. The traveler in the train station will recognize his counterpart by a password, "Zeno of Elia." Zeno was the early Greek philosopher who stressed indivisibility—"the one"—in contrast to the school of Heracleitus, whose basic principle was flux—a continually moving and divisible reality. The password is exchanged but not the suitcases, and the narrative yields to a succession of similarly unfinished stories: the seeming triumph of flux and disunion and the denial of Zeno's principle.

The seventh reader in the library is permitted the last word. Beginnings and endings as such are not important; "the ultimate meaning to which all stories refer has two faces: the continuity of life, the inevitability of death." Back with Ludmilla, the Reader plans to finish Calvino's book. He cannot finish the first story called "If on a Winter's Night a Traveler," but he can finish the book of the same name, which is not, after all, a pastiche of many books but a complete narrative of his own initiation as a Calvino reader, that is, a reader who has learned not to demand what the author cannot or will not give him. The main story, his own, ends happily with his marriage to Ludmilla, which has produced one whole reader, one whole life. Zeno's principle is reaffirmed—if one allows for what Samuel Taylor Coleridge liked to call "unity in multeity." The artist has made a whole out of seemingly disparate parts, a whole symbolized by the union of the two Readers.

Critical Context

Well before he wrote this novel, Calvino demonstrated an interest in modern critical approaches such as the semiotic theory of the Swiss linguist Ferdinand de Saussure and structural linguistics, especially as advanced by Roman Jakobson. One branch of structuralist criticism has emphasized reading as a creative, unrestrained response to writing, an idea endorsed, with reservations, in *If on a Winter's Night a Traveler*. Calvino defies the reader's expectations because they impede a creative response. Refusing to travel down literary ruts, the author leaves the ten stories to the reader to finish—or not finish. This strategy marks what is sometimes called the antinovel, whose best known practitioner, Alain Robbe-Grillet, has gone much further than Calvino in obliterating the familiar benchmarks of the novel.

It is Calvino's awareness of this modern shift in critical emphasis from writing to reading, then, that differentiates him from Chaucer. Whereas Chaucer portrays an author struggling to master the art of writing, Calvino depicts the reader wrestling with the demanding art of reading. Both involve impatient audiences, but Calvino challenges his audience's motives. Reading demands respect for the writer's art, but the reader must respect the art of reading, too, which calls for more active involvement, more creativity, than the lazy reader can summon. To cite Coleridge again:

> The reader should be carried forward, not merely or chiefly by the mechanical impulse of curiosity, or by a restless desire to arrive at the final solution; but by the pleasureable activity of mind excited by the attractions of the journey itself.

In Calvino's book the journey is not that of a character in a railroad station but of the Reader—a journey to which any reader can aspire.

Sources for Further Study

Cannon, JoAnn. *Italo Calvino: Writer and Critic*, 1981.

De Lauretis, Teresa. "Narrative Discourse in Calvino: Praxis or Poiesis?" in *PMLA*. XC (1975), pp. 414-425.

Olken, I. T. *With Pleated Eye and Garnet Wing: Symmetries of Italo Calvino*, 1984.

Salvatori, Mariolina. "Italo Calvino's *If on a Winter's Night a Traveler*: Writer's Authority, Reader's Autonomy," in *Contemporary Literature*. XXVII (Summer, 1986), pp. 182-212.

Sorapure, Madeleine. "Being in the Midst: Italo Calvino's *If on a Winter's Night a Traveler*," in *Modern Fiction Studies*. XXXI (Winter, 1985), pp. 702-710.

Robert P. Ellis

ILL SEEN ILL SAID

Author: Samuel Beckett (1906-   )
Type of plot: Antistory
Time of plot: Unspecified
Locale: Unspecified; a generalized rural location
First published: Mal vu mal dit, 1981 (English translation, 1981)

> *Principal character:*
> "SHE," the protagonist, and perhaps the narrator, an old
> woman who is nearing her end

The Novel

While he is best known as a playwright, Samuel Beckett's devotion to fiction and the novel predates by many years his involvement with the theater and has proceeded in tandem with it, giving to his entire output a unity and continuity which his plays, when taken alone, do not provide. It may be argued that the serious student must confront Beckett's fiction in order to attain full exposure to the intellectual and aesthetic range and challenge of this twentieth century master.

Evidence of his commitment to fiction is perhaps most impressively provided by the series of works written in the 1970's and 1980's. The term "series" is used here merely for descriptive convenience: The author himself does not apply it to his later fiction, for reasons which readers familiar with the Beckett persona will readily understand. Having come to an apparent standstill imaginatively in his fiction with *Comment c'est* (1961; *How It Is*, 1964), and having conducted a number of crucial fictional experiments thereafter, notably in *Imagination morte imaginez* (1965; *Imagination Dead Imagine*, 1965), Beckett inaugurated the series in question with *Pour finir encore et autres foirades* (1976; *Fizzles*, 1976).

Ill Seen Ill Said is typical of the author's later work in a number of ways, and these ways in turn constitute the critique of fiction which is an underlying preoccupation of these works and which links them to Beckett's earlier fiction. In terms of locale, for example, the fewer features provided, the truer the text is to its minimalist, terminal spirit. The countryside is unpromising, infertile, and menaced by the ring of stones which surrounds it. Sheep graze, but only in order to underline the insistently antipastoral character of the place. Seasons take their round, but with little discernible effect. Translated into human terms, the protagonist's cabin is furnished with the bare essentials, though among them is the apparent luxury of curtains, required by the rituals of sighting and perceiving which occupy a large portion of the solitary protagonist's time.

Just as such traditional fictional expectations as "social milieu" and "material representation" are confounded in *Ill Seen Ill Said*, so is the concept of action. The protagonist, marked by the restlessness which is characteristic of Beckett's characters, journeys back and forth to a grave. These irresistible treks, which the gravestone seems to command, are performed without issue, without acknowledged purpose, and without end. "She" is in the grip of an action rather than in command of one. The result is that the stone—a stylized outcrop of the terrain—has more power and meaning than anything the protagonist or the reader can create for it. In addition, as though to complete, or to make consistent, the ethos of dearth around which the fiction is structured, the protagonist is prevented from attaining significance for herself or from attaching it to the territory beyond herself. The subjects of *Ill Seen Ill Said*, therefore, are ignorance, emptiness, and untranslated sensory experience.

Stylistically, *Ill Seen Ill Said* is painfully simple and direct, minimally punctuated yet resourceful, and even, on occasion, amusing. The narrative exhibits a superficial sense of continuity, but continuity is of less significance than contiguity, circularity, repetition, and inconclusiveness. Such strategies oblige the reader to come to terms with a text rather than to perform the more familiar exercise of reading a story. The unlikely collaboration between language and nonentity once again is both product and source of a Beckett work.

The Characters

The protagonist of *Ill Seen Ill Said* is, surprisingly for Beckett's fiction, a woman. Superficially, the protagonist suggests a specific feminine archetype. With her long white hair, black dress, waxen pallor, and remote habitat, "she" appears to be a witch. Nevertheless, such a figure seems to be suggested only in order to help the reader discover that the association is of no interpretive assistance. The inference is that attempts to decode and enlarge upon the protagonist's existential poverty are misleading. This conclusion seems to be underlined by her lack of other feminine connotations, as suggested by the barrenness of her surroundings and her childlessness. "She" is a woman in order that gender be rendered inconsequential.

The protagonist's most salient feature, her eye, has nothing to do with her putative femininity. This obdurate organ is what connects her with a perceivable world. It admits light and the objects that light illuminates, and its unflinching operation lends its owner a Cyclopean power and fixity. As in the case of the protagonist's femininity, however, the nature of the eye is not natural. The connections, facilitated by the optic nerve, between world and thinking mind are nonexistent in this case. Instead of an interaction between perceiver and perceived, Beckett depicts a disjunction between them. The protagonist, therefore, maintains a fidelity to a world which she cannot comprehend—the world of stone. At the same time, she exists in a realm of mental processes which occur without the immediate or obvious stimulus of external phenomena. In effect, the protagonist is less a character, or a woman, than she is an eye. In addition, she is less an eye than she is an instrument of process, even if the process in this case is denoted by its rarity.

A reading which suggests that "she" consists of two disparate zones—one unthinkingly in thrall to the world of things, the other submerged in the world of mind—seems more consistent than one claiming that there is more than one character in *Ill Seen Ill Said*. Nevertheless, the text does seem to support the latter reading as well. Some of this evidence is provided by the presence of a narrative voice which intermittently interjects advice and encouragement during the course of the narrative. The unexpected prominence of such a presence does not necessarily argue for the existence of what might be called an "independent narrator," an authority similar to the omniscient narrator of more conventional fictions, but one who has let slip the mask of his omniscience. The manner in which the narrative voice is introduced at the beginning of the work seems calculated to alert the reader to the existence within the text of two different, mutually exclusive subjects. The first considers the realm of phenomena; the second deals with imaginative resources.

The protagonist's reality, or destiny, is to shift unknowingly from one of these areas to the other in a manner which seems apprehensible only to the reader, not to "she" herself. For her to know the form she inhabits would bring a deceptive certainty and stasis to her condition—deceptive since, in the interests of stability, it would suppress all that can undermine it. Thus the protagonist is a persuasive embodiment of uncertainty and irresolvability, an embodiment of the auxiliary "may," which needs a verb to achieve itself but which is not deprived of its meaning when standing alone. "She" convinces the reader of the reality of her existence. Near as she is to a condition of finality—death—the protagonist is not there yet and so may exemplify only the antithesis of finality.

Themes and Meanings

In the course of his career, Beckett's name has become virtually synonymous with certain themes and with the absence of absolute, definite meanings. Among his themes are the absurdity of human existence, the difficulty (if not impossibility) of communication, the dissonance inevitably produced by attempts to harmonize thought and deed, heart and head. Such themes, together with the author's predictably mocking misgivings about anything as localized and specific as a theme are once again present in *Ill Seen Ill Said*. Nevertheless, in the case of an author as philosophically sophisticated and aesthetically adventurous as Beckett, themes are at least as important for the way in which they are presented as for what they say, and may not be abstracted from the work without defacing it.

A preoccupation of *Ill Seen Ill Said* which forces itself upon the reader with particular emphasis concerns matters of completeness and finality. The novel's insistence on a closed setting, and on the apparent singularity of its protagonist, does not, paradoxically, negate the depiction of totality. Instead, Beckett sets up an ostensibly self-sustaining presence—the old person engaged in mindless though absorbing routines of time-killing is used here, as elsewhere in both his fiction and drama—which Beckett then proceeds to consider problematically. The noncharacter is a tissue of abstractions, knowable primarily because of its existence within the most minimal dimensions of space and time. Typically, however, Beckett refuses to accept the model's success and flaws appear: options, choices, changes, needs. Since neither space nor time is necessarily static, there is no justification for equipping their symbolic embodiment with stasis. Without stasis, however, there is imperfection, mutability, failure—the human lot. The protagonist, and indeed the title, of *Ill Seen Ill Said* are further reminders of Beckett's lifelong concern with such preoccupations.

It seems difficult, therefore, and also unwise, to elicit definitive meanings from this or any other Beckett text. Yet it should be noted that the work offers a number of approaches to meaning, some more promising than others. There are a number of cultural and intellectual references—to "the rigid Memnon pose," for example, and to Michelangelo. Such references offer areas of speculation beyond the text and briefly break its claustrophobic enclosure. A numerological interpretation seems possible because of the prominence of the number twelve in the text, and this approach may be associated with the astral traffic vaguely reported as relevant to the protagonist's outlook. Perhaps, however, the quest for meaning in this or any other Beckett text is most appropriately undertaken with the author's use of language in mind. Its rhythmic variety and poise, its lexical range, and its spareness all speak eloquently of the novel's portrayal of the unspeakable, yet communicable, vicissitudes of existence.

Critical Context

Beckett's reputation as one of twentieth century literature's most impenitent, and perhaps eccentric, innovators was assured long before he embarked on the short novels of his career's later years. As well as being as inventive and filled with integrity as any of his earlier works, they also provide, in a more lyric, chaste, distilled form, many of the philosophical and aesthetic concerns of a writer who has devoted his career to performing the burial rites of Romanticism.

Ill Seen Ill Said is an expression of an extraordinary singularity and consistency of artistic vision—so much so, in fact, that it is tempting to regard it, together with the two other central works of the series, *Company* (1980) and *Worstward Ho* (1983), as constituting a redaction of the critically acclaimed trilogy, *Molloy* (1951; English translation, 1955), *Malone meurt* (1951; *Malone Dies*, 1956), and *L'Innommable* (1953; *The Unnamable*, 1958). Such a view, however, is not necessary. *Ill Seen Ill Said* can readily be appreciated as a work which speaks for itself in the artistic tone and philosophical idiom which has made Samuel Beckett an important voice in modern literature.

Sources for Further Study
Bair, Deirdre. *Samuel Beckett: A Biography*, 1978.
Ben-Zvi, Linda. *Samuel Beckett*, 1986.
Coe, Richard N. *Beckett*, 1964.
Knowlson, James, and John Pilling. *Frescoes of the Skull: The Later Prose and Drama of Samuel Beckett*, 1980.
Pilling, John. *Samuel Beckett*, 1976.

George O'Brien

I'M NOT STILLER

Author: Max Frisch (1911-)
Type of plot: Existential mystery
Time of plot: The mid-twentieth century
Locale: Switzerland, Europe, and the United States
First published: Stiller, 1954 (English translation, 1958)

> *Principal characters:*
> ANATOL LUDWIG STILLER, the protagonist, who insists that he
>   is James White
> JULIKA STILLER-TSCHUDY, his wife
> ROLF, his public prosecutor and his friend
> SYBELLE, Rolf's wife, who has an affair with Stiller
> DR. BOHNENBLUST, Stiller's defense counsel

The Novel

I'm Not Stiller is the story of a man's fight to deny his past and to create a new identity for himself. At every juncture he is forced to confront the image of the man he once was and does not want to be. Anatol Stiller's story is told in two parts: in the accounts recorded in seven notebooks written by Stiller/ White in prison, and in a postscript written by Rolf, Stiller's public prosecutor and friend.

On one level, the prison notebooks reveal the story of Anatol Stiller, a failure trying to be a hero. After proving himself a coward in the Spanish Civil War, the mediocre sculptor Stiller, insecure about his masculinity, marries a ballerina, Julika, a beautiful but frigid woman. Unsuccessful in his attempts to bring out the "woman" in his wife, the restless and moody Stiller embarks on an affair with Sybelle. Meanwhile, his tubercular wife is confined to a sanatorium in Davos. Haunted by guilt and abused by his mistress, Stiller jumps a ship to the United States. After several years of drifting through the American wasteland, Stiller tries to put a bullet through his head, narrowly escaping suicide. Confronted by an inexpressible presence, which he calls his angel, Stiller considers himself reborn and returns home to Switzerland, where he is arrested and put on trial to prove to him his identity.

On another level, Stiller's notebooks document his struggle to maintain his fabricated identity as James White, a smuggler, wife murderer, and American soldier of fortune, who rescues women from burning huts, survives volcanoes, and murders millionaires in the heart of the jungle. In order to make him accept his old identity, the court presents Stiller with irrefutable evidence: photo albums, testimony from his wife, verification by his former mistress, and corroboration by five of his friends. Stiller is taken back to his favorite restaurants, to the sanatorium where he deserted his wife, and finally, to his former studio, which he physically demolishes as he pleads with his wife to accept him as his new self. In the end, the court condemns him to be Anatol Stiller and he acquiesces.

In the second part, Rolf, Stiller's public prosecutor, recounts the years after Stiller's trial. Stiller reclaims Julika as his wife and settles down as a potter in a ramshackle farmhouse in Glion. The marriage, however, self-destructs; Julika is hospitalized, and Stiller, obsessed with becoming her savior, sees himself once again as her murderer. On Easter Monday, Julika, who had always been dead in Stiller's eyes, dies. The novel ends on an ambiguous note: "Stiller remained in Glion and lived alone."

The Characters

I'm Not Stiller is a novel about characters seeking freedom—the freedom to accept themselves as they are. Stiller always casts himself in the role of a hero, thus setting impossible tasks for himself. Trying to be a hero, he finds himself to be a coward. Attempting to re-create his wife, he symbolically becomes her murderer. Only when he examines his life can he come to terms with his failures. Armed with this knowledge, Stiller refuses to accept his old identity. In his path toward freedom, he moves toward self-acceptance but finds himself once again pursuing the impossible task of saving his wife. After her death, Stiller withdraws from the world and falls silent. Whether his silence signifies the true inner freedom of self-acceptance or reveals the resignation of a man absorbed in his own despair is one of the haunting questions of this novel.

Like Stiller, Rolf hides behind a false persona, trying to create an open marriage that would allow him and his wife to engage in extramarital affairs. Only by coming to grips with his true feelings is Rolf able to see that there is no freedom without commitment. Sybelle, Rolf's wife, seeks to challenge her husband by freely engaging in an affair, which leads her into open promiscuity. Only when she leaves Rolf to earn her own living in America is she able to gain freedom. In the end, Rolf and Sybelle are reunited.

Julika, unfortunately, is never able to be free. Although Stiller continually molds her into a "graven image," not allowing her to be herself, she remains with him, unable to see that she is compelled to play the part of a victim. After seven years of health and prosperity, she returns to Stiller, once again becoming a childlike victim instead of a mature, independent woman. In the end, her inability to free herself and face responsibility costs her her life.

Dr. Bohnenblust, Stiller's defense counsel, is the typical patriotic Swiss who sees freedom in terms of laws, rights, and institutions. He questions nothing, always appeals to common sense, and offers Stiller a middle-of-the-road path of self-sacrifice, connubial obligations, and public responsibility. His is a life based on shallow, external appearances. Inwardly he is empty— an inauthentic man, imprisoned in a sterile system which he has created.

Themes and Meanings

I'm Not Stiller clearly follows in the existentialist tradition, which holds that individuals must define themselves rather than allow themselves to be defined by others. When five of Stiller's friends visit him, each sees a different Stiller, but none can see the true one. In his visit to America, Stiller observes a black family at a refined social gathering in which the blacks are reduced to a parody of middle-class whites. As destructive as defining one's self in the eyes of another is basing one's life on a false code. For example, Stiller tries to live by a Hemingwayesque code of masculinity even though he has a feminine personality, and Rolf bases his marriage on a false code which forces him to deny his emotions.

In Stiller's world, it is difficult to find one's true self. In an age of mass communications, replications have replaced authentic experiences, and the life of the modern individual is a collage of secondhand experiences gleaned from newspapers, books, and television. In Stiller's dream, even the act of crucifying an individual has been reduced to the ceremony of nailing that person's photograph to a tree. *I'm Not Stiller* speaks to a modern audience living in a world in which prefabricated images are confused with human personalities. As Stiller points out, the human soul cannot be discovered in a photo album, nor can a person's inner being be found in a résumé.

Critical Context

I'm Not Stiller is a mixture of many literary styles. On one level, it can be viewed as a *Bildungsroman* in which Stiller makes self-discoveries and finally comes of age. The book also follows the tradition of romantic realism in the vein of Leo Tolstoy's *Anna Karenina* (1875-1877; English translation, 1886), a novel often mentioned in the text, for it examines in detail the psychological torments of modern relationships, but *I'm Not Stiller* goes beyond realism, using many of the techniques of the late modernist. The narrative structure is fractured so that incidents appear out of chronological order. Stories are filtered through several narrators; Stiller tells the story of Rolf's marital problems as they are related to him by Rolf and narrates his own actions in the third person. The same incidents are related from the viewpoints of two or three of the involved parties. Many times there are conflicting accounts. Sybelle and Rolf relate different versions of their last confrontation before Sybelle leaves for America.

In keeping with the modernist tradition, *I'm Not Stiller* creates a montage effect, interweaving dreams, fabrications, fanciful stories, and eyewitness accounts. Anticipating the postmodernist tradition, *I'm Not Stiller* introduces parody into a serious novel. For example, Stiller's adventures can be seen as a pastiche of several Ernest Hemingway narratives. Stiller fights in the Spanish Civil War (*For Whom the Bell Tolls*, 1940), reenacts the bravura of bullfights (*The Sun Also Rises*, 1926), falls in love with a nurse/medic (*A Farewell to*

Arms, 1929), and becomes obsessed with an act of cowardice ("The Short Happy Life of Francis Macomber," 1936). Moreover, Stiller is a parody of a Hemingway hero living in a Kafkaesque world in which the bureaucratic machinery of the state puts him on trial, primarily to prove to him that he is really himself. *I'm Not Stiller* is the novel which established Max Frisch's reputation, not only in German-speaking countries but also around the world. It stands in the forefront of the postwar renaissance of the German novel.

Sources for Further Study
Adamson, G. L. *The Contemporaneity of Max Frisch's Novels*, 1973.
Butler, M. *The Novels of Max Frisch*, 1976.
Peterson, C. *Max Frisch*, 1972.
Probst, G., and J. Bodine. *Perspectives on Max Frisch*, 1982.
Weisstein, Ulrich. *Max Frisch*, 1976.

Paul Rosefeldt

THE IMMORALIST

Author: André Gide (1869-1951)
Type of plot: Psychological realism
Time of plot: 1900
Locale: Northern Africa, Italy, France, and Switzerland
First published: L'Immoraliste, 1902 (English translation, 1930)

> *Principal characters:*
> MICHEL, the narrator and a historian of pagan civilizations
> MARCELINE, his wife
> BACHIR, a young Arab boy toward whom Michel feels an
> intense physical attraction
> CHARLES, a young Norman farmer who also attracts Michel
> MENALQUE, a French intellectual and hedonist with whom
> Michel is on intimate terms

The Novel

Told in the first person by Michel, the central character, *The Immoralist* is a retrospective account of the three years of his life directly preceding the opening of the novel—three years during which his father dies, he marries Marceline, he nearly dies from tuberculosis and undergoes a profound psychological transformation, and Marceline dies. Although Michel tells his own story, the reader receives it secondhand from a friend to whom he has told it; thus Michel's narration is framed, at beginning and end, by this friend's voice as he writes to his brother, an important French official, and pleads with him to secure for Michel a position in the French government. The friend's plea seems charitable, coming as it does before he recounts Michel's narration; by the end of the novel, after the reader has witnessed the murderously shrewd, calculating, and self-centered Michel "the immoralist" (he would call himself an amoralist), the idea of him working for any government seems, without question, immoral.

A published, polyglot historian and self-professed "learned Puritan" at the age of twenty-four when his father becomes fatally ill, Michel says that he decided to marry Marceline because it would comfort the old man to know that his son would not be alone in the world (Michel's mother had died when he was fifteen). Michel says, furthermore, that he did not love the twenty-year-old Marceline when he married her, but "at least I had never loved any other woman. That was enough, I assumed, to insure our happiness. . . ." His lack of love for her explains, in part, why their marriage is not consummated until several months after the wedding. Married in Paris, they set out on what is to become a three-year journey, interrupted only by relatively brief sojourns in various places of Michel's choosing. Unfortunately, in her goodness and naïveté, Marceline fails to see that Michel does not love her and that he forces her into the latter half of their journey, at least, because he knows that it will kill her. Initially, their travels are for the purpose of Michel's historical research at various ancient ruins, but Michel's interest in the past diminishes in direct proportion to the growth of his increasingly intense and ultimately hedonistic involvement in the present.

From Paris, Michel and Marceline travel to Marseilles, where they board a ship bound for northern Africa; they are traveling to Sousse by way of Tunis. As the couple nears Sousse late at night, Michel begins coughing up blood so profusely that his handkerchief and hands are covered with it. He decides not to tell Marceline, who is asleep beside him, yet, when she awakens and notices nothing abnormal (he has hidden his handkerchief from her), he is overcome by an irrational anger because she has not also had to suffer. Once they are situated in a hotel room, his anger compels him to make her suffer too, so he tells her in a brutally direct way about the blood; the news causes her to faint. Suddenly he is sorry to have upset her, and he asks himself, "Wasn't it enough that *I* should be sick?"

He has already answered this question with his actions, as well as proved to himself and the reader that Marceline is totally malleable beneath the force of his will—even when he is seriously ill with tuberculosis. Indeed, she becomes his servant not only during his illness, but also after he recovers determined to be a different person and "make the thrilling discovery of life." One significant discovery that he makes, after she begins to bring children from the streets of Sousse to their room to keep him company, is that he prefers the companionship of young males far more than that of his wife—so much more, in fact, that, even before he is completely recovered from his illness, he begins to see Marceline as an impediment to his sensual, essentially homosexual quests.

While before his illness Michel devoted himself to intellectual pursuits, one significant result of his infirmity is that he becomes obsessed with his physical being, with "voluptuous gratification," and with living for the moment; thus, when he and Marceline travel to the ruins located in Syracuse, Italy, he realizes that the past now represents for him "that immobility, that terrifying fixity, of . . . death." Since he now feels a horror of death, he decides to abandon his profession, giving himself up instead to "myself, to things, to existence, which seemed to me divine."

Interested mostly in developing within himself his "authentic" and "perfectible being," he decides that he and Marceline must travel to Ravello. Once there, he spends his days on the shore of Paestum without her, sunbathing nude and admiring the emergent beauty of his body and "new being"—a being, it should be noted, that he enjoys concealing from his wife, so the image she has of him "grew falser day by day." Marceline herself, however, is tired of traveling and tells her husband that she wants to settle in one place. He agrees to this, but then he persuades her to travel to Rome, Florence, Naples, Ravenna, and Paris before he decides that they will settle for a time in Normandy on a farm that he has inherited from his mother.

A week after they have settled at the farm, Marceline informs Michel that she is pregnant, and although he says that he "spent almost every moment of the day with her," he becomes intensely attracted to Charles, the son of Bocage, the elderly caretaker of the farm. Once again, Michel's actions contradict his words, for he spends almost all of his time with Charles, walking or riding or, in one instance rich in Freudian symbolism, wading through a muddy and recently drained pond to catch eels. In Africa, Michel had most enjoyed himself with the young males (such as Moktir, a petty thief) when Marceline was absent, and when he is with Charles, he is again thankful for his wife's absence, because "she might have spoiled our fun a little." Nevertheless, Charles must return to school, Michel is left "alone" with Marceline once again, and the cool, late autumn weather arrives. Michel decides that they must move to Paris, where he has been offered a temporary position as a lecturer based on his past research. His decision to accept the job in Paris, it should be understood, is made neither because he needs a salary (his father's estate left him wealthy) nor because he wants to teach: Michel takes this course of action as another way to secure for himself whatever distractions he can find from his marriage and his growing responsibilities.

Once in Paris, Michel devotes himself to the acquisition of material possessions, but this devotion lasts only until he realizes that their value is lost for him with the first blemish, for then they become "things stained, things infected by disease and somehow marked by mortality." Unfortunately for Marceline, her difficult pregnancy—made more difficult by the couple's ceaseless socializing, most of it caused by Michel—becomes another loathsome mark of mortality for her husband. Perhaps this makes it easier for Michel to leave her, at a time when she is extremely ill, and spend an entire night with Menalque, a hedonist who has challenged his friend to prove that he is not a man of "principle." When Michel returns to Marceline in the morning, he finds that she has had a miscarriage. When, during the weeks that follow, she suffers from phlebitis, and the consequent congestion of her lungs, his perception of her takes a turn that will prove fatal to her: "Sickness had entered Marceline, henceforth inhabited her, marked her, soiled her. She was a tainted thing." Thus begins the part of their journey together that is clearly devoted to "cleansing" Michel's life with death.

They return to his farm in Normandy for a brief period, and Michel enjoys spending most of his time with Pierra, a migrant farmhand, and Alcide, Bocage's second son. Meanwhile, Marceline's illness worsens, and Michel decides that they should travel to Paris, and then on to Neuchâtel, where they are forced by her condition to stop for a longer period of time than he would like. While at Neuchâtel, a doctor diagnoses Marceline's illness as tuberculosis and recommends that the couple travel to Switzerland for her health. They are there only two months before Michel, bored by the Swiss, convinces his wife that they should travel to Italy.

In Milan, Marceline's condition becomes worse; in Rome, and then in Naples, she shows no improvement. Michel becomes bored with Naples, so they return to Rome, and four days later they set out for Sorrento. There the weather is cold; they return to Naples for a few days before sailing to Palermo, remaining only five days before moving on to Taormina. In Taormina, Michel is so attracted to a carriage driver that he kisses him and then spends several days searching for the young man without finding him again. Afterward, they return to Syracuse for eight days before traveling first to Tunis and then to Biskra, where he finds Moktir. Michel persuades the thief to travel with him and Marceline, and they set out for Touggourt.

Marceline, according to Michel, "wasn't feeling well; I couldn't tell what was happening to her." On their first night in Touggourt, Michel leaves Marceline alone in their room and spends most of the night drinking and dancing with Moktir. Upon his return, he finds her covered with blood and near death. Rather than going to find a doctor, Michel sits in the room and watches as Marceline slips in and out of consciousness, intermittently coughing up more blood, until she dies. True to himself, Michel tells his friend everything "without a quaver in his voice, without an inflection or a gesture to reveal that any emotion whatever disturbed him."

The Characters

To understand the existential doctrine that Michel hungrily embraces after his brush with death is to understand a mercilessly self-serving and hedonistically Machiavellian idealogue. To a significant extent, Michel lived by this doctrine even before his illness. Regardless of what he says (for he is a masterfully duplicitous and thus unreliable narrator), his marriage to Marceline is as much a result of his selfish beliefs as her death later proves to be.

As Michel is recuperating from his illness, he decides that, in the future, "recovery alone must become my study; my duty. . . my health; I must consider Good, I must call Right, whatever [is] healthy for me; must forget, must repulse, whatever [does] not cure." After he has recovered his health, however, the doctrine changes. He considers "Good" and "Right" whatever pleases his senses or makes him feel youthful, beautiful, and seemingly immortal. In short, he embraces a type of hedonism that is unethical, because it is Michel-centered and completely exclusive of the rights and well-being of others, particularly of Marceline. Indeed, he married her less to comfort his dying father than to provide for himself a surrogate protector with limited rights. When they marry, his health is "delicate," and—even though he had "acquired ideas about the stupidity of women" and felt absolutely no love for Marceline—compared to him, she "seemed quite strong."

It is Marceline's strength and devotion to Michel that saves his life, but in his eyes, "my salvation depended on no one but myself." When she tells him she has prayed to God for his recovery, he reproaches her and insists that he does not want her prayers because they would leave him "indebted" to God: "It makes for obligations; I don't want any." Marceline, unfortunately, fails to see the extent to which Michel's denunciation of obligations might affect her, just as she fails to see the real man behind her ideal image of Michel.

Ironically, at the moment that their marriage is consummated, it is also symbolically ended, for Michel regards the act as proof that he has become stronger than his wife and has "possessed" her. After this moment, she seems to him "delicate," all of her grace "a kind of fragility." Even in the best of health, she is barely tolerable to him as he pursues "delicious" sensations. Once her health truly begins to fail, she becomes repugnant and "like rest to a man who is not tired." Michel never acknowledges the fact that her health is broken by carrying his child; not once does he offer, or even seem to feel, any sympathy, when she is nearing death at the age of twenty-three. Instead, he literally rushes her toward death, demanding that they move more and more frequently the weaker she becomes. When Marceline tells Michel that his "doctrine" for living "eliminates the weak," he replies, "As it should." He absolutely believes that "only the strong deserve sympathy."

Just as Marceline has value for Michel only as long as she can serve his needs or desires, the same is true of the other characters to whom he is attracted. His homosexual yearnings are stimulated by the "animal grace" and physical beauty of Bachir, by the beauty and cunning of Moktir, and by the "supple and well built" body of Charles. Because Menalque is an educated embodiment of Michel's amoral doctrine of existence, Michel needs the older man as both a teacher and an intimate strong enough to force him to prove that he is capable of denouncing all principles. (Menalque is the ultimate hedonist and has been banished from France's polite society for his lifestyle. "I create each hour's newness," he tells Michel, "by forgetting yesterday completely.")

Michel proves himself to be deserving of Menalque's society when he leaves Marceline, pregnant and seriously ill, and accepts his mentor's invitation to spend the night. Thus, after his encounter with Menalque, the qualities Michel finds attractive in certain males, and for which he chooses to become intimate with them, go beyond mere physical attractiveness. For example, he becomes attached to Pierra because the farmhand is not only handsome but also "guided solely by instinct; he did nothing save on the spur of the moment, yielded to every passing impulse."

Themes and Meanings

When André Gide's *The Immoralist* was first published in 1902, many of its readers vilified Michel. As Gide stated in his preface to the novel, much of the public's indignation "overflowed" onto the author, because many readers identified Michel with his creator (a frequent consequence of first-person narration). Gide claimed, furthermore, that he took care not to pass judgment on Michel. That might, if the author's efforts at neutrality were successful, partly explain why readers could transfer their negative reactions so easily. Within Michel's narrative, Gide succeeds in remaining unobtrusively neutral, but he did choose to frame his protagonist's story with Michel's voice of the unnamed friend who is writing to his brother. As powerfully engaging and believable as Michel is, Gide did not need to use a narrative frame. So why did he do it?

The most obvious reason involves the extent to which moral principles are essential not only to sustaining civilization but also to making civilization possible. The novel is entitled *The Immoralist*, which both explains and justifies Gide's use of the frame, as it is not the author himself who calls Michel the immoralist but Michel's friend. Nevertheless, with both the title and the frame, Gide primes his readers with a preconception about the story's "hero." He anticipates his readers' indignation over Michel's essential inhumanity, and with the incorporation of the friend's voice, Gide goes one step further and allows one of the story's readers (although an imaginary one) to speak *and* pass judgment.

By providing the verdict as a deductive premise and then drawing his readers into a masterfully duplicitous narrative that both undercuts the verdict and requires readers to rely upon inductive rather than deductive reasoning, Gide forces thinking individuals to ask questions of Michel and themselves. One of the hardest of these questions concerns principles and the extent to which the existence (needs, desires, and interests) of Self can supersede the existence of Other before civilization completely collapses.

Michel's specialty is, significantly, ancient and failed civilizations, and he proves by his seemingly aimless and clearly self-serving wanderlust that he feels neither fidelity nor responsibility to his own civilization, whose future, as in any society, depends upon familial continuity. Indeed, Michel indirectly destroys his own child before deliberately destroying his wife, the mother of that child. Superseding the well-being and survival of other human beings, and civilization itself, according to Michel, is the libido-driven Self: "I had been born to make undreamed of discoveries; and I grew almost fanatical in my quest, for whose sake I realized the seeker must abjure, must disdain culture, propriety, rules."

Finally, one should not overlook the implicit irony of the novel's title, which Michel's friend presumably pens: While he is obviously disturbed and unaccepting of the "cruelty" he faces in Michel's narrative, he is nevertheless pleading with his brother, a powerful official in the French government, to secure a job for "the immoralist." Isn't the friend also an immoralist? After all, the man is depending upon a person of power to provide for Michel, whose own will to power has destroyed both human life and moral principles in order to validate itself. The friend, then, in the face of his knowledge and his own moral reaction to it, also turns his back on principle to help Michel find a secure position in the government. Thus Gide's professed neutrality is hardly that at all, especially with Michel's friend and the reading public. Both constitute Michel's audience, and both are implicitly judged immoral as long as they disregard the inhumanity of an individual such as Michel.

Critical Context

When Gide's *The Immoralist* was first published, the philosophy of Friedrich Nietzsche was enjoying great popularity in France, and Gide's journals indicate that he wrestled intellectually with Nietzsche's thinking for many years. It is not surprising, therefore, that much of Michel's thinking duplicates that of Zarathustra, the main character in Nietzsche's *Also sprach Zarathustra* (1883-1885; *Thus Spake Zarathustra*, 1896).

Zarathustra expresses only contempt for Christianity, morality, conscience, and altruism. He, like his creator, considers these things to be human weaknesses, and he deplores weakness of any kind, claiming that "the will to power" is the highest good. Since Nietzsche's philosophy is essentially optimistic, one can understand how it came to be popular in France, where idealism and optimism were strong and would remain so until 1914, when the German empire was destroyed and France was devastated. Furthermore, since Nietzsche advocated the cultivation of a race of "supermen," individuals physically powerful, unscrupulous, and merciless, one can perhaps understand how his writings could be used as a philosophical justification for Nazi doctrines of racial and national superiority.

Addressing the "herd" devoted to a "slave morality," Zarathustra says that "my will to power walks with the feet of your will to truth!" Gide wrote in one of his journals that he was often "torn" by what he called an ongoing "conflict [within himself] between the rules of morality and the rules of sincerity." In *The Immoralist*, the conflict is resolved by Michel's "sincerity" to his "perfectible being," to his will to power, and to his disdain for essentially Protestant moral precepts (embodied in Marceline) which limit the self-actualization of the individual. Yet, although Gide accomplished an artistic resolution of the conflict between puritanically intolerant attitudes and the individual's search for his own nature, he remained ambiguous about the ethical ramifications of Michel's philosophy. At the end of the three years, the narrative recounts, Michel tells his friend, "I am at a moment in my life past which I can no longer see my way." As for Gide, after *The Immoralist*, he would go on to project the conflict between the wish for self-fulfillment and the barriers of convention into semiautobiographical fiction: *La Porte étroite* (1909; *Strait Is the Gate*, 1924) and *Les Faux-monnayeurs* (1925; *The Counterfeiters*, 1927). While Gide is never as ambiguous in his writing as is

Nietzsche, philosophically both writers are forerunners of the existential movement, which emphasizes, among other things, the complete freedom of the will, as well as the individual's ability to create his own destiny.

Sources for Further Study

Ames, Van Meter. *André Gide*, 1947.

Brennan, Joseph Gerard. *Three Philosophical Novelists: James Joyce, André Gide, Thomas Mann*, 1964.

Cordle, Thomas. *André Gide*, 1969.

Fowlie, Wallace. *André Gide: His Life and Art*, 1965.

Ireland, George William. *André Gide: A Study of His Creative Writings*, 1970.

Mann, Klaus. *André Gide and the Crisis of Modern Thought*, 1943.

O'Brien, Justin. *Portrait of André Gide: A Critical Biography*, 1953.

Weinberg, Kurt. *On Gide's "Prométhée": Private Myth and Public Mystification*, 1972.

David A. Carpenter

IN SICILY

Author: Elio Vittorini (1908-1966)
Type of plot: Philosophical memoir
Time of plot: The 1930's
Locale: Sicily
First published: Conversazione in Sicilia, 1937, serial; 1941, book (English translation, 1948)

Principal characters:
SILVESTRO FERRAUTO, the narrator
CONCEZIONE FERRAUTO, Silvestro's mother
COSTANTINO FERRAUTO, Silvestro's father

The Novel

Narrated in the first person, *In Sicily* concerns a few days in the life of a thirty-year-old Sicilian, Silvestro Ferrauto, who returns to the village of his youth after having spent half of his life working as a Linotype operator in northern Italy. His account begins, just prior to that visit, while he is enduring a winter in which he feels "haunted by abstract furies": Despite his certainty that an imminent calamity will seal mankind's doom, he can summon no emotion. Existence seems a dream without content, and his one desire is to surrender utterly to despair. Not even his wife and daughter can relieve his fascination with nullity.

Then, one day, an envelope arrives addressed in handwriting he recognizes as his father's; strangely, it bears a postmark from Venice, not Sicily. After some hesitation, he opens the letter and reads that his father has turned his back on his marriage in order to launch a new career and to live with a new woman. The father's motive in writing the same letter to each of his five sons has not been to ask their forgiveness or understanding—after all, he reasons, in leaving home he is only doing what they had done many years before; moreover, he has assigned his full monthly pension to his wife. Rather, his purpose is to urge his sons to ease their mother's loneliness by visiting her on her birthday.

Silvestro's childhood suddenly floods back to him. Memories—of his father, an amateur actor, reciting from William Shakespeare, of the smell of prickly pears, of the sight of the mountains, of the taste of home-baked bread—all become more vivid than any experience he has had in the fifteen years since his departure. The idea of making the journey down the whole length of the peninsula seems too impractical to consider; while on a walk to mail a birthday card to his mother, however, he sees an advertisement for reduced fares to Sicily. That night, unable to fathom quite how it has come about, he finds himself on the train south. Even so, he professes indifference as to his final destination and, after crossing the strait, tries to prove the point by buying a ticket for Syracuse, a route opposite to the one leading to his village. A day of idling in the big city brings no satisfaction, however, and so, upon discovering that the birthday card is still in his pocket, he sets out on the tortuous mountain roads to his mother's house.

As soon as he arrives, Silvestro is overcome by the feeling that he has emerged from a vacuous dream into the intense experience of life as a two-fold reality. He is simultaneously boy and adult, and his mother Concezione's age and role magically change as his mental perspective flickers. This shimmering sense of reality produced by the superimposition of the past on the present (and of the present on the past) is especially keen when the conversation concerns the broader implications of his parents' sexual relationships.

Concezione harbors no bitterness because of her husband Costantino's desertion or even because of his periodic escapes into the valley with various women—indeed, she admits to being rather attracted by that sort of masculine swagger and romantic impulsiveness—but she resents that, although he wrote lyrics to the "dirty sows" who were his paramours and called them queens, he treated her as uninspiring and ordinary. Silvestro, sensing an opportunity to satisfy his curiosity, asks: "Were you a dirty sow when you did the thing with other men?" His mother quickly defends herself. There were only two, she says, and one was a mistake, the result of confusion caused by an earthquake. The other—the one who counted—was a wayfarer who had traveled across Sicily; after he praised the smell and taste of her freshly baked bread, she "wanted to see him sated, and it seemed a Christian and charitable act to appease his hunger and thirst for other things." "Blessed old sow," her son thinks to himself.

The ironic juxtaposition of these parental infidelities has a humorous aspect, but it serves a further purpose as well. The wayfarer acted as a substitute for Costantino, whom he resembled in temperament, and his attention to Concezione restored the pride in herself as a woman that her husband's neglect had undermined. Now, many years later, when it is age and loneliness that beat against that pride, another man who aches with emptiness, her son, has traveled to her across Sicily; in reawakening him to the goodness of life, she is also revitalized.

On the second day of Silvestro's visit, the denial of death through the sensual affirmation of life becomes even more explicit. When Concezione, who earns a meager living by giving injections, takes her son with her on her rounds of patients suffering from tuberculosis or malaria, she enjoys observing the attractive middle-aged women quicken with excitement as they expose their flesh in his presence; at the same time, she delights in seeing that her son is also aroused. Silvestro, however, remembers a young girl from his childhood who died. She, too, had had injections for her illness; she, too, had removed her chemise in front of him. Suddenly, he has had enough of the game. Death, he states, is real and must be acknowledged. What is unstated but implied in several complex ways is his confrontation with the inevitability of his mother's death—and his own.

In the next section, while Concezione continues to make her calls, Silvestro befriends a knife grinder, who introduces him to a variety of tradesmen. One of them, a harness maker, sees in Silvestro a fellow initiate in a fundamental truth: "The world is big and beautiful, but it has been greatly outraged. Everyone suffers, each for himself, but not for the world that has been outraged, and so the world continues to be outraged." The sentiment quickly becomes a chorus in the conversation of these workers, who repair to a tavern to assuage their suffering. In an obvious reference to the New Testament (John 4:10-11; 7:38-39), the tavernkeeper calls the wine they drink "living water." The allusion to Christ's restoration of the faithful is extended in the company's singing in praise of the blood of the "Holy Wine Bottle." A draper, however, denies that the wine has any such property, and he urges the men not to forget the world; "Don't have illusions," he keeps repeating. Silvestro embraces the message. As he walks to his mother's house, he thinks of this one night as many: "the nights of my grandfather, the nights of my father, the nights of Noah, the nights of man, naked in drink and defenceless, humiliated, less of a man than even a child or a corpse."

The last of the novel's five main sections begins with Silvestro's meditation on his father, who, by playacting Shakespeare's poetically ennobling lines from *As You Like It* about the transformation of man, tried to subdue the pain of the world's unremitting insult to him. This memory leads to a hallucination of his brother Liborio as, at once, an eleven-year-old boy and a soldier killed in Italy's war for national glory. Liborio speaks of the cemetery in which they meet as a theater where, every night, the suffering dead re-create the deeds that shaped history but have been left unsung by any Shakespeare.

The next morning, while great flocks of crows, birds of death, gather around the Ferrauto hillside, a woman interrupts the conversation between mother and son; Silvestro hears the woman say only two words, "Fortunate Mother," and he knows that she has brought the news of Liborio's death in battle. After an ironic passage in which Silvestro tells Concezione that her son's death pays her honor and has earned for her a place in history (one must remember that Elio Vittorini wrote knowing his words would be read by the Fascist authorities), he starts weeping, uncontrollably, for his brother, for his mother, for Sicily, for the world, and for no one. Eventually, he finds himself standing under a monumental bronze statue of a naked woman. The "conversation in Sicily" ends with her "clanging laughter."

A short epilogue deals with Silvestro's farewell to his mother, whom he finds washing the feet of an old man. Although the man hides his face, Concezione intimates that he is Silvestro's father. The son draws close. Surely, he thinks, the man is too old; perhaps he is his grandfather, or even the wayfaring lover who ate his mother's bread so long ago.

The Characters

Although more than a dozen men and women play a role in the novel, the story revolves around only three people. Silvestro derives from the same mold that supplies so many protagonists to twentieth century literature. Disaffected, uprooted from his ancestral culture, and tired of a life that neither interests the intellect nor wrings joy from the emotions, he recalls the citizen of T. S. Eliot's *The Waste Land* (1922) and seems a direct forerunner of Albert Camus' Meursault in *L'Étranger* (1942; *The Stranger*, 1946). Even though the type is well established in a number of national literatures, Silvestro's depiction has an especially Italian cast. Culturally and economically, Italy's deepest division is between north and south. Silvestro, like the author, is not only a southerner but also a Sicilian who, for exactly half his life—the dessicated part—has been the product of the industrialized, modern north. The return to his origins represents a renewal of life that draws nourishment from its essential tragedy.

More than Silvestro's mother, Concezione is an Earth Mother, an embodiment of the female principle. She is associated with the Virgin Mary (whose name day is the Feast of the Immaculate Conception, whence comes Concezione's name), but she is also a vegetation goddess (her sons believed she produced melons from her womb), and the epithet "old sow" alludes to an archetypal representation of the life-giving, nurturing mother. At the same time, however, the regeneration she symbolizes implies the circularity of life and death. Yet before the reader interprets Concezione's role as a figure for Female Mystery, he is fascinated by Vittorini's masterly creation of a complicated flesh-and-blood woman who wrestles for dignity and life itself against an ultimately indomitable adversary.

Costantino directly enters the narrative only in the epilogue—and then as a veritable ghost. Even so, through the memories of his son and wife, he is seldom far from the story's meaning. To the same extent that Concezione is the Female, he is the Male. Exuberant and fatally attracted to illusion in his search for affirmation of life, he is a *puer aeternus* destined never to understand his failure.

Themes and Meanings

Because the novel was produced by an avowedly political writer under the tyranny of Benito Mussolini, there has been a strong tendency to read it as an anti-Fascist allegory, as a veiled history of Italy, or even as a poetic, Marxist version of the development of civilization. Certainly, the novel contains some elements of each, but its force is profoundly mythic and its unity depends upon the kind of cohesion one finds in the patterns of poetry. (Vittorini's fiction bears a basic resemblance to the poetry and aims of his brother-in-law Salvatore Quasimodo.)

The central theme concerns the quest for the "living water" that redeems life. Wine, offered as the living water in the tavern, provides only illusion, but so does Concezione's experience with the wayfarer, which, significantly, occurred at Acquaviva—literally "living water" in Italian. Finally, Silvestro sees both his father and his mother defeated by life's dreadful reality, yet the commitment to the illusion has a transcendent meaning.

Critical Context

Written in 1937, the novel derives from Vittorini's own return to Sicily from Milan four years earlier. In this respect, as in several others, it is fundamentally autobiographical, even though a note prefacing the story states that the protagonist is not the author, and that the locale is Sicily merely because it has a more harmonious sound than Persia or Venezuela. Yet if the disclaimer is patently a dissimulation at one level, at another it is accurate, for the author has treated his materials in such a way as to render them as myth.

Vittorini can be usefully compared with Cesare Pavese, his only peer among Italian fiction writers of their generation. Both were translators and remarkably astute critics who made Italians aware of the giants of American literature; their own work clearly shows the influence of Herman Melville, Sherwood Anderson, John Steinbeck, and William Faulkner. Both were politically situated on the Left and were active opponents of Fascism; their humanistic sympathies, clothed in the politics of their period, are similarly evident in their works. Whereas Pavese amassed a relatively large body of excellent fiction, however, Vittorini's output was inconsistent. His fiction in the early 1930's suffers under the burden of bearing an unmediated political and social message; the postwar work lacks the moral urgency that had driven his better writing. Beyond a doubt, *In Sicily* is his masterpiece, and even though it is not a perfect novel (some of the later sections are either too clouded or too obvious in their straining for significance), it ranks among the finest achievements in European fiction of the twentieth century.

Sources for Further Study

Heiney, Donald. *Three Italian Novelists: Moravia, Pavese, Vittorini*, 1968.

Lewis, R. W. B. "Elio Vittorini," in *Italian Quarterly*. IV (Fall, 1960), pp. 55-61.

Pacifici, Sergio. *A Guide to Contemporary Italian Literature: From Futurism to Neorealism*, 1962.

Schneider, Marilyn. "Circularity as Mode and Meaning in *Conversazione in Sicilia*," in *Modern Language Notes*. XC (1975), pp. 93-109.

Frank Gado

IN THE LABYRINTH

Author: Alain Robbe-Grillet (1922-   )
Type of plot: New Novel
Time of plot: World War II
Locale: A French city
First published: Dans le labyrinthe, 1959 (English translation, 1960)

> *Principal characters:*
> THE NARRATOR, a doctor
> A SOLDIER, a young man whose life the narrator tries and fails
> to save
> A WOMAN, who shelters the wounded soldier
> A BOY, who helps the soldier find a street
> A LAME MAN, who is shamming his lameness to avoid fighting
> in the war

The Novel

Traditional terms of literary analysis such as "plot" and "character" do not apply comfortably to the New Novel form credited to Alain Robbe-Grillet. In a series of essays collected under the title *Pour un nouveau roman* (1963; *For a New Novel*, 1965), Robbe-Grillet describes such terms as "several obsolete notions":

> We are so accustomed to discussions of "character," "atmosphere," "form," and "content," of "message" and "narrative ability" and "true novelists" that it requires an effort to free ourselves from this spider web and realize that it represents an idea about the novel (a ready-made idea, which everyone admits without argument, hence a dead idea), and not at all that . . . "nature" of the novel in which we are supposed to believe.

With this warning in place, Robbe-Grillet describes his New Novel, in which the act of writing is the form itself, and in which the minute description of objective reality is intertwined with fanciful conjecture, dream states, feverishly subjective distortions, and pure invention, none of which answers to any chronological sequence as assumed in the traditional novel. Nor is character defined in the same way, since no psychologically recognizable or three-dimensional portraits are proffered by the writer. The novel is peopled instead by rather vaguely identified and often amorphous creatures, ambiguous and unstructured, about whom the reader knows only the external details of their lives.

In the Labyrinth, Robbe-Grillet's fourth novel, stands as his most fully realized example of the theories he only partially succeeded in illustrating in his previous novels. Unraveling the events, which twist and turn in a labyrinthine way, the reader understands that a young soldier is wandering the streets of a French city, seeking to deliver a shoe-box shaped package to the family of another soldier, who died in a hospital. The contents of the package, a mystery which holds the reader's interest, prove to be unimportant personal belongings, not the bomb or the secret papers suggested by the intrigue of the novel.

The soldier, seen from the perspective of a narrative observer whose own physical position relative to the soldier is open to question, is fevered; much of what is reported can then be seen as the hallucinations of the soldier himself. He enlists the help of a local boy who (depending on the whim of the narrator at various points) skips happily through the snow, holds an umbrella in the rain, or hides the soldier after he has been shot by enemy soldiers. A woman, possibly the boy's mother, helps the soldier, trying to learn the correct name of the street he seeks and tending his wounds.

In the meantime, the narrator is alone in his room (possibly), where every detail of the mantel, the circular stains made by the ashtray, the fly walking on the lampshade, and the crack in the ceiling is described dispassionately and scientifically. At one point, the narrator looks at a small engraving of a tavern scene, which works itself into the narrative pattern, and describes the scene down to the facial expressions and direction of the gaze of each person in the tavern. The two realities nevertheless blend together; for example, the tavern scene includes a young boy clutching a brown box like the one the soldier carries through the streets of the city. Finally, dying on a bed that may be the woman's (except that the narrator's crack on the ceiling is discerned), the soldier is given a third injection of painkiller by the doctor, who refers to himself as "I," thus identifying himself as the narrator of the entire novel.

In one sense a subjective recounting of real events, and in another sense a conjectural reconstruction, invented in the quiet of the doctor's room (possibly based on conclusions drawn from the box of letters and insignificant items left behind by his dead patient), the novel never retreats to the traditional forms established by such great French writers as Honoré de Balzac and Gustave Flaubert. Instead, it remains in a descriptive mode, devoid of "meaning" or "signification," refusing all attempts to place a grid of symbolic or universally understood images over the objective descriptions.

The Characters

The reader knows least about the central character, the narrator. He (or she) cannot be described in psychological terms, since it is only as an observer and as a maker of stories that the narrator is available for scrutiny. The narrator is, in turn, the subjective inventor of the other characters in the book, giving them external traits and stances, clothing them, perhaps even adding occasional dialogue, but avoiding any internalization or explication of their motives. Of the woman, the reader learns that she wears an apron;

that, unlike her neighbors, she does not run at the sight of the injured soldier; that she has a son; that her husband is feigning his lameness. From this information, the reader is free to draw conclusions.

Because of the objective description of every detail, the narrator's view is extremely subjective, since everything available to the reader is filtered through this one sensibility. If the narrator could be considered a reliable one, several inferences about the characters could be drawn, but the narrator himself reverses his observations, "erasing" with a "no" the twist or turn that leads nowhere. Thus the soldier may or may not be a spy, a traitor, a coward, or a hero, depending on the narrator's description of his overcoat, its insignia, and other details of the soldier's experiences, all of which must be either conclusions drawn from the detective-like observations of the narrator or purely fictive constructions created to fill in details where no evidence is present.

In either case, the term "character" is inaccurate when discussing the traits of a person seen only from the outside and in a convolution of the time frame that disallows even a cause/effect relationship leading to analysis of character. Robbe-Grillet has succeeded in writing a novel without characters in the traditional sense, while at the same time "photographing" in excruciating detail a small group of figures possibly embroiled in subversive activities or possibly living out their lives in helpless innocence.

Themes and Meanings

If the reader has difficulties identifying a plot, discerning characters, and making sense of the chronological sequence of events, an even more difficult task awaits anyone who seeks meaning in what Robbe-Grillet has said is a novel without "signification." The descriptive style in this piece has as its purpose the stripping away of all metaphor, all symbolism, all universality, to reduce (or, some critics would say, return) all objects to their objectivity. According to the principles of writing that Robbe-Grillet follows, the universe is "neither significant nor absurd. It *is*, quite simply."

Given the scholar's predilection, however, for finding meaning in all literary utterances, it is clear that there are several labyrinths, a structure ubiquitous in Western literature from the time of Theseus and the Minotaur, in the landscape of Robbe-Grillet's novel. The most obvious labyrinth in the novel, the city streets, is the site of most of the soldier's and boy's actions; a minor labyrinth, the hallways and doorways of private dwellings, completes the landscape. Less obvious, but apparent on closer inspection, is the meandering of the chronological sequence, which is further confused by the narrator's use of the present tense, linking events only with such ambiguous phrases as "and now."

Yet the act of inventing or constructing a life story, the activity of the narrator, is also the act of writing a novel, and the labyrinth closest to being understood in this metaphorical sense is the limitless ability of the author himself to turn the events of his novel in any direction that suits him. In fact, in many ways the entire novel is a discussion of the process of writing a novel. The narrator often gives signals, such as "this scene" or "again," that indicate that he is returning to a point in his narrative at which corrections or variations are required and that demonstrate the flexibility of his invention.

Finally, Robbe-Grillet's whole theory of novel-writing returns to this simple point: Writing is an artificial activity in which stories are constructed with complete fluidity, answering neither to scientific physical principles nor to historical traditions of "plot," "character," and the like. The novel is a creation, unique and irreproducible, which takes its form from its own facticity. In this regard, the New Novel of Robbe-Grillet is the correct form for telling the existential world its own story. More than an exercise in the destruction of traditional forms, Robbe-Grillet's novels offer a fresh view of the phenomenological universe, discernible (by definition) only through perceptions, void of signification beyond—but infinitely variable and fascinating within— the senses.

Critical Context

The first responses to Robbe-Grillet's novels were mixed. His detractors condemned the purposelessness they saw in the disorder of events, the randomness of detail, and the failure to engross the reader in some emotional or even intellectual way. They pointed to the cinematic techniques, especially the camera-like perspective of the unreliable narrator, as a bastardization of the novel form which allows for multiple perspectives. Other critics praised this "demystification" of the novel, however, and saw Robbe-Grillet as bringing the art of fiction writing into the twentieth century. Several other writers were already dealing with perspectivism, the retelling of the same story from the perspective of several characters. The most successful of these experimenters was William Faulkner in such novels as *The Sound and the Fury* (1929). Samuel Beckett's novels, which move forward without benefit of narrator, as an internalized voice recounts and retells the story of the immobile narrative figure, bear some resemblance to Robbe-Grillet's work, but the physical details, the measurable shapes and so forth, are usually absent in Beckett, replaced by a denuded gray landscape almost antithetical to Robbe-Grillet's meticulously detailed world.

Robbe-Grillet has been accepted in the literary world as a representative of a group of writers seeking to objectify the experiences of their narrators in a reaction against the romantic or emotional novels of the popular culture. His films, notably *L'Année dernière à Marienbad* (1961; *Last Year at Marienbad*, 1962), have also enhanced his reputation, despite some critics' objections that the cinematic techniques of the novel are diluted by the overly obvious camera's eye. In the wake of the postmodernist movement and the postmodern novel, Robbe-Grillet's experiments with the narrative objectifier are seen as the forerunner to the personalized narrator/writer in the novels of William Gass and Raymond Federman.

It is ironic that, despite Robbe-Grillet's insistence that his novels bear no signification, they should be dissected by scholars seeking hidden patterns of "symbols" and "codes." Before choosing a literary career, Robbe-Grillet was a naturalist; the detailed descriptions in his novels have often been compared to the botanist's minute description of specimens found in nature. Perhaps the best way to understand his work is to see him as a careful observer in the field of human activity, neither drawing conclusions nor interpreting findings but rather reporting exactly what he sees.

Sources for Further Study
Carrabino, Victor. *The Phenomenological Novel of Alain Robbe-Grillet*, 1974.
Morrissette, Bruce. *Intertextual Assemblage in Robbe-Grillet*, 1979.
_____. *The Novels of Robbe-Grillet*, 1975.
Robbe-Grillet, Alain. *For a New Novel*, 1965.
Stoltzfus, Ben F. *Alain Robbe-Grillet and the New French Novel*, 1964.

Thomas J. Taylor

INDIAN SUMMER

Author: Adalbert Stifter (1805-1868)
Type of plot: Bildungsroman
Time of plot: The 1820's
Locale: Vienna, the Austrian Alps, and the subalpine countryside
First published: Der Nachsommer, 1857 (English translation, 1985)

>*Principal characters:*
>HEINRICH DRENDORF, the narrator, a budding scientist
>BARON GUSTAV VON RISACH, a gentleman farmer, the owner
>   of the Asper estate (the Rose House), and the mentor of
>   young Heinrich
>MATHILDE TORONA, the owner of the Sternenhof estate
>NATALIE, Mathilde's daughter, who lives with her
>GUSTAV, Mathilde's son, who is under the tutelage of Baron
>   von Risach
>KLOTILDE, Heinrich's young sister

The Novel

Indian Summer is a leisurely paced novel whose chief attribute is its serenity. The plot, deliberately lacking in dramatic incidents, tensions, and struggles, charts the almost imperceptible growth of a young man toward the humanistic ideal of a harmoniously shaped individual who is able to master life and live it in a model environment. His union with a young girl, similarly reared, in the end establishes a potentially perfect family, founded within a circle of like-minded relatives and friends in an idealized, Edenic landscape.

The first of the novel's three books introduces the reader to the young narrator, Heinrich Drendorf. He presents his model family: the father, a respectably affluent merchant, a self-made man of humble origin who, by sheer dedication and industriousness, has accumulated an extensive collection of art and antiques; the mother, noble and pious, a woman who is totally absorbed in her family duties; Heinrich himself, a docile and obedient son; and his young sister, Klotilde, who is strongly attached to her brother. Surrounded by love and understanding, the young man is initially molded by the patriarchal high moral standards of the family. From his maternal granduncle, Heinrich receives an independent income, which he prudently manages. As an ambitious and industrious student, he takes seriously his studies of mathematics and then natural sciences, geology in particular. In order to study these subjects, he makes various excursions into the different parts of his country, especially the Alps.

On one of his outings, seeking shelter from a storm which he believes is rapidly approaching, Heinrich reaches an estate of a noble-looking older gentleman. The man contradicts Heinrich's prediction of a thunderstorm but hospitably invites him to his home. Encountering this man, Baron Gustav von Risach, the owner of the Asper estate, proves to be crucial to the narrator's character and education. The exemplary order with which the estate is governed and the aesthetic principles by which the buildings, antique furnishings, paintings, and a classical Greek marble sculpture are arranged have a great effect on the young man. A wall of stunningly beautiful roses together with the gardens, orchards, and fields presents an ideal and harmonious realm under the guidance of the wise, Prospero-like Baron von Risach. In spite of the cordiality between the young man and his host, names are not exchanged or immediately learned. After several days spent admiring the estate and having every detail explained to him, inspecting workshops where artists are restoring old masterpieces and creating new ones, and looking at cacti lovingly cultivated by the chief gardener, Heinrich meets a young boy, Gustav, who is tutored by the old gentleman.

Upon his departure from the Rose House, as he now prefers to call the estate, Heinrich encounters a carriage with two ladies and is so impressed by the younger one's face that he decides that from now on he should sketch human faces in addition to stones and minerals. The stay at the Asper estate and the enlightening discourses by its owner on subjects varying from husbandry to science and art have lasting consequences for young Heinrich. Invited to return, he makes frequent visits which are attuned to the seasons of the year; he spends winters in the city with his family, but when spring arrives, he breaks out on his exploratory journeys which regularly bring him back to the Rose House.

While in the city, he continues to further his systematic education. Now, wiser from his aesthetic and ethical experiences at the Baron von Risach's estate, he becomes more sensitive to things that he previously overlooked or ignored. During a performance of *King Lear*, for example, he is so moved by William Shakespeare's discernment of what Heinrich calls "ultimate reality" that he instinctively looks around for a kindred soul in the theater and sees the sympathetic eyes of a young girl who shares his deep emotion.

While on his second visit to Baron von Risach's estate, he encounters Gustav's mother and sister, who have arrived to witness the exalted moment of the blossoming of the roses. Mathilde Torona, the boy's mother, owns property, the Sternenhof estate, in the immediate surroundings, and his sister, Natalie (the same girl who was in the carriage and in the theater, as is later revealed), is the embodiment of exquisite charm. Though Heinrich sees that there is intimacy between Mathilde and Baron von Risach, he is kept in the dark about the true nature of their relationship until almost the end of the novel.

A gradually developing mutual, though unexpressed, attraction begins to grow between Heinrich and Natalie. While crucial to the novel, the love of these two young people is treated rather circumspectly. Aside from occasional flights into solitude and mild restlessness, the young people go on without a wordy display of romantic impetuosity. Instead of being an impediment, their budding love is a further impulse toward their shared ideal of steady maturation. It is book 2 that emphasizes the holistic approach to the development of a full personality and a humanistic ideal characteristic of a *Bildungsroman*.

Heinrich has to learn that only through patient submission to the "gentle law" of natural order and measured receptiveness to new experiences, especially of aesthetic nature, will his being and his personality grow to understand and appreciate a life led on a higher moral plane. He therefore willingly subjects himself to the further guidance of Baron von Risach as well as of his father and thus sees things around him in their proper perspective. The art collection of Baron von Risach awakens in Heinrich the sympathetic understanding of his own father's art collection and thus brings father and son closer together. The new insights help Heinrich look at older people with different eyes, seeing in them a ripe beauty of which he was previously unaware. Thus, a chance remark by Baron von Risach that older women are like roses slightly faded holds new meaning for him, especially when he looks at Mathilde. The declaration of love between Natalie and Heinrich, which occurs in the last chapter of the second book, does not constitute a dramatic climax of the novel; instead, it is only another augmenting experience in the ennobling process that the two young people undergo.

The third book continues with the unfolding of the already established harmony existing in the young couple. Their potential union is validated when both Natalie and Heinrich inform their respective parents and obtain their consent. By including their parents in the "secret" of their mutual attraction, they broaden the base on which to found their future happiness, which could blossom only in an atmosphere of honesty and harmony.

In two further chapters, "The Confidence" and "The Communication," Heinrich finds that, while he had always been accepted and affectionately treated by all concerned, Baron von Risach, Gustav, and Mathilde now treat him with a new feeling of attachment and there is a new sense of mature intimacy in his own family. Only his sister, Klotilde, is initially unhappy about the prospect of losing him.

Heinrich's father charts now the course toward the orderly sanctioning of Heinrich's union with Natalie. First, he and Heinrich will go back to their village in order to achieve a better understanding of their roots, and Heinrich will have to undertake a two-year educational trip through Europe. Before that happens, however, Heinrich will have to be initiated by Baron von Risach into the secret of his relationship to Mathilde. In the fourth chapter, entitled "The Look into the Past," the narrator describes this ritual submersion in the past in order that the present can be fully comprehended. This chapter constitutes the center of the whole moral and pedagogical structure of the novel. In a flashback, the reader learns not only about Baron von Risach's past but also about how he became what he is now. He discloses why, when one acts rashly with youthful excess, prompted only by egotistical passions that require immediate fulfillment, one inevitably ruins every promise of happiness and may destroy oneself in the process.

Coming from a poor family, the young Gustav Risach was engaged, on a wealthy estate, as a tutor to a young boy whose sister was Mathilde. When Gustav and Mathilde, attracted to each other, exchanged passionate vows by swearing eternal love, Mathilde's mother rejected their union as unsuitable because of Mathilde's immaturity and youth. Gustav accepted her judgment, but Mathilde, hurt by the disclosure of their secret, spurned him as a weakling for obeying her mother's dictate. After a period of total despair and thoughts of suicide, Gustav entered the government services. Upon learning that Mathilde had married another, Gustav married a woman whom he did not love. He advanced in his service, was made a baron, and, following the death of his wife, resigned from service and bought an estate in the lower Alps. Having never forgotten Mathilde, he constructed a wall of roses on his estate in her memory, recalling similar roses grown on her family estate. Mathilde, herself now a widow with two children, arrived at the estate attracted by the wall of blooming roses. Past mistakes cannot be rectified, and the two, now old, have matured into a state of resignation and acceptance. While they can no longer enjoy the summer of their youthful love, they have settled down for a prolonged "Indian summer" of gentle, platonic affection. Mathilde bought a neighboring estate, Baron von Risach became the foster father of Mathilde's son, Gustav, and Natalie, her daughter, learned to tread a different path from her mother, yielding not to the moment of abandoned passion, but accepting the slow, ripening process of more enriching love.

The concluding chapter describes the preparation of Heinrich's family to enter into the close relationship with his bride's family. With a newly acquired carriage, they travel first to the Rose House, then to Mathilde's Sternenhof. There is a promise of an unclouded happiness which will spread from the young couple to the estates, which now number three, since Heinrich's father has forsaken the city for an estate in the same area.

The Characters

Adalbert Stifter has a visual imagination which disposes him to call the reader's attention to the dark eyes and brown hair of Natalie and Gustav, for example, as well as to the characters' clothing. Typically, however, he suggests rather than describes. All the main characters are what human beings could be under ideal conditions; this precludes any real individualization. The most impressive character is Baron von Risach, who possesses the proverbial wisdom, kindness, and serenity of old age and whose present sphere of activity is large enough to allow him to realize all of his formerly unfulfilled dreams. Mathilde's beauty reflects the grace and calm resignation which she personifies. Heinrich is a model son and brother, Klotilde is the ideal daughter and sister, and Gustav is an exemplary youth. So much perfection in the main characters would be unbearable without the human failings shown in the flashback and some hints at the dangerous depths of human nature that are revealed in two minor characters in the novel, the vagabond zither player Joseph and, especially, Eustach's brother, the artist Roland.

Themes and Meanings

In *Indian Summer*, the antagonism between the classic and the romantic is resolved; the polarity is caught in the depictions of Natalie, dignified, calm, and displaying perfect form, and Mathilde, first rapturous and yearning and later mystically renouncing. Yet these two are naturally linked as mother and daughter. Natalie, through education, has developed strength of character and a noble spirit. Her being is classical in its balance just as her appearance is classical in a form such as that of Greek maidens. Natalie and Gustav are incarnations of the Greek ideal of *Kalokagathie*, the fusion of the beautiful and the good. Heinrich, a youth on the way to becoming a man, gradually assumes the contours of Baron von Risach, the man of action. Heinrich's attainment of full and perfect manhood is the theme of the novel. He progresses from innocence and latency to sophistication and realization without ever falling into serious error. His education, while awkward at times, is never arduous. All the major characters mature without rebellion or friction between generations. The mark of their nobility is their naturalness and simplicity. Love does not overpower them; instead, it becomes clear to them gradually, like the growing appreciation of the beauty of a classical marble statue which emerges from the protective cover of plaster. To suit his didactic purpose, Stifter places restraints on the relationship between the two lovers in order to contrast it with Baron von Risach and Mathilde's story. This restraint is in keeping with the whole tenor of the book. Heinrich and Natalie are always in close communion with nature, and they are always at one with themselves. These characters have no inclination to show off or appear brilliant. This prevents the young people from having real friends outside their own circle. For Stifter, genuine education is possible only through association with greater and more mature minds. Yet the aesthetic and ethical unity which informs the characters in the foreground and presents them as ideals does not redeem the secondary characters, who remain inferior.

Critical Context

Indian Summer has often been criticized for its length, its elaborations, and its many details. The critic Walter Muschg describes this work as a sacral, didactic poem which represents a spiritual order constructed from hieratic symbols. Another critic, Keith Spalding, reads the novel as an illustrated code of law that sets down the guidelines for perfection in life. It certainly seems true that Stifter is, in the characters, landscapes, and human relationships of *Indian Summer*, concerned with aesthetic and ethical implications. In many ways, the book is utopian. The Rose House is the nucleus of an ideal society engaged in agrarian management and the restoration of historic art objects. Restraint is the tenor of this society, as is close communion with nature. In this blueprint, the classical ideal of full and realized humanity is set forth.

The degree of autobiography in the novel is difficult to determine; certainly much of the depiction of Baron von Risach's childhood and early adulthood corresponds to Stifter's early life, but largely this is a presentation of the ideal life as dreamed by its author.

Sources for Further Study

Gump, Margaret. "*Der Nachsommer*," in *Adalbert Stifter*, 1974.

Naumann, Ursula. "*Der Nachsommer*," in *Adalbert Stifter*, 1979.

Oertel Sjögren, Christine. *"The Marble Statue as Idea": Collected Essays on Adalbert Stifter's "Der Nachsommer,"* 1972.

Pascal, Roy. "Adalbert Stifter: *Indian Summer*," in *The German Novel*, 1956.

Steffen, Konrad. "*Der Nachsommer*," in *Adalbert Stifter*, 1955.

Frank S. Lambasa

INFERNO

Author: August Strindberg (1849-1912)
Type of plot: Autobiographical expressionism
Time of plot: 1894-1897
Locale: Pariś, Germany, and Sweden
First published: 1897 (English translation, 1912)

> *Principal characters:*
> THE NARRATOR, Strindberg's alter ego
> HIS WIFE, who carries on a love-hate correspondence with
> him
> CHRISTINE, his daughter, who inspires him
> HIS MOTHER-IN-LAW, who comforts him

The Novel

In *Inferno*, the psychologically disturbed narrator sets forth on a journey through an earthly hell and emerges purified of his sins. Leaving his wife and child liberates him but also fills him with guilt. Living alone in Paris, he rejects love in order to pursue knowledge and with the aid of signs and portents discovers carbon in the element sulfur. At the same time, the narrator, believing that his life is being controlled by an unknown power, withdraws from the world of loose living, only to be whipped by prostitutes and harassed by ruffians, who punish him for his sins. When his scientific experiments leave his hands bleeding and incapacitated, he enters the St. Louis Hospital, where he is surrounded by decay, disease, and death. Once there, however, his relationship with a motherly nun revives him and teaches him to bear his sufferings.

Although he receives financial aid for a time, his suffering increases. After dabbling in black magic by trying to cast a spell on his child, he finds himself plagued by three Scandinavian women playing three separate pianos in the rooms next to him. Fleeing to the Hotel Orfila, the narrator continues his grandiose experiments, trying to produce gold from lead. Incidents which he perceives as strange omens continue to plague him, as he discovers a man who looks like his wife, letters displaying his wife's maiden name, and an envelope addressed to a Dr. Bitter.

Undergoing a series of mystical experiences, the narrator sees his life as a purgatory in which he is threatened by his enemy Popoffsky, betrayed by his friend the Danish painter, and persecuted by the Devil, who turns over his glass, flicks soot on him, and leaves him in a world of excrement and filth. Doubting the efficacy of his scientific experiments and choked by noxious gases, he opens his window and sees the North Star beckoning him northward.

Fleeing from one location to another only increases his torments. He feels electric shocks running through his body, sees infernal machines being built above his room, and prepares himself for death by reading Psalms. Even in the wholesome atmosphere of his friend's family at Dieppe, the demoniac spirits continue to persecute him. Seeking refuge with a doctor increases the intensity of his sufferings and leaves him convinced that he is living in Hell. Only when visiting his daughter and mother-in-law does he find temporary consolation, although he continues to look out on a world filled with disease and evil. Eventually, he feels vultures trying to tear out his heart and he vainly cries out to God.

Finally, he settles in Sweden, believing that his torments have purified him. Embracing Roman Catholicism and Swedenborgian mysticism, he accepts a life of repentance and seeks refuge in a Belgian monastery. In the end, he holds up his life as a warning to those who think that they can shape their own destiny in an earthly hell which is controlled by an "Invisible Hand."

The Characters

In *Inferno*, the narrator is the only complex character. All the others are projected to the reader through his ego. On one level, he is a disturbed individual trying to maintain his sanity by seeking both rational and irrational answers for his sufferings. On another level, he becomes an archetypal scapegoat thrust into a cosmic drama. At first, he sets himself up as a Promethean rebel who is condemned to eternal punishment for revealing the secrets of the universe. Later, he envisions himself as Job, the innocent victim whom God has turned over to Satan in order to show the wicked that a just man must endure his suffering. Like Job, the narrator suffers from skin ulcers, endures poverty, is rejected by friends, and is surrounded by excrement. Also, he questions God but never receives a satisfactory answer to the meaning of human suffering. Then the narrator assumes the role of a mock Christ figure, suffering the stigmata of bleeding hands and bearing on his shoulders the sorrows of the world. Finally, the scapegoat hero becomes God's fool—a laughingstock to teach humanity the vanity of worldly ambitions.

On his path through the inferno, the narrator encounters several false friends: Popoffsky, a former compatriot who now wants to murder him; a Danish painter who double-crosses him; a mysterious friend who wants him tried for witchcraft; a doctor who becomes his tormentor. All human relationships deteriorate, and the narrator must face his agonies alone. Women also play an important role in the narrator's enlightenment. He often sees women as temptresses and defilers of his purity. Sensual women, such as prostitutes, constantly abuse him. Feminists are seen as maenads trying to ruin him and tear him to pieces. Only the mother figure offers him consolation. The nun in the St. Louis Hospital, his mother-in-law, and her sister show him love and teach him to bear his sufferings. His daughter, Christine, the pure virgin, becomes his Beatrice and directs him on the path to a higher love. Finally, it is the Virgin Mary, embodying both the qualities of purity and maternity, who becomes his protectress. Her presence recurs throughout the novel, as she is raised to the status of a goddess, more powerful even than the crucified Christ.

Themes and Meanings

Inferno deals with humanity's powerlessness in a world of torment, evil, disease, and death. Surrounded by criminals and sinners, forced to witness death and decay, confronted by excrement and filth, persecuted by diabolical machines, and driven to the brink of insanity, the narrator depicts a world of unremitting agony. Rebellion is futile, for it leads to pride and retribution. Those who pursue wealth and fame find that their goals inevitably become the instruments of their torture. Love turns to hate, friends become enemies, and virtues are transformed into vices.

Grappling with the age-old dilemma of Job, August Strindberg at times sees human suffering as a means of purification; occasionally, he also sees a direct connection between sin and suffering. He even holds that people can suffer for sins committed in another life. Intermingling Catholic and Protestant theology, Buddhist ideals, Swedenborgian mysticism, and occultist theory, Strindberg creates more paradoxes than explanations. He consoles those afflicted with mental anguish by telling them that they are God's special people. Lurking behind Strindberg's divinity, however, is a capricious and inexplicable God who can turn the proud into beggars, the wise into fools, and the prophets into charlatans, and who can ultimately reduce human existence to a joke.

Critical Context

Inferno documents Strindberg's mental breakdowns and emotional crises from 1894 to 1897. The narrator's chemical experiments, the places where he stayed in Paris, and the people he mentions can all be traced back to Strindberg's experiences. Yet documentation shows that *Inferno* is not an accurate autobiography. Events in Strindberg's life have been rearranged to construct an almost poetic novel which treats more than a single individual's bout with mental illness.

Inferno was a watershed work for Strindberg, for in it, he came to terms with his crisis of faith and emerged with a new vision, an expressionistic vision which sounded the death knell of literary naturalism. In *Inferno*, one can see the nascent development of expressionism in the outcast hero, the nameless characters, the solipsistic universe, the pilgrimage motif, the macabre images, the dreamlike episodes, the infernal machines, and the apocalyptic visions. After *Inferno*, Strindberg would create his dramatic masterpieces, such as *Ett drömspel* (1902; *A Dream Play*, 1912) and the three-part *Till Damaskus* (1898-1904; *To Damascus*, 1913), refining these expressionistic techniques and ultimately influencing the development of German expressionism as well as of modern absurdism.

Sources for Further Study
Brandell, Gunnar. *Strindberg in "Inferno,"* 1974.
Johannesson, Eric. *The Novels of August Strindberg*, 1968.
Lagercrantz, Olof. *August Strindberg*, 1984.
Lamm, Martin. *August Strindberg*, 1971.
Meyer, Michael. *Strindberg: A Biography*, 1985.

Paul Rosefeldt

THE INQUISITORY

Author: Robert Pinget (1919-   )
Type of plot: New Novel
Time of plot: c. 1960
Locale: In and around the village of Sirancy, France
First published: L'Inquisitoire, 1962 (English translation, 1966)

> *Principal characters:*
> THE INTERROGATOR, a magistrate or similar official
> THE INTERROGEE, an old man who does most of the talking

The Novel

The Inquisitory has no beginning, middle, or end. It does not take a group of characters and lead them through a series of complications to a resolution of any kind. Instead, the entire novel is a series of questions and answers that begins abruptly, develops no patterns of theme or conflict, and ends inconclusively. No authorial commentary is provided to establish a context, and there is no punctuation except for an occasional comma in the longer answers. After a few pages, the reader becomes aware that the interrogator is an officer of the law who is questioning an old man about the disappearance of a servant who, like the old man, had been employed at Château de Broy, the estate of two unnamed "gentlemen." The fate of the servant, however, is soon lost in the welter of wide-ranging questions and detailed answers. Beyond this bit of abortive plot—little more than the device for setting the interrogation in motion—the reader is constantly frustrated in his attempts to find a thread of narrative to follow in the labyrinth of text. Furthermore, the old man is deaf, and the questions are apparently written out for him and transcribed by a recorder.

The title of the novel is itself unusual. The French word *inquisitoire* is apparently a neologism, translated by the obsolete English word "inquisitory"—in effect, another neologism. The intensity of the protracted interrogation is perhaps best suggested by translating *inquisitoire* as "grilling" or "third degree."

Despite the plotlessness of the old man's rambling testimony, however, the overwhelming accumulation of detail—page after page of street layouts, room furnishings, and so forth—begins to produce its own effect, especially as the foibles and personal entanglements of various local figures are quickly sketched. It is as if a gifted dramatist had created an enormous set, crowded with the minutiae of daily life, and put an endless sequence of walk-ons in the background, while the audience waits restively for a protagonist who never appears. Gradually, the audience shifts its attention to the elaborate scene painting and the petty minidramas of the walk-ons.

Although the official's ostensible purpose in the interrogation is to investigate the servant's disappearance, he reveals a salacious preoccupation with the habits of the two gentlemen at the Château de Broy. The two men are apparently homosexuals—although their servant balks at discussing this fact—and their bohemian soirees are always sybaritic, often orgiastic. Moreover, the gentlemen's lives are colored by a faintly expressed suspicion that their prosperity derives from transactions in drugs and prostitutes. Nevertheless, the man is discreet about his employers' predilections and remains loyal to them. The questioner's insistent prodding eventually elicits a panorama of the life around the village of Sirancy and the nearby town of Agapa. More than six hundred inhabitants are named, and some of them star in their own brief dramas as re-created by the old man.

The interrogee's own life provides by far the most interesting vignette. Halfway through the interrogation, he reluctantly discloses that he was married for ten years and has fathered a son. The son, Claude, succumbed to meningitis when he was eight, and two years later, the wife, Marie, also died. He has now been a widower for ten years. The tale of their married life is bizarre. While working for an eccentric couple, the Emmerands, he and his wife had been drawn into their employers' spiritualist practices. Mme Emmerand was a medium, and the old man suspects her of having caused Claude's death simply to have a dead child with whom to talk. The old man is just as superstitious as the Emmerands, and he is sure that he caused their deaths by pricking several photographs of them with pins.

The old man's tales about the villagers frequently have a scandalous sexual element. His account of the Emmerands leads him, for example, to tell of an adulterous affair between two of the couple's friends, M. d'Eterville and Mme Flammard. Although the old man phrases his story prissily, with apologies for the more lurid details, it is clear that he took a Peeping Tom's pleasure in what he observed. M. Flammard overlooked his wife's liaison with the influential d'Eterville because Flammard wanted to curry favor with her lover. The old man sensed this and kept a close eye on the romance, even spying through the window on the couple's lovemaking.

The old man's voyeurism is only a mild perversion compared to the criminal compulsions visited upon Johann, a servant of the Grossbirke family. Johann talked a weak-witted young man named Stoffel into helping to plot the murder of his own girlfriend, and then joined him in committing necrophilia. Johann then repeated his criminal acts upon two other young women before the police finally dug up the three corpses in the vacationing Grossbirkes' cellar. The story of Johann is related in the context of a long summary of sexual misdoings in the neighborhood, a summary in which the questioner obviously takes a lively prurient interest.

The *pièce de résistance* of the rambling chronicle is probably the recollection of the elaborate evening party hosted by the man's two gentlemen. He tells the whole story, including the provisioning of the party with about seventy bottles of Johnny Walker whiskey, mountains of forcemeat balls, and a dish made of brains and rice with mushrooms. The old man remembers all the preparations and adorns his story with digressions and asides ("perhaps I did take a swig at Fifine's Rue des Trouble-Fête yes perhaps I did, the poor woman had been very lonely since Florent died"). The questioner's zeal for information about the fête extends to such questions as "How many statues are there along the main drive," a query that leads to a long recital of the statues of Jupiter, Diana, and the malapropistic "Mynerve the patron saint of philosophers." Such epic recall is redeemed from tedium largely by the old man's colloquial garrulousness, and it gives a compensating intricate texture to a social history deprived of structure.

The Characters

The old man dominates the novel. Everything is seen through his eyes, and by the time he has finished his long ordeal (actually the novel simply ends—there is no reason to think that the questioner is necessarily through with his subject), he has taken on considerable life. He is a shrewd, superstitious countryman whose long experience has taught him much about human nature. He apparently has the instincts of a born gossip, a faculty that gives his testimony vitality and insight. He witnesses the goings-on at the château with curiosity, but if he feels any disapprobation about the values and behavior of the two gentlemen, he seldom reveals it. Only an intelligent man could recall so many details with such precision, and he is remarkably articulate and well versed in such matters as the names of the gods represented in the statues. At the same time, he is capable of such gross malapropisms as "peddermint" for "pediment" and "Cubid" for "Cupid." Ultimately, perhaps, he is a congeries of attributes that do not always fit together convincingly, but as a narrative voice for a chronicle of social history, he is generally appealing and satisfying.

Themes and Meanings

As is clear from *The Inquisitory*, Robert Pinget is not the kind of novelist who interlards his narrative with didactic commentary or burdens it with symbols and allegory. In one respect, however, he is a very old-fashioned novelist with a truly conventional appeal: The careful depiction of life in his chosen microcosm, the region around Sirancy and Agapa, makes *The Inquisitory* a kind of novel of manners. It is a portrait of French life in the tradition of Honoré de Balzac and Marcel Proust, an art that builds on the amassing of realistic detail. Yet whereas the earlier novelists used their social settings as a backdrop for the development of powerful characters such as Vautrin and Swann, for Pinget the backdrop is all. Although some of his other novels are set in the same locale, they are not all realistic in technique.

The Inquisitory makes occasional sly use of names. The American ladies' man, for example, is called Douglas Hotcock, and the local bishop is Monseigneur Bougecroupe, or "Budgebottom." The place-names are sometimes coarsely humorous, and one of the Sirancy priests tries to provide euphemistic etymologies for them. This kind of wordplay is a familiar device of fiction, and it lightens a stream of narrative that often amounts to little more than a listing of the common facts of mundane reality.

Pinget's refusal to cast his social history of Sirancy and Agapa in a conventional novel form is in itself a statement of theme and purpose: to describe a world in which events do not reveal patterns of plot and meaning. The old man insists that life unfolds as it does, and one should accept it and not try to draw conclusions. For him, life's only purpose is to be lived. Life may be inscrutable, even meaningless, but with luck, it can be survived, and often it can be enjoyed. His cheerful anticipation of what the next day always brings affords the only moral to be found in *The Inquisitory*.

Critical Context

Pinget is one of several French writers of the 1950's and 1960's known as the New Novelists. The other most notable practitioners are Alain Robbe-Grillet, Michel Butor, and Nathalie Sarraute. The New Novelists are generally phenomenologists—that is, they reject an objective view of reality and find what is "real" to be only the subjective vision of things imposed on life by the mind. Thus, the world outside human perception has no fixed referents but is instead always succumbing to interpretation. This metaphysic has its accompanying radical aesthetic: The reasoning is that because the usual structure of Aristotelian beginning, middle, and end suggests an outward order that is illusory, then the proper aesthetic approach for a novelist is one that transcribes events in their true disorderliness and refuses to stamp any given interpretation of these events as "true."

The New Novel is, then, in its own view of things, relentlessly realistic, and it is probably for precisely this reason that it cannot be a popular art. Whatever the truth, if any, about subjects and objects, the average reader seeks a story that gives shape to the lives of people and things. Indeed, the mind cannot help its compulsions: Give it two facts and it will make a story out of them. It does not necessarily follow, however, that the best art is one that turns this story-making impulse entirely over to the reader.

The New Novelists would reject Stendhal's description of a novel as "a mirror walking down a road," with its assumption that there is a world out there to be reproduced. Such an aesthetic of mimesis is identified with a bourgeois commonsense philosophy and deserves to be replaced by an elitist art. Thus, objections to the New Novel can be parried by references to a naïve audience whose appreciation is made impossible by its simplistic epistemology.

At least in *The Inquisitory*, the radical technique comes to little. Once the reader discovers that he is being denied the courtesy of punctuation (and punctuation practices begin elsewhere than in epistemology), he quickly adjusts to supplying it himself and goes on about the business of finding a story. When the persistent reader finishes the book, he will probably find that what he has enjoyed most are the short stories of sex and violence embedded in the long series of answers. It is ironic and amusing that after all the critical polemics occasioned by the New Novel, the appeal of one of its foremost examples lies in its discovery of sex and violence as topics.

Sources for Further Study
Bann, Stephen. "Robert Pinget," in *The London Magazine*. IV (October 7, 1964), pp. 22-35.
Cismarie, Alfred. "Robert Pinget: An Introduction," in *American Benedictine Review*. XIX (June, 1968), pp. 203-210.
Henkels, Robert M., Jr. *Robert Pinget: The Novel as Quest*, 1979.
Knapp, Bettina, ed. *French Novelists Speak Out*, 1976.
Mercier, Vivian. *The New Novel from Queneau to Pinget*, 1971.
Oppenheim, Lois, ed. *Three Decades of the French New Novel*, 1986.

Frank Day

THE INSULTED AND THE INJURED

Author: Fyodor Dostoevski (1821-1881)
Type of plot: Romantic realism
Time of plot: The mid-nineteenth century
Locale: St. Petersburg
First published: Unizhennye i oskorblyonnye, 1861 (*Injury and Insult,* 1887;
 better known as *The Insulted and the Injured*)

Principal characters:
 IVAN PETROVITCH, the narrator, a brilliant but penniless author
  in whom everyone confides, in love with Natasha
 NATASHA NIKOLAEVNA ICHMENYEV, a beautiful and passionate
  young woman, in love with Alyosha
 NIKOLAI SERGEYITCH ICHMENYEV, Natasha's father, who
  disowns her when she goes to live with Alyosha
 ALYOSHA PYOTROVITCH VALKOVSKY, a naïve and weak-willed
  young aristocrat
 PYOTR ALEXANDROVITCH VALKOVSKY, Alyosha's father, a
  fortune-hunting prince who is scheming for Alyosha to
  marry Katerina
 KATERINA FYODOROVNA FILIMONOV, an idealistic young heiress
  who eventually marries Alyosha
 ELENA (NELLIE) SMITH, a little girl whom Ivan rescues from
  destitution

The Novel

The Insulted and the Injured unfolds the emotional tragedy of a young
woman who abandons her family and her good name for the sake of a grand
passion. The story is related in a flashback as a chain of events that began in
St. Petersburg a year before the book opens. The narrator is a penniless
young author, Ivan Petrovitch, who becomes the confidant of all the other
characters and is therefore able to explain their thoughts and motivations.

Ivan has been hailed as a genius, but his self-denying concern for everyone
else's problems prevents him from finishing his second novel, the proceeds
from which would help him pay off his creditors. Orphaned in childhood, he
has been brought up by Nikolai Sergeyitch Ichmenyev, a once-wealthy landowner now in reduced circumstances, and his wife, Anna Andreyevna Ich-
menova. Ivan is in love with their daughter, Natasha Nikolaevna Ichmenyev.
Natasha at first returns his feelings but soon confesses that she has fallen passionately in love with Alyosha Pyotrovitch Valkovsky, the weak-willed, naïve
son of Prince Pyotr Alexandrovitch Valkovsky.

The Ichmenyevs are devastated when Natasha leaves home to live with

Alyosha. They feel not only dishonored but also humiliated, for the Prince, who was once Nikolai's patron, has become his bitter enemy, and the two men are locked in conflict in a lawsuit. Nikolai disowns Natasha. The Prince is also opposed to Alyosha's liaison with Natasha; he forbids their marriage and cuts off his son's allowance. The Prince is scheming to have Alyosha marry a wealthy heiress, Katerina Fyodorovna Filimonov, and contrives to bring him constantly in contact with her.

Throughout the novel, Alyosha, an innocent victim of his father's machinations, is torn between his fascination with Katerina's youth and idealism and his love for Natasha. As he spends more of his time away from her, Natasha becomes sick with anxiety, and Ivan supports and comforts her.

Ivan also spends much time consoling the Ichmenyevs, especially when Nikolai loses his lawsuit and becomes almost insane with despair. Ivan has acquired a further responsibility by rescuing a young, destitute girl, Elena Smith, from the clutches of a brutal procuress, Madame Bubnov. Elena, who insists on being called "Nellie," is an epileptic and is suffering from a high fever as a result of her experiences.

While Ivan is nursing her back to health in his dingy lodgings, she reveals, in several poignant passages, that her mother, like Natasha, had sacrificed everything for love. The lover, unnamed until the final chapter, had abandoned Nellie's mother and tricked her out of her family fortune. In addition, Nellie's grandfather had cursed his daughter and refused to help her. The mother and child had survived by begging in the streets of St. Petersburg until the mother died of tuberculosis, nearly a month before Ivan's intervention. When Ivan leaves Nellie for a time to comfort Natasha, who is distraught because Alyosha has been spending several days in Katerina's company, Nellie reacts sullenly to his attentions to Natasha.

One evening, the Prince pays a surprise visit to Natasha and Alyosha, with Ivan present. The Prince tells them that he has changed his mind and is now eager for them to marry, and he restores Alyosha's allowance. Alyosha is delighted, but Natasha is suspicious. At a subsequent meeting, she accuses the Prince of pretending to consent to the marriage in order to play on Alyosha's indecisiveness, making him yearn for the freedom to visit Katerina at will.

The Prince is furious; he invites Ivan to have supper with him and taunts him by describing at length his philosophy of self-interest and by pouring scorn on those whose sense of honor has placed them in his power. He unfolds further plans to humiliate Nikolai and to engineer Natasha's complete downfall. Later, the Prince visits Natasha and insults her by offering to "place" her in society as mistress to an elderly aristocrat. When Ivan arrives at her apartment, the Prince has left, and Natasha, knowing that she has lost Alyosha to Katerina and deeply humiliated by the Prince's proposition, is completely distracted.

Ivan rushes back to his lodgings and persuades Nellie to go with him to the Ichmenyevs and tell them her story. As the frightened child pours out the tragic tale, Anna is reduced to tears and Nikolai, resistant at first, becomes filled with remorse for his harshness toward Natasha. He is about to go to his daughter when she bursts in and begs his forgiveness. Nellie remains in the household, much loved by everyone but in failing health. Ivan learns, through an intermediary, that the man who wronged Nellie's mother was, in fact, Prince Valkovsky, and that Nellie, as the Prince's daughter, has a claim to all of his wealth. The child dies before there is a chance of restitution, however, and the Prince remains secure. As the novel closes, Ivan and Natasha talk nostalgically together of their lost chance of happiness.

The Characters

Most of the novel's characters are ruled by a conventional morality and a fierce sense of pride. Nikolai Ichmenyev is implacable in his adherence to high moral principle. Even Nellie, who has experienced the depths of degradation, proudly upholds her mother's dictum that it is nobler to beg from strangers than to be beholden to acquaintances. When Natasha, like Nellie's mother earlier, attempts to break with convention, the consequences are disastrous. Her intelligence and honesty are no match for the Prince's philosophy of pure self-interest.

Alyosha's naïve, butterfly personality and his eagerness to please make him the perfect instrument for his father's schemes. His breathless actions and his excited, ingenuous explanations to Natasha about the time he spends with Katerina are like those of an engaging young child. The rivalry of two intelligent women for the love of so weak a character would have stretched credulity to the breaking point if he had not been so persuasively drawn.

Fyodor Dostoevski works diligently to make Natasha's relationship with Alyosha convincing. For example, Natasha attempts to analyze the quality of her love. "People say about him," she tells Ivan, "that he has no will and that he's not very clever. And that's what I loved in him, more than anything else." Nevertheless, she wonders if she would have loved him less if he had been "like other men."

Alyosha's behavior as a childlike adult contrasts with Nellie's as a "real" child growing into adulthood. Her willfulness and her pride, her sudden changes of mood, and her developing sexual feelings (which she cannot wholly understand) are observed with great insight and tenderness. In addition, Dostoevski's own experiences as an epileptic appear in his descriptions of her illness.

Ivan's character—modest and conscientious and deeply sensitive to the suffering of others—emerges as much from other people's reactions to him as from his comments as he tells his story. In addition, the novel's tragic mood is intensified by his foreboding that he has not much longer to live. His self-sacrificing love for Natasha is paralleled by her belief that Alyosha would be happier with the youthful and idealistic Katerina. Both these beliefs are proved false. Toward the end of the novel, Natasha learns that Alyosha has not found fulfillment with Katerina, and finally, she asks Ivan, "Why did I destroy your happiness?"

The Prince's dark spirit hangs over the novel like a malevolent cloud. The suddenness of his appearance at Natasha's apartment adds great dramatic force to their confrontation, while his theory of egotism, expounded to Ivan in forthright and often crude terms, is the key to the whole novel. "All is for me," he tells Ivan, "the whole world is created for me. [I] have long since freed myself from all shackles. I only recognise obligations when I have something to gain by them. You, of course, can't look at things like that, your legs are in fetters."

In addition to the major characters, Dostoevski peoples the novel with a host of vividly drawn minor characters. Madame Bubnov, for example, stands in contrast to the Prince, whose eloquent self-justification is countered by her unthinking and more physical exploitation of other people's weaknesses in the lower depths of St. Petersburg.

Themes and Meanings

Natasha is not the first fictional woman to come to grief for the sake of a consuming passion. Nevertheless, in *The Insulted and the Injured*, Dostoevski uses this familiar situation to subvert its more usual implications. The Prince is the first in a long line of Dostoevski's self-willed men, men who choose to live for their own gratification. Through the Prince's character, the author pursues a theme that dominates much of his subsequent work: the ascendancy of the self-willed man over those who limit themselves by living within the confines of morality and honor. By the end of the book, although almost everyone else has suffered greatly, the Prince's egoism ensures that he remains unscathed.

As well as boasting about his own achievements, the Prince mounts a rumbustious attack on idealism. He sneers at Ivan, calling him a "novelist of the naturalistic school," and deals a satirical blow at those he calls "Schillers," the dreamers and idealists in the Russian intelligentsia of the mid-nineteenth century. The Prince rants to Ivan about his hatred for "these vulgar and worthless naiveties and idyllic nonsense." The Prince's anti-idealism is echoed in a different setting, when Alyosha gives his excited and largely incoherent account of his days with Katerina and her visionary young friends and their plans for saving the world. Clearly, Dostoevski, through the medium of Ivan's narrative, is poking fun at the high-minded dreamers of this world. Indeed, throughout the novel, he engages in many other literary and philosophical controversies of the period.

The ingenious construction of the plot, with most of the characters pouring out their souls to Ivan, overcomes the limitations of a first-person narrative and also enables the author to sustain suspense by controlling the flow of information.

Critical Context

Dostoevski's early involvement with a group of Utopian socialists came to an abrupt end in 1849, when he was arrested for expressing anticzarist ideas, sentenced to death, and reprieved at the scaffold. Instead of death, he suffered ten years of banishment, imprisonment, and enforced military service before returning to the world of literature. *The Insulted and the Injured* was his second novel after his return. It is a transitional novel, indicating Dostoevski's rejection of his earlier idealism—personified to some extent by Ivan—but not yet achieving the refined and complex psychological studies of the self-willed man which characterize much of his mature work.

As well as tracing Nikolai Gogol's influence on *The Insulted and the Injured*, critics have sometimes described the novel as Dickensian, pointing to the grim realism of its description of the St. Petersburg underworld, its ebullient characterizations, and its emotional tone. Neither Natasha nor Katerina, however, has the sentimentality and archness associated with Charles Dickens' female characters, and the novel's heightened romantic emotionalism is used to convey a pessimistic (non-Dickensian) assessment of human motivation.

Sources for Further Study

Fanger, Donald. *Dostoevsky and Romantic Realism: A Study of Dostoevsky in Relation to Balzac, Dickens, and Gogol*, 1967.
Jones, John. *Dostoevsky*, 1985.
Mochulsky, Konstantin. *Dostoevsky: His Life and Work*, 1966. Translated by A. Minihan.
Wasiolek, Edward. *Dostoevsky: The Major Fiction*, 1964.
Woodhouse, C. M. *Dostoevsky*, 1974.

Nina Hibbin

INTER ICE AGE 4

Author: Kōbō Abe (1924-   )
Type of plot: Science fiction
Time of plot: The near future
Locale: Tokyo
First published: Daiyon kampyōki, 1958-1959, serial; 1959, book (English
   translation, 1970)

Principal characters:

PROFESSOR KATSUMI, the narrator, a computer scientist at the
   Institute for Computer Technique
TANOMOGI, his assistant
WADA KATSUKO, a young female assistant
DR. YAMAMOTO, in charge of the electronic and diagnosis
   room at Central Welfare
PROFESSOR YAMAMOTO, his brother, in charge of Yamamoto
   Laboratories

The Novel

Inter Ice Age 4 is narrated by a scientist, Professor Katsumi, who is
attempting to overcome bureaucratic interference so that his institute can
build a supercomputer capable of predicting the future. Katsumi soon loses
sight of this goal, however, as mysterious events threaten his safety. He un-
covers a plan by a group of industrialists and government officials to develop
mutant humans, called aquans, capable of living in undersea colonies. In this
respect the novel merges several genres, including science fiction, the detective novel, and the novel of ideas.

The novel begins with a cryptic prelude describing a huge tidal wave head-
ing for the Japanese coast. The significance of this event—a harbinger of the
eventual flooding of the earth—is not clear until much later.

Professor Katsumi's narrative, divided into two program cards, an interlude, and a blueprint, explains that he and his research staff are building a
forecasting machine in response to the Soviet computer Moscow I, which can
predict events in the immediate future. Suddenly, however, the Russians
announce a new and more powerful computer, MII, which predicts the end
of capitalism by the year 2080. The United States responds that it deplores
such an application of scientific resources and refuses to use its own computer to predict political events. The Japanese government, influenced by the
United States, tells Katsumi not to apply his computer to political events.

The staff at the institute, however, wishing to test the Soviet hypothesis,
soon discover that practically any prediction has political overtones, and they
let the computer decide how to proceed. The machine suggests choosing a

private individual and predicting his future; the man must not know that he is being observed. Katsumi and his assistant, Tanomogi, decide on an anonymous man in a café, who seems to have been stood up by a date. They observe him wandering aimlessly and making phone calls; eventually they follow him to a woman's apartment, where Tanomogi reports hearing a mysterious thud. The next morning Katsumi discovers that the man, an accounting superintendent, has been strangled by his mistress.

The research staff decide to proceed with the study, connecting the dead man's body to the computer. The computer reveals that the accountant was curious about how the secretary in whose apartment he was killed could have afforded a large purchase; she told him that she had been paid to have an abortion at a special laboratory. The dead man's memory, visualized through a computer monitor, also reveals that the woman was not in the apartment when he was killed. Katsumi is worried that suspicion will fall on himself and Tanomogi. Throughout their investigation, a strangely familiar voice on the phone warns Katsumi to stop asking questions.

Mysterious and threatening events escalate: The murder suspect commits suicide; Katsumi's wife is forced to have an abortion; Tanomogi hints about a special laboratory that enables mammal fetuses to evolve into underwater animals with gills; Katsumi recognizes the threatening voice as his own, reproduced by the computer.

Finally, in the chapter entitled "Program Card No. 2," the truth is revealed to the protagonist. At Professor Yamamoto's laboratory, a group of scientists, including Katsumi's assistants Tanomogi and Wada, have been working on a project to develop mammals for work in undersea colonies, using the premature fetuses from abortions. To keep the project secret, Tanomogi had to murder the accountant; Katsumi himself will have to be killed because he resists the change demanded by his own creation, the forecasting machine. At the lab, Katsumi sees the living fetus of his own son, as well as groups of other aquan children bred to live underwater. An assistant explains that a fourth ice age is about to flood most of the Earth's surface and that a group of businessmen and government officials has formed the Society for the Development of Submarine Colonies in order to prepare society for the catastrophe.

In the final chapter, "Blueprint," a computer shows the future state of Japan after the flooding—a society dominated by the aquans. As the novel ends, Katsumi hears the footsteps of his assassin outside the door. In the postscript, the novelist states that his purpose has been to confront his readers with the cruelty of the future that lies before them.

The Characters

Unaware of the undersea project at the beginning of the novel, Professor Katsumi represents the individual's ignorance of the future and the difficulty one has in confronting such drastic change. The professor's belief that he is in charge, that his machine is serving him, undercuts the notion that one can act freely or independent of social, political, and technological realities. One key example of this ignorance is Katsumi's inability to recognize that his own voice (generated by the computer) has been making the telephone warnings. When he does recognize the voice, he assumes that someone else has manipulated the computer, not that the computer—which he initially programmed—has taken charge of the situation. The reader sympathizes with Katsumi nevertheless, sharing the same ignorance and despair. Not until the end of the novel does Katsumi discover the double roles that the others have been playing, or that he himself has been manipulated to serve the undersea project, even to the extent of contributing his own son to the colony. Throughout the course of events he believes that his colleagues are reliable; his discovery that his assistant Wada was responsible for his wife's abortion and that Tanomogi is a murderer underscores the real separation between himself and others.

Since the novel focuses on the alienation and lack of awareness of its narrator, Professor Katsumi, most of the other characters are rather opaque to the reader. This opacity contributes to the ambivalence of the novel. In the postscript, Kōbō Abe remarks that the novel leaves not only the reader but also the writer with many doubts. Consider, for example, the motives of Tanomogi: Is the assistant a greedy capitalist, a revolutionary seeking to bring about a new society, or a reformer manipulating the capitalists in order to bring about a beneficent change? The conspirators are certainly intelligent, resourceful, and practical, and yet as a group they appear sinister and threatening. Whatever the motives of Tanomogi, Wada, or Professor Yamamoto, the reader is likely to feel distanced from them; although they are real characters and not simple abstractions or symbols, they remain mysterious and aloof.

Themes and Meanings

In the guise of a science-fiction novel, *Inter Ice Age 4* speculates on a number of themes: the impact of computers and technology on everyday life, the limitations on human freedom imposed by one's ability to predict the future, the conflict between the individual and society or government, the difficulty of facing change, and the question of whether a stable identity is possible. The novel's attitude in each of these cases is remarkably open, as the novelist's remarks on the character of Tanomogi might indicate, leaving the reader with questions rather than answers.

The ability of computers to predict the future would seem to encroach dangerously on freedom and individuality; if one can predict with certainty the outcome of world events, then no individual has the freedom to choose between alternatives. Such a power would not only curtail drastically an individual's choices but would also limit any moral system based on free choice and responsibility. Certainly Professor Katsumi's confidence in the benign power of the machine is subverted by the events that befall him—the forced abortion on his wife and the taking of his son, his own assassination for the good of the project.

Yet, as the novel shows, Katsumi's free choice has been an illusion from the start; he has always been a pawn of the undersea project, whether he knew it or not. Furthermore, his insistence on being in control is not necessarily justifiable, for the outcome of the project may benefit humanity as a group, even if the individual must suffer in the short run and self-serving capitalists profit from the venture. The ultimate enemy, after all, is the impervious force of nature, and Katsumi's refusal to cooperate with the project is, in effect, a refusal to accept an inevitable change. The chapter "Blueprint" explains the individual's hesitancy to accept change itself: In the computer's prediction of a world largely submerged by water, a young aquan swims to a small island and climbs onto land, feeling great happiness before perishing on the rocks.

The flooding itself is a key metaphor for the ineluctable erosion by time and change of a familiar, comfortably knowable world. Two responses are possible: accepting and even exploiting the inevitable, as the Society for the Development of Submarine Colonies does, or resisting this change—a futile effort, as Katsumi discovers. The first attitude seems cold and pragmatic, the reader finding little to recommend the scientific detachment and inhumane methods of the researchers; the novel's plot and point of view lead the reader to sympathize instead with Katsumi's more human response to change. The novel does not glorify Katsumi as a hero, however, any more than it unambiguously portrays Tanomogi as a villain. Rather, the novel emphasizes Katsumi's frustration in order to develop the theme of the limitations of any individual's understanding.

Katsumi, then, embodies any individual who attempts to impose an orderly explanation on the modern world. The search may seem to make sense, but this sense is valid only insofar as the searcher remains ignorant of his limitations. Katsumi faces this reality only after it is too late to change direction—only after he has been sentenced to death, ironically by his own computer. The researcher's fundamental blind spot is his ignorance of his own identity. Believing that he transcends the world he investigates, that he possesses a godlike objectivity, Katsumi fails to recognize his own voice on the telephone. When he remembers that he programmed his voice into the computer, he believes that someone else has manipulated the computer voice, refusing to admit that the computer could take on a life independent from himself, or from any other human. The abduction of Katsumi's son by the Society and the infant's metamorphosis into an aquan further underscores Katsumi's lack of control over his identity.

Unlike its protagonist, the novel *Inter Ice Age 4* does not impose an a priori judgment or interpretation on its subject matter. Curiously ambivalent, the novel presents conflicts without taking an easy side in favor of the individual or the society, without deciding in favor of either change or tradition.

Critical Context

Kōbō Abe's novels stand apart from the tradition of earlier modern Japanese fiction in their unpolished prose and loose structure, in their experimentation with genre (often employing popular genres such as science fiction and the detective novel for conveying more abstract ideas), and in their emphasis on portraying philosophical conflicts, often at the expense of a sense of place and time. *Inter Ice Age 4*, for example, undermines the emphasis on subjectivity inherent in the Japanese "I novel," thematically by representing the limits of the narrator's understanding of the world around him, and structurally by concluding the novel with the first-person narrator's anticipation of his imminent assassination, the realization of which makes the reader suddenly aware of the narrative apparatus and its artificiality—if the narrator is about to be killed, how can he pass this information on to the reader? The addition of a prelude and a postscript further define the limits of the narrator's subjective perceptions. For the novelist, neither objectivity nor subjectivity holds the key for understanding the world, if any such key does exist.

Inter Ice Age 4, like many of Kōbō Abe's novels, owes more to modern Western literature, particularly the novels of Franz Kafka, than to Japanese models. Like Kafka, Abe uses a protagonist whose search for meaning assumes that his own search is meaningful and will necessarily yield a solution. The disparity between the searcher's confidence in his abilities to solve the riddle and the baffling complexity of the world suggests the absurdity of any search for a transcendent answer, a theme echoed in the modern dramatic movement known as the Theater of the Absurd. Like the French New Novelist Alain Robbe-Grillet, Kōbō Abe uses the form of the detective novel—a genre characterized by the search for intelligibility—to point out the ultimate unintelligibility of the world. More philosophical than its Western models, the work of Kōbō Abe nevertheless takes its place among them as an example of how modern literature tends to explore the world while at the same time refusing to accept its explorations as definitive or even valid, except insofar as they are able to question their own validity.

Sources for Further Study

Hardin, N. S. "An Interview with Abe Kōbō," in *Contemporary Literature*. XV (1974), pp. 438-456.
Kimball, Arthur G. *Crisis in Identity and Contemporary Japanese Novels*, 1973.

Williams, Phillip. "Absurdity and Kōbō Abe's Art," in *Journal of the English Institute*. III/IV (1972), pp. 129-143.
Yamanouchi, Hisaaki. *The Search for Authenticity in Modern Japanese Literature*, 1978.

Steven L. Hale

THE INVESTIGATION

Author: Stanisław Lem (1921-   )
Type of plot: Philosophical detective mystery
Time of plot: The 1960's
Locale: London and its environs
First published: Śledztwo, 1959 (English translation, 1974)

> *Principal characters:*
> GREGORY, a well-educated young detective at Scotland Yard
> SHEPPARD, a chief inspector and Gregory's superior
> SCISS, a statistics genius who sometimes aids the police

The Novel

The Investigation is a detective novel. Several corpses have apparently become reanimated while awaiting burial, and some have disappeared. As Gregory, of Scotland Yard, investigates the cases, he and his associates must deal with such problems as how to distinguish the normal from the miraculous, how to develop explanations for any phenomena, and how to distinguish facts from interpretations. The narration follows Gregory's work on this case, playfully manipulating the conventions of detective fiction.

The novel opens with various experts studying the details of several cases in which corpses have been disturbed or have disappeared. The presumed crimes have been perfectly executed, for there is no evidence to identify their agent, nor is any motive indicated. Sciss, the statistician, finds a pattern in the occurrences. They are moving, like a wave, away from a central point. He successfully predicts the probable location of the next occurrence.

The central section of the novel details Gregory's investigation of what turns out to be the last in the series of disturbances. Gregory's analysis of the scene moves him toward concluding that a naked male corpse has come back to life, left its coffin, climbed out a window (even though the door was unlocked), and crawled through new-fallen snow to the back door of the mortuary, before finally succumbing. The sight of the reanimated body climbing through the window probably caused the constable on special guard duty to panic, and as a result, the only eyewitness to one of these events ran wildly into the road, where he was struck down by a passing car. Having suffered a fractured skull, the constable remains unconscious and near death during the investigation.

In addition to fulfilling the pattern of location discovered by Sciss, this event shares with the others the time of occurrence, between midnight and dawn; the presence of a small dead animal, a cat, at or near the scene; and foggy weather.

The detective's problem is to find the person who is causing these events to happen, which involves finding some intelligible motive for producing these phenomena. The police begin with the natural idea that a madman is the perpetrator, but no known form of madness would lead to these acts. When Chief Inspector Sheppard assigns the case to Gregory, no solution seems possible. Together, however, the two men consider several possibilities. Gregory finds the inhuman perfection of the incidents most disturbing, as it suggests that there is no agent. Sheppard points out that a fanatic attempting to start a new religion might try to imitate Christ's resurrection, in which case the perfection of the incidents would be the goal rather than merely a means of escaping detection. Sheppard also suggests the possibility that these are real miracles, without a human or natural cause.

As Gregory works on the case, he circles among such alternatives. A well-trained detective, he is trapped intellectually by the problem. Detection requires that the human cause be found, but it also requires the right answer. The very self-criticism that should lead him to the right answer moves Gregory away from a human cause. Yet the detective is above all else a materialist, like David Hume. Hume defines a miracle as a violation of the laws of nature; nevertheless, Gregory eventually finds himself saying, paradoxically, "anything is possible if it frees me from the necessity of believing in miracles."

Having irrationally chosen Sciss as a suspect, Gregory follows him and converses with him and his associates. Sciss has discovered a statistical correlation between the reanimations and the incidence of cancer in the region, which suggests that something about this area prevents cancer from developing in its normal way. As a result, whatever agent causes cancer—defined in this story as a producer of disorder within the usual order of the human body—has metamorphosed into its opposite, an agent that temporarily restores a kind of order to dead bodies. Although possibly correct, this hypothesis remains unexplored, requiring as it does scientific rather than police investigation. The investigators' ability to construct alternative explanations creates increasing uncertainty.

Sciss and his associates seem to convince Gregory that the real difference between the normal and the miraculous is the frequency of occurrence. In making such an argument, they follow Hume more rigorously than Gregory does. For example, when Gregory objects that the "virus" seems too intelligent, one of Sciss's associates points out that meteor showers exhibit a similar kind of intelligence. Yet because there are reasonable explanations for the behavior of meteor showers, they are not thought intelligent. If dead bodies were temporarily reanimated every day in the same way that dropped apples always fall, the event would be considered normal and not mysteriously caused by any intelligence, even though the common understanding of the force of gravity is no greater than the investigators' understanding of the power which makes the bodies return to life. Sciss explains that what is common and has been described is often generally thought to be understood, when, in fact, humanity continuously encounters the inexplicable.

The belief that most normal phenomena have been explained stems from Newtonian physics; from Victorian optimism, as expressed in classical detective fiction; and from the human need for an orderly mental environment and the interpretation of facts. The detective lives by faith, whether he knows it or not—the faith that there are laws of nature that a miracle might violate.

Gregory eventually entertains other hypotheses. Perhaps Sciss insanely creates interesting statistical events. Perhaps an extraterrestrial civilization is studying the human body. Perhaps a scientist is secretly testing a new chemical.

Finally, the injured constable regains consciousness and gives testimony before he dies. He says he saw the body return to life and try to come out through the window. Gregory can simply reject such testimony under the circumstances as unreliable, even though it is perfectly consistent with his observations of the scene. As Hume argued, testimony for miracles is inherently unreliable.

Faced with the apparently impossible, Sheppard fabricates a human explanation which Gregory agrees to accept. A distribution company moves empty trucks by night through the affected area. One driver was recently killed in a train accident. His profile and schedule would allow the police to associate him with all but one of the occurrences. If that one is classified separately, they can construct "the story" of these occurrences and close their case.

As Sciss's novelist friend points out, the police mind requires a perpetrator. The police, in effect, create a fiction, committing a kind of crime themselves, so that this crime may not go unsolved. Thus, they mirror the "cancer virus" that metamorphoses into its opposite when absolutely prevented from performing its natural function. Even though Sheppard and Gregory have come to accept Sciss's interpretation intellectually, they cannot let it rest and still continue to play their roles as detectives.

The Characters

Stanisław Lem uses his characters to manipulate the conventions of the detective plot and to toy with the reader. This playfulness directly serves Lem's theme. Gregory proves a subtle and effective detective, yet his methods often seem incompetent. When the case is turned over to him, his first step is to play a game of his youth, taking random rides on the Underground. This action leads him to think, mistakenly, that he sees one of the reanimated bodies on a train. In fact, several times, Gregory takes a random direction that fortuitously leads him to an apparently significant clue which, in turn, proves to be a red herring for the reader. One purpose behind this aspect of Gregory's technique is to show the reader that significant information about the case may be found as effectively by random search as by systematic search, for even though these "leads" prove fruitless, they are no more so, for his purposes, than the "real" ones.

Gregory tends to suspect the people that he encounters who seem to hold back information from him, and the only two suspects that he finds are Sciss and Sheppard. Each man has a murky private life about which he does not want to talk. Yet Gregory himself has such a problem. His landlord seems to spend the entire night in the room next door, making unidentifiable noises, and Gregory is irrationally reluctant to investigate these sounds that keep him awake most nights. As a result, he wants to keep this side of his life secret. Gregory, the landlord, Sciss, and Sheppard all remain essentially mysterious characters. Their idiosyncrasies remain unconnected and largely unexplained, while in a classic detective novel they would be related in some way to one another and to the crime.

One reason behind this aspect of Lem's use of character is that human beings continuously manifest inexplicable behavior, often with quite banal explanations, that appears to be deeply mysterious when viewed in the absence of a fuller picture. The reader never knows why Sheppard has pictures of executed people on his wall at home or how he always seems to know where Gregory is or why Gregory is ashamed to spy on people. Sciss's idiosyncrasies are probably explained by his search for sadomasochistic sex with young girls, and the landlord's noises are probably the result of chronic illness, but these explanations are never fully confirmed.

Themes and Meanings

Humanity knows much less than it thinks it does. Armour Black, the writer who joins Sciss, Gregory, and McCatt (a scientist) in a conversation, explains the central idea of the novel. The universe presents the mind with facts, but the mind is not content with facts. To take in a fact is to interpret it, to create, assume, or "observe" its connections with other facts. It is not merely the detective's methodology that demands a perpetrator for these events, for all methodologies require the interpretation of facts. As McCatt observes in a later conversation, a human being must use the mind; it has no other way to play the game.

Similarly, the reader must use his mind, for there is no other way to play the reading game. Lem's manipulation of detective conventions gives the reader an experience parallel to Gregory's. All the central mysteries remain unexplained, though revelations often seem imminent.

An important implication of this limitation is that humans always read themselves into the universe. At the beginning of his investigation, Gregory meets in an arcade a familiar-looking stranger who will not let him pass. On the verge of violence, Gregory discovers that he is before a disguised mirror—he is in conflict with himself. This incident is paradigmatic here and in many of Lem's works.

Critical Context

The Investigation combines the techniques of Sir Arthur Conan Doyle and Franz Kafka, using the conventions of detective fiction to undermine the metaphysics of the genre. Doyle and his followers present orderly worlds in which knowledge is possible. Lem, like Kafka, challenges such worldviews.

This novel differs from many of Lem's other works because of the interest he shows in it about the mystery of human character. Lem must present his characters rather fully in order to reveal how incomprehensible they are. As a result, his characters seem more rounded here than in many of his works. *The Investigation* is unique among Lem's works that have been published in English, being neither science fiction nor a discursive extrapolation on technology or philosophy. Nevertheless, it shares with most of Lem's work the major themes of the human hunger for absolute knowledge and the limits of the ability of the human mind to understand.

Sources for Further Study

Engel, Peter, and John Sigda. "An Interview with Stanisław Lem," in *The Missouri Review*. VII (1984), pp. 218-237.

Lem, Stanisław. *Microworlds: Writings on Science Fiction and Fantasy*, 1984.

Occhiogrosso, Frank. "Threats to Rationalism: John Fowles, Stanisław Lem, and the Detective Story," in *Armchair Detective*. XIII (1980), pp. 4-7.

Potts, Stephen. "Dialogues Concerning Human Understanding: Empirical Views of God from Locke to Lem," in *Bridges to Science Fiction*, 1980.

Ziegfeld, Richard E. *Stanisław Lem*, 1985.

Terry Heller

THE INVINCIBLE

Author: Stanisław Lem (1921-   )
Type of plot: Experimental science fiction
Time of plot: The distant future
Locale: Planet Regis III in the outermost quadrant of the Lyre Constellation
First published: Niezwyciężony i inne opowiadania, 1964 (English translation, 1973)

> *Principal characters:*
> HORPACH, the commander of the spaceship *Invincible*
> ROHAN, the navigator, from whose point of view much of the narration proceeds

The Novel

The Invincible is ostensibly a traditional science-fiction adventure novel whose tight and engaging plot describes an investigatory expedition to a distant planet. It is, in addition, a parabolic commentary upon the difficulties of human and nonhuman communication.

The narrative begins with the landing of the spaceship *Invincible* on the planet Regis III in the outermost quadrant of the Lyre Constellation. The goal of the crew, led by Horpach, the spaceship commander, with the assistance of Rohan, the navigator, from whose perspective subsequent events are recounted, is to retrieve a lost spaceship, the *Condor*. Satellite photographs reveal a series of geometric formations suspected to be abandoned cities. These prove instead to be lifeless, impenetrable, metallic mounds of wiry tangles supported within by huge pillars which intersect innumerable rods and folded layers of honeycomb structures.

The crew also locates the *Condor*. Its interior is in shocking disarray, and dead crewmen are scattered in and about the ship. It appears that the *Condor* crew died of natural causes, although one *Invincible* scientist suggests mass insanity. Rohan leads a second squad to the abandoned "cities" but is ordered to return to the *Invincible* when a member of another investigative group returns to the craft a helpless amnesiac. A prospecting expedition under the command of Regnar sets off to analyze minerals but instead comes in contact with "furiously dancing . . . sparkling black iron crystals" that form an immense cloud and swallow up the expedition's scout. Dispatched to rescue this party, Rohan finds most of Regnar's men in a confused stupor. Four of the team's members—Regnar, Benningsen, Korotko, and Mead—have disappeared.

Lauda, a physicist, proposes that intelligent life from the Lyre Constellation may have brought robots and computers to Regis III in an unsuccessful effort to escape an exploding supernova. While the voyagers died, their robots adapted and flourished. A process of machine evolution took place, however, in which solar energy and miniaturization enabled the predecessors of the "tiny pseudo insects" to triumph. The ruins of the "cities" found earlier are the remains of the inanimate self-reproducing structures that lost the battle for existence to the "insects."

Rohan and his party return to the *Invincible*, having been attacked by a swarming black cloud which killed one man and left the remainder infantile. From samples captured by Rohan, it is learned that the "insects" are Y-shaped with tiny wings and crystalline structures. When joined together, these "insects" can fly, generate heat, and produce electrical or magnetic fields to protect themselves.

Horpach sends a huge robot ship, the *Cyclops*, to track down the four missing men. The "insects" attack it. In defending itself, the *Cyclops* produces an enormous and devastating conflagration. The *Cyclops* emerges outwardly unscathed, but the *Invincible* crewmen quickly realize that it has lost its bearings and is wandering aimlessly around the planet. Subsequently, the defeated *Cyclops* attacks the *Invincible* and is destroyed by a tremendous shot of energy from the mother ship. Following the attack, Horpach, who now appears quite human and frail, admits that he is unsure whether to leave or to remain on the planet and asks Rohan to make the decision. Rohan resents this abdication of responsibility but grudgingly agrees to search for the missing men in what will be a very dangerous solitary mission.

In the course of the one-man reconnaissance, the cybernetic "insects" attack Rohan, but by remaining immobile he experiences no ill effects. He stumbles upon the bodies of three of the four men, witnesses strange behavior by the "insects," and becomes convinced that the expedition should leave Regis III. Rohan finds an abandoned vehicle which carries him safely to the *Invincible*.

The Characters

The Invincible has elements of both the classic detective novel, in which the characters investigate some unusual event, and the futuristic adventure story, in which there is no convenient or unequivocal solution to the problem at hand. While the setting is not as conventional as that offered in *Śledztwo* (1959; *The Investigation*, 1974) or *Katar* (1976; *The Chain of Chance*, 1978), the detective genre laced with Stanisław Lem's ubiquitous irony and sense of play serves the characters well. The quest of Horpach and Rohan for their missing comrades proves to be an exploration of man's ethical dilemmas made tortuous and bitter by an alien contact that can be pursued only from the narrow perspective of human understanding.

Horpach and Rohan emerge as distinctive characters during this enterprise. Horpach, the unrepentant rationalist and conqueror, is technologically confident, grimly certain of the rightness of contact, and determined to overcome the cybernetic creatures of Regis III. On the other hand, Horpach is also courageous and, within the sphere of technology, quite resourceful. He expresses the themes most critics agree are central to Lem's work: the tension of living in a universe of "chance and order" in which the natural desire to gain knowledge of the world often becomes an arrogant need to dominate and control what is discovered.

Rohan, in contrast, is a struggling, suffering character whose human limitations are brought to the surface by a confrontation with the unknown. Lem's central characters are often loners who display a range of personalities. While Ijon Tichy, for example, of *Dzienniki gwiazdowe* (1957; *The Star Diaries*, 1976), is a genial amateur and unpredictable Gulliver who indulges in intellectual high jinks, Rohan, like Kelvin in *Solaris* (1961; English translation, 1970), is outwardly self-assured and inquisitive about the cosmos, but often psychologically unguarded. For example, he is initially confident about the meaning of the mission to Regis III and seemingly subscribes to Horpach's ideals and values, but as the cybernetic "insects" inflict one humiliating defeat after another on the crew of the *Invincible* and their formidable hardware, Rohan's assessment of the mission is clouded by anxiety, sleeplessness, and uncertainty.

Rohan is very much a typical Lemian protagonist. Despite the horrific specter of fellow humans stripped of experience, knowledge, and personality by the cybernetic swarms, Rohan comes to see that the alien creatures have a right to exist apart from human expectations and that conquering them or seeking revenge is pointless and illusory. He makes a painful but authentically ethical decision that humans have no business on Regis III and should simply leave.

Themes and Meanings

The Invincible treats the theme of human contact with alien life in the context of profound doubts about human sovereignty and self-determination. Lem has looked about the universe and found that humans are not the measure of it. The cosmos is essentially a mystery, and rational models of it are futile gestures of anthropocentricity. Lem asks how an individual may be sure of itself or know, as Istvan Csicsery-Ronay has said, "anything other than itself" in a universe in which there are no closed reference systems and no possibility of knowing either the self or anything outside it without a "standard that transcends both the self and the Other." Human beings are trapped, according to Lem, in institutions, relationships, and limited, self-deceiving frames of reference which they impose unsuccessfully on a random and enigmatic universe.

A corollary theme, here and in many of Lem's writings, is the relationship between man and machine. The "insects" on Regis III have a primitive form of consciousness. They can remember to reassemble themselves into a defensive system. They frustrate humankind's romantic appropriation of the universe and dispel the heroic illusion of unlimited conquest of nature, projected into space, which demands contact with aliens as an expression of ultimate understanding. The evolution of the cybernetic cloud and its eclipse of human supremacy, while ironically raising the issue of the blurred boundary between the natural and the artificial, suggest from Lem's perspective a rough equality among all sentient entities.

The Invincible warns, as Lem himself has said, that the time of "seamless, unified philosophical systems" is over. Science and technology have failed to bridge the enormous gap between human knowledge and the universe, and encounters with "the Other" continue to expose human ways of understanding as illusory. Ursula K. Le Guin has interpreted Lem's work as emphasizing the need for human beings to continue to act, in spite of this lack of understanding, because actions "retain, in the very depths of the abyss, their unalterable moral value." Rohan's impossible and unfulfilled excursion on behalf of the missing crewmen, climaxed by his renunciation of unbridled heroics and his redemption through an individual ethical decision, suggests that one may still attribute worth and purpose to human activity.

Critical Context

In pre-1956 Polish material such as *Astronauci* (1951; the astronauts), *Sezam i inne opowiadania* (1954; "Sesame" and other stories), and *Obłok Magellana* (1955; the Magellan nebula), Lem demonstrated an untempered faith in science, human reason, and the inevitable triumph of a just and classless society marked by ubiquitous love, humane sentiments, and beneficent technology. After 1956, Lem became concerned with the alienated individual in the cosmos and how that individual comes to know not only the world of familiar experience but also the larger universe. This led inevitably to an examination of a standard science-fiction theme: human and nonhuman encounter.

Lem has explored this theme brilliantly in *Solaris*, *The Invincible*, and *Fiasko* (1986; *Fiasco*, 1987). All three of these novels are parables about humankind's thirst for meaning in an apparently meaningless and random universe and the concomitant difficulties of communication with nonhuman life-forms; all three reveal the consequences of technological hubris. Finally, for all of their dizzying range of speculation, all three suggest that human consciousness is the chief riddle of the universe.

Sources for Further Study

Barnouw, Dagmar. "Science Fiction as a Model for Probabilistic Worlds: Stanisław Lem's Fantastic Empiricism," in *Science-Fiction Studies*. VI (July, 1979), pp. 153-163.
Engel, Peter. "The World of Stanisław Lem, Cybernetic Moralist," in *The*

New Republic. LCXXXVIII (February 7, 1983), pp. 37-39.
Jarzebski, Jerzy. "Stanisław Lem, Rationalist and Visionary," in *Science-Fiction Studies*. IV (July, 1977), pp. 110-126.
Le Guin, Ursula K. "European SF: Rottensteiner's Anthology, the Strugatskys, and Lem," in *Science-Fiction Studies*. I (Spring, 1974), pp. 181-185.
Science-Fiction Studies. XIII (November, 1986). Special Lem issue.
Ziegfeld, Richard E. *Stanisław Lem*, 1985.

James B. McSwain

INVISIBLE CITIES

Author: Italo Calvino (1923-1985)
Type of plot: Magical realism
Time of plot: From the thirteenth through the twentieth centuries
Locale: The garden of Kublai Khan's palace; a series of cities perhaps real, perhaps imaginary, in his empire
First published: Le città invisibili, 1972 (English translation, 1974)

> *Principal characters:*
> MARCO POLO, a Venetian traveler, now resident in the court of Kublai Khan
> KUBLAI KHAN, the Tartar emperor

The Novel

    Invisible Cities consists of a series of dialogues between Marco Polo, the famous Venetian traveler, and Kublai Khan, the legendary conqueror. The two sit in Kublai Khan's garden, and Marco Polo recounts, or perhaps invents, descriptions of a multitude of fabulous cities. Since these cities are never actually seen, but only described, they are invisible to the emperor; since they might not even exist, they may be literally unknown to everyone but the reader, who is entranced by the shimmering, haunting evocations of Marco Polo / Italo Calvino.

    There is no action in the novel, merely conversation, but the reader is carried along by the descriptions of the cities, and by their careful relationship in an intricate, philosophically oriented pattern. *Invisible Cities* is a carefully crafted, jewel-like work which moves on at least three different levels: the verbal pictures of the cities, the philosophical interpretations, and the artistic reflections.

    The cities are divided into eleven categories. There are connections between cities and memory, desire, signs, eyes, names, the dead, and the sky. There are also kinds or types of cities: thin cities, trading cities, continuous cities, and hidden cities. Marco's description of each place corresponds meticulously to its inherent nature.

    The city of Melania, for example, is among the "cities of the dead," and its inhabitants are not living human beings but unknowing representatives of the stock types found in literature: the hypocrite, the sponger, the king's son fallen to low estate and awaiting recognition. All the residents of the city play roles, and while the roles gradually shift and might multiply, they remain static and stereotypical, and thus, dead. "Melania's population renews itself: the participants in the dialogues die one by one and meanwhile those who will take their places are born, some in one role, some in another."

    Theodora, on the other hand, is among the hidden cities, and what was long concealed in its memories and libraries is unwittingly revealed by the actions of its citizens. Determined to rid their homes of vermin, they painstakingly eradicate all pests—rats, fleas, spiders. No sooner is this accomplished, however, than "the other fauna" come back to light: "Sphinxes, griffons, chimeras, dragons, hircocervi, harpies, hydras, unicorns, basilisks were resuming possession of their city."

The Characters

At first, it would seem that Kublai Khan and Marco Polo are the only characters in Calvino's novel; other persons, when mentioned at all, are described only briefly, and purely as stock figures. In one sense, Calvino has deliberately reduced his work's personnel to a bare minimum, yet, between them, Kublai Khan and Marco Polo may be seen to represent the entire population of the Khan's empire. Kublai Khan is master of much of the world; Marco Polo is a well-traveled voyager in it. Together they encompass, at least through experience and observation, most of the world's events and persons. In this respect, Calvino's message and techniques reflect the old duality of man and universe as images of one another: The microcosm of the individual captures and repeats the macrocosm of the great world. Society contains nothing not present in the individual, and this is especially true of cities, in which the diversity of the multitude is only the complexity of the individual written large.

At times, Calvino hints, Kublai Khan and Marco Polo seem to be the only characters in the entire world of *Invisible Cities*, and all the fabled townscapes merely images in their minds. Indeed, they themselves may be self-created fictions or artifices of illusion:

> Perhaps this dialogue of ours is taking place between two beggars nicknamed Kublai Khan and Marco Polo; as they sift through a rubbish heap, piling up rusted flotsam, scraps of cloth, wastepaper, while drunk on the few sips of bad wine, they see all the treasure of the East shine around them.

Because of the nature of *Invisible Cities*, it does not matter if Marco Polo and Kublai Khan are speaking of real or imaginary cities, with actual or ghostly inhabitants, in an empire that may or may not exist. In a novel concerned with artifice and illusion, it is enough that the voice speaks and the mind believes.

That speaking voice brings to life the most varied and interesting of the novel's characters, the cities themselves. Whether they are thin cities or trading cities, whether they are cities connected with memory, or signs, or the sky, or the dead, all of them are unique and memorable. Calvino carefully suits the odd, yet believable, aspects of each city to a philosophical concept, which adds to the layered texture of the work. At the same time, however, each place has the particular feel, sight, and even odor of a real city, which makes them seem to exist, no matter how exotic or implausible they are. All of these cities are unique yet odd, and all are in some particular way enchanting. It is certainly no accident that Calvino has given each of them a woman's name.

Themes and Meanings

Calvino's vivid and haunting descriptions make up a large part of the charm of *Invisible Cities*, and Calvino's travelogue of wonders, his evocations of cities suspended on ropes over chasms, or constructed entirely of pipes and inhabited by water sprites, are part of the narrative tradition of the fantastic that may be traced back to *The Arabian Nights' Entertainments*.

This travelogue is only part of the interlocking nature of the book, however, for layered above and below it are philosophical and artistic considerations. Do the cities described by Marco Polo exist, even in the fictional empire of the great Kublai Khan? Does that empire itself have any substance beyond the evanescent words used by the traveler to beguile the weary emperor? What is the nature of reality, and how can one recognize it? These questions, perhaps playfully put, are nevertheless important, and form the substantial core of Calvino's seemingly light entertainment. Despite the bright, sometimes bizarre settings, then, *Invisible Cities* has a serious side, one which reflects Italo Calvino's preoccupation with the interaction of reality and art.

"Perhaps, Kublai thought, the empire is nothing but a zodiac of the mind's phantasms." Those phantasms are created by human beings, and the zodiac is fashioned by the artist. The seemingly paradoxical interaction of fantasy with reality is Calvino's main concern in this book. Cities, as much as the books describing them, are artificial creations, and descriptions of imaginary cities are a further remove from what people conventionally assign to the realm of reality.

Still, as Marco Polo and Kublai Khan reveal in their discussions, the boundaries between reality and illusion are shifting and indistinct. All the cities described in the novel may be one and the same city and merely taking on different aspects according to the whim of the traveler. This possibility is caught well by Calvino. The city of Zemrude gets its form, the reader is told, simply from the mood of the beholder. Despina, on the other hand, can be approached from the sea or across the desert, and each side presents a totally different face to the traveler; direction determines vision.

All these descriptions of cities are fantastic and exotic, but beyond that, they are all mutable. The shifts in the urban landscapes, the changes in streets, buildings, and even inhabitants, are caused by the presence of the observer. Calvino's marvelous cities are affected by a phenomenon well documented in anthropology and sociology, and notorious, since the early part of the twentieth century, in physics as the "uncertainty principle."

Simply put, the presence of the observer changes the thing which is observed. An anthropologist viewing the rituals of an isolated tribe is not merely one more item in that tribe's universe but an alien presence which profoundly, if subtly, alters that universe. In physics, one can know either the direction of an electron's spin or its velocity, but not both, because merely to measure one fundamentally alters the other. Human and physical science seem to reveal that contact with reality at its most basic levels is both relative and uncertain.

The same message is presented in *Invisible Cities*. Those who live in the cities perceive one aspect of them; those who visit discern another; Marco Polo, in his talk in Kublai Khan's evening garden, presents a third; and the printed form of Calvino's novel further multiplies these images of reality and unreality. Both Calvino and Marco Polo are in the position of the artist who must persuade others to trust the tale but cannot compel their obedience. As Marco Polo says in *Invisible Cities*, "If you choose to believe me, good."

Critical Context

Calvino's novels typically concern themselves with the complex interplay of art and reality, life and artifice. Generally, his writings move toward a more open and openly delighted display of technique and literary skill, and in several of his later works he demonstrates his ability to hold the reader's attention while ignoring or deliberately subverting the traditional expectations of plot and character development.

Invisible Cities is just such a work, and fits well into other Calvino novels such as *Il castello dei destini incrociati* (1969; revised 1973; *The Castle of Crossed Destinies*, 1977) and *Se una notte d'inverno un viaggiatore* (1979; *If on a Winter's Night a Traveler*, 1981). In these later works, Calvino deliberately sets himself what would seem to be unpromising and even annoying conditions for his writing. The underlying schemes are elaborate, highly artificial, and seemingly inflexible. *The Castle of Crossed Destinies* bases its plot on two decks of tarot cards; *If on a Winter's Night a Traveler* is a series of ten novels which begin, advance to an exciting, critical point, and then abruptly end; *Invisible Cities* is the record of a dialogue that may never have taken place about towns which never existed.

Still, in all these works Calvino demonstrates that he is a master, even a wizard, with language and thought, equally adept at creating a fantastic city and revealing its philosophical nuances. On the surface, *Invisible Cities* seems a glittering bauble of a book, all fantasy and show. Underneath, however, the startling inventions and sly humor reveal a thoughtful meditation on life, art, language, and humanity—and their tangled relationships. On one level, the book delights the seeker of novelty and entertainment; on another, it rewards the serious, but not solemn, thinker.

   Invisible Cities is a key work in Calvino's later career, and one of his most inventive and enjoyable books. If art is a mirror held up to nature, as some would have it, then *Invisible Cities* is a mirror held up to itself, creating a bright and dazzling interplay of lights and reflections. For the perceptive and sympathetic reader, the book is its own best critical commentary.

Sources for Further Study

Andrews, Richard. "Italo Calvino," in *Writers and Society in Contemporary Italy: A Collection of Essays*, 1984. Edited by Michael Caesar and Peter Hainsworth.

Calvino, Italo. *The Uses of Literature*, 1986.

Carter, Albert Howard. *Italo Calvino: Metamorphoses of Fantasy*, 1987.

Olken, I. T. *With Pleated Eye and Garnet Wing: Symmetries of Italo Calvino*, 1984.

Michael Witkoski

INVITATION TO A BEHEADING

Author: Vladimir Nabokov (1899-1977)
Type of plot: Dystopian parable
Time of plot: The future
Locale: The capital of a fictional European country
First published: Priglashenie na kazn', 1935-1936, serial; 1938, book (English translation, 1959)

Principal characters:
CINCINNATUS C., a condemned prisoner, who awaits death
PIERRE, his jolly executioner
RODION, the turnkey
RODRIG IVANOVICH, the director of the prison
EMMIE, his twelve-year-old daughter
ROMAN VISSARIONOVICH, Cincinnatus' court-appointed attorney
MARTHE, Cincinnatus' faithless wife
CECILIA C., Cincinnatus' mother

The Novel

Invitation to a Beheading is a metaphysical, dystopian novel set in a nameless, timeless, and nightmarish land. The hero, Cincinnatus C., a neurasthenic young teacher of defective children, has been condemned to death for the crime of "gnostical turpitude," the perception and knowledge of forbidden things in a world where all things are already named and known to all. More concretely, his offense is being opaque in a society whose citizens are all transparent, devoid of fresh perceptions, lacking dark, secret corners in their minds or souls. Cincinnatus is "different."

The novel opens with the pronouncement of Cincinnatus' sentence and his return to the hilltop prison, where he is to await the unknown day of his beheading. The plot is simple. Cincinnatus, the only prisoner in the vast fortress, sits in his cell, where he is attended to by the bluff jailer, Rodion, who serves the prisoner his food and cleans; Rodrig Ivanovich, the frock-coated prison director, who makes official calls; and his lawyer, Roman Vissarionovich, who encourages Cincinnatus to pursue pointless legal formalities. Apart from discovering the date of his execution, Cincinnatus is chiefly interested in arranging a last visit with his beloved but unfeeling and promiscuous wife, Marthe. Both events are incomprehensibly elusive, as are most things in the story. On the morning of Marthe's supposed visit, Cincinnatus, amid great fanfare, is instead introduced to a new prisoner and soon-to-be executioner, the fat and jolly Pierre. As the days pass, Pierre forces his odious friendship on the condemned man. Pierre seems to enjoy strange privileges and comes to visit Cincinnatus frequently.

Cincinnatus spends much of his time writing private thoughts in his diary. Haunted by the sense of his own uniqueness, that which sets him apart from all other members of his society, he writes, "I am the one who is alive—not only are my eyes different, and my hearing, my sense of taste—not only is my sense of smell like a deer's, my sense of touch like a bat's—but most important, I have the capacity to join all of this into one point." Equally strong is his belief that he "know[s] a paramount thing that no one here knows." Cincinnatus senses that he is in his prison world by mistake and that his true home is a bright, radiant universe peopled by others like himself. His diary probes this other universe and, by implication, the problematic nature of death as a possible gateway between worlds. He increasingly doubts the reality of the world in which he has spent his wretched existence.

Meanwhile, Cincinnatus receives a series of callers, each more bizarre than the last. In addition to the unwelcome visits from Pierre, Cincinnatus at last receives a theatrical visit from Marthe, accompanied by her new lover and her entire grotesque family. The scene is an exercise in absurdist black humor. The condemned man, reared in an orphanage, is also visited by his mother, Cecilia C., whom he barely knows. Although he doubts her authenticity (as he does that of almost all of his surroundings), he is struck by her comment that his father, a nocturnal passing stranger, was like him. A final "guest," Emmie, the prison director's daughter, is often in and out of his cell and childishly talks of a rescue.

As the nights pass, Cincinnatus hears digging sounds. Finally, the cell wall splits open and Pierre and Rodrig burst through with gales of laughter. They force Cincinnatus to crawl back through their tunnel to Pierre's cozy cell, where they have tea and Cincinnatus is treated to a showing of the headsman's ax. Crawling back toward his own cell, Cincinnatus unexpectedly finds himself free, on a cliffside. Emmie appears and leads him through a door which, alas, leads to the director's apartment, where Rodrig and Pierre are having dinner. It has all been an elaborately staged hoax. There is, however, one more theatrical event. It is a bizarre custom for the condemned man and his executioner to attend a gala dinner given by the town fathers on the eve of the execution. There, Cincinnatus and Pierre are treated to an elaborate light show which spells out their initials on a distant hillside.

The morning of the ceremonial public beheading arrives. As Cincinnatus leaves the prison with Pierre, his cell slowly starts to disintegrate. As they are driven through the streets, further signs of dissolution appear. Cincinnatus mounts the scaffold and places his head on the executioner's chopping block, but the crowd becomes increasingly transparent and the scene confused. The ax falls, and "amidst the dust, and the falling things, and the flapping scenery, Cincinnatus made his way in that direction where, to judge by the voices, stood beings akin to him."

The Characters

Invitation to a Beheading is not a realistic novel, and author Vladimir Nabokov has not attempted to create rounded, believable characters. Most are frankly caricatures. Cincinnatus is the exception. Blond, thin, physically slight, he is a dreamy, unassertive young man of morose, reflective temperament. He is absorbed in the past, in nature, and in literature. His senses and his unworldly perceptions are extraordinarily acute, for Cincinnatus is an artist—although his diary is the only tangible expression of his talent and unique intuitions. He is the only "real" person in a false universe with its totalitarian society and imperceptive, philistine citizens.

Pierre, the executioner, is the character most directly opposed to Cincinnatus. The two are contrasted in many ways. Cincinnatus is delicate, slender, and neurasthenic. Pierre is robust, plump, and jolly. The contrasts continue: deep integrity/shallow vulgarity, artist/philistine, victim/executioner. This dichotomous relationship comes to a head at the gala dinner party, where the initials of the two men are intertwined in colored lights. In the original Russian text, the paired initials are revealed as inverted mirror images of each other, reflecting the characters' relationship to each other—an effect that is lost in the English translation. Pierre is the essence of his banally trivial totalitarian society, just as Cincinnatus is the embodiment of that remote, ideal world which he intuits. The unctuously evil Pierre with his plump white hands and smelly feet is one of the great characters of Russian literature.

The trio of Rodion, Rodrig, and Roman constitutes a set of somewhat sinister puppets, evoking a comic opera combining the Marx brothers and the Three Stooges. The three are carefully individuated: Rodion, the fat turnkey with his red beard, cornflower-blue eyes, and bass-baritone voice; Rodrig, the pompous, frock-coated prison director with his pitch-black toupee and fruity bass tones; and Roman, the fidgety, lean lawyer with his harelip and tenor voice. By following their ominous antics, the careful reader will soon discover that the three performers sometimes exchange roles and identities, along with their costumes, wigs, and makeup. Even the paternity of young Emmie is uncertain, for at times she is referred to as the director's daughter, and at others, Rodion's.

Emmie, at twelve, is a nymphet in a sinister, make-believe world. Fey, ballerina-like, and ethereal but with erotic undercurrents, she tantalizes Cincinnatus with hints of escape: first with a series of crude, cartoonlike drawings depicting an escape and then, even more explicitly, with a suggestion that they should flee and be married. She, too, proves to be part of the hoax.

Only two characters have realistic qualities. Cecilia C. pays a visit to her doomed, illegitimate son, whom she has seen only once since his birth. Cincinnatus suspects her, as he does all those who surround him, of being a mere puppet and regards her with doubt even after she tells him the secret of his "different" father. As she is about to leave, however, Cincinnatus catches in her gaze "that ultimate, secure, all-explaining and from-all-protecting spark that he knew how to discern in himself also." Another more realistic, though almost incidental, character is the taciturn prison librarian, who brings Cincinnatus treasures from the past. As Cincinnatus mounts the scaffold before the festive crowd, the librarian sits on the steps, doubled up and vomiting. Together with Cincinnatus, these two are the only characters with an inkling of another world, a higher reality.

Themes and Meanings
The central theme of *Invitation to a Beheading* is the plight of the artist, someone with a personal vision of the world and a unique way of conveying it to others. The writer lives at the center of a paradox; he possesses his own language, the only one adequate to the expression of his vision, but his language is incomprehensible and, thus, suspect to his audience, his fellow citizens. Cincinnatus' prison is thus dual. On one level, he is in an actual prison for crimes against the totalitarian state, and, on a deeper level, he is in the prison-house of language.

Cincinnatus' prison is only one of the novel's worlds for which he dimly visualizes a replacement, an ideal world in which he is a free citizen among people who speak his tongue. The novel's structure is cast in terms of these two opposing worlds: the world of the prison and the totalitarian society that it represents, and Cincinnatus' ideal world, the free world of his imagination. This thematic dichotomy manifests itself in many ways, but most important is the frequent juxtaposition of the terms "here" (that is, this world) and "there" (that world). This distinction defines the novel's metaphysical, moral, and political geography.

Invitation to a Beheading is a tightly, almost schematically structured work. It opens with the pronouncement of Cincinnatus' death sentence and ends with his "execution." With only minor variation, each of the twenty chapters—which begin with Cincinnatus' morning awakening and end with lights-out—corresponds to one day in the death countdown.

The writing is saturated with intricate stylistic games involving letter shapes which form patterns, hinting at the presence of "the other world," in this case, the controlling hand of the author. Almost every chapter has its own dominant motif: a clock tolling off the remaining hours of Cincinnatus' life, an otherworldly draft that wafts a fake acorn on Cincinnatus' bed, and Cecilia C.'s *nonnons*, grotesquely twisted, unrecognizable objects which become familiar and pristine when reflected in artfully distorted mirrors—a parable of the relationship between the perverted world of the novel and the ideal world of art.

Critical Context

Invitation to a Beheading is Nabokov's most artifice-saturated and technically sophisticated novel. Together with *Dar* (1937-1938, 1952; *The Gift*, 1963), the last of his Russian-language novels, it stands at the pinnacle of his Russian oeuvre. With his emigration from France to the United States in 1940, the trilingual Nabokov began writing only in English. *Invitation to a Beheading* is Nabokov's earliest major statement of "the two-world theme," which underlies so much of his work. The gifted heroes in their wretched, illusory, fictional worlds sense, from intricate patterns around them, that an ideal and meaningful world exists, the world of the all-powerful author. The point of transition between the two worlds is death. Death is at the center of much of Nabokov's writing, despite the fact that he is the author of two comic masterpieces, *Lolita* (1955) and *Pale Fire* (1962). The two-world theme, with its focus on death, extends from *Invitation to a Beheading*, written in 1934, to Nabokov's last completed novel, *Look at the Harlequins!* (1974).

Vladimir Nabokov's fiction is a unique literary phenomenon. An absolute master of two languages, he made contributions to both Russian and English literature that place him among the greatest literary figures of the twentieth century.

Sources for Further Study

Alter, Robert. "*Invitation to a Beheading*: Nabokov and the Art of Politics," in *TriQuarterly*. XVII (Winter, 1970), pp. 41-59.

Johnson, D. Barton. "The Two Worlds of *Invitation to a Beheading*," in *Worlds in Regression: Some Novels of Vladimir Nabokov*, 1985.

Peterson, Dale E. "Nabokov's *Invitation*: Literature as Execution," in *PMLA*. XCVI (1981), pp. 824-836.

Rampton, David. "*Invitation to a Beheading* and *Bend Sinister*," in *Vladimir Nabokov: A Critical Study of the Novels*, 1984.

Stuart, Dabney. "All the Mind's a Stage: The Novel as Play," in *Nabokov: The Dimensions of Parody*, 1978.

D. Barton Johnson

THE ISLAND OF CRIMEA

Author: Vassily Aksyonov (1932-   )
Type of plot: Historical fantasy
Time of plot: The late 1970's
Locale: The Crimea, Moscow, the countryside near Moscow, and Paris
First published: Ostrov Krym, 1981 (English translation, 1983)

> *Principal characters:*
> ANDREI ARSENIEVICH LUCHNIKOV, the editor of the *Russian Courier* and a politician with the aim of reuniting Crimea with the Soviet Union
> ARSENY NICHOLAEVICH LUCHNIKOV, Andrei's father, a scholar and former colonel in the White Army during the civil war period
> ANTON LUCHNIKOV, Andrei's son, a member of the political group Yaki, which advocates a free Crimea
> MARLEN MIKHAILOVICH KUZENKOV, a Russian who is the head of the Foreign Division of the Central Committee, torn between duty to the Soviet state and the democracy of Crimea
> TATYANA LUNINA, a Soviet athlete and KGB agent, who is Andrei's mistress
> COLONEL SERGEEV, a KGB official in charge of the Foreign Division

The Novel

The Island of Crimea is a fantasy about a state which has remained free and democratic for sixty years. It is the story of democracy and socialism clashing over the tiny country of Crimea. The principal character, Andrei, is the catalyst bringing about "The Idea of Common Fate," a movement to reunite Crimea with the Soviet Union.

The novel begins with Andrei Luchnikov driving along a modern, Westernized roadway to visit Kakhova, the mountain estate of his father, Arseny. Andrei is a middle-aged, attractive, and powerful man, who is not only the editor of the nation's only Russian-language newspaper but also a leading political figure in Crimea. Arseny has uncovered a plot to assassinate Andrei for his efforts toward reunification with the Soviet Union. Andrei considers the threat idle and continues writing columns on the glories of the Soviet Union and the need for Crimea to reunite with her historic past.

Crimea has become a multinational democracy filled with Western-style capitalism. The traditional Crimean people have intermarried with foreigners, creating a cosmopolitan culture. The younger generation has created a language called Yaki, which is a conglomeration of English, French, and Russian. These young people have traveled and consider themselves part of a world community. Andrei sees this as a passing fad, although his son Anton participates in the Yaki movement.

The novel follows Andrei on trips to Paris and Moscow, where characters are introduced who are either opponents or advocates of Crimean reunification. In Paris, at a cocktail party, Andrei is greeted by a Western film director who agrees with the idea of reunification because he anticipates a film spectacle. The Soviet émigrés at the party either avoid Andrei or talk to him under the assumption that reunification is a radical idea but not a serious issue. The first attempt on the hero's life occurs when he leaves the party, but he continues with his schedule of events and meetings. Andrei prepares for his trip to Moscow by buying presents and goods not available in the Soviet Union, including clothing for his mistress, Tatyana Lunina.

Although he speaks fluent Russian, Andrei is given a state interpreter in Moscow. He is allowed to visit only a few places and is constantly followed by Colonel Sergeev's KGB operatives. Andrei meets Tatyana at a cocktail party where she is escorted by her husband, Sasha. Sasha was a member of the Soviet Olympic team, as was Tatyana; both are now sportscasters. Andrei accompanies them home and a scene ensues. He believes himself in love with Tatyana and wants her to come away with him. She chooses to stay with her husband.

The trip changes dramatically at this point and becomes a revitalizing experience for Andrei. He slips away from his KGB guards and, in the company of a dissident rock group, wanders throughout the Soviet Union. Marlen Kuzenkov, a member of the Central Committee, plays an important role in allowing Andrei to see the real Soviet Union. Kuzenkov is torn between loyalty to the Soviet state, the Communist Party, and the Crimean democracy. Although he allows Andrei to slip away, he reports to the Central Committee that he can control the outcome of the Crimean election. Kuzenkov does not try to help the Soviets, nor does he interfere with the election, assuming wrongly that the Crimeans would prefer democracy to a police state.

Andrei returns to the Crimea after three weeks of travel, having crossed into Sweden with Benjamin Ivanov, a member of the rock group. Instead of being appalled by the way the Russian people live, Andrei rejoices in their tenacious hold on life. He enters the Crimean Car Rally with his friend Count Novosiltsev, a professional auto racer; they hope to score a victory for "The Idea of Common Fate" and gain votes for reunification in the upcoming election. Tatyana joins Andrei in Crimea to lend her support to the cause of reunification. Another assassination attempt is made against Andrei; though Tatyana warns Andrei, Novosiltsev is killed. Andrei wins the race and uses his victory as a political platform. He realizes, however, that

Tatyana is a KGB agent and blames her for Novosiltsev's death; she leaves. The novel then moves very quickly toward a conclusion. The Crimeans vote to reunify with the Soviet Union and are immediately invaded. Kuzenkov commits suicide, realizing the enormity of his sin in not interfering with Andrei. Arseny and Tatyana are killed, and Andrei's son Anton, his wife, Pamela, and their newborn son, Arseny, leave by boat for Turkey and freedom. Andrei is left at a church burying his dead while Colonel Sergeev of the KGB looks on.

The Characters

Andrei Luchnikov is aloof from the realities of day-to-day existence. He is part of Vassily Aksyonov's own generation of intellectuals who believed that the Stalinist legacy was dead and that a new, freer Russia would emerge. As the intellectuals of the late 1960's were disappointed, so is Andrei. The character becomes involved in the destruction of his own country. Andrei sets the wheels of change in motion only to be crushed under them.

Andrei cannot understand his father's love, nor his attachment to an independent Crimea. Arseny sees the problems of reunification. He sees reunification as a retreat from historical reality. He himself has retreated to his mountain home, Kakhova, named after the battle in which Crimea won her independence from Soviet Russia. This retreat from political life and Andrei's inability to value his father's views are themes similar to those in Ivan Turgenev's *Ottsy i deti* (1862; *Fathers and Sons*, 1867). Arseny is killed during the Soviet invasion when the Volunteer Army, the old men who served during the civil war, approach the Soviets to lay down their rusty weapons.

Anton, Andrei's son, offers Aksyonov's view of a younger generation participating in the community of humanity regardless of nationality. There is more than a generational conflict between father and son. Anton is not a political activist but believes that all people should have freedom. He joins the Yaki movement not to antagonize Andrei but to feel a part of a group. In the end, Anton is saved along with his wife and son by Benjamin Ivanov, the man who led Andrei out of the Soviet Union.

Andrei's mistress, Tatyana Lunina, is the major female character of the novel. She is expected to entrap Andrei for the Soviets through her sexuality. Instead, she creates a trap for herself. Tatyana must either submit to the will of the Party or she and her family will have none of the advantages acquired by her liaison with Andrei. Tatyana is a product of the Soviet mentality. To retain her material well-being she must prostitute herself for the Party. Tatyana attempts to delude herself that she loves Andrei, but she is incapable of sustaining any human relationship, as exemplified by her divorcing Sasha in order to be free for Andrei. She subsequently leaves Andrei for a rich, elderly American businessman, ensuring her eventual murder by the KGB.

Tatyana is the link between Andrei and Colonal Sergeev, as well as between Andrei and Marlen Kuzenkov. Sergeev is a Party hack, doing as he is told without question. He is an example of the worst excesses of Stalinism. Kuzenkov is a Soviet intellectual. He questions the Party and is, at times, at odds with it. Kuzenkov speaks to Andrei at the end of the novel, begging him to understand the consequences of reunification with the Soviet Union. Sergeev is beneath Kuzenkov but has him under surveillance, proving that no one is outside the reach of the KGB.

There are many minor characters who add flavor and liveliness to the novel. Kuzenkov meets an old Russian soldier of the civil war period, who tries to justify the collectivization of agriculture and Stalinism. Andrei has a group of friends with whom he went to the Czar Alexander II school, who are all high-ranking officials in the Crimean government, businessmen, or military officials. These men join with and support "The Idea of Common Fate." They are representative of the 1917 revolutionaries and are all murdered by their own revolution. The character Vitaly Gangut is a Soviet dissident film director. He comes out of his obscurity to film the reunification of Crimea, which turns into a very real invasion. Aside from Tatyana, the women in the novel play sexual roles and are primarily mannequins without human emotions.

Themes and Meanings

The theme of generational conflict underpins this novel. As in Turgenev's *Fathers and Sons*, Andrei and Arseny cannot understand each other's political reasoning. Aksyonov adds a new dimension with the grandson, Anton, who is misunderstood by his father but who finds a sympathetic ear in his grandfather. Arseny is representative of the victory of the mythical Crimea over the Soviet Union: He is a fighter. Andrei is the intellectual who sees the Crimea as an extension of the Soviet Union, although they have been separated by sixty years of history. He greets the Soviet Union as representative of Lenin's ideals, not Stalin's brutalities. Anton is the twentieth century ideal: youth, which knows no allegiance or boundaries but which is interested in all humankind. The elder Arseny's death is symbolic of the death of the country, while the birth of his great-grandson Arseny, on the same day, is a new beginning for Crimea.

The Soviet political system is the other major preoccupation of the novel. The independent country of Crimea highlights the Stalinist past and present of the Soviet Union and illustrates an alternative, what "might have been." A sense of Russian nationalism causes the Crimeans to vote for the reunification. The people are blissfully unaware of the political realities of the Soviet state until the military invasion takes place. Aksyonov plays democracy off against socialism by creating a situation in which the Russian past seems more alluring than the present realities of a post-Stalin Soviet Union. The

Crimea buries itself in an unwillingness to look across its border. Andrei tells the Crimeans that their economy will only be enhanced by the Soviet Union instead of being destroyed. The people listen and give their democracy its final blow in voting to join the Soviet Union, and with that Andrei realizes the enormity of his political naïveté.

Nowhere in the novel is Aksyonov's political theme more eloquently stated than in Andrei's article on the one hundredth anniversary of Stalin's birth. Aksyonov calls Stalin a nonentity with no redeeming value. The article proceeds in building a colossus whose power and control over the Russian people continues. Aksyonov sees two choices for the Soviet Union: Either the Soviet Union breaks the shackles of Stalinism or the terror of Stalinism will live on, fueled by other nonentities to come, who will build on the grave of Stalin and feed on his decaying bones.

Critical Context

The major context of this novel is the disenchantment of Soviet intellectuals with the Revolution. A major factor in this process was the Prague Winter, which followed the invasion of Czechoslovakia by Soviet troops in 1968, replacing "socialism with a human face" with an approach more acceptable to the Kremlin. *The Island of Crimea* provides a close parallel to the events of 1968.

Aksyonov is one of a group of Soviet writers who question whether the Soviet Union will be able to rid itself of the specter of Stalin and the police state he created. Aksyonov was forced to emigrate to the West in 1980, after *Ozhog* (1980; *The Burn*, 1984) was published in Italy. His political stance stems from the time he spent in internal exile with his mother, Evgenia Ginzburg, the author of *Krutoi marshrut* (1967, 1979, two volumes; *Journey into the Whirlwind*, 1967; also as *Within the Whirlwind*, 1981).

The Island of Crimea is one of Aksyonov's mature works, leaving behind the identification with Soviet youth that he showed in such works as *Kollegi* (1960; *Colleagues*, 1962). *The Island of Crimea* portrays the stagnant, repressive state of the Soviet Union during the years under Leonid Brezhnev.

Sources for Further Study

Johnson, John J. "Introduction: The Life and Works of Aksenov," in *The Steel Bird and Other Stories*, 1979.

Meyer, Priscilla. "Aksenov and Soviet Literature of the 1960's," in *Russian Literature Triquarterly*. VI (1973), pp. 447-463.

_____. "A Bibliography of Works by and About Vasily Pavlovich Aksenov," in *Ten Bibliographies of Twentieth Century Russian Literature*, 1977. Edited by Fred Moody.

Mozejko, Edward, Boris Briker, and Per Dalgard, eds. *Vasiliy Pavlovich Aksenov: A Writer in Quest of Himself*, 1986.

Slobin, Greta. "Aksenov Beyond 'Youth Prose': Subversion Through Popular Culture," in *Slavic and East European Journal*. XXX (Spring, 1987), pp. 50-64.

Linnea Burwood

THE ISSA VALLEY

Author: Czesław Miłosz (1911-   )
Type of plot: Initiation
Time of plot: 1904-1918
Locale: Poland
First published: Dolina Issy, 1955 (English translation, 1981)

> Principal characters:
> THOMAS DILBIN, the protagonist of the novel, who matures in a rural valley
> GRANDFATHER SURKONT, Thomas' teacher and guide while his parents are absent
> ROMUALD BUKOWSKI, the hunter who initiates Thomas into his world

The Novel

The Issa Valley is the tale of a rural boyhood from the turn of the century to World War I. The place is Poland, but the part of Poland that was formerly the nation of Lithuania. The Issa Valley may be secluded, but there are conflicts between those who wish to restore Lithuania and those who support Poland. The main character of the story is Thomas Dilbin; he is living with his Grandfather and Grandmother Surkont, members of the landed gentry, while his father and mother are away. The novel follows Thomas from his earliest years to the age of fourteen. During those years, Thomas is initiated into the larger world and comes to terms with the historical situation and the diverse characters who surround him.

The setting of the novel is a combination of the pastoral and the rural; there are idyllic descriptions of the forest, the lakes, and the river, but there are real peasants in that forest with their folklore and tales of demons. Thomas is influenced by the pastoral and rural elements as well as the social, religious, and political environment. Some of the conflicts between these aspects can be seen when Thomas has to curtail his visits to a peasant family and the fishing expeditions and adventures because of his studies. The political and nationalistic conflicts are apparent when Thomas is sent to learn to write Polish from Joseph, a peasant who is an ardent Lithuanian nationalist. Another conflict can be seen in his friendship with a poor boy, Dominic Malanowski. Dominic is a free spirit and shocks Thomas by slicing a Host he received at Mass; Thomas is shocked not only by the sacrilege but also by a revelation that his own existence is transitory. As a result, Thomas, for the first time, wonders about his curious state with his mother and father absent and the former solidity of his world threatened.

In contrast to the threat to Thomas' sense of self, there are chapters in the novel that describe and discuss his ancestors and their world, especially the heretic Hieronymous Surkont. Surkont denies the Trinity in favor of the one God of the Bible and joins the Swedish king in an attempt to reestablish the nation of Lithuania. Obviously, he represents both independence of thought and something of the absurdity of betraying his country, Poland, in order to bring back his ancient Lithuanian heritage. Many of the characters in the novel are faced with similar absurd choices.

Living characters also influence Thomas' view of the world. For example, Romuald Bukowski introduces him to the world of hunting in the forest. Thomas had earlier wandered about the woods as an observer, naming trees and birds, but now he is an active pursuer. He hunts adders, deer, and ducks with the gun that Romuald has given him. There are, however, both contrasts and conflicts caused by this relationship with Romuald. His grandfather, for example, brings Thomas back to the world of books by giving him *The History of Lithuania*. Furthermore, Thomas is both a reluctant and an inefficient killer in the forest.

A historical conflict between classes also appears in the novel; Thomas' grandfather is a large landowner and is subject to the division of the large estates to give the peasants their own land. Grandfather Surkont tries to avoid that appropriation of land by placing his daughter Helen into the cottage of the forester Balthazar; by doing this, he will be able to hold on to twice as much property. This, however, leads to a conflict with Balthazar, who has been paranoid since an encounter with a German soldier. Balthazar, in an attempt to hold on to what he has, ends up burning his place down and killing a villager, ultimately being killed himself.

Death brings about the most important changes in Thomas. First, the death of his Grandmother Dilbin makes him question the nature of death; was it inevitable? Why did people accept it as a necessity and not fight against it? He begins to see: "What looked so simple could not be so simple." Death in the forest also affects Thomas. He is an eager killer at first, but the touch of the first duck he kills surprises him. He is angry when he panics when the birds are flushed, but when he shoots a squirrel he begins to question his earlier values. He regrets killing the animal, and the world of the forest that had seemed to be his preserve is now "gutted." Later, he has a chance to kill a buck and refuses; he even forgets about his gun.

The novel ends with other changes in Thomas. He begins to judge his elders rather than merely accept them. He wonders whether Grandmother Surkont's self-containment and aloofness are proper, and he is shocked to find that his mother, Tekla, has not fulfilled a vow because it is inconvenient. He even begins to perceive his possible vocation when he tentatively tells the elders that he may become a priest. The final movement of the novel is a departure from the Edenic land of the Issa Valley to the city. The last view the reader has of Thomas is sitting in a wagon bound for the city to an unknown future: "Your future can only be guessed, for no one can predict how you will be shaped by the world that awaits you."

The Characters

One of the most important aspects of Czesław Miłosz's method of characterization is that Thomas is the only character who really changes or develops. This, however, does not mean that the characterization is not successful. His portrayal of Grandfather Surkont is masterful; Miłosz uses physical characteristics and sounds to portray him. The two grandmothers are also impressively and differently characterized. Grandmother Surkont is indifferent to everything but herself and her immediate comforts, while Grandmother Dilbin seems to be involved in everything.

Balthazar is the most important and interesting of the peasant characters. He actively feels the presence of the demons as they take over and control his actions. He is not a typical peasant but a complicated and divided character who cannot decide whether to follow the traditional ways or rebel and preserve his land and cottage. This division destroys him. Romuald Bukowski is a typical character; he is the independent male who cares for such masculine pursuits as hunting and fishing. Yet Miłosz does reveal other aspects of Romuald's character; he is very gentle when he teaches Thomas how to hunt, and he is understanding when Thomas fails. He also shows that he is not a prisoner of his class when he marries a poor woman, although the motivating factor in his decision is that the new wife will allow him to continue his male pursuits and comforts.

Themes and Meanings

The most important theme of the novel is the maturation of Thomas; that maturation takes place in a special world and in special circumstances. First, Thomas does not have a mother or a father to guide him or introduce him to the world. He is taught by surrogates such as his grandfather, the peasants, and Romuald. He is a product of the entire valley, not only one part.

While this world that makes up the Issa Valley may seem on the surface to be a timeless place, the outside world does impinge upon the valley. The history of Lithuania touches nearly every character in the book, including Thomas. The war and the division of the land are also outside influences which change the lives of the upper and lower classes. Balthazar is driven mad because of these changes, and the former position of the Surkonts is about to change.

Another theme of the novel is the natural world. Miłosz lovingly describes the valley and its flora and fauna, its soil and its lazy river, and, above all, its forest. Characters are defined by how they relate to the land. Romuald, for example, lives by killing the animals within the forest. Grandfather Surkont will do whatever he can to hold on to the land his ancestors possessed.

Magdelana, who commits suicide after an affair with the local priest, is said to be haunting the land. Thomas is, however, singled out for his responsive relationship with the land; he is described as being "wild" about the spring flowers and is said "to immerse his gaze in them." He learns from the forest by observing everything within it and by drawing a map of his "kingdom" and filling a notebook with names and pictures of birds and flowers. He also acquires a moral sense from nature when he has regrets over killing a squirrel and when he refuses to kill a buck. Nature is a substitute for his absent father and mother and is his best guide and friend.

Critical Context

The Issa Valley, hailed as a masterpiece, has been compared by critics to works by Ivan Turgenev and to Leo Tolstoy's *Detstvo* (1852; *Childhood*, 1862) and *Otrochestvo* (1854; *Boyhood*, 1886). It has a simplicity and power that is rare in this postmodern age, and Michael Irwin in *The Times Literary Supplement* has compared it to such great nineteenth century works as Charles Dickens' *David Copperfield* (1849-1850) and George Eliot's *The Mill on the Floss* (1860). Thus, not only is Miłosz's novel an exceptional work, but it is also not a representative late twentieth century novel. Paul Zweig, in one of the few negative reviews of the book, touches on this aspect of the novel; he finds the book to be ahistorical, since "history prowls helplessly at the edges of the timeless valley." Yet while Miłosz's novel is not postmodernist or even modernist, it certainly does not exclude history but instead presents it as a force that drives and alters the characters and world of the Issa Valley. The absence of Thomas' parents, the division of the land, and the unsettled situation of Lithuania are all aspects of this historical force that is at the heart of the novel.

Miłosz, a Nobel Prize-winning poet, wrote *The Issa Valley*, one of his few prose works, in a lyrical style which evokes unforgettably the natural setting. The novel has been justly praised by John Bayley in *The New York Review of Books* for its "solidity" and its concentration on "things" rather than "consciousness." A companion book to *The Issa Valley* is Miłosz's *Rodzinna Europa* (1958; *Native Realm: A Search for Self-Definition*, 1968), which gives a factual but no less interesting description and history of Polish Lithuania and discusses such topics as "The City of My Youth," "Catholic Education," "Marxism," and "Russia." It is clear from *Native Realm* that *The Issa Valley* is at least partially autobiographical. The chapter "The City of My Youth" deals with urban Wilno and not the Issa Valley; it also deals with a later stage in Miłosz's life and is much more objective and detached than this intimate and compelling novel.

Sources for Further Study

Bayley, John. "Return of the Native," in *The New York Review of Books*.

XXVIII (June 25, 1981), pp. 29-31.

Irwin, Michael. "Across the Dark Era," in *The Times Literary Supplement.* July 24, 1981, p. 827.

Miłosz, Czesław. *Native Realm: A Search for Self-Definition*, 1980.

_____. "The Nobel Lecture, 1980," in *The New York Review of Books.* XXVIII (March 5, 1981), pp. 11-15.

Stone, Judy. "Interview with Czesław Miłosz," in *The New York Times Book Review.* LXXXVII (June 27, 1981), pp. 7, 16, 17.

Zweig, Paul. "Czesław Miłosz, Child and Man," in *The New York Times Book Review.* LXXXVII (June 27, 1981), pp. 7, 29.

James Sullivan

JACQUES THE FATALIST AND HIS MASTER

Author: Denis Diderot (1713-1784)
Type of plot: Philosophical comedy/satire
Time of plot: The third quarter of the eighteenth century
Locale: France, both countryside and town, possibly Paris
First published: Jacques le fataliste et son maître, 1796 (English translation, 1797)

Principal characters:
THE NARRATOR, identified with but not necessarily the same as the author
JACQUES, the valet, lackey, and general servant to an aristocratic master
THE MASTER, unnamed, often a foil for Jacques
THE INNKEEPER'S WIFE, who tells one of the main stories within the narrative

The Novel

Jacques the Fatalist and His Master is deceptively simple in plot. The two title characters travel through an unidentified French landscape telling each other stories, which are interrupted by various adventures and misadventures. Usually, Jacques does the talking, for his master has an insatiable appetite for stories, and Jacques is a compulsive talker. Throughout the novel, Jacques tells his master the story of his falling in love, though he is bedeviled by constant interruptions, mishaps, separations, and other people's stories: his master's, the innkeeper's wife's, and a host of other minor characters'. Taking precedence over all the voices is that of the narrator, himself interrupting the characters and addressing the reader.

On the first page, the reader learns that Jacques has joined the army after a quarrel with his father, has adopted his captain's fatalistic philosophy— "Everything which happens to us on this earth, good and bad, is written up there"—has been wounded in the knee, and has fallen in love. The master asks for the story of his love, and Jacques begins, in frustratingly minute detail for the master (and possibly the reader), to tell of how he was wounded, left for dead in front of a farmhouse, found by the farmer's wife, treated by surgeons, of what they said, how much they drank, and the day-to-day progress of the healing. His story is punctuated throughout by the narrator's comments on how novels should or should not be written and by the master's interruptions to argue with his servant's views on fate, life, and love.

After spending the night (the narrator says he is not sure where) the master discovers that he has left his watch behind, and Jacques his purse. There is a digression into how Jacques recovers their property and a tribute to his ingenuity which is reminiscent of Sancho Panza's shrewd peasant intelligence in Miguel de Cervantes' *Don Quixote de la Mancha* (1605, 1615). While he waits for Jacques, the master has his horse stolen, although the narrator says that they spent most of their time walking and talking, possibly leading the horses. This inconsistency is the least of the novel's purposeful contradictions.

Jacques begins his story again, but not for long. The narrator intrudes with a digression on the dullness of truthful and faithful narratives, unless in the hands of a genius, and tells, as an example, the tale of the poet whom he advised to go to Pondicherry (a French outpost in India) to make his fortune, in order that he could afford to continue to write bad verses, since he was incapable of writing good ones. Then Jacques disgresses into the story of his brother Jean, who left the Carmelites, going to Lisbon only to perish in the earthquake of 1755. The two travelers then pass a funeral procession which Jacques is sure is his captain's. After a number of reflections on death and destiny by the master, and on novelistic coincidence by the narrator, Jacques again resumes, only to be interrupted with another story by the narrator. The new horse, which Jacques is riding, keeps leading him to gibbets, and the master reflects that Jacques's destiny may be hanging. Jacques tells his captain's story—he had a close friend but one with whom he was driven to duel compulsively. The narrator interrupts with a similar experience and two further unrelated narratives (though they do continue with the themes of love and betrayal). Jacques's horse then suddenly insists on going to a certain house, injuring Jacques in the process. He is treated with extreme kindness, only to discover that his benefactor is the town executioner.

Persistent, Jacques begins his story of love again, only to have the narrator interrupt with two brief anecdotes, one about Socrates, and two more stories linked to the ones he has told earlier. Finally, the companions arrive at an inn and settle down for the evening with Jacques's love story, only to be interrupted by the innkeeper's wife, who tells them the story of Madame de La Pommeraye and the Marquis des Arcis, the latter also a guest at the inn. Madame de La Pommeraye is a virtuous woman who finally yields to the Marquis. He then falls out of love with her, and she seeks revenge, plotting a year of ingenious deception during which he will marry a whore. This, the centerpiece of the novel, was often reprinted separately as a narrative of high morality. The innkeeper's wife herself is interrupted almost two dozen times before she completes the narrative, in which the Marquis forgives his wife when Madame de La Pommeraye confronts him with the truth, thus depriving her of her revenge. A lengthy debate follows the story on the relative morality of all the characters.

At last, Jacques introduces the young woman with whom he is to fall in love, but this time the interruption takes the form of a quarrel between

Jacques and his master over Jacques's obedience and who, indeed, is master. The innkeeper's wife arbitrates the quarrel and reconciles them, defining their positions permanently. As the two men leave the inn, they fall in with the Marquis des Arcis and his secretary, and hear the story of how the latter was forced to leave a monastic order after he unmasked his wily and lecherous superior, Father Hudson.

Jacques then gives a Rabelaisian account not only of how he lost his virginity, but also of how he sported with two farmer's wives who thought he was still an innocent. (It is this episode that became a major target for subsequent censors.) Then the master tells his own love story, a somber tale of betrayal by his best friend, imprisonment, and final responsibility for a son who was not his. It is this son whom they are traveling to see, in order to put him to a trade. Jacques, as they travel, almost finishes his story, when suddenly the false friend arrives to see the child's mother and he and the master duel. The former friend dies, the master flees, panic-stricken, and Jacques is jailed. On this gloomy note, the narrator stops, saying that this is the point at which his manuscript stops. Then, he discovers a few more paragraphs, and at the last moment, an old friend of Jacques (the one he tricked when he lost his virginity) appears, releasing him from jail, and finally all are reunited— Jacques, friend, master, and Jacques's love, whom he marries. One is not sure, finally, if the sudden happy ending, typical of a number of popular eighteenth century novels, is a satire on both novels and readers, or if a somber ending is not ultimately in keeping with the tone and general philosophical stance of the novel. Considering the latter, it may well be both.

The Characters

There are four major characters: Jacques, the master, the narrator, and the innkeeper's wife. The narrator sets the mood and tone of the novel from his opening staccato series of questions and answers: "How did they meet? By chance like everyone else. What were their names? What's that got to do with you? . . . Where were they going to? Does anyone ever really know where they are going to?"

This voice recurs throughout the narrative, haranguing the reader and upsetting expectations at every turn. Though he is identified with the author, it is important to recognize the distinction between the narrator's persona and the actual Denis Diderot, who had considerable life outside the novel. Diderot himself cautioned readers to seek an author not in one of his characters but in his entire body of work. The reader, also a minor character, is a creation representing a group of typical readers' attitudes and not necessarily those of the actual reader. Twentieth century readers are less likely to insist on the rules of literary composition (in particular, unity) and less likely to question the use of earthy vernacular. Otherwise, the insistence on romantic adventure, impossible coincidence, excessive action, wealthy and highborn characters; the impatience with the slow-moving, philosophic, and "realistic"; the insistence on inconsequential detail and description rather than on gestures and nuances of the spoken word; and above all, the passion for love stories—all are quite timeless.

Diderot emphasized the particular and individual, and each of his characters is fully realized, even his very minor ones. Though Diderot was an art critic with a strong sense of the visual, he often ridiculed extensive physical description. He preferred to use his knowledge of the stage to portray characters by action and dialogue, rather than by description. For example, a number of dialogue passages are written as a play, simply identifying the speakers. For all this individualizing, however, very few of the characters have names, and the major voices belong to Everyman: servant ("Jacques" was often a name for "peasant") and master, author and reader. Though with unique voices, they speak for a variety of representative points of view. The master is conservative and traditional in politics and religion, morals and literary style; in Jacques can sometimes be heard hints of the revolution to come. The major quarrel between master and man is precipitated as much by Jacques's statement that a Jacques is a man as much as any other man and the master's contradicting him, as by Jacques's insolence. Yet in the give and take of argument, the master can be more liberal, Jacques more conservative; nor does Jacques consistently maintain his fatalism. Ideas as well as persons are almost literally characters in *Jacques the Fatalist and His Master*; remove them, and there would be very little narrative remaining.

This is not to imply that the novel is abstract. Far from it. As the innkeeper's wife tells her story, the interruptions—the mail, the friar almoner, the cooper, the straw chandler—build up a picture of life in an eighteenth century inn. The narrator's asides describing where and how the characters are sitting, the number of bottles of wine consumed and in what manner, all give substance to the scene. During one of the innkeeper's wife's absences, Jacques and his master observe that in the way she tells her story, she reveals that she was not born an innkeeper's wife. Beyond acknowledging the truth of the assertion, she refuses to digress into her own history. Jacques's godfather and his son are two earthily Chaucerian portraits, and the amoral Father Hudson has a kinship with Molière's Tartuffe.

Themes and Meanings

Despite its title, the theme of fatalism may function in the novel somewhat as Jacques's love story functions as a narrative device. Early in the novel, the narrator observes that the question of whether man has free will has been debated for two thousand years "without getting one step further forward." Eventually, Jacques arrives at the end of his love story, but the reader is left with more than a few unanswered questions and much to consider. The same is true of the discussions of fatalism, love and betrayal, masters and servants.

Diderot's treatment of fatalism is, in part, a satire of Benedictus de Spinoza's philosophy. Nevertheless, Diderot also points out the difficulties and inconsistencies in applying any philosophy to life. The idea of all things being written "up there" can be consoling when things go wrong, but in terms of practical action, human volition also becomes important. In one argument, Jacques asks his master if he can will himself to fall off his horse. Then Jacques loosens the girth so that his master will fall but catches him. He is not injured, because it was written "up there"—and also, according to Jacques, because of the servant's foresight. Jacques has a prayer in which he resigns himself to fate, but he admits that his own actions are often "inconsistent and violent." Yet the satire is in the genial Horatian mode rather than in the bitter Juvenalian one. The novel suggests that one needs to examine all sides of the question, all sides of life, including the dark ones, yet also to try to keep uppermost a genial, tolerant, and open mind.

With his interest in medicine, the human body, and the relationship of biology to psychology, coupled with his iconoclastic view of institutions, it is not surprising to find Diderot an advocate of open and natural sexual relationships. For late twentieth century readers, Diderot's treatment of the sexes does not seem to be as advanced as his own contempories believed it to be. There is no equality between the sexes; women must still resort to cleverness, wit, and subterfuge in order to survive. Jacques and his master quarrel about women; Diderot pairs innumerable opposite adjectives—good/wicked, stupid/clever, unfaithful/faithful—without saying which character asserted which adjective, concluding "and they were both right." Thus, Diderot does make fun of stereotyping; the episodes involving women may well reflect the attitudes of the times.

As Diderot examines the relationships of men and women, master and servant, novelist and reader, and of whoever "wrote up there" to those whose lives are written, the major themes become interrelated and multifaceted. These relationships are all in a state of flux and ambiguity, and truth, if it be arrived at at all, is found through the examination and tension of opposites. Master and servant may seem to be a constant, but Jacques and his master have a unique relationship, and just after the innkeeper's wife settles their quarrel forever, the master observes to the Marquis des Arcis that Jacques is his master rather than the opposite. Actually, they are interdependent, but when Jacques refers to Oliver Cromwell and the death of Charles I and is about to continue with what people in France are saying now, the master abruptly changes the subject.

The novel's structure reflects another major theme: the nature of the novel itself. Parallels are constantly implied between the novelist's writing and whoever is writing what is written "up there." In its loose, episodic structure, with its narrator's interruptions, and in its satiric tone, *Jacques the Fatalist and His Master* resembles Laurence Sterne's *The Life and Opinions of Tristram*

Shandy, Gent. (1759-1767). Sterne and Diderot met and then corresponded, and at the end of his novel, Diderot introduced a passage that he said was taken word-for-word from Sterne's novel, leaving gracefully and humorously open who found it first. Much has been written about Diderot's possible plagiarism, but imitation was an accepted eighteenth century literary device, and Diderot's novel is quite different from Sterne's.

Diderot's narrator at one point insists that he is writing a true story and not fiction, which is why the story is not written as a novel should be. At another, he observes that "the person who takes what I write for the truth might perhaps be less wrong than the person who takes it for a fiction." The truth, Diderot may be saying, as far as people can know the truth of anything, may be that all things need to be called into question.

Critical Context

Unpublished until 1796, twelve years after Diderot's death, *Jacques the Fatalist and His Master* was not initially received with great enthusiasm. Of Diderot's contemporaries, Voltaire and Jean-Jacques Rousseau recognized his creative genius, though Rousseau later broke with Diderot, and neither man lived to read the novel. Nevertheless, Catherine the Great of Russia not only admired the philosopher's work but also purchased his library and papers, leaving him their use during his lifetime and also providing him with a small monthly stipend. Many of these materials are still in Leningrad.

Johann Wolfgang von Goethe and Johann Christoph Friedrich von Schiller both admired the novel, but French critics found the book disordered, inconsequential, and, in some cases, offensive. In the first half of the nineteenth century, the response was more favorable. The novel was dramatized in 1832 and again in 1847. Stendhal, Honoré de Balzac, and Eugène Delacroix were among Diderot's nineteenth century admirers in France. In Great Britain, Thomas Carlyle thought the novel brilliant, though he deplored its obscenity, and Karl Marx wrote to Friedrich Engels recommending both *Jacques the Fatalist and His Master* and *Le Neveu de Rameau* (1821, 1891; *Rameau's Nephew*, 1897). In Germany, the philosopher Georg Wilhelm Friedrich Hegel, in a discussion of the master-servant relationship, spoke admiringly of Jacques and his master.

Although an edition of Diderot's complete works was compiled in France between 1875 and 1877, Diderot's place in intellectual history for both Continental and British readers was not high. Considered more an editor, translator, and compiler than an original thinker and a novelist, he was assigned to the lesser ranks of Enlightenment figures and was known mainly for his editorship of the monumental *Encyclopedia* (1751-1772). Critical reaction to *Jacques the Fatalist and His Master* continued to be indifferent or unfavorable until 1912, when observation of the bicentenary of Diderot's birth started to gather momentum. Then, critics began to reread and reevaluate Diderot's works. As Peter France has observed, in the twentieth century, not only did Diderot become appreciated, but diverse groups began to claim him for their own as well. The Soviet Union saw him as a major precursor, as did the French Communist Party. Liberals saw in him an early humanist; Romantics, an aesthetic forerunner; existentialists found in him some of the roots of their philosophy; and modern writers, too, claimed him as their own for his irony and for his unconventional approach to the novel.

One of the more telling contemporary comments on Diderot is the exiled Czech writer Milan Kundera's adaptation of the novel for the stage, *Jacques et son maître: Hommage à Denis Diderot* (1981, 1985). Inspired by Diderot's novel as Diderot was by Sterne, Kundera saw the novel as a milestone on the road taken by travelers from Don Quixote to Godot, a refreshing voice of reason and comedy in a much more irrational age. By overlapping and counterpointing the love stories, which can be performed by the same actors taking a number of parts, Kundera emphasizes Diderot's questioning mind, his paradoxes of freedom and fate, masters and servants, author and characters. Using Diderot's own technique of dialogue and gesture, of demonstrating rather than explicating, Kundera demonstrates that *Jacques the Fatalist* still has much to offer successive generations of readers.

Sources for Further Study

"Diderot's Great Scroll: Narrative Art in *Jacques le Fataliste*," in *Studies on Voltaire and the Eighteenth Century*. LXXXVIII (1975).

Fellows, Otis. *Diderot*, 1977.

France, Peter. *Diderot*, 1983.

Fredman, Alice Green. *Diderot and Sterne*, 1954.

Loy, J. Robert. *Diderot's Determined Fatalist: A Critical Appreciation of "Jacques le Fataliste,"* 1950.

Katharine M. Morsberger

JEALOUSY

Author: Alain Robbe-Grillet (1922-   )
Type of plot: New Novel
Time of plot: After World War II
Locale: A house on a banana plantation
First published: La Jalousie, 1957 (English translation, 1959)

> *Principal characters:*
> THE NARRATOR, a person unidentified as to age or sex
> A . . . , a woman who lives in the house
> FRANCK, the owner of a neighboring plantation

The Novel

Jealousy, Alain Robbe-Grillet's third published novel, takes place in a house on an isolated banana plantation somewhere in the Western Hemisphere, perhaps on an island, perhaps on the South American mainland. The book opens with the description of a shadow cast by one of the house pillars and then moves to a description of A . . . and her activities, then to a railing, then back to A . . . , then to the general physical surroundings of the plantation. The tone of the novel is now set; a calm, detached, almost scientific description of what the narrator sees and hears. The passages that describe the most important observations of the narrator are repeated at various times throughout the book and in no discernible chronological or spatial order.

At least in part because the title of the book is *Jealousy*, most critics believe that the narrator is a man and married to A . . . . According to their reading, he is insanely jealous of A . . . and suspects her of having an affair with Franck. Nevertheless, one notable critic, Maurice Blanchot, states that the narrator is not a person but only a pure, anonymous presence. Such an interpretation would be more in keeping with Robbe-Grillet's theories on literature as expressed in his *Pour un nouveau roman* (1963; *For a New Novel*, 1965). It must be noted that the original French title is *La Jalousie* and that a "jalousie" in French—and also in British English—is a venetian blind. There are, in fact, venetian blinds on the windows of the house, and the narrator spends a good part of the time peering through them. Then, too, Robbe-Grillet posed for the photograph that appears on the cover of the Grove Press 1965 combined edition of *Jealousy* and *Dans le labyrinthe* (1959; *In the Labyrinth*, 1960), and that photo shows him looking through a venetian blind.

While Robbe-Grillet's first book, *Les Gommes* (1953; *The Erasers*, 1964), has a plot, and his second *Le Voyeur* (1955; *The Voyeur*, 1958) has at least part of a plot, *Jealousy* has only a series of scenes that may roughly be divided into two groups: connecting scenes and critical scenes. In the first category, there are, for example, passages in which the narrator defines the shape and size of the various parcels of land where the banana trees have been planted and counts and recounts the number of trees that have been cut or replanted. There are also those that describe workmen replacing (or getting ready to replace) a log bridge and servants coming and going. In short, they are descriptions that do not advance what could be considered to be a story.

In the second category, those scenes which may be considered to be critical to the development of a plot, there are two that are repeated several times and are believed to demonstrate that the book is about a jealous husband. The first shows the three people in the book sitting on the veranda after dinner at night. The chairs of A . . . and Franck are in close proximity and that of the narrator is placed so that observing them and overhearing their conversation is difficult. The second involves Franck's decision to make a trip to town and A . . .'s desire to accompany him in order to make some unspecified purchases. Since there is no linear time in the book, the reader does not know just when they decided to make the trip, the trip being recounted at various times both as though it were still in the planning stage and as though it had already happened. The reader does learn, however, that they did not come back the same day, that they spent the night in town, and that A . . . made a totally insignificant purchase.

For those readers who find a jealous husband in the book, there is one additional critical scene. The three protagonists are at the dinner table when A . . . sees a centipede, an insect that she mortally fears. Franck gets up from the table and mashes it against the wall, leaving there the outline of part of its body, and then steps on the remains that fall to the floor. Both this incident and a description of the outline on the wall are retold several times in descriptions that range from the very brief to the very detailed. This insistence on the mark left by the death of the centipede is alleged to show increasing jealousy and obsessive behavior on the part of the narrator. At one time, the narrator is seen trying to remove the outline. Even though it is in the shape of a question mark, putting both the significance of the scene and the meaning of the centipede very much in doubt, this mark is now considered to be a symbol both of Franck's dominant sexual role and a stain on the narrator's honor.

Two scenes are given only once. In the first, a hand is seen clutching at sheets in a hotel room bed and Franck gets out of the bed. In the other, Franck is driving his car at night and there is an accident. It should be noted that the narrator never leaves the house and therefore could not have witnessed those events, that the reader sees Franck after the trip to town and knows that he did not have such an accident, and that A . . . and Franck are not positively seen together in the two scenes.

The Characters

While the description of the characters in *The Erasers* and *The Voyeur* was summary by traditional standards, it is all but nonexistent in *Jealousy*. In his critical articles, already mentioned, Robbe-Grillet states his belief that a change in the very nature of the protagonist is necessary if the novel is to be revitalized. Instead of the conventional hero with a name, face, and background, the new hero must be a simple *il* ("he" or "it") and serve as the "subject of the action expressed by the verb." Thus, information that would allow the reader to identify personally with the characters of the book should be absent from the work or at least reduced to a minimum. It seems obvious that Robbe-Grillet has reached his goal in writing *Jealousy*.

The narrator of the novel never speaks and is never spoken to in the way that normally occurs in novels. French grammar is so constructed that it is possible to identify the gender of unidentified speakers simply by checking the endings of adjectives. Thus a person who says "je suis fatigué" (I am tired) is male, while "je suis fatiguée" identifies a female. Yet this narrator is never quoted, nor do A . . . and Franck address the narrator directly; thus this person cannot be identified as to gender.

As for Franck, Robbe-Grillet tells the reader only that he has a wife and child (who never appear in the book), that he mistrusts native drivers, and that he eats like an American. That is, after cutting his meat, he shifts his fork from his left to his right hand.

Then there is A . . . . She has long legs, long hair, and green eyes, and is very efficient at running the house. As with some of the characters in *The Erasers*, there is a strong indication that she is not to be seen as a real person. Robbe-Grillet says that her eyes are very big, that she always keeps them as wide open as possible, and that she never blinks—no matter what the intensity of the light. He adds that they are in fact so big that one seems to see both of them at the same time, even when she is in profile. It would appear that the reader is faced with a mannequin or perhaps a painting by Pablo Picasso.

Themes and Meanings

Just as it is impossible to talk about the characters of *Jealousy* in the traditional manner, so is it impossible to treat its themes and meanings in that way. This is true because the book is static; there is movement but no progress. There is a clue, perhaps, as to how the book should be seen, a clue that occurs near the beginning, when the narrator describes his observations as being an exercise. If the reader takes observation and description to be the main purpose of the book, then he or she can make sense of it.

There are several passages in the novel in which the narrator is, as usual, looking through a window. The glass in the window is of poor quality and there are serious imperfections in it. The narrator then plays the same game that everyone has played at one time or another; "he" deliberately distorts what "he" observes. Upon finding an imperfection, the narrator moves so that the imperfection is between "him" and the object that "he" is observing. The result is that the object is totally distorted from what it is in objective reality. The narrator makes things change location and even disappear completely. The object still exists, but the narrator's perception of it depends not on its objective existence but on how "he" chooses to consider it.

Applying this point of view to the stain left by the centipede, it would seem that the reason that the mark grows or shrinks during the various descriptions is less a sign of rampant jealousy on the part of the narrator than an indication that Robbe-Grillet is doing what all artists do: practicing his craft. Artists, painters in particular, rework the same compositions over and over in the search for total perfection. The centipede, described with the fidelity of an anatomical plate, now joins the famous segment of tomato from *The Erasers* as a masterpiece of description.

This interpretation, that the subject of the book is the art of observation and writing, can be justified by a close reading of another passage in the book. A . . . and Franck are reading a novel that is set in Africa. The narrator notes that never do they talk about the quality of the writing, preferring instead to discuss the characters as though they were living people whom they might have known or about whom they might have heard. They go so far as to imagine what might have happened *if*, only to be faced with the fact that the book exists as it is despite their modifications. The narrator then notes that things are what they are, one cannot change reality. The only reality here is the book itself, exactly as Robbe-Grillet wrote it, and nowhere in *Jealousy* does Robbe-Grillet say that there is a jealous husband.

Critical Context

As a general statement, it can be said that Robbe-Grillet is one of the proponents of the French New Novel, a disparate group that includes such well-known authors as Samuel Beckett and Claude Simon, as well as the lesser known, to Americans, Nathalie Sarraute and Claude Ollier. The New Novelists are no real "school," since each follows his, or her, particular bent. Nearly all that they have in common is the suppression of linear time and space in their stories. The reader may already be familiar with the screen-plays written by several of these artists which give visual expression to the lack of linear development. The best are, probably, *Hiroshima mon amour* (1959; *Hiroshima mon amour: Text by Marguerite Duras for the Film by Alain Resnais*, 1961) and *L'Année dernière à Marienbad* (1961; *Last Year at Marienbad*, 1962) by Robbe-Grillet. They also show, in general, a devotion to art as opposed to the politically and socially engaged stance of their imme-diate predecessors, Jean-Paul Sartre and Albert Camus. Nevertheless, Alain Robbe-Grillet really differs from the others in that there is no story, in the traditional sense, in *Jealousy*. This book stands alone, considered by both Robbe-Grillet's admirers and detractors to be the highest expression of his art. It will not be repeated because it cannot be. Were Robbe-Grillet to attempt another *Jealousy*, the result would be not a triumph but a parody.

Sources for Further Study

Barthes, R. "Objective Literature: Alain Robbe-Grillet," in *Two Novels*, 1965.

Blanchot, Maurice. *Le Livre à venir*, 1971.

Lanes, Jerrold. Review in *Saturday Review*. XLIII (January 2, 1960), p. 16.

Minor, A. "A Note on Jealousy," in *Two Novels*, 1965.

Morrissette, Bruce. *The Novels of Robbe-Grillet*, 1975.

Peyre, Henri. Review in *The New York Times Book Review*. LXIV (November 22, 1959), p. 5.

Robbe-Grillet, Alain. *For a New Novel*, 1965.

Sturrock, John. *The French New Novel: Claude Simon, Michel Butor, Alain Robbe-Grillet*, 1969.

Robert R. Brock

JOB
The Story of a Simple Man

Author: Joseph Roth (1894-1939)
Type of plot: Parable
Time of plot: The early twentieth century
Locale: Zuchnow, the Ukraine, and New York City
First published: Hiob: Roman eines einfachen Mannes, 1930 (English
translation, 1931)

Principal characters:

MENDEL SINGER, a teacher of Hebrew and the elements of the
  Bible
DEBORAH, his wife
JONAS and
SCHEMARJAH, his sons
MIRIAM, his daughter
MENUCHIM, Mendel's son, who is born early in the novel and
  is apparently afflicted with epilepsy
MAC, Schemarjah's friend in New York
SKOWRONNEK,
MENKES,
ROTTENBERG, and
GROSCHEL, Mendel's friends and counselors in New York

The Novel

Mendel Singer teaches Hebrew in Zuchnow, a small Ukrainian village.
His life is sparse and meager, but he is healthy and eats well, and he loves his
wife, Deborah, and his children. Still, his prospects are not good in this
impoverished region. Then, Deborah bears a fourth child, Menuchim.

For a year Menuchim seems to develop normally, but in the thirteenth
month a change comes over him, affecting his breathing, color, and shape. At
first Mendel worries little; after all, he is an upright man. When the doctor
from the inoculation commission examines Menuchim, however, he declares
the boy an incurable epileptic. With little other hope, Mendel increases his
devotions. Deborah invokes the spirits of her dead forebears.

One day, Deborah takes Menuchim to Klucysk to visit the rabbi. Singling
her out from the throng of the afflicted, he pronounces that Menuchim will
become sound, though not soon, and that his parents should never lose hope
or abandon him.

Deciding that the older children should help with Menuchim, Deborah
makes them carry him around with them. Hating this burden, they eventually
drop him in a ditch filled with water in which he nearly drowns. Yet he some-

how manages to survive. Life continues, punctuated only by Menuchim's first word, "Mama." That, however, remains his only word.

Ten years pass. The children grow up, although Menuchim changes very little. Suddenly, the daughter, Miriam, begins to wander in the evenings, delighting in arousing the Russian soldiers. When the two healthy boys are taken for military training, Deborah rages at Mendel for doing nothing about it, then she rushes out to spend the night in the graveyard praying.

She decides to seek help from a middleman, leaving Mendel with the children. Mendel loves these quiet hours with Menuchim; yet, after vainly trying to teach him to read, Mendel sinks into despair. Meanwhile, Deborah discovers that her meager hoard of cash can buy only one exemption, for her son Jonas. Nevertheless, Jonas declares that he wants to enlist. Early the next morning, he leaves home, although he does not join the service immediately.

Shortly thereafter, the son Schemarjah is taken for duty. Led out to replace the outpost guard at the border, the new recruits come under fire; they desert, by morning arriving at a town at which they are taken into custody. For a while, the Singer family hears nothing of Schemarjah, although Jonas writes occasionally.

A few years later, a foreigner appears at the Singer home. He brings a letter from Schemarjah, who is in New York, where he has gone into business with this man, named Mac. Now calling himself "Sam," Schemarjah has married and invites his family to visit him in the United States. Unfortunately, the family's traveling is limited by Menuchim's disabilities.

Mendel attends the New Moon ceremony, after which he lingers, rapt in thought. Unseen, he watches a Cossack soldier and a Jewish girl in a familiar yellow shawl making love. Back home, he asks after the absent Miriam, only to learn that she has gone walking. He prays and contemplates all night, concluding that his daughter is in danger. He confides in Deborah.

She resolves on action. Breaking out her carefully hidden hoard of cash, she urges Mendel to buy the necessary papers for traveling. They await only the passage money from Schemarjah. Deborah nearly balks at leaving Menuchim because of the rabbi's stipulations. Yet she realizes that her daughter's only hope is to be taken away from Cossack temptation. They find a young couple to live in their house and care for Menuchim. On the last day, Deborah can hardly bear to be torn from her ten-year-old baby, and Mendel is wracked with doubts. Still, they bend to necessity, and the journey passes uneventfully. New York teems with streets full of hot, hurrying, dusty people. Mendel is struck dumb to discover that he has abandoned home and son for pandemonium.

At first, the exchange seems ill-advised. For the aging couple, life is a struggle in the new land, as it was in the old. The younger generation, however, seems to thrive in the superficial glitter. Schemarjah promises to send for Menuchim as soon as the child is able to travel. Mendel resigns himself wearily to this new, meaningless life. Then things suddenly change. One day, two letters arrive: Menuchim has miraculously learned to run and speak, and Jonas has finally joined the army.

Mendel grows old; he lives only in the hope of seeing Menuchim again. Mac plans to go to Russia and bring Menuchim back, but suddenly the long-threatened war breaks out. News from the war zone is scarce. Nothing is heard of Menuchim, and Jonas is declared missing in action. Then the United States joins the war, and Schemarjah and Mac volunteer. Miriam, who has been going with Mac, takes to seeing other men. Before long, Mac returns, bearing Schemarjah's watch and his final good-bye. Deborah begins to sing a lullaby for a dead child but collapses, and before help can arrive, she dies.

After a week of mourning, Miriam's latest companion calls on Mendel. When Mendel goes to her, he sees that remorse over her infidelity has driven her insane. She is committed to an asylum and pronounced incurable.

From the depths of his misery, Mendel renounces God and burns all of his sacred objects except for one small purse. He declares that he is burning God. His neighbors gather to console and pacify him, but he rejects their counsel; he believes that he has not deserved this treatment. Not even the example of Job can offer him relief.

Mendel's anger smolders within him while he leaves his home and pursues a meaningless routine as an assistant in Skowronnek's music shop. Everything about him grows shabbier and older. Even the end of the war brings no satisfaction. Nevertheless, Mendel decides to celebrate like everyone else. Alone in the music shop, he plays a record on the gramophone. It works like a magical balm on him; for the first time during his suffering, he begins to weep. Mendel asks the name of the record; it is "Menuchim's Song." Mendel identifies it with his own lost Menuchim.

During a special Passover concert by a European orchestra, Mendel decides to sneak into his old home to retrieve Deborah's hoarded money. He needs the money to search for Menuchim. The next day, he learns that the new tenant is looking for him, and he fears that his robbery has been discovered. He also learns that the director of the orchestra, a young musical genius named Alexej Kossak, seeks him. Preoccupied with his mission, Mendel declines to meet with him.

The following day, Mendel is to take the Passover meal with the Skowronneks. At the point in the ceremony when the door is opened to let in the prophet Elijah, a stranger knocks to be admitted. It is Kossak. After the meal, he reveals that he is from Zuchnow. He tells Mendel that the man who had taken Mendel's house has died of typhus, the woman has gone back to her parents, and the house has been taken over by soldiers. Kossak bought the house and has now brought Mendel the money.

After inquiring everywhere for Jonas, Kossak has learned only that he fled to Poland, thereafter fighting in a resistance unit. Still, Kossak has hopes, and his inquiries continue. He then tells something of his own life: A sickly child, he was placed by his parents in an institute, where he developed a remarkable gift for music.

Mendel is desperate to ask about Menuchim, but in his despair, he cannot speak. Instead, Mrs. Skowronnek brings out the question, and Kossak declares that Menuchim is still living. Mendel is overwhelmed. Kossak adds that Menuchim, now a young man, has become completely normal. Finally, he announces that he himself is Menuchim. After the entire neighborhood joins in the celebration, the restored Menuchim leaves with his father for the Astor Hotel.

There, the splendor of the decor and of the lighted city below makes Mendel feel as if he has been swept to heaven. He and Menuchim reminisce over family history. This reminds them of Miriam and the others; Menuchim suggests that one miracle, his restoration, may beget others. Mendel agrees to go wherever his son leads. He has a vision of reunion and restoration, in the manner of Job. At that moment, a dove flies below the marquee of the terrace. Mendel allows Menuchim to put him to bed, where he dreams of his family while his son prepares for their journey back to their home in the Ukraine.

The Characters

Mendel Singer is the dominant figure in this book. Joseph Roth develops him in detail and in depth. He is seen awake and asleep, at work and at prayer, most often with his family, who constitute the center of his consciousness and his life.

Superficially, this seems to be poor narrative strategy, for Mendel Singer is neither remarkable nor distinguished, in no way exciting. In this "story of a simple man," Roth centers on the kind of shabby, nondescript figure most readers would not look at twice, the common man shambling through dusty lanes without a significant life of his own. Yet this figure stays in the memory; it is easy to attach an identity to it and thus to identify with it. Roth capitalizes on this; he makes one wonder what could happen to such a man and makes one put oneself in his place. The "simple man" becomes Everyman. His simple, repeated actions become the routine of daily life.

Like Mendel, the other characters are typecast. Deborah is the devoted, devout, and superstitious mother, suffering in the absence of her children; Roth even describes her as a wife like other wives, sometimes driven by the Devil. Jonas and Schemarjah are typical first and second sons, the former a bit more daring, the latter a bit luckier at landing on his feet. In her headstrong desire to follow her sexual inclinations, Miriam seems more individualized, yet she is essentially identified with that single trait. Menuchim, on the other hand, is a literal grotesque, but even in that, he is one-dimensional, the incarnation of the "baby" of the family. Roth uses simple, homely details to invest all these typed characters with particularity. It is significant that all are driven by forces which they cannot control.

Themes and Meanings

Roth typecasts his characters both to promote easy identification and to focus on his themes. The title discloses his primary intention; by using the title of the most parabolic and paradoxical book of the Old Testament, Roth directs the reader's attention to the problem of human suffering. The subtitle extends the intention; unlike the heroic Job, Mendel Singer is the "simple man," and the problem becomes not only unjustified suffering but also the common suffering of the poor and the neglected. To that extent, *Job* is an updating of the old story. The hero becomes mankind, and his problems are universalized. The Old Testament writer attempted to reconcile the sufferings of the worthy with the concept of a just and loving God. Roth expands that dilemma to include all suffering.

Roth generalizes further by presenting Mendel with the dream and the promise of the United States, the brave new world which held forth for generations of European peasants the hope of escaping the poverty of an exhausted land and the tyranny of absolute rulers and entrenched bureaucracies. The fortunes of Schemarjah attest this: Sent to apparent slaughter by executive mandate, he escapes by blind luck, stumbles to the United States, and becomes wealthy in the insurance business. The contrast between the two worlds appears in a significant detail. Schemarjah's letter includes the trivial gift of ten dollars, yet that amounts to a tenth of the total "fortune" which Deborah has accumulated after twenty-odd years of scraping. The promised land, however, proves a lure and a deception. The country is rich, but life is poor in many significant ways, and Mendel loses everything that makes his life meaningful. Material prosperity is not the antidote or antithesis to suffering; in the end, what remains of the Singer family is returning home.

Critical Context

The novel *Job* is a transitional work in Roth's career. In his earlier works, he was primarily concerned with establishing a homeland for the dispossessed, a cultural center in the autocratic world of post-World War I Central Europe. Later, he concentrated on problems of personal freedom and on combatting the racial hatred of totalitarian Nazism. In this work, Roth is at his most universal: Mendel is Everyman, only accidentally (or incidentally) Jewish. For that reason, *Job* has become the most enduring of his works; fifty years after Roth's death, it is more widely read now than when it was originally published. Because of the simplicity of his style—a trait he shared with Hermann Hesse—and a minimalist quality of representing the complexities of life by sparse selection of telling details, he has been linked with the primitivists. The fairy-tale-like atmosphere created by this technique is perfectly suited to his transmutation of the most timeless of parables.

Job can hardly be considered a Jewish novel; yet it captures with great charm the essence of Jewish village life in turn-of-the-century Europe. This is almost incidental to the vision at the center of the story and the skill with which Roth creates a nearly perfect marriage of theme and style. The remarkable achievement of *Job* has led to a belated recognition of Roth's other works, raising Roth to a secure place in the German literature of the early twentieth century.

Sources for Further Study

Bell, Robert F. "The Jewish Experience as Portrayed in Three German Exile *Novellen*," in *South Atlantic Bulletin.* XLII (1977), pp. 4-12.

Powell, Ward H. "Joseph Roth, Ironic Primitivist," in *Monatshefte.* LIII (1961), pp. 115-123.

Sanger, Curt. "The Experience of Exile in Joseph Roth's Novels," in *Exile: The Writer's Experience*, 1982. Edited by John M. Spalek and Robert F. Bell.

James Livingston

THE JOKE

Author: Milan Kundera (1929-   )
Type of plot: Comic realism
Time of plot: 1947-1965
Locale: Czechoslovakia
First published: Žert, 1967 (English translation, 1969, revised 1982)

Principal characters:
> LUDVIK JAHN, the protagonist, whose anti-Party joke earns
> for him six years of hard labor
> MARKETA, his girlfriend and fellow student, to whom he sends
> the joke
> PAVEL ZEMANEK, another fellow student, Party Chairman of
> the Division of Natural Sciences
> HELENA, another student, later Zemanek's wife and a feature
> reporter for radio
> LUCIE SEBETKA, an angelic young woman, Ludvik's girlfriend
> during part of his imprisonment
> KOSTKA, Ludvik's Christian friend, a university lecturer and
> later a hospital virologist
> JAROSLAV, Ludvik's hometown friend, a devotee of Moravian
> folklore

The Novel

Set in Communist Czechoslovakia, *The Joke* relates the serious consequences of a frivolous message that a university student sends his girlfriend by postcard: "Optimism is the opium of the people! A healthy atmosphere stinks of stupidity! Long live Trotsky! Ludvik." *The Joke* is divided into seven parts, with each part narrated in the first person by one of the main characters except for part 7, which is narrated alternately by three characters.

Parts 1 and 2, both brief and set in 1965, show Ludvik Jahn and Helena preparing for their rendezvous in Ludvik's unnamed Moravian hometown. The rendezvous is the result of an elaborate plot whereby Ludvik plans to take revenge on his enemy Pavel Zemanek by seducing Helena, Zemanek's wife. Part 3, narrated by Ludvik, shows his motives for seeking revenge, describing the highly politicized school years after the February, 1948, Communist revolution and recounting the story of the notorious postcard. Although a Communist student leader himself, Ludvik sends the joking message to Marketa, his naïve girlfriend, when they are separated during the summer of 1949—he with an agricultural brigade, she at an ideological training session. Mocking what Marketa is being taught, Ludvik means simply to shock her as a joke, but the effect is far greater than he intended. The message is intercepted by the Communists, who, led by Zemanek (supposedly a friend), oust Ludvik from the Party and from the university. The Party's wrath, however, is still not sated. Soon Ludvik is drafted into the military and assigned to a group with black insignia (that is, a penal unit).

Ludvik does his national service at Ostrava, where a typical day consists of work in the coal mines followed by indoctrination, punitive tasks, and bedtime. Provided they behave, the soldier-prisoners are allowed out of the guarded, fenced-in camp one day each month. Usually they go on a wild spree together, but one time when Ludvik is by himself, he meets the shy Lucie Sebetka, a factory worker. They fall in love, and she begins appearing at the camp fence daily with flowers for him. Their relationship provides the emotional support that Ludvik and apparently also Lucie deeply need, but Lucie refuses to have sex with him, even after Ludvik goes to considerable trouble and takes serious risks to arrange their trysts. Finally Ludvik resorts to force, which Lucie resists ferociously and successfully. In frustration, Ludvik screams at her to get out, but Lucie leaves town entirely. Then, realizing what he has lost, Ludvik goes AWOL to find her, gets caught, and has ten months of jail added to his time. When his military service ends, lest more hard time be added, he volunteers for three more years in the mines as a civilian worker.

Part 4, narrated by Jaroslav, Ludvik's hometown friend, is an interlude from the main action, replete with discussions of Moravian folk music and folk celebrations. This part traces Jaroslav's relationships with Ludvik, his wife Vlasta, and his son Vladimir. All these relationships have been deteriorating, paralleling the Communist government's once-enthusiastic but nowdeclining support of Moravian folklore, as epitomized in the upcoming event, the annual Ride of the Kings, which this year (1965) Jaroslav has had to organize almost single-handedly in the face of uncooperative authorities.

Part 5, narrated by Ludvik, returns to the main action with a vengeance. Helena meets Ludvik in his hometown, and Ludvik proceeds with his revenge plot. He recounts in detail how he plies her with drink and seduces her in a monumental sex scene. Yet his satisfaction is short-lived. As soon as the seduction ends, Helena, now drunkenly maudlin, tells him that she and Zemanek have been estranged for years and continue to live together only for the sake of their daughter. Thus Ludvik's elaborate revenge is meaningless: He has succeeded only in becoming romantically entangled with Helena, whom he decides that he detests.

If Ludvik has won Helena, he has forever lost the loving Lucie. This fact is driven home in part 6, which, narrated by Ludvik's Christian friend Kostka, again recounts past events, particularly Lucie's flight from Ostrava. She fled all the way to western Bohemia, where Kostka, himself expelled form a university teaching post for his Christian beliefs, was working on a collective farm. There, living in the woods like a fairy, stealing the farmers' milk and eating food set out by children, Lucie becomes a subject of local folklore. Finally captured by kindly authorities, she is put to work on the collective farm and rehabilitated by Kostka. Yet her life, too, is blighted: She eventually marries a man who is unfaithful and beats her. They settle in Ludvik's hometown, where Lucie works in a barbershop, and Ludvik in 1965 at first fails to recognize her when she shaves him.

The novel comes to a climax in part 7, set on the day of the 1965 Ride of the Kings. Zemanek appears at the festival with his attractive young girl-friend, Miss Broz. After Helena privately tells him how things stand between her and Ludvik and offers a divorce, Zemanek—obviously pleased to get rid of her so easily—is smug and congratulatory toward Ludvik, whom he hails as an old friend. In return, Ludvik can only suffer his unvented frustration. Time and change have cheated him of his hatred, which has dissipated, and meanwhile Zemanek has become a liberal critic of the regime, a person who shares Ludvik's own views. Ludvik's only recourse is to be honest with Helena and tell her that he does not want to see her again. In shock, Helena tries to kill herself by swallowing what she thinks is a bottle of analgesics, but they are actually laxatives. She is thoroughly purged of any romantic feelings toward Ludvik.

The sorrowful Ludvik wanders down by the river, where he comes across the equally sorrowful Jaroslav lying in the grass. Earlier in the day, Jaroslav was duped by his wife and son into thinking that the son was playing the role of the disguised king in the Ride of the Kings, when actually young Vladimir had left for the motorcycle races. In despair, Jaroslav broke all the kitchen china and furniture into a heap in front of his wife. Now he is on his way with his violin to perform in the traditional cimbalom band. Ludvik, a clarinetist, joins him, and before a tavern crowd they play music together as in the old days. Playing the music lifts Ludvik emotionally, but it brings the realization that he and his friends have led devastated lives. Then even the music ends when Jaroslav has a heart attack during the performance. He will recover, but he will always be a diminished, if not a devastated, man.

The Characters

Although *The Joke* centers on the story of Ludvik, the novel could be subtitled "Ludvik and His Friends." In a highly complex novelistic structure, the stories of Ludvik's friends weave in and out of his story, supplementing and complementing it. All of their stories, as Ludvik realizes at the end, tend to reinforce—sometimes comically, sometimes sadly—a sense of loss or "devastation." /

Ludvik's life comes apart with the foolish joke and its horrendous consequences—ejection from the Party and the university; the wasted years in the military penal unit, prison itself, and the mines; and the difficulties of returning to civilian life in the Communist society that suspects him. The worst consequence is the effect of his experiences on Ludvik himself, on his character and on his personality. A dedicated and joking fellow, he becomes a stunted, shallow, and suspicious person, unable to maintain any solid beliefs or relationships. He provides a prime example of the division between body and soul that Milan Kundera maintains is the theme of the novel. In effect, he has lost his soul, reducing love to sex (with Lucie) and sex to revenge (with Helena). Hope appears, however, in the understanding of himself that he finally reaches.

Some of the other main characters could almost be considered symbolic of aspects of Ludvik. The angelic Lucie and the Christian Kostka represent the soul that Ludvik has lost—the possibilities for love and belief. Lucie herself exemplifies the other side of the body/soul division. As a result of belonging to a youth gang that treated her as a sexual plaything, raping her repeatedly, Lucie cannot tolerate sex. It is significant that Kostka, not Ludvik, reintroduces her to sex (and thereby becomes guilt-ridden himself). The brokenhearted Jaroslav is identified with Ludvik's cultural roots: "Jaroslav too (more than anyone, actually) represented the devastated values of my life. . . ." Like Ludvik also, Jaroslav is the object of some rather dark, mordant, ironic humor.

Much of the lightness in *The Joke* comes from contrasting or minor characters. Obviously contrasting with Ludvik, and eventually arousing Ludvik's jealous admiration, is the opportunistic Zemanek, a type apparently found in all political systems, able to ride each new tide to popularity. The raucous, heavy-breathing Helena just as obviously contrasts with Lucie; both are female types found in later Kundera novels. Like these contrasting characters, the numerous minor characters in *The Joke* are typed; for example, those in Ludvik's penal unit could substitute for characters in a television situation comedy.

Themes and Meanings

Milan Kundera has objected to attempts to give his novels narrow political readings. For example, he begins the preface to the 1982 edition of *The Joke* as follows:

> When in 1980, during a television panel discussion devoted to my works, someone called *The Joke* "a major indictment of Stalinism," I was quick to interject, "Spare me your Stalinism, please. *The Joke* is a love story!"

Apparently the point of Kundera's objections is that his novels are not merely political novels, not merely salvos in the Cold War, but much more. In the main tradition of the novel, Kundera is most concerned with the personal destinies of his characters in *The Joke*.

Yet the personal and the political are never far apart in Kundera. Ludvik's awful experiences clearly result from doctrinaire Communist overreaction, and the "devastation" suffered by the other main characters (except possibly for Lucie, whose troubles seem to originate with her family) is also linked to the Communist takeover of Czechoslovakia. As Kundera goes on to say in his preface, Ludvik and his friends are victims of "the joke history has played on them"—something of a sick joke, to be sure. The devastation visited on the individual characters has spread over the whole society—much like the blight in *Oedipus Rex*, a work prominently mentioned in a later Kundera novel, *L'Insoutenable légèreté de l'être* (1984; *The Unbearable Lightness of Being*, 1984)—and become cultural. The cultural devastation is specifically manifested in the attack on Christianity, which Kostka finds compatible with true Communism, and the decline of folk culture, as seen in the folk music and the Ride of the Kings and symbolized by Jaroslav's heart attack. Christianity and folk culture are being replaced by a barren youth culture: Rather than be king, Jaroslav's son prefers to go to the motorcycle races. Communism has preserved poor Czechoslovakia in body but not in soul.

Critical Context

With its complex but controlled structure, cast of characters, and symbolism, *The Joke* is an impressive first novel, reflecting Kundera's experience as a writer of poetry, plays, criticism, and short stories. Before writing novels, Kundera was also a professor of film studies in Prague—indeed, an inspirer of Czech New Wave cinema—and this experience too can be seen in the cinematographic quality of *The Joke*, particularly in the final section set against the Ride of the Kings festival. In most of these features, as well as in its humor and irony, *The Joke* hints of Kundera's later masterpieces, *Le Livre du rire et de l'oubli* (1979; *The Book of Laughter and Forgetting*, 1980) and *The Unbearable Lightness of Being*.

Kundera protested the first English translation of *The Joke*, which included rearranged and omitted text. For example, a large portion of material on Moravian folk music, so important to the novel's symbolism, was cut. (In the liberal Czechoslovakia of 1967, the novel was published uncensored.) American scholar Michael Henry Heim, who also translated *The Book of Laughter and Forgetting* and *The Unbearable Lightness of Being*, published a new English translation of *The Joke* in 1982 that Kundera approved.

Sources for Further Study

Donahue, Bruce. "Laughter and Ironic Humor in the Fiction of Milan Kundera," in *Critique: Studies in Modern Fiction*. XXV (Winter, 1984), pp. 67-76.

Harkins, William E., and Paul I. Trensky, eds. *Czech Literature Since 1956: A Symposium*, 1980.

Kundera, Milan. Preface to *The Joke*, 1982. Translated by Michael Henry Heim.

Lodge, David. "Milan Kundera and the Idea of the Author in Modern Criticism," in *Critical Quarterly*. XXVI (Spring/Summer, 1984), pp. 105-121.
Podhoretz, Norman. "An Open Letter to Milan Kundera," in *Commentary*. LXXVIII (October, 1984), pp. 34-39.

Harold Branam

JOSEPH AND HIS BROTHERS

Author: Thomas Mann (1875-1955)
Type of plot: Comic epic
Time of plot: c. 1400 B.C.
Locale: Canaan and Egypt
First published: Joseph und seine Brüder, 1933-1943 (English translation, 1934-
1944, 1948): *Die Geschichten Jaakobs*, 1933 (*Joseph and His Brothers*, 1934;
also as *The Tales of Jacob*, 1934); *Der junge Joseph*, 1934 (*The Young
Joseph*, 1935); *Joseph in Ägypten*, 1936 (*Joseph in Egypt*, 1938); *Joseph, der
Ernährer*, 1943 (*Joseph the Provider*, 1944)

> *Principal characters:*
> JACOB, the blessed son of Isaac
> RACHEL, Jacob's favorite wife
> JOSEPH, their beloved son
> MUT, Potiphar's wife, who tries to seduce Joseph
> IKHNATON, the Pharaoh of Egypt

The Novels

In his four Joseph novels, Thomas Mann explores the roots of Western
civilization by elaborating on the stories of Abraham's descendants, which
are recorded in the last half of the book of Genesis. The first novel in the tetralogy, *Joseph and His Brothers*, explains how Joseph's ancestors developed
and bequeathed to him a profound desire to serve only the Highest, the One,
the Living God. In obedience to his God, Abraham had nearly sacrificed his
son Isaac before God told him to put a ram on the altar instead. When Isaac,
old and almost blind, bestows the divine blessing, he is tricked into giving it
to Jacob, his smooth son, rather than Esau, the hairy one, after their mother
dresses her favorite in goatskins.

Jacob leaves home to herd sheep for Laban, with whose lovely daughter
Rachel he soon falls deeply in love. For seven years he labors for the right to
marry her. Then, on the wedding night, Laban pulls a trick by sending his
older daughter Leah to Jacob's bed instead. Before daylight reveals the sub-
stitution, they have consummated the nuptials nine times, conceiving a son,
Reuben. Leah bears Jacob several more children before Jacob's subsequent
union with Rachel produces Joseph and later Benjamin, whose birth proves
fatal to Rachel.

One of Jacob's tales concerns his famous dream of a stairway to Heaven,
where he wrestles from an angel a blessing that his numerous posterity will
be called Israel after him. By two wives and two concubines he begets twelve
sons, whose descendants form the tribes of Israel. He also has a daughter,
Dinah, who is wooed and kidnapped by and then married to the Prince of
Shechem. Her brothers devise a gruesome revenge. In negotiations with her

abductor, they secure a promise that Shechemites will adopt certain Hebrew customs, including circumcision. Then, while all the men of Shechem are recovering from their wounds, Joseph's brothers fall upon the city and massacre them. The shepherd king is horrified by his sons' violence, especially the excesses of Simeon and Levi.

In the second novel, *The Young Joseph*, Joseph's brothers turn on him. More beautiful, imaginative, and virtuous than they, Joseph faces problems with self-absorption and the envy of others. His brothers' resentment is exacerbated by Jacob's favoritism, particularly evidenced by his giving to Joseph the coat of many colors, an elaborately embroidered garment worn by Leah on her wedding night. Joseph further chafes them by reporting his dreams of angels, heavenly bodies, and sheaves of wheat bowing down to him. In chagrin, the brothers withdraw from Jacob's tents and pitch camp a few miles away, until Jacob sends Joseph to retrieve them. When he arrives, they beat him and dump him into a pit. Reuben saves his life by deflecting the brothers' blows and later returns in secret to pull him out of the pit. He finds it empty: Joseph has been rescued by traveling salesmen, who pay twenty pieces of silver for him and lead him into Egypt. The brothers present the torn and bloody coat to Jacob, allowing him to think that his favorite son has been devoured by wild beasts.

The third novel, *Joseph in Egypt*, deals with slavery and sex. Joseph is sold to Potiphar, a high government official and friend of Ikhnaton, the Pharaoh of Egypt. At birth, Potiphar was castrated in an act of religious piety by his parents, but he is nevertheless yoked with Mut in ceremonial wedlock. The upright Mont-kaw, his overseer, recognizes Joseph's genius and arranges an introduction to his owner. Joseph soon wins Potiphar's favor with a charming discussion of artificial pollination. He is promoted from gardener and dumbwaiter to majordomo, but obstacles persist. The malicious dwarf Dudu thwarts him by helping Mut make sexual advances to Joseph. Often she orders Joseph to attend her privately in the palace, but Joseph always turns these sessions into business briefings on his work in the household. Eyebrows are raised around the palace after a ladies' party where, while they are peeling oranges with sharp knives, Mut calls Joseph in to pour the wine. Such is his beauty that the ladies gasp and cut their fingers. Years of frustration culminate when Mut nearly bites through her tongue and implores Joseph, "Thleep—with me!" After she suggests that they kill Potiphar, Joseph flees as she tears off his jacket. Dudu stirs Potiphar's suspicion, and Mut lodges a false charge of rape. Potiphar transfers Joseph to Pharaoh's prison, ordering the snitch Dudu to bear the expected physical punishment instead.

The fourth novel, *Joseph the Provider*, is a spectacular success story. The warden Mai-sachme puts Joseph in charge of the other prisoners, including Pharaoh's chief baker and chief wine steward, recently implicated in an unsuccessful coup attempt. When they are troubled by strange dreams, Joseph explains their meanings: that the wine steward will be found innocent and the baker guilty, and so they are. A reputation for dream interpretation brings Joseph to Pharaoh's attention. Joseph wins the boy-king's heart in long conversations on theology, governmental administration, and dreams. Pharaoh had dreamed of seven skinny cows consuming seven fat ones and of seven withered ears of corn swallowing seven full ones. Joseph deftly leads Pharaoh to see in the dreams a prophecy of famine. To avert disaster, he makes Joseph his chief administrator. By Joseph's wise governance, an enormous grain surplus is amassed and the great landowners and neighboring district kings are brought under Pharaoh's thumb as the crops fail and assets must be liquidated.

Meanwhile, Joseph's sister Tamar manages "to squeeze herself into the history of the world." As a girl she had absorbed wisdom at Jacob's knee. Then, one after another, she weds two of Judah's sons, both of whom soon die, leaving her a childless widow. Jacob will not let her marry Judah's third son, so she masquerades as a temple prostitute and seduces Judah himself, thus founding the line of descent leading to the Messiah.

Famine forces Joseph's brothers to come to Egypt for grain. Shorn and clothed as an Egyptian official, Joseph is not recognized by his half-brothers, who bow down to him now as he had dreamed. On the pretext that they are spies, he takes Simeon hostage, thus forcing them to bring Benjamin to him. On their return, he reveals his identity but takes Benjamin hostage in order to lure Jacob to Goshen. On their way home, the brothers worry about how to break the news to their aged father, whose grip on life might be jolted by either revelation: that Joseph is alive or that Benjamin is being held hostage. The task falls to the musical girl Serah, whose glad song penetrates Jacob's understanding without breaking his heart. He consents to be carried to Goshen, and there he is finally reunited with his beloved son. Joseph asks forgiveness, but instead Jacob bestows the blessing on Judah and adopts Joseph's two sons as his own, since Joseph's achievement is so worldly and so Egyptian.

The Characters

The story begins and ends in Jacob. His spirit presides over the whole tetralogy. One of the original God-dreamers, his "mild and pensive piety" is a pure, if not simple, expression of his somewhat timid yet profoundly thoughtful nature. Still, he plays the rogue. He tricks Esau out of his birthright. He gets the better of Laban when dividing the flock by settling for lambs of mixed color and then causing the ewes to conceive such offspring. Near death, he confuses everybody by crossing his hands as he settles blessings on the heads of Joseph's sons. Yet Jacob maintains his resolute morality to the end. Disgust for Egyptian customs is the lodestar of his morality. Since revelry, prostitution, and bestiality have there been raised to the level of religious rite, Jacob considers Egyptian society to be a version of Hell, based on bondage, error, and death. It is profoundly ironic that, before being laid to rest in the tomb of his fathers, Jacob's body is mummified in Egyptian fashion.

Retelling history's oldest story of personal love, Thomas Mann drew a most feeling portrait of Rachel. More is made of her emotions and inner feelings than her outward beauty. In her selfless suffering, she attains archetypal significance. Her chaste beauty and noble charm survive in Joseph. Her affection for Jacob helps Judaism become a religion of love; Jacob's fondness for her seems as ardent as his faith in God when he gazes into her black eyes brimming with tears of joy and sorrow. Rachel shares Jacob's antic spirit, once taking revenge on her father by absconding with his precious household idols. Just as delicate as she is lovely, Rachel suffers mental anguish in childlessness and physical pain in childbirth. Dying in labor, she typifies the savior whose death brings life.

Joseph is the most complex and compelling character of all. As he walks through the streets, women mount the housetops and throw their rings down to him. His godlike beauty, eloquence, and charisma astound all whom he meets and his chroniclers as well; even the account in Genesis lingers on his legend. Yet in Mann's story, Joseph's personal development overshadows his natural gifts. As a boy uniquely beloved, he expects people to love him more than they love themselves. His dreamy egotism is shattered by his fall into the pit. Realizing his folly, Joseph allows the energies of his ego to flow from arrogance into the common weal. He accepts that his lot in life is to play out an ancient pattern, to undergo a tragic withdrawal before returning to glory. His bondage in Egypt replays the pattern. There, Joseph develops the virtues on which his triumph depends. His chastity, loyalty, and sympathy are tested and proved.

Joseph is altogether more modern in outlook than Jacob: more volatile and witty, less single-minded, and more practical. His manner is far from patriarchal. Joseph's complexity is epitomized in the epithet *tam*. Originally it meant one who is upright, a dweller in tents, but it came to connote the intellectual agility of a wanderer who loves God, the kind of man who can handle the glad and sorry aspects of a double-sided life.

In his portrayal of Mut, Mann developed the personal, as opposed to the mythical, side. Although she had been well-adjusted to her role as the official wife of Pharaoh's eunuch, she begins to find her personal life empty. Understandably, her passions take human shape when Joseph enters her life, as a slave, hers to command. For two years, she tries to conceal desire behind polite conversation, but her womanhood has been aroused, and all reserve thaws. On a holiday when the house is almost empty, she throws herself at Joseph, is rebuffed, and recoils in panic. Her happiness could have been ruined, but everyone seems to understand, and her husband's even-handed disposition of the affair restores their intimacy.

The brothers are a mixed lot. Collectively, they represent the ordinary people who do not appreciate the heightened artistic sensibilities of a man such as Joseph. Six are born to the dog-headed Leah: Zebulun, who hates herding sheep and longs for adventure at sea; bony Issachar, who loves the quiet life; the violent "twins" Simeon and Levi; Judah, a sensitive soul of leonine lust; and Reuben, the eldest, a big, soft, excitable man, who loses his birthright through shameful intercourse with his father's concubine. Two are born to Leah's maid, Zilpah: sweet-toothed Asher, a seeker of pleasure, and the forthright Gad, as stubborn as a butting goat. Two are born to Rachel's maid, Bilhah: subtle Dan, a stickler by nature, with a judicious turn of mind, and the fleet Naphtali, who has the gift of gab. Only Rachel's son Benjamin delights in his remarkable brother Joseph. Tied to the apron strings, he receives from Jacob more protection than affection, never knowing the effusive love and hate that Joseph experiences.

Themes and Meanings

The Joseph story suggested to Mann almost everything important in life, so for sixteen years, from 1926 to 1942, he kept amplifying, reinventing, and explaining it until he had created an epic forty times longer than its source in Genesis. It immerses one more deeply in its own fictional world than a brief account could, and the reader emerges with a feeling of familiarity with life as it was lived in Jacob's tents or eighteenth-dynasty Egypt. Yet Mann was not primarily concerned with historical realism. Like John Milton in *Paradise Lost* (1667, 1674), Mann sought to explain the highest matters to modern minds by interpreting biblical lore.

The tetralogy could be called a *Bildungsroman*, since it traces the growth of Jacob and of Joseph from boyhood to manhood. Its scope, however, is more ambitious. *Joseph and His Brothers* is about the growth of Western civilization itself. In the way Joseph outgrows his puerile vanity and harnesses his energies for the common good, the direction of cultural evolution is discerned, from the early tribal patriarchies to modern megastates. As Joseph and Pharaoh transcend the violence and bestiality of polytheism, so civilization rises from barbarity to refinement. A dreamy and artful shepherd boy becomes administrator of a powerful empire. In him, the individual and the collective, the artistic and the political, are reconciled. Joseph is not a mere portrait of the artist but a paradigm of the progress of civilization. He learns his lessons well at Jacob's knee but does not stop there. He gains wisdom from Babylonian and Egyptian traditions as well, blending in himself the Hellenic, Hebraic, and other Near Eastern elements of Western civilization.

The progress of civilization is linked with the developing concept of God. Abraham, Isaac, and Jacob build their ideas of the Most High from primitive beginnings in Yahu, "a troublesome sort of hobgoblin," and Jewhe, who spits fire and snorts steam. They know a spiteful and lonely deity who is jealous of his bond with man and prone to fits of fury, once nearly destroying the earth and all that was in it by flood. The patriarchs' "labour upon the godhead" leads to a more comprehensive and exalted Lord, in whose thought "all the manifold shapes of things were first present" and by whose words creation was ordained. Vast as all space, He includes everything, "not the Good, but the All."

Mann asks whether Abraham should be called the Father of God for having "thought Him into being" and whether man was made in God's image to be used as a mirror, a tool of God's self-knowledge and, thus, His evolutionary progress. So much is made of Joseph's egotism because the germ of the idea of God can be seen in it. "The claim of the human ego to central importance," Mann says, "was the precondition for the discovery of God," the notion of self being wrapped up with the idea of unity or of the whole. Thus, a belief in the sanctity of God leads to a belief in the dignity of the individual and the dignity of humanity. Joseph's progress from dreamy conceit to imperial power is a mythical formula of that whole religious and cultural transformation.

Joseph comes to Egypt at a time of great religious upheaval. The rigid religion of Amun, based on fear and brute force, is losing its hold. The new Pharaoh hates war and resents the principles of the priests of Amun, leaning instead toward worship of the loving lord of the sun, Aton. Under Joseph's influence, he moves from polytheism toward monotheism, even changing his personal name from Amenhotep to Ikhnaton. In Egypt Joseph proves that his keen understanding of God could alter the destinies of empires as well as of families.

Mann once called myth the way old men think about young humanity. His mythical way of thinking is reinforced by the theme of correspondence, which pervades all four novels. As if in tune with the celestial music of the revolving spheres, images, thoughts, and events are correlated by the correspondence of present with past, nature with spirit, and the world below with the world above. Joseph learns that a spiritual abstraction such as numeration can control the enormous forces of nature and time, so he delights in the mysteries of the 360 degrees in a circle, the five extra days in the year, or the magic of threes and sevens. Insight into the correspondence of moral worlds above and below makes Joseph's triumph possible, for he realizes that what appears sunny refers to the underworld. His mythical mind sees all human life as a kaleidoscope which produces changing patterns from the same materials. Thus, Mut's ripping his jacket mythically corresponds with the shredding of the coat of many colors and with the dismemberment of the Egyptian god Osiris.

Correspondence renders even slight details rich with symbolic meaning.

The ram, for example, signifies God's bond with man after being substituted on Abraham's altar of sacrifice. In his death throes, Isaac pathetically thinks he is turning into a ram. Jacob gets rich through uncanny skill in breeding the animal. Joseph imagines Jacob's disgust at a ritual in which the daughters of Egypt yield themselves to rams. Rachel's name means "mother sheep," and her son is called an inspired lamb by Pharaoh. Joseph is mythically linked with the moon as well. A nomad in its course among the heavenly bodies, the moon symbolizes the inner qualities of the *tam* wanderer. The nomadic man must negotiate fortune and misfortune, favor and disfavor. The ever-changing moon typifies such mediation, receiving light from the sun and giving it to earth. Playing female to the sun and male to the world, the moon is special to lovers, who, like Jacob and Rachel, save their most meaningful moments for moonlight. Joseph associates the moon with Ishtar, the goddess of love. Though his father once rebukes Joseph for baring himself to the moonlight during his midnight meditations, his dreamy moon musings confirm the mythological cast of his mind in his early youth. Much of the meaning and method of this mythical epic are recapitulated in one of its sentences: "For we move in the footsteps of others, and all life is but the pouring of the present into the forms of the myth."

Critical Context

A work such as *Joseph and His Brothers* occurs seldom in literary history. So extraordinary and idiosyncratic an undertaking deserves the epithet "unique." Formal literary categories shed less light on such singular achievements than most, yet Mann's tetralogy belongs on the shelf with other modern comic epics in prose, such as John Bunyan's *Pilgrim's Progress* (1678-1684), Miguel de Cervantes' *Don Quixote de la Mancha* (1605, 1615), and Laurence Sterne's *Tristram Shandy* (1759-1767). It fits the epic formula, which calls for a hero of superhuman capacity and transnational significance, an episodic structure, divine intervention, and a sustained elevated style.

Although a tone of high seriousness and didactic purpose pervade it, *Joseph and His Brothers* is a comic masterpiece. In tragedy, things do not work out for the better, but they do here. Tragedy involves the loss or lack of something at a crucial moment, but here is God's plenty of everything. For example, time is abundant: Tragedy tends not to happen until, somehow, time runs out; here, there is time for everything. Events have plenty of time not only to happen, but to recur in the mythical cycle and to be remembered *ad infinitum*, as well. There is always time for retelling, for savoring the ironies of intent and event, and for ridiculous magnification or reduction through interpretation. In its use of time, handling of detail, vast repetition, and cosmic perspective, the whole manner of *Joseph and His Brothers* is comic rather than tragic.

Acutely sensitive to irony and nuance, Mann's comic genius saturates episode, dialogue, and description. The reader delights in the orange-peeling party, the vignette of the city of cats, the satire on impish Dudu, the sly retorts, and the sharp epithets. Joseph considers the artful jest as God's best gift to man, "the profoundest knowledge we have of that complex, questionable thing we call life." Jacob's roguery and Joseph's felicitous rapport enable them to achieve their serious purposes. Where would either have got without the comic sensibility to pull it off time after time?

Had it been composed by a tranquil scribe in placid times, this epic would be astonishing. That it came down from the most turbulent time in its author's life and the history of Europe is even more impressive. The work was received quite propitiously. Mann was awarded the Nobel Prize in Literature in 1929 while still working on *Joseph and His Brothers*. Early the next year, he toured the Near East, storing up memories of scene and lore which come to life in the Egypt novels. He returned to Germany and there finished *The Young Joseph* and began *Joseph in Egypt* before leaving Germany again on a trip from which he would never return. Exiled by the Nazis, Mann became a wanderer like Joseph and his ancestors. His daughter managed to recover the manuscript from their home, which Adolf Hitler had confiscated.

Completed in the United States in 1942, the tetralogy celebrates a victory of enlightenment over darkness. The conflict in Egypt between followers of Amun and Aton reflects the division of public opinion in Europe on Nazism. The cult of Amun uses fear and bloodshed to enforce a policy of reactionary nationalism, just as the storm troopers did. Certain salient characteristics of Nazi officialdom are parodied in the portraits of the vicious dwarf Dudu and the high priest Beknechons. Mann later compared Joseph and his administration with Henry Wallace and Franklin D. Roosevelt's New Deal. Both administrations succeeded in feeding the poor and dominating foreign powers. Both radically altered the relationship between the government and the economy.

The Joseph novels prophetically urge Western civilization not to take the road of Fascism toward bondage, lies, and death. It is significant that Mann found a higher road—toward life, prosperity, and love—in the tradition of the Jews, whom Hitler persecuted. Mann's epic sought to restore the blessings of civilization by enlightening Europe in its darkest hour.

Sources for Further Study
Bab, Julius. "*Joseph and His Brothers*," in *The Stature of Thomas Mann*, 1947.
Hamburger, Käte. *Thomas Manns Roman "Joseph und seine Brüder*," 1945.
Hatfield, Henry. "Myths Ancient and Modern," in *From the Magic Mountain: Mann's Later Masterpieces*, 1979.
Mann, Thomas. "The Joseph Novels," in *The Stature of Thomas Mann*, 1947.

Van Doren, Mark. *"Joseph and His Brothers*: A Comedy in Four Parts," in
Thomas Mann: A Collection of Critical Essays, 1964.

John L. McLean

JOURNEY TO THE CENTER OF THE EARTH

Author: Jules Verne (1828-1905)
Type of plot: Science fiction
Time of plot: The 1860's
Locale: Hamburg, Germany; Iceland; the subterranean strata; and Stromboli, Italy
First published: Voyage au centre de la terre, 1864 (English translation, 1874)

Principal characters:
AXEL LIDENBROCK, the narrator, the nephew of Otto Lidenbrock
OTTO LIDENBROCK, a professor of mineralogy at a college in Hamburg
HANS BJELKE, an Icelandic eider hunter
GRAUBEN LIDENBROCK, Otto's seventeen-year-old ward and Axel's fiancée

The Novel

Journey to the Center of the Earth is the story of a secret expedition beneath the earth's surface, down through geologic space and time to an imagined subterranean world. Narrated by Axel Lidenbrock, one of the three adventurers, it tells how he, Professor Otto Lidenbrock, and their guide, Hans Bjelke, descend the chimney of an extinct volcano near Reykjavík, Iceland, proceed to unknown regions, and then, miraculously, survive a volcanic eruption which shoots them to the surface again from the mouth of Mount Etna.

The novel begins in the spring of 1863. Otto accidentally discovers a mysterious manuscript written by Arne Saknussemm, a sixteenth century Icelandic heretical philosopher and alchemist. Days pass as Otto wracks his brain endeavoring to decipher the cryptogrammic code of the manuscript, not realizing that Axel has done so already and has learned of Saknussemm's startling claim to have found a passageway to the center of the earth. Axel believes the claim is either a hoax or a legend, unworthy of scientific investigation; besides, knowing his uncle's obsessive temperament, he fears the consequences if Otto should learn the secret. Eventually, he does tell Otto, however, and just as he suspected, the professor decides to test the truth of the theory. Otto is convinced that the downward journey is feasible; moreover, unlike the majority of scientists of his day, he believes that the earth's core is not fiery liquid but solid, and relatively moderate in temperature. Thus, after hasty preparations and a brave farewell to pretty Grauben—who promises to marry him on his return—Axel sets forth with Otto on the train and sea journey which brings them to Iceland.

There they hire a reliable guide, Hans, who agrees to accompany them wherever they go. Climbing to the crater on Mount Snaeffels—identified by Saknussemm as his starting point—they begin their descent. At the bottom of the volcano's chimney, they proceed along one of several galleries, lit by the natural light of quartz crystals. "It was as if the spirits of the underworld were lighting up their palace to receive earthly guests," the romantic Axel reflects. The gallery ends abruptly and they must retrace their steps, almost dying of thirst in the process. Luckily, Hans finds an underground stream which not only revives them but also becomes a "familiar genius . . . guiding us through the earth." They descend more quickly now, moving spiral-fashion horizontally and vertically downward. Some six weeks after beginning, then, they have penetrated (according to Otto's calculations) to a depth of ninety miles and are about six hundred miles southeast of Iceland.

Finally, after more weeks of traversing tunnels of silent, gray rock they come upon a sea (promptly named "the Lidenbrock Sea") around which grow forests of antediluvian origin. Otto decides to explore the sea, hoping to find a new avenue of descent, and orders Hans to build a raft. During the next days their voyage carries them through waters filled with huge fish and reptiles, "marine monsters" of prehistoric ages. Suddenly a storm rises, driving their craft forward out of control at a stupendous speed. They are shipwrecked on a rocky coast only to discover that they have been returned to their starting point on the shore.

While Hans patiently reconstructs the raft, Otto and Axel explore the coastline. They wander into an immense "ossuary" composed of mineral, vegetable, and animal debris from countless ages, amid which they find the fossilized remains of a Caucasian humanoid of the Quaternary era, seeming proof of the antiquity of man. Their most striking discovery is a Renaissance-period "poniard," or dagger, marked with the initials "A.S." Otto is exultant; the old Icelandic's message was no hoax. In his honor, Otto dubs that part of the coast "Cape Saknussemm."

Balked in their attempt to sail again by adverse winds, the members of the party try to reenter the tunnel which led them to the sea, only to find that it has been sealed by rock during the recent storm. They try to unblock the passage with explosives, but this action causes an earthquake which exposes a fissure through which they are drawn on their raft. Now, surely, thinks Axel, they are doomed. In total darkness they seem to be rising; the temperature rises as well. Otto surmises that they have inadvertently triggered a volcanic eruption and that they are now standing on the perilous point of a shaft of water and lava surging upward through the earth's crust. The fact that they manage to survive their final spinning exodus from the spout of Etna and to land safely on the mountain's side is amazing. As they make their way to the quiet rural town of Stromboli, Axel is conscious that it was here, in days of old, that "Aeolus had held the winds and tempests in chains."

Back in the world of men, news of their "marvelous journey" spreads far and wide. Although they did not reach the center of the planet, Otto is justly praised for his achievement. As for Axel, he is content to write the popular narrative of the expedition—and then to marry his beloved Grauben.

The Characters

The two principal characters are typical Verne creations. Otto is described by Axel as "a learned egoist" and "a hoarder of knowledge"—"there really are professors of this kind in Germany," he adds. Fifty years old, a distinguished academic and a remarkable linguist, Otto is restless, impulsive, secretive, eccentric, and, at times, foolishly irrational. He is less sympathetic than the scholarly Professor Aronnax of *Vingt Mille Lieues sous les mers* (1870; *Twenty Thousand Leagues Under the Sea*, 1874) and rather more like the fascinating, demoniac Captain Nemo of that great book. Axel is entirely Otto's antithesis; youthful, romantic, knowledgeable enough about scientific fact and theory to challenge his mentor's assumptions, he is the perfect foil to his uncle. While always loyal and respectful to Otto, Axel's privately expressed anxieties and wistful reflections mark him as a more fully human protagonist than his companion.

Of the minor characters, Hans is the most important. He seldom speaks, never complains, and stolidly accepts his role as guide and general handyman to the expedition. His sole demand that he be paid his wages at regular intervals strikes the reader as mildly absurd, given the dangers of the enterprise. Yet Hans's physical strength and manual skills lend plausibility to the story and complement the intellectual natures of Otto and Axel. He is Verne's common man. Grauben has little to say or to do, underlining the fact that in a Verne novel there are no strong roles for women. The remaining minor characters—the Lidenbrock housekeeper, a professor in Reykjavík, and a few more—are merely functional figures of no intrinsic interest. One should not ignore, however, the ghostly presence of Arne Saknussemm, hovering over events from first to last. His intriguing testament is both a spur to action and a constant reminder of the resourceful human imagination and courage the author so evidently admired.

Themes and Meanings

A work of science fiction seeks to unify two quite different approaches to life: the scientific and the imaginative. To succeed, such a work must convince the reader, as Samuel Taylor Coleridge would say, to suspend disbelief in order to accept an imaginary excursion into realms of space and time beyond the known or predictable; yet, that journey of thought must seem absolutely probable, scientifically feasible. On purely scientific grounds, the reader could quarrel with Verne's assumption that subterranean regions are habitable; that mine-like tunnels enseam layers of basalt and granite; that spacious caverns, forests, and seas exist there; or that anyone could survive being in a volcanic eruption. Once the reader accepts Verne's premise that such things are possible, however—and Verne does treat those events as credible—he can then enjoy the narrative as the fictional adventure it is.

The idea of the journey itself is an ancient fictional motif. To sustain that motif, Verne develops three interlocking themes which are equally ancient, and effective: the underground as an underworld, man's hubris in daring to venture there, and the capriciousness of Nature. Allusion has been made to Axel's mythological imagination. For him, the journey is not unlike a descent to the underworld, fraught with all the hellish overtones that accompany the archetypal descent. Axel experiences vertigo as he is about to enter "the fathomless pit that was to swallow me." Later he is bemused by the "troglodytic life" he is leading. After he and Otto discover the fossil man, he ponders whether a race of "men of the underworld" still exist. Indeed, he becomes so enthralled by his experience that, just before the final ascent, he is even more desirous than Otto of reaching the center of the earth. Verne presents him as a latter-day knight errant who must undergo an ordeal before he can wed his princess, Grauben.

A second theme is shown by Otto's hubris in defying conventional wisdom in undertaking the journey. At one point he imagines himself as a Columbus of the nether regions, who by sheer "will" shall conquer its mysteries. What ultimately saves him and his companions from disaster is Nature's capriciousness. Nature often appears to be their antagonist, determined to prevent her secrets from becoming known: The sea rises up to shipwreck the explorers; the earth will not abide the intruders but expels them back to the surface through a volcano. In seeking to disclose Nature's secrets, these hubristic humans are reminiscent of yet another myth: that of Pandora and her box. When her curiosity conquered her faithful obedience to higher powers, she loosed death and destruction upon the world. Verne's tale, however, takes a more optimistic ending: Nature is shown "red in tooth and claw" (to borrow the metaphor of one of Verne's contemporaries, Alfred, Lord Tennyson) and offers death "in so many. . . forms," but Nature also spares the group, even in the throes of a violent eruption.

Clearly, Verne was first and foremost a skilled storyteller, who succeeded in translating a fascinating idea into a novel that continues to be read and enjoyed for its sheer capacity to entertain. In addition, he was able to exploit traditional motifs and themes that speak to the human condition, thereby examining in a modern/speculative context the age-old questions of man's place in the universe—the hallmark of great science fiction.

Critical Context

Journey to the Center of the Earth is the second of Jules Verne's "voyages extraordinaires," a vast project entailing nearly a score of novels about adventures on, beneath, and above the earth and seas. He virtually invented the modern school of science fiction, influencing authors as diverse as H. G. Wells and Arthur C. Clarke. By combining diligent research into scientific fact and hypothesis with his natural bent as a storyteller, he molded a popular form of narrative which appealed to his nineteenth century audience's appetite for tales of wonder. Often erroneously thought of as a juvenilist (such as his contemporaries R. M. Ballantyne, G. A. Henty, and W. H. G. Kingston), his work surpasses theirs in its appeal to adult readers as well, and in terms of credibility of detail, atmosphere, and subtlety of characterization. Unfortunately, Verne has not always been served well by translators, and the full extent of his remarkable accomplishment is only now beginning to be appreciated.

It should also be noted that Verne wrote his books when the revolutionary theories of Charles Darwin and Charles Lyell were reshaping man's knowledge of the physical history and processes of the natural world, and when new mechanical inventions and technologies were transforming every aspect of social and economic life. Initially, he welcomed these changes and held optimistically to the view that knowledge was good in and for itself, and that man was ennobled in his attempts to search out new experiences. Gradually, his books show, he came to share some of his heroes' distrust about the capacity of mankind, generally, to live in harmony with these advances. In a paradoxical fashion, then, he anticipated both the hope and the skepticism of the nuclear age concerning man's very survival.

Sources for Further Study
Amis, Kingsley. "Starting Points," in *New Maps of Hell: A Survey of Science Fiction*, 1960.
Jules-Verne, Jean. *Jules Verne: A Biography*, 1976.
Miller, Walter James. "A New Look at Jules Verne" and "Jules Verne, Rehabilitated," in *The Annotated Jules Verne: "Twenty Thousand Leagues Under the Sea,"* 1976.
Rose, Mark. "Space," in *Alien Encounters: Anatomy of Science Fiction*, 1981.

Eric Thompson

JOY OF MAN'S DESIRING

Author: Jean Giono (1895-1970)
Type of plot: Mystical realism
Time of plot: The 1930's
Locale: The Grémone Plateau, a farming region in France
First published: Que ma joie demeure, 1935 (English translation, 1940)

>   *Principal characters:*
>   BOBI, the central character, whose mystical unity with his
>   surroundings bonds all the other characters together
>   JOURDAN, Bobi's host, a farmer
>   MARTHE, his wife
>   AURORE, the daughter of the widow, Madame Hélène
>   JOSÉPHINE, the wife of Honoré

The Novel

The opening sequence of *Joy of Man's Desiring* quickly establishes man's relationship with the earth, a sense of being pervaded by all of nature. Jourdan, a farmer, finds himself inexplicably restless one late winter night: The night is virtually alive, pulsing with creation. Into this animate darkness Jourdan takes his horse and plow and begins to turn over the land. He is proceeding row by row when he sees a stranger standing on a hill, set against the stars.

Calling himself Bobi, the stranger strikes up a conversation with Jourdan as naturally as if the two men have known each other all of their lives. Strangely drawn to Bobi, Jourdan invites him back to the house, where Marthe, Jourdan's wife, prepares breakfast; the three talk cryptically about happiness and the living earth. Bobi has already broached the idea of turning over part of Jourdan's farm to wildflowers.

Later, Bobi and Jourdan set out on a visit to the neighboring farms. Like Jourdan, the farmers accept Bobi at once; though he is often laconic, strangely distant, he is at the same time as natural with them as are the members of their own family. He soon becomes part of the Grémone community, a sage, gentle man with an inexpressible fund of loneliness.

Bobi's influence on the community, and on Jourdan and Marthe particularly, awakens a sense of joy among them. Bobi convinces Jourdan that the wheat Jourdan is storing could better be given to the birds—as a sort of first step in the cure of the leprosy of unhappiness which afflicts all men. In a major scene closing the first part of the novel, Jourdan and Marthe pile up a great amount of wheat, and birds flock to feed on it. Surrounded by birds, husband and wife share a moment of mystical joy.

Meanwhile, Bobi has gone into the Grémone forest, returning with a wild stag which he has named Antoine. The stag is wondrously tame, and Bobi admits that he has communed with the animal, showing it his love, trust, and understanding. The stag thus becomes not so much Bobi's pet as a symbol of the mysteriousness of life and of the link between living things and the living earth. Antoine remains on Jourdan's farm, though at complete liberty. Fascinated, the Grémone community visits the stag. He is of particular interest to Aurore, the beautiful daughter of the widow Hélène. Aurore has seen the deer from her window and felt her kinship with it as it gamboled about her house.

The following Sunday, the community celebrates with a feast. Their joyful surrender to the innocent pleasures of food and drink and to one another's company exhibits an almost pagan naturalness, an unaffected, spontaneous love for the things of earth. It is at this feast that Joséphine, the wife of Honoré, having fallen in love with Bobi, almost seduces him with the same pagan candor, which is as passionate as it is natural. Aurore, too, loves Bobi for his wholesomeness, but she becomes angry when he does not understand her attraction to him.

The following spring, the Grémone farmers, inspired by Bobi, set out to catch some does for Antoine. The hunt through the forest is one of joy and an odd peacefulness, the does almost allowing themselves to be captured in the nets.

The community united now as it had never been, Bobi proposes doing away with individual wheat fields and planting instead one communal field, uniting the labors of all in achieving the greatest joy. Grémone ignites to the idea and the climax sees all Grémone as one. In the end, the one field is plowed and Bobi senses that his purpose has been fulfilled. Sadness, even despair, closes in on him, however, when he learns that Aurore, having taken Jourdan's revolver, has gone into the woods and killed herself. The people of Grémone bring her body home, and Bobi leaves in a thunderstorm. In the final scene, he is struck by lightning as he ponders the nature of desire and joy.

The Characters

Bobi's first appearance in the novel is as beautiful as it is mysterious. Seen against the bright horizon of evening stars, he is a creature at home in the natural world, comfortable amid the elemental forces of wind and rain and the eternal round of seasons. He is a latter-day Pan, emerging in the late winter to pipe in for Grémone the mysterious joys of spring, the symbol of resurrection.

Yet Bobi is far from naïve. Unlike Pan, he is also a twentieth century man, afflicted with a modern sadness, a loneliness that keeps him apart from those who love him. Though he can guide the farmers into a joyful search for meaning through submission to nature, he himself is enigmatically unhappy, unfulfilled, as if knowing the futility of such a search. Though he evokes passion in Joséphine and deep love in Aurore, his love for them is peculiarly nonsensuous.

Jourdan is also a man of ambivalent moods. Himself restless, yearning for the mysterious peace that has eluded him, he is at heart the practical farmer and typifies the shrewd, successful peasant, a man in tune with the seasons primarily because such congruence means a better farm and a better physical existence. Yet Jourdan is ductile, mysteriously open to Bobi's Pan-like influence. Sensing that his well-being has not made him any happier, he becomes a sort of first apostle for Bobi's pagan evangelism.

Marthe is also in search of peace and joy, but she is content to follow her husband's actions, to trust his decisions. Nevertheless, when the birds come to eat the wheat she has her private moment of joy and can relate with the other wives as a woman with her own ideas and intentions.

Just as Marthe remains a vital part of the Grémone community, Aurore maintains a privacy which keeps her at the virtual edge of the group. Like Bobi, Aurore has a special kinship with nature; she shares a stronger relationship with the deer of the forest than she does with her own family. She is a kind of nymph, a counterpart to Bobi's Pan, and her attraction to him is thus easily explained as a confluence of kindred spirits.

Though characterization in the novel is really subservient to Jean Giono's epic theme, Aurore is the most stereotypical and least successful character in the work. Her delicate beauty is all attenuated flesh and blood, not really physical but ideal. When Bobi spurns her, not fully realizing the intensity of her love, she reacts as a real woman would—in anger and perhaps in jealousy. Her suicide is melodramatic, however, emphasizing her character as a figure of romance and myth.

By contrast, Joséphine is as corporeal as Aurore is ethereal. She is described in purely physical terms, a woman of full breasts and large passionate eyes. Joséphine is unashamedly sensuous, but her refusal to give herself fully to Bobi illustrates her peasant morality, her strength and loyalty. Her refusal underscores, as well, the basically solitary nature of man.

Themes and Meanings

For all of its lyricism, *Joy of Man's Desiring* is often a richly ambiguous work. Though it clearly postulates the need for man to still his yearning for peace and joy with a willing surrender to nature, the basic sadness surrounding the lives of the characters makes that surrender futile or at least questionable. A recapitulation of the plot of *Joy of Man's Desiring* sounds absurd without an awareness of both the lyrical quality of the novel—the full details of nature and peasant life—and the tension, the conflict inherent in the surrender of one's personality to the world spirit.

In the novel, there is a pantheistic view of such a world, yet such a world is controlled by a unity that brings each of the characters closer. Nevertheless, the characters never come close enough to one another to become truly happy. The community's members discover their own aloneness, symbolized by Jourdan's restlessness and Joséphine's silent conviction that Bobi will one day return to Grémone. As for Bobi, he leaves with a sense of failure: Despite his effect on Grémone, he has been unable to communicate his deeper feelings, his almost poetic sense of the mysteriousness of life.

Critical Context

Joy of Man's Desiring is Giono's fullest expression of the poetic nature of peasant life. Always a writer who glorified the natural human emotions, who chose the instinctual over the rational, Giono reacted against the more cerebral, psychological novels of his contemporaries and deliberately mined his own ground, the ruggedly beautiful region of Provence and its people. *Le Chant du monde* (1934; *The Song of the World*, 1937) was the final tale in a trilogy which protested the victimization of modern man by mechanized civilization. *Joy of Man's Desiring* is the summation of that protest. Longer, richer in detail, more poetically realized than its predecessors, the book is nevertheless written in Giono's most characteristic manner.

After World War II, he produced works in a new style: laconic, sparsely detailed, containing less poetry and more story. Some of these later works, such as *Le Hussard sur le toit* (1951; *The Hussar on the Roof*, 1953; better known as *The Horseman on the Roof*, 1954), are more reminiscent of the realistic tradition of Stendhal than of the poetic/mystical vein of the earlier Giono. *Joy of Man's Desiring* is thus a crucial book in Giono's canon.

Sources for Further Study
Goodrich, Norma. *Giono: Master of Fictional Modes*, 1973.
Nadeau, Maurice. *The French Novel Since the War*, 1967.
Peyre, Henri. "Jean Giono," in *French Novelists of Today*, 1967.
Redfern, W. D. *The Private World of Jean Giono*, 1967.
Smith, Maxwell A. *Jean Giono*, 1966.

Edward Fiorelli

KANGAROO

Author: Yuz Aleshkovsky (1929-　　)
Type of plot: Satire
Time of plot: 1949-1956
Locale: Moscow, Yalta, Munich, and an unnamed labor camp
First published: Kenguru, 1981 (English translation, 1986)

Principal characters:
　FAN FANYCH, an international gangster
　KIDALLA, a KGB investigator
　JOSEF STALIN, the General Secretary of the Communist Party
　　of the Soviet Union
　CHERNYSHEVSKY, a labor camp prisoner and a Party loyalist

The Novel

Kangaroo begins with a fatal phone call in 1949. Fan Fanych, alias "Etcetera," crook extraordinaire, has been living and working both in jail and out on time borrowed from the MVD (KGB). When he hears the phone ring, he realizes that he is finally being called to account. Kidalla, the KGB investigator in charge of monitoring Fan's activities, likes to keep tabs on the technological front and offers him a choice of computer-generated crimes. Fan discards various assassination attempts, Pan-Armenian plots, counterfeit bank note schemes, and a production of *The Brothers Karamazov* at the Central Theater of the Red Army. The option which attracts his attention is the bizarre case of Gemma the kangaroo, or, in official parlance, the "case of the vicious rape and murder of the aged kangaroo in the Moscow Zoo on the night of July 14, 1789, and January 9, 1905." It is not surprising that this is the case which Kidalla has already chosen for him. They proceed to negotiate the conditions for Fan taking the fall: Fan's terms include foreign newspapers in his cell, current films, and women.

Fan, as agreed, finds himself in a cozy private cell with potted geraniums and a private tutor. Professor Bolensky, age seventy-nine, has arrived to prepare Fan for his role as a violator of kangaroos, but the two are soon distracted by a parade of nubile young "stewardesses" and "waitresses"—KGB trainees seeking to pass their exams in "Obtaining Information During Foreplay with Enemies of the People." In the month that they spend together in the cell, Fan learns his lessons in kangaroo physiology and the Professor learns his in sex and female psychology. In the process, the Professor falls in love with a six-foot-six basketball player, and she with him, and so bids a fond and grateful farewell to Fan.

More machinations follow, in the course of which Fan is reconditioned as a male kangaroo and meets "Kooler," the inventor of the computer.

Drugged, Fan passes out and awakens in a courtroom at his own trial. He, along with the rest of the spectators, is stunned by a film documenting the entire crime: pathetic shots of the murdered Gemma and the baby kangaroo in her pouch, of the sleeping watchman and the hordes of Muscovites combing the nearby woods in search of clues, of Gemma's funeral escort replete with Australian and Soviet flags, and of Fan Fanych's final desperate escape attempt inside an East German cow. The audience is alternately outraged and tearful, and so is Fan Fanych, especially since he is beginning to believe that it is he himself on the big screen. Only when the surrogate sneezes (something Fan never does) does Fan realize that he has been replaced.

Fan's death sentence is never carried out, and he undergoes another experiment, a tinkering with his sense of time. That too fails, and he is led away—to be shot, he thinks. Instead, he finds himself in the back of a truck, dressed like a convict and headed for a labor camp. In the camp he encounters chief guard Dziuba, who claims to have shot 1,937 men in honor of the year 1937, and a gaggle of Old Bolsheviks—true believers who periodically dispatch their plans, resolutions, and suggestions to Vyacheslav Molotov or Lazar Kaganovich in the hope of vindication and who eagerly question Fan on "the enthusiasm of the masses and the international situation." Fan takes a break from this "human zoo" of camp life to tell his invisible audience of one, Kolya, about his encounters with Adolf Hitler's wallet and Josef Stalin's feet. After a miserable decade or so of killing rats, the loyal comrades are set free, one by one. Only Chernyshevsky, their spokesman, and Fan are left. They while away the time by playing cards; Fan loses everything to Chernyshevsky (his bread ration until the KGB's fiftieth anniversary and his soul until Stalin's one hundredth) but survives—Chernyshevsky, too, is taken away.

Fan is freed shortly thereafter. Confused and hungover, he wakes up to a different world—one that is not, however, different enough. Stalin is dead but not out of the mausoleum yet. Slogans still overhang the streets. Fan returns to his communal apartment, falls in love, and goes to the KGB headquarters to find out what is happening. Kidalla, supposedly, is no longer there. Fan has been falsely accused and is scheduled to be rehabilitated and sent to the writers' colony at Peredelkino to serve as a consultant on labor camp life for those authors unfortunate enough to miss out on this fashionable form of exile. Puzzled, he refuses, and returns to the scene of his supposed "crime." He demonstrates the truth of his third eye, developed in the labor camp to hunt rats, to the same old drunken watchman and discovers that although Gemma really was murdered, she has been replaced by her baby. An eccentric Australian millionaire has left Fan a fortune for executing kangaroos, but the state takes most of it, and Fan and his drinking buddy Kolya are left with a piddling sum, which they use to drink to life and to tell Fan's story.

The Characters

The hero of *Kangaroo* is a thief, a pickpocket, and occasionally a liar. His is also—with the exception of his invisible listener Kolya, and Josef Stalin's right foot—the only truly honest voice in the book. That Fan's monologue constitutes the book makes no difference, because in *Kangaroo* Yuz Aleshkovsky is not experimenting with reliable versus unreliable narrators or with point of view. The reader is not expected to delve into the whys and wherefores of Fan's (or Stalin's) criminal behavior. Fan Fanych, grown and full-blown, is to be taken at his word—at face value, however grotesque that face might be.

In a sense, word is more important than face, because Aleshkovsky's characters, like Fyodor Dostoevski's, begin with a voice and end with a body. Physical description is not particularly important, although physicality itself is. Fan's language itself identifies him as a member in good standing of the criminal underworld, a world with its own laws and its own language—both of which stand in complete opposition to "socialist legality" and authority. In this case (all meanings apply here), his opposite number is Kidalla, the almost anonymous KGB agent who protects him for years in order to charge him with the crime of the century: kangaroo rape. Kidalla himself has no personality; he seems anonymous because his largest part in the narrative is as an outside force, a disembodied voice through the intercom in Fan's cell. Even face-to-face meetings provide no physical description. Ironically, though, Kidalla comes closer to speaking Fan's language than do the other major characters: He may be rotten to the core, but at least he has no illusions about international justice and the uses of force.

Not so Chernyshevsky, Fan's barracksmate and spokesman for the Old Bolsheviks in the camp. In this phantasmagoric world, he is both the nineteenth century radical critic Nikolay Chernyshevsky and a walking composite of the revolutionary Party elite purged by Stalin in the 1930's. A creature of ideology and dogma, he garbles his slogans and garbles his mind: "Doesn't the Central Committee understand that revisionism has to be crushed at birth? Say, Citizen Jailer, did you send Kaganovich our scheme for infiltrating the ranks of the U.S. Republican Party and the British Conservative Party?" When he plays cards with Fan and wins away all of the latter's food ration, he distracts his opponent by constantly humming the "Internationale." His words have no relation to anything outside their own sterile constructs, so when the rules dictate that he stop playing cards with Fan he does so, with no thought that Fan is about to starve to death and needs a chance to win his own life back.

Aleshkovsky deals with Stalin in a different way. First, word and action conspire to expose the old conspirator: As Fan watches from his cellar hideout in the Livadia palace, Stalin arrives. There is an old shoemaker in the palace courtyard, a Muslim who seems to resemble Stalin's father. Interested and sympathetic at first, Stalin is carried away by his own paranoid clichés, and he orders the man's arrest. That action in itself might contribute to the myth of Stalin's character as mysterious, arbitrary, and all-powerful, but Aleshkovsky proceeds to demystify the Great Man in the best tradition of Russian literature: Like Nikolai Gogol before him, he renders a world—here a man—ridiculous by reducing him to his component parts. Where Gogol divided polite Petersburg society into waists and mustaches sauntering down Nevsky Prospect, or chronicled a correspondence between two dogs, or separated a would-be snob and his oversized nose, Aleshkovsky puts Stalin's best foot forward. Stalin's right foot begins to object, criticize, and swear like a trooper. It mocks him, threatens, pleads—even plays footsie with Franklin Roosevelt under the Yalta conference table.

Aside from any extended punning on left and right deviations (charges during the purge trials), the whole episode with Stalin's foot is part of Aleshkovsky's discussion of human nature. Stalin, although tempted at least at some points to listen to what his body is telling him ("My foot is giving me trouble"), finally ignores it and retreats into dogma, just like his victim, Chernyshevsky.

This, then, is what makes Fan the unlikely hero of the tale: A crook, a thief, and a liar, he is what he is out of self-interest, not ideology. That may not be particularly good, but it is at least better and more natural than the alternative. His multiple aliases and identities, aside from marking him as a criminal, also make him a kind of perverse Soviet Everyman. He cons the system as best he can, not so much for profit as for survival, and his instinct for life encompasses an understanding of others' survival, too. What makes him a true character—never mind good—is his consistent mercy and compassion for his fellow creatures, whether they be human or animal. "Human suffering," Fan says, "is no better by a single tear or scream or faint than a butterfly's or a cow's or an eagle's or a rat's. That's the only thing I'm sure of."

Themes and Meanings

What is Aleshkovsky satirizing? Nothing more and nothing less than both the Soviet State and the Soviet state—the state of being and mind that the State engenders. Nothing and no one escapes: slogans and slogan-mouthers (which is almost everyone), beer and beer-vendors, communal apartments and their omnivorous cockroaches. In his range of targets he resembles other satirists such as Aleksandr Zinoviev or Venedikt Erofeev or even Edward Limonov, whose seamy and often obscene grotesques subvert official optimism. The poles of Aleshkovsky's fantastic tale, however, are truth and falsehood, art and artifice, natural (read here divine) and unnatural order. Language itself is one of the chief gauges of those extremes.

The trial is the core of the novel. A trial is, in theory, a mechanism for getting at what has really happened. Here it becomes an elaborate machine to obscure what has happened or, more precisely, to create what never happened at all: a collective fiction. Difficult as it might seem to top the clownish evil of Stalin's show trials, Aleshkovsky does so, from the parody of establishing the exact time of the crime ("on the night of July 14, 1789, and January 9, 1905") to the accused's sincere disgust at himself for perpetrating (or appearing to have perpetrated) such a heinous crime. During the purge trials, some people speculated that hired actors might have stepped in for the most prominent defendants: Here Fan only realizes that there is an actor portraying him at the end of the film.

Why does Aleshkovsky (and his hero, given the possible charges, for that matter) pick this particular crime? Why rape, why an aged kangaroo? The key is not only in the sheer idiocy of the accusation but also in the genuine perversity of the crime. One of Stalin's favorite epithets for his ideological victims was "unclean"—their crimes were "obscene," "foul." Aleshkovsky gives his readers an even stiffer dose of vile stuff—a real outrage for the righteous public to swallow.

It is not only the purge era at which Aleshkovsky aims in the novel. Like Fyodor Dostoevski's characters, Fan is not guilty by association but is still responsible for himself and his fellow creatures. He has his own sins to atone for, "for his own [case], the real one, the biggest case of all." The KGB and its computer are a Russian Frankenstein and his monster—the utopian nightmare of the infinite perfectibility of man. The crime is concocted by a machine, the product of reason alone: It is not that Fan is blameless, but that he is not to blame for this crime. Gemma the kangaroo, however, is blameless in a way that no human ever could be. She cannot compromise with her jailers or tacitly acknowledge the truth of those "objective conditions" which have put her behind bars. Nor can she lie to herself or others; she can only be her own kangaroo self—with no goal, no rationale, no ideology to justify her existence other than those ordained but unspoken by God and nature. Using her to make a moral point and then killing her to prop up a false accusation is the real perversion of the novel.

Fan's rueful memories of his rebellious suit of clothes also serve this point. His suit is worn out, ready for the ragbag, but Fan will not let it die a natural death and forces his own will on the material; he takes it to a tailor. Turn a suit inside out, turn a man into a kangaroo, turn a way of life upside down— it is all social engineering.

> "We should never turn anything, Kolya. Let them live and die at their appointed hour, or at least from natural misfortunes—forests, jackets, states, shoes, literature, overcoats, mountains, cats, mice, neckties, and people. . . . I certainly don't want to get to the Last Judgment to find me and Karpo Marx accused of trying to change the world."

Fan's lyrical flights and swoops when he drinks to both animal and human zoos, to "every captured, crucified butterfly, and to beetles," when he pities even the rats he is forced to hunt (except for the chief rat, Jean-Paul Sartre) are a counterpoint to the dark, manic humor of his foul but uncorrupted language. His use of *mat* (the Russian family of expressions both exceedingly profane and exceedingly inventive), or prison argot, and of street slang is his last line of defense against the deadly conformity of acceptably pretty literary diction and heroic officialese. Crooked, con-man vernacular, like Fan himself, can only be true to itself; live, spontaneous language cannot support dead theory.

Critical Context

Before he left the Soviet Union in 1978, Yuz Aleshkovsky was known officially as a children's writer and unofficially as the author of scurrilously funny (therefore subversive) songs. At least one of those songs has become part of national folklore, witness to Aleshkovsky's ear for the spoken language: Of all the ears inside and outside the Soviet Union, his is probably the one closest to the ground.

His novels and stories belong to the narrative tradition called *skaz*, which is an untranslatable term for the type of yarn told in the first person by an unself-conscious narrator whose language draws at least as much attention to the teller as to the tale. That language may be dialect, it may be slang, or it may be purely idiosyncratic. Its effect may be satiric, but its objects is itself, and it can carry the reader far beyond what passes for a plot. His satire mocks not only a social system but also the human folly that produced it.

Like Dostoevski's Underground Man, Aleshkovsky's protagonists carry on a monologue which is really a dialogue with themselves or some other, invisible audience. Those protagonists may already be schizophrenic, as in the psychiatric ward of *Sinen'kii skromnyi platochek* (1982; modest blue kerchief) or the interrogation rooms of *Ruka* (1980; the hand), or may become that way by living a massive lie, as in *Kamufliazh* (1980; camouflage). They may be singled out for extraordinary adventures because of some prodigious physical trait: Nikolai Nikolaevich, the hero of a novella by the same name (1980) is chosen as chief donor for a sperm bank; Sergei Ivanovich, the hero of *Bloshinoe tango* (1986; a tango for fleas), wields a phenomenal sense of smell.

Whatever their other and numerous sins may be, they all share both physical and spiritual intuition. This raunchy crop of thieves and derelicts has a clear sense of good and evil, although, in proper Dostoevskian fashion, that sense does not always rule their actions. They are all men in extremis, at the end of their rope—or someone else's. This moral finality takes Aleshkovsky's work beyond social satire to philosophy, and then faith. Seen by some as a purveyor of bad jokes and worse taste, he is one of the most serious moralists of twentieth century Russian literature; he bellies up to the bar with Job, and what the rest of the customers hear is, as Joseph Brodsky puts it, the sound of "Jeremiah—laughing."

Sources for Further Study

Brown, Edward J. "Truth Through Obscenity," in *Russian Literature Since the Revolution*, 1982.

Meyer, Priscilla. "*Skaz* in the Work of Juz Aleskovskij," in *Slavic and East European Journal*. XXVIII (Winter, 1984), pp. 455-461.

The New York Times Book Review. Review. XCI (April 27, 1986), p. 9.

The New Yorker. Review. LXII (April 28, 1986), p. 120.

Jane Ann Miller

KLINGSOR'S LAST SUMMER

Author: Hermann Hesse (1877-1962)
Type of plot: Künstlerroman
Time of plot: c. 1919
Locale: The countryside and small towns of Italy
First published: Klingsors letzter Sommer, 1920 (English translation, 1970)

> Principal characters:
> KLINGSOR, a famous painter
> LOUIS, his friend, also a painter
> HERMANN (TU FU), Klingsor's friend, a writer

The Novel

This loosely structured, episodic novella relates the last passionate, troubled, exhilarating summer of the middle-age Klingsor, a leading European painter. It begins with a preface, in which the narrator reports that Klingsor died in the fall. No one knows the circumstances of his death; there are rumors that he went mad and that he committed suicide. He was always known for his heavy drinking. The narrative then moves on to vivid, impressionistic snapshots of Klingsor's life during that last, wild summer.

He is first seen at night, on the balcony of his studio, situated in the lush Italian countryside. He is strained by overwork, lack of sleep, and intense, voluptuous living. Still, he is accustomed to extravagance. He thinks of his girlfriend Gina, a girl half his age, and he studies the work he has accomplished during the day.

In the next episode, Klingsor receives a visit from his old friend, a fellow painter whom he calls Louis the Cruel or Louis the Bird. Together, they argue good-naturedly about the respective callings of work, art, and sensual enjoyment. Louis is a *bon viveur*, and he and Klingsor spend the day together in a nearby town with Louis' beautiful woman friend. After some days pass, Louis leaves suddenly, as is his custom. He was always happier when traveling.

With a group of artistic friends, including the writer Hermann, whom Klingsor calls Tu Fu, Klingsor visits the village of Kareno. He walks through mountain paths and lush vegetation, with a view of lakes and forests. There is a philosophical discussion about death and the passage of time, and Klingsor reflects passionately on the need to live in the present. The group reaches a tiny village at the summit of the mountain path, where Klingsor is captivated by the sight of one of the local women. He later meets another sensual young woman whom he calls the Queen of the Mountain; he sees her through his visionary, artistic eyes. Continuing the journey, Klingsor is in good spirits; at dinner in a grotto he drinks wine freely, fondles the women, sings, and tells tales. It is a picture of bacchanalian enjoyment and excess.

After an interlude which includes a letter written by Klingsor to his friend Edith, the narrative restarts in late July. From this point, Klingsor's awareness of death is mixed more insistently with his sense of the ecstasy of life. Tu Fu visits him with an astrologer from Armenia. Over the ever-present wine, they discuss ways of overcoming melancholy. The astrologer believes that it can be conquered and banished forever through one intensive hour of concentration. They discuss freedom of the will, the transcendence of time, and the approach of death.

The narrative then moves to an evening in August. Klingsor reflects on the fullness of his life and his many experiences. Yet he now hears the "music of doom." He meets a peasant woman from the valley who remembers him as the famous painter. They make love.

Before the final, climactic episode, there are two diversions from the narrative. First, Klingsor writes a letter to Louis. In it, Klingsor says that he still feels creativity exploding within him; he must go on working because the world is inexpressibly beautiful. Second, a poem by Klingsor which he sends to his friend Tu Fu is included. Klingsor is waiting for death, but he mocks death by singing drunken songs far into the night.

The final episode describes the painting of Klingsor's self-portrait in the first days of September. It was the crowning glory of his tempestuous summer. The narrator briefly flashes forward and describes how the portrait, after Klingsor's death, has been seen by others. Some perceived tranquillity and nobility, others saw madness, and still others saw a confession or a self-glorification. It was not a naturalistic portrait. Returning to the present, the narrator describes the intense and ecstatic few days of painting. Sleeping and eating little, but drinking as usual, Klingsor had seen many faces in himself, from the child to the libertine, and finally to the doomed man who accepted his fate. Somehow, he managed to compress his entire life's experience, with all of its differing shades, into his portrait. It was a terrible struggle, but he had faith that what he was doing had some universal significance beyond his small individual life.

When the painting was finished, he locked it in the unused kitchen, showed it to no one, and resumed his normal life. The story ends with Klingsor making a visit to town, buying fruit and cigarettes to give to his girlfriend. The reader is left to puzzle over the reason for the death reported in the preface, since the narrator chooses to give no explanation, except to say that the rumors of suicide or madness had no foundation.

The Characters

Klingsor is to some extent an autobiographical figure. He was born, like Hermann Hesse, in 1877, and he embodies some of the conflicts of Hesse's own life. Hesse also took up painting. Impulsive and intense, Klingsor prides himself on being totally receptive to life, living more fully and perceiving the world more richly than the next man. In his youth, he had been a manic-depressive; his spells of ecstasy were followed by pain and deprivation. It was like a continual cycle of death and resurrection. Yet he had dared to do new things, even though he knew that the intensity with which he lived would burn him out shortly. His creativity had flamed too violently, too overwhelmingly, for it to endure. He does not believe in tomorrow and acts as if every day were his last. He fails not because of the poverty of his spirit, but because he reaches for too much, wanting what the world cannot give.

Klingsor is also the archetypal romantic. He places enormous importance on his feelings. He wants to experience every emotion fully, even negative ones, which he does not believe are bad. To wrong even one feeling, he writes to his friend Edith, is to extinguish a star.

He knows the futility of all of his enterprises. Life is short and irrevocable and his preoccupation with death, which he both wants and fears, becomes more pronounced as the summer passes. As the Armenian astrologer puts it, he sits singing in his burning house.

His friend Louis, the only other character who is portrayed in any depth, is a reflection of the sensual side of Klingsor's personality. He is also a famous painter, the only man who fully understands Klingsor's art and whose own is its equal. He is a wanderer and a sensualist who would sooner have his favorite girl on his lap than spend his time painting. We only paint when we have nothing better to do, he teases Klingsor. He believes that painting reduces and limits nature and does not enhance it. Klingsor sees the force of Louis' argument, but, typically, he wants both worlds—the pure creativity of the mind as well as the joys of the senses. Both are equally valuable in his eyes as long as the burning intensity of life and love is in both.

Other characters, including a number of sensual women (Klingsor is an incorrigible womanizer) flit in and out of the narrative. A doctor friend remarks on death and prompts Klingsor to affirm the paradise of the moment, more precious because it is never to return. Tu Fu, the writer, pops up from time to time with some appropriate verses on death. Yet, appropriately enough for a man who wishes to absorb all things into himself, the focus always remains on Klingsor.

Themes and Meanings

Style, point of view, symbolism, and theme combine to bring out the central meaning of the story: Klingsor's search for the eternal, all-embracing, and universal nature of the individual self. The exaggerated and extravagant style, including the frequent use of apostrophe, reflects the passionate, luxuriant nature of Klingsor's own personality, his way of seeing the world. Here, for example, are some of Klingsor's typical thoughts:

Ring high and blast your trumpet, cadmium! Boast loudly, lush crimson lake. Laugh glaringly, lemon yellow! Come here, you deep-blue mountain in the distance. Come to my heart, you matt dusty-green leaves. How tired you are, how you let your pious branches droop submissively. I drink to you, lovely things of the world!

The fact that the story is told entirely from Klingsor's point of view by a sympathetic third-person narrator only adds to the force of Klingsor's egocentricity, his need to subjugate the world. Other characters are seen only in terms of how he responds to them.

A central motif is that of the mirror. Klingsor's life is referred to as a hall of mirrors; he tends to seek his own likeness in others, and he paints the environment as a reflection of his own image. His painting of a mountain, for example, looks like a crazy, masked face. Whenever he looks outward, he sees himself.

Along with this quest to find the self in everything, to expand his own individuality, is the quest for eternity—though, basically, the two quests are one and the same. Klingsor aims to abolish time and annihilate death through his art, and he complains about the very existence of time: "Why always this idiotic succession of one thing after another, and not a roaring, surfeiting, simultaneity?" He wants "the whole full symphony" playing at once, and he is temperamentally inclined to see totalities in things, multiple possibilities. A woman to whom he is attracted, for example, is "everything: mother, child, mistress, animal, madonna." He also longs to paint so as to reveal simultaneously the totality of opposites in nature: birth and decay, God and death. Klingsor gets as close as he has ever got to the "whole symphony" in his self-portrait, which is the culmination of his quest. In a few days of glorious torment and ecstasy, he paints a thousand faces in the one face. The face blends with the natural environment; the hair is reminiscent of leaves and the bark of trees and the eye sockets are like clefts in rock. The portrait expresses not only the totality of his own life but also European man at this point in evolution, at once "Faust and Karamazov, beast and sage." There are yet more faces, stretching through eons of past time, "as if the last man on earth in the moment before death were recalling once again with the speed of dream all the forms of past ages when the universe was young."

Critical Context

Klingsor's Last Summer was the collective title given to the three stories which Hesse published in one volume in 1920. The others are *Kinderseele* (*A Child's Heart*, 1970) and *Klein und Wagner* (*Klein and Wagner*, 1970). The title story is by far the richest of the three, and it has received the most critical attention.

The story contains strong autobiographical elements. Hesse sometimes described his own calling as that of a magician, and Klingsor is the name of a powerful magician in Wolfram von Eshenbach's medieval romance *Parzival* (c. 1200); the name also occurs in Novalis' *Heinrich von Ofterdingen* (1800), a work which Hesse admired.

Klingsor's search for simultaneity, for the annihilation of time, is common to many of Hesse's heroes. In *Siddhartha* (1922; English translation, 1951), for example, the protagonist eventually learns that there is no such thing as time, and this is a crucial aspect of his enlightenment. Goldmund in *Narziss und Goldmund* (1930; *Death and the Lover*, 1932; better known as *Narcissus and Goldmund*) also resembles Klingsor in his belief that the purpose of art is "to save what little we may from the linked, never ending dance of death."

Klingsor's Last Summer was followed two years later by *Siddhartha*, another story about the search for the self. Like *Klingsor's Last Summer*, *Siddhartha* affirms the value of both the material and spiritual aspects of life. Stylistically, however, the romantic extravagance of the earlier story is replaced with a simple classical structure, and the final outcome is also very different. Siddhartha succeeds where Klingsor fails; he wins serenity through a quiet contemplation of life, whereas Klingsor's intoxicated moments of illumination are accompanied by self-torture and fear of death. Klingsor actively attempts to force life into his own mold, while Siddhartha waits and is passive.

Klingsor's Last Summer represents an intense, idiosyncratic attempt to conquer the forces of psychic chaos in one romantic, dizzy, sensual assault. Hesse was soon to declare that this was not the answer, but when viewed as a stage on the journey, the story has its value. It vividly captures the torments and frustrations of the self as it attempts to push beyond its boundaries and capture the transcendental harmony of the world.

Sources for Further Study
Field, G. W. *Hermann Hesse*, 1970.
Heiney, Donald. Review in *The Christian Science Monitor*. LXIII (December 30, 1970), p. 9.
Henel, E. G. Review in *Library Journal*. XCV (October 1, 1970), p. 3304.
Hill, Susan. Review in *New Statesman*. LXXXII (September 10, 1971), p. 340.
Rose, Ernest. *Faith from the Abyss: Hermann Hesse's Way from Romanticism to Modernity*, 1965.

Bryan Aubrey

LADIES' HAIRDRESSER

Author: I. Grekova (Yelena Sergeyevna Ventsel, 1907-   )
Type of plot: Post-Socialist Realism
Time of plot: The 1960's
Locale: A large, provincial Russian city
First published: Damskii master, 1963 (English translation, 1973)

> *Principal characters:*
> MARYA VLADIMIROVNA KOVALEVA, a Soviet career woman with
>   two sons who live at home while attending college
> VITALY, a ladies' hairdresser, age twenty
> GALYA, Marya's secretary, age twenty-three

The Novel

I. Grekova's good-humored but pessimistic novella, *Ladies' Hairdresser*, uses the Socialist Realist tradition of focusing on the workplace and work relationships as the core of the individual's life. In the Soviet tradition, work is the very best part of life, and there is no such thing as an undignified or boring job. The narrator, Marya Vladimirovna (more formally, "Professor Kovaleva," when she is pulling rank), appears to belong to the elite of Soviet society: She is the head of a computer institute and (like the author) a recognized mathematician. Yet she lives, almost literally, in a pigsty. When she calls her lazy, good-humored sons "pigs," they slyly and literally agree with her, quoting from a standard reference work: " 'Female pigs are not as irritable as males, but are just as courageous. Though their small fangs cannot inflict serious wounds they are no less dangerous than hogs, since they will not let go of the object of their wrath. . . .' " At work, Marya is surrounded by coworkers of whom she is very fond, but who are of no help whatsoever.

One evening, exhausted and exasperated, she goes out to have her hair done. Even though the wait will be a minimum of two hours, for a "sheepskin" permanent wave, Marya is prepared to sit patiently. Always keenly interested in people, she makes delicate psychological observations of the other customers, speculating about their lives, based on scraps of conversation and details of their appearance. For the reader, she is an expert guide to the nitty-gritty of Soviet life.

An apprentice hairdresser, Vitaly calls challengingly for his next customer, with the warning: "I am . . . capable of disfiguring you." Marya is game even for that. Thus she becomes acquainted with a member of her own society who might as well be from another world.

Vitaly would seem to be a natural, though somewhat fey, Socialist hero: He approaches his work with tremendous seriousness, as though it were an abstruse branch of science. For a time, he dresses the hair of Marya's secretary free of charge, in part as a favor to Marya, in part because the young woman's beautiful, honey-colored hair has an "interesting texture." His work is so exquisite that the bewildered mathematician is moved to poetry to do it justice. On the job, Vitaly's professionalism, indeed genius, is frustrated by everything: his superiors, his clients, his coworkers, and the system itself, with its production quotas, complaint books, and graft (which must be paid even to keep a humble hairdressing job). The novel ends with the surprising announcement that this supreme artist of hairdressing has taken a job as an apprentice metalworker. After all of his tribulations, the young man himself is overjoyed at going into a new field (though one wonders whether his devotion will not be frustrated all over again—as are Marya's best efforts, in her more privileged arena). The irreplaceable loss to the women of Russia is left unremarked.

The Characters

Marya Vladimirovna Kovaleva observes people, especially the young, from a nonjudgmental and deeply compassionate viewpoint. Though a representative of an establishment which prides itself on bringing up a socially responsible younger generation, Marya is putty in the hands of her bright, idle, impossibly spoiled sons: her "dear, dear fools." They are accustomed to getting by on charm, and their mother does not seriously attempt to change them.

Instead of being subjected to heavy-handed criticism, the privileged boys' weaknesses are highlighted by their contrast to young Vitaly, already self-supporting, whose harsh and shrunken life has killed much of his potential. A sensitive artist, his talents have become narrowly focused: His innate sense of visual beauty has been reduced to hairdressing; his intense feeling for music has been reduced to whistling.

Galya, the sweet but totally incompetent secretary whom Marya introduces to Vitaly, falls in love with him. Vitaly, however, has no response. Sexual neuroses and homosexuality are taboo topics in Soviet literature. Thus, Marya never speculates about Vitaly's sexual makeup. She does deftly convey the sexually seething atmosphere of the beauty-salon milieu. Vitaly's nonresponsiveness to Galya is put in the context of his nonrecognition of love in general: His life has been so emotionally starved, he does not know what love is. He only knows that marriage requires a decent apartment, something that neither he nor Galya has any chance of getting. In reply to Marya's definition of love, he soberly concludes that he does not feel it for Galya.

Galya is not portrayed in depth, but she symbolizes the problems of many young, single Russian women: Though an attractive twenty-three-year-old, she already finds that Russian men prefer girls still younger; the boyfriend who had seemed perfect turns out to be a married man; and Vitaly, the first young man with a serious outlook on life, is only interested in her hair.

Marya exclaims: "Oh you girls, you poor girls. The war's long been over, another generation has grown up, and there are still too many of you."

Themes and Meanings

Despite its humorous tone, *Ladies' Hairdresser* has a basically pessimistic message: The individual is prevented from achieving self-realization in Russian society. Moreover, since Grekova's individualists strive for perfection through socially desirable channels—original achievement in higher mathematics; making people look and feel better than they had dreamed possible—the loss is much greater for society than for the frustrated innovators. Both Marya and Vitaly refuse to become bitter (though Vitaly breaks down and weeps silently). Yet one wonders how long they can go on striving to do their best, with no encouragement or reward.

A secondary theme is conveyed by details that casually hint that the society is unhealthy or even decadent. Every detail of personal life indicates that families are in great disarray. While at work, Marya is handed an "urgent" official document which she tosses aside as routine: "On being brought to the police station Citizen Popov [an employee of the Institute of Computers] relieved himself against the wall and the surrounding area. . . ." When they are at home, Marya's sons, both bright college students (the future elite), are always in their underwear, wipe the table with their clothes, leave beer bottles everywhere. The Komsomol organizes a young people's party at the Institute, and a near riot ensues from a foolish party game. When Marya attempts to set a good example by organizing a clever party around sophisticated computer gadgets, it is accepted lackadaisically, without interest or enjoyment. In Grekova's society, people are not happy and apparently do not know how to be.

Critical Context

While the official school of Soviet literature, Socialist Realism, degenerated into self-parody during the Stalinist era, Russian writers after 1958 have in some cases been able to pick up the pieces and forge a vigorous new literature. This post-Socialist Realism leaves out the facile faith and optimism of the old school. The most useful part of the old legacy of writing novels to order to spotlight different industries, is that work, any occupation under the sun, has become the fully naturalized environment of Soviet literature. The supreme post-Socialist Realist novel may be *Rakovy korpus* (1968; *Cancer Ward*, 1968), also written by a professional mathematician, Aleksandr Solzhenitsyn, in which life, work, and the human soul are so compellingly intertwined that all three are made more meaningful. Grekova's *Ladies' Hairdresser* is an important bridge to that level.

Also anticipating the later Solzhenitsyn, Grekova makes women and their particular concerns (not simply woman as Communist, woman as worker, woman as war heroine) into a much more fully naturalized part of Soviet Russian literature. Both men and women lose their aura of Soviet heroism and become more believable. From the past, Grekova embraces Mikhail Zoshchenko's tradition of apolitical yet gentle irony. Even more than Zoshchenko, Grekova brings out the malaise beneath the foibles.

Sources for Further Study
Friedberg, Maurice. Introduction to *Russian Women: Two Stories*, 1983.
Grekova, I. *The Hotel Manager*, 1983.
Library Journal. Review. CVIII (November 15, 1983), p. 2171.
Publishers Weekly. Review. CCXXIV (November 25, 1983), p. 58.
Virginia Quarterly Review. Review. LX (Summer, 1984), p. 97.

D. Gosselin Nakeeb

LAFCADIO'S ADVENTURES

Author: André Gide (1869-1951)
Type of plot: Psychological satire
Time of plot: The 1890's, during the pontificate of Leo XIII
Locale: Various locales in France and Italy
First published: Les Caves du Vatican, 1914 (*The Vatican Swindle*, 1925; better known as *Lafcadio's Adventures*, 1927)

Principal characters:

LAFCADIO WLUIKI, the bastard son of Juste-Agénor de Baraglioul

JULIUS DE BARAGLIOUL, a writer, Lafcadio's half brother

JUSTE-AGÉNOR DE BARAGLIOUL, a wealthy aristocrat, the father of Julius and Lafcadio

MARGUERITE DE BARAGLIOUL, the wife of Julius

GENEVIEVE DE BARAGLIOUL, the daughter of Julius and Marguerite

ANTHIME ARMAND-DUBOIS, Julius' brother-in-law

VERONICA, Anthime's pious wife

AMÉDÉE FLEURISSOIRE, a simple, pious man

ARNICA, his wife, the youngest sister of Veronica and Marguerite

GASTON BLAFAPHAS, the lifelong friend of Amédée Fleurissoire

PROTOS, an adventurer and former schoolmate of Lafcadio (also known as DEFOUQUEBLIZE, a professor of law)

CAROLA VENITEQUA, Protos' accomplice

The Novel

A complex novel of contrapuntal development, *Lafcadio's Adventures* is divided into four interrelated parts. In the first book, André Gide introduces the reader to a scholarly—indeed pedantic—freethinker and would-be scientist. Anthime Armand-Dubois, crippled by rheumatoid arthritis, is physically grotesque yet intellectually vigorous. Because of his misshapen body, he retreats into abstruse scientific research. Unlike his pious Catholic wife, Veronica, Anthime is driven in his studies to demolish the religious superstructure that, in his judgment, obscures reason and promotes superstition. A Freemason, he plans to publish in scientific journals his minor, often cruel, experiments involving animal vivisection and abuse. Then suddenly, he experiences a religious conversion. After his young niece prays for the forgiveness of his sins, Anthime has a vision of the Virgin; coming to his senses, he appears to be healed from his pain, throws away his crutch, and swears devotion to the Church.

In book 2, Gide treats the sophisticated, somewhat smug novelist, Julius de Baraglioul, who has just received a troubling letter from his distinguished father, Juste-Agénor de Baraglioul. The dying gentleman wants Julius to report to him information concerning the actions and intentions of a young stranger, Lafcadio Wluiki. With some misgivings, Julius visits Lafcadio's shabby lodgings, reads the youth's enigmatic diary, then is startled by the arrival of Lafcadio himself. Shortly thereafter, the two men, of vastly different temperaments and stations in life, discover their link to each other: They are half brothers.

In book 3, Gide introduces Julius' gentle and ingenuous brother-in-law Amédée Fleurissoire. Quite comfortable with the routines of his bourgeois life and his bland marriage to Arnica (Marguerite de Baraglioul's younger sister) Amédée is startled into heroic enterprise after learning a terrible secret. Through the intervention of Father Salus and the Countess de Saint-Prix, Arnica passes on to her husband the information that Pope Leo XIII has been imprisoned and that a false Pope has taken His Holiness' place.

In book 4, Amédée, flushed with religious enthusiasm, begins his absurd journey to discover for himself the truth. With great discomfort, he travels to Rome, then—convinced by Protos (an adventurer who earlier disguised himself as Father Salus) into believing that the plot is a true conspiracy—agrees to secure from his wealthy brother-in-law letters of credit to ransom or release the supposed captive.

Lafcadio, the young adventurer, who has just inherited an annual income of forty thousand francs from his father's estate, happens upon Amédée in a train compartment. To Lafcadio, Amédée is a complete stranger who nevertheless inspires a sudden thought: Why not commit a perfect crime—a gratuitous act for which there is no logical explanation—by pushing this innocent man from the train? Cool and emotionless except for the exhilaration of having committed an unprovoked, motiveless crime, Lafcadio later reads an account, while in Naples, of a mysterious accident that occurred recently near Capua, of a "Crime, Suicide . . . or Accident?" according to the newspaper headline. While in Naples, he also meets his half brother Julius, and the two discuss the import of the event. For Julius, the theme of an unmotivated crime would be perfect for his new novel. For Lafcadio, the game of discussing the subject but not revealing his own role in it is dangerous but entertaining. The game becomes truly dangerous, however, when Protos, disguised now as a pedantic law professor named Defouqueblize, confronts Lafcadio with incriminating cuff links that connect him with the crime; Protos blackmails the youth into cooperation.

Fortunately for Lafcadio, Protos himself is vulnerable: He has murdered his mistress Carola Venitequa, and the police soon have him in custody and charged with Amédée's murder as well. Now Lafcadio has a moral dilemma. Should he confess to his part in the crime, or should he follow the advice of

Julius' daughter Genevieve (who is in love with him), and allow Protos to pay a double penalty, since he is already doomed? The choice is life with dishonor but with the promise of love and redemption, or death. The reader must guess which one Lafcadio will choose.

The Characters

Most of the characters in this ironic novel of deception and betrayal are either simpletons or sophisticates. Chief among the first group are the "wise fools," Amédée Fleurissoire and his friend Gaston Blafaphas. Because of their innocence, they are easy victims of knavery. Nevertheless, they are "wise," for their simple piety protects them from cynicism in a world of ambiguous moral choice.

Similarly, most of the sheltered women in *Lafcadio's Adventures* are innocent to the point of simplicity: Veronica Armand-Dubois, Marguerite de Baraglioul (and her daughter Genevieve), and Arnica Fleurissoire. All are conventionally religious, unimaginative, and complaisant in the round of their domestic obligations. They are also notably lacking in sexual passion, with the possible exception of Genevieve, who is romantic yet untried. More sexually experienced, though also inherently simple in spirit, is Carola Venitequa, who sacrifices herself in defense of her unlikely hero, Amédée. Also included, with some qualifications, among the wise fools is Anthime Armand-Dubois. A fanatic, whether of science or of religion, he is a true believer in absolutes. He sways back and forth between extreme intellectual positions, mistaking absolute reality for the temporary resiliency of his bones and joints. He muddles through life, never fully comprehending a reality apart from his own prejudices and superstitions.

At the opposite pole are the sophisticates, among them, Julius de Baraglioul, a novelist with a shrewd sense of human psychology who nevertheless cannot understand reality when he confronts it; Lafcadio Wluiki, the truly "free" man of the novel, capable of nearly every excess but also a victim of his own calculation; and finally, Protos, a confidence man utterly unscrupulous when he thinks logically but also careless in his passion. These sophisticates are thus "foolish" despite (or because of) their cunning. Masters of expediency, they are betrayed by inner weaknesses: Julius by vanity, Lafcadio by self-confidence, Protos by cruelty. In the end, the test of reality exposes their weaknesses: Julius, who steals Lafcadio's concept of the "gratuitous crime" for the purposes of his fiction, fails to recognize in his half brother the actual criminal; Lafcadio, who has imagined himself to be superior to other men because of his disinterested isolation, finally recognizes that he is the least of men, a murderer; finally, Protos, who has always defined people as being of two types, the "slim" (the tricksters who carry no moral baggage) and the "crusted" (the tricked), ends up in the hands of the police, charged with a murder—that of Amédée—he observed but did not commit.

Themes and Meanings

Just as Gide counterpoints fools and sophisticates, so in his themes he contrasts religion with science, conventional morality with immorality, reality with illusion. A skeptic, he treats religious excess as a metaphor for irrationality. Anthime vacillates between the false gods of scientific and religious fanaticism. As a scientist, he is cruel; as a devout Catholic, he is self-abnegating. In both devotions his zeal is excessive. To Gide, science is suspect, because intelligence itself lacks moral direction. The intelligent Julius mistakes appearance for reality, and the cunning Lafcadio uses intelligence as a weapon, supposing himself to be a superman exempt from moral laws. Finally, the near-knave (for in Gide's world, no absolute evil exists) Protos manipulates ignorant people with the most outrageous, absurd swindle conceivable—he pretends that the Pope in Rome has been kidnapped by Freemasons and other rogues. Master of protean disguises, he conceals reality so that only the illusion (the hoax) appears to be true. He befuddles the hapless Amédée but confounds others as well. In Gide's world of ambiguous moral choices, conventional religion offers no sure guide. Every man is on his own. Every man is either a potential victim of swindle or a potential swindler.

Critical Context

Published in 1914, *Lafcadio's Adventures* presented for the first time in Western literature the concept of a "gratuitous act," a motiveless crime for which the perpetrator suffers neither a guilty conscience nor a sense of moral responsibility. Previously, important writers had described crimes of passion and violence; crimes committed for flimsy or even absurd reasons; crimes premeditated or sudden. Before Gide's novel, writers had not concerned themselves with a crime committed solely for caprice, for no purpose except amusement—an act against a victim hitherto unknown to the criminal, simply to satisfy a curiosity about what might happen as a consequence. In Fyodor Dostoevski's classic analysis of murder in *Prestupleniye i nakazaniye* (1866; *Crime and Punishment*, 1886), the student Raskolnikov imagines himself to be a superior person who can commit a crime with impunity, but he later suffers from guilt and is punished for his crime, as much through his own conscience as through imprisonment. In another classic crime, that exposed in Joseph Conrad's *The Secret Agent: A Simple Tale* (1907), Mr. Verloc attempts to blow up the Greenwich Observatory, an utterly absurd action that would create havoc among civilized people. At least Verloc's intended crime has a motive: He is an anarchist and has been ordered by his superiors to commit the act.

Lafcadio's crime, in contrast, is motiveless as well as meaningless. Although he believes himself to be morally superior in committing murder, he suffers no subsequent guilt. Thus his action is philosophical as well as capricious. Only within the framework of a society lacking a moral law can such a gratuitous act be imagined. Because Gide's novel takes place in such a society which operates according to loose principles of ethical relativism, his protagonist's actions are pre-existential. Lafcadio makes a decision that he believes is a correct one for him, no matter what other people may think. In a sense, he is a perfectly "free" man—one bound neither to circumstances of birth nor to nationality; neither to religious affections nor moral principles. Because he is a bastard who feels equally at home in any nation, he is not tied to place or condition of class; because he lacks religious or moral scruples, he is free to act as he wishes. He defines his own morality.

In addition, as a comic character who is mobile within a closed society, he counterpoints his respectable, conventional half brother, the humorless Julius. As a writer, Julius is concerned with art and life, but he confuses the two. After he learns from Lafcadio the concept of a gratuitous crime, Julius wishes to apply that theme to his next novel, but he fails to connect Lafcadio with the crime itself. Thus Julius' projected novel is a parody of a metafiction: a novel that tells the reader how the author wrote his book.

Indeed, the whole of *Lafcadio's Adventures* is a parody of the traditional novel. Unlike conventional fiction of the time, Gide's novel lacks a genuine hero, lacks romantic involvement, lacks a "moral." Lafcadio is at best a rogue-hero; his romance with Genevieve is contrived; and his fate is left up in the air. Will he agree to marry Genevieve, burying the evidence of his crime in order to live the life of a reconstructed bourgeois? The reader is free to draw his own conclusion—but beware Lafcadio's leer.

Sources for Further Study
Breé, Germaine. *Gide*, 1963.
Cordle, Thomas. *André Gide*, 1969.
Fowlie, Wallace. *André Gide: His Life and Art*, 1965.
Guerard, Albert Joseph. *André Gide*, 1969 (revised edition).
Perry, Kenneth. *The Religious Symbolism of André Gide*, 1969.

Leslie Mittleman

THE LAMB

Author: François Mauriac (1885-1970)
Type of plot: Tragic fable
Time of plot: 1921
Locale: Larjuzon, a French country home outside Paris
First published: L'Agneau, 1954 (English translation, 1955)

> *Principal characters:*
> XAVIER DARTIGELONGHUE, a young seminary student
> JEAN DE MIRBEL, a jaded and cynical landowner
> MICHÈLE, Jean's wife
> BRIGITTE PIAN, Michèle's stepmother
> DOMINIQUE, Mme Pian's secretary
> ROLAND, an orphan staying with the Mirbels
> THE CURÉ OF BALUZAC, a hardened and cynical priest

The Novel

Although not a sequel, *The Lamb* includes three of the main characters in François Mauriac's critically acclaimed novel *La Pharisienne* (1941; *A Woman of the Pharisees*, 1946) which appeared thirteen years earlier. Ten years older, the sadistic Jean de Mirbel, the domineering Brigitte Pian, and her stepdaughter Michèle are reintroduced to play a crucial role in the tragic destruction of the young man Xavier, the lamb of the work's title.

Although the narrative portion of the novel focuses on the seduction and sacrifice of Xavier, it is interspersed with sections of dialogue between Jean and Michèle in which, after Xavier's death, they discuss their responsibility for the young man and become reconciled to each other as husband and wife. In fact, these interchapters reveal the result of the sacrifice of Xavier, primarily the change of Jean from a cynic to one who understands the nature of love but does not fully understand the meaning of Xavier's death.

The narrative begins with Xavier on his way by train from Bordeaux to Paris, where he will begin seminary training. He becomes fascinated with a couple on the train platform; later, when the departing man enters his compartment, he finds out that the man, a well-known local landowner named Jean de Mirbel, has left his wife. Perhaps because of what he believes to be his priestly calling, Xavier is compelled to reunite them. When Jean discovers that Xavier is about to enter the priesthood, he mocks the clergy and takes advantage of Xavier's desire to help by convincing him to postpone his entrance into the seminary and to come with him back to his home.

When they arrive at Jean's villa, they join not only his wife Michèle but also her stepmother Brigitte Pian, Mme Pian's secretary Dominique, and a young boy named Roland whom Michèle has taken home from an orphanage to adopt. Xavier's meeting with Dominique and the romantic and sexual attraction she has for Xavier makes him doubt his plans to enter the priesthood and to wonder if she is the real reason he has been brought to Jean's house. He also is drawn to the child Roland after discovering that neither Jean nor Michèle wants the boy. After several days during which Xavier and Dominique spend time together—mostly in company with Roland, who worships Dominique—the budding romantic situation is ended by an argument between Jean and Mme Pian as both of them maneuver for possession of the two young people—Mme Pian for Dominique and Jean for Xavier.

Although Xavier is distressed by Mme Pian's storming out of the house and taking Dominique with her, the most distraught is Roland. Xavier decides to stay on at the villa to serve as Roland's protector, knowing that Jean hates Roland and wishes to send him back to the orphanage. When Roland becomes hysterical at Dominique's departure and Jean locks him in the library, Xavier finds a ladder and climbs into the boy's room to watch over him.

Xavier goes to a local priest at Baluzac to make confession, but he finds that it is the priest who needs spiritual help more than Xavier himself. When Xavier talks of the love of Christ and the brotherhood of man, the priest angrily sends him away. Finally, Xavier draws up a will leaving his entire estate to the foundling Roland and makes arrangements with Dominique to have Roland taken in by another guardian. When Jean discovers Xavier's plans, he drives to Baluzac to stop him. On the way there he runs into Xavier, who is on his way back to the villa on a bicycle, and kills him. The novel ends with Jean and Michèle discussing the meaning of Xavier's death and finally coming to the conclusion that they and all the others—the priest, Roland, Dominique, Brigitte—were partially responsible for the sacrificial death of the young lamb Xavier.

The Characters

Because of the fablelike nature of this short novel, the reader is given little insight into the psychological complexity of the residents of Jean's villa. Jean himself is a cynical, somewhat sadistic, figure who plays the satanic role of trying to seduce Xavier away from his plans to enter the priesthood. He seems incapable of love and interested only in destroying those around him. Michèle is even less fully delineated; like Jean she seems primarily dominated by the need to possess others and by her own petty jealousies.

Brigitte Pian is perhaps the most possessive of all, determined to control her young secretary Dominique and cynical about the relationship between Xavier and Jean. Dominique is little more than the object of Xavier's romantic and sexual attraction. Roland, although unloved by Jean and Michèle, is a relatively unlovable character who is jealous of Dominique's attraction to Xavier. The Curé of Baluzac is, like Jean, jaded and cynical and lacking in faith. All in all, these characters are fairly flat and stereotypical, existing more for the sake of the role they play in the death of Xavier than as individualized characters.

It is into this nest of pettiness, cynicism, jealousies, and ennui that the young and innocent Xavier is drawn. Xavier is primarily characterized by his initial doubt about entering the priesthood and then by his desire to help the helpless. After he meets Dominique he begins to feel that she is the key to his life as a man, and he has second thoughts about his seminary plans. Although his priestly motives are scorned by Jean and he is suspected of homosexual desires, first by Mme Pian with Jean and then by Jean with Roland, as the novel progresses he seems to be characterized by nothing more than a pure and selfless love.

The mystery of his death revolves around the question of whether he committed suicide because of his apparent failure at becoming a priest, whether Jean murdered him, making him a sacrificial victim of a Christlike love, whether he was pushed by Satan himself, or whether he willingly died to make sure that Roland would have his estate. This final question is never resolved; the answer to it depends on whether one reads the story as a psychological novel of the young innocent, or whether one sees it as a symbolic novel of Christlike sacrifice. The tone and characterization of the work suggest this latter symbolic reading.

Themes and Meanings

The theme of this simple story seems relatively clear; it is a modern version of the Christ story, with Xavier in the role of a saintlike figure who is sacrificed to rekindle the sense of love in those fallen cynics who surround him. When Xavier first postpones his plans to enter the seminary and go home with Jean, he does so because he is strangely drawn to those who he senses need his help. After he arrives he becomes the object of both desire and jealousy of all of those in the house. Jean is jealous because Xavier is drawn to Roland; Michèle is jealous because Xavier is drawn to Dominique; Roland is jealous because he fears losing Dominique to Xavier; and Brigitte is jealous because she fears losing her control over Dominique to Xavier.

Throughout, Xavier remains pure and blameless, perhaps too pure in his saintliness; the only "human" aspect he reveals is his attraction to Dominique. His love for Roland is selfless, pure and Christlike. On the night that Jean locks the boy in the library, Xavier walks through thorns and pinecones to find a ladder so he can comfort Roland. His feet are bloodied and he leaves tracks of blood behind him—an obvious symbolic image of Christ's crucifixion.

At the end of the novel, the reader is asked to believe that Xavier's death has effected a change in those around him. The Curé believes that Xavier was indeed a saint; Mme Pian has masses said for the young man; and, most important, Jean and Michèle appear to be reconciled with each other. Jean himself has become someone quite different from the unbelieving self he has been throughout the narrative. Indeed, in the final section of dialogue between the husband and wife, they shed tears of remorse, knowing now that love does exist in the world, even though it is "crucified." Jean feels that he is suffering as he has never suffered, even though at the same time he is at peace. Now he believes what Xavier believed, for he has been given the peace that Xavier had.

The central irony of the novel is obvious: Xavier has been able to achieve a much more Christlike success in "saving" the "lost" Jean de Mirbel by not having become a priest than he would have had he continued on his journey and entered the seminary. In Xavier's encounters with Jean the novel presents a classic antithesis between good and evil, in which, as is typical of the parable form, both these absolutes are ultimately mysterious. In making himself a willing sacrifice to aid the lonely Roland and to demonstrate the nature of love to Jean, Xavier becomes an embodiment of God's divine grace, an instrument of salvation to the lonely and the lost.

Critical Context

Because of its brief length, its unity of time and place, its small cast of characters, and its dependence on dialogue, *The Lamb* shares many of the characteristics of drama, as is typical of the tradition of the short novel form. Also, characteristic of the short novel, the work focuses on a tragic figure caught in a metaphysical dilemma and involved in a symbolic drama of philosophic complexity. Because of these characteristics it falls into the tradition of such works in American literature, from Herman Melville's nineteenth century *Bartleby the Scrivener* (1856) to Saul Bellow's twentieth century *Seize the Day* (1956), and in European literature from the short novels of Fyodor Dostoevski to those of Albert Camus.

Although *The Lamb* has been considered a tour de force by critics, both thematically, in its realization of a modern religious fable of Christlike sacrifice and love, and technically, in its use of a split plot line in which the novel begins with the dialogue between Jean and Michèle and then moves back and forth between dialogue and narrative, it is generally not considered to be one of Mauriac's greatest novels.

Mauriac, who received the Nobel Prize in Literature in 1952, gave up writing fiction after the publication of *The Lamb*, blaming the poor critical reception of the book for his decision. A number of critics, however, in contrast to the majority opinion, argued that the novel transcended many of his earlier works about the priesthood by incorporating a saint, rather than a mere priest, while others admired the book for its ultimate theological mystery. If the work is not considered to be the finest in the Mauriac canon, it is nevertheless thought to be his most spiritual fictional parable.

Sources for Further Study
Iyengar, K. R. Srinivasa. *François Mauriac: Novelist and Moralist*, 1963.
Jenkins, Cecil. *Mauriac*, 1965.
Maloney, Michael F. *François Mauriac*, 1958.
Smith, Maxwell A. *François Mauriac*, 1970.

Charles E. May

THE LAST OF THE JUST

Author: André Schwarz-Bart (1928-   )
Type of plot: Bildungsroman
Time of plot: From the early 1900's to 1943, with a prologue covering the
    period from 1185 to 1792
Locale: Zemyock (Poland), Berlin and Stillenstadt (Germany), Paris, and
    Auschwitz
First published: Le Dernier des Justes, 1959 (English translation, 1960)

Principal characters:
THE NARRATOR, who presents himself as a friend of Ernie
ERNIE LEVY, one of the thirty-six Just Men
MORDECAI LEVY, Ernie's grandfather
MOTHER JUDITH, Ernie's grandmother
GOLDA ENGELBAUM, Ernie's fiancée

The Novel

Although the bulk of *The Last of the Just* deals with Ernie Levy, it begins
with a brief episodic history of his family from 1185 to 1792, for tradition held
that God had granted the Levy family, in each generation, one *Lamed-
Vovnik*. The *Lamed Vov*, the thirty-six Just Men, absorb the world's suffering: "[I]f just one of them were lacking, the sufferings of mankind would poison even the souls of the newborn, and humanity would suffocate with a
single cry."

Through the centuries the Levys wandered and suffered as did all the
Jews. A Levy finally settles in Zemyock, a small and isolated Polish town.
When, soon after World War I, the town is captured by White Guard
Cossacks, the refugee Levys find a place in Stillenstadt, Germany. The patriarch, Mordecai, and his wife, Mother Judith, are supported by their son
Benjamin's tailor shop. Then, the almost unreal, idyllic charm of Stillenstadt
is shattered by Nazi violence. Benjamin's second son, Ernie, experiences this
tragedy with particular intensity; after concluding that he is a *Lamed-Vovnik*,
he attempts suicide.

The Levys become refugees again, managing to find a niche in Paris.
While Ernie enlists in the army, the Vichy government rounds up Jews; the
Levy family, except for Ernie, is interned and then sent to their deaths. For a
time, Ernie sinks into—indeed wallows in—a deliberately unhuman life
focused on food and lust, but when a sympathetic Christian refers to his
"Jewish eyes," he once again becomes capable of feeling. The twenty-year-
old Ernie returns to the Jews left in Paris and falls in love with Golda
Engelbaum. When she is taken to the internment camp at Drancy, he follows
her. He rides with her and a group of frightened children in the boxcar to

Auschwitz. Having comforted and calmed them, as the door of the gas chamber closes, "he knew that he could do nothing more for anyone in the world. . . ."

The Characters

While the novel concentrates on Ernie, several others are also developed in detail. His grandfather, Mordecai, is large and tough, and traditionally learned and pious; when Nazis come to burn Torah scrolls, Mordecai charges them, swinging an iron bar. He is an archetype, the Patriarch, as Judith is the archetype of Mother. Lesser characters, such as Benjamin Levy, are finely crafted, their essential personalities explicated in their idiosyncratic approaches to life. Even Golda, whose late appearance in the novel gives her only scant space, is a fully developed character; the swift and mutual love between her and Ernie has no aspect of literary contrivance. Myriad other minor characters are each etched with a sure hand in taut and beautiful prose.

From his birth, Ernie is distinctive: Second to his older brother in size and courage as well as age, smaller even than his younger brother, he has flashes of insight into others' souls, a magic realistic concept of the world. Preoccupied with his destiny as a *Lamed-Vovnik*, he fantasizes about protecting all the Jews; only after his family's deportation does he attempt to escape his role by means of a Rabelaisian but despairing life-style. His return to humanity and the Jews of Paris signals a return to life and love and the working out of his destiny as a Just Man.

Themes and Meanings

André Schwarz-Bart uses various distancing devices to detach the reader from an immediate emotional identification with the characters. The narrator himself speaks with a detached and often ironic tone. Frequently, he refers to or apparently quotes historical records and witnesses. Interspersed with vague chronological references are specific names, places, and dates. The calm and objective narrative is broken only by flashes of irony, but the detachment begins to thin as the narrator approaches the twentieth century. The Levy Just Men become more and more fully developed characters to whom the reader responds, and the novelistic detail intensifies.

Zemyock, where the Levys had originally come to rest, is in almost magical isolation from the brutal realities of the world. Its atmosphere is to be recreated by the author, from time to time, in each of the later places inhabited by the Levys, from Berlin to Auschwitz. This vision is projected often for Stillenstadt, "Quiet City," where Ernie grows up. The pervasive charm of the town provides the magical background for Ernie's discovery of himself as a *Lamed-Vovnik* and for his attempted suicide as well. Later, in Paris, the charm of a spring day in a park is set against the certainty of the deaths of

Ernie and Golda, just as the internment camp rises amid the suburban tranquillity of Drancy. The final reality of Auschwitz seems itself unreal, with an orchestra playing on the route taken to the gas chambers by the prisoners. Ernie's tears of blood seem merely an acceptable response.

The narrator or a child is usually the medium by which these magic-realist episodes are described. Stillness, the contrasts of light and shadow, the interpenetration of dream and reality, violence and rescue, all produce not only a narrative but also, and more incisively, a vision of a world of ambiguity and anguish. Schwarz-Bart's prose is never bitter, but his thesis is clear: Jewish suffering through the ages is the responsibility of a Christianity which turns the Cross upside down, wielding it as a sword against innocent victims.

While the thrust of the novel is clear, the author's stance is sometimes ambiguous. Ernie is the last Just Man, yet he dies in Auschwitz. There have been previous ironic comments, such as Mother Judith's, "'What a great God is ours, . . . and how oddly he runs the world!'" There has also been Benjamin Levy's cry, "if God did not exist . . . where does all the suffering go?" In addition, the novel concludes with an anguished prayer interspersed with the names of concentration camps: "And praised. *Auschwitz*. Be. *Maidanek*. The Lord. *Treblinka*. And praised. *Buchenwald*. Be. . . ." The last word, however, is less ambiguous:

> Yes, at times one's heart could break in sorrow. But often too, preferably in the evening, I can't help thinking that Ernie Levy, dead six million times, is still alive somewhere, I don't know where. . . . Yesterday, as I stood in the street trembling in despair, rooted to the spot, a drop of pity fell from above upon my face. But there was no breeze in the air, no cloud in the sky. . . . There was only a presence.

Critical Context

It is probable that the self-educated André Schwarz-Bart was influenced in the 1950's by the work of Jorge Luis Borges, and possible also that during that same period Gabriel García Márquez was influenced either by Schwarz-Bart or by similar literary tendencies, which have characterized much modern Latin American literature as well as its European counterpart.

Upon its publication, *The Last of the Just*, while provoking a teapot tempest of criticism, garnered the prestigious Prix Goncourt and major critical acclaim. Thereafter, it fell from notice: It was viewed as outside the French literary mainstream; as Holocaust literature, it was frequently considered in critical categories other than the literary.

Schwarz-Bart has since published, with his wife, two novels following *The Last of the Just*, *Un Plat de porc aux bananes vertes* (1967; a plate of pork with green bananas) and *La Mulâtresse Solitude* (1972; *A Woman Named Solitude*, 1973), each with a black woman as protagonist. In them, the authors bridge the centuries of Jewish agony and the Holocaust, and the centuries of black enslavement, with an explication and a perception of humanity's sufferings. *The Last of the Just* stands not merely as the first of a trilogy, however, but as a major work on its own merits, a work of French literature, of Jewish and Holocaust literature, and of modern Magical Realism.

Sources for Further Study

Adams, Phoebe. Review in *Atlantic Monthly*. CCVI (December, 1960), p. 120.

Kahn, Lothar. "The More Recent Writers," in *Mirrors of the Jewish Mind*, 1968.

Menton, Seymour. "*The Last of the Just*: Between Borges and García Márquez," in *World Literature Today*. LIX (Autumn, 1985), pp. 517-524.

Morton, Frederic. Review in *The New York Times Book Review*. LXV (October 23, 1960), p. 4.

Popkin, Henry. "Around a Prize-winner, a Paris Literary Storm," in *The New York Times Book Review*. LXIV (December 20, 1959), p. 1.

Marsha Kass Marks

THE LAST TEMPTATION OF CHRIST

Author: Nikos Kazantzakis (1883-1957)
Type of plot: Philosophical realism
Time of plot: A.D. 30-33
Locale: Jerusalem and the surrounding countryside
First published: Ho teleutaios peirasmos, 1955 (English translation, 1960)

> *Principal characters:*
> JESUS, a carpenter from Nazareth who assumes a messianic
>   role in and around Jerusalem
> MARY, Jesus' mother, who cares for Jesus' paralyzed father,
>   Joseph
> JUDAS ISCARIOT, a member of the Zealot faction, bent on
>   overthrowing Roman rule
> PETER, a fisherman who leaves his profession to become a
>   follower of Jesus
> SIMEON, a rabbi, the uncle of Jesus and father of Mary
>   Magdalene
> MARY MAGDALENE, a cousin of Jesus, a prostitute in the town
>   of Magdala
> MATTHEW, a tax collector who becomes a follower of Jesus
>   and begins writing about him while traveling with the
>   group of disciples

The Novel

The Last Temptation of Christ is a fictionalized account of the life and death of Jesus. In it, Nikos Kazantzakis concentrates on the human aspects of Christ, tracing his adult career from his departure from home in Nazareth, through his famous temptation in the desert and his public ministry in the company of his disciples, to his final passion and death. Jesus' life is seen as a perpetual conflict between temptations of the flesh or the intellect and the desires of the hero to fulfill his destiny as Savior.

The novel opens in Nazareth, where young Jesus the carpenter is being pursued by a demon whose identity is unclear: Is this tempter the Devil, or is it God? Wracked by uncertainty, Jesus continues his work—building crosses for the Romans to use to crucify Zealots who are trying to overthrow the invaders from the west.

Finally, uncertain how to reconcile the conflicting passions he feels within himself, Jesus leaves home. His wanderings take him to Magdala, where he confronts his cousin Mary, the village prostitute and daughter of the rabbi to whom Jesus often turns for advice. Their meeting is a crisis for Jesus, as Mary accuses him of spurning her and of avoiding his responsibilities to his mother and family. Dejected and confused, he travels into the desert, settling with a band of ascetic monks who want him to succeed their dying abbot as the leader of their commune. Realizing that to do so would be to abandon the world, Jesus leaves the monastery and wanders alone into the desert. There, the Tempter appears to him in various forms (a lion, a woman) and offers Jesus ease from his confusion, appealing first to his senses, then to his intellect. Jesus is able to reject these temptations.

Strengthened in his purpose to help save humankind, Jesus returns to Galilee and begins assembling his group of disciples. The ragtag collection of fishermen and ne'er-do-wells is willing in spirit but weak in intellectual prowess and lacking in determination in the face of obstacles. Only Judas, a Zealot who has been sent by his band to infiltrate the group and murder Christ, has inner strength. Once converted to Jesus' side, he alone has the courage to support his adopted master in a crisis.

The band travels throughout the villages near Jerusalem, moving toward the holy city as Christ comes to understand the meaning of the visions he has had: He must sacrifice himself to save humankind, to show them the way to achieve salvation for themselves. Those with whom he comes in contact are swept away by his sincerity and by his knowledge of both the Jewish Law and of human nature. Jesus establishes an especially close relationship with Mary and Martha, two women who take him into their homes and for whom he raises their brother Lazarus from the dead.

In Jerusalem, Jesus comes to the attention of the Jewish leaders, who see him as a threat. While the authorities plot to have Jesus killed, he is formulating his own plan: He takes Judas aside and asks for Judas' help in carrying out his destiny. Eventually, Jesus is taken into custody, condemned to death, and led to Golgotha to be crucified. On the cross, swooning in pain and suffering the last agonies of a man who believes that he may have been abandoned and condemned for naught, he suddenly finds himself freed, taken away, and allowed to live a full life, marrying and fathering children. In his advanced age, he meets an itinerant preacher, Paul of Tarsus, who argues with him about the differences between the life Jesus has led and the legend Paul is creating about Jesus in order to lead others into the growing fold over which Paul has sway. Jesus realizes that abandoning the cross was wrong— and, at that instant, he becomes aware that he has been dreaming and he is still on the cross. With a cry of triumph at overcoming this last temptation, he dies.

The Characters

Kazantzakis is at his most daring in his portrayal of characters in this novel. Drawing almost exclusively on biblical narratives, he transforms the participants in the drama of Christ's life and passion into men and women who possess twentieth century intellectual and psychological attributes. The format of the novel allows him to expand the sparse accounts found in the

Gospels and thereby achieve a certain complexity of characterization. As a result, the main figures in *The Last Temptation of Christ* appear to be more human than they do in the Bible—a quality that directly contributes to the controversy that has surrounded the novel since its original publication.

No character is more humanized than the hero of the work, Jesus. From the reader's first meeting with the young carpenter of Nazareth, Jesus is presented as a man uncertain of his future, afraid of the demands that God is placing on him, unsure if he is being called to greatness or simply being tempted by the Devil to commit the greatest of sins, that of pride. He also is tempted by desires of the flesh: The scene in which Jesus confronts his cousin Mary Magdalene in her home in Magdala, where she entertains male travelers, is overtly sensuous, forcing the reader to see how voluptuous the young woman can be and how much effort it takes for Jesus to resist her. It is Kazantzakis' special strength that he is able to present Jesus as a human being without appearing to be blasphemous, although readers who are uncomfortable with extrabiblical narratives may be disturbed by the portrait of Christ in this novel.

Kazantzakis is equally iconoclastic in his portrayal of the apostle Judas Iscariot. The villain of the biblical account of Christ's betrayal and crucifixion, Judas in *The Last Temptation of Christ* becomes a hero. A strong man committed to the overthrow of the Roman invaders in his homeland, Judas is the one apostle whom Christ can trust to help him redeem humankind through his death. At first Judas expects Jesus to lead a political revolution; eventually, however, he comes to accept the kind of redemption Jesus offers and the necessity of Christ's death. Thus, Judas' actions in turning Christ over to the Jewish authorities are portrayed as a necessary and admirable part in this drama of salvation. The relationship between these two characters dramatizes one of Kazantzakis' central philosophical ideas: that God needs human beings to complete the act of salvation, as much as human beings need God to be saved.

The women in the novel are portrayed in a fashion consistent with Kazantzakis' belief that woman is by her nature a temptation of the flesh that man must overcome if he is to be saved. Mary Magdalene is most clearly such a temptation. She entices Christ first with her body, then with pleas that he abandon his mission as Redeemer and settle down as a husband and father. Jesus' mother, Mary, and the sisters of Lazarus, Mary and Martha, offer similar temptations, encouraging Christ to be like other men, to achieve immortality by fathering children who will remember him and carry on his name.

A host of other characters appear in the novel in roles similar to those they have in the biblical narratives. The apostle Peter is a blustering, impetuous rouster whose genuine love for Jesus is matched in intensity only by his insistence on speaking before he thinks. The tax collector Matthew, who joins the Apostles after Christ befriends him, begins writing his narrative of Jesus' life and works, only to have Christ accost him for slanting the facts of his life to parallel the Old Testament prophesies. This, implies Kazantzakis, is how legends are made.

Themes and Meanings

As in his other works, Kazantzakis displays his basic belief in existential philosophy in *The Last Temptation of Christ*. The central theme of the novel is that of the suffering hero's struggle to achieve meaning for himself in a world where the meaning of existence is not clear. Though the characters are drawn from a religious work, readers should not confuse the religious aims of the biblical originals with the philosophical issues with which Kazantzakis' characters struggle. Kazantzakis himself describes his story as emblematic of the constant struggle between God and humans. Each individual, he posits, must rise above his or her animal nature to achieve "salvation"—that is, achieve the perfection that inheres in all human beings.

One of the major aims Kazantzakis sets for himself in *The Last Temptation of Christ* is to show how the Gospel story must grow and be adapted if it is to continue to be relevant. Thus, his Jesus is constantly challenging not only Old Testament values but also the accounts of miracles and parables as those have been handed down in the New Testament. For example, Jesus and Nathanael discuss the story of the wise and foolish virgins, which in the Bible ends with the foolish virgins being turned away from the wedding feast. Jesus forces Nathanael to acknowledge that true Christian spirit requires that these women be pardoned. That lesson and others like it characterize Kazantzakis' version of this Christ story.

The novel presents another theme central to Kazantzakis' outlook: As much as man needs God to be saved, so does God need man. Influenced by the German philosopher Friedrich Nietzsche, Kazantzakis attempts to explore the implications of Nietzsche's observation that "God is dead," that is, God is irrelevant now to those who no longer need the concept of the deity as an ideal or a motivator for doing good or living well, because that world has been rendered meaningless by the discoveries of science and psychology. Is it possible, Kazantzakis wonders through the characters and incidents of this novel, that the concept of God can be sustained in the modern world? To keep God "alive" as an inspirational force that will lead the majority to better themselves, there must be those people—Kazantzakis calls them heroes—who will perpetuate the ideals of, even the very notion of, God. This they must do even when they know that there is no certainty in belief, no guarantee of any salvation beyond death. Such iconoclastic ideology has been a source of difficulty for many who have attempted to confront Kazantzakis' works from traditional viewpoints, and many have turned away disappointed, even outraged, that the author has turned traditional religion on its head.

Critical Context

The Last Temptation of Christ is one of two novels in which Kazantzakis treats the theme of the suffering hero by relying on the outline of the Christ story. In the other, *Ho Christos xanastauronetai* (1954; *The Greek Passion*, 1953; also known as *Christ Recrucified*, 1954), he offers as his Christ figure a young Greek shepherd who is chosen to play Jesus in the annual passion play and who assumes the role in a more literal fashion. Both novels depict the struggle of the hero to overcome temptations of the flesh and achieve spiritual salvation. That theme dominates Kazantzakis' most famous novel, *Vios kai politela tou Alexe Zormpa* (1946; *Zorba the Greek*, 1953), which tells the story of an ascetically minded young man who comes to appreciate the joys of life through his relationship with the jack-of-all-trades Alexis Zorba.

As a retelling of the life of Jesus, *The Last Temptation of Christ* is part of a tradition that stretches back to medieval European literature. The dramatic differences between Kazantzakis' work and other novels are, however, significant. One need only compare *The Last Temptation of Christ* with Lloyd Douglas' *The Robe* (1942), which also has Christ for its hero, to see how little heed Kazantzakis pays to conventional attitudes toward biblical characters and situations.

Sources for Further Study

Chilson, Richard W. "The Christ of Nikos Kazantzakis," in *Thought: A Review of Culture and Ideas.* XLVII (1972), pp. 69-89.

Hoffman, Frederick J. *The Imagination's New Beginning: Theology and Modern Literature*, 1967.

Lea, James F. *Kazantzakis: The Politics of Salvation.* 1979.

Levitt, Morton P. *The Cretan Glance: The World and Art of Nikos Kazantzakis*, 1980.

Laurence W. Mazzeno

LAUGHTER IN THE DARK

Author: Vladimir Nabokov (1899-1977)
Type of plot: Ironic romance
Time of plot: The late 1920's or early 1930's
Locale: Berlin, the south of France, and Switzerland
First published: Kamera Obskura, 1932 (*Camera Obscura,* 1936; revised as
  Laughter in the Dark, 1938)

> *Principal characters:*
> ALBERT ALBINUS, a wealthy patron of the arts and minor art
>   critic
> MARGOT PETERS, a sometime artists' model, prostitute, and
>   cinema usherette, who becomes Albinus' mistress
> AXEL REX, an unsuccessful but talented artist, Margot
>   Peters' lover
> PAUL, Albinus' brother-in-law

The Novel

Albert Albinus, a bland wealthy supporter of the arts, happily married and the father of an eight-year-old daughter, Irma, whom he idolizes, lacks only one thing in his comfortable life: He has never experienced a grand sexual passion. The novel opens with Albinus about to embark on such an adventure, and the narrator announces in the first short paragraph that Albinus will abandon his wife for a mistress, that he will love her but will not be loved in return, and that his life will end in disaster.

After such dismissive contempt for the tradition of keeping the plot secret, the narrator tells the reader that Albinus has already met the woman who will be his downfall and is thinking vaguely of her, while also thinking about a film project using the services of an artist, Axel Rex, who is, as the novel begins, away in the United States. Rex will, ironically, be partially responsible for Albinus' final disaster.

Albinus has encountered a pretty young woman working as an usherette in a Berlin film house and has become infatuated with her. Margot Peters, whose life is aimless but filled with dreams of becoming a film star, takes up with Albinus, determined to use his money and connections to launch her career. She finds him attractive but does not love him, and she quickly draws him away from his wife and child, determined not only to make him pay for his pleasures but also to marry him, and later, if her film career is successful, to abandon him. Albinus, ashamed of his treatment of his family, is quite helpless and yet so deeply enchanted by Margot that he cannot resist her. He does finance a minor film in which Margot is given a secondary role, and they live together in his old apartment without any attempt on Margot's part to hide the impropriety of their relationship.

Rex, the wandering artist, appears, and impresses Albinus deeply. He is even more impressive to Margot, since he is, in fact, her first lover and the one man who has any power over her; they join forces to make use of Albinus for their mutual benefit. Rex pretends to have homosexual tastes in order to disarm any suspicions that Albinus may have about his attentions to Margot, and he is so charming and amusing that he joins the lovers on a vacation in France.

By chance, Albinus discovers the truth about Margot and Rex. Margot manages to convince her lover-victim that it is all a joke, but he refuses to stay with Rex, and in driving Margot away from their resort hotel, distressed and confused, he wrecks his car. Margot is only slightly injured, but Albinus is blinded, seemingly permanently. Margot takes him to a quiet Swiss chalet to recuperate. He does not realize that Rex has come along, having been informed that Rex has gone back to the United States. Albinus, fragile, depressed, and tormented by his suspicions of Margot, is helpless in her hands, and systematically the two conspirators coerce him into signing over large amounts of money to them and plan to cheat him into selling his property and paintings for their advantage. In a few months, they plan to abandon him, leaving him alone and penniless. Even more cruel is their mocking of the poor man before his very (sightless) eyes, and Rex is particularly amused at being in the same room with him, worrying him with faint noises and actions which Albinus cannot understand, since Margot assures him that only she attends him.

Albinus' brother-in-law comes to see him and reveals the trick. He takes Albinus back to Berlin and his forgiving wife, but Albinus is determined to kill Margot. He has a chance to do so when she returns to Berlin to sack his apartment, but in the scuffle between the blind, betrayed lover and the greedy mistress, Albinus' own gun is turned on him, and he is killed. Margot, seemingly unhurt, flees the room.

The Characters

The first paragraph, with its casual indifference to any pretense of realistic suspense, is the key to this novel. Nabokov is not interested in originality but in "making new" the age-old tale of the foolish, middle-aged male drawn to disaster by the heartless, gold-digging siren. Albinus fulfills all the qualifications for a bad film (in fact, his story often formed the plot of motion pictures of the 1920's and 1930's). Indeed, the film in which Margot so unsuccessfully acts has the same kind of lachrymose plot of sexual betrayal. Margot, reared in working-class squalor (with its hints of violence and vulgarity), cunning without being intelligent, and well aware of the monetary value of her brash prettiness, is Nabokov's deliberate parody of the film vamp, just as Albinus is the feckless, stupid "fool for love." When Albinus discovers the truth, he reacts as the film dupe would do: He is determined to blow out Margot's brains. The blind man groping silently for his victim in a closed room, the roar of the pistol, the scuffle to the death are all of a piece with the overripe cinema of the period. Significantly, the last words of the novel are set in the language of a motion-picture script.

Rex, however, is more than a simple parody of a cinema villain, and he is the most interesting character of the three. He is an artist of considerable talent and some reputation, and he is dangerously intelligent. Moreover, he is doubly connected in the love triangle: in the obvious way as Margot's lover and coconspirator, and also as the man with whom Albinus wants to work in bringing to film the idea, which he has taken from a novelist, Udo Conrad, of a cartoon in which great paintings can be animated. Rex is also a man with a philosophy of life and art, and it is his idea of manipulating life as if it were art that is to be the moving force in Albinus' ultimate tragedy. Albinus may be presumptuous in planning to turn fine art into the lesser art of cinema, but his ambitions pale before Rex's determination to turn life into art, as he does both before and after Albinus is blinded because it amuses him. In that arbitrary play with people's lives, he is more villainous than the film cads, who usually have some simple ambition behind their nastiness; as such, he—like Albinus and Margot—is also a parodic figure, but not a simple one, since a complicated intellectual structure informs his machinations.

Themes and Meanings

The relation between reality and art lies at the bottom of this peculiar manipulation of a banal tale of a wandering husband destroyed by his love for a worthless woman. From the beginning, Nabokov builds the story up to something more than its plot, and at the same time, tears it down, showing the reader that it is "just a story" with which he, as artist, can do as he pleases. Coincidence occurs throughout the novel, undermining its credibility. Conrad, the novelist, provides the idea which brings Albinus into contact with Rex, and later it is Conrad, met by chance, who precipitates Albinus' discovery of Rex's betrayal. Rex happens to be Margot's great love, although she does not know really who he is, or even where he is, until he suddenly appears at a dinner party given by Albinus. The poster outside the motion-picture theater in which Margot works prefigures Irma's experience of watching the man from the open window. There are several of these doublings, all placed cleverly, and without comment, throughout the novel. Indeed, this cleverness is part of the point of the novel, which uses a story that ought not to have any aesthetic power at all.

Real life is not romantic enough for Albinus; he must have the kind of romantic adventure which occurs only in films. Appropriately, he has modest connections with the films, Margot wants to be a film star, and Rex has the technical skills to provide Albinus with his dream film. It is, quite deliberately, too coincidental and too often full of cinematic echoes. The reader is made aware of the way in which Nabokov "dresses" the set, and the seemingly awkwardly and irrelevantly placed objects against which the characters act; Rex, in particular, cooperates with the author in manipulating the environment, much as a film director might do. Nabokov is exaggerating and pointing out the role of the author in making the tale as theatrical as possible. If Albinus wants drama in his life, he truly gets it, and then some: The agony is literally piled on at the death of his innocent daughter, who dies of natural causes but with a hint that she died of a broken heart while waiting to see her father; in the various ways he is betrayed and made a fool; in his accident and blindness; and in the ultimate cruel joke of his being killed by his own gun.

Nabokov makes art out of the fast shuffle of art and life, and where one begins and the other ends is unclear. If Albinus, the betrayer of the family, deserves his punishment, there is also a sense that he receives more than he deserves. Albinus, the man of feeling, comes up against Rex, the man of coldly amused sensations, and is torn to pieces. This result may be the obvious, simplistic moral of the story, but the reader is left with a nagging sense that such excessive punishment is almost irrelevant, that Nabokov does not really care about such a pious idea. In a sense, the title is a guide to the intellectual indifference that pervades the novel. Albinus is a fool to think that this young girl could love him, and his blind love makes it impossible for him to see the real relationship between Margot and Rex. Albinus is, in a sense, no blinder after his accident than he was before it.

The way in which Nabokov works out parallels and patterns is also important. Albinus wants to be an artist, but he must use another man's ideas, and he is not, as he thinks, even a very good critic of art. Rex is amused, for example, by the fact that one of his forgeries hangs in Albinus' house. Margot is also inclined to be an artist but proves to be a terrible actress. Rex has the talent, but not the determination, and he fritters away his gift in his cruel teasing of undistinguished Albinus.

Yet the pattern is complete only if Udo Conrad and Paul are remembered. It is Conrad's idea that Albinus would use, it is Conrad who sets Albinus on the scent of the guilty conspirators, and it is Conrad who lives a sober—even boring—life, making real art, rather than playing at it. Paul, the sensible, long-suffering, unattractive brother-in-law, rescues Albinus from the dream turned into a nightmare. Nevertheless, Albinus cannot resist the grand gesture of the romantic lover betrayed and is killed for his presumption.

Critical Context

Laughter in the Dark is a reworking of an earlier story, originally written in Russian and translated into English under the title *Camera Obscura*. That earlier tale is denser in detail than the later work, but it, too, explores the idea that fiction is not quite the same as reality, that there is always an aspect of parody to a work of art. Most writers attempt to hide the fact that they are imitating life; Nabokov often directs the reader's attention to the imitation. *Laughter in the Dark* uses variations of common devices seen in many of his works. The use of the fable frame, the love triangle, the interest in mixing art forms, the seeming disinterest in moral values, and the sophisticated slyness of the tale are all characteristic of Nabokov as storyteller. The old cliché that "love is blind" takes on a cruel edge of wittiness in the hands of this master of the proposition that the way in which the story is told is more important than the story itself. With this novel, Nabokov came to artistic maturity.

Laughter in the Dark is sometimes called one of the "dream" novels. It was followed by two other works in which dreams come true, and the consequences are not quite what was expected: *Otchayanie* (1936; *Despair*, 1937, revised 1966) and *Priglashenie na kazn'* (1938; *Invitation to a Beheading*, 1959). The idea of male infatuation of a forbidden, destructive kind is common in Nabokov, however, reaching its most famous expression in *Lolita* (1955).

Sources for Further Study

Appel, Alfred, Jr., and Charles Newman, eds. *Nabokov: Criticism, Reminiscences, Translations, and Tributes*, 1970.

Field, Andrew. *Nabokov: His Life in Art*, 1967.

Fowler, Douglas. *Reading Nabokov*, 1974.

Lee, L. L. *Vladimir Nabokov*, 1976.

Moynahan, Julian. *Vladimir Nabokov*, 1971.

Charles Pullen

THE LEFT-HANDED WOMAN

Author: Peter Handke (1942-   )
Type of plot: Philosophical realism
Time of plot: 1975-1976, from winter to spring
Locale: An unnamed city in West Germany
First published: Die linkshändige Frau, 1976 (English translation, 1978)

> *Principal characters:*
> MARIANNE, the woman of the title, a thirty-year-old
>   translator
> BRUNO, her husband, a sales manager for a porcelain firm
> STEFAN, their eight-year-old son
> JÜRGEN, Stefan's friend and schoolmate
> GRANDFATHER, Marianne's father, a writer, who comes to visit
> FRANZISKA, Marianne's friend and Stefan's schoolteacher
> ERNST, a publisher who gives Marianne employment
> THE CHAUFFEUR, Ernst's driver
> THE ACTOR, an unemployed film actor who falls in love with
>   Marianne
> THE SALESGIRL, who sells Marianne a sweater and later
>   attends Marianne's party

The Novel

Peter Handke tells the story of a woman determined to break with her husband and her past and to form a new life for herself. Marianne, a mother and hausfrau in her thirtieth year, begins to examine her life keeping house in the suburbs of a large industrial city in West Germany. Her husband, Bruno, who works as sales manager for a porcelain company, is due to return from an extended business trip to Scandinavia. Her eight-year-old son, Stefan, is a student who is working on an essay entitled "My Idea of a Better Life." The theme of his essay apparently becomes the theme of the novel. Since the story is told from a detached, objective, dramatic point of view, however, this possible connection is left for the reader to make.

Mother and son drive to the airport to meet the returning father. The story opens in winter, at an unspecified time after Christmas. Returning from Helsinki, the father is exhausted but happy to be back in Germany with his family. He explains that he was "afraid of going mad with loneliness" in Finland, where he did not understand the language.

Bruno's key statement introduces the contradictory logic that dominates the story. After telling his wife that he loves her and feels bound to her, he adds, "I now feel I could exist without you." The statement has more meaning for his wife than he might guess. There is a slight suggestion that Bruno might have been intimate with his German-speaking interpreter in Finland, "a woman with a child and no husband."

After sending their son to bed, Bruno takes his wife to a hotel for a festive dinner, then gets a room for the night. The next morning, the woman tells her husband about "a strange idea" she had, a discovery, an "illumination." The idea is that they should separate, that her husband should leave her. Surprised, Bruno agrees to a separation, thinking it may be only temporary.

The rest of the novel concerns the woman's attempt to adjust to her life as a single parent. She discusses her new status with her friend Franziska, who is also Stefan's schoolteacher. Marianne once worked as a translator at a publishing house and knows that she can earn money translating books. Franziska invites her to join a women's group, but when she approaches the group, she apparently is not interested. She is an enigmatic and private person. When Bruno comes to take his belongings, he begins to show resentment about his wife's decision. The child seems to be absolutely neutral concerning the separation.

Some days later, Bruno confronts his wife on the street as she, seeking employment, goes to mail a letter. He treats her roughly, shoving her into a telephone booth. He accuses her of being mentally ill, burns her photograph in protest, then offers her money. Back home, she rearranges her furniture, an attempt, presumably, to put her new life in order. Eventually, the publisher Ernst, a weary man of fifty for whom Marianne once worked, brings her the autobiography of a young Frenchwoman to translate at home.

Marianne and Stefan visit Bruno at his office, and Bruno shows his son how he intimidates people who come into his office. The husband's frustration is shown by the fact that "he hammer[s] his face with his fist" after they leave. Some time later Bruno visits Marianne at home and threatens to break down the door. He insults her in his anger, saying "I've never known a woman to make a lasting change in her life." Apparently he feels out of control and defeated by her resolve.

The everyday details of Marianne's new life alone are described meticulously: the long hours spent at her typewriter, the long walks she takes. She seems to be determined to master her loneliness on her own terms. Although Franziska urges her to attend one of the meetings of her women's support group, Marianne prefers to be alone. At times she is even irritated by the presence of her son and his fat friend Jürgen.

Marianne's father comes to visit. He was once a successful writer. They have their pictures taken and meet a man whom the father recognizes as an actor. He criticizes the unemployed actor for holding back and not taking risks, which may denote approval of his daughter's behavior. Some time after the father returns to his home, the woman again meets the actor, by chance, at a café. The actor is fascinated by Marianne and has been following her. He confides in her, perhaps following her father's advice about not holding back.

He confesses that he desires her, then runs from the café in embarrassment.

Bruno telephones one night to invite himself to Marianne's house with Franziska. Ernst also comes to call and is invited in with his chauffeur. Then a salesgirl from whom Marianne has purchased a sweater for Bruno, arrives. The actor is also invited. A fight breaks out between the jealous Bruno and the actor, who is sitting in Bruno's chair. Later on, they reconcile, play Ping-Pong, then leave together.

The party ends, the guests leave, and Marianne reflects to herself: "You haven't given yourself away. And no one will ever humiliate you again." The novel ends with an epilogue from Johann Wolfgang von Goethe, stating that "one goes on living as though nothing were wrong."

The Characters

Handke's characters are fairly conventional but extremely abstract and oddly presented in a detached and absolutely external manner. In fact, the novelist, who had previously written two film scripts for Wim Wenders—including the script adapted from his own novel *Die Angst des Tormanns beim Elfmeter* (1970; *The Goalie's Anxiety at the Penalty Kick*, 1972)—first imagined his story as a motion picture and went on to direct a film version.

The novel, which differs in some particulars of setting and action from the film, was written as a challenge. As Handke has explained in his notes for the film production, "I wanted to try a kind of prose in which the thinking and feeling of the individual characters would never be described—in which, instead of 'she was afraid,' the reader would find; 'she left,' 'she walked over to the window,' 'she lay down next to the child's bed.' . . . —And I felt this form of limitation actually acted as a liberating force on my literary work."

The reader senses the psychology behind the characters' motivation, in spite of the generally dramatic framework, stripped of soliloquizing or internal monologues. At first the characters are simply described by function: the woman, the boy, the schoolteacher, the publisher, the actor, and so on. The woman's name is not mentioned in the first quarter of the narrative. The publisher's name is not given until the last quarter.

Despite this purposeful detachment, the characters are vividly delineated. Bruno, the husband, is very traditional in his understanding of his role as husband and father. An establishment figure, his politics tend toward the right wing; his business affairs have conditioned him to intimidate other people; in dealing with frustration, his tendency is to become abusive, first toward Marianne, later toward the actor, whom he considers a rival.

The narrative is totally lacking in sentiment. Marianne's "strange idea" of liberating herself from a domineering husband, her "illumination," as she calls it, causes her to redefine her other relationships as well. Her friend Franziska and, later, the actor offer her companionship, but she prefers to be a loner and hold to her own notion of independence. The actor's sentimental desire to possess her is no more appealing than her husband's advances when he returns from Finland in the novel's opening section.

She is not entirely antisocial, however, as shown at the party in the novel's closing section, but she is determined that the people who gather at her home be on an equal footing. For that reason, the publisher's chauffeur is invited as an equal. As he says to his employer at the party, "[t]omorrow you won't speak to me anyway." Marianne gives the man a taste of liberation.

Marianne has a talent for breaking down barriers between other people, but she will not give herself away and she will only accept people on her own terms. At the end of the novel, after her visitors have left, she articulates this point, adding, "no one will ever humiliate you again." Before, Bruno treated her as a possession and humiliated her in public. She has now redefined her life, purposefully, choosing loneliness as a consequence of independence.

The other characters exist only to give definition to Marianne and her rebirth. The boy is cared for, but there seems to be no close sentimental attachment between mother and son. Handke offers a bleak design for living in this story, strongly suggesting that self-dependency is necessary to lead a well-balanced life in the industrial world. The novel's title (which is never explained in the text) would seem to be ironic, attaching the stigma of social awkwardness to Marianne, who first seems to be a withdrawn, social misfit. Despite the apparent bleakness of her chosen life, however, as critic J. Hoberman wrote, the story is strangely "affirmative, without being sentimental." There is something admirable in Marianne's strength of character.

Themes and Meanings

The themes of Handke's novel are independence, integrity, loneliness, self-preservation, and dignity. Although written by a man, *The Left-Handed Woman* is very much a woman's story, convincing, no doubt, because the themes transcend gender. Marianne apparently has not been abused by her husband before she decides to leave him, but she has not been allowed much justification for self-respect in her married life. She seems determined to prove herself.

Though Handke is careful not to reveal Marianne's feelings, one supposes that there may be some personal satisfaction as a consequence of her finding employment and being able to provide for herself and her son. She is also able to establish relationships on her own terms after her liberation. She rises above emotional ties to her father, her son, her closest friend, her ex-husband, and the actor who is enamored of her.

Once she has liberated herself from male dominance, she avoids emotional entanglements. She extends friendship, but that is all. Her editor, an older man, seems to respect her. She earns that respect from the reader as well, for she has acted courageously. There is no evidence that she has thought through her position, but that is partly a consequence of the novel's point of view. She appears to behave on instinct. The mystery of human motivation is therefore established and maintained, to the degree that the novel conveys an almost documentary feeling, except that the subject never confides in others. That is the source of her mystery; that is the cause of the reader's fascination. She neither seeks nor accepts support. Her privacy is inviolate and protected.

Critical Context

Peter Handke may be regarded as an avant-garde inconoclast reacting against accepted narrative traditions and criticizing the complacency of the generation of German writers who preceded him. Handke first gained notoriety in 1966 when he challenged the "realistic" achievements of the prestigious Gruppe 47 writers who represented the establishment. Distrustful of language and of conventional notions of reason, Handke's early works were an assault against the literary establishment of his time. His plays, one of which bears the title "Offending the Audience," were antitheatrical *Sprechstücke* (literally, pieces of speech) that assailed time-honored conventions of drama.

His first novel, *Die Hornissen* (1966; the hornets), was recognized as a German equivalent of the French New Novel and enhanced his reputation as an experimental writer. In addition, his alliance with Wim Wenders connected him with a new generation of filmmakers who were revitalizing the German cinema.

For Handke, characters take precedence over the story being told. Interviewed in 1979, he said "What is 'story' or 'fiction' is really always only the point of intersection between individual daily events." He described narrative as "an 'I' . . . writing a narrative poem about the time in which he lives, about the self, and about others."

The psychology of the central characters of both *The Goalie's Anxiety at the Penalty Kick* and *The Left-Handed Woman* is irrational and mysterious, but, unlike Marianne, the central character of *The Goalie's Anxiety at the Penalty Kick* is apparently quite mad. Both characters, however, are responsible for their extreme actions, and both are threatened by the consequences.

Because Handke distrusts language and its deceptive nature, his writing is sparse and primarily descriptive and his point of view dramatic or objective, with the narrator assuming the perspective of a mobile film camera, picturing the action, but not interposing to mediate or to interpret the story or the characters for the reader.

Novelist John Updike has noted that Handke writes "from an area beyond psychology," and the point is well taken, if a little obscure. Handke does not put the reader in touch with the minds of his characters, but he does suggest something about Marianne's psychology through what she says and through the way she responds to what she reads (while translating the autobiography of a Frenchwoman, not unlike herself) and to what others say. Though motives are not fully explained, the advantage is that psychology is not simplified to banal and manageable levels.

Writing in *The Yale Review*, Maureen Howard described *The Left-Handed Woman* as "a tale of modern perversity," a "novel about the unsaid," documenting "solitary pain" and "deranged loneliness." Howard claims that the characters lose their names as their identities recede in the mind of the central character, but one could argue the opposite, for as Marianne (who is not herself named until the narrative is well in progress) comes to grips with her new identity and her existential rebirth, those characters who are meaningful to her are called by their Christian names. Bruno is always Bruno, moreover, and Franziska, her closest friend, is always Franziska.

The stance is one of defensive integrity, an ideal that is approached toward the end, as Marianne grows into her intense individualism and her sense of self-preservation eclipses the danger of self-destruction. At the novel's end, Marianne seems relatively in control of her life, having found employment and having advanced beyond the self-doubts that accompanied her decision to separate from her husband. Reading this novel requires more than a little patience, but the work is extremely well crafted, and the development goes beyond the potential banality of another mid-life crisis. Handke is able to take an ordinary life and make it interesting.

Sources for Further Study

Gray, Paul. "A Formidable and Unique Austerity," in *Time*. CXIV (June 19, 1978), p. 80.

Hoberman, J. "*The Left-Handed Woman*," in *The Village Voice*. XXV (April 7, 1980), p. 27.

Howard, Maureen. "*The Left-Handed Woman*," in *The Yale Review*. LXVIII, no. 3 (March, 1979), pp. 439-441.

Klinkowitz, Jerome, and James Knowlton. *Peter Handke and the Postmodern Transformation*, 1983.

Pawel, Ernest. "Sleeping Beauty as a Housewife," in *The New York Times Book Review*. LXXXIII (June 18, 1978), p. 10.

Updike, John. "Northern Europeans: Discontent in *Deutsch*," in *Hugging the Shore: Essays and Criticism*, 1983.

James M. Welsh

LETTER TO LORD LISZT

Author: Martin Walser (1927-   )
Type of plot: Social realism
Time of plot: Mid-June, the early 1980's
Locale: Southwest Germany, near Lake Constance
First published: Brief an Lord Liszt, 1982 (English translation, 1985)

> *Principal characters:*
> FRANZ HORN, a department head at Chemnitz Dentures
> ARTHUR THIELE, the owner of Chemnitz Dentures and Fin
>   Star
> DR. HORST LISZT, Horn's colleague and rival

The Novel

Written six years after *Jenseits der Liebe* (1976; *Beyond All Love,* 1982), this short novel returns to the main character of that earlier work, Franz Horn. Here and in the previous work, Martin Walser studies the psyche of a moderately successful contemporary businessman. Horn is no economic dynamo; in fact, he considers himself worthless when compared to his more successful rivals—and in this case, everyone is a rival. Horn bemoans the fact that the only two men who could be his friends are his boss, Arthur Thiele, and his rival, Dr. Horst Liszt.

On the Friday before the Whitsuntide holiday, the department heads of Chemnitz Dentures are called together for an announcement of the suicide of their main competitor, Benedikt Stierle. Since Franz Horn hoped to quit his job and apply for a position with Stierle, this event occasions his reflections on his life and work as set forth in a letter (with nineteen separate postscripts) to his colleague and rival, Dr. Liszt.

Expected at his mother's home for her name-day celebration (his wife and daughters await his arrival), Horn is incapable of movement. He slumps at his desk and begins a letter of apology to Liszt, citing their most recent disagreement at a local inn while waiting for Arthur Thiele to pick them up in his sailboat. From Horn's behavior and responses on that day, it has become evident to Liszt that Horn has never liked him; as they are leaving the restaurant, Horn insists on separate taxis, an obvious insult to Liszt. Liszt himself must always be in the right, must constantly project his personality over his subordinates and colleagues, hence the appellation "Lord" in the title.

Since Liszt has not responded in the intervening week to Horn's apologetic note, Horn now wishes to write again, pleading for forgiveness. Yet as night progresses and the letter grows in volume, Horn clarifies for Liszt (and for himself) the true nature of their relationship. They have not been friends, but in the light of the coming merger of their small company with the giant Bayer conglomerate, perhaps they should now band together for their mutual protection and survival.

The letter and its numerous postscripts gradually reveal the recent chronology of Horn's life: his position at the Internal Revenue Service prior to assuming the new post with Chemnitz Dentures; his immediate rise to favor with Arthur Thiele; his estrangement and departure from his wife and two daughters, followed by an eventual suicide attempt; and, finally, his rehabilitation over the past four years, including the adversarial relationship with Liszt. Now the impending merger and subsequent division of personnel threaten Horn's vulnerable ego and precarious security. The inner circle will move with Thiele to concentrate on the new factory for surfboards, while the expendables will remain at the present site under the observation of efficiency experts, who will soon discover that Horn sleeps at his desk while Liszt drinks at his; that both will thus soon be replaced is obvious to Horn.

Following this all-night exertion, Horn finds that he can neither send the letter to Liszt nor bring himself to destroy it. He finally files it away in a secret drawer and, relieved, discovers that he can now continue his life. He showers and gets in the car for the early morning drive to his mother's, ready to celebrate her name day properly.

The Characters

As an isolated work, *Letter to Lord Liszt* will perplex most readers, for its main, in effect its only, character is briefly sketched here. In Walser's earlier work *Beyond All Love*, Franz Horn's personality was solidly established, his life and increasing difficulties thoroughly portrayed, including the unsuccessful suicide attempt. For a reader without benefit of the earlier novel, Horn's present dilemma will require attention to detail and nuance; even then, its meaning may escape the reader's comprehension, for the work is short and the narrative perspective enigmatic.

Franz Horn is a complex character, competent yet full of self-hate. As the product of an unsophisticated, petty bourgeois family, he inherited all the motivation for success but none of the requisite confidence in his abilities. His self-esteem is therefore nonexistent and must be created or substantiated through his work. That this approach has not been successful can be seen in his suicide attempt; on that fateful evening, he was, unfortunately, saved by his boss, Arthur Thiele, and thus is further in Thiele's debt and in his shadow. In the intervening years since the suicide attempt, Horn seems to have mellowed somewhat, though he can no longer create a positive self-image through achievement. He is pushed aside in the firm, first by Liszt and then by the merger and impending reorganization of the firm; also, with Stierle's death, a comparable and desirable position has disappeared.

Horn rationalizes that it is not ability but attitude and personality that determine success in business. One must willingly defer to one's superior so that the individual's successes are primarily attributed to the boss. One must also have a personality in harmony with the expectations of those with whom one works. Horn has long been troubled by the disparity between his own sense of himself and the image that his fellow workers have constructed of him; his strongest desire is to cultivate a personality that reflects his innate attitudes while simultaneously mirroring those traits perceived by his colleagues.

Yet self-realization and economic competition do not lend themselves to a harmonious resolution. Horn can find no way out of his dilemma; in fact, he is paralyzed by its growing intensity. He is no longer capable of suicide, yet he can find no viable alternative. Instinctively, he grasps for paper and pen, initially to grovel once again at Liszt's feet. With each succeeding page, however, he gains perspective and courage, while describing his problems more accurately. He is, moreover, not alone, for Liszt will soon be in the same predicament within the firm.

Finally, Horn arrives at the letter's conclusion, or at least at the final postscript. With each addendum, he has more clearly defined his life. He gradually gains the strength to curse, to revolt, and to hate as well as to love—and eventually to accept his existence, come what may. His letter to Liszt serves several purposes: It is an apology and an explanation of what has occurred and what is about to occur within their professional lives; consequently, it is Horn's personal enlightenment and, perhaps, salvation; and, ultimately, it is an attempt to reach out, as an equal, to his long-standing rival, so that they can brave the storm together.

Themes and Meanings

Since the novella is basically a monologue (comprising Horn's long letter, the postscripts, and a minimum of narrative text), the reader has primarily one point of reference: Franz Horn. Horn recalls incidents and conversations, presumes individuals' reactions, and even fictionalizes certain events (the two floating saints and the fantasy of Gerhild and Viktor, for example). It is uncertain whether his perceptions are accurate, whether Horn is telling the truth. The reader is forced to accept basic events as given and must interpolate the rest. The question is constantly present: How self-serving and how objective are Horn's statements?

The irony of this letter lies partly in the fact that it is neither sent nor destroyed; it exists, therefore, only for Horn, its author, the only person who is aware of it. The letter seems to serve the function of literature as therapy, a concept Walser himself has repeatedly proclaimed as his own motivation for writing. In this regard, the act of expressing one's troubles, of writing them down, can be therapeutic; once verbalized, the problems have been distanced from their author, and the author is less vulnerable to them. Conversely, to digest such a confession can also be cathartic for the reader, for through such an experience the reader, too, gains greater objectivity in his own, similar problems. Hence, one must be curious about this letter's possible benefits for Liszt, if he is indeed experiencing the stress that Horn posits.

A further irony, however, lies in the characters' relationships to one another. Just as Horn had replaced a Mr. Bull in the firm by making him a laughingstock, so Liszt displaced Horn several years before this novel begins. The reader is led to suspect that Liszt is experiencing the same fate in the presence of the Austro-Finn Rynännen, Thiele's latest prodigy. Thus a letter such as Horn's could have been written by any number of people under like conditions in this firm. Indeed, Walser presents a strong case that similar stress may occur at any time and on a widespread basis; he has established a cycle that appears to be endless in the booming European business climate, and its consequences may prove destructive to sensitive souls such as Franz Horn.

Critical Context

Martin Walser has admitted that all of his fictional works are located in his native region (approximately the triangle between Stuttgart, Zurich, and Munich) and therefore could justifiably be considered "regional literature." Among the most notable are several novel cycles, each revolving around a recurring main character, such as the so-called Kristlein trilogy, which features Anselm Kristlein and comprises *Halbzeit* (1960; half-time), *Das Einhorn* (1966; *The Unicorn*, 1971), and *Der Sturz* (1973; the crash). The work at hand belongs to yet another cycle, which portrays three male relatives as they grapple with their respective mid-life crises: Gottlieb Zürn of *Das Schwanenhaus* (1980; *The Swan Villa*, 1982), Xavier Zürn in *Seelenarbeit* (1979; *The Inner Man*, 1984), and Franz Horn of *Beyond All Love* and *Letter to Lord Liszt*. Since Walser frequently describes aspects of his own life in his fiction, the reader should be alert to—and may possibly be amused by—autobiographical details.

While both Xavier and Gottlieb Zürn struggle successfully to overcome their insecurities, constipation, and inertia, Franz Horn must deal with an existential crisis of great magnitude, as evidenced by his suicide attempt. Because his self-hate is so extensive and his attitude so pessimistic, the two works in which he is the main character have not received as much popular or critical acclaim as the others. These two works are so extreme that they preclude most readers' identification with Horn's fate. Because of their unremitting seriousness, Walser's immensely successful use of irony, his optimism, and his light sense of humor are absent here.

Not politically active like his contemporaries Heinrich Böll and Günter Grass, Martin Walser has, in fact, subdued his early social criticism; as a result, several critics have declared that Walser does not want to risk his popularity as a writer of politically harmless best-sellers. In spite of these attacks, Walser is arguably one of the most widely known contemporary German writers, especially for his recent depictions of middle-aged males and their inner lives. Since the mid-1970's, Walser's fiction has grown increasingly popular, while spawning a growing body of critical literature as well. His insights into human nature have produced many unforgettable characters, and his almost casual narrative style has attracted an international audience. Several of his works have been adapted for the screen, and his novella *Ein fliehendes Pferd* (1978; *Runaway Horse*, 1980) is already considered a classic of the genre.

Sources for Further Study

Doane, Heike A. "Martin Walsers Ironiebegriff," in *Monatshefte*. LXXVII (1985), pp. 195-212.

Kaes, Anton. "Porträt Martin Walser," in *The German Quarterly*. LVII (1984), pp. 432-449.

Parkes, K. S. "Crisis and New Ways: The Recent Development of Martin Walser," in *New German Studies*. I (1973), pp. 85-98.

Parkes, Stuart. "Martin Walser: Social Critic or *Heimatkünstler?*" in *New German Studies*. X (1982), pp. 67-82.

Thomas, R. Hinton. "Martin Walser: The Nietzsche Connection," in *German Life and Letters*. XXXV (1982), pp. 319-328.

Waine, Anthony Edward. *Martin Walser*, 1980.

Todd C. Hanlin

THE LIFE AND EXTRAORDINARY ADVENTURES OF PRIVATE IVAN CHONKIN
and PRETENDER TO THE THRONE

Author: Vladimir Voinovich (1932-   )
Type of plot: Sociopolitical satire
Time of plot: Summer, 1941
Locale: Krasnoe, a fictive village in rural Russia
First published: Zhizn i neobychainye priklyucheniya soldata Ivana Chonkina,
    1975 (English translation, 1977); *Pretendent na prestol,* 1979 (English
    translation, 1981)

> *Principal characters:*
> IVAN CHONKIN, the eponymous hero, who is sent to the village
>   of Krasnoe to guard a small plane
> NYURA BELYASHOVA, the postmistress and Chonkin's lover
> IVAN GOLUBEV, the chairman of the collective farm
> KUZMA GLADISHEV, a pseudoscientist who is raising hybrid
>   potato-tomato plants
> CAPTAIN MILYAGA, the head of the local "Institution" or
>   "Right Place" (a euphemism for the NKVD, the precursor
>   to the KGB)
> LIEUTENANT FILIPPOV, the man who replaces Milyaga
> MAJOR FIGURIN, the man who replaces Filippov
> KAPITOLINA "KAPA" GORYACHEV, the NKVD secretary and
>   the paramour of Milyaga and Figurin
> BORIS ERMOLKIN, the editor of *Bolshevik Tempos*
> PAVEL EVPRAKSEIN, a prosecutor

The Novels

Vladimir Voinovich's novel *The Life and Extraordinary Adventures of Private Ivan Chonkin* and its sequel, *Pretender to the Throne,* are caustic satires of Soviet-Russian society which lampoon the labyrinthine bureaucracy, banalities, and ineptness of the NKVD, the forerunner of the KGB, the Soviet "secret" police.

After a small plane of the Soviet Air Force makes a forced landing on a field near the village of Krasnoe, Ivan Chonkin, a soldier, is dispatched to Krasnoe to guard the plane. Chonkin is a poor excuse for a soldier, with his short torso, jug ears, and peasant physiognomy. His posting, however, serves the double purpose of getting rid of an untrainable recruit and a potentially embarrassing situation, for Chonkin has already incurred the wrath of his unit's political commissar for asking, in the presence of others, whether Joseph Stalin has had two wives.

Chonkin, however, proves to be a true soldier and diligently and conscientiously guards the plane. After a few days, having exhausted his meager rations, he ventures toward the outskirts of the village and strikes up a conversation with Nyura Belyashova, the local postmistress. Nyura takes a liking to him, and soon the two become lovers. In order to guard the plane and, at the same time, be near his Nyura, Chonkin pulls the light plane, with Nyura's help, into her garden.

Despite his blissful life with Nyura, Chonkin is concerned that he has not received any further orders from headquarters. With this in mind, therefore, he turns to Nyura's neighbor for advice. Kuzma Gladishev is known in the village as a learned man, for he not only reads books but also engages in scientific research: He grows hybrid plants whose roots, supposedly, will produce potatoes and its branches, tomatoes. Gladishev's garden is taken up by these mysterious plants, which are fertilized with a concoction of animal and human feces. Gladishev's house is permeated by the abominable smell of this nutritive nostrum, which he keeps in jars, despite the constant fretting and fuming of his wife.

When Chonkin comes to his house, Gladishev shows him his plants, and Chonkin, in all the simplicity and naïveté which had caused him trouble earlier, asks Gladishev whether the same plants can also be made to produce tomatoes on the bottom and potatoes on the top. Gladishev, however, considers the question not stupid but challenging and proceeds to help Chonkin, his newfound friend who appreciates "scientific" problems. Together they draft a letter to Chonkin's superiors requesting further clarification of his situation as well as additional rations and a new uniform.

In the meantime, Ivan Golubev, the chairman of the local *kolkhoz* (collective farm), suspecting that Chonkin is not merely a simple soldier but rather a government agent planted to spy on the locals and uncover Golubev's unsavory deals, decides to visit Chonkin and confront the "spy." When he enters Nyura's house and greets Chonkin, Golubev notices on the table Chonkin's letter to headquarters, which Chonkin has not mailed yet. The letter confirms Golubev's suspicions that Chonkin has written a report on the questionable practices and deception of the *kolkhoz* staff regarding the annual grain harvest and milk production. Golubev returns to his office and resigns himself to the fate that awaits him: prison. He does not despair, however, for in prison he will have three meals a day, and the government will take care of him.

When Nyura returns home from her mail route, she finds Chonkin's letter and tells him that she will mail it for him. She never mails it, however, fearing that headquarters may order Chonkin to another post and that she will lose her beloved. Thus life continues, until Chonkin, upset by rumors that before his arrival Nyura was sleeping with Borka, her hog, has an argument with her and leaves, once again taking up his post at the plane. Nyura tries to convince him of the stupidity of such malicious rumors but to no avail.

Meanwhile, rumors that the Germans have invaded the Soviet Union be-gin to circulate in the village of Krasnoe. Everyone panics, not so much out of fear or ideological concern, but because of greed and concern about indi-vidual welfare: The peasants want to hoard and stock supplies of necessities for the duration of the war. The provisions of the local store are up for grabs, with the villagers engaging in a melee of slapstick dimensions. During this fracas, Chonkin and Nyura find themselves under a heap of human bodies vying for bars of soap and cubes of sugar. The encounter rekindles their love, and once more Chonkin moves in with Nyura.

One day, Nyura asks Chonkin to fetch her cow from the field. On his way, he is distracted by the loudspeakers announcing that the Germans have actu-ally invaded the country. Because of the announcement and subsequent dis-cussion among the villagers, Chonkin forgets his errand and returns home to face an angry Gladishev, whose plants have been trampled and devoured by the cow. Chonkin tries to calm and mollify Gladishev by promising to replant the garden, without success. Gladishev is ready for revenge: He writes an anonymous letter to the local "Right Place" (a euphemism for the NKVD), accusing Chonkin of being a deserter and a hooligan.

Having read Gladishev's letter, Captain Milyaga, the head of the Right Place, dispatches Lieutenant Filippov with six men to Krasnoe to arrest Chonkin. When the seven men arrive, they find Chonkin guarding the plane. Chonkin challenges them and warns that he will shoot if they come near his post. Eventually, Chonkin, with the help of Nyura, takes all seven men pris-oner, ties them up, and locks them up in the house. He and Nyura take turns watching the captives. After a few days, not having heard from Filippov, Milyaga decides to look into the Chonkin affair himself and rides out to Krasnoe. When he arrives at Nyura's house, he too is taken prisoner by the overzealous Chonkin.

Several days later, the district secretary of the Communist Party calls Milyaga and learns that Milyaga has disappeared. This mystery, coupled with rumors of advancing German troops, prompts the secretary to investigate. Rumors have it that Milyaga and his soldiers have fallen victims to "the Chonkin gang," a dangerous group which is quite active in the area. Immedi-ately, the secretary contacts the army. A regiment is sent to deal with the Chonkin gang.

In the meantime, after a drinking bout of epic proportions with Golubev, who has now befriended him, Chonkin falls asleep; Milyaga escapes. As Milyaga runs toward safety, however, he is knocked out by a soldier from the regiment which was sent to deal with Chonkin's gang. Thinking that the un-conscious man might be a German spy, the regiment's commander directs one of his subordinates to interrogate Milyaga in German. Confronted with a Russian lieutenant speaking in German, Milyaga believes that he has been captured by an advance German unit, musters his best high school German, and answers in kind. The Russian lieutenant, whose knowledge of German is rudimentary to say the least, is convinced that Milyaga is actually Milleg (a Germanized form of the name Milyaga). His convictions are strengthened when Milyaga, in his attempt to ingratiate himself with the "German" interrogator, yells "Heil Hitler and death to Stalin." The regimental commander, now convinced that Milyaga is a spy, has him shot.

Meanwhile, a hilarious battle rages around Nyura's house, as an entire regiment tries to encircle Chonkin. Finally, Chonkin is subdued and taken prisoner. When General Drinov, the commander of the operation, realizes that Chonkin was rightfully guarding the plane as ordered and has kept the regiment at bay by himself, he decorates Chonkin for heroism. Later, however, Drinov rescinds the decoration when Filippov shows him the warrant for Chonkin's arrest. Chonkin is taken away to prison, all the while reassuring Nyura that he will be back.

In *Pretender to the Throne*, the reader finds Chonkin languishing in prison, futilely trying to convince his incredulous fellow inmates of his adventures and his heroic defense of the plane. Official correspondence regarding Chonkin's fate is indecisive, and the case is shelved, for the war is now of more importance. Nevertheless, Nyura will not let the case rest and mounts a personal campaign to free Chonkin, who is, as Nyura's expanding girth testifies, an expectant father. Her inquiries, however, lead her into a bureaucratic nightmare, and she is shunted from one important person to another. Her queries become suspect, for no one raises questions without an ulterior motive. Consequently, the diligent Filippov, who after the ignominious death of Milyaga became the head of the district secret police, scrupulously pursues Chonkin's case and reopens the soldier's file. During his investigation, Filippov learns that Chonkin was also known in his village as the "prince," the apellation deriving from the fact that his mother had become pregnant by a young officer named Golitsyn soon after the Russian Revolution. This Golitsyn was somehow related to the venerable Russian family of princes of the same name, and when Chonkin was born the villagers, in jest, called him prince. It is this "fact" that heightens Filippov's suspicions that Chonkin might be a despicable blue blood and an enemy of the people. Filippov's subsequent reports become a catalyst for a maze of suspicion, to such an extent that even Stalin learns about the "prince," while in his wartime headquarters deep inside Moscow's subway tunnels. The secret police are so convinced that Chonkin is truly a prince that his name is erased and replaced by the name Golitsyn in the records.

In the meantime, a German agent named Kurt (curiously called "Hans" in the English translation) is reputed to be working in the Krasnoe area. One rumor leads to another, and Filippov is accused, unjustifiably, of being the German agent. He is forced to sign his "confession" and then is summarily shot as an "enemy of the people." Major Figurin replaces Filippov as head of the local secret police and immediately sets out to restore the dignity of the police by declaring Milyaga to be a true Soviet hero. Soldiers are sent to locate his remains, but since they cannot find them, they return with a casket filled with the bones of a horse. During the funeral procession, Boris Ermolkin, one of the pallbearers, trips and falls, the casket comes open, and the horse's bones are spilled out onto the pavement. Figurin nevertheless decrees that the horse's elongated skull is truly that of Milyaga, and his "remains" are buried in all solemnity.

Meanwhile, the hysteria of the witch-hunt for enemies of the people continues, and many citizens are incarcerated and "confess" to their crimes. Finally, Chonkin himself is brought to trial; Pavel Evpraksein, the prosecutor, accuses him of being an agent of the Germans and the defunct royal family, because he is, after all, a prince. Chonkin is condemned to death and returned to his cell. The Germans are informed by their agent in place that a certain prince with pro-German sentiments is languishing in prison. Adolf Hitler orders his armies to circumvent Moscow—their original target—and save the prince, whom Hitler will then install on the throne of Russia. At the same time, Drinov, the general who had earlier decorated Chonkin, leads his division against the Germans reportedly camping outside Moscow. He does not know, however, that the German army has obeyed Hitler's orders; when he arrives, he finds no Germans. Drinov attributes this absence to a natural fear of Russians on the part of the Germans. The Russians celebrate their "victory," and Drinov is invited to Stalin's subterranean headquarters and is decorated. Drinov's pangs of conscience urge him to tell Stalin about the heroism of a simple Russian soldier: Ivan Chonkin. Since by now the name Chonkin has been replaced officially by that of Golitsyn the Prince, Stalin, unaware of the connection, directs Beria, the NKVD chief, to order Chonkin's release.

When Figurin returns to his office, he finds a note from Kapitolina, his secretary, who confesses that she was the German agent. He also finds two sets of conflicting orders: one to execute and another to release Chonkin. Calling headquarters to assess the situation, Figurin hears German voices on the line. Realizing that the Germans have taken over the district, he decides to flee, but, true to his bureaucratic soul, he orders one of his subordinates to let Chonkin go, with the understanding that the subordinate will then kill the escaping Chonkin. Thus both conflicting orders will be followed.

Figurin's subordinate, however, has a change of heart and lets Chonkin go without harming him. Chonkin eventually makes his way to Krasnoe to see Nyura. When he arrives, he is taken by surprise: In front of the *kolkhoz* office stands a German officer, who is addressing the gathered villagers; next to the German, with his legs planted far apart, is Gladishev, clapping his hands. Chonkin backs away and leaves the village.

The Characters

Although the characters seem to be merely caricatures of real human beings, they do lend an epic aura, for Voinovich does not stress plot development; instead, he concentrates on the characters and lets them act and speak for themselves in much the same manner as Homer had done in his epics. The plot is simple: In the village of Krasnoe (the Russian word for "red"; the village serves as a microcosm of the Soviet Union), there suddenly appears a soldier who becomes the unwitting catalyst to the unmasking of the characters with whom, directly or indirectly, he comes in contact. Voinovich's characters become the victims of their own greed, ineptness, or paranoia. Just as Homer's heroes are thematic—they represent human strengths and weaknesses, virtues and vices—so Voinovich's characters unveil their paranoia, chicanery, greed, and absurdities. Gladishev, with his hybrid potatotomato, is a mockery of the agronomist Trofim Lysenko, whose spurious theories on genetics crippled Soviet science during the 1940's and 1950's.

In Boris Ermolkin, the editor of the *Bolshevik Tempos*, Voinovich parodies the Soviet bureaucrat who, in deference to canonical Communism and an unequivocal belief in Stalin, has abandoned his family; like a recluse, he works endless hours editing in his office. His is an isolated, monastic existence, not much different from the secluded life of medieval monks copying and correcting liturgical texts in their cells. Furthermore, when Ermolkin faces temptation, in the form of a young lady of negotiable virtue, he dispels the evil and cleanses his soul by yelling "I'm a Communist!"—an act similar to that of a medieval monk invoking the name of Christ in order to abjure wicked enticement.

Pavel Evpraksein, the prosecutor, is indecisive and Hamlet-like: A brooding, introspective character with the Russian predisposition to elegiac and expansive rhetoric, he is, at heart, a libertarian, but in his capacity as prosecutor he can be absolutely ruthless. In the end, he ineptly commits suicide. The most virulent aspersions are cast on the NKVD as represented by the three succeeding heads of the local organization: Captain Milyaga, Lieutenant Filippov, and Major Figurin. Milyaga is an ingratiating coward, Filippov is a paranoid automaton, while Figurin is a peacock in repose whom everyone calls "Idiot Idiotovich" (Idiot the son of an idiot).

Chonkin and Nyura represent the common folk—the salt of the earth. In their unadulterated simplicity, honesty, and earthiness, they are the elemental force and, perhaps, the only hope of the Soviet Union.

Themes and Meanings

Voinovich's main goal is to debunk the Kafkaesque Soviet bureaucracy and the banality of the secret police. In doing so, however, he draws on the rich history and folklore of the Russian people. When Ermolkin, for example, is told that a horse will prove to be his undoing, Voinovich alludes to the death of Prince Oleg, who was bitten by a snake which came out of the skull of his dead horse. Moreover, in the person of Mukhin, a minor character who is the local laureate of children's poetry, Voinovich parodies a famous incident in the life of Fyodor Dostoevski: Mukhin is awaiting his execution, when suddenly he is handed a note saying "Just kidding. J. Stalin."

The confessions of some of the characters allude to Stalin's purges in the 1930's when the country was swept by terror and paranoia, which resulted in thousands being executed or sent to Siberia. Finally, the allegation that Chonkin is actually a prince alludes to a real historical situation of the early seventeenth century, when Russia was going through the "Time of Troubles": A number of false pretenders to the throne arose who were backed by various foreign interests, just as in Voinovich's book, Hitler wants to locate the prince and use him. Moreover, "Prince Golitsyn" is based on the real Prince Golitsyn, a pro-Western Russian personage of the late seventeenth century.

Critical Context

Voinovich is a caustic satirist in the tradition of other Russian writers such as Nikolai Gogol, Ilya Ilf and Evgeny Petrov, and Mikhail Zoshchenko, though much more direct and scatological in his approach. The latter fact is probably because these novels first circulated in samizdat (underground self-publishing in the U.S.S.R.) and then were published abroad. The books were not therefore subjected to rigorous Soviet censorship. Much in the manner of Gogol, the narrator-author of the novels is not omniscient but rather an unwitting bystander who happens to eavesdrop on his characters. Moreover, the unfolding of the novels is reminiscent of Voltaire's *Candide* (1759), whose eponymous hero is not much different from Chonkin, the simple, unsophisticated, and naïve waif. On the other hand, Voinovich's novels remind one of Jaroslav Hašek's Josef Shweik, the bungling and simpleminded "good soldier" whose actions frustrated and hindered various schemes of the Austro-Hungarian war machine in World War I.

Voinovich began the saga of Ivan Chonkin in the 1960's and circulated it in samizdat. Finally, the saga was published abroad in Russian in 1975 (*The Life and Extraordinary Adventures of Private Ivan Chonkin*) and 1979 (*Pretender to the Throne*). The open-ended conclusion of the second work suggests that a sequel is forthcoming. Although he had won critical acclaim for his earlier writings, Voinovich was expelled from the Russian Writers' Union in 1974 and was not allowed to publish in the U.S.S.R. because he had incurred the wrath of the authorities for having vociferously criticized government policies and for protesting Aleksandr Solzhenitsyn's expulsion from the Writers' Union. In 1980, Voinovich emigrated to West Germany.

Sources for Further Study
Brown, Deming. *Soviet Russian Literature Since Stalin,* 1978.

Brown, Edward J. *Russian Literature Since the Revolution*, 1982.

Prescott, P. S. Review of *Pretender to the Throne: The Further Adventures of Private Ivan Chonkin* in *Newsweek*. XCVIII (August 31, 1981), p. 63A.

Sheppard, R. Z. Review of *The Life and Extraordinary Adventures of Private Ivan Chonkin* in *Time*. CIX (January 3, 1977), p. 80.

Terras, Victor. *Handbook of Russian Literature*, 1985.

Nicholas Vontsolos

THE LIFE AND OPINIONS OF KATER MURR

Author: E. T. A. Hoffmann (1776-1822)
Type of plot: Künstlerroman
Time of plot: The late eighteenth and the early nineteenth centuries
Locale: Siegharsweiler (a town), Sieghartshof (a court), and the Abbey of
  Kanzheim—all in Germany
*First published: Lebensansichten des Katers Murr, nebst fragmentarischer
  Biographie des Kapellmeisters Johannes Kreisler in zufälligen
  Makulaturblättern*, 1819-1821 (*The Educated Cat*, 1892; better known as
  *The Life and Opinions of Kater Murr, with the Fragmentary Biography of
  Kapellmeister Johannes Kreisler on Random Sheets of Scrap Paper*, 1969)

> *Principal characters:*
> MURR, a literate tomcat living, loving, and writing in
>   Sieghartsweiler with Meister Abraham Liscov, and later
>   with Johannes Kreisler
> JOHANNES KREISLER, a conductor, composer, and music tutor
> FÜRST IRENÄUS, the former ruler of a small principality who
>   continues to hold court in Sieghartshof
> MEISTER ABRAHAM LISCOV, an inventor, organ builder,
>   magician; the counselor to Fürst Irenäus, and mentor of
>   Kreisler
> BENZON, a widow in her thirties, the former lover and present
>   manipulator of Irenäus
> JULIA, her daughter, who is in love with Kreisler but is
>   engaged to Irenäus' idiot son, Ignatius
> PRINCESS HEDWIGA, the hypersensitive daughter of Irenäus,
>   who is engaged to Prince Hector, whom she loathes

The Novel

E. T. A. Hoffmann, who introduces himself as the editor of Murr's manuscript, informs the reader in the preface that this novel consists of the reminiscences of Murr the cat, interrupted at seventeen places by pages from an anonymous biography of the composer Johannes Kreisler which was used by Murr as scratch paper and sent to the printer by mistake. While the Murr material runs in a straightforward if interrupted chronology, the Kreisler biography (which constitutes more than half of the novel), supposedly torn at random from the book by Murr, lies like a jigsaw puzzle in need of reconstruction by the reader. For example, the first section to be read belongs chronologically with the material of book 3 of the novel, which Hoffman did not live to complete. In summarizing the events, it will be necessary to deal with the two biographies separately.

Murr's "Life and Opinions"—the title reflects the influence of Laurence Sterne's humorous novel *Tristram Shandy* (1759-1767)—is divided into four parts. In "Existential Feelings: Boyhood Months," Murr tells of his being saved from drowning by Meister Abraham Liscov, of his learning to read and embarking on a literary career, and of his friendship with the poodle Ponto and his subsequent mastery of poodle language. Murr's love affair with the cat Miesmies, which ends when she betrays him for another tomcat, forms the central episode in the second chapter, "The Life and Experiences of the Youth." In the next chapter, Murr is saved from philistinism by his friend Muzius and becomes a "Bursche." (Hoffmann is parodying the student organization called the "Burschenschaft," or "brotherhood," which tried to liberalize German society.— He successfully fights a duel with Miesmies' seducer. The brotherhood is crushed by dogs and their human masters, who kill Muzius. The final chapter, "The Maturer Months of Manhood," shows Murr visiting the "higher world" of canine social gatherings, a privilege granted him through his fame as a poet and through his friendship with Ponto, whose transfer from one master to another as a result of his discovery of an adulterous liaison is narrated at great length. In a final note, the "editor," Hoffmann, informs the reader that "bitter death has snatched away the clever, educated, philosophical, poetical Kater Murr in the middle of his beautiful career," and that the projected book 3 will contain the rest of Kreisler's biography, together with reflections and comments from the later period of Murr's life, when he lived with Kreisler.

A double triangle forms the basis of the Kreisler plot: Kreisler feels a conscious though idealized attraction to the musically talented Julia and an unpleasantly physical attraction—described as an electric shock when their hands touch—to Princess Hedwiga. Both women love Kreisler but are condemned to arranged marriages: Fürst Irenäus engages Hedwiga to the handsome but murderous Prince Hector so that he can perhaps regain a principality to rule; the widow Benzon, in order to gain the patent of nobility, which is her sole desire, convinces Irenäus to let her daughter, Julia, marry his son Ignatius, who has the mental capacities of a seven-year-old and could hence scarcely consummate the marriage.

Prince Hector, on the other hand, who harbors the secret that he has murdered his brother in a spar over a woman (coincidentally the illegitimate daughter of Benzon and Irenäus), is powerfully attracted to Julia. Kreisler defeats Hector's attempt at seduction by transforming their tête-à-tête into a recital in which he accompanies Julia at the piano. He finally chases Hector away by showing him a portrait of his brother, given to Kreisler by Meister Abraham for just such a purpose. Infuriated, and frightened by Kreisler's knowledge of his fratricide, the prince sends his adjutant to kill the composer. The shot misses, and Kreisler fatally wounds the assassin, escaping afterward to the Benedictine cloister at Kanzheim, where he composes for the musical monks. The Abbot Chrysostomus, on instructions from Benzon, who has perceived her daughter's attraction to the musician, attempts without success to convince Kreisler to enter the order. When the fanatically ascetic monk Cyprianus arrives and denounces Kreisler's music as impious, Kreisler defends himself by showing the monk the portrait, thus indicating that he is aware of a connection between Cyprianus and Hector. Indeed Cyprianus is the murdered brother, saved by a miracle.

Though the reader cannot be certain what ending Hoffmann would have given the novel, it is clear that the scene would have returned to Sieghartshof and that the plot would have centered on foiling the planned double marriage. It seems likely that mistaken origins would be cleared up: that the dark-skinned Hedwiga would have been revealed to be of Gypsy origin, swapped as a baby for Julia, who would then be the rightful daughter of Irenäus. Kreisler, who was reared by an aunt and later an uncle and remembers nothing of mother or father, might also be of royal blood, perhaps Julia's brother or half brother. Hoffmann would thus have been able to resolve Kreisler's attraction to Julia while at the same time preventing a marriage which is taboo for the Romantic artist. There are also some indications that Kreisler would have entered a period of insanity.

The Characters

Kater Murr is a parody of the self-proclaimed literary genius whose every sentiment, poem, and idea reads as cliché or plagiarism. Indeed, the editor sometimes intervenes to point out passages which Murr has quoted verbatim from William Shakespeare or from Kreisler. Through such citations, however, Murr is made to appear the very paradigm of the Romantic artist: He is singularly unsuccessful at practical life, unable even to venture into the city without getting lost, and all of his love affairs—including an incestuous relationship with his own daughter—end unhappily.

Hoffmann uses the contrast between Murr and Ponto to turn the distinction between feline independence and canine servitude into an analysis of two basic human types, which he might have called "artistic" and "bourgeois." Ponto obtains everything that he desires by self-humiliation and flattery without regard to his own freedom or to moral considerations. When his first master, tricked into believing him degenerate by a wife whom Ponto had exposed as an adulteress, starts to beat him, Ponto has no qualms about going to the wife's lover, Baron von Wipp, or carrying the lovers' billets-doux under his collar. Dogs are thus identified in general with the upper classes, the police, and the whole repressive social system of Hoffmann's Germany. Murr, whatever his failings, remains free and unhypocritical and hence evokes a certain sympathy in the reader. Even the egotism which is his most striking trait reveals a frankness that other geniuses lack.

Kreisler shares with Murr an essential freedom and detestation of hypocrisy and an inability to integrate himself fully within society. As opposed to Murr, everything about him is unique and original, but it is precisely that originality—particularly the ironic brilliance of his rhetoric, always verging on nonsense—which prevents anyone besides Meister Abraham, who has been his teacher since childhood, from knowing him. Kreisler is perceived by Julia as the essence of goodness, by Hedwiga as the essence of sensuality, by Benzon as a danger, and by almost everyone else as a madman. Indeed, Kreisler's greatest fear is of being destroyed by the madness which he senses is pursuing him. Insanity for Kreisler is embodied in the figure of the mad painter Ettlinger, whom Kreisler resembles and whom he at one point sees as literally stalking him in the famous *Doppelgänger* motif. Similarly, Kreisler was created by Hoffman as a more bizarre version of himself: Kreisler's inserted narration of his childhood is a thinly disguised autobiography of Hoffmann.

Most of the other characters are archetypes: Meister Abraham is the omniscient good fairy, providing the hero with magic weapons at the appropriate moments; Hedwiga, who spends most of the novel in fits and trances, represents the mysterious drives of the unconscious; Benzon is the scheming parvenue contrasting with the buffo role of Irenäus. Finally, Julia is the chaste damsel in distress whom Kreisler loves from afar. *The Life and Opinions of Kater Murr* then presents the reader with a remarkable variety of character types, drawn from fairy tales, from romance, from theater and opera, and from Hoffmann's own Romantic imagination.

Themes and Meanings

Music is not only a major theme of this novel but also a plot device, a motif, a meaning, a linguistic style, and practically a character. One could speak of the musical structure of the work as a whole, in which the harmony of the Murr episodes alternates with the dissonance of the Kreisler episodes— rather than assume that there is any logical connection between them. (The problem of how to tell a story is thus an implicit theme of the novel, which presents a tour de force of narrative possibilities.) The language of the novel is imbued with musical terminology. For example, Kreisler characterizes Prince Hector as "a damn [tritone] which must be resolved." To understand the power of this vituperation, one must know that the tritone is the most dissonant interval in the twelve-note scale, often referred to as the "devil in music." Music appears at every crucial point in the novel: Julia and Hedwiga first meet Kreisler on a walk through the park, when they perceive him singing a wild song; at a point of crisis, the two women again take a walk and hear a hymn which Kreisler had composed. They embrace and say to each other, "It was he." In other words, Kreisler *is* his music, which means that his personality is indefinable.

Here, music stands for art in general. Hoffmann—who always believed that he would be remembered for his musical compositions rather than his writings—shared the Romantic perception of music as the highest art form because it was the most abstract. The philosopher Arthur Schopenhauer would later characterize music as an embodiment of pure will, and something of this meaning inheres in *The Life and Opinions of Kater Murr*: The deepest, most meaningful exchanges between characters are always musical ones, inaccessible to language. Language itself acts as a barrier between classes, between male and female, and between cat and human. Music thus expresses the dark, ineffable side of the human personality which always concerned Hoffmann and which is embodied here in several major characters: Kreisler, Meister Abraham (and his wife, the seer Chiara), and Hedwiga.

Music is also the art form best capable of resolving the conflict between mechanistic and individualistic theories of art and of personality. Though music is the most profound expression of emotions or of the will, the beauties of Western harmony are nevertheless explicable in mathematical terms. This conflict between a mechanistic, scientific, or Enlightenment view of society and the Romantic concept of desire and the unconscious as the foundation of human psychology is embodied in the two disparate narrative strands of the novel. The *Bildungsroman* which the Murr material parodies depends upon Enlightenment concepts of education and human perfectibility. The *Kreis* (circle) in Kreisler's name, on the other hand, hints at the eternal recurrence of desire, of man's being an incorrigible prisoner of his passions. Music, with the release that it gives from chronological time and with its transformation of individual sexual desire into general artistic passion, is perhaps the only reconciliation of these conflicting views, but it is evanescent.

Critical Context

Hoffmann gained world fame through his short fiction; his efforts in the novel form, begun late in his career, have received less attention. *The Life and Opinions of Kater Murr*, however, besides its central if ambiguous position in the history of the *Bildungsroman* genre (and of its variant, the *Künstlerroman*), is also a brilliant and influential representative of the possibilities of *Tierdichtung* (animal literature), of the relation between music and literature, and of Romantic narrative art in general.

The autobiographical figure of Kreisler, developed first in "Johannes Kreislers des Kapellmeisters musikalische Leiden" (1810; the musical sufferings of Johannes Kreisler the Kapellmeister), is one of the best and most influential representations of the Romantic hero and artist. As the quintessential individual, he stands in conflict with society, and Hoffmann used this novel as he had rarely used his novellas to satirize almost every aspect of German civilization. Each location of the novel thus centers on one of the three estates of German society and its failures: the triumph of form over feeling in the aristocratic world of Sieghartshof, the aesthetic epicureanism of the monks at Kanzheim, the hypocrisy and self-importance of the burghers and academics in Murr's Sieghartsweiler. Finally, opposed to these there is the world of nature, home of the irrational and of artistic inspiration, appearing to Hedwiga as an absolute danger and to Kreisler as a refuge.

The Murr section manages to satirize nearly every aspect of contemporary German politics and history: the student movements that had played an important role in Germany's struggle for independence and unification; *Philistertum* (middle-class stagnation); and, most prominently, practically every poetic, scientific, and moral writing of the age, from the Enlightenment to Romanticism, from the educational theories of Johann Heinrich Pestalozzi to the genre of the *Bildungsroman*.

The Life and Opinions of Kater Murr represents an absolute negativity, an irony which ironizes even itself, the final bitter outpouring of a man who had been disappointed in love, in art, and in politics and who could already feel the paralysis which would kill him a year later. Yet remarkably, the bitterness of *The Life and Opinions of Kater Murr* is completely transcended by its wit, its highly suspenseful plotting, and the brilliance of its language. In short, it is the "musical" masterpiece that Hoffmann always dreamed of composing.

Sources for Further Study
Hewett-Thayer, Harvey W. *Hoffmann: Author of the Tales*, 1948.
McGlathery, James M. *Mysticism and Sexuality: E. T. A. Hoffmann, Part Two: Interpretations of the Tales*, 1981.
Negus, Kenneth. *E. T. A. Hoffmann's Other World: The Romantic Author and His New Mythology*, 1965.
Rosen, Robert S. *E. T. A. Hoffmann's "Kater Murr": Aufbauformen und Erzählsituationen*, 1970.
Taylor, Ronald. *Hoffmann*, 1963.

Thomas Beebee

LIFE IS ELSEWHERE

Author: Milan Kundera (1929-   )
Type of plot: Satiric *Künstlerroman*
Time of plot: c. the 1930's and the 1940's
Locale: Prague, Czechoslovakia
First published: La Vie est ailleurs, 1973 (English translation, 1974)

> *Principal characters:*
> JAROMIL, the poet as a spoiled child and young man
> MAMAN, the poet's smothering mother
> THE POET'S FATHER, who is killed by the Nazis when the poet is a child
> THE JANITOR'S SON, the poet's only school friend, later a security policeman
> THE ARTIST, the poet's instructor and briefly Maman's lover
> XAVIER, the poet's romantic, adventurous alter ego in his daydreams
> THE REDHEADED GIRL, the poet's unattractive lover
> THE BEAUTIFUL FILMMAKER, whom the poet would like to love
> THE MIDDLE-AGED MAN, the redheaded girl's confidant and other lover

The Novel

Life Is Elsewhere narrates the fictional biography of Jaromil, showing the stages of his development and along the way parodying many of the clichés surrounding the romantic figure of the poet (documented by intermittent references to numerous actual poets). For example, Jaromil could have been conceived on a park bench, on a soiled bed, or in a romantic forest near Prague. His mother, Maman, who plays an overwhelming role in molding the young poet, decides that it was in the romantic forest. Other circumstances of Jaromil's premarital conception, however, are not so auspicious. His father, a poor young engineer, wants Maman to abort the fetus, but Maman's well-to-do parents intervene and arrange the couple's marriage; afterward they move to the top floor of her parents' home, where Jaromil is born.

Relations between the couple never return to their original warm temperature, although they have sex and make a home together. Resentful of her husband, Maman directs all of her affection to little Jaromil, watching carefully over his eating and bowel movements and recording all of his first sayings (editing them for better effect). When he uses a rhyme, she is convinced that her child is a budding poet, and her subsequent efforts go into developing his artistic talents. Little Jaromil thus becomes convinced from an early age that he is a special person with special gifts.

When he begins school, his schoolmates are not as easily convinced; in fact, they heartily detest him. The perfect student, Jaromil has only one school friend, the janitor's son, another pariah. Otherwise Jaromil is something of a loner, staying at home and daydreaming about his alter ego, Xavier (to whose heroic and romantic exploits an entire section of the novel is devoted). These experiences merely reinforce his artistic inclinations, which are further developed when Maman signs him up for lessons with an artist. Maman receives her own lessons free when she has an affair with the artist, but she soon breaks it off, fearful of her deepening emotional commitment. Her husband's arrest by the Nazis (World War II is raging, and Czechoslovakia is under German occupation) reconfirms her loyalty to him, and when he dies in a concentration camp she virtually enshrines his memory. Later, after Maman learns that the Nazis arrested him because of his longstanding affair with a young Jewish woman, the shrine comes down.

In high school Jaromil finally comes into his own. He learns that some girls—unfortunately, generally the frumpier ones—are attracted to sensitive, poetic young men. He is so sensitive, however, that, even though obsessed by thoughts of sex, he cannot take the final plunge when he gets an amorous university student naked in bed with him. Obviously he has a major problem, but the problem is quickly solved by a redheaded store cashier, who takes him to her apartment and starts making love to him before he has time to think about it. The redheaded girl is skinny, freckled, and plain, if not ugly, but Jaromil is proud to call her his girl because she loves sex and gives such a tremendous boost to his ego.

Jaromil's ego also hitches a ride on the successful Communist revolution of 1948, which overturns the old order and gives him and other social misfits their chance to shine (one of the others is the janitor's son, who joins the security police). Jaromil's fluency enables him to hold forth at political meetings, and his poetic talents are in demand for ideological poems. As these appear in party newspapers and magazines, Jaromil begins to build a reputation. One of his admirers is the janitor's son, who invites him to read his poems at the police academy with other prominent poets. At the poetry reading, Jaromil is the hit of the evening, winning enthusiastic applause and the attention of a beautiful young filmmaker (whose work is also subsidized by the police academy). Unhappily, Jaromil has to pass up the opportunity to spend the night with her because he is embarrassed to be wearing old-fashioned, dirty shorts. The beautiful filmmaker reappears later—this time, with Maman's excited cooperation, wanting to make a film about Jaromil. The film is duly made, though Maman dominates the show and Jaromil's voice has to be dubbed.

Meanwhile Jaromil has become less and less proud of his redheaded girlfriend and has begun treating her cruelly. He slaps her and becomes jealous at the mere thought of her with another man, even an examining physician or her brother. Actually, unknown to Jaromil, she has been seeing another man, a middle-aged man who is both her confidant and her lover. Returning from him one day, she is late for a rendezvous with Jaromil, who flies into a jealous rage. To assuage him, the redheaded girl concocts a story about being late because she was trying to persuade her brother not to flee the country illegally. Immediately Jaromil sees his citizen's duty and a way to test her love: They must go to the police together and inform on her brother. The redheaded girl is shocked and confused by this proposal, so Jaromil does not wait for her agreement. The next day he visits his friend in the security police, the janitor's son, and informs on the redheaded girl's brother. That same day, the redheaded girl and her brother are arrested and interrogated (which Jaromil takes morbid pleasure in imagining). Both are sent away to prison, the redheaded girl not reemerging until three years later.

Shortly after the redheaded girl's arrest, Jaromil attends a party at the beautiful filmmaker's apartment, where he hopes to consummate his relationship with her. Instead he gets into an argument with another man at the party, who characterizes Jaromil's poetry with a scatological remark. When Jaromil tries to fight, the man picks him up by the collar and the seat of his pants and deposits him outside on a highrise balcony in the cold. Too proud to return to the party after his humiliation, Jaromil stays outside on the balcony and contracts a deadly chill. Finally arriving at home, he catches pneumonia and, just before his twentieth birthday, dies in Maman's arms.

The Characters

The great bard William Shakespeare, noted for his generous, gentle manner, is evidence that poets do not have to be unstable personalities or total egotists, but Shakespeare himself observed (through one of his characters) that "The lunatic, the lover, and the poet/ Are of imagination all compact." Such statements, plus the examples of the lives of numerous poets such as those to whom Milan Kundera refers in this novel, inform the romantic view of the poet that Kundera parodies in the figure of Jaromil. It is unclear how much credence Kundera (himself once a poet) gives this romantic view, but certainly enough to satirize it and to consider it dangerous. It is also unclear how much real talent Jaromil is supposed to have (the examples of his poetry quoted in the novel do not inspire confidence) and how much he is a pseudopoet, an imitation of a poet. Part of Kundera's point may be that some would-be poets believe that they must live up to a romantic image, that living up to the image makes them poets, or that the image justifies their personal behavior.

The outlines of the image are fairly clear—a sensitive child is born, shows talent early, is shunned by classmates, retreats into self, produces masterpieces while failing at personal relationships, and dies young. Jaromil fits the outline except for the masterpieces. The outline is subsumed and given unity by Jaromil's leading trait, his egotism. His self-absorption is indicated by the lack of names for the other main characters, by his fantasies about Xavier, and by his sex life—his masturbation, impotency, and relationship with the redheaded girl. "Life is elsewhere" for Jaromil in the sense that other people and the world exist only as they relate to him in his solipsistic vision.

Yet Jaromil is also the product of Maman, who shares his existential problem. She is wrapped up in her own romantic vision, and Jaromil is little more than a projection of herself, her creation, a substitute for her disappointed hopes. Through him she can live out the romantic life she missed. When real life and romance offer themselves to her, she, like her son, fails to meet them halfway. For Maman, too, "life is elsewhere," but exactly where is hard to say.

Themes and Meanings

To Kundera, it is immaterial whether Jaromil has poetic talent or is only a pseudopoet. Although Kundera explores the nature of the poetic personality in *Life Is Elsewhere*, his main interest is the "lyrical attitude," which both poets and nonpoets can hold. In particular, he has noted in several places that the lyrical attitude is typical of revolutionaries, such as the Communist revolutionaries of his own Czechoslovakia. Poets and revolutionaries have the lyrical attitude in common, which is why poets are attracted to revolutions and revolutions need poets—why Jaromil is attracted to the Communists and ultimately hits it off with the security police.

Jaromil thus illustrates the reasons Kundera distrusts the lyrical attitude, which is characterized by enthusiasm and emotion rather than rationality. In poets the lyrical attitude can lead to fine poems, but in revolutionaries it can lead to fanaticism, excesses, and disregard for human life (much as it can destroy the personal life of the poet and those around him). Jaromil, the "sensitive" poet, demonstrates the horrible potential of the lyrical attitude by his treatment of the redheaded girl and his trip to the security police to inform on her brother.

Critical Context

Kundera finished *Life Is Elsewhere* in 1969, the year after the Russians invaded Czechoslovakia and reinstituted Communist "normalization" following a period of liberalization that had culminated in the Prague Spring of 1968. The title is taken from a revolutionary slogan of French students who were demonstrating in Paris at the time against the French government. No doubt Kundera found the slogan ironic in view of the situation in his country.

Soon after he finished the book, the slogan and title could have applied to Kundera's own life. He was expelled from the Communist Party (for the second time), as well as from his university teaching position, and his books were banned. *Life Is Elsewhere* was not published in his own country; instead, it was first published in France in 1973 in a French translation, appearing in Czech as *Život je jinde* only in 1979. Although usually considered Kundera's weakest novel, *Life Is Elsewhere* is vitally important for understanding his position on the "lyrical attitude."

Sources for Further Study

Donahue, Bruce. "Laughter and Ironic Humor in the Fiction of Milan Kundera," in *Critique: Studies in Modern Fiction*. XXV (Winter, 1984), pp. 67-76.

Fuentes, Carlos. "The Other K," in *TriQuarterly*. LI (Spring, 1981), pp. 256-275.

Harkins, William E., and Paul I. Trensky, eds. *Czech Literature Since 1956: A Symposium*, 1980.

Harold Branam

THE LIFE OF AN AMOROUS MAN

Author: Saikaku Ihara (Hirayama Tōgo, 1642-1693)
Type of plot: Picaresque
Time of plot: The early seventeenth century (during the Tokugawa period, 1603-1867)
Locale: Japan
First published: Kōshoku ichidai otoko, 1682 (English translation, 1964)

> *Principal character:*
> YONOSUKE, the protagonist, a man whose life is dedicated to pleasure

The Novel

   The Life of an Amorous Man is an episodic account of the life of a seventeenth century Japanese adventurer who explores the pleasures of the flesh. It follows the wanderings of Yonosuke (Man of the World) from his childhood, when he reveals at age seven a gift "for sensual things," through his profligate, unregenerate youth and comfortable, sophisticated, even celebrated, manhood to his final voyage in search of the legendary "isle of Nogo." The driving passion of Yonosuke's life is the pursuit of sensual pleasure, which he finds primarily, but not exclusively, in the company of *tayu,* the courtesans in entertainment houses who were the prototypes of geishas. The book details Yonosuke's liaisons with countless women as he pursues some sort of final sensual fulfillment on trips back and forth across the island of Japan, through the gutters of this primitive world and into its most stately pleasure domes. *The Life of an Amorous Man* is a remarkable document not for its depiction of a man driven by the pursuit of pleasure but for its revelation of the lives of the common people during the early years of the Tokugawa period and, particularly, for its vivid portraits of women.

   The novel is divided into two parts, each of which chronicles roughly half of Yonosuke's life. His extreme sensitivity to "sensual nuances or suggestions" is in part a matter of heritage, for his father was a man of considerable wealth who spent many years pursuing "the charms of beautiful women and the pleasures of wine," and his mother was a celebrated courtesan before her marriage. Yonosuke writes love notes, courts women and girls, and forms definite opinions about the inseparability of proper etiquette and pleasure even before he reaches puberty. He makes his transition to manhood in the arms of a youth bound into service as a male whore, and soon Yonosuke is receiving advice from an elderly confidant about seduction and the management of illicit affairs. From this point forward, the novel consists of one brief chapter after another dealing with Yonosuke's encounters with women or men of the "gay world," a polite name for the world of harlots, courtesans,

innkeepers, entertainers, and pleasure houses. His father tolerates his philandering as long as Yonosuke makes some effort to keep one foot in the respectable world of business. Yet, "profligate and intractable, he [becomes]
an unregenerate playboy" whose governing thought is: "Tomorrow will be
tomorrow, so why not spend the evening as if this were my last night upon
earth?" By the time he is nineteen, Yonosuke is disowned by his father and is
physically exhausted and debilitated by constant dissipation.

For a while, he repents his dissolute ways and becomes a monk, but after
a superficial questioning and dismissal of the "promised hereafter," he sells
the "coral beads of his rosary" and turns again to "the life of the flesh." He
supports himself in a variety of ways, from being the "business master" of
young, itinerant homosexual whores to selling "whalebone ear scratchers" to
working as a wandering minstrel. Yonosuke is self-conscious enough to see
an "image of himself in [the faces of cheap, itinerant entertainers], in their
cheap parasitical way of living, . . . in the few tricks they performed for one
night's pleasure in a harlot's arms." Yet, in spite of self-knowledge, poverty,
and misery, the lure of amorous women never fails to attract him.

Yonosuke becomes a connoisseur of the gay world and is befriended by
wealthy men who appreciate his worldliness and sophistication. Although he
is poor, Yonosuke is offended by courtesans who have no "subtlety, no graciousness." His travels take him from one city to another, and soon he can
distinguish among the strengths, the weaknesses, and the styles of the courtesans of Kyoto, Edo, Osaka, or Inari-machi. He seduces village maidens,
city wives, nuns, Shinto oracles, mothers, hardened whores, and refined
courtesans; he is driven by a restless desire to experience more women, more
sophistication, more pleasure.

Although he serves some time in prison for the attempted rape of a married woman and begins to be troubled by bad dreams about women he has
abused in some way, Yonosuke remains as committed as ever to the pursuit
of pleasure. Because he is now acknowledged as a "much traveled expert on
promiscuous women," Yonosuke is taken into service by a number of the idle
rich, who use him "to recommend new sources of pleasure." After a few
more years, haunted by his dreams and feeling a bit jaded by his life of dissipation, Yonosuke resolves to become an ascetic and embarks on a pilgrimage to a holy hermit. Yet his resolve lasts only until he receives news that his
father has died and left him a great fortune. Immediately, he reverts to his
"old sensual philosophy" and dedicates his wealth "to all the lovely courtesans of this country."

While the first part of *The Life of an Amorous Man* details Yonosuke's
experiences in the dark alleys and poorer quarters of the gay world, the second part charts the wanderings of the now-wealthy libertine through the
brightly lit and gorgeously adorned upper reaches of the same world.
Yonosuke's first adventure as a respectable citizen is marriage. He courts,

wins, buys, and then marries a renowned hostess, Yoshino. Soon, Yonosuke begins to wander from the "home-fire hibachi," for in his opinion, "domestic bliss is at best routine . . . [and] the spirit is restless, lured by recurrent visions of fresh adventures." Yonosuke embarks on a campaign of "fresh adventures" that for any but the wealthiest and most decadent of men would be merely "visions," the stuff of fantasy. For example, he travels to Murotsu, where the courtesans are said to be "superior to any that flourished in olden times." There he asks for and receives the eighty most highly praised women of the city, selects the seven most refined and beautiful, and then finally chooses one to entertain him. In appreciation of her charms and services, he buys her freedom and sends her home.

Yonosuke begins to focus his attention on only the most renowned of courtesans. He has interesting, challenging, and pleasurable encounters with the finest and most beautiful hostesses of every major city: Washu, gentle Kindayu, and "Hatsune, the nightingale," of Osaka; Yoshida, "the rising star," "the peerless Takao," and Komurasaki, "the hardest of all courtesans to see," of Edo; Yoshizaki and Takahashi, "the one courtesan whom all men admired," of Kyoto; and Kaory, the leading courtesan of Kambayashi. He becomes the most celebrated patron of Japan's gay world.

Age brings few changes to Yonosuke. He does, however, decide to "propitiate the gods, for one can never tell"; consequently, he showers the Buddhist temples and Shinto shrines with money and gives money to those who are less fortunate than himself, "especially those within the periphery of his pleasure-seeking world." He even prepares an elaborate gift for the courtesans of distant Nagasaki—a gift so extravagant that it becomes the centerpiece of a museum devoted to the fashion and beauty of the gay world:

> 44 huge full-robed dolls: 17 likenessess of noted Kyoto courtesans, 8 of Edo, and 19 of Osaka. . . . Almost everyone in Nagasaki came to see and sigh over these wondrous things of beauty. They satisfied, even if vicariously, the secret yearning of every normal man.

Rather than waiting for death to come to him, Yonosuke embarks on one final, daring, doomed adventure. He has a lovely and luxurious ship built stocked with delicacies, and he sails beyond the horizon with a few old companions in search of a mythical island inhabited solely by beautiful and refined women.

The Characters

Yonosuke's escapades are the focus of virtually every page, but Yonosuke is not a particularly interesting or complex individual. Saikaku Ihara was much more concerned with using Yonosuke as a device with which to examine all corners of the gay world than with studying his psyche. Yonosuke is a flat and static character whose commitment to the gay world dominates his life. He is distinguished by his sensitivity to the nuances not only of sensuality but also of etiquette, style, and graciousness. Yonosuke becomes more sophisticated, experienced, and celebrated as he grows older, but he never changes in any essential way. He does go through a few periods of questioning and self-reproach, even of bad dreams and despair, but these moments of doubt pass quickly and seem to have no lasting effect. For all of his sophistication, Yonosuke is finally a superficial, "whimsical, and aimless" man, content to live in and for the moment.

A modern writer might wish to examine the causes of Yonosuke's ceaseless quest for the new and the pleasing, but Saikaku is content simply to record Yonosuke's capers and to allow him to enjoy himself. Yonosuke's "invincible determination," his resourcefulness, his unquenchable appetite, and the ingenuity and imagination that he employs in the pursuit of pleasure are admirable. In addition, he repeatedly proves to be a generous and pleasant-spirited, though somewhat solipsistic and callous, man. Yonosuke is incorrigible but charming.

The most interesting characters in the novel are the many briefly sketched inhabitants of the gay quarters. Saikaku, with a few deft strokes, gives vivid life to a gallery of courtesans, male and female. The stoical youth to whom Yonosuke loses his virginity graphically reveals what it is like to be bound into service as a male whore: "We cannot refuse any man, no matter if his body is covered with sores or if he has never used a toothpick in his life. We must endure everything he does throughout the long autumn night." Yonosuke's wife is truly "gentle and courteous and big of heart." She wins the approval of his haughty family quite graciously. She deals with his philandering with tolerance and civility and then ends the marriage with dignity. Miskasa, a courtesan with whom Yonosuke has a prolonged affair, is a woman of "deep feeling" and great strength of character, with a capacity for genuine commitment. She is literally willing to die for Yonosuke. Her love is wasted on him, for he is incapable of sustained commitment. When Yonosuke finally arranges to spend an evening with the famous Hatsune, he realizes as soon as he is in her presence that he is "no match for this astute courtesan in witty conversation." Hatsune's superior intelligence justifies her conviction that "men are fools"; yet she must spend her nights entertaining one man after another. Perhaps the most endearing portrait of a courtesan is that of brilliant Komurasaki, who, through her perceptiveness and generosity, saves the life of Juzo, a tailor, "just another man from another city."

The novel is also peopled with numerous nameless but nevertheless memorable creatures of the dark world of rural poverty and moral decay: a priestess who lives in shadows and who sells "strange drugs and secret accommodations," "cheap itinerant entertainers . . . living just this side of the beggar's lot," the myriad poor of country villagers who "exploit one another just to keep body and soul together," nuns who have "long since degenerated into a state of semi-prostitution," humane grave robbers, and many others. Although he is not concerned with, or particularly skilled at, creating a central figure of great range, depth, or complexity, Saikaku is quite adept at drawing sharp, interesting character sketches.

Themes and Meanings

Although *The Life of an Amorous Man* entertains more than it educates, Saikaku's novel can be seen as a critique of the moral and spiritual degeneration that accompanied the decay of the feudal system and the growth of modern popular culture. During the Kamakura-Muromachi era, which extended from approximately the thirteenth to the sixteenth century, the aristocratic samurai warrior controlled the political and economic worlds and the Buddhist priest was the leader of the spiritual and the intellectual worlds. During the peaceful and prosperous years of the Tokugawa shogunate, however, the Bushido code of the warrior fell into disuse, and the ardor and integrity of the Buddhist and Shinto faithful diminished. As the world became more comfortable, strict spiritual and ethical codes became less important.

In *The Life of an Amorous Man*, Saikaku reveals a rural world of genuine corruption where virtue is the exception: samurais turned bandits or male whores; base cozeners posing as Shinto oracles and Buddhist monks; nuns who live by whoredom; and villagers who value nothing more than survival and live by theft, deception, self-prostitution, or the exploitation of others. The urban world is more prosperous and more pleasant than this rural world, but it, also, is morally empty. In the society of Saikaku's cities, the emphasis is on form rather than substance. The trappings of medieval aristocratic aesthetic ideals exist in the sophisticated gay world, but the focus is on surface beauty. The traditional concerns of promoting virtue and reproving vice, of forging a bond between inner and outer beauty, and of living an honorable life have given way to a preoccupation with questions of fashion, style, and reputation. The merchant class virtue of *iki* (smartness) has supplanted such venerable ideals as *giri* (ties of obligation) and *ninjo* (human feeling).

Saikaku has no illusions about the moral and spiritual quality of life in the gay quarters, but neither does he seem particularly disturbed by what he sees. He is not a satirist or a reformer; he is a storyteller whose chief interest is in a faithful and engaging representation of life. Saikaku, like Yonosuke, is not interested in the deeper implications of his story. He does, however, have a genuine awareness of and sensitivity to the full humanity of women and to the tragic dimensions of their plight in a male-dominated world. He is a sensitive, witty, and good-humored writer with, given his class and historical setting, an exceptional sympathy for women and others who suffer inordinately because of the inequities of the world.

Critical Context

Saikaku Ihara was a vivacious, witty, and energetic member of the merchant class. Although he was neither a learned man nor a sophisticated craftsman, he founded a popular school of writing and is now recognized as one of Japan's most successful authors. Literacy was widespread in seventeenth century Japan, printing was efficient, and books were cheap; consequently, there was a large and somewhat unrefined reading public hungry for entertaining literature. After an unsuccessful beginning as a composer of haiku, Saikaku turned to writing novels. His fast-paced, witty, realistic, and often salacious sketches of contemporary life and manners were so successful that they came to serve as models for future generations of Japanese writers. Although he did write some moral and instructional tales, he is particularly remembered for the licentiousness of his novels; some are reputed to be too explicit for translation. He was a prolific writer who left the world numerous volumes of tales, novels, and sketches. *The Life of an Amorous Man* and its companion piece, *Kōshoku ichidai onna* (1686; *The Life of an Amorous Woman*, 1963), are among his best-known works.

Sources for Further Study

Hamada, Kengi. Introduction to *The Life of an Amorous Man*, 1964.

Hibbett, Howard Scott, Jr. *The Floating World in Japanese Fiction*, 1959.

_____. "The Japanese Comic Linked-Verse Tradition," in *Harvard Journal of Asiatic Studies*. XXIII (1960/1961), pp. 76-92.

_____. "Saikaku and Burlesque Fiction," in *Harvard Journal of Asiatic Studies*. XX (June, 1957), pp. 53-73.

"Kôshoku Ichidai Otoko," in *Introduction to Classic Japanese Literature*, 1948. Edited by The Kokusai Bunka Shinkokai.

Hal Holladay

THE LIME WORKS

Author: Thomas Bernhard (1931-   )
Type of plot: Philosophical realism
Time of plot: c. 1970
Locale: An abandoned lime works near Sicking in Upper Austria
First published: Das Kalkwerk, 1970 (English translation, 1973)

> *Principal characters:*
> KONRAD, an eccentric scientist who is working on the
>   definitive work on the sense of hearing
> HIS WIFE (née ZRYD), a cripple and Konrad's chief experi-
>   mental subject, whom he murders
> THE NARRATOR, an obscure insurance salesman who gathers
>   information about the Konrad couple
> FRO and
> WIESER, estate managers who provide much of the
>   information about the Konrad couple

The Novel

During the night of December 24, an eccentric scientist named Konrad murdered his crippled wife at their residence, an abandoned decaying lime works in Upper Austria. He used a carbine that she kept strapped to her wheelchair. After dragging the body around, searching for a way to dispose of it, he propped her up in her wheelchair again and left the house. A few days later, the police found him cowering half-frozen under the rotting planks of the lime works's manure pit, his shoes "bloated with liquid manure"; he was arrested and brought to the Wels district prison to await his trial.

The greater part of the novel, of which 230 pages are written in one continuous paragraph, tries to shed light on the circumstances of the monstrous crime and the bizarre personal lives of the Konrads. A faceless narrator, an insurance salesman who frequents the local taverns to peddle his policies, gathers information in order to piece together the Konrads' story. Since the narrator's "evidence," however, consists of little more than a mass of hearsay and gossip gathered at the taverns, the reader is presented with conflicting versions. It is second- and third-hand information at best, gained principally from two estate managers, Fro and Wieser, who frequently report statements attributed to Konrad himself.

The picture that emerges is one of a man on the brink of madness. He is totally obsessed with his life's work, *The Sense of Hearing*, which is to become a definitive study. After decades of unremitting brain work, he claims to have the entire book in his head but is unable to commit it to paper. He has awaited the auspicious moment when everything would come together just once so that he could write it in one continuous flow. At propitious moments, however, he is invariably disturbed by something, as though everything and everyone were in conspiracy against his writing.

After years of continuous and torturous worldwide travels with his crippled wife, he became convinced that the abandoned lime works, which had been in the family for centuries, was the only place where he could possibly live and do his scientific work. Hence, he moved heaven and earth to possess it, paying an exorbitant price to his nephew, who for decades had taken a sadistic delight in Konrad's desperate efforts to acquire the property.

It was accessible only from the east. To the north, it was surrounded by water, on the south by ramparts of rock. By planting the tallest-growing thickets he could find, Konrad succeeded in hiding the estate from view. By installing countless bars and locks, he turned it into a heavily barricaded fortress to protect himself and his wife against burglars and, in general, against what he called outsiders. He was intent on severing all ties to the outside world, a world which in his view was merely marking time anyway. In particular, he sought to flee the destructive consumer society "with its chronically irritating and ultimately ruinous effect on everything in the nature of intellectual effort." So it came about that for five years Konrad and his wife lived in almost total self-imposed isolation in what resembled a dungeon or a prison.

At the lime works, which his wife detested, Konrad continued to conduct hearing experiments to fill up the time until the moment arrived, as he confidently and unwaveringly believed it would, when he would finally write his book. He subjected his wife to an excruciating series of hearing experiments, sometimes for seven to eight hours a day. He produced copious notes on his experiments but usually destroyed them immediately so that no one could deduce his methods from his notes. His wife started to suffer from pains in her ears which gradually spread to her whole head as he intensified the experiments. When they were not busy with the exercises, they tormented each other in many different ways. For example, when she wanted him to read aloud from Novalis, her favorite Romantic poet, he deliberately read to her from his favorite, the Russian anarchist Pyotr Alekseyevich Kropotkin, whom she detested. She, on the other hand, took a malicious pleasure in sending him down from her second floor room to the basement every few minutes for a glass of cider, insisting that he bring her each time only one glass, which she then proceeded to pour out.

For decades they had lived off a sizable inheritance, but in time the capital dwindled and Konrad, behind his wife's back, sold off nearly all of their possessions and incurred enormous debts. Shortly before the murder, he owed at least two million to the bank, and a forced auction of the lime works was imminent. He lived in constant fear that the man from the bank might come knocking on the door, so he no longer opened the door and no longer left his room. After months of neglect, he came to look like a derelict, filthy from top to bottom.

Initially, Konrad had thought that if he could just get a few sentences down on paper, then the rest of the book would gradually write itself, but at the peak of concentration it always fell apart. The more obsessed he became, the more impossible it became for him to write his book. Toward the end, he welcomed any distraction at all; nothing was too trivial or too insignificant to take him away from his task. He wore himself out brooding over the most absurd notions, all pretexts for not writing, for not facing the fact that he was simply unable to write his book. Just before the murder, he must have realized that there was no ideal moment or place to write the book, that he had fallen victim to a mad dream like thousands before him. He would never write the book, not at the lime works, in prison at Stein, or in the mental institution at Niederhardt.

The Characters

Since the narrative provides conflicting information assembled by an obscure narrator from many different, often unreliable sources, it is treacherous to make any definitive statements about the central characters, Konrad and his wife. Even Konrad's extensive self-revelations, reported by Fro and Wieser, that constitute a sizable portion of the novel are highly contradictory. Konrad, depending on whose testimony one is to believe, is a genius, a madman, or a fool. He himself likes to think of himself as a brilliant scientific philosopher. Similarly, it is unclear whether his crippled wife is cared for or shamelessly used by her husband

As far as Konrad is concerned, it is safe to say that he is a misanthropical monomaniac who has totally lost himself in what was to become a major "medico-musico-metaphysical-mathematical" study. Much of the novel reflects his convoluted, compulsive thought processes, which invariably return to his unrealized study. He tries to create favorable conditions for writing and, upon failing to write, tries to justify his inability to commit his thoughts to paper. He alternately blames his failure on interruptions from the outside world, on nature, on the lime works, and on his wife, but all these justifications are negated in time. The most likely cause for his foiled aspirations is mentioned at the very end of the novel, where Konrad is said to have lacked courage, decisiveness, intellectual audacity or, what was perhaps the most important quality of all, "fearlessness in the face of realization, of concretization."

Konrad's wife and half sister, whose maiden name is Zryd, is only referred to as Mrs. Konrad or the Konrad woman. Once a tall and stately beauty, she was almost totally crippled by an accident and, the reader is told, by decades of the wrong medications. She has for years pitted herself against her husband's work, because she considered it nothing more than a delusion and told him so whenever he reached the point of utter defenselessness. In fact, one theory has it that Konrad killed his wife because she had once too often called him a fool, a madman or, her favorite expression, "a highly intelligent mental case." Earlier, she had made every effort to sabotage their move to the lime works; she had even bribed the nephew into not selling the estate to her husband. Once at the lime works, she too exhibited compulsive behavior patterns. She set about knitting mittens for her husband, who loathed mittens, as she knew very well. She worked on them for months on end and had him try them on only to unravel them as soon as they were done. As time wore on, she simply sat in her chair, half asleep and in a state of deepest depression, unless she was subjected to his increasingly torturous hearing exercises. Over the years, she slumped over more and more in her wheelchair until her dependence on him was absolute.

The two central characters are caught in a beneficial yet destructive symbiotic relationship. As Thomas Bernhard put it so aptly, by marrying they moved "from the purgatory of loneliness into the hell of togetherness." For years, they managed to save themselves from total despair only by lies. In some ways, they are exact opposites. She would like to live in her idyllic hometown, Toblach, and he prefers the isolated, delapidated lime works. She craves contact with friends and relations, whereas he insists on severing all contact with the world. Yet they are very much alike in other ways. Both seem capable simultaneously of slavish obedience and the utmost cruelty toward each other. He, for example, threatens to withhold food from her, to prolong the exercises, or not to air her room in order to get his way. She nags him incessantly about his criminal record and prevents him from writing by demanding his constant attention. The true motive for the murder—if there is one at all—is not revealed.

The other individuals in the novel—for example, the rather obscure narrator, Fro and Wieser, the public works inspector, the forestry commissioner, and the handyman Hoeller—are minor figures whose main function is to provide conflicting information about the Konrad couple.

Themes and Meanings

The Lime Works is a difficult work by any standard. It defies easy answers; in fact, one of its central themes is precisely that "nothing can be elucidated with any finality, ultimately." The uninitiated reader will find the novel about as forbidding and inaccessible as the casual visitor finds the lime works. The passages describing the labyrinthian structure from which the novel derives its name apply to the novel as well. Everyone seeing the lime works for the first time is immediately dumbfounded by it. Even those with exceptional alertness quickly tire and eventually succumb to deep exhaustion. They are bound to suffer immediately every kind of disappointment, because every assumption, every preconception, every actuality is likely to be erroneous, to be quite the opposite, in fact. The whole construction of the lime works, and thus of the novel, is said to aim at total deceptiveness so that one is likely to fall into a trap every time. Both the lime works and the novel leave the impression of hopeless confusion. It should come as no surprise then that the mystery of the shooting is never completely resolved; it is never clearly established whether the shooting constituted a case of impulse killing or premeditated murder, whether it was the act of a madman, an accident during the cleaning of the gun, or perhaps a case of mercy killing.

Since the first few short paragraphs contain an unusually large number of clearly marked contradictory statements, the reader notices immediately that none of the statements in the novel can be taken at face value, that they all have to be weighed and compared with one another. That process reveals very quickly that for every assertion there is sure to be a counterassertion somewhere else: The lime works is shown to be both a refuge and a prison, the best and worst place for Konrad's work; he shows all of the characteristics of a genius and all those of a fool; he is said to be a fanatic about truthtelling, yet he tells his wife nothing but lies. All of this serves to reinforce the central premise that nothing can be stated unconditionally, that one's very existence is probably pure self-deception.

The Lime Works is an account of a scholar's failed attempt to explore a complex natural phenomenon (the human ear) and thus to triumph over a hostile nature; it is the tale of an artist's maddening inability to write, to put his thoughts into words; it is also the infinitely sad story of a marriage. In a more general sense, however, the novel describes the futile and dangerous attempt of a thinking man to search for the ultimate truth, to lend some meaning to his existence—a futile and dangerous task, because "the thinking man always moves alone into an intensifying darkness." Konrad, striving for completeness, universality, totality, and the absolute, is doomed to fail as he reaches the very limits of human knowledge and linguistic capabilities. As one critic correctly stated, in the strange ramblings of this solitary philosopher can be heard "something of the eternal hopelessness and loneliness of the human condition."

Critical Context

Thomas Bernhard, whose work defies easy categorization, is perhaps the most widely discussed and controversial Austrian author of the 1970's and the 1980's, comparable only to Peter Handke in stature and productivity. His oeuvre, highly original and always provocative, has found increasing acceptance. For the *Lime Works*, which now ranks as one of the finest experimental novels in postwar German literature, Thomas Bernhard was awarded the prestigious Georg Büchner Prize and the Prix Seguier. Critics link him with Franz Kafka and Samuel Beckett and are quick to note the striking affinities to Arthur Schopenhauer and Ludwig Wittgenstein.

If Thomas Bernhard's numerous plays and prose works enjoy considerable popularity in spite of their decidedly depressing subject matter, it is largely because of their seductive language. Bernhard, an accomplished stylist and a trained musician, takes the German language to its limits. By working extensively with repetition, variation, modulation, intensification, and leitmotif, he has developed a distinctive, highly musical style that is very captivating. Words and phrases are repeated over and over; they are combined and recombined, varied and intensified, which gives his language its famed relentlessness and compulsiveness. The most distinctive feature, however, is the frequent occurrence of hyperbole. Bernhard's world is no less extreme than his language. It is a cold and gloomy world of illness, suffering, pain, decay, anger, hatred, crime, failure, insanity, and above all else, death, from whose vantage point all human endeavor ultimately becomes ridiculous.

Sources for Further Study

Craig, D. A. "The Novels of Thomas Bernhard: A Report," in *German Life and Letters*. XXV (1970/1971), pp. 343-353.

Dierick, A. P. "Thomas Bernhard's Austria: Neurosis, Symbol, or Expedient?" in *Modern Austrian Literature*. XII (1979), pp. 73-93.

Fetz, Gerhard. "The Works of Thomas Bernhard: Austrian Literature?" in *Modern Austrian Literature*. XVII, nos. 3/4 (1984), pp. 171-192.

Goodwin-Jones, Robert. "The Terrible Idyll: Thomas Bernhard's *Das Kalkwerk*," in *Germanic Notes*. XIII (1982), pp. 8-10.

Lindenmayr, Heinrich. *Totalität und Beschränkung: Eine Untersuchung zu Thomas Bernhards Roman "Das Kalkwerk,"* 1982.

Rossbacher, Karlheinz. "Thomas Bernhard: *Das Kalkwerk* (1970)," in *Deutsche Romane des 20. Jahrhunderts: Neue Interpretationen*, 1983. Edited by Paul M. Lützeler.

Schwedler, Wilfried. "Thomas Bernhard," in *Handbook of Austrian Literature*, 1973. Edited by Frederick Ungar.

Sorg, Bernhard. *Thomas Bernhard*, 1977.

Judith Ricker-Abderhalden

LOCAL ANAESTHETIC

Author: Günter Grass (1927-   )
Type of plot: Social criticism
Time of plot: 1967
Locale: West Berlin
First published: Örtlich betäubt, 1969 (English translation, 1969)

> *Principal characters:*
> EBERHARD STARUSCH, a forty-year-old teacher of German and
>   history
> THE DENTIST, who is currently treating Starusch's
>   prognathism
> PHILIPP SCHERBAUM, a student in Starusch's class
> VERO LEWAND, Scherbaum's girlfriend, also a student
> IRMGARD SEIFERT, a teaching colleague of Starusch

The Novel

As the forty-year-old bachelor Eberhard Starusch undergoes protracted treatment for a protruding lower jaw, he uses the sessions not only to deal with his dental problems but also to address a variety of present and past issues which are exceedingly painful to him. While part of the narrative consists of a straightforward reconstruction of his dialogues with the dentist, it is Starusch's psychic projections of present and past events onto the screen of the television set which the dentist uses to distract his patients that lend the novel its characteristic filmic quality and surrealistic fluidity. Reality and fantasy intertwine as Starusch confronts the actual and the repressed, the pains of the present and the psychic wounds of the past, which intersect with and reflect German history and the contemporary political climate.

Starusch is a man profoundly unhappy with his life and plagued by festering psychic sores caused by past failures, the chief of which being the engagement broken off several years before by his fiancée, Sieglinde Krings. Although he feigns indifference, Starusch was profoundly angered and humiliated by Sieglinde's rejection of him in favor of another man, and that anger now expresses itself in the form of murderous fantasies projected onto the blank television screen. Horrified by Starusch's violent visions, the dentist provides the metaphorical link between the external action (the cleansing of Starusch's teeth) and the psychic projections on the screen when he states:

> Your tartar is your calcified hate. Not only the microflora in your oral cavity, but also your muddled thoughts, your obstinate squinting backward, the way you regress when you mean to progress, in other words, the tendency of your diseased gums to form germ-catching pockets, all that—the sum of dental picture and psyche—betrays you: stored up violence, murderous designs.

The theme of compensatory violence and obsession with past failures is also represented in the figure of Sieglinde Krings's father. Modeled after the historical Field Marshall Schörner, Krings was one of Adolf Hitler's most stubborn generals, always willing to fight to his last man but never willing to admit error or defeat. Upon his return from Russian captivity in 1955, General Krings spends most of his time staging mock warfare in a sandbox, a vain attempt to win lost battles. The introduction of General Krings into his novel is a clear example of Günter Grass's intent to link the personal biography of his fictional protagonist with the broader context of German history and suggests that Starusch's psychological mechanism of converting "calcified hatred" caused by past failures into fantasies of violent revenge might provide a key to the understanding of twentieth century German history. Would history have been changed, Starusch muses, if Hitler had not been denied admission to the Viennese Art Academy?

Among his present concerns, Starusch is most troubled, apart from his teeth, by the plans of his favorite student, Philipp Scherbaum, to douse his dog, Max, with gasoline and set him ablaze in front of the cake-munching ladies in Kempinski's restaurant on Berlin's fashionable Kurfürstendamm Street. Scherbaum wants to shock them into understanding the effects of napalm on living beings. He has already rejected the notion of self-immolation as ineffective; the sensibilities of the Berliners to human suffering have been dulled, but their love of dogs is legendary.

Although at Scherbaum's present age of seventeen Starusch was himself the leader of an anarchist youth gang in wartime Danzig—familiar to readers of Grass's *Die Blechtrommel* (1959; *The Tin Drum*, 1961) as the "Dusters"—experience and "the sadness of [his] better knowledge" have turned him into an opponent of genuine violence (his harmless fantasies in the dental chair notwithstanding). A reformist rather than a revolutionary, Starusch is determined to dissuade Scherbaum from an act which he views as futile and potentially self-destructive, but at the same time he admires his student's unspoiled idealism and is not at all comfortable in disabusing him of it.

Scherbaum is no ideologue driven by a romanticized vision of the possibilities of revolutionary action but rather "a thin-skinned kid who feels the wrongs of the world, not only when they're close to him, but also when they're far away." He is not the least bit interested in explaining the war in Vietnam in ideological terms. Instead, "he sees human beings burning and he's made up his mind to do something about it." Though Scherbaum's radical girlfriend, Vero Lewand, accuses Starusch of having the effect of a "reactionary tranquilizer" on him, it is more accurate to view him as a kind of local anaesthetic, easing the pain while attempting to find a more appropriate response to its cause. With the help of the dentist and to the profound disappointment of Irmgard Seifert, who sees Scherbaum's proposed action as redemption for the moral failures of her own youth, Scherbaum eventually drops his plan to burn his dog and takes on the editorship of the school newspaper instead. Though his editorials cannot cure the world's ills in the short run, it is possible that they will contribute to the process of gradual reform. Still uncomfortable with the idea that this may indeed be all that is possible, Starusch notes in a kind of afterword from the perspective of two years later that he feels a fresh growth of tartar (hate, anger, frustration) on his teeth, and the novel concludes with the observation: "There will always be pain."

The Characters

Eberhard Starusch shares many biographical traits with the author, including date and place of birth, having experienced wartime captivity by the Americans, and an extended residence in the Rhineland following his release and before settling in West Berlin. More important, however, Starusch represents the political philosophy which Grass evolved in the late 1960's, an extremely turbulent period in German politics. It is a philosophy of skepticism, commitment to the values of the Enlightenment, and such profound distrust of ideological systems and pat answers that, at least in Starusch's case, it leads to a large measure of self-doubt and tends to express itself through an equivocating on-the-one-hand-but-on-the-other-hand approach. Starusch recognizes that nothing is ever simple or unambiguous, that contradiction and paradox are inescapable and that progress must be painfully slow. Nevertheless, the former radical gang leader whom experience has transformed into a moderate, reflective, middle-aged schoolteacher "in spite of everything regards himself as progressive."

If Starusch is plagued by doubts about the correctness of his moderately liberal views, the dentist represents complete faith in the power of reason, science, and technology to ameliorate, if not completely eliminate, man's pain. He has no patience with action lacking a rational basis, calling it "active stupidity" and comparing it with "the precipitate extraction of teeth, this mania for creating gaps that no longer hurt." Progress may come only at a snail's pace, but it is inevitable if pursued rationally. Thus, he supports the more mature Starusch (even as he works on his "wisdom" teeth) in the latter's resolve to dissuade Scherbaum from his plan.

On the other end of the political spectrum from the dentist is Vero Lewand. She represents the view popular in some quarters of West German society, particularly in the late 1960's, that society is too corrupt to be reformed and must be violently swept aside before any real progress is possible, even if there is no clear vision of the society that will replace it. Vero is used more as a foil for Grass's devastating criticism of the radical left than as a serious rival for Scherbaum's political soul, however, for Scherbaum speaks contemptuously of Che Guevara as "Vero's pin-up" and notes that "she reads Mao like my mother reads Rilke."

Irmgard Seifert, dubbed "the arch angel" by her students, is obsessed with the guilt she incurred as a teenager when, as a leader in the Nazi league of German girls, she helped to instruct young boys in the use of bazookas and denounced a peasant for refusing to allow military maneuvers on his land. Unable to come to terms with her past in any constructive way, she fails to regard her pain as "an instrument of knowledge," as Starusch does, and she looks upon Scherbaum as a personal savior while investing his proposed sacrifice with redemptive significance. Although she means to encourage him with her verbal self-flagellation, Seifert ultimately helps to dissuade Scherbaum from his plan. The dentist proves to be correct in observing to Starusch: "Your colleague's enthusiasm will suggest to your student what kind of supporters his action is likely to attract. The more she raves the harder it will be for him to light a match."

Philipp Scherbaum represents extreme sensitivity and political innocence. When Starusch takes him to visit the scene of his proposed action, Scherbaum reacts to the sight of the fur-coated women gorging themselves against the backdrop of Kurfürstendamm Street, with its materialistic excesses, by vomiting uncontrollably. The irony of Scherbaum's plight is apparent in his comment: "I'm not supposed to throw up, they are, when Max burns." His protest against insensitivity presupposes a degree of sensitivity similar to his own.

While Starusch admires Scherbaum's purity and innocence, he realizes that they are possible only because his ideals have never been tested against reality. In the real world, matters are never simply black and white but shades of gray, and compromise, the loss of political innocence, is always required for progress to be made. Neither Grass nor Starusch appears entirely comfortable with this truth, but there is no help for it: "There will always be pain."

Serving as mouthpieces for particular philosophical positions and attitudes and presented to the reader solely through the eyes of Starusch, a most unreliable narrator, the characters in *Local Anaesthetic* clearly do not appear as fully developed, realistic human beings. Through all Grass's caricaturing and distortion, however, important archetypal patterns of human thought and experience are recognizable.

Themes and Meanings

At the most fundamental level, *Local Anaesthetic* is a novel about political maturation, the growth through experience from a state of innocent idealism to a state of ambivalence and acceptance of limitations and contradictions. While the novel conveys a pervading sense of sadness over the fact that the gaining of wisdom involves a certain disillusionment, surrender of utopian ideals, and dulling of sensitivity, it concludes that there is no choice but to accept mankind's inability to eliminate all the painful aspects of human existence. Ultimately, Grass would agree with the dentist that to eliminate human failings would be to eliminate man. Thus, the best that one can do to alleviate the pain is to continue the Sisyphus-like struggle for rational remedies (rather than "creating gaps that no longer hurt") and to resort to the judicious use of "local anaesthetics," a term which obviously refers to both pharmacological and psychological painkillers within the context of the novel.

The extensive metaphorical use of the language of dentistry is one of the most striking stylistic features of *Local Anaesthetic*, and Starusch's sessions in the dentist's chair lend the novel its narrative backbone. From that center, however, the story wanders freely through the present and the past, the real and the imagined, as seen through the unreliable and sometimes confusing filter of Starusch's conscious narration and subconscious thoughts. The theme of contradiction, paradox, and uncertainty finds its appropriate reflection in Grass's liberal use of oxymoron as the most adequate linguistic representation of reality. Even the relationship between Starusch and Seifert, for example, is described as "distinguished by passionate moderation." Thus the novel's unconventional, nonlinear structure as well as its inconclusive, often contradictory language must be seen not as a flaw but as an inevitable consequence of the themes which Grass seeks to present.

Critical Context

After the overwhelming critical success of the Danzig trilogy which includes *The Tin Drum*, *Katz und Maus* (1961; *Cat and Mouse*, 1963), and *Hundejahre* (1963; *Dog Years*, 1965), *Local Anaesthetic* was not warmly received. Many critics longed for the comic and grotesque aspects of the earlier works and their baroque richness of plot, detail, and characterization. Whereas the earlier novels shared the theme of "coming to terms with the past" and allowed themselves a narrative view from below or outside society, *Local Anaesthetic* focuses on the present and places its characters within society. It is a reflection of the author's concern and involvement with contemporary political questions and is best read in conjunction with his nonfiction political essays and speeches of the same period, *Über das Selbstverständliche* (1968; partially translated in *Speak Out!*, 1969).

To be sure, *Local Anaesthetic* lacks the dynamism of the earlier works, but that is hardly surprising in a novel in which one of the dominant themes is expressed in the line: "Keep up your dialogue with the boy. Dialogue prevents action." To a considerable degree, the turning away from an obsession with the past toward the concerns of the present can be seen not only as representing the political maturation of the author but also as coinciding with that of West Germany. While never losing sight of the fact that the seeds of the present lie in the past, Grass's novel seriously and imaginatively considers difficult questions which, though clearly tied to the West Germany of the late 1960's, are certain to remain of interest to a wider readership.

Sources for Further Study

Hayman, Ronald. *Günter Grass*, 1985.

Hollington, Michael. *Günter Grass: The Writer in a Pluralist Society*, 1980.

Lawson, Richard H. *Günter Grass*, 1984.

Miles, Keith. *Günter Grass*, 1975.

Thomas, Noel. *The Narrative Works of Günter Grass: A Critical Interpretation*, 1982.

Dennis McCormick

THE LONG VOYAGE

Author: Jorge Semprun (1923-   )
Type of plot: Historical realism
Time of plot: From 1936 to 1945
Locale: A train carrying prisoners across France to a German concentration
    camp; the French countryside; and the camp itself
First published: Le Grand Voyage, 1963 (English translation, 1964)

Principal character:
> MANUEL (GÉRARD), the narrator, a twenty-year-old Spanish
> exile, now a philosophy student working for the Maquis

The Novel

The opening of *The Long Voyage* compels total attention, as the narrator begins speaking about a nightmare journey in progress. From his first words, "There is the cramming of the bodies into the boxcar, the throbbing pain in the right knee. The days, the nights. I force myself and try to count the days, to count the nights," a mood of extraordinary psychological intensity is set. The narrator—his name, background, personality, and occupation a mystery—reports that he is confined among 120 men "stacked in on top of one another" in a freight car moving across occupied France in 1943. It is apparent from his description and the terse tone of his speech that the conditions of physical stress and psychological horror which he is experiencing will require an exceptional effort of mind and body for survival. At first, the details that he presents force the reader to concentrate on the purely physical demands of the situation; then, as the narrator begins to demonstrate the ways in which he uses the powers of his mind and imagination to combat these pressures, it becomes apparent that even the strongest body will not have sufficient strength without a complementary mental fitness. In a further widening of scope, the narrator employs associative images from the unfolding present, the long inland voyage of the title, to provide connections to the past and projections into the future beyond the completion of the journey.

During the five days that the German prison train carrying members of the Maquis (the legendary French underground) moves toward its destination, the narrator, a so-called Spanish Red who has fled from the Basque country into exile in France, describes his life in the Resistance, his capture and transportation to the camp, some fragments about his existence in the camp, his reflections upon his liberation at the end of the war, and his reasons for waiting sixteen years to write about his experiences. The surging core of the narrative is the journey, so intense and desperate, so completely absorbing, that sporadic relief is necessary for the reader as well as for the narrator. Consequently, like a motif in a musical composition that recurs as a point of departure and return, the dreadful trip continues, interrupted strategically by related episodes that progressively reveal more about the narrator and his life.

Driven from his home in Barcelona when he was thirteen years old by Francisco Franco's Fascist forces, the narrator, Manuel (who is known to his colleagues by his nom de guerre, Gérard), was studying philosophy in France when that country was conquered by the Germans. Choosing to become a member of the Resistance, he was active in partisan operations until betrayal led to his capture. He begins the journey to the concentration camp in Weimar with the same attitude with which he approaches every new situation. He has consciously trained himself, in accordance with his vocation as a scholar-philosopher, to attune very closely the responses of his mind to any occurrence. He has already prepared a basic series of precepts and principles for any course of action. In addition, although he seems very focused on the self, he maintains a sympathetic curiosity about his colleagues' behavior and is prepared to work with them for the welfare of all. These characteristics serve him well in the chaos of the boxcar, in which survival depends on attention to detail (where one stands, how one drinks, whom one trusts), and Manuel, although only twenty years old, has had considerable experience with conditions demanding rapid action, physical endurance, and quick wit.

As the voyage continues, Manuel is reminded of incidents in his life previous to his capture. His commitment to freedom is shown in its formative stages as he enthusiastically tests his ideas against those of his fellow students; then his faith is given actuality in the emerging practical strength that enables him to maintain his sanity while other men crumble. His belief that he fights not as a "patriot" but to maintain his (and the world's) essential humanity is tested by the bestial acts of the SS but is reinforced by contact with German conscripts. The understated heroism of his colleagues in the Maquis lives in his mind as an inspiration, but each individual death is a unique, surprising, and unsettling experience, sometimes so bizarre that a kind of gallows humor must be used to alleviate his rage at the Nazis, which might further threaten any rational action.

On the fourth night of the voyage, the story unfolds into the future, as Manuel introduces events following the war, which, as they occur, lead him back to the trip itself. The entire sequence of events following his liberation in April, 1945, is an example of the disjunction of differing perceptions. He cannot share in the banter of the liberating soldiers, nor can he adjust to the "normal" routine of official procedures. He carries his awareness of the camp with him into the world; he remains distant (thus, paradoxically, more attractive) when his mates are flirting with women; he has become intensely interested in others on the "inside," especially the Jews who have known suffering beyond his own. This interlude, even though it is rife with uncertainty, is nevertheless a relief from the trip, which becomes more harrowing with each digression.

As the men are tested with increasing severity, the interludes become less a leavening of tension and more a complement to it, changing its magnitude, but not its awful persistence. During this period, instead of imagining a positive existence to counterbalance the present, Manuel, in writing about it, makes the trip somewhat more bearable by juxtaposing its worst moments to even more terrible visions of evil. The story of the arrival and subsequent slaughter of a group of Jewish children and the story of the disappearance of his friend Hans (a German Jew known as "Phillipe") are attempts to confront the worst obscenity with its only antidote, the most unusual and purest heroism. The journey moves to its conclusion with the death of "the guy from Semur," Manuel's soul mate for the five days which have become a lifetime. The last moments of the trip are described while a rush of imagery streams through the narrator's mind, the focus narrowed again to the physical trial of the men now at or beyond the limits of sanity, at the threshold of death.

Although the voyage is concluded, the novel continues in a brief second book, almost a coda, in which the narrative perspective shifts to the third person, gradually increasing the distance that the narrator maintains from the experience and placing the story into the context of history. As Manuel enters the camp where he will spend the remainder of the war, his thoughts turn to his greatest fear and his most significant motivation to survive and record his exploits: "Gérard tries to engrave all this in his memory, meanwhile vaguely thinking that it is well within the realm of possibility that the impending death of all the spectators may efface forever the memory of this spectacle." As "the certainty of this idea takes hold of him," his resolve to persevere, after the horror of the long voyage, is very strong. The thought that he is about to "leave the world of the living" pulses like a throbbing image of the monstrous reality he must face. The novel itself is his testament to the effects of the awful experience and the possibilities of enduring to continue the fight against Fascism.

The Characters

Not only is Manuel the one character of any dimension in the book; it is actually his *mind* that is the novel's focal point, the novel's primary character. Some of the other people whom Manuel meets are momentarily striking in his description of them (particularly the man he rides literally pressed against for the entire train trip, called "the guy from Semur"), but none of them has any real existence beyond those moments when that person is in the narrator's presence. These characters are not reduced to caricature or type—Jorge Semprun is particularly adept at capturing character with a short remark and at suggesting complex psychological dimensions in a brief conversation—but their primary function is to reflect or react to Manuel's mood. Manuel's mental processes are so important because Semprun has written

The Long Voyage to demonstrate that the mind is the source of a person's strength and to show that the inner working of a person's mind is the best way to know his spirit and soul.

Semprun believes that integrity of character comes from clarity of thought and openness to the challenge of contradictory ideas. His commitment to the absolute freedom of expression stems from his hatred of the enclosures that any totalitarian system places over the minds of its subjects. Manuel is a warrior whose weapon is his mental agility, which permits him to act effectively in situations that present no easy solution and to endure situations in which effective action is not possible.

Manuel's derision for SS methodology is separate from his hatred for their butchery. He sees the SS as the ultimate expression of a state that cannot adjust to spontaneity and that hates and fears the unexpected and the uncontrollable—precisely those qualities of life which Manuel regards as essential to the democratic society he defends. Manuel's refusal to hate Germans is part of his struggle to see people as individuals, not as abstractions, and to forge a world in which a man's existence is determined by an inner sense of continuing discovery.

Manuel's ability to dissociate himself temporarily from unpleasant surroundings and to live in a created realm enables him to handle stress well, and his facility for reconstructing the sensory impact of a vital, life-enhancing scene supports him by revivifying the best elements of the life that he is struggling to preserve. The closing pages of the novel, written in the form of an extended paragraph to evoke the rush of sensations in his mind as the long journey concludes, are like a final fusion of mental assessment and physical reaction. The simultaneous assimilation of data and expression of intent affirms Manuel's methods and the possibility of his survival. Much too intelligent and experienced to have any illusions of romantic heroism, Manuel is an archetype of the existential hero made popular by Albert Camus—a hard man in a hard world whose heart and soul are still humanity's best hope.

Themes and Meanings

Semprun's essential task in *The Long Voyage* is to bear witness to the atrocity that permanently altered the *spiritus mundi*, to show the kind of person who could live through the horror and still retain some semblance of humanity, and to demonstrate that the qualities of character that made survival and resistance possible are also crucial to the construction of a society in which such evil would not be possible. The distortion of reason in the twisted, lockstep logic of the SS is constantly presented in contrast to the pure reason of the truly free man. Nevertheless, for all that reason can do, there are some things beyond its capabilities, some actions so terrible that anyone "imbued with the prejudices, the realities of the past"—that is, normal life—will find them impossible to imagine. Where *The Long Voyage* goes beyond even the authentic, convincing description of incarceration and torture is in Semprun's understanding of the effect of these experiences on the camp survivor. When Manuel, at twenty a historical scholar, a philosopher, an athlete, and a linguist, is driven beyond reason, his mental reconstruction can serve as a guide to psychic survival in the modern age.

The most significant manifestation of Manuel's temporary psychosis is his changing response to his experiences. At first, he resolves to report what he has seen so that no one will be able to say, in stupefied amazement after it is too late, "What do you know about that?" Then, as horror piles upon horror, he decides that he will tell no one, believing that he is now beyond the comprehension of people who have not shared his trials. He has also decided that he must somehow forget, regardless of whether he will ever be ready to remember. For sixteen years, he says nothing, and during that time, his life is sporadically and uncontrollably interrupted by a sudden rush of painful memory, as an image or thought triggers recollection. At these moments, he is convinced that he is eternally alone, the ultimate exile, not only without a country (Franco is still in power in Spain) but also, and perhaps worse, no longer comfortable in the mental landscape which he once inhabited with joy. He thinks, repeatedly, "I'm all alone, when I remember this voyage. The solitude of this voyage is probably going to prey on me for the rest of my life."

The passage of time and the effect of thoughts that he cannot suppress enable him finally to move beyond the prison of the self. He realizes that he can rejoin humanity by recognizing that in indulging his own suffering he is claiming, falsely, a unique and unjustifiable place of importance for himself. Almost of its own accord, the powerful apparatus for deliberation that he has constructed works: He realizes, recalling the death of the Jewish children, that he has kept this dreadful vision to himself out of a kind of perverse pride. It is his mark of singularity that only he has seen such horror. Watching postwar children who are reaching their adolescence, he decides that he has no right to keep to himself a story that "concerns everyone, especially the children who are sixteen today," the children who were not murdered during the war. His resolution to act, to tell the story of the voyage, is based on Albert Camus' contention that to choose action creates meaning, even if life cannot, rationally, be shown to have any meaning. Thus, in a final triumph of the rational mind that Manuel loves, combined with a faith that carries one across the void which logic cannot leap, he has found a way to combat the horror of the Holocaust. In this way, he has validated his intellectual and instinctive reactions to the world and demonstrated that the freedom he treasures is resilient enough to survive the consequences of tyranny. In addition, he has shown that his humanity, expressed in his love for his comrades, can never be broken. As he says, in an unusual but justifiable moment of sentiment when two young partisans permit an SS officer to live, "But I'm happy that these two young partisans have committed this foolish act . . . [that they] who have knowingly opted for the possibility of dying, who . . . so often faced death in a war that showed them no quarter, can emerge from this war clean and pure of heart."

Critical Context

Jorge Semprun, a survivor of Buchenwald, has committed his life and his art to the building of a world in which such atrocities can never happen again. *The Long Voyage* belongs with the works of such writers as Primo Levi and Elie Wiesel as a record of what the Holocaust was actually like, and as an account of the effect of that terrible moment in history on the minds and souls of those who lived through it. In collaboration with Alain Resnais, Semprun wrote the screenplay for *La Guerre est finie* (1966) a film which shows a man returning to Spain to continue the struggle against Franco; Semprun also helped Constantin Costa-Gavras to adapt the novel *Z* (1966; English translation, 1968) into the film of the same title which was released in 1969. Under the pseudonym Federico Sánchez, he published *Autobiografía de Federico Sánchez* (1978; *The Autobiography of Federico Sanchez*, 1979), a history of the Communist underground in Spain, which continues to demonstrate that a man of the Left in Europe can also be, like George Orwell, against all forms of totalitarianism.

Sources for Further Study

Boyers, Robert. "The Voyage of Jorge Semprun," in *Atrocity and Amnesia: The Political Novel Since 1945*, 1985.

Butor, Michel. *Passing Time*, 1960.

Géniès, Bernard. "L'Expérience de J. Semprun à Buchenwald," in *La Quinzaine Littéraire*. CCCXXI (March, 1980), pp. 24-25.

Schmigalle, Gunther. "Jorge Semprun's *Kritik des Kommunismes*," in *Iberoamerica*. XII (1984), pp. 3-21.

Sinnegen, J. *Narrative and Ideology*, 1982.

Leon Lewis

THE LOSER

Author: George Konrád (1933-   )
Type of plot: Psychological realism
Time of plot: The 1980's
Locale: Budapest and other areas in Hungary
First published: A cinkos, 1980 (English translation, 1982)

> *Principal characters:*
> T, the narrator and protagonist, a Jewish Communist and a
>   writer and scholar
> HIS WIFE
> DANI, his brother
> TERI, Dani's girlfriend

The Novel

The Loser begins and ends in the Hungary of the 1980's, when the revolutionary fervor of the Hungarian Communists, who had welcomed the Russians as liberators both from the older hierarchical regime and from the Nazis, has been replaced by disillusionment. The narrator, known only as T, who is upper-class by birth but a Communist by conviction, has spent much of his life in forced labor camps, in military service, or in prison. Always somewhat alienated because he is Jewish, always suspect because of his intellectual independence, in his later years he has been confined in a mental institution.

In the first section of the novel, T describes life in the asylum, which becomes a metaphor for life under Communist rule, where, as he says to the director, the people presumed to be insane are actually permitted more freedom of thought and speech than anyone else. At the end of the section, T is released; with his marriage destroyed and his career in suspension, however, he has little interest in life.

The next three sections of the novel trace the narrator's history in chronological order. The second section begins with T's farewell to his younger brother Dani, who is leaving that night for the West. Dani, an energetic, irrational young man with a dangerous appetite for excitement, says that he no longer trusts himself with his temperamental, whorish girlfriend, Teri, who is as destructive and untrustworthy as the present political system. If he cannot free himself from the system and from her, Dani says, he may kill either Teri or himself.

After Dani leaves, T recalls his youth: the prosperous, secure environment in which he grew up; his kindly shopkeeper grandfather whose honesty and charity denied the usual assumptions about greedy, bourgeois Jews; his lusty, devoted grandmother. He remembers his delicate mother and roistering father, the nursemaid and the young aunt who initiated him into sexuality, and other characters who were part of a world which seemed destined to endure forever.

In section 3, T relives the collapse of that world. First comes World War II and Fascist domination. Perhaps T's detachment from life begins with the torture of his mistress, Sophie. He likes to think that it is his loyalty to the other Communists which keeps him from talking and thereby saving her, but perhaps he is only indifferent. At any rate, she is sacrificed and dies at Auschwitz, uselessly, since their comrades are betrayed in any case. During their sufferings, however, the Hungarian Communists dream of revolution and of rescue by their Russian comrades. Thus the narrator escapes from forced labor for the Fascists to fight with the partisans, then flees to the Russian lines. There he is shocked to find that the Russian Communists have no sense of brotherhood with the Hungarian Communists. In the months which follow, T is recaptured by the Germans and then taken by the Russians, who use him to persuade Hungarian soldiers to surrender. Bitterly, he comments on his later sense of guilt, when those trusting Hungarians return to their country only after ten years in the labor camps of the Russians, who had called them to be comrades.

The fourth section of the novel deals with T's gradual disillusionment with the ideals for which he has worked and fought. When Budapest is "liberated" in 1945, the Communists expect a state ruled by poets and scholars, with free speech, a free press, and an enlightened society. Instead, there is repression. Yearning for the freedom which has been their dream, the Hungarians rise up in 1956 but are defeated by Russian tanks. Once again, T goes to prison, but this time the repressive society is a Communist state. At this point, T seems to have two choices: to leave Hungary for the West or to toady to the authorities by producing noncontroversial research—playing the academic game but actually abandoning both the search for truth and the expression of his own opinion. Like George Konrád himself, however, he chooses rather to stay in Eastern Europe, where he has invested so much of his life, circulating his writings privately and accepting the periodic knock on the door, the house search, the prison term.

The final part of the novel focuses on T's relationships with the two most important people in his life, his wife and his brother. For two decades, the relationship with his wife has withstood uncertainty and separation. Finally, however, after his confinement in the asylum, T finds that his desire for solitude is stronger than his love for his wife. As he withdraws from intimacy, she finds someone else and the marriage disintegrates. Dani's relationship with his own girlfriend, Teri, is also unsatisfactory. Just after T has decided to return to the asylum, which he prefers to outside society, he learns that Dani has killed Teri and is being hunted for murder. Returning once again to action, rather than detachment, the narrator finds his brother and helps him to hang himself.

The Characters

T and the other Hungarian Communists, like Konrád himself, had hoped for a new freedom which would enable people of all classes to assert their individual wills, as T's prosperous parents and grandparents, and others of their class, had been able to do in a hierarchical society. They were disillusioned to discover that the Communist society in practice allowed freedom to no one. The characters in this novel are divided between those who insist on being themselves, even in a repressive society, and those who submerge their personalities and structure their utterances, even their thoughts, in order to seem like everyone else.

T is by nature an intellectual, a person who examines every event and every theory in the light of reason. His willingness to envision change makes him a revolutionary; when the new society develops, however, based on unthinking acceptance of simplistic theories and the practice based upon them, T has no place in it. Throughout the novel, T contrasts himself with those who choose not to question, such as the director of the asylum, and the academics who would teach him how to succeed without doing any significant thinking. T cannot surrender his mind, even to preserve his physical self. Unfortunately, as he lives more and more in the mind, he loses the capacity to live in the heart, and thus his marriage is the final sacrifice to a society that has driven its brightest members into conformity or into themselves.

T's wife is a bright, outgoing person who is similarly stunted. Generous and imaginative, she cannot be at ease in a society where secretiveness is a necessity. When T can no longer reach out to her or to anyone else, she finds a young lover and abandons the effort to reach her husband.

Dani, T's untrustworthy younger brother, has been both a revolutionary and an informer, just as he has been both the lover and, finally, the murderer of his beloved. Adventuresome, emotional, unstable, he seems to court death as the final adventure. Needing freedom as much as his older brother needs it, he responds to deprivation with violence. When he learns that Teri has informed on him in order to prevent his leaving the country, he knows himself to be imprisoned by her and by his society. He had predicted that if he did not make it to the West and freedom, he would explode. He does, murdering Teri and then killing himself.

The other characters in the novel are presented through T's eyes as well as through their own words and actions but appear and depart as he recounts his life story. Sometimes, like the Cossack of World War II, the character will reappear in order to reveal his fate. The Cossack, unlike T, is a successful adapter. Twenty years after his initial encounter with T, he is a successful Soviet politician. When he encounters the protagonist once again, it is to define freedom, which, he says, is the ability to lie in bed, drink vodka, and chase women, while convincing everyone that you are superior. Such characters as the director of the asylum, the Cossack, the lieutenant colonel who conducts the house search, and the brand bank manager, whom T sees as a double at the end of the story, cannot understand those who refuse to conform to society's demands. Thus they provide a significant contrast to the individualists: the narrator, his wife, and his brother.

Themes and Meanings

The title *The Loser* could be applied to T, who at the end of the novel has lost his freedom, his work, his wife, and even that dream of a better society for which he has been willing to give his life. Certainly his fellow academics, the director of the asylum, and other characters who have fitted their expectations to the possibilities which their society affords are puzzled by what seems to be T's insistence on losing. His desire to retreat to the asylum is another version of his brother's impulse toward violence and death.

The title could surely be plural, as well, for a society which brands its subtlest, most rigorous thinkers as enemies of the state, which fetters their minds and imprisons their bodies, which denies them publication and expels them from libraries and from universities, is a society of losers. Konrád suggests this interpretation with a number of metaphors. For example, he contemplates the closed ward in the mental institution, which is not unlike an Eastern European Communist country. In order to protect society, supposedly, one begins by locking up those who threaten to harm themselves. Soon one moves to those who are troublesome or who annoy someone in power. Finally, those who are not locked up become so nervous that they wish to be, in order to avoid responsibility. While this argument is supposedly the director's justification for his asylum, the passage is clearly Konrád's vision of his own society. Cynically, the director points out that Hungary has a history of defeat and occupation and that Hungarians have learned to be losers who do whatever is necessary in order to survive: to lie, to cower, to fawn.

T, however, cannot be content with existence on those terms. He understands another metaphor, Dani's identification of Teri with the regime which Dani must flee. The obsessive love, the changeable emotions, the flagrant infidelity which are exhibited by Teri are also characteristic of the Communist state, which seems to punish or reward by whim. Although at any given moment there is only one approved opinion, that opinion will change as the political power shifts, and thus an individual who hopes to stay in power must be an intellectual whore not unlike the changeable Teri, who, significantly, is perfectly willing to betray Dani rather than to lose him. Like her society, however, Teri loses what she crushes with her possessiveness.

In this new society, progress is halted by the constant pressure toward conformity and either repression or destruction of the self seems to be inevitable. It is not surprising that T, who is a loser in his own country, should consider leaving. Yet he does not flee. One reason is that he loves his country; as he says, he has his whole life invested in it. Another may be, as the director of the asylum comments, that from time to time the pressure is relaxed, and T can talk to foreign correspondents or travel abroad, where his works have been published and where he has a considerable following. A more important reason may be suggested when T thinks about his periods in prison. There, he says, his inner self is tested. There he can discover whether he has a core of integrity which cannot be destroyed. Again, the metaphor is obvious. Communist Hungary is a prison from which, understandably, many have made every effort to escape. Having decided to remain, one must use it as a testing place. Sadly, in his need to remain true to himself, T has had to withdraw from human distraction, even from love. Ironically, as he preserves his own self while waiting for death, he must once more enter the world in order to save his brother from execution by helping him to kill himself.

Critical Context

With the publication of *A látogató* (1969; *The Case Worker*, 1974), Konrád was recognized in Hungary as an outstanding writer. *A városalapító* (1977; *The City Builder*, 1977) and *The Loser*, which are clearer attacks on the repressive system into which Communism has evolved, were circulated by the process called samizdat (self-publishing, or private circulation), while being officially published outside Hungary. With each book, Konrád's reputation has grown; yet each book has its strengths and its weaknesses.

The Case Worker is a poignant and universal story of a social worker's involvement with a defective child, whose parents were driven to suicide by their hopeless situation. The book was praised because of its effectiveness within its narrow focus. On the other hand, *The City Builder* is far more diffuse, lacking a forward-moving plot and seeming to some critics to be simply an exploration of the consciousness of the protagonist, a city planner who has become disillusioned as the dream of progress deteriorates into a fearful and stagnant bureaucracy. Although Konrád's descriptive passages have always been admired, in *The City Builder* there seems to be no development in plot or character to relate those vivid passages. With *The Loser*, Konrád combines the development of *The Case Worker* with the scope of *The City Builder* to produce a gripping novel.

In all of his works, as the critics have pointed out, consciousness is primary. The world is seen through the eyes of a single narrator, who is also the protagonist. An educated, sensitive person with an intellectual's capacity for independent thought, the narrator can relate events to the movements of history as well as to his own experience. It is interesting that, as the works progress, the narrator seems to become more detached, even from his own emotions. In critical response to *The Loser*, there has been some disagreement as to whether T's aloofness is meant to represent a personal reaction or the final destruction of any self in the repressive state. There is also disagreement as to whether the protagonist is a sympathetic figure or a satirical target. In any case, the clear structure of the novel leaves no confusion about the events which shape the protagonist. That his character is complex enough to cause such critical discussion may be an indication of Konrád's mastery of his form.

Sources for Further Study

Blake, Patricia. Review in *Time*. CXXI (January 17, 1983), p. 70.

Koger, Grove. Review in *Library Journal*. CVII (September 15, 1982), p. 1769.

Publishers Weekly. Review. CCXXII (August 6, 1982), p. 58.

Sennett, Richard. Review in *The New York Times Book Review*. LXXXVII (September 26, 1982), p. 1.

Solotaroff, Ted. "The Weight of History," in *The New Republic*. CLXXXVIII (February 14, 1983), pp. 28-33.

Rosemary M. Canfield-Reisman

THE LOST HONOR OF KATHARINA BLUM
How Violence Develops and Where It Can Lead

Author: Heinrich Böll (1917-1985)
Type of plot: Social realism
Time of plot: February 20, 1974, through February 24, 1974
Locale: An unnamed German city (probably West Berlin)
First published: Die verlorene Ehre der Katharina Blum: Oder, Wie Gewalt entstehen und wohin sie führen kann, 1974 (English translation, 1975)

> *Principal characters:*
> KATHARINA BLUM, the protagonist, a victim of the police and the press
> WERNER TÖTGES, a *News* reporter
> LUDWIG GÖTTEN, a suspected "terrorist" who becomes Katharina's lover
> HUBERT BLORNA, a lawyer and one of Katharina's employers
> TRUDE BLORNA, "THE RED," his wife
> ALOIS STRÄUBLEDER, a wealthy industrialist in pursuit of Katharina
> ELSE WOLTERSHEIM, a friend of Katharina
> KONRAD BEITERS, a former Nazi and Else's lover
> ERWIN BEIZMENNE, a police commissioner
> PETER HACH, the public prosecutor and the Blornas' friend
> WALTER MOEDING, Beizmenne's assistant

The Novel

The Lost Honor of Katharina Blum examines, as Heinrich Böll's subtitle suggests, "how violence develops and where it can lead." The novel, narrated in what purports to be responsible journalistic prose, begins by "objectively" describing Katharina Blum's murder of Werner Tötges, a reporter for the irresponsible *News*, and then attempting to account for that murder by exploring the four days between Katharina's meeting with Ludwig Götten, a suspected terrorist, and Tötges' murder. As a responsible journalist, the narrator carefully identifies the sources of his "report": "doctored" transcripts of police interrogations and the testimony of Hubert Blorna, an attorney, and Peter Hach, the public prosecutor. In the course of his narrative, he also quotes extensively from stories in the *News*, which bears a strong resemblance to the *Bild-Zeitung*, a German mass-circulation tabloid with which Böll had feuded about journalistic practices.

After listing his sources and explaining his narrative method, the narrator presents the brutal "facts": Four days after meeting Ludwig Götten, Katharina killed Tötges in her apartment and turned herself in to Walter Moeding, the crime commissioner. The balance of the novel concerns not the murder, the "lowest of all levels," but the "higher planes" of motivation and meaning that transform a so-called political murder into an act of integrity.

The story begins with Katharina's attendance at a carnival party at the home of her friend Else Woltersheim; there she meets Ludwig, the subject of police surveillance and, after dancing exclusively with him, takes him to her condominium, where they spend the night.

The next morning, the police storm her apartment and when they cannot find Ludwig, they interrogate her, search the apartment, and take her to the police station for further questioning. As she leaves with the police, a photographer from the *News* takes several pictures of her (the least flattering and most suggestive of her "criminality" is the one subsequently printed in the *News*), and the narrator uses the occasion to introduce the recurrent theme of collaboration between the press and the police.

After making her statement and being interrogated by the police, Katharina is escorted to her apartment by a sympathetic Moeding, who cautions her not to use the telephone (it has obviously been "bugged") or to look at the news (or the *News*). His warning proves justified; her later conversation with Ludwig is tapped, and the *News* indicts and convicts her of being Ludwig's mistress and accomplice, though Ludwig has not yet been convicted of a crime. By distorting Hubert Blorna's answers to seemingly innocuous questions and by using innuendos about Katharina's gentlemen visitors and the purchase price of her condominium, the *News* successfully converts Katharina's virtues—her desire to protect Alois Sträubleder, a wealthy industrialist, and her diligence and thrift—to vices.

When Katharina returns for more interrogation, the police commissioner, Erwin Beizmenne, confronts her with two tangential items gleaned from an exhaustive search of her apartment: inordinately large gasoline receipts, which she dismisses accurately but unconvincingly as having been the result of aimless driving, and an expensive ruby ring, which she refuses to identify (it is a gift from Sträubleder, who is pursuing Katharina unsuccessfully). Beizmenne also interrogates Else Woltersheim and some of her guests at the Wednesday night party.

While there is no official police case against Katharina, police collaboration with the press provides an unofficial case against her. The *News* tries her in the press, convicts her, and, as Hubert's wife, Trude Blorna, predicted, ruins her life.

Tötges visits Katharina's sick mother, manufactures damaging statements, and quite possibly causes the old woman's death, which the *News* ironically blames on Katharina's behavior. The unscrupulous and resourceful Tötges also uses derogatory comments from Katharina's loutish ex-husband to defame her further.

Because, as Katharina states, everyone reads the *News*, the events that follow the lurid newspaper accounts are predictable: She receives obscene calls and letters, some of which allude to her Communist views, and she is shunned by her neighbors. In response, Katharina proceeds, methodically, to smash the contents of her immaculate apartment, a symbol of her life which has now been invaded and destroyed by the press. The Blornas, her friends, also suffer from the *News*'s coverage of Katharina because they refuse to abandon her. Trude, known as "the Red" because of her hair, is referred to as "Trude the Red," with Communist implications; Hubert, a lawyer for Sträubleder's companies, loses money, prestige, and position because he and Trude support Katharina and because Trude insults Sträubleder.

The police, who have traced Ludwig's call to Katharina, finish interrogating her and capture Ludwig at Sträubleder's resort home, where he has been hiding. (Katharina gave him the key that Sträubleder had given her.) Nevertheless, Katharina becomes more composed. When she meets the Blornas in the afternoon, they unsuccessfully attempt to dissuade her from going through with her planned Sunday interview with Tötges. Unfortunately for Tötges, Katharina reads his Sunday *News* story, which blames Katharina for her mother's death. The story triggers Katharina's decision to get a gun and to find Tötges. When she cannot find him, she returns to her apartment and waits. He enters, calls her "Blumikins," and asks for a "bang"; she pulls out the pistol and repeatedly shoots him, ironically giving him the "bang" he has requested.

Böll's novel, which begins with an "objective" murder, concludes appropriately with Katharina's first-person subjective account of her emotions, attitudes, and motives at the time of the violent crime. The violence of Katharina's act is not, however, the only violence suggested by Böll's subtitle, though her violence certainly does have both personal and political repercussions. The "violence" to which Böll alludes also refers to Tötges' attack on Katharina, for his persecution of her effectively destroys her "honor" in almost a sexual sense: He "penetrates" the innocent Katharina psychologically and emotionally, and when he attempts to make his metaphorical rape literal, his violent action leads to his own destruction.

The Characters

In order to elicit the sympathies of his readers, Heinrich Böll presents Katharina Blum, his protagonist, as an innocent victim of press and police collaboration. She is the "nun," linked through her name and superficial similarities to Saint Catherine of Alexandria, but she is a saint in a post-Christian world marked by secularism and materialism. The exemplar of her capitalistic society, she is the independent career woman whose industry, thrift, and independence are rewarded by the condominium that is the symbol of her economic success. She gains sympathy as a victim, but she also forfeits sympathy because she is an uncritical participant in the society that destroys her. Despite her incarceration, for example, she has plans for investing her accumulating capital in a restaurant; she seems to have learned little about the society that persecuted her because of her loyalty, independence, and political vulnerability (neither the "Christian'" businessman Sträubleder nor the former Nazi Konrad Beiters is attacked).

Although she seems—until she kills Tötges—passive in the face of the relentless persecution, her passivity is, Böll suggests, caused by her faith in justice and in the system. Appropriately enough, her only "resistance" is semantic, for she shares the narrator's emphasis on linguistic precision and what he calls "reportorial obligations." Katharina insists that "gracious" rather than "nice" be used to describe the Blornas' conduct, and she distinguishes between "advances" and "becoming amorous" when speaking of her ex-husband. Like the *News* reporter, the police do not share her linguistic sensitivity and are cavalier about the relationship between language and meaning.

To her persecutors, Katharina is a potential object of exploitation: Sträubleder wants to exploit her sexually, Beizmenne wants to use her politically, and Tötges wants to exploit her both journalistically and sexually. Their actions are brutal, violent, and insensitive; Sträubleder repays her loyalty to him by stating that she stole the key, Beizmenne attacks her honor by referring to her relationship with Ludwig in graphically obscene terms, and Tötges (his name derives from the German *töten*, meaning "to kill") destroys her reputation before attempting to seduce her. In fact, he causes his own death through his deceitful manipulation of language; so successful is he in distorting Katharina's image that he mistakes Katharina for his media creature and acts accordingly. Like Sträubleder, he is an opportunistic capitalist intent on exploitation.

Katharina's allies are simply no match for her adversaries. Ludwig is actually a thief, not a romantic terrorist allied with a revolutionary movement. The Blornas, who seem to belong to the capitalistic class allied to press and police, find that their position is quite tenuous, given their leftist orientation. Since they initially pose no real threat to the system, their "radical" views are accommodated, but when their intervention on Katharina's behalf threatens Sträubleder, they find that they are, like Katharina, expendable. They are social liberals who cannot confront their incompatibility with the system intellectually. (Böll may also be suggesting that they are not really incompatible with that system.)

Themes and Meanings

Böll's title suggests that Katharina's "lost honor" is an individual example of how people are destroyed by the violence in contemporary German society, and his subsequent disclaimer about the similarity between the fictional *News* and the *Bild-Zeitung* implicity identifies the press as the source of that violence. The press not only collaborates with the police and with business but also serves to express the neo-Fascist views of a repressive coalition dedicated to maintaining, through repressing dissidents, the status quo. That control may be exerted through the misuse and abuse of language will come as no surprise to those familiar with George Orwell's "Politics and the English Language," an essay that demonstrates how government may use language to mask reality and discourage critical thought.

By calling attention to Katharina's "lost honor," Böll also relates sex to violence and language, and he develops this idea early in the novel. When he first questions Katharina in her apartment, Beizmenne uses language to attack her: "Well, did he f—— you?" Such language is not intended to elicit information, but to offend, to hurt, to dehumanize. Tötges unwittingly duplicates Beizmenne's linguistic aggression when he asks her, "How about us having a bang for a start?" Katharina is aware of the irony when she pulls out the pistol and thinks, "Bang, if that's what you want." Since feminists have shown how pornography and obscenity are related to violence against women, Katharina's response is practically self-defense, an act of integrity and independence.

Because Tötges is so cavalier with language (at one point he explains his lies as an attempt to "help simple people express themselves more clearly"), the narrator attempts to demonstrate proper journalistic prose. By beginning with a "factual" account of the murder, the narrator, unlike Tötges, spares his readers the lurid details; as the narrator continues his account, he identifies his sources, checks secondhand information, corrects himself, and uses the word "allegedly" when he is not certain of his facts. Knowing the story is complex, he advises his readers that the story should "flow" but that certain "blockages," like tensions or pressures, may interfere. Those "blockages" do occur as the narrator is drawn, almost against his will, into Katharina's plight, and he does modify his "objective" tone as he becomes scathingly ironic and bitterly attacks such governmental methods as wiretapping. In effect, the narrator is compelled to abandon reportage for propaganda and to become the novelist.

Critical Context

The Lost Honor of Katharina Blum has its immediate origins in Böll's own battles with the *Bild-Zeitung*, which he had censured for its irresponsible reporting on the Baader-Meinhof Group, the object in Germany of a national manhunt in 1971. Böll was attacked for his defense of the Group—he had really only defended justice—and harassed by the police. Another victim of the *Bild-Zeitung* was Professor Peter Brückner, who was falsely accused of aiding the Group and was subsequently subjected to Katharina-like treatment by the media. Because Böll wrote the novel in response to governmental attacks on individual civil liberties, it is regarded as the most overtly political of his novels, and when it was successfully adapted to film by Volker Schlöndorff and Margaretha von Trotta in 1975, it became his most controversial work.

Despite its topicality, *The Lost Honor of Katharina Blum* does resemble Böll's other work; his criticism of governmental exercise of power has continued throughout his career. Having experienced National Socialism at first hand as a soldier in Adolf Hitler's army, Böll, in writing about the present, is affected by the past, which he sees reflected in what he regards as contemporary Fascism, with its totalitarian emphasis on the rights of the state over the rights of the individual. Of Böll's other novels, many concern the Fascist legacy in German life: *Haus ohne Hüter* (1954; *The Unguarded House*, 1957; also as *Tomorrow and Yesterday*), *Ansichten eines Clowns* (1963; *The Clown*, 1965), and, most notably, *Gruppenbild mit Dame* (1971; *Group Portrait with Lady*, 1973), which traces, through its protagonist, events in Germany beginning in 1922. *The Lost Honor of Katharina Blum*, however, has come to be regarded as his most successful novel.

Sources for Further Study
Conrad, Robert C. *Heinrich Böll*, 1981.
Heinrich Böll: On His Death, 1985. Translated by Patricia Crampton.
Magretta, William R., and Joan Magretta. "Story and Discourse: Schlöndorff and von Trotta's *The Lost Honor of Katharina Blum* (1975)," in *Modern European Filmmakers and the Art of Adaptation*, 1981.
Williams, Rhys W. "Heinrich Böll and the *Katharina Blum* Debate," in *Critical Quarterly*. XXI (1979), pp. 49-58.
Zipes, Jack. "The Political Dimensions of *The Lost Honor of Katharina Blum*," in *New German Critique*. XII (1977), pp. 75-84.

Thomas L. Erskine

LOUIS LAMBERT

Author: Honoré de Balzac (1799-1850)
Type of plot: Philosophical realism
Time of plot: 1811-1824
Locale: Vendôme, France
First published: 1832 (English translation, 1889)

> *Principal characters:*
> LOUIS LAMBERT (PYTHAGORAS), a prodigy, mystic, and thinly
>   disguised version of the young Balzac
> THE NARRATOR (THE POET), an older version of Balzac
>   recounting his youth
> PAULINE DE VILLENOIX, Lambert's fiancée and caretaker

The Novel

An autobiographical fable of self-identity, *Louis Lambert* is one of a few principal works in his multinovel epic *The Human Comedy* (1829-1848) that Honoré de Balzac explicitly called philosophical studies. Like most works in this genre, *Louis Lambert* lacks either action or plot development in the usual sense and reflects, rather, the intellectual growth of its protagonist from his childhood as a prodigy through his days at the Collège Vendôme to his insanity and death. In tracing his own spiritual growth and passion for mysticism, Balzac reorders and rearranges his own experience into a fiction that both reflects his actual development as a thinker and organizes its presentation so that it resembles but does not equal the facts of his life. Balzac distances himself, however, by making Louis a philosopher, not a writer of fiction, and also by telling his story from the viewpoint of another character, the narrator, rather than in the first person.

The novel opens with a description of Louis' intellectual childhood, his biblical reading to probe the mysteries of Scripture and his omnivorous reading of any other book that he could beg or borrow. Providentially encountering Madame de Staël, he is saved from a life of service in the army or in the Church and is to be educated at her expense. The bulk of the novel describes that education in the school of the Oratorians at Vendôme, an education that Louis (nicknamed "Pythagoras") and the narrator (nicknamed "the Poet") achieve despite the ignorance and malice of their instructors and classmates.

Balzac's descriptions of a highly regimented life at boarding school emphasize the uniformity of thought and performance that was its goal, and they also highlight the alienation of those who seek an education beyond the confines of a banal and structured curriculum. Ironically, Louis and the narrator are punished at every turn for not keeping up with the assigned studies that are, compared to the philosophical studies that they clandestinely pursue, dull and elementary. These secret studies, writings, and discussions occur at the risk of corporal punishment from the instructors and ridicule from the other schoolboys. When one of the fruits of Louis' studies, "Treatise on the Will," is discovered, it is indeed ridiculed, and both Pythagoras and the Poet continue to suffer the indignities and wretchedness of school for a short time longer until the narrator leaves the college.

The final phase of Louis' life begins in Paris with a brief story, in which he discovers the vanity and inconsequence of Parisian life before he returns to Blois. Once in Blois, Louis courts Pauline de Villenoix and, on the eve of his wedding, is so overcome by the prospect of marrying the angelic Pauline that he becomes utterly insane. This madness is foreshadowed from the novel's beginning and seems to be the inevitable outcome of a life devoted to exploring will, thought, and mysticism. It is the unfolding of the time-honored superstition that madness is the natural result of a life spent in study and meditation.

The narrator reenters Louis' life by chance, having met Louis' uncle and learned of his friend's unfortunate state. His encounter with the mystically mad Louis and his caretaker-fiancée, his recording of aphorisms, and his reverence for Louis lead the narrator to wonder whether his friend is truly mad or is in a constant state of ecstasy.

The Characters

Louis occupies center stage for most of the narrative, with the other characters taking up a necessarily small place in the novel. The narrator, for example, is intent upon filling in only enough background about Louis' family, uncle, and fiancée to add continuity to his tale, which showcases the mental life of his friend. Each of the characters is sharply drawn and carefully described with the characteristic realism that Balzac developed in his fiction. None, however, including the narrator, distracts the reader from focusing on Louis, and all exist in the narrative only in relation to him.

Balzac has noted that this novel was among his most difficult to write, because it contains so much of himself and embodies the research he had done on mysticism, both ancient and modern. Louis, indeed, replicates that research, converses about it with the narrator, writes of it in letters to his uncle, and infuses it into the letters he writes to his "angel," Pauline, who later records twenty-two fragments of his lucidly mad thoughts. These fragments, complemented by fifteen more that the narrator recalls, sketch out Louis' notions of the divine, of flesh becoming word, of the animate existence of thought and will, and of the relation of motion to number and of all to unity.

Louis Lambert, then, exists primarily as the spokesman for Balzac's reflections on spiritual matters and their intersection with the physical world. Yet Balzac undercuts his character by making him so thoroughly obsessed with the world of ideas that he is incapable of functioning in any practical way. The man of genius is also the victim of that genius; the thinker is ultimately unable to voice his thought; the spiritual man, by neglecting the physical world, is not equipped to survive in it. Like many protagonists of Romantic fiction, Louis is a seeker after something that does not exist, or, if it does exist, does so imperfectly. This fruitless quest is the burden of Balzac's treatment of character and the viewpoint that Louis personifies: Genius is self-destructive.

Balzac's irony extends to Pauline, who not only refuses to accept Louis' madness but also believes that he is sane, and who herself is nearly mad. She believes that Louis is in direct communication with a spirit world and that he is the medium through which eternal truths are spoken. For all of her blindness, Pauline is one of Balzac's great creations, a model for his other characters who exemplify a particular virtue. Her steadfast devotion to Louis and her self-sacrifice to care for him make her a remarkable antithesis to him. He has sacrificed himself for ideas and lives catatonically; she has devoted herself to him and can survive despite the burden she has undertaken.

Each of the minor characters—Louis' parents, his uncle, some schoolmates and masters—is drawn with such fidelity to detail and habit of speech, with such realistic rendering of situation, that, like the characters of most great writers, they have their own existence. While they enter and exit as needed to illustrate Louis' conditions and reflections, each could, like the narrator, reenter at any time to give his or her account of this man of genius.

Themes and Meanings

Balzac combines the forms of personal recollection, letters, and fragmentary speeches in order to portray the man of genius overcome by his own quest for knowledge. The direction of this particular genius is mystical and scientific, as Louis seeks to integrate the thought of Pico della Mirandola, Blaise Pascal, Emanuel Swedenborg, Louis-Claude de Saint-Martin, Franz Mesmer, and others into a theory that would explain the mysteries of human life, thought, will, and the physical and spiritual universe. That the formulation is, by its nature, impossible does not diminish the importance or attractiveness of this quest.

It should be emphasized that *Louis Lambert* does not contain a systematic statement of a clearly articulated philosophy. Rather, Balzac presents suggestions, hints, proclamations of theories, ideas, and propositions that he has gleaned from the arcana of the spiritual writing popular in his era. Electricity in the blood and other bodily fluids, phrenology, galvanic activity, mesmerism, angels, and the expansion of the soul all find a place in Louis' intellectual world. Indeed, the theories about the physical and metaphysical world are so important in this novel that they overshadow both action and character development. This is a philosophical novel in which the ideas count for more than any other thing. That the ideas are not wholly realized or worked out is important; were they fully presented, Balzac would have no need to end with Louis' madness. It is characteristic of Romantic thought and writing that incompleteness is preferable to closure.

In filling out his portrait, Balzac touches upon many themes common to the literature of the Romantic rebellion. The central issue of education hinges upon the notion of perfectibility and carries on the work begun by Jean-Jacques Rousseau in opposing the more traditional conception of education with an unsystematic but superior exploration of the universe of knowledge. The child prodigy, a staple of Romantic poetry and prose, encounters one of the foremost actual proponents of Romanticism, Madame de Staël, and becomes her spiritual heir. Personal tragedy, sentimentalized and exalted, is another of Romanticism's sublime and noble burdens.

Each of these themes coalesces in the central figure, who is the ultimate Romantic hero. Louis is, supremely, one of the splendid isolates of Romanticism. The theme of alienating isolation is worked out in the child's separation from his parents, his eventual isolation from his uncle (himself a social outcast), his parting from the narrator after college days spent isolated from the other students, and his isolation in madness on the eve of his marriage, which was to unite him with another human being. Indeed, in his last phase, it is evident that he is unaware of the existence of anyone but himself; thus, he is the personification of subjectivity.

Critical Context

Louis Lambert was the product of a new and growing tradition of French Romanticism and added to that tradition; it was also an important work in Balzac's own estimate of his career, although it is not ranked among his generally acknowledged masterpieces. The more well-known precedents for the novel include Jean-Jacques Rousseau's *Émile: Ou, De l'éducation* (1762; *Emilius and Sophia: Or, A New System of Education*, 1762-1763), Benjamin Constant's *Adolphe* (1816; English translation, 1816), Étienne de Sénancour's *Obermann* (1804; English translation, 1910-1914), and Chateaubriand's *René* (1802; English translation, 1813). Similar concerns with human nature's physical and spiritual dimensions are evident in Mary Shelley's *Frankenstein* (1818), Johann Wolfgang von Goethe's *Die Leiden des jungen Werthers* (1774; *The Sorrows of Werther*, 1779; better known as *The Sorrows of Young Werther*) and *Faust: Eine Tragödie* (1808; *The Tragedy of Faust*, 1823), and Lord Byron's *Manfred* (1817). Balzac's contribution to the tradition is the acute observation and detailed description of the actual state of persons, places, and segments of society (the school, village life, Parisian life), and the penetrating examination of the life of a mind overloaded with facts, suppositions, theories, and intuitive mysticism.

Although the novel has not fared well in the late twentieth century, it was well received in Balzac's time and remained one of his favorites. He had begun writing in a philosophical vein—the entire body of his work may be viewed as explorations in philosophy—early in his career, but his chief philosophical works include, along with *Louis Lambert, Le Peau de Chagrin* (1831; *The Wild Ass's Skin*; also as *The Fatal Skin*), and *Melmoth reconcilié* (1835; *Melmoth Converted*, 1900). Of the nearly ninety novels in *The Human Comedy*, which range from scenes of private and provincial life to scenes of Parisian life, political life, military life, and country life, Balzac particularly favored *Louis Lambert* because it is his most autobiographical work.

The master of analysis, having at last analyzed this critical period in his own life when he himself underwent a crisis of mysticism, built an even firmer foundation for his speculations based on observation of human behavior. While engaged over a three-year period in writing and rewriting this novel, Balzac was also at work on several other volumes, including his best-known masterpieces, *Eugénie Grandet* (1833; English translation, 1859) and *Le Père Goriot* (1835; *Daddy Goriot*, 1860; also as *Père Goriot*).

Sources for Further Study
Besser, Gretchen. *Balzac's Concept of Genius*, 1969.
Curtius, Ernst R. *Balzac*, 1933.
Evans, Henri. *Louis Lambert et la philosophie de Balzac*, 1951.
Le Yaouanc, Moïse. *Nosgraphie de l'Humanité balzacienne*, 1959.
McCormick, Diana Festa. *Honoré de Balzac*, 1979.

John J. Conlon

THE LOVER

Author: Marguerite Duras (1914-   )
Type of plot: Psychological realism
Time of plot: The early 1930's
Locale: Saigon
First published: L'Amant, 1984 (English translation, 1985)

> *Principal characters:*
> THE NARRATOR, a young French girl
> HER LOVER, a wealthy young Chinese man
> HER MOTHER
> HER OLDER BROTHER
> HER YOUNGER BROTHER

The Novel

The main plot of *The Lover* is the story of a fifteen-and-a-half-year-old French schoolgirl's love affair with the son of a rich Chinese businessman in Saigon during the 1930's. The novel is narrated by the girl herself, now an old woman and a successful writer. At the time of their first meeting, the girl's father has been dead for about ten years. Her two brothers, seventeen and eighteen years old, live with their impoverished mother, who is the head-mistress of the girls' school in Sadec. In the novel's first fully developed scene, in which the slightest details are described minutely, the girl is return-ing to Saigon—where she attends the French high school and stays at a state boarding school—after spending a school vacation with her family in Sadec. She is standing near the native bus she has been riding as it is being ferried across a branch of the Mekong River, as is the chauffeur-driven limousine of the young Chinese man, who is twelve years older than the girl and has just returned from spending two years studying in Paris. The young girl, "dressed like a child prostitute" in a red silk dress with a very low neck, gold lamé high heels, and a man's fedora, excites the young man's interest, and he immedi-ately offers to take her to wherever she wants to go in Saigon.

He shows up every day to pick her up at the high school and drive her back to the boarding school. One Thursday, he drives her instead to his flat in Cholon, the Chinese capital of French Indochina, where they make love for the first time. As time passes, the lovers become more deeply involved, though the relationship can never go beyond sexual intercourse: An inter-racial marriage would never be accepted by his father, who has already arranged that his son marry a young Chinese heiress, and the girl has no desire to marry at all. Sometimes she spends the night with him; sometimes she stays away from school all day. In the evenings, they dine at expensive Chinese restaurants, and when her mother and brothers come to Saigon, they all dine out together. Her family is too poor to refuse the evenings out at the young man's expense but also too convinced of his racial inferiority to consider that the affair could be anything but a disgrace and a scandal for the girl and her family. They never acknowledge his presence or speak to him, not even to say hello or to thank him for the dinners. During these evenings the young girl finds herself acting toward him just as her family does. Her schoolmates, with the exception of Hélène Lagonelle, also begin to avoid her as the affair becomes more widely known. The Chinese man in turn is constrained to hide the affair from his father, who is in control of all of his money and who would disinherit him if he were to marry a white girl.

The relationship ends after a year and a half, when the young girl leaves for France to finish her education. Sometime later, the young man obeys his father's orders and submits to an arranged marriage with the wealthy Chinese girl. In the last scene of the novel, the young man, visiting Paris with his wife many years after World War II, telephones the narrator, now a well-known author, and tells her that he still loves her.

The novel also introduces several subplots in addition to the main story of the lovers, the two most important of which are the study of the relationships among the members of the girl's family and the presentation of scenes and characters from occupied France during the war, particularly of the social life of some people who collaborated with the German forces.

The Characters

The Lover is at least partly autobiographical, representing Marguerite Duras' personal recollection of and confession about her childhood and her first love affair. The dates and places given in the novel correspond very closely to those facts known about her life, as does the makeup of the girl's family. Among the few characters whose names are mentioned in the book are the mother and the "younger" brother (in fact two years older than the girl), who have the same names as Duras' own mother and younger brother. The anonymous first-person narrator is now a writer very much like Duras, has had some of the same experiences in later life (involvement in political activities, struggle with alcoholism), and has written similarly about her early life and her family. Yet because so many of the characters are left nameless and because the names given are so seldom used, there is a suggestion that the novel should not be read simply as a thinly veiled autobiography.

The distance between Duras and her protagonist is reinforced stylistically by the narrator's frequent references to herself in the third person; the young girl often seems to be merely an observer of her own actions, directed by more powerful forces than her own conscious decisions. The ambivalent relationships presented in the novel similarly resist simple and direct analysis. The young girl's erotic passion for the Chinese man is genuine but is accompanied by—and perhaps intensified by—the attraction of the forbidden, the violation of the cultural taboo against miscegenation. She is also aware that the young man's wealth constitutes part of his attractiveness, and her ready acceptance of expensive clothing and a diamond ring places her in the role of prostitute at the same time that she is lover, alien, and, as an underage virgin, victim.

Duras sees all passionate relationships as ambivalent in this way, and the young girl's intense love for and hatred of her mother are shown to be nearly equal forces. Her mother in turn alternately accepts her daughter's behavior sympathetically and rejects her as a prostitute. The mother and daughter find another area of conflict apart from the Chinese man in the girl's two brothers, the mother preferring the elder to her other children, while the daughter sees him as the younger brother's victimizer. (The daughter goes so far as to blame him, along with their mother, for the younger brother's death during the Japanese occupation of Indochina.)

Several less central characters also play important roles in the novel, especially Hélène Lagonelle, a schoolmate for whom the young girl has erotic longings, and a small community of French collaborators during the war. Barely mentioned, but significant for that reason in this novel of family and gender relations, are the narrator's father, husband, and son.

Themes and Meanings

As is always the case in Duras' work, personal relationships are symbolically related to larger political and philosophical issues. The inextricably mingled pleasure and pain of the love affair between the French girl and the Chinese man, a relationship clearly doomed to failure from the beginning, is complete at one level as the story of an adolescent girl's initiation into sexual love. Nevertheless, it is also both a parable of French colonialism and a metaphor for the hopelessness of the universal human struggle against loneliness and despair. This interpenetration of the political and personal extends to the subplots: Those who collaborated politically with the enemy during the war are seen in a somewhat sympathetic light as private individuals (a point that troubled some reviewers), and conversely, the private family circle is seen in terms of the political realm. As Duras' narrator remarks, "I see the war as I see my childhood. I see wartime and the reign of my elder brother as one."

Yet in Duras' works, belief in political commitment is mere superstition; personal problems and relations are of transcendent importance, a valorization which persists despite the marked absence of any examples of enduringly successful relationships in her writings. The realistic presentation of the social and historical contexts of prewar French Indochina and occupied France is always subordinate to the story of the lovers and the interplay between passion and destruction, between erotic attraction and xenophobic repulsion.

Critical Context

Duras is often included in the group of French New Novelists, along with writers such as Michel Butor, Alain Robbe-Grillet, and Nathalie Sarraute, and their work does share some important features. The cinematic feeling of her work is characteristic of these writers, and *The Lover* is composed of a comparatively small number of carefully detailed short scenes, alternating between the time of the affair and various later periods up to the narrator's present, often repeated with slight variations or from different points of view and following one another without transitions. Nevertheless, her emphasis on exploring feelings rather than ideas clearly diverges from the more theoretical concerns of these other New Novelists.

Although it is a very short novel, *The Lover* manages to introduce most of the major concerns that have dominated Duras' writings: erotic love and its close relation to destructiveness, the pain of familial relations, and the interrelatedness of personal problems and political beliefs. The reception of *L'Amant*, the original French version of *The Lover*, was perhaps the greatest triumph of Duras' long and distinguished career, which has included nearly fifty novels, film scripts, and plays, as well as film directing. The novel was both a popular and a critical success, selling more than 700,000 copies and winning France's most prestigious award for fiction, the Prix Goncourt. Most American reviewers reacted with comparable enthusiasm. Although *The Lover* was not as popular in the United States as in France, it spent several weeks on the best-seller lists and became, for the American public, Duras' best-known work since her screenplay for Alain Resnais' film *Hiroshima mon amour* (1959).

Sources for Further Study

Cismaru, Alfred. *Marguerite Duras*, 1971.

Kristeva, Julia. "The Pain of Sorrow in the Modern World: The Works of Marguerite Duras," in *PMLA*. CII, no. 2 (1987), pp. 138-152.

Murphy, Carol J. *Alienation and Absence in the Novels of Marguerite Duras*, 1982.

Solomon, Barbara Probst. "Indochina Mon Amour," in *The New Republic*. CXCIII (September 9, 1985), pp. 26-32.

Willis, Sharon. *Marguerite Duras: Writing on the Body*, 1987.

William Nelles